Excavations at the Lower Palaeolithic site at East Farm Barnham, Suffolk, 1989-94.

D0303146

Edited by Nick Ashton, Simon G. Lewis and Simon Parfitt

with illustrations by Phil Dean

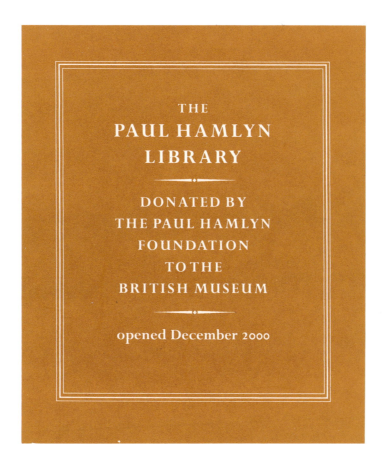

BRITISH MUSEUM

OCCASIONAL PAPER   NUMBER 125

EXCAVATIONS AT THE LOWER PALAEOLITHIC SITE AT EAST FARM, BARNHAM, SUFFOLK 1989-94

Edited by
Nick Ashton, Simon G. Lewis and Simon Parfitt,
with illustrations by Phil Dean

BRITISH MUSEUM OCCASIONAL PAPERS

Publishers: The British Museum
                   Great Russell Street
                   London WC1B 3DG

Production Editor: Josephine Turquet

Distributors: British Museum Press
                   46 Bloomsbury Street
                   London WC1B 3QQ

Occasional Paper No. 125, 1998

Excavations at the Lower Palaeolithic site at East Farm, Barnham, Suffolk, 1989-94
Edited by Nick Ashton, Simon G. Lewis and Simon Parfitt,
with illustrations by Phil Dean

ISBN 0 86159 125 9
ISSN 0142 4815

Front cover: Reconstruction of the Barnham landscape, contemporary with its use by humans, showing the underlying stratigraphy (see p. 265)

For a complete catalogue giving information on the full range of available Occasional Papers
please write to:
The Marketing Assistant
British Museum Press
46 Bloomsbury Street
London WC1B 3QQ

Printed and bound in the UK by the Short Run Press

CONTENTS

CONTRIBUTORS

Nick Ashton
Department of Prehistoric & Romano-British Antiquities, British Museum, Franks House, 38 Orsman Road, London N1 5QJ

D.Q. Bowen
Department of Earth Studies, University of Wales Cardiff, Cardiff CF1 3YE

Caroline Cartwright
Department of Scientific Research, British Museum, Great Russell Street, London WC1B 3DG

Nick Debenham
Quaternary TL Surveys, 19 Leonard Avenue, Nottingham NG5 2LW

Randolph E. Donahue
Department of Archaeological Sciences, University of Bradford, Bradford, West Yorkshire BD7 1DP

J. Alan Holman
Michigan State University Museum, East Lansing, Michigan, USA 48824-1045

Chris Hunt
Department of Geographical & Environmental Sciences, University of Huddersfield, Queensgate, Huddersfield HD1 3DH

Brian G. Irving
Solway Rural Initiative, The Resource Centre, King's Street, Aspatria, Cumbria CA5 3ET

Rob Kemp
Department of Geography, Royal Holloway, University of London, Egham, Surrey TW20 0EX

Simon. G. Lewis
Department of Geography & Geology, Cheltenham & Gloucester College of Higher Education, Francis Close Hall, Swindon Road, Cheltenham GL50 4AZ

John McNabb
Institute of Prehistoric Sciences, University of Liverpool, Brownlow Street, Liverpool L69 3BX

Simon Parfitt
Institute of Archaeology, University College London, 31-34 Gordon Square, London WC1H 0PY, *and* Department of Palaeontology, Natural History Museum, Cromwell Road, London SW7 5BD

E.J. Rhodes
Research Laboratory for Archaeology and the History of Art, 6 Keble Road, Oxford OX1 3QJ, *formerly* Department of Geography, Royal Holloway, University of London, Egham, Surrey TW20 0EX

Clive Roberts
School of Applied Sciences, University of Wolverhampton, Wulfruna Street, Wolverhampton W1V 1SB

M.B. Seddon
Department of Zoology, National Museum of Wales, Cathays Park, Cardiff CF1 3NP

John R. Stewart
McDonald Institute, University of Cambridge, Downing Street, Cambridge CB2 3ER

Francis Wenban-Smith
Department of Archaeology, University of Southampton, Southampton SO17 1BJ

John Wymer
The Vines, The Street, Great Cressingham, Thetford, Norfolk IP25 6NL

PREFACE

John Wymer

When I first saw the old brickearth pit at Barnham in 1979 it was a veritable jungle of trees, mainly dead, scrub and nettles. It was almost impenetrable and it took two days before my small team could cut our way through to where I estimate Paterson had dug in the 1930's. He had already established the basic stratigraphy and the prolific nature of the site, but it was uncertain whether any archaeological levels remained. This fortunately proved positive, and a considerable number of flakes and cores were recovered from the test section, beneath the colluvial deposits, some in primary context and others within solifluction layers below. This fitted Paterson's published sequence and it was clear that much more was there than I had suspected. This was all I wished to know for my brief note on the site in my book on *The Palaeolithic sites of East Anglia.*

It was great pleasure to me, and adequate justification for the cutting of the test section, that Nick Ashton chose this site for part of the project by the Quaternary Section of the British Museum Department of Prehistoric and Romano-British Antiquities: a project with the specific aim of conducting investigations at sites which would enhance the understanding of the palaeoliths in their collections. This splendid report does exactly that.

Already, G. de G. Sieveking of that department, had emphasised the great potential of some of the sites in East Anglia. He had made numerous trial excavations at known palaeolithic sites between the valleys of the Lark and Little Ouse, and conducted a series of excavations at High Lodge, Mildenhall. The latter were concluded in 1988 and enigmatical and controversial stratigraphy was gradually resolved. The astonishing sequence of glacial transportation of the raft of interglacial deposits into the Anglian till being beyond earlier conceptions. The major, profound result of this was the proof that people had been in East Anglia prior to the Anglian Stage glaciation, some half a million years ago. This all began to fit in with other investigations taking place on the pre-Anglian river systems of the Midlands and East Anglia by Jim Rose, Colin Whiteman and other Quaternary scientists. Palaeoliths were known to have come from gravels on this time from Lakenheath to Warren Hill at Mildenhall. Previous excavations at Hoxne by Richard West and Charles McBurney of the University of Cambridge, and later by myself at Hoxne for the University of Chicago, indicated occupation during the latter part of the interglacial after the Anglian. What better site to establish what was happening at the beginning of this same interglacial than at Barnham. Clacton and Swanscombe already showed that there had been human activity along the Thames/Medway in this earlier part of the Hoxnian interglacial.

The great advance in Quaternary studies during the last few decades has seen the application of an interdisciplinary approach to Palaeolithic excavations go from lip-service to reality. This can be seen from the growing number of reports now published on major Palaeolithic sites in Britain, of which this is the latest. A new generation of specialists actually work on or visit sites, rather than study samples brought to them in their laboratories. High standards have been set and will be undoubtedly perpetuated. However praiseworthy this may be, if palaeolithic archeology is to advance, all the intensive labour and organisation it requires has to be balanced against prosaic questions. What has been achieved? What is known that was not known before? It does not take long when reading this report to discover that the answer is plenty. Moreover, I think that the results at Barham epitomises a new, wider approach to the subject. Stratigraphy, context and sequence must all be clearly established, as here it mainly was; refits and spatial distributions of artefacts give some idea of what people were doing, but the real need in current thought on the matter, is to learn how people had adapted to different habitats, i.e.: the landscape. In recent history, one can write of *The Making of the Landscape*, as per the excellent series published for Norfolk, Suffolk and England as a whole, but for palaeolithic studies it is the 'changing of the landscape'. Climate, erosion, let alone glaciations have rendered areas of Britain to change from lush forest to barren steppe through time. We need to know what the landscape was like for people at particular times. At Barnham, we do. We know that they were active around a sheet of fresh water. The earliest people around it were probably there soon after the disappearance of the ice, to judge by their flint tools and debitage sludging down the slopes towards the water. The later people who sat on the cobble layer probably enjoyed a much more pleasant climate, in fact the presence of pond tortoise suggests it was warmer than the present day. Wet sieving on the grand scale (some nine tons of sieved sediment) has produced impressive lists of the smaller animals around the water: ducks, frogs, voles, birds, fishes. Remains of large mammals are scanty, but there are enough Hoxnian sites in southern England that have produced them to know that there would have been elephants, rhinos, deer, bovids and other beasts in the vicinity.

ACKNOWLEDGEMENTS

It is nine years since the excavations were initiated at Barnham, and there are many organisations and people to thank. The excavations were primarily funded by the British Museum, the British Academy and the Society of Antiquaries, but additional grants were received from the Royal Archaeological Institute, the Geologists' Association, the Thetford Industrial Committee and Center Parcs. Thanks are also due to those who supported the grant proposals and the project as a whole, namely Clive Gamble, Derek Roe and John Wymer, and those from my own department, Ian Longworth, Tim Potter and Jill Cook. Permission to excavate was kindly granted by the landowner, the Duke of Grafton, and by the tenant farmer, David Heading.

The excavations were initiated with the help of, and assisted throughout by Simon Lewis, John McNabb and Simon Parfitt. Working on the excavations were: Dan Adler, Sue Ashton, Louise Austin, Matthew Baker, Judy Bell, Mark Berger, Barbara Bláhouá, Nina Bridges, Dave Bridgland, Louise Byrne, Simon Chamberlain, Richard Champion, Celine Chantier, Tim Clark, Jakub Cząstka, Nick Debenham, Daniel Dean, Phil Dean, Mike Field, Richard Fisher, Sharon Gerber-Parfitt, Philip Greenwood, Richenda Gurney, Jill Guthrie, Ian Heading, Ival Hornbrook, David Hunt, Pat Hunter, Sophie Hunter, Brian Irving, Simon James, Mervin Jones, Tudor Bryn Jones, Dave Johnston, Cathy Lewis, R.J. MacRae, Indira Mann, Lisa Marlow, Kathleen McCulloch, Paul McCulloch, Jamie McKenzie, Melanie McQuade, Siòbhan Murphy, Debbie Musman, Sarah Newcombe, Eva Pache, Karen Perkins, Paul Pettitt, Kristina Pillai, Caroline Powell, Cath Price, Eddie Rhodes, Danielle Schreve, Pierre Schreve, Chris Steward, John Stewart, Jules Tipper, Micky Tipper, Steve Trow, Frank Wenban-Smith, Lee White, Mark White, Sara Wild. Cath Price undertook the photography on site, and Phil Dean and Cath Price drew the sections. The post-excavation finds and sediment processing were undertaken with the help of Sharon Gerber-Parfitt, Pat Hunter, Brian Irving, John McNabb, Danielle Schreve, Pierre Schreve and Dorli Williamson. Refitting was achieved with the assistance of John McNabb, Pierre Schreve and Felicity Woor. I thank them all.

Individual contributors have also received help. Simon Lewis thanks Neil Cousins for laboratory work, and David Bridgland for reading earlier drafts of Chapter 4. Clive Roberts (Chapter 5) is grateful to Cheltenham & Gloucester College of Higher Education for a grant towards the geophysics. Al Holman (Chapter 9) would like to thank the National Geographic Society for a grant (61-6063) to study the herpetofauna. Simon Parfitt thanks the staff of the mammal section (Department of Zoology - Natural History Museum, London) for access to comparative osteological material in their care, and to the Photographic Department (Natural History Museum, London) for printing the SEM photographs. He also thanks Andy Currant (Department of Palaeontology - Natural History Museum, London) and Thijs van Kolfschoten (University of Leiden) for helpful discussion and advice. He also thanks John Stewart and particularly Adrian Lister for commenting on drafts of Chapters 7 and 11. Chris Hunt (Chapter 13) thanks Richard Hubbard, Sarah Hall and John Wymer for discussion, and Richard Hubbard, Sarah Hall and Jean-Luc Beaulieu for access to unpublished data and discussion. The fluorescence microscopy technique emplyed for the palynology was developed and tested by Sarah Hall, while most of the samples were prepared by David Philpot. The manuscript was much improved by constructive refereeing by Rob Scaife. Rob Kemp (Chapter 6) thanks Jerry Lee for making the thin sections and for helping to collect the original samples, and Margaret Onwu for doing the organic carbon analysis. I thank John McNabb and Mark White for commenting on several drafts of the flint chapters. I also thank Josephine Turquet, the Occasional Papers Editor, for commenting on and proof-reading the draft of the volume, and to Stephen Crummy for assistance in the printing out of the final copy.

Throughout the excavations we have been helped enormously by the kindness and generosity (and at times tolerance) shown by the people of Barnham. This was continually displayed in the Grafton Arms, in particular by Wendy and Ginnie Grove with their staff, providers of excellent food and much beer.

Finally, our greatest thanks must go to the Heading family - David and long-suffering Margaret and their sons Edward and Richard - who not only provided free camping and showers on the farm, but above all gave enthusiastic support and encouragement for the project. Without their help the project would have faltered many years ago. Thank you.

Nick Ashton
1.10.98

1. INTRODUCTION

Nick Ashton

In February 1989 a brief excursion was made to East Farm, Barnham, while checking survey details at the nearby site of High Lodge. This visit confirmed that the former clay pit was still accessible and that Pleistocene deposits were still in place around its edges. Although completely overgrown, the weathered section on the south side of the pit, cut by Wymer in 1979, could still be located. Six months later the first of six seasons of digging was initiated and the results of that work are presented in this report.

The clay pit (TL 875787) lies on farmland, 500m to the south of Barnham village, Suffolk (Figs 1.1-1.2). The discovery of artefacts around the turn of the century, while the pit was still in active use, led to more detailed fieldwork by T.T. Paterson from 1932-36 (1937, 1942). His interpretation of several Clactonian industries being overlain by an Acheulian industry, combined with his geological interpretation of the Breckland sequence, led to the site being regarded as one of the flagships of the British Lower Palaeolithic (see Chapter 2). Subsequent fieldwork by Wymer in 1979 recovered an industry in primary context, interpreted as Clactonian, with one group of refitting flakes and a core (see Chapter 20).

The previous fieldwork led naturally to the main aims of the 1989-94 excavation. It was hoped initially to recover more of the core and flake industry in primary context (a rarity in the British Lower Palaeolithic) in an area adjacent to Wymer's section. Through more extensive excavation it was also hoped to locate Paterson's Acheulian industry (never clear from his publications) and, if found, to relate it directly to the core and flake industry. Finally, through fieldwork both within and outside the pit, it was intended to provide a detailed geological context for the site, that could be related to the regional stratigraphic sequence. As part of this programme it was hoped that environmental information would contribute, particularly as there were records from the *Geological Memoir Survey* (Whitaker *et al.* 1891) of shells being located within the pit, and personal accounts of larger fauna being recovered while the clay pit was still active (Paterson 1937).

Through the excavations these aims have been achieved and the results have contributed a wealth of information about the industries and the geological and environmental background to the site. The geology (Chapter 4), together with the geophysical investigations (Chapter 5) and micromorphology (Chapter 6) have provided a detailed description and analysis of the deposits both within the pit, and within the Barnham area, giving a complete glacial-interglacial sequence, that can be directly linked to the British Quaternary stratigraphic framework.

As part of this sequence, the fossiliferous channel deposits in the base of the pit have yielded a rich fauna (Chapters 7-12) together with pollen and charcoal (Chapters 13-14) that chronicle the change from cool to fully temperate conditions (Chapter 15), mirroring the shift from a slow-flowing fluvial environment, to still-water, and finally a dry landsurface.

The mammals (Chapter 11) also provide a means of supporting the geological correlation of the site, with other determinations given by amino acid racemisation (Chapter 16), thermoluminescence (Chapter 17) together with optically-stimulated luminescence and electron spin resonance (Chapter 18).

These studies provide the stratigraphical and environmental context for the flint industries at the site. Analyses of the taphonomy (Chapter 19), technology (Chapter 20), raw material (Chapter 21) and microwear (Chapter 22) contribute to an understanding of the variety of human activities at the site and help to generate models of human behaviour in the landscape (Chapter 23).

Above all, this volume attempts to demonstrate that a multidisciplinary approach to sites of this period, not only contributes individual studies of the geology, fauna and flora, but, as an integrated package, also provides the critical backdrop of environment and landscape, against which variation in the stone tool industries, and the behaviour they reflect, can be interpreted.

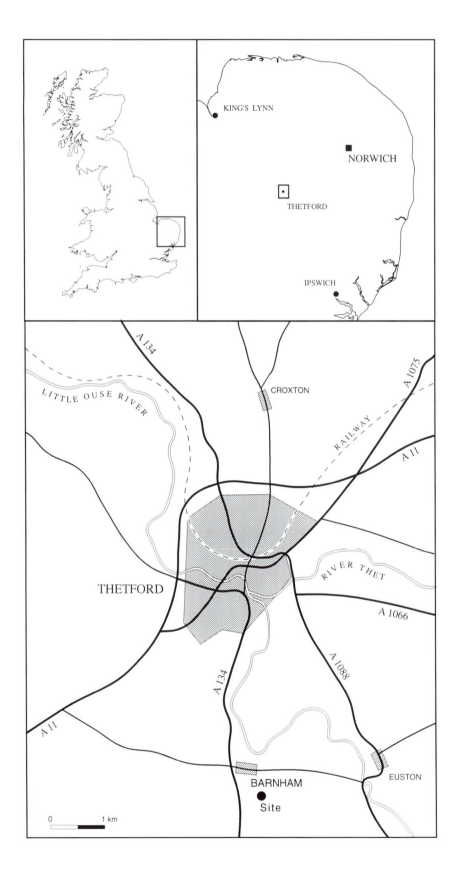

Fig. 1.1. The location of Barnham.

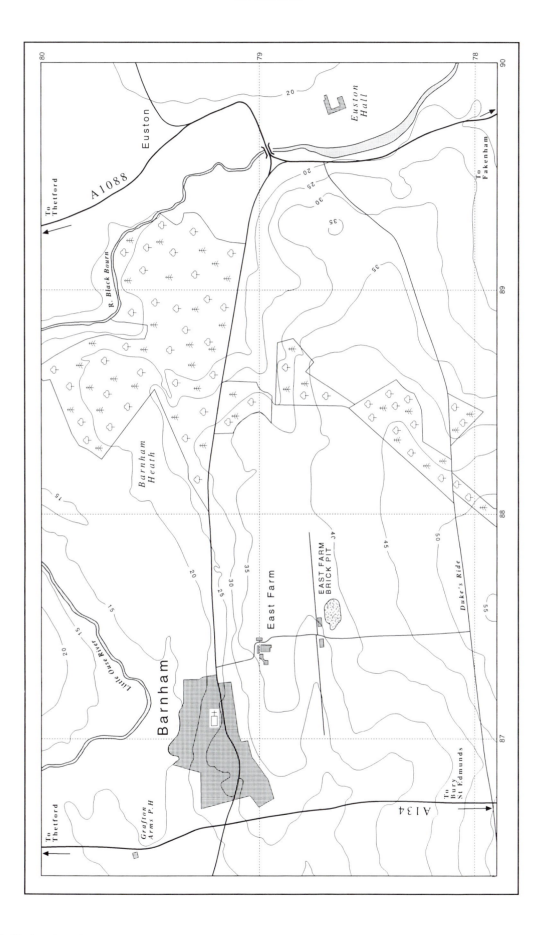

Fig. 1.2. The location of East Farm Pit and the Barnham area.

2. THE HISTORY OF INVESTIGATIONS AT EAST FARM PIT, BARNHAM

John McNabb

EARLY INVESTIGATIONS

Prior to the second decade of this century Barnham St Gregory was not known as a prolific producer of 'palaeoliths'. The East Farm Pit was cited as a locality of geological and palaeontological interest by the *Geological Survey Memoir* (Whitaker *et al.* 1891). The authors describe brown sandy loam with a black layer at the base, resting on clay, which in the centre of the section rests on a boss of iron-stained sands. In the western end of the pit dark grey clay contained shells and bones. In the same report pointed bifaces (Chellean) are described as coming from gravel deposits in the vicinity of the village. W.G. Clarke (1913) ascribed them to a gravel pit east of the village, and it is clear that this is not the East Farm Pit.

In his report on 'Some Barnham Palaeoliths' Clarke (1913) described a section recorded by H. Dixon Hewitt in 1912 in East Farm Pit. From the top this consisted of a stony layer passing into a sandy brickearth and a narrow dark band (to 2ft), more brickearth and a second narrow dark band (to 4ft), and brickearth becoming stonier at the base (to 12ft).

In the same report Clarke noted records of artefacts being found by among others H. Muller. These come from two locations, the first being a clay pit near the brickyard (beneath the present day RAF accommodation (TL 877794) to the east of the village), and the second a pit 'half a mile' south-east of Barnham church. This latter he attributed to East Farm Pit. Six of the artefacts were bifaces, all of them described as ovates (and hence attributed to the Acheulian and not to the Chellean), two of them twisted, and all with ocherous staining. Three are illustrated by Clarke (1913, pl. LXV), the smallest of which experienced a brief period of re-employment since it was used to clean the clay off the workmen's spades. A scraper is also described which has its proximal end worked. Although it is not entirely clear whether the scraper edge is the worked proximal end, if it is not then it is the first instance of a composite tool at Barnham, a scraper and a flaked flake on the same blank. This is a common phenomenon at Barnham and also other British Lower Palaeolithic assemblages (McNabb 1992).

Clarke and Dixon Hewitt also found at least eight flakes in the pit between 1912 and 1913, with at least six being from the brickearth, and all of them being described as Mousterian. One flake is described as having '...two bulbs of percussion and one reverse bulb in a space of ¾in., evidence of attempts at flaking' (Clarke 1913, 302).

This is a clear description of an inversely flaked flake. Other pieces were described as striated, as were many from the current excavations. Of further interest, within the geological section described by Clarke (recorded by Dixon Hewitt - see above), was a 'line of flakes' at 3ft below the surface.

It is clear that Clarke felt that Barnham and the East Farm Pit were important because an industrial succession could be demonstrated from the typological character of the implements. The range encompassed Chellean, Acheulian, and Mousterian, while towards the end of the paper Aurignacian and Solutrean were also described. Only Magdalenian was absent from the complete Palaeolithic sequence of the day. The publication date of 1913 is interesting, as it was in 1912 that Smith and Dewey (1913) excavated in the Barnfield Pit, Swanscombe. Their stated aim was to find just such a chrono-cultural sequence that could be used as a framework for dating the various developmental phases, reflecting the work of the French paleontologist Gabriel de Mortillet (1883), and believed to be present in the British Lower Palaeolithic (McNabb 1996b). It is against this background that the sequence suggested by Clarke should be seen.

In a summary of a meeting of the Prehistoric Society for East Anglia in Norwich Museum in 1919 (Caton 1919) artefacts tentatively associated with the East Farm Pit are described. They consisted of stained flakes, a large scraper and an ovate. The biface had a lustrous patination and a few striations, and was noted by Paterson as being identical to material he excavated from the gravels (Paterson 1937, fig. 16:4; see below).

PATERSON'S INVESTIGATIONS 1933-1936

The investigations of T.T. Paterson (1909-94) in the East Farm Pit were conducted from 1933-36, as part of a Cambridge University PhD (1942), a course that took him from the icy shores of Baffin Island (where a fjord is named after him) to India and South Africa. His Barnham work was set against a global background, in which he sought to model the direct links between climate change, environment, material culture, and evolution in hominids. His work is an intriguing window on the archaeological world of the 1930s, and it is important to set his Barnham work against the integrated world view that he promoted. A brief overview of Paterson's theories are included in order to set the geological, archaeological, and cultural development at Barnham in its proper context.

CYCLE		East Anglia	Barnham	Cultures
UPPER PLEISTOCENE	arctic 5th Glac.	sands, silts	15	Upper Palaeolithic
		erosion--------------------		
U3	cold	sands, gravels	14	Middle Palaeolithic
		erosion--------------------		
	cold 4th Glac.	Upper Boulder clay	13	
C3	cold	current-bedded sands	12	
U2		erosion--------------------	11	
	temperate	loams gravels		Upper { Acheul
U1	cold	solifluxion--------------		Clacton
	temperate	loams silts		
		sands gravels		
		erosion--------------------		
	cold 3rd Glac.	Middle Boulder Clay	10	
MIDDLE PLEISTOCENE	cold	Current-bedded gravels	9	Middle { Acheul (F)
M2		erosion------------------	8	Clacton (D-E)
	warm	loams gravels	7	
C2	cool	solifluxion, erosion---	6	
M1	warm	silts		Lower { Acheul
		sands gravels	5	Clacton (A-C)
		heavy boulder gravels		
		erosion------------------	4	
	cold 2nd Glac.	Lower Boulder Clay	3	
LOWER PLEISTOCENE		erosion------------------	2 / 1	Abbevillian (pre-Acheul) pre-Clacton Cromerian
L2	warm	Forest Bed		
C1		estuarine		
L1	cold 1st Glac.	shallow water		
		Red Crag		

Fig. 2.1. The European geological and cultural sequence, based on Paterson (1941-42). Barham industries are in brackets in right-hand column

Background to the geological work

Flying in the face of convention Paterson refused to embed his system within the commonly accepted Alpine sequence of Penck and Bruckner (1909), arguing that it was only of local significance. Instead he chose the Geike system (1894) of five Pleistocene glaciations, which depended on the identification of world-wide climatic patterns. Within this system, Paterson recognised three major cycles of sedimentation during the Pleistocene (C1-C3), each corresponding to the Lower, Middle and Upper Pleistocene respectively (Fig. 2.1). Within each major cycle were further sub-cycles, characterised by alternate deposition and erosion. The Lower and Middle Pleistocene were each subdivided into two phases (L1-L2 and M1-M2), and the Upper Pleistocene into three (U1-U3) (Fig. 2.1). Paterson's own contribution to this was the recognition of the repetitive character of sedimentation at both the major and sub-cycle levels, irrespective of geographical location. This provided Paterson with the key to long distance correlation.

He argued that large-scale synchronous erosive events were the result of major changes in climate. As deeply incised river channels were found in parts of the world where there were no large-scale earth movements (such as South Africa), Paterson argued that precipitation, rather than uplift or glacially generated erosion, was the major driving force behind regional and inter-regional erosive events.

To develop a direct link between observable end products and their causes, Paterson (1940-1) invoked the concept of power volume, the potential of a river to produce sediment, itself dependant on changes in precipitation, or position within a river system. At its simplest level, he argued that increased precipitation led to an increase in power volume, which itself led to increased erosion. Conversely, a decrease in precipitation and power volume led to sedimentation. Erosion was principally recognised from the escarpments of terraces. In Asia, Africa, and Europe he consistently identified five terrace escarpments within major drainage basins, thus identifying five main increases in precipitation from the middle of the Middle Pleistocene.

However, erosion and sedimentation would also be affected by the position within a river system, so that erosion in the upper reaches of a river would be reflected by sedimentation in the lower reaches. Only by looking at the complete river system, through the study of erosion and sedimentation, could changes in precipitation be understood. Importantly for the Barnham sequence, Paterson argued that cold episodes were associated with aggradation, particularly in the middle reaches of a river, due to decreased precipitation and winter and spring freezing. In contrast, solifluction was generally associated with increased precipitation, and hence erosion.

The interpretation of the geological history of Barnham

Paterson's interpretation of the Barnham sequence is summarised in Figure 2.2, information for which is largely drawn from his thesis (Paterson 1942). The sequence is also summarised in the site report (Paterson 1937), and in a brief overview of the Brecklandian sequence (Paterson 1939). The fieldwork, conducted between 1933 and 1936, not only looked at exposures within East Farm Pit, but also examined sections in a series of pits (pits 8 to 19, Fig. 2.3) in the Barnham area. Many of the critical relationships were seen within these exposures and at times supplemented by surface augering. It is also clear within the scheme that several relationships were inferred, rather than directly observed. The following sequence should be read in conjunction with Figure 2.1 as well as the schematic diagram in Figure 2.2 and the map in Figure 2.3.

1. Steep sided channels were cut into the Chalk at both Barnham and Euston.

2. Some 150ft (45m) of gravel was aggraded into the channel at Euston.

3. A blanket of blue till (grey after weathering) covered the landscape, including the gravels at Euston. The absence of Bunter quartzites and the identification of northern erratics indicated a northern and eastern source for the till. This till was created by the first ice advance in East Anglia (Lower Boulder Clay) and was the second glacial period of the Geike system.

4. The blue/grey till was extensively eroded, but in the Barnham area survived as patches around the channel. Any till that may have been deposited in the Barnham channel was eroded out at this stage.

5. A second series of gravels (up to 65ft, 19.5m) was aggraded within the Barnham channel. The absence of Bunter quartzites, his yardstick for the second ice advance in the region, showed that the gravels predated this second glaciation. This and the identification of stratification within the gravels suggested to him that this was fluvial deposition in a temperate climate (as opposed to glacial outwash). The final phase of this aggradation was contemporary with occupation by Clactonian knappers of Industries A-C.

6. A colder and wetter phase ensued, marked by solifluction of the gravel surface deposits, which striated and rolled the artefacts of Industries A-C. The gravel surface was occupied by more Clactonian knappers (Industries D and E) whose artefacts were unstriated and unrolled.

7. Subsequently, the countryside was extensively carpeted by brown coloured loams indicating marshy and damp conditions in a warm climate. At Barnham these loams contained molluscs, fauna, and also biface assemblages indicating the presence of a new knapping tradition (Industry F).

8. After the channel had become choked by the brown loams, the river switched direction, flowing to the north of its former course, to the north of East Farm, virtually in its present position. This shift was accompanied by downcutting to within 10ft (3m) of the present level of the River Little Ouse. This formed the basis for the modern topography of the Barnham area, since the Chalk ridge on which East Farm stands was created by the change of direction, and the downcutting initiated the modern river valley.

9. This new channel was infilled with some 55ft (16.5m) of current-bedded gravels heralding the onset of glacial conditions. However this aggradation was not sufficiently high to top the Chalk ridge and was therefore contained to the north of it. Bunter quartzites from the Midlands within the gravels differentiated them from the earlier gravels.

10. The second ice sheet to cover the region (3rd glacial period of Geike) spread a brown till (Middle Boulder Clay) over the area, the colour originating from the loams over which the ice sheet passed. Again, the presence of Bunter quartzites within this till clearly demarcated it from the earlier (blue/grey) till. The effect of this ice advance was to depress the overall level of the countryside by 150ft (45m). It is clear from Paterson's writings that the relationship between the till and the outwash gravel (X, Fig. 2.2) was not seen, only inferred.

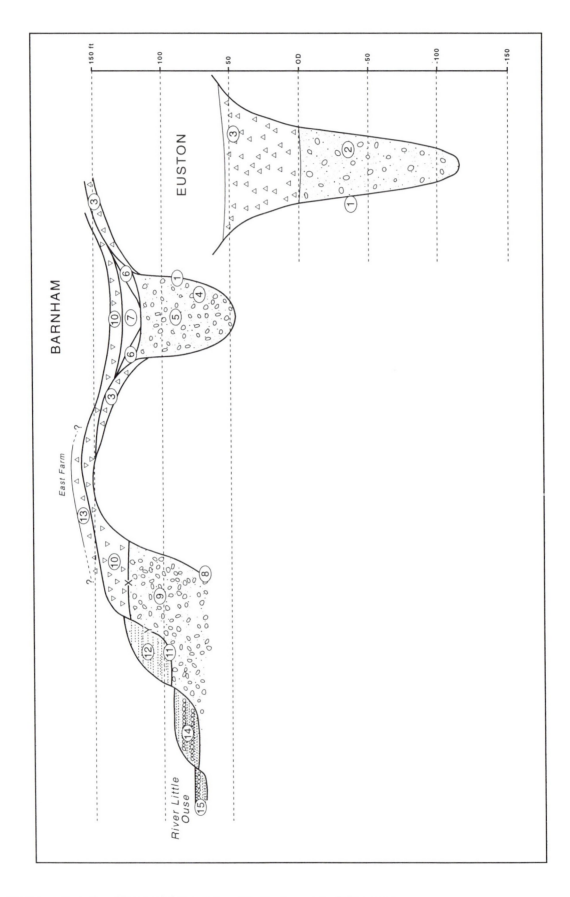

Fig. 2.2. Schematic section of Paterson's interpretation of the Barnham geological sequence.

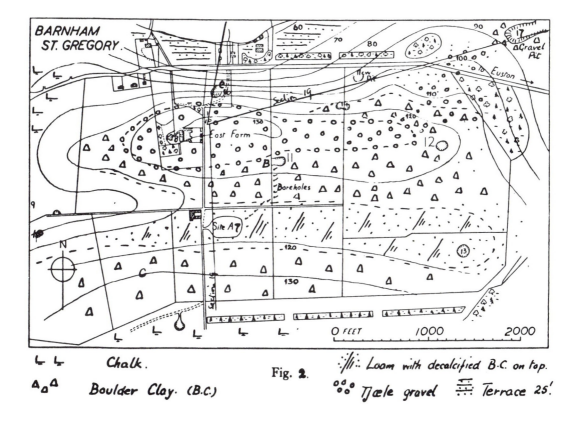

Fig. 2.3. Location of Paterson's Pits around East Farm reproduced from Paterson (1942). Note that the numbering of pits 11 and 12 has been corrected to fit Paterson's description. Also see Fig. 4.3.

With the retreat of this second glacier, downcutting occurred as the land began to recover its former height inducing the erosion of the Middle Boulder Clay. This occurred within an interglacial period, mirroring the preceding one, except much shorter. Within the Breckland region there was widespread deposition of sediments in the newly re-cut river channels. At Barnham there was little evidence of this interglacial north of the Chalk ridge, but it was well represented at Elveden (Paterson & Fagg 1940).

11. The next phase at Barnham was the end of this interglacial and the subsequent 3rd ice advance (4th glaciation of Geike - (13) below). Erosion cut into the former current-bedded gravels and the succeeding brown till, as the climate began to deteriorate.

12. Chalky current bedded sands to the north of the ridge, which contained a cold adapted flora, mark the onset of the glaciation. However, the exact relationship between these deposits and the outwash gravels (9) was not seen but inferred from the height of the deposits (Y, Fig. 2.2).

13. Deposits from the third glacial advance were not as marked at Barnham as the previous two. The boulder clay was heavily decalcified and weathered, and in places had been soliflucted over adjacent areas. It post-dated the chalky sands because in Pit 17 it overlay them in the form of a green, weathered, decalcified unit. As decalcified flinty sands this unit also capped the Chalk

ridge, and it was soliflucted over the northern slopes of this ridge.

14. After the retreat of this glacier, downcutting occurred to below 25ft (7.5m) above the Little Ouse, forming the bench for the higher of the terraces present in the modern landscape.

15. A later phase of downcutting and aggradation formed the lower or 10ft (3m) terrace.

Paterson's interpretation of the Barnham sequence illustrates how field observations were translated into world correlations. Big picture systems were very much the vogue of the 1930s and 1940s (for example Breuil 1932; for discussion see Dennell 1990), based on a genuine belief in the ability of science and logical method to achieve any goal, with theory empowering and structuring supposedly independant empirical observation. Paterson's approach is a reflection of this in his recognition of synchronous events in distant parts of the world. In identifying persistent difficulties in correlation at both the empirical and theoretical level, and attempting to resolve them by field testing a theoretical model, Paterson's work is, in spirit, not dissimilar to research strategies of today.

9

Background to the archaeological work

It is clear from Paterson's writings that the interpretation of the archaeological assemblages formed an essential pillar to his chronological framework. In common with others working at the time (eg Breuil 1932) he believed in the chronologically parallel development of different traditions of toolmaking (parallel phyla), in particular the Clactonian and the Acheulian. Each was represented by Lower, Middle and Upper industries, with additional sub-phases, all being clearly delineated in geological time (Fig. 2.1). This approach was rooted in one of the common assumptions of the era and was part of an unquestioned *zeitgeist* that there existed a direct link between stone artefacts, culture, and biological development in humans. This was the fundamental truth behind the ability to practice what modern archaeology has come to call culture history.

'...by regarding man as an animal, cultural changes in effect represent the evolution of the brain of man, that part of his anatomy that is most clearly hominid as distinct from the anthropoid. Furthermore, he is mobile and there is no reason to doubt that he migrated as speedily as any other mammal, and therefore his cultural horizons would be synchronous in the geological time sense.' (Paterson 1940-41, 374).

This view of history may be called 'progressive time'. It was the mechanism by which Paterson and his contemporaries could combine stone tools in a one-to-one relationship with biological change. It is nowhere better illustrated than in Paterson's ideas on core development. Core forms and their corresponding flakes in 'Lower Clacton' times showed an inability on the part of the knappers to pre-determine flake shape. This was a cognitive shortcoming which was being expressed through material culture, whereby '...the capacity for conceiving the future flake had not yet been developed.' (Paterson 1940-41, 382). However, 'Upper Clacton' core reduction was almost entirely geared to consistently producing flakes of a pre-conceived design (see below).

The excavation technique

A brief description of the method of excavation is given in the 1937 site report, and is notable for the exacting character of the digging technique. An area of 25m² was laid out on the southern side of the pit where the gravels rise to the surface. The excavated area was undisturbed by quarrying since it was necessary to remove a few inches of the overlying brickearth. This area may have been located in the current excavations, where a square cut trench was found on the north side of Area I (see Chapter 3).

The upper part of the gravel was dug in five 3-4in spits to a depth of about 2ft (0.6m). Everything was retained for examination, and material was only discarded after it had been deemed unstruck. A 4ft (1.2m) section was cleaned up adjoining the main area, which showed that artefacts occurred sparsely down to about 4ft (1.2m) below the surface of the gravel. A local 'Jack of all trades', Wattie Woods from Thetford, was engaged to excavate a well adjacent to this section, which showed that the gravel was at least 65ft (19.5m) in depth. No artefacts were found below the top of the gravel in the well.

The interpretation of the archaeological history of Barnham

Six different industries were identified at the site, beginning with the lowest - A. For the first five industries the divisions were based on patination and surface colour. The sixth was the biface assemblage from the overlying brickearths/loams. The lowest industries, A and B, were heavily striated, a feature that Paterson attributed to solifluction resulting from the period of increasing precipitation, contemporary with the final phases of aggradation in the gravel channel (see above). Striation was less frequent in the later industries. Industry C was largely characterised by a milky looking surface discoloration overprinting cream or blue patina. The interpretation of the industries provided confirmation of his overall chronological framework. Industry A was assigned to the Lower Clacton A, Industries B and C to Lower Clacton B, Industries D and E to the Middle Clacton A, while Industry F was attributed to the Middle Acheul.

The impression given in the report, and commonly held through received wisdom is that the first five of these assemblages were stratified throughout the depth of the upper portion of the gravel. This is not quite the case. Industry A was found lower in the profile, but B and C were intermingled throughout the upper 3ft (0.9m) of the gravel. Paterson separated flakes between them, primarily on the grounds of surface appearance only. Industries D and E were found together on the surface of the gravel, and again it was surface appearance that distinguished between them. Precise provenancing for Industry F was not given, except as being from various depths within the brickearth.

The time-progressive nature of Paterson's overall ideas on cultural development are clearly seen in the changes that occur through time from Industry A to E. He describes advances in the technique of core working, as the knappers become more adept at controlling their medium. From Industry C onwards cortex is less frequent on flakes - indicating their ability to remove it prior to knapping flake blanks, and flakes become more regular and standardised. Platform angles (between butt and ventral face) gradually decrease while the bulbs of flakes become deeper. Greater incidences of parallel flaking on the cores, and the introduction of more specialised core forms further attest to the incremental advances made by the knappers.

Advances in retouching techniques parallel this trajectory. Tools were divided into single or multiple forms, the latter being the occurrence of two different kinds of tool on the same flake. The impression given is that the shape of the retouched edge was deliberate, and that edge character was tied to function. The most developed of the industries was E, conversely the industry which showed the least amount of retouch. With typical Paterson logic he showed that this was a clear indication of technical development since the knappers were able to conceive of and execute the forms of flake they wanted. Therefore considerable quantities of modifying retouch was unnecessary, simplicity implying achievement, contrary to the usual assumption of simple = crude = early.

To modern eyes all this seems rather incongruous; almost all of the retouch illustrated on flake tools by Paterson is natural, acquired during transport, and even a brief glance through the 1939 report shows that all the cores and flakes illustrated for each of the industries are virtually identical.

For industry F, Paterson described not only the pieces he found during his own excavations but also those recovered by earlier workers. It is curious to note the differences in patination and surface appearance that exist in the small biface sample he described. The two bifaces found during the excavation are irregular and asymmetrical. Both have white to cream coloured patina, whereas the two in the Muller Collection have a blue/green patination.

It is possible that the bifaces from the loam were originally from the surface of the gravels. The thin deposit of 'loam' that was removed by Paterson, is likely to be the same as the yellow silty sand in the current excavation. He also notes that some of the flakes from Industry F are striated. This is also the case for the Caton biface which because of its condition was placed by Paterson in Industry D. In the current excavations several striated flakes were recovered from within the yellow silty sand, and have been interpreted as being derived from the cobble layer (the top of Paterson's gravel). Finally, there are pieces from Industry E that are illustrated by Paterson (1937) and reminiscent of biface manufacturing flakes on the basis of their form and dorsal scar patterning (Figs 17.1, 17.2, 17.3, 18.2). Flakes have also been noted from the yellow silty sand in Area 1 in the current excavation that might be interpreted as biface manufacturing debitage (see Chapter 20).

Paterson's interpretation of the Barnham industries reflects the assumed link between cultural and biological evolution and illustrates the interdependent nature of culture history. Reduction processes offered a window from which a number of different sources of evidence could be addressed, all made possible by the view of progressive time. It is not difficult to see how a generation in the grip of modernism could so easily follow such a chain of reasoning especially when embedded in the brand of social Darwinism prevalent in the middle decades of this century which espoused incremental progress over time (McNabb 1996b). The clear psychological bridge between material culture and biology would only have served to reinforce a Darwinian view of change.

WYMER'S INVESTIGATIONS IN 1979

There was no further fieldwork at Barnham until 1979, when following excavations at Hoxne, John Wymer took the opportunity to cut a section in the East Farm Pit (Wymer 1985). The section was located in the centre of Area I of the current excavations on the southern side of the brick pit, and uncovered essentially the sequence of deposits illustrated in Figure 4.6 (Chapter 4).

In the 40 years after Paterson's work, there were many changes in the interpretation of the British geological framework. Not least of these was the view (still current) that there had been only one glaciation in East Anglia, represented in the Barnham area by the Lowestoft Till. Consequently Wymer, assisted by Jim Rose, adopted a much simpler interpretation of the geology. On the basis of his own section, the publications of Paterson, and field notes of Baden-Powell, he argued that Lowestoft Till lay at the base of the sequence (although this was not seen). It was incised by a 20m deep channel, which was infilled with outwash gravels and solifluction at the top. This whole sequence was covered by brickearth, with the artefacts coming from the base of the brickearths and the top of the solifluction gravel. He also identified a black clay towards the base of the brickearths and it was tentatively interpreted as a palaeosol by Rob Kemp (see Chapter 6). The broad essentials of this interpretation have changed little through the current work, although his interpretation of the Farm ridge being on outwash gravels was based on Baden-Powell's misinformed notes; these were supplied by Paterson, but Paterson himself quotes borehole records that clearly show the ridge to be of Chalk with only a capping of sands and gravels (1942).

Archaeologically the small scale-excavation was highly successful. Wymer was the first to confirm that the assemblage from the gravel surface (Industry E of Paterson) was *in situ* by discovering a refitting core and 13 flakes (see Chapter 20, Fig. 20.3). Together with the remainder of Wymer's material, it is clearly an integral part of the assemblage excavated from the surface of the cobble layer and from within the yellow silty sand in the current work. Wymer was also the first to interpret Paterson's Industries A to E, as being technologically inseparable, the only distinction lying in the condition of the artefacts. He interpreted these assemblages as being Clactonian. There was no sign, however, of Paterson's overlying biface industry.

DEVELOPMENTS SINCE 1979

In a major article in *Current Anthropology*, Ohel (1979) referred to Barnham, among other sites, with the contention that the flaking debris left by Clactonian knappers was the residue of biface roughing out activities, the bifaces being removed for finishing and use elsewhere. A further article specifically on the Paterson material from Barnham (Ohel 1982), using metrical analyses, suggested that the material from the surface of the gravels was slightly different to the material from within the gravels. He also suggested, as an alternative interpretation to his technological argument, that Barnham was neither unambiguously Clactonian, nor Acheulian, possibly a mixture of both. This suggestion is interesting as a few biface manufacturing flakes may have been identified during the current excavations in Area I (see Chapter 20). Ohel

also alluded to flaked flakes in the Paterson assemblage (in this case inverse proximal detachments), suggesting they are at odds with traditionally interpreted Clactonian assemblages using the definition of Breuil (1932). He alluded to the possibility that these are Acheulian patterns.

SUMMARY

The first 80 years of fieldwork at Barnham clearly showed the importance of the site for creating and supporting the British archaeological and chronological framework. It was one of only two sites (the other being Swanscombe) where it was argued that Clactonian industries were stratified below Acheulian. Equally, the suite of geological deposits formed an important sequence that contributed to the interpretation of the East Anglian chronological framework. From the above descriptions it is also clear that several of the interpretations remain unclear or unresolved. Was the much simpler interpretation of Wymer correct, or did Paterson's field observations justify his much more complex sequence? From where were the few enigmatic bifaces really coming? It is against this background and with many of these issues in mind that the current excavations are set.

3. DESCRIPTION OF EXCAVATIONS 1989-94

Nick Ashton

The aim of this chapter is to provide a key to the specialist reports in the remainder of the volume. Not only is a detailed description given of the fieldwork, but also a rationale for the way the excavation was undertaken. As such, it is critical for a full understanding of the excavation. To avoid confusion, the nomenclature used for the geological units, is the same as that subsequently adopted and used throughout the rest of the volume, but not necessarily that used in the field. For comparison with previous publications (Ashton *et al.* 1994a, 1994b) Table 3.1 lists any changes in nomenclature. A full description of the geology is given in Chapter 4.

Unit	Description	Faunal area	Ashton *et al.* 1994a, 1994b
7	brown silt and clay "brickearth"		brown clayey silts
6	black clay		dark brown silty clay
5e	yellow silty sand		grey silty sand
5d	grey/brown stony clay		
5c	grey silt and clay	gritty clay	silts and clays
		shelly clay	
		black clay	
		brown-grey clay	
		laminated shelly clay	
		basal silt	
5b	grey chalky clay		
5a	brown silt and clay		
4	cobble layer		cobble layer
3	brown diamicton		brown diamicton
2	chalky diamicton		chalky diamicton
1	sand and gravel		sands and gravels

Table 3.1. Geological unit numbers and descriptions used in this report and in Ashton *et al.* (1994a, 1994b).

Prior to excavation, the pit at East Farm was completely overgrown with a combination of elder, dog-rose and hawthorn with several more substantial oaks and other deciduous trees (Pl. 3.1a). The pit was 130m by 70m in it's maximum dimensions, and had been largely untouched since the work of Paterson in 1933, although a large amount of 'carrot-earth' had been dumped over the north west edge of the pit in the 1950s, concealing the edge of the pit for 50m. On the south side, the 2m wide section, excavated by Wymer in 1979, was still clearly visible. It was on the basis of the work by Paterson in the 1930s and by Wymer in 1979 (see Chapter 2), that the current project was initiated.

From the outset, there were three main aims: (1) to investigate the relationship between the Clactonian and Acheulian industries, described by Paterson; (2) to recover more of the refitting Clactonian material, that had been discovered by Wymer; and (3) to place these industries in a secure geological and environmental context.

THE 1989 SEASON

The initial season in 1989 aimed to re-expose Wymer's 1979 section, to assess the potential for further excavation in that area, and to locate other areas within the pit that might merit more thorough investigation. The work took place over four days in August with a team of five people.

The 1979 section (Area I; Fig. 3.1) was cut back to reveal a cobble layer at the base, overlain by 25cm of yellow silty sand, 10-20cm of black clay and up to 2m of brown silt and clay or 'brickearth' (see Wymer 1985, 117). This was overlain by a brown sand and topsoil. The section was deepened by 0.9m in a 1m x 1m area at the base of the section to expose the underlying deposits, which consisted of sand and gravel at the base, overlain by a brown diamicton (see Chapter 4 and Figure 4.6 for a full description of the sediments). The deepening of the section indicated that the sequence was more complex than that described by Wymer (1985, 117) who interpreted the cobble layer as the top of the sand and gravel, revealed by Paterson. The current work showed that a new deposit, brown diamicton, lay between the cobble layer and the sand and gravel. All the deposits in the area were decalcified, and samples taken for the recovery of fauna proved to be sterile.

One core and seven flakes were recovered from the top of the cobble layer, in the same stratigraphic position as Wymer's refitting material. In addition a single flake was found in sand at the base of the sequence.

An augerhole, 10m to the south of Area I in the field, showed the same sequence of deposits down to the brown diamicton, but revealed chalky diamicton at the base. This was interpreted as Lowestoft Till (see Chapter 4). Neither Paterson or Wymer had located deposits of this nature in the East Farm Pit, although Paterson revealed similar sediments in several of his pits around East Farm. The location of Lowestoft Till, provided the first opportunity to relate the other deposits in the pit, to a regionally important, stratigraphic unit.

A test section 25m to the north-west of Area I was excavated on the edge of the former cart-track into the pit. It was hoped that the deposits beneath the cart-track would be *in situ*. Unfortunately the section revealed disturbed clay, sand and silt, and was abandoned at a depth of 1.2m. A core and seven flakes were recovered, of which two are in the same condition as those from Area I, and may be Lower Palaeolithic, but the remaining five are probably later prehistoric.

THE 1990 SEASON

Following the work in 1989, the main priority of the season was to excavate a large trench (Area II) in the field adjacent to Area I (Fig. 3.1). It was hoped that this would reveal in section the relationship between the higher units at the site and the chalky diamicton. In addition, it would provide fresh exposures to sample for both the geological and environmental work. Finally, an assessment could be made of the potential for the recovery of undisturbed archaeology in the field. The work took place over two weeks in August with seven people.

At ground level Area II was approximately 5m x 5m and reached a total depth of 4.9m. Two steps were cut at 1.5m and 2.8m below ground surface, reducing the size of the trench to 3m x 3m and 1m x 3m at each step. At the base the area was little more than 0.4m x 1m due to sloping sections and because a further step was cut at a depth of 4m on the north side. The top 1.5m was excavated by JCB, while the remainder was excavated by hand. The sections revealed broadly the same sequence of deposits as the augerhole, but with more detail. Chalky diamicton lay at the base, overlain by brown diamicton, a thin spread of cobbles, yellow silty sand, black clay, a large thickness of brown silt and clay, and a brown sand (see Chapter 4, Fig. 4.19). The topsoil was up to 0.8m thick. Within the brown silt and clay, several darker bands were visible. Samples were taken from the sequence of brown silt and clay and have been examined for particle size, and organic carbon, iron and manganese content (see Chapter 4). Equivalent bands within Area I have been examined through micromorphology (see Chapter 6).

The only artefacts to be found were on and within the thin cobble spread. In total there were 46 artefacts, most of which were in a rolled and abraded condition. This unit was at the same depth and occurred in the same stratigraphic position as the cobble layer in Area I. In this area, however, it was much more sparse, in terms of both cobbles and artefacts, and appeared to be thinning out to the south. For this reason it was decided not to pursue any further excavation in the field in future seasons.

Further work was also undertaken in Area I (Pl. 3.2a). The 1m x 1m test pit at the base of the section was expanded to 1.4m x 1.6m and was taken to a depth of 1.5m below the base of the section. This exposed further sand and gravel underlying the brown diamicton (see Chapter 4).

Also in Area I, a narrow strip, 30cm wide and 3m long, was carefully excavated on the east edge of the test pit. This was taken down through the black clay, yellow silty sand and the cobble layer. The artefacts were recorded three dimensionally, triangulated in from two grid pegs. This information has since been transferred into the system first deployed in 1992 (see below). From the base of the yellow silty sand, the surface of the cobble layer and from within the cobble layer, a total of 89 artefacts were excavated. Some were in very fresh condition, while others had been considerably rolled (see Chapter 19).

Beyond the pit, a total of 15 geological test pits (TP1-TP15) were excavated by JCB (see Chapter 4, Fig. 4.3). Several were located adjacent to the exposures that Paterson described, to relate his composite interpretation of the local stratigraphy to the East Farm Pit, while others were located between these areas and the East Farm Pit. From these it was clear that the two tills, recognised by Paterson (in different exposures) were the same, and that these underlay the sequence of silt and clay in the East Farm Pit (see Chapter 4).

A temporary benchmark was surveyed in from a benchmark on Barnham Church, to a position on the barn 100m to the north-west of the pit. It was situated in the main entrance on the east side, on the concrete base of the southerly entrance post, having a height of 34.45m OD.

THE 1991 SEASON

The 1991 season was the first major season and took place over four weeks in August with between 15 and 20 people, as did the three subsequent seasons. The main aim was to continue the geological investigations and to excavate a large area of *in situ* archaeology.

The previous season had established that there was still a high concentration of artefacts in Area I. The area was expanded to the east and to the west, creating two areas each approximately 3m x 4m (Area I East and Area I West). The sterile upper units were removed by a mini-excavator down to the top of the black clay. For safety reasons an 80cm wide step was cut halfway down the section. The underlying deposits were then excavated carefully by hand down to the upper part of the cobble layer. Artefacts were recovered from the base of the yellow silty sand and from the surface of, and within, the cobble layer. The position of each artefact was recorded three dimensionally within metre grid squares. The grid squares were numbered 10 to 19 along the east axis with letters D to G along the north axis. In subsequent seasons the system was adapted, and all locational details have been altered to the new system (see below). In addition to this, any flakes with a maximum dimension greater than 4cm had their maximum dip and orientation noted (see Chapter 19).

The artefacts consisted of flakes, chips, cores and flake tools of which 298 came from the base of the yellow silty sand, and 83 from the cobble layer. In general those from the cobble layer were more rolled and abraded than those from the yellow silty sand, but there was also clearly intermixing of artefacts between the two units (see Chapter 19). Although Area I West and Area I East displayed essentially the same stratigraphy, there was a much thinner spread of yellow silty sand over Area I West. Consequently, a greater proportion of the artefacts were from the cobble layer in Area I West and it was excavated to a greater depth.

On the north edge of Area I West, a 40cm deep trench was located which was approximately 5m x 5m in size. This is now thought to be Paterson's excavation area, the location of which had not been recorded previously (Fig. 3.1). At this point the yellow silty sand would have been completely truncated by clay pit digging which explains why the vast majority of Paterson's artefacts are rolled and derive from the cobble layer or below.

To the north of Area I a trench was excavated in the base of the pit, alongside a pre-existing bluff, to expose the sand and gravel beneath the brown diamicton (see Chapter 4, Fig 4.7). Two sections were cut into the bluff on the south and east sides to a depth of 1.9m. In a shallow trench on the surface of the clay pit, the brown diamicton could be traced from Area I to the Area I (gravel section) (see Chapter 4). During the sampling of the Area I (gravel section) and while cutting the shallow trench from Area I, 27 artefacts were recovered from the brown diamicton. Most of these were rolled, except two flakes in a much fresher condition (see Chapter 19).

Three further sections were cut around the edge of the pit. The first (Area III, west section) was cut at the extreme western end of the pit (Fig. 3.1; Pl. 3.1b). It was 3.6m wide and 3.0m deep, with a step midway down the section. At the base lay a chalky diamicton (see Chapter 4, Fig. 4.14), which was overlain by up to 2m of brown silt and clay. Eight flakes were found while cutting the section, or were recovered while

eroding out of the weathered section in subsequent seasons. They came from various heights within the brown silt and clay. A shallow trench was also cut, extending out from Area III (west section), eastwards into the centre of the pit. It was 1m wide, 45cm deep and 12m long. In the section a series of sand, silt and clay deposits were identified which all dipped into the centre of the pit, stacked up against the chalky diamicton in Area III (west section). The uppermost units in the east of the trench were found to be calcareous and contained fragmented shells. A series of augerholes (91/1 - 91/4) up to 20m further east into the pit established that the sand, silt and clay reached a maximum depth of 6.8m, overlying chalky diamicton.

A 1m wide section (Area III, south section) was cut 10m to the south-east of the extension trench on a bluff, preserved by the disused trackway into the pit (Pl. 3.3a; also see Chapter 4, Fig. 4.13). Again the sediments consisted of clay, silt and sand, and were also dipping to the east. Most of the sediments were decalcified, but a pocket of calcareous sediment survived halfway down the east side of the section and also contained fragmented shells (see Chapter 12).

A third section (Area IV(3)), 1.5m wide and 3.6m deep, was cut in the north-eastern end of the pit. Here, brown silt and clay overlay black clay and decalcified grey silt and clay (see Chapter 4, Fig. 4.23). Augering established that chalky diamicton lay at a depth of 1.6m below the base of the section (see Chapter 4).

During February 1992 ten pits were excavated by JCB for the farm, to find the best location for a potential reservoir within the hectare of field across the farm track to the west of East Farm Pit (see Chapter 4, Fig. 4.3). These were recorded and listed as TP16 to TP25. Although the recording conditions were not ideal, and could only be viewed by surface inspection, they generally revealed that brown silt and clay on the slightly higher ground to the south, overlay chalky diamicton. Sand and gravel was seen in pits in the dry valley bottom to the north, but their relationship with the brown silt and clay or the chalky diamicton was not clear.

THE 1992 SEASON

The aims for 1992 were to continue and expand Area I, investigate further Area III, and to link these two areas by a slit trench to provide a better understanding of their geological relationship.

Area I West had been completed in 1991, but Area I East was continued and extended to form a total area of approximately 4m x 9m. This season an EDM was used to locate the artefacts, using as a base the same grid as the previous season. Whereas in the previous season, a letter and number combination had been used to locate a grid square, this was all converted to numbers, so that the south-west corner of square D10 was given a grid coordinate of 100.00, 000.00 to the nearest cm, or the south-west corner of square E11 was 101.00, 001.00. In this way the entire pit was encompassed by the new grid system. In addition, for flakes with a long axis greater than 4cm, the orientation of the dip was computed by recording the high and low points of the maximum dip. All the previous methods of recording (see above) were adapted to this system, which itself was maintained for all subsequent seasons.

As with the previous season the black clay was largely sterile, with the exception of one biface found at the interface of the black clay and the underlying yellow silty sand. No other debitage was found in association. Two pieces of unworked burnt flint were also found in the black clay, and a further piece in the underlying yellow silty sand. These have since been used for thermoluminescence dating (see Chapter 17). All the other artefacts lay towards the base of the yellow silty sand (721 pieces) or were from the cobble layer (193 pieces). By the end of the season the top of the cobble layer had been exposed and partially excavated across the whole area.

A series of monoliths were taken through the brown silt and clay ('brickearth'), black clay, yellow silty sand and brown diamicton for micromorphological work (see Chapter 6).

Area III (south section) was extended by 5.5m to the south west making the total section 6.5m long and up to 3.5m deep with a step half way down the deeper part of the section (Pl. 3.3a). Chalky diamicton was located in the bottom west corner, and above this the sand, silt and clay units that had been observed in 1991 could be seen more clearly to be dipping to the north-east (see Chapter 4, Fig. 4.13). Towards the top of the section at the junction of a grey/brown stony clay and the overlying black clay, six small biface manufacturing flakes were excavated in the section. They were spread out in a line with only 75cm between the first and the last and were clearly the edge of an *in situ* scatter. The area behind the section was left untouched for further investigation in 1993.

To relate the deposits in Area III to those in Area I, a 1m wide trench was excavated between the two areas (Fig. 3.1). So the nature of the deposits in the centre of the pit could be seen, the trench already started in 1991 from Area III was continued eastwards into the centre of the brick pit, then turned south towards Area I (gravel section). Due to the dense vegetation and also to avoid, where possible, previous disturbance from brick pit digging, there were several additional twists in the direction that the trench took. The surface deposits were removed by mini excavator which revealed that the uppermost units consisted of grey silt and clay. It also showed that large quantities of these had been removed

by brick pit digging forming a regular series of pits along the line of the trench. The pits had been backfilled mainly with a mixture of topsoil and the brown sand found at the top of the sections around the brick pit edge, clearly differentiating the *in situ* material from the backfill. This backfill was removed to reveal sections through the grey silt and clay and underlying deposits. As the grey silt and clay thickened towards the centre, so the pits deepened to a maximum of 2.4m in the centre. The pits were numbered 1 to 13, starting at the western end (Fig. 3.1). Pits 1 to 9 revealed a series of sections normally between 1m and 2m apart. In Pits 10 to 13, however, the clay digging had been much more extensive, so that the pits were considerably longer (up to 12m in length).

From the sections in Pits 1 to 9 it was clear that the grey silt and clay dipped into the centre of the brick pit, and consequently that the deposits revealed in the upper part of the sections became progressively younger towards Pit 9. From Pit 10 to 12 the same grey silt and clay could be traced to the south, but became decalcified in Pit 10. In Pit 12 it was seen to thin out and rise to the south where it overlay a brown diamicton. At this point it was truncated at its surface by clay digging. The brown diamicton could be traced to Area I (gravel section) where it overlay the sand and gravel (see Chapter 4, Figs 4.7, 4.19).

A total of 8 augerholes (92/1 - 92/8) in the base of Pits 1 to 13 established that the fine sediments reached a maximum depth of 6.8m in this part of the pit, overlying chalky diamicton. The fine sediments were the infillings of a depression, one edge of which could be traced to the south and west.

It soon became clear that the basal units within the depression (reached through augering), despite being calcareous, were largely sterile, but the top 2-3m contained an abundant fauna in a very good state of preservation. Two column samples were excavated in Pit 4 and Pit 9, being 0.5m x 0.25m in surface area and taken down 1.7m and 1.2m respectively (see Chapter 7, Figs 7.1-7.2). Context was recorded by unit and within each unit by 10cm spits. In effect the column sample from Pit 4 lay stratigraphically beneath that from Pit 9, although the precise relationship was not clear (see Chapter 4). Larger bones were excavated and recorded *in situ*, while all the sediment was later sieved off-site at 0.5mm mesh size (see Chapters 8 - 11). Each of the samples from the columns was later subdivided to provide samples for the molluscan analysis (see Chapter 12). In addition to the faunal material, two flakes and a core were recovered from the grey silt and clay, all of which were in an exceptionally fresh condition, were barely patinated and completely unstained (see Chapters 19-20).

Plate 3.1a. View of East Farm clay pit from the north; b. Area III (west section) showing till at the base (photos: C. Price).

Plate 3.2 a. Area I, excavated down to the cobble surface; b. Area IV(4), excavated down to the cobble surface (photos: C. Price).

Plate 3.3 a. Area V excavation area, with Area III (south section) below; b. Area III (faunal area) (photos: C. Price).

THE 1993 SEASON

The main aims of the 1993 season were to complete the excavation of Area I, to open up a new area adjacent to Area III (south section) for the recovery of further biface manufacturing debitage, and finally to excavate an area of the grey silt and clay in Area III for the recovery of larger fauna.

Excavation continued in Area I down through the cobble layer. By the end of the season at least one spit of cobbles was removed from the whole area. Over a limited part (4m x 3m) on the western side, a further spit of cobbles was removed to reveal the underlying brown diamicton. In total 416 artefacts were excavated from the yellow silty sand and 272 artefacts from the cobble layer (see Chapter 19).

A new 4m x 4m area (Area V; Pl. 3.3a) was opened on the south side of Area III (south section) (Fig. 3.1; see Chapter 4, Fig. 4.13). The previous season's excavation had revealed six biface manufacturing flakes in the section lying on the surface of a grey/brown stony clay, immediately beneath a black clay. Up to 1m of topsoil and brown silt and clay ('brickearth') was removed by mini-excavator. The remaining 20-30cm of brown silt and clay and 10-15cm of black clay were removed by hand down to the top of the grey/brown stony clay. An undulating surface was uncovered, generally dipping to the north-east. On the surface a total of 53 artefacts were excavated of which 17 were biface manufacturing flakes all in fresh condition. The remainder consisted of flakes and cores, the majority of which were again in fresh condition, although others were considerably rolled. The fresh artefacts appeared to be *in situ* with the majority in the northern part of the area. However, there were no discrete concentrations or clear knapping scatters. The underlying deposits were not examined.

A new 2m x 3m area was selected (Area III, faunal area; Pl. 3.3b) adjacent to Pit 9 for excavation of the grey silt and clay, with the metre squares labelled A to F (Fig. 3.1; see Chapter 7, Fig. 7.3). The area was excavated carefully in 10cm spits, with the bone, antler and flint recorded where possible *in situ*. As large samples of small vertebrates had already been collected from the column samples, the primary aim was to collect larger vertebrates. For this reason all the sediment was collected and sieved at 5mm mesh, except that from square C, which was sieved at 2mm mesh size as a control. Four spits were removed during the season through the top part of the grey silt and clay (gritty clay), from which a total of 153 bone or antler fragments and 29 flint artefacts were excavated *in situ*.

Samples for pollen were taken alongside the column sample in Pit 4 and also from Pit 9 (north) adjacent to the excavation in Area III (see Chapter 4, Fig. 4.28; Chapter 7, Fig. 7.1). In addition, a sample containing

charcoal was taken from a black clay at the top of the grey silt and clay in Area III (see Chapter 14).

A further series of nine test pits (TP26-34) was excavated by mini-excavator in the centre of the clay pit (Fig. 3.1; see Chapter 4, Fig. 4.4). These revealed that the grey silt and clay was also present further into the centre of the pit, and was overlain by black clay and brown silt and clay. These were thought to be equivalent to the black clay and brown silt and clay in Area I. Augering in the base of the pits established that chalky diamicton lay beneath the sand, silt and clay at over 7m in depth from ground surface in TP34. This was plugged and temporarily abandoned until the following season.

Two sections (Area IV(1) and Area IV(2)) were cut on the northern edge of the pit (Fig. 3.1). Although the colour of the sediments varied between the two sections due to differential decalcification, they showed essentially the same sequence (see Chapter 4, Figs 4.21, 4.22). This consisted of grey silt and clay overlain by black clay and then by brown silt and clay. All the units were dipping sharply to the south. No artefacts were found in either section.

A further 1.5m wide section was cut on the south-east edge of the pit (Area IV(4); Fig. 3.1; Pl. 3.2b). A similar sequence to that in Area I was revealed; sand and gravel was overlain by a cobble layer, yellow silty sand, black clay and over 2m of brown silt and clay (see Chapter 4, Fig. 4.8). On the surface of and within the cobble layer, 47 artefacts were excavated of which 30 were biface manufacturing flakes (see Chapter 19).

THE 1994 SEASON

With the discovery of biface manufacturing flakes in Area IV(4) the main aim of this season was to expand and fully excavate the area. In addition, it was aimed to complete the excavations in Area III and Area V.

Area IV(4) was expanded to the west to form approximately a 7m x 3m area (Fig. 3.1; Pl. 3.2b). As with Area I, a 0.8m step was cut halfway down the section for safety reasons. The overlying brown silt and clay was removed by mini-excavator and the black clay and the yellow silty sand were removed rapidly by hand down to the top of the cobble layer (see Chapter 4, Fig. 4.8). The top of the cobble layer was carefully excavated and then removed as a further four spits of *c.*4cm each. The cobbles had been truncated on the northern edge of the area by clay digging, with the edge running parallel to the side of the pit. In total 634 artefacts were excavated from the area of which 238 were biface manufacturing flakes. In addition, a small biface was excavated from spit 4 on the final day. The remainder consisted of flakes, cores and flake tools. The condition of the artefacts was similar to those from Area I, varying from fresh to rolled (see Chapter 19).

A 1.5m x 1m area in the north-eastern part of Area IV(4) was taken down a further 50cm to reveal sand and gravel dipping to the north, underlying the cobble layer (see Chapter 4, Fig. 4.8). No artefacts were found from this context.

A further test pit and section (Area IV(5)) were cut midway between Area I and Area IV(4) to relate more closely the stratigraphies in the two areas (Fig. 3.1; see Chapter 4, Fig. 4.9). The same sequence of deposits was exposed, from sand and gravel at the base to the brown silt and clay at the top. However, in this area the lower units were dipping steeply to the north, suggesting that the location was further into the centre of the depression. Although 61 flakes and cores were found on and in the cobble layer, they were all considerably rolled and abraded, and there was no evidence of *in situ* knapping.

A test pit (TP35; Fig. 3.1) 16m to the west of Area IV(5) revealed backfill to a depth of 2m, but augering established that chalky diamicton lay at a depth of 4m overlain by grey silt and clay. After the season a 70cm wide trench was excavated between Area IV(5) and TP35 to relate the sand and gravel to the chalky diamicton (Fig. 3.1), but the relationship was not clear in this section (see Chapter 4 for a discussion of this relationship, Fig. 4.11).

In Area III (faunal area) the excavation continued through the grey silt and clay. Between two and four further spits (spits 5 to 8) were removed across the entire area through the gritty clay, the number of spits being dependant on the depth of the deposit within a particular square. An underlying shelly clay was only removed from the two central squares (C and D) as three spits (spits 8 to 10). As the unit was largely devoid of bone or antler, only Square C was retained for sieving. The underlying black clay was abundant in bone, and was removed as a single spit (spit 11) from both these squares and sieved. A total of 203 fragments of bone and antler and 24 flint artefacts were recorded *in situ* from the area (see Chapters 19, 20, 22 and 23). In addition, further mollusc samples were taken from the section on the west side of the area from the shelly clay (see Chapter 12).

In the 1993 season, Area V had been excavated down to the surface of the grey/brown stony clay. In 1994, a further 82 artefacts were excavated from this surface, of which 14 were biface manufacturing flakes. The grey/brown stony clay was then taken down a further 10cm across the whole area. Although 59 artefacts were recovered, the majority were rolled and only one was from biface manufacture. As the concentration of artefacts in both seasons had been on the northern edge of the area, the excavation was extended in two approximately 1.5m x 1.5m areas to the north-east and north-west (Fig. 3.1). An additional 33 artefacts were excavated from the surface of the grey/brown stony clay in these areas including 12 biface manufacturing flakes (see Chapter 20). The area was not excavated further.

Between Area V and Area III (west section), a third 4m x 1.5m area (Area V West) was excavated to trace the surface of the grey/brown stony clay. Again, the undulating surface could be clearly identified with a total of six artefacts recovered, including two biface manufacturing flakes.

The augerhole that had been started in TP34 the previous season, was continued with extra rods. This revealed fine grained sediments down to 15.7m below ground surface which were sitting on chalky diamicton, indicating that the channel was considerably deeper at this point (see Chapter 4, Fig. 4.4).

To the north-west of the clay pit, a series of test pits (TP36 - TP40) were excavated by JCB, parallel to the farm track (see Chapter 4, Fig. 4.3). These contributed to the understanding of the glacial sediments within the dry valley. This augmented the geophysical work undertaken between 1992 and 1995 (see Chapter 5). Additionally, throughout the six years new sections were regularly recorded at active gravel pits in the area. These included three pits to the east and north-east of East Farm Pit (Tilbrook's 1st, 2nd and 3rd pits - see Chapter 4, Fig. 4.3). Three sections were also cut in the Kidney Plantation Pit (see Chapter 4, Fig. 4.33).

4. QUATERNARY GEOLOGY OF EAST FARM BRICK PIT, BARNHAM AND THE SURROUNDING AREA

Simon G. Lewis

INTRODUCTION

In Chapter 2 a brief review is given of the history of research into the Quaternary geology and Palaeolithic archaeology of the Barnham district. Of particular importance in the development of ideas concerning this sequence is the work of T.T. Paterson, who conducted systematic excavations in the East Farm Pit and who also described a large number of adjacent exposures (Paterson 1937, 1942). This work enabled the main archaeological site (East Farm Pit) to be viewed within a stratigraphical framework for the area, which in turn contributed to the overall geological sequence for the Brecklands put forward by Paterson (1939) on the basis of his work over a wider geographical area.

The reinvestigation of this locality provides an opportunity to re-evaluate the work of Paterson in the light of current ideas concerning the Quaternary geological succession of East Anglia and the interpretation of Lower Palaeolithic artefact assemblages. A number of objectives for geological aspects of the 1989-1994 excavations were therefore identified: (1) to establish the precise sequence of deposits within the brick pit itself; (2) to locate the archaeological material within that sequence; (3) to investigate other nearby localities described by Paterson that were critical to the interpretation of the Brecklands sequence, (4) to establish the nature of the depositional processes that have operated at the site as a basis for the interpretation of the artefact assemblages, and (5) to place the archaeological site within the wider stratigraphical framework of the Barnham district, and in particular its relationship to the glacial sequence of the area, which arguably, since it probably relates to a single glacial episode within the Pleistocene, provides the best regional lithostratigraphical marker.

Geological investigations were undertaken at the site throughout the 1989-94 excavations. Numerous sections were created within the brick pit itself, and the details of the development of the excavation are provided in Chapter 3., In addition to these large sections a number of test pits were dug, both within and outside the brick pit, in order to investigate the lateral continuity of the various deposits. A total of ten test pits were dug within the old brick pit (TP 26-35), with a further 20 pits dug on other parts of East Farm (TP 1-15 and 36-40). Also within the brick pit a total of 21 hand-auger holes were completed. These were located over the floor of the pit, often in the base of test pits, as a significant thickness of back-fill covered the floor of the pit. Most of these auger holes reached chalky diamicton, but the thickness of this deposit could not be proved with this augering method. These data were supplemented with other records from temporary exposures created over the five-year period (TP 16-25 and TP 41-54) and by sections excavated in the few remaining small pits in the area (originally described by Paterson (1942) and numbered 9-17) and by larger exposures in three gravel pits that were operational between 1989 and 1994.

In addition to this work, a programme of geophysical investigations was undertaken in order to determine the geometry of the Chalk bedrock surface beneath the site. The details of this work are reported in Chapter 5.

REGIONAL CONTEXT OF THE SITE

The site lies within a part of East Anglia known as the Breckland. It is some 4km south of Thetford, and lies on the Euston Estate, within the limits of East Farm. The Breckland is an area of western Suffolk and Norfolk approximately bounded to the south by the River Lark, to the north by the River Wissey and to the west by the Fen edge and extending some 30km eastwards (Fig. 4.1). It is a low plateau that rises occasionally above 50m OD on the highest parts, and is generally between 30-50m OD. The adjacent low-lying Fen basin lies generally at 3-7m OD. The Breckland is dissected by a number of rivers which form a radial drainage pattern from central East Anglia. The major rivers draining the Breckland westwards into the Fen basin are the Rivers Lark, Little Ouse and the Wissey (Fig. 4.1).

The area is underlain by Cretaceous Upper Chalk, with Upper Jurassic Oxford Clay and Gault in the west of the region flooring the Fen basin (Fig. 4.2). The regional dip of the strata is at a low angle towards the east. There is a discontinuous cover of Quaternary sediments over the region; however the area has not been mapped in detail since the end of the last century (Whitaker *et al.* 1891). The heathland soils and vegetation that characterise the Breckland are a consequence of the tills, sands and gravels and extensive, but thin, coversands that cover much of the area.

The site itself lies within the valley of the Little Ouse River, which flows westwards into the Fens, close to the confluence with the Black Bourn, a small south bank tributary that joins the Little Ouse River on Barnham Heath. The site lies 1km to the south of the river and it is separated from it by a west-east running Chalk ridge, 35-39m OD on which East Farm stands.

The brick pit lies at the head of a small dry, re-entrant valley that slopes to the west, although the site itself lies slightly to the south of the axis of the dry valley (Fig. 4.3). The ground surface at this point is *c*.38m OD.

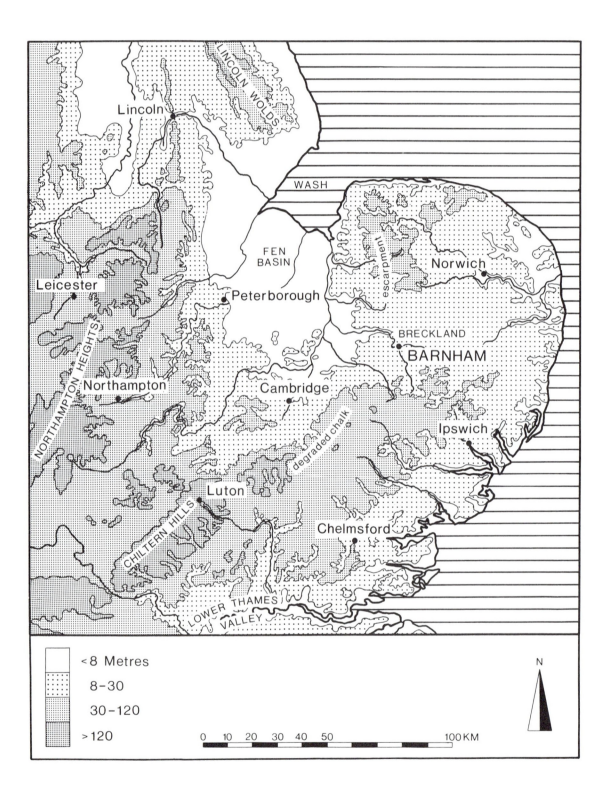

Fig. 4.1. Relief and drainage of eastern England.

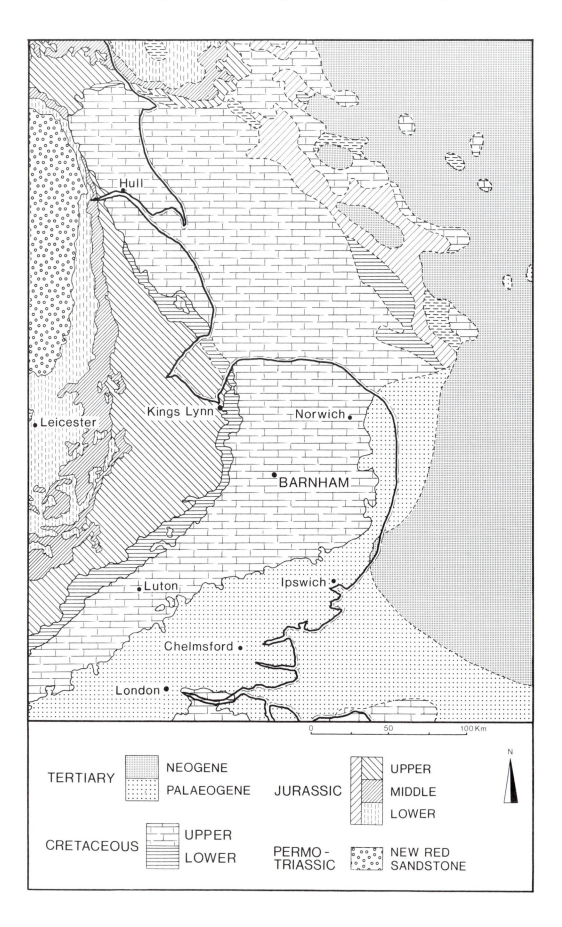

Fig. 4.2. Geology of eastern England and the adjacent parts of the North Sea basin.

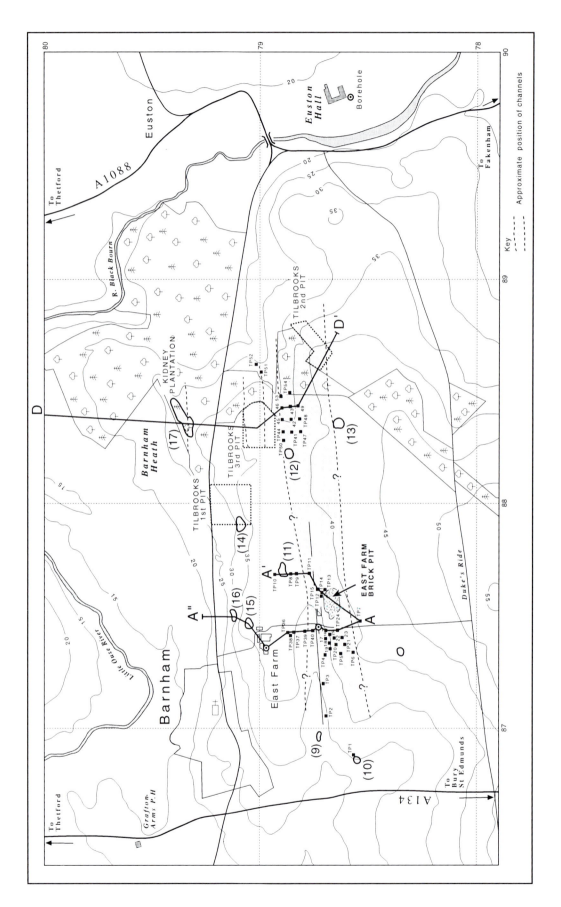

Fig. 4.3. Map showing position of East Farm Pit and sections, test pits, old pits (numbered following Paterson 1942) and gravel quarries investigated during the course of the 1989-94 excavations in the area of East Farm. Dashed lines show the approximate position of the channel margin

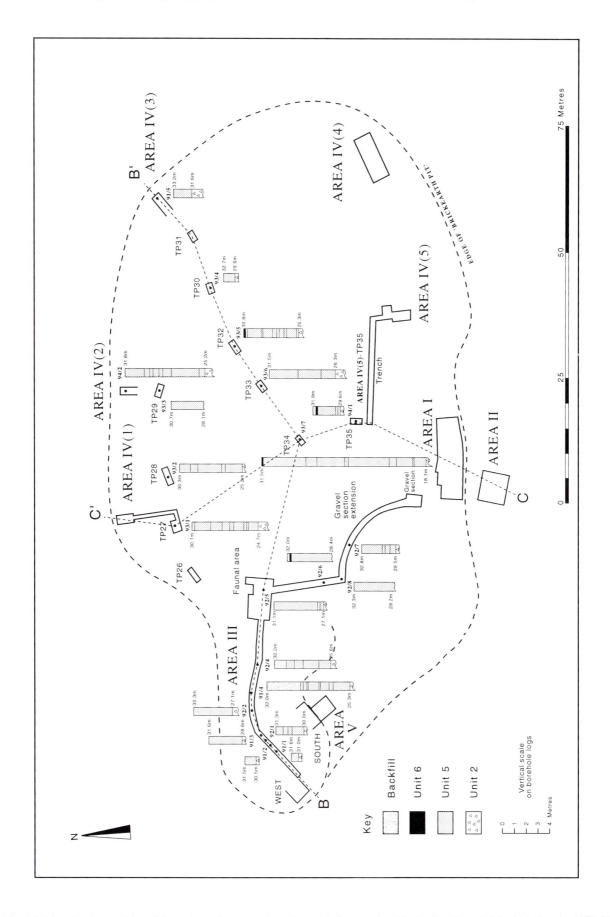

Fig. 4.4. Map showing position of the main sections, test pits and auger holes completed in the East Farm brick pit during the 1989-94 excavations.

THE GEOLOGICAL SEQUENCE OF EAST FARM PIT - A HISTORICAL CONTEXT

T.T. Paterson's excavations in the brick pit, conducted in 1933 and reported in 1937 (Paterson 1937), revealed a sequence of Quaternary deposits on the south side of the brick pit. Further details on the site are given in his PhD thesis (Paterson 1942). The basic succession that was established from this work for East Farm brick pit (using Paterson's bed lettering system) is:

(f)   dark red coarse sand, with many pieces of flint (*c.* 0.6m),

(e)   reddish-brown loam (*c.* 3m), containing Acheulian artefacts,

(d)   grey-brown sandy loam (*c.* 1m),

(c)   yellowish sandy clay, with dark brown to black seams (*c.* 0.3m),

(b)   grey brown sandy clay (*c.* 0.3m),

(a)   gravel, flint pebbles with coarse sand, the gravel surface dips towards the north-east, many flakes were recovered from the upper layers of gravel and from its surface, the gravel was proved to a thickness of *c.*19.5m in a hand dug well, but was not bottomed.

These observations generally accord with those of Skertchly (in Whitaker *et al.* 1891), who also records the presence of shells and bones in the sediments.

It is worth noting at this point how Paterson integrated this site into his geological sequence for the Brecklands as a whole. Paterson (1937) illustrates a schematic sequence for the Barnham area, based upon his research in the East Farm Pit and observations in other adjacent pits. In this sequence, the deposits containing artefacts and faunal remains, and considered by Paterson to have been formed during an interglacial, are sandwiched between two 'boulder clays' (tills). This is one of the cornerstones of Paterson's interpretation and is based upon the differentiation of two distinct till units: the first (lower, blue coloured till) lacking Bunter (quartzite and quartz) erratics and the second (brown coloured till) which contains many Bunter pebbles. The lower till underlies the 'loams' (Paterson's beds (d) and (e), see above), a relationship which was inferred from the observation that the 'loams' in the East Farm Pit overlie gravel which contains no Bunter pebbles and from observations of gravel similar to bed (a) in the brick pit overlying 'blue boulder clay' (the lower till) in a pit (his pit 10; Fig. 4.3) some 700m to the west. The brown, Bunter pebble-bearing till was considered to post-date the loams and their associated archaeology on the basis of: (1) the incorporation of loam into the till giving it its brown colour; and (2) the assertion that this till could be traced from the top of the ridge to the north of the brick pit to a point a few metres from the edge of the pit where it passed laterally into 'coarse red brown sand with angular grains and flints' (Paterson 1942, 14), which was equated with bed (f) in the brick pit sequence. It should be noted that this relationship was demonstrated only by hand-augering down the slope, not through excavated sections. Nowhere were these two tills seen in direct superposition in a single section, though they were observed in close proximity in pits 9 and 10 to the west of the brick pit (Paterson 1942, 22).

Paterson (1939) developed these ideas and illustrated the interpretation of the Breckland sequence as a whole. In this stratigraphy the brown till at Barnham was referred to as 'Middle boulder clay' and the Barnham sequence formed the lower part of a complex geological succession comprising three 'boulder clays' (tills) and two interglacial sequences. The lower was represented at Barnham and the upper at Elveden, a site some 7km to the west of Barnham (Paterson & Fagg 1940). This was the basis on which the Barnham and Elveden sequences and their contained archaeological material were differentiated. The interpretation of the Barnham sequence by Paterson, in particular the recognition of two tills at this locality separated by temperate 'loams', was therefore crucial to his overall interpretation of the geological sequence of the Breckland and to the interpretation of the archaeological record of the region.

Subsequent work on the chalky tills of East Anglia by Baden-Powell (1948), who visited the Barnham locality with Paterson in 1939, attempted to incorporate Paterson's succession into the regional scheme. Baden-Powell (1948) suggested that the uppermost of the three glacial deposits at Barnham was equivalent to the Gipping till which was believed to be present in eastern Suffolk. The middle 'brown boulder clay' was tentatively equated with the Lowestoft till and the lower 'blue boulder clay' with the Cromer till. All three were considered to predate the Hunstanton glaciation. The widely held view currently, that there is only one chalky till in eastern England (Bristow & Cox 1973; Perrin *et al.* 1979), has created a problem in the Breckland where a number of sites have been considered to show two chalky tills separated by non-glacial (temperate) deposits. Among these, High Lodge (Lewis 1992) and Beeches Pit (Preece *et al.* 1991) have been reinvestigated and the presence of an upper till has been examined. In both cases no convincing evidence for an upper till can be found. East Farm, Barnham is another such site where two chalky tills were postulated by Paterson (1942).

THE GEOLOGICAL SEQUENCE FROM THE 1989-1994 EXCAVATIONS

A number of areas were excavated within the old brick pit (Fig. 4.4). These sections (Fig. 3.1), together with test pits and augers holes in the pit (Fig. 4.4) and information from the surrounding area (Figs 4.3, 4.5) provide the basis for the following account of the Quaternary succession.

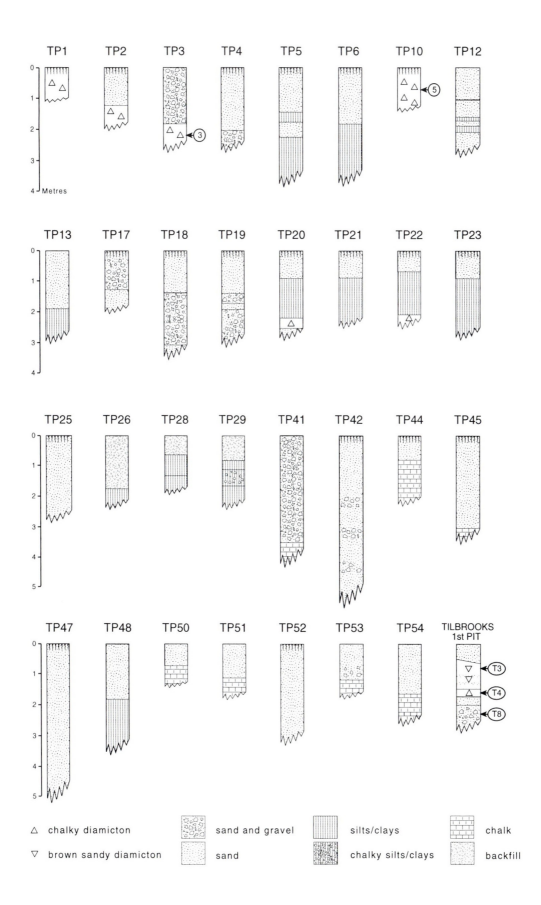

Fig. 4.5. Logs of trial pits not shown elsewhere and log of section in Tilbrook's 1st Pit. For locations of sections see Figs 4.3 and 4.4.

The work carried out between 1989 and 1994 has added significantly to the available data on the East Farm Pit succession and has indicated that a more complex sequence exists both vertically and laterally within the pit. It is now possible to recognise 7 major units present within the old brick pit. These are:

Unit 7	brown silt and clay ('brickearth')		
Unit 6	black clay		
		Unit 5e	yellow silty sand
		Unit 5d	grey/brown stony clay
Unit 5	silt and clay	Unit 5c	grey silt and clay
		Unit 5b	grey chalky clay
		Unit 5a	brown silt and clay
Unit 4	cobble layer		
Unit 3	brown diamicton		
Unit 2	chalky diamicton		
Unit 1	sand and gravel		

The sequence within the pit is highly variable and the complete stratigraphy, indicated above, cannot be observed in any one section. However, using the available sections, trenches, test pits and auger holes the stratigraphical succession can be established. The exact relationship of the lowest two units, the chalky diamicton and the sand and gravel, remains problematic however. This will be discussed further below.

Morphology of the Chalk surface

Chalk bedrock was nowhere exposed within the old brick pit. It is therefore not possible to determine in detail the geometry of the Chalk surface beneath the Quaternary sediments in the pit. The available information from the auger holes, completed during the current investigations (Fig. 4.4) and from other sources, confirms that a thick series of Quaternary deposits is present beneath the brick pit. The deepest auger hole within the pit (BH 93/7) proved some 13.5m of fine-grained material (Unit 5), ending in chalky diamicton (Unit 2); the thickness of the latter unit was not proved. This, together with the uncorroborated report of a hand-dug well commissioned by Paterson (1942, 12) to determine the thickness of the gravel, which was sunk some 20m beneath the floor of the pit, indicates that the Chalk surface at this point must lie below 25.6m OD (BH 93/7), and probably several metres lower. A water well adjacent to farm buildings close to the brick pit (Fig. 4.3) proved Chalk at *c*.16m OD (Paterson 1942). A further well on top of the ridge at East Farm (Fig. 4.3), 300m north of the brick pit, proved Chalk at *c*.38m OD (Woodland 1942). Chalk is also found at or near the surface 400m to the south of the site, where there is an old Chalk pit. These data indicate that the deposits exposed in the brick pit occupy a deep depression in the

Chalk bedrock, that is aligned in a west-east direction, coincident with the alignment (though not necessarily the slope) of the dry valley in which the East Farm brick pit sits. The geometry of the Chalk surface has been investigated using geophysical methods, and the details of this work are discussed elsewhere in this volume (Chapter 5). The suggested position of the channel in the Chalk surface is shown in Figure 4.3.

Unit 1: sand and gravel

Unit 1 has been recorded within the brick pit in Area I, beneath the excavated surface (Fig. 4.6) and in the gravel section adjacent to the main part of Area I (Fig. 4.7). It has also been exposed in Area IV(4) (Fig. 4.8) and Area IV(5) (Fig. 4.9). Outside the brick pit, sand and gravel was seen in a number of test pits (TP 3, 4, 16, 17, 18, 19, 25, 37 and 38) and in an old pit on the northern side of the 'Farm ridge' (Paterson's pit 15) (Fig. 4.3). The geometry of this unit and its relationship to Unit 2 is poorly understood. In the interim report on these excavations, Ashton *et al.* (1994a) suggested that the lowest unit in the sequence was a chalky diamicton. In that report a cross section through the deposits in the brick pit showed the sand and gravel to overlie the chalky diamicton, and occupy a deep, steep sided channel feature of unknown depth to Chalk. Paterson (1937, 1942) also considered that the sand and gravel, which is believed to be at least *c*.20m in thickness, post-dated the diamicton (his lower 'blue boulder clay'), though there was no section in which this could be conclusively demonstrated (except possibly pit 9).

Given this interpretation, the geometry of the sand and gravel unit within the brick pit remains problematic because of the considerable thickness of the unit, established by Paterson (1942), to be some 20m, and the limited lateral extent of the unit that this interpretation allows. Investigations during the 1993-94 seasons demonstrated that if this gravel indeed occupies a channel cut into the chalky diamicton, this can be no more than 30-40m wide, its margins lying between Area II and TP 35 (Fig. 4.4).

An alternative interpretation of the sequence that is consistent with the available information is that the main part of the sand and gravel underlies the chalky diamicton and is a more extensive unit beneath the pit and outside its bounds, overlain by chalky diamicton. The latter deposit was proved in many auger holes, but could not be penetrated due to its very stony and consolidated nature. Chalky diamicton was observed to lie directly on Chalk in only one place: TP 39 (Fig. 4.3), which is in a marginal position to the channel feature. Sand and gravel was observed to overlie chalky diamicton only in the trench linking Area IV(5) with TP 35 (Fig. 4.11), where it consists of *c*.1m thick unit of gravel, which thins out completely towards the east

sample number	qtz	qtzte	sst	glauc sst	Carb chert	Rhaxella chert	flint	chalk	lst	soft sst	ironst	Jurassic shell	ign	meta	other	n
Unit 1	**sands and gravels**															
3	1.7	2.7	0.0	0.0	0.7	1.2	92.5	0.0	0.0	0.0	0.5	0.0	0.0	0.0	0.5	402
21	2.0	2.4	1.6	0.0	2.0	0.8	87.1	0.0	0.0	0.4	0.4	0.0	0.0	0.0	3.5	255
22	4.0	3.8	0.5	0.0	2.4	1.2	86.2	0.0	0.0	0.0	0.0	0.0	0.0	0.0	1.9	421
25	3.2	7.9	2.0	0.0	1.6	0.8	83.4	0.0	0.0	0.0	0.0	0.0	0.0	0.0	1.0	495
26	5.1	10.0	2.6	0.0	2.3	0.3	76.8	0.0	0.0	0.0	0.0	0.0	0.3	0.0	2.6	311
148	0.0	1.2	1.2	0.0	0.0	0.0	16.3	81.4	0.0	0.0	0.0	0.0	0.0	0.0	0.0	172
	0.0	*6.3*	*6.3*	*0.0*	*0.0*	*0.0*	*87.5*	*(437.5)*	*0.0*	*0.0*	*0.0*	*0.0*	*0.0*	*0.0*	*0.0*	
245	2.6	5.5	1.2	0.0	3.2	0.3	83.3	0.0	0.0	0.0	0.6	0.0	0.0	0.0	3.5	347
501	1.5	5.4	0.0	0.0	0.0	0.0	89.3	3.9	0.0	0.0	0.0	0.0	0.0	0.0	0.0	205
	1.5	*5.6*	*0.0*	*0.0*	*0.0*	*0.0*	*92.9*	*(4.1)*	*0.0*	*0.0*	*0.0*	*0.0*	*0.0*	*0.0*	*0.0*	
504	4.1	5.4	0.0	0.0	0.4	0.0	74.8	13.5	0.2	0.0	0.0	0.0	0.0	0.0	1.7	539
	4.7	*6.2*	*0.0*	*0.0*	*0.4*	*0.0*	*86.5*	*(15.7)*	*0.2*	*0.0*	*0.0*	*0.0*	*0.0*	*0.0*	*1.9*	
505	5.2	9.8	0.0	0.0	1.9	1.0	61.8	15.2	2.4	0.0	0.5	0.5	1.0	0.0	0.8	594
	6.2	*11.5*	*0.0*	*0.0*	*2.2*	*1.2*	*72.8*	*(17.9)*	*2.8*	*0.0*	*0.6*	*0.6*	*1.2*	*0.0*	*1.0*	
508	6.8	13.5	0.0	0.9	3.6	0.0	72.1	0.0	0.0	0.0	0.0	0.0	0.9	0.5	1.8	222
514	3.0	4.5	0.7	0.0	2.2	1.5	78.7	0.0	0.0	0.0	0.0	0.0	0.7	0.0	8.6	267
515	1.1	0.8	2.1	0.0	2.7	2.4	86.9	0.0	0.0	0.0	0.0	0.0	0.0	0.0	4.0	373
516	1.2	4.1	0.5	0.0	2.4	1.2	79.1	0.0	0.0	0.0	0.0	0.0	0.0	0.2	11.3	417
517	3.7	8.7	0.8	0.0	0.8	0.8	81.9	0.0	0.0	0.0	0.0	0.0	0.4	0.0	3.1	518
518	8.9	9.9	1.0	0.0	2.5	0.0	77.2	0.0	0.0	0.0	0.0	0.0	0.0	0.0	0.5	202
Unit 2	**chalky diamicton**															
1	0.7	2.2	1.5	0.0	0.7	0.0	14.0	74.3	3.7	0.0	0.0	2.9	0.0	0.0	0.0	136
	2.9	*8.6*	*5.7*	*0.0*	*2.9*	*0.0*	*54.3*	*(288.6)*	*14.3*	*0.0*	*0.0*	*11.4*	*0.0*	*0.0*	*0.0*	
2	1.3	3.4	0.5	0.0	0.6	0.2	27.9	49.2	0.2	0.0	2.1	0.0	0.0	0.0	14.6	616
	2.6	*6.7*	*1.0*	*0.0*	*1.3*	*0.3*	*55.0*	*(96.8)*	*0.3*	*0.0*	*4.2*	*0.0*	*0.0*	*0.0*	*28.8*	
4	19.9	21.9	0.3	0.0	1.9	0.0	25.2	26.3	0.4	0.0	1.8	0.0	0.0	0.0	2.4	739
	27.0	*29.7*	*0.4*	*0.0*	*2.6*	*0.0*	*34.1*	*(35.6)*	*0.6*	*0.0*	*2.4*	*0.0*	*0.0*	*0.0*	*3.3*	
10	0.0	0.0	0.0	0.0	0.0	0.0	6.6	89.5	1.3	0.0	0.0	2.6	0.0	0.0	0.0	76
	0.0	*0.0*	*0.0*	*0.0*	*0.0*	*0.0*	*62.5*	*(850.0)*	*12.5*	*0.0*	*0.0*	*25.0*	*0.0*	*0.0*	*0.0*	
12	1.1	0.7	1.1	0.2	0.0	0.4	23.6	39.4	2.0	0.0	0.2	0.7	0.0	0.0	30.6	457
	1.8	*1.1*	*1.8*	*0.4*	*0.0*	*0.7*	*39.0*	*(65.0)*	*3.2*	*0.0*	*0.4*	*1.1*	*0.0*	*0.0*	*50.5*	
37	0.6	0.0	0.2	0.3	0.2	0.1	7.0	89.0	1.1	0.0	0.9	0.2	0.0	0.0	0.5	1026
	5.3	*0.0*	*1.8*	*2.7*	*1.8*	*0.9*	*63.7*	*(808.0)*	*9.7*	*0.0*	*8.0*	*1.8*	*0.0*	*0.0*	*4.4*	
502	2.5	5.6	0.2	0.0	0.7	0.0	12.0	77.3	0.3	0.0	0.3	0.0	0.0	0.0	1.1	1045
	11.0	*24.9*	*0.8*	*0.0*	*3.0*	*0.0*	*52.7*	*(340.9)*	*1.3*	*0.0*	*1.3*	*0.0*	*0.0*	*0.0*	*5.1*	
503	3.5	5.4	0.2	0.0	1.3	0.2	47.9	39.8	0.0	0.0	0.8	0.0	0.0	0.0	0.8	997
	5.8	*9.0*	*0.3*	*0.0*	*2.2*	*0.3*	*79.7*	*(66.2)*	*0.0*	*0.0*	*1.3*	*0.0*	*0.0*	*0.0*	*1.3*	
506	0.3	1.4	0.7	0.0	1.0	0.0	11.8	75.1	0.7	0.0	0.0	1.4	0.0	0.0	7.6	289
	1.4	*5.6*	*2.8*	*0.0*	*4.2*	*0.0*	*47.2*	*(301.4)*	*2.8*	*0.0*	*0.0*	*5.6*	*0.0*	*0.0*	*30.6*	
507	0.3	0.4	0.9	0.0	0.3	0.0	9.3	87.1	0.4	0.0	0.9	0.3	0.1	0.0	0.0	680
	2.3	*3.4*	*6.8*	*0.0*	*2.3*	*0.0*	*71.6*	*(672.7)*	*3.4*	*0.0*	*6.8*	*2.3*	*1.1*	*0.0*	*0.0*	
Unit 3	**brown diamicton**															
11	1.3	3.1	3.1	0.6	0.6	3.1	80.5	0.0	0.0	0.0	0.0	0.0	1.3	0.0	6.3	159
20	4.2	4.2	4.9	0.0	3.5	0.0	77.5	0.0	0.0	0.0	0.0	0.0	0.0	0.0	5.6	142
166	1.4	1.4	2.8	0.0	4.2	1.4	64.8	0.0	0.0	2.8	16.9	0.0	0.0	0.0	4.2	71
244	8.6	3.1	9.8	0.0	3.7	0.0	73.0	0.0	0.0	0.0	0.6	0.0	0.0	0.0	1.2	163
511	3.9	4.5	1.5	0.0	1.8	0.6	85.9	0.0	0.0	0.0	0.0	0.0	0.2	0.1	1.5	1089
512	2.5	3.3	1.2	0.0	1.8	0.9	89.2	0.0	0.0	0.0	0.1	0.0	0.1	0.1	0.9	1291
513	2.9	3.7	1.3	0.0	2.5	1.3	87.3	0.0	0.0	0.0	0.0	0.0	0.3	0.0	0.7	944
Unit 5d	**grey/brown stony clay**															
164	3.5	1.7	0.3	0.0	1.2	0.6	92.2	0.0	0.0	0.0	0.0	0.0	0.0	0.0	0.6	346
167	3.7	6.1	0.0	0.0	2.1	0.8	87.2	0.0	0.0	0.0	0.0	0.0	0.0	0.0	0.0	374

Table 4.1. Clast lithological analysis of deposits at East Farm Barnham. 11.2-16.0mm size fraction counted from sands and gravels, 8.0-16.0mm fraction counted from diamicton units. Percentages calculated excluding the non-durable chalk component are also shown (in italics) for those samples containing chalk pebbles.

of the section and has also been truncated to the west and is not present in TP 35 (Fig. 4.11). The lack of data concerning the configuration of the Chalk rockhead and the geometry of Units 1 and 2 allows only a tentative conclusion to be drawn concerning their relationship. This revised interpretation may be preferred because: (i) it can better accommodate the significant thickness of sand and gravel suggested by Paterson and proved in the water well adjacent to the barn (*c.* 15m); (ii) it obviates the need for a rather complex geometry to be invoked for this unit to explain its distribution in and around the brick pit; and (iii) it is in accord with the reconstruction of the bedrock geometry determined by geophysical investigations (Chapter 5) and the nature of the sediments infilling the channel, which appear to be dominantly coarse grained sand and gravel facies.

Within the brick pit the character of the sand and gravel is quite variable. In Area I, the unit occurs at the base of the exposed sequence (Figs 4.6, 4.10), where it consists of beds of medium to coarse gravel typically 20-30cm in thickness and thinner facies of medium-coarse, occasionally pebbly sand. The beds are inclined, in some cases steeply, towards the north-east, with evidence of displacement and near-vertical contacts. The apparent disturbance of the units has largely obscured any primary bedding in these deposits though in places the sand units are clearly sorted. In the adjacent section, Area I (gravel section) (Fig. 4.7), the gravel is better exposed, and shows similar properties including a uniform dip of the beds towards the north-east. Again evidence of sorting of the finer sediment is visible. The colour of the sand facies and interstitial sand in the gravel facies is variable ranging from light olive brown (2.5Y 5/6) to dark brown (7.5YR 3/4). The upper contact of the unit is complex. In Area I (gravel section) the upper contact dips steeply towards the north-east. In the main part of Area I the contact with the overlying units shows displacement and disturbance, again with a general dip towards the north-east (Fig. 4.10).

The particle size distribution of the unit shows considerable variability. The gravel facies range from very coarse cobble gravel with little interstitial sand to sandy gravel (Fig. 4.12), the gravel fraction ranging from 35.4-97.9%, with 0.7-59.75% sand. All samples have only a very small proportion of fine (<0.063mm) material. Sandy facies within this unit also show a variable particle size distribution (Fig. 4.12), being generally well-sorted and consist predominantly of medium sand. Occasional beds of fine sand also occur within the unit (sample 181).

Analysis of the clast lithology of the gravel (11.2-16mm fraction; Table 4.1) indicates that it is dominated by flint (72-93%). The other frequently occurring lithologies are quartz, quartzite, sandstone, chert (probably Carboniferous) and *Rhaxella* chert (Table 4.1). Chalk (which, as a non-durable, locally-derived rock type has been excluded from the calculation of percentages shown in italics in Table 4.1) does not occur in any of the samples of this unit from within the brick pit itself.

Sand and gravel has been observed in test pits elsewhere on East Farm (Fig. 4.3). In these exposures it is again medium to coarse and flint-dominated gravel. The clast lithology (samples 501, 504, 505) is very similar to the gravel within the brick pit, though chalk is present in these samples. Sample 505 was obtained from poorly exposed gravel in an old pit on the northern side of the 'Farm ridge'. This pit was described by Paterson as showing coarse conglomerate gravel, with flints up to 30cm in diameter. On the basis of its different character and topographic position, this may be a different unit to the sand and gravel seen in and around the brick pit.

This sand and gravel unit is interpreted as of fluvial origin. Given the paucity of good, undisturbed exposures in this unit, detailed consideration of its mode of deposition and palaeoflow direction is difficult. However, on the basis of the sedimentology of the deposits, the clast lithology and the association with a deep, steep-sided channel cut into the underlying Chalk, a glaciofluvial origin seems likely. Lithologically the gravel is typical of glaciofluvial gravel in the region, which contains a characteristic suite of lithologies indicative of glacial inputs to the region (Bridgland & Lewis 1991; Lewis 1992; Bridgland *et al.* 1995). These include *Rhaxella* chert, derived from Jurassic rocks from north Yorkshire, reworked shell fragments and limestones from Jurassic outcrops in the Midlands, glauconitic (Spilsby) sandstone from the Lower Cretaceous in the area of the Wash basin and occasional igneous and metamorphic rocks. The absence of chalk clasts in the samples from Area I may be the result of decalcification.

The gravel fills a deep channel in the Chalk bedrock, which may have formed as a result of sub-glacial meltwater erosion. Such 'tunnel valley' features are common in East Anglia (Woodland 1970) and are frequently extremely deep, reaching depths several tens of metres below Ordnance Datum (for example a borehole at Euston (TL 898786) showed till and sand and gravel to a depth of -50m OD; Woodland 1970) and are also often characterised by an undulating long profile, probably the result of the high hydrostatic pressures of sub-glacial meltwater. It is possible that the feature at Barnham is a continuation of that at Euston, some 2.5km to the east, though Paterson considered that they were two separate features, the incision of which was separated by the deposition of a till unit.

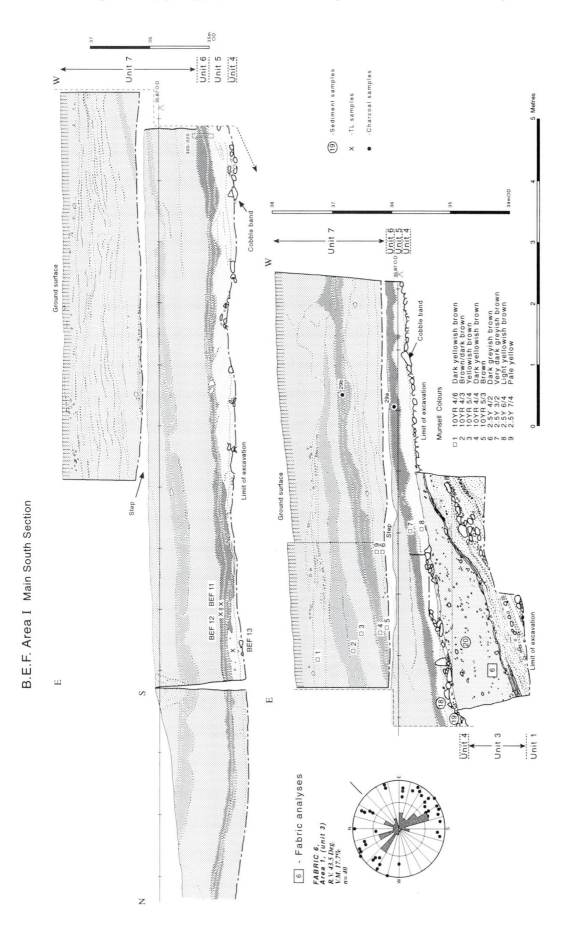

Fig. 4.6. Area I main south section.

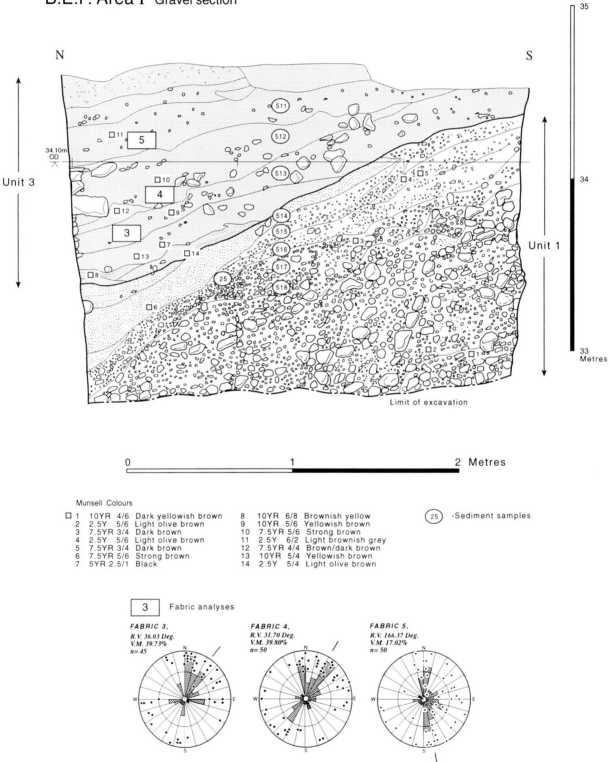

B.E.F. Area I Gravel section

Fig. 4.7. Area I gravel section.

Munsell Colours

1	10YR 4/6	Dark yellowish brown	8	10YR 6/8	Brownish yellow	
2	2.5Y 5/6	Light olive brown	9	10YR 5/6	Yellowish brown	
3	7.5YR 3/4	Dark brown	10	7.5YR 5/6	Strong brown	
4	2.5Y 5/6	Light olive brown	11	2.5Y 6/2	Light brownish grey	
5	7.5YR 3/4	Dark brown	12	7.5YR 4/4	Brown/dark brown	
6	7.5YR 5/6	Strong brown	13	10YR 5/4	Yellowish brown	
7	5YR 2.5/1	Black	14	2.5Y 5/4	Light olive brown	

(25) - Sediment samples

3 Fabric analyses

FABRIC 3,
R.V. 36.03 Deg.
V.M. 39.73%
n = 45

FABRIC 4,
R.V. 31.70 Deg.
V.M. 39.80%
n = 50

FABRIC 5,
R.V. 166.37 Deg.
V.M. 17.02%
n = 50

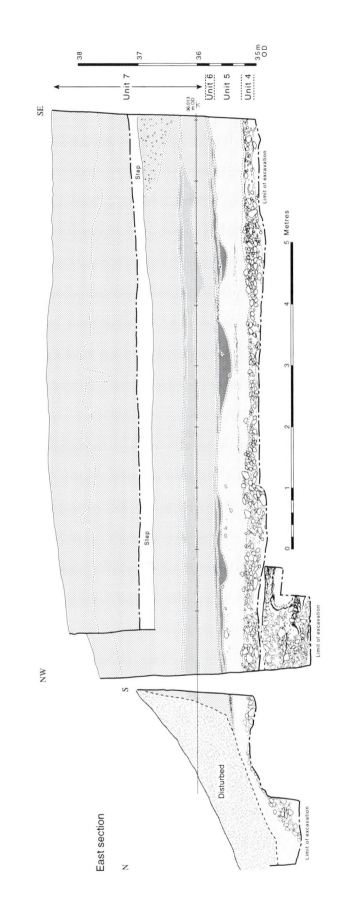

Fig. 4.8. Area IV(4) main section and east section.

Unit 2: chalky diamicton

This unit consists of predominantly chalk and flint pebbles in a calcareous clay-rich matrix. The base of this unit was not seen in any exposures or auger holes within the pit, and it was seen to rest on Chalk bedrock in only one test pit (TP 39; Fig. 4.3). Chalky diamicton has been observed in a number of sections in and around the brick pit and in test pits and auger holes. Within the brick pit itself, chalky diamicton occurs in section only in Area III (south and west sections) (Figs 4.13, 4.14). Augering in the base of the brick pit has recovered material that resembles chalky diamicton from varying depths beneath a cover of silts and clays (Unit 5), (though the problems of recovering sufficiently large samples using this method make a confident interpretation of the material difficult).

To the south of the pit chalky diamicton occurs 5m below the surface immediately adjacent to the pit in Area II. Some 100m to the south of the brick pit, in TP 7 (Fig. 4.3) chalky diamicton occurs close to the surface, and is at the surface for some distance to the south of this point, though Chalk bedrock crops out by the time the Duke's Ride is reached. To the north of the site chalky diamicton has been proved at depth in a number of test pits. TP 8, 9 and 10 near the crest of the 'Farm ridge' all showed chalky diamicton near the surface (beneath plough soil), and TP 11 at the foot of the slope proved chalky diamicton 1.7m below the surface. The traverse (A-A^1) of test pits from the top of the ridge to the brick pit (Fig. 4.15) is in a very similar position to the auger hole traverse reported by Paterson (1942). This was critical in the differentiation of two 'boulder clay' (till) units at the locality, and is discussed further below. West of the brick pit chalky diamicton is again encountered in TP 1, adjacent to Paterson's pit 10, in which 'blue boulder clay' was recorded (Paterson 1942), and again in TP 2 and 3 (Fig. 4.3).

On the basis of the available evidence it is possible to conclude that the surface of the chalky diamicton forms a depression aligned west to east, coincident with the alignment of the dry valley (Fig. 4.16). Within the brick pit the surface of the chalky diamicton slopes from the northern and southern edges, with the deepest point identified in BH 93/7 at 18.1m OD (Fig. 4.16). More generally over the area of the pit the diamicton surface lies at between 26-29m OD, rising steeply at the flanks of the pit; on the southern side it is present at 34.3m OD in Area II and at *c*.33m OD in Area III (west). On the northern side the surface rises to 31.6m OD beneath Area IV(3) (Fig 4.16).

The matrix of the diamicton is variable in colour, being dominantly of 2.5Y hues and generally pale yellow (2.5Y 8/4) to brownish yellow (2.5Y 6/4) in colour. In TP 10 the matrix is pale brown (10YR 7/4). Apart from this observation, no clear distinction can be made between 'blue' and 'brown' facies as suggested by Paterson (1942). In Area III (west) the upper part of the diamicton is decalcified, forming a sub-horizontal layer and also infilling a vertical 'pipe' feature (Fig. 4.14). This decalcified facies is dark yellowish brown (10YR 3/4) in colour.

The particle size distribution of the chalky diamicton shows a generally poorly sorted character (Fig. 4.17) indicating that the unit is a silt/clay diamicton with gravel sized material in a sandy silt/clay matrix, with mean values of 13.4% gravel, 30.0% sand, 32.4% silt and 24.3% clay. Samples 2 (from TP 2) and 4 (from TP 9) show remarkable similarity in their particle size distribution, though the sampling points were some 750m apart (Fig. 4.3). Apart from this there is little discernible pattern in these data.

The clast lithology (8-16mm fraction) of the chalky diamicton (Table 4.1) shows that the deposit is dominated by locally derived flint and non-durable chalk pebbles. Among the other lithologies present are quartz (up to 27%, though more typically between 1.8-11.0%), quartzite (up to 29.7%, though more typically between 1.1-9.0%), sandstone, Carboniferous chert, *Rhaxella* chert, limestone, ironstone and Jurassic shell fragments (Table 4.1). Two samples have high proportions of quartz and quartzite, ultimately derived from Triassic rocks in the Midlands (samples 4, 502).

Two fabric analyses of 50 pebbles each were undertaken on this unit in Area II (Fig. 4.19). Sections in Area III were deemed unsuitable because of the evidence of solution and disturbance which may have affected the disposition of clasts. Fabrics 1 and 2 in Area II both show a strongly developed pattern (Fig. 4.19), with resultant vectors (and vector magnitudes) of 110.5° (80.4%) and 116.6° (73.6%) respectively. Both these results are statistically significant at the 0.01 level. Both fabrics show a unimodal distribution with most of the down-dip orientations clustered in the 090°-180 ° quadrant (Fig. 4.19). The fabric data is consistent with the regional pattern of ice movement established by West and Donner (1956), in particular the west to east direction of movement may be related to the earlier of two distinct phases of ice movement, referred to as the Lowestoft advance by West and Donner (1956). Similar regional patterns were reported by Ehlers *et al.* (1987).

On the basis of this information the chalky diamicton is interpreted as a glacial deposit, most probably a lodgement till formed at the base of a glacier moving across the location in a west-north-west to east-south-east direction. The limited information on the diamicton recovered from the auger holes allows only a tentative inference to be made, that this material was deposited by the same process as the chalky diamicton seen in Areas II and III. The ice-sheet deposited till over the entire area, on top of the sand and gravel which fills the sub-glacial channel.

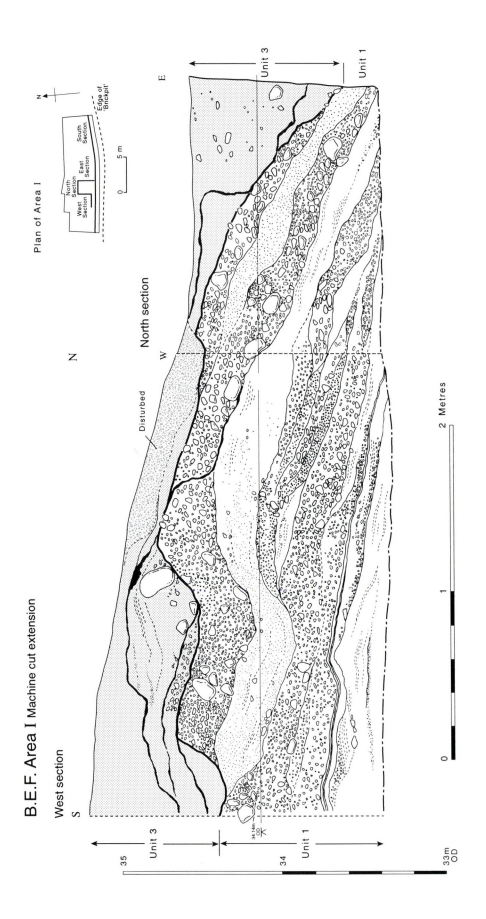

Fig. 4.10a. Area I machine cut extension, west and north sections.

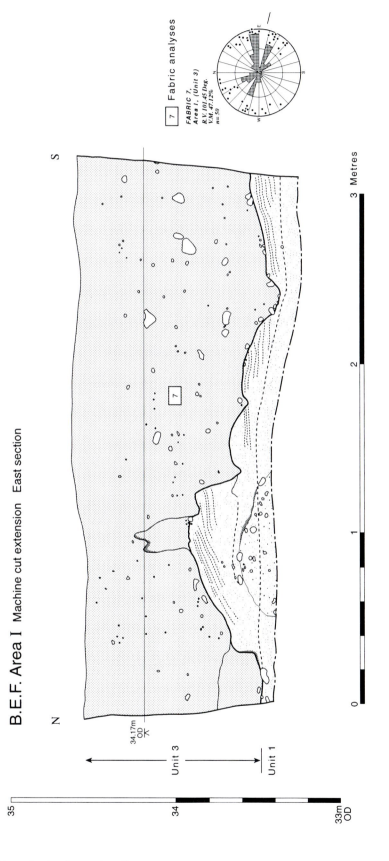

Fig. 4.10b. Area I machine cut extension, east section.

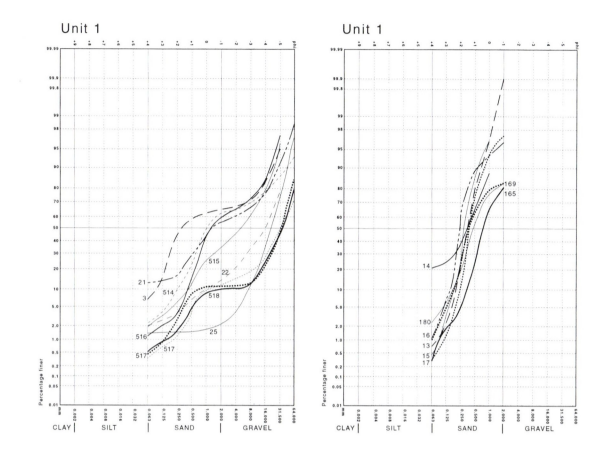

Fig. 4.12. Particle size distributions, Unit 1.

Paterson (1942) argued that two facies of chalky till could be differentiated at Barnham, one blue without Bunter pebbles, the other brown, with Bunter pebbles. On the basis of this evidence it is possible to confirm only that a facies of till containing a greater proportion of Bunter quartz and quartzite (though they are present in the majority of the samples) can be identified (samples 4 and 37), and that this facies appears to occur on the northern side of the dry valley, occurring mainly towards the top of the 'Farm ridge'. However, it is not possible to differentiate consistently two separate units on the basis of colour or texture. The clast lithological variations may be evidence of changing source areas for the ice sheet that deposited the till, with a more westerly, Midlands, component becoming important as glaciation progressed. Alternatively there is a series of quartzite and quartz rich gravel in central East Anglia, the Ingham sand and gravel (Clarke & Auton 1982, 1984; Rose 1987; Lewis 1993), which is also known to occur along the Chalk outcrop on the eastern margin of the Fen basin. This may have provided a more local source for these lithologies, the nearest outcrop of such deposits being around Maidscross Hill, Lakenheath (Flower 1869; Rose 1987; Lewis 1993). Contrary to

Paterson's (1942) interpretation, the stratigraphical evidence also indicates that it is not possible to trace this Bunter-containing facies from the top of the ridge southwards down the slope to pass laterally into a decalcified stony sandy clay and overlie the interglacial sequence in the brick pit. A more reasonable interpretation of the evidence is that the till which outcrops on the crest of the ridge can be traced to the foot of the slope and continues beneath the silts and clays and 'brickearth' in the pit, as suggested by cross-section A-A[1] (Fig. 4.15).

The chalky diamicton (Unit 2) at Barnham was therefore deposited as a single lithostratigraphic unit, within a single glacial event, albeit with clast lithological variations that may reflect changes in the source areas of the ice sheet or erosion and transport of pre-existing quartzose gravel in western Norfolk and Suffolk. It was deposited by an ice-sheet moving from the west-north-west. The deposition of till probably continued the infilling of the sub-glacial valley that had been partly filled with sand and gravel (Unit 1), though no sections or boreholes in the brick pit showed sand and gravel underlying the till.

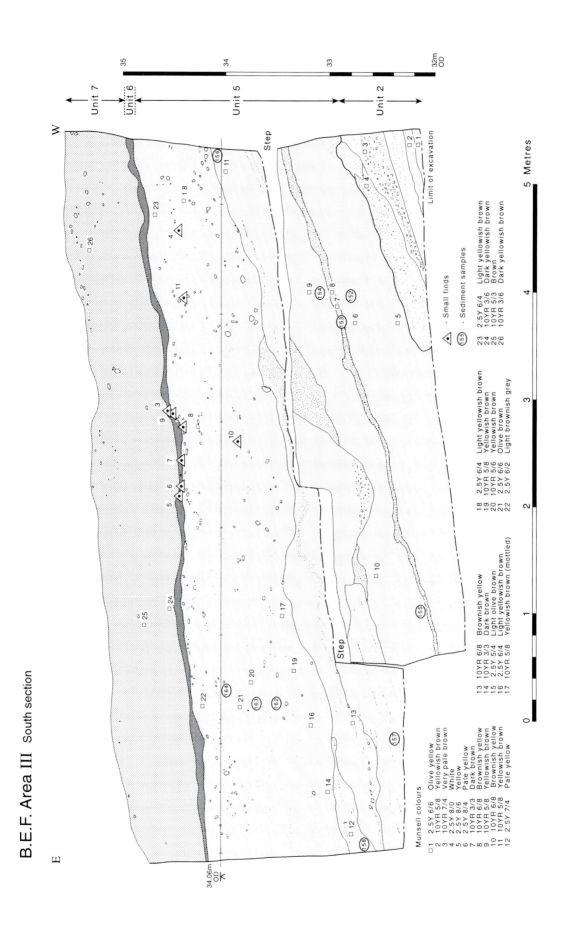

Fig. 4.13. Area III south section.

B.E.F. Area III   West section

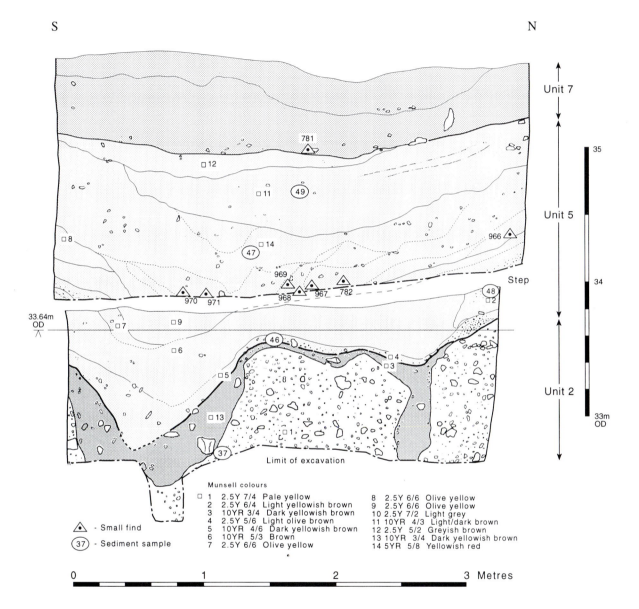

S   N

Unit 7

Unit 5

Step

Unit 2

33.64m
OD

Limit of excavation

Munsell colours

□	1	2.5Y 7/4	Pale yellow
	2	2.5Y 6/4	Light yellowish brown
	3	10YR 3/4	Dark yellowish brown
	4	2.5Y 5/6	Light olive brown
	5	10YR 4/6	Dark yellowish brown
	6	10YR 5/3	Brown
	7	2.5Y 6/6	Olive yellow

8	2.5Y 6/6	Olive yellow
9	2.5Y 6/6	Olive yellow
10	2.5Y 7/2	Light grey
11	10YR 4/3	Light/dark brown
12	2.5Y 5/2	Greyish brown
13	10YR 3/4	Dark yellowish brown
14	5YR 5/8	Yellowish red

⚠ - Small find

㊲ - Sediment sample

0   1   2   3 Metres

Fig. 4.14. Area III west section.

Unit 3: brown diamicton

The next unit in the sequence consists of mainly brown-coloured diamicton. This unit has a very restricted occurrence and has been observed in Areas I and II. It overlies the sand and gravel (Unit 1) in Area I (Figs 4.6, 4.7), Area I (gravel section extension) (Fig. 4.18) and also overlies chalky diamicton (Unit 2) in Area II (Fig.

4.19). The unit attains a maximum observed thickness of *c*.1m. It consists of dipping beds of stony sandy clay, generally towards the north-east, into the centre of the depression in the surface of the underlying deposits. The facies within this unit are generally massive, with occasional thin and discontinuous units of fine-medium sand. The matrix colour is variable but is generally brown, with dominantly 7.5YR and 10YR hues and colour ranging from strong brown (7.5YR 5/8) to light brownish grey (2.5Y 6/2). The matrix is non-calcareous.

The particle size distribution of this unit is variable, but generally poorly sorted, consisting of gravel sized material in a silt/clay matrix (Fig. 4.17), with mean values of 31.5% gravel, 32.6% sand, 10.5% silt and 25.5% clay. The coarser elements of the unit occur in Area I (gravel section) (samples 511, 512 and 513), where they overlie coarse sand and gravel (Unit 1). Somewhat finer facies occur in Area I (main section) and Area II, shown by samples 11 and 20, which have very similar particle size distributions. Sample 166 in Area I (gravel section) also shows a similar distribution. The clast lithology (Table 4.1) of the brown diamicton (8-16mm fraction) shows that the unit is dominated by flint clasts (64.8-89.2%). Other rock types present as minor constituents include quartz, quartzite, sandstone, Carboniferous chert, *Rhaxella* chert, ironstone and igneous rocks. Chalk is not present.

Three sets of clast macrofabric measurements were taken from this unit in Area I (gravel section) (Fig. 4.7). The results show a north-south preferred orientation of gravel-sized particles, with resultant vectors from samples 3, 4 and 5 of 36.0°, 31.7° and 166.4° respectively (Fig. 4.7). Two further macrofabric analyses were undertaken on Unit 3 in Area I (Fig. 4.10). The results show a weakly developed preferred orientation with resultant vectors of 43.5° and 101.5° (Fig. 4.10). The reliability of fabrics 6 and 7 may be limited as there is evidence of displacement and disturbance of the unit in that area.

This unit is interpreted as the result of decalcification and mass-movement of material down the sides of the valley towards the centre of the depression in the surface of the chalky diamicton (Unit 2). The north-south preferred orientation in Area I (gravel section) is consistent with this. The more east-west movement suggested by fabric analyses from Area I (main) may reflect the local slope at that point or it may be a result of post-depositional disturbance of the deposits.

The brown diamicton is probably derived from two main sources: decalcification of chalky diamicton to produce the finer, brown coloured facies seen in Area I (main) and in Area I (gravel section - extension), and secondly from the sand and gravel (Unit 1), which provides coarse flint gravel to the greyish brown diamicton in Area I (gravel section).

The lithological composition of the unit clearly indicates derivation from the underlying glacial and glaciofluvial deposits. The conditions under which deposition of this unit took place cannot be determined. However, it is likely that mass movement processes would have been initiated during the cold climate conditions that immediately followed deglaciation, and may have continued into the subsequent temperate episode.

Paterson (1942) did not recognise this diamicton unit in his excavation, possibly due to its discontinuous nature, though the upper part of the gravel sequence was thought to have undergone solifluction, possibly as a consequence of increased precipitation (Paterson 1942, 22) and the surface of the gravel dipping gently to the north-east. Paterson noted the presence of artefacts in the upper part of the gravel (Chapter 2), which had scratches on their surface and were interpreted as the result of solifluction processes.

Unit 4: cobble layer

This unit is a prominent layer of coarse flint cobbles, present in Area I and also in Area IV(4) and Area IV(5). The cobble layer either forms the upper surface of the sand and gravel (Unit 1) or it overlies brown diamicton (Unit 3), where the latter is present in Area I, (Fig. 4.6). Where Unit 3 is present, the cobble layer is a very distinctive coarse layer in between two fine grained units. The flint cobbles are generally 10-20cm in diameter, occasionally larger. This is considered to be a separate unit because of its distinctive character and archaeological significance. The cobble layer is gently inclined over much of the exposed surface of Area I, and dips towards the north-east (Fig. 4.6). In Area IV(4) and IV(5) the cobble surface dips steeply northwards into the pit (Figs 4.8, 4.9). The recorded height range of the cobble layer across the three exposed surfaces is between 35.6m and 32.5m OD. The cobbles are almost exclusively flint. Some have clearly been rolled and battered, while others are more nodular, suggesting little transport since they were liberated from the Chalk.

The cobble layer is thought to be the result of accumulation of large clasts eroded from the underlying and adjacent sand and gravel, and diamicton, but which could not be transported in a generally low energy environment. The cobbles form a layer that may be likened to a lag-deposit in as much as they are the coarse particles that could not be transported. The cobble layer is in a marginal position in relation to the centre of the channel and was probably only periodically inundated by slow flowing water when fine-grained sediment was winnowed from the surface of the gravel and/or diamicton leaving the coarser component in place.

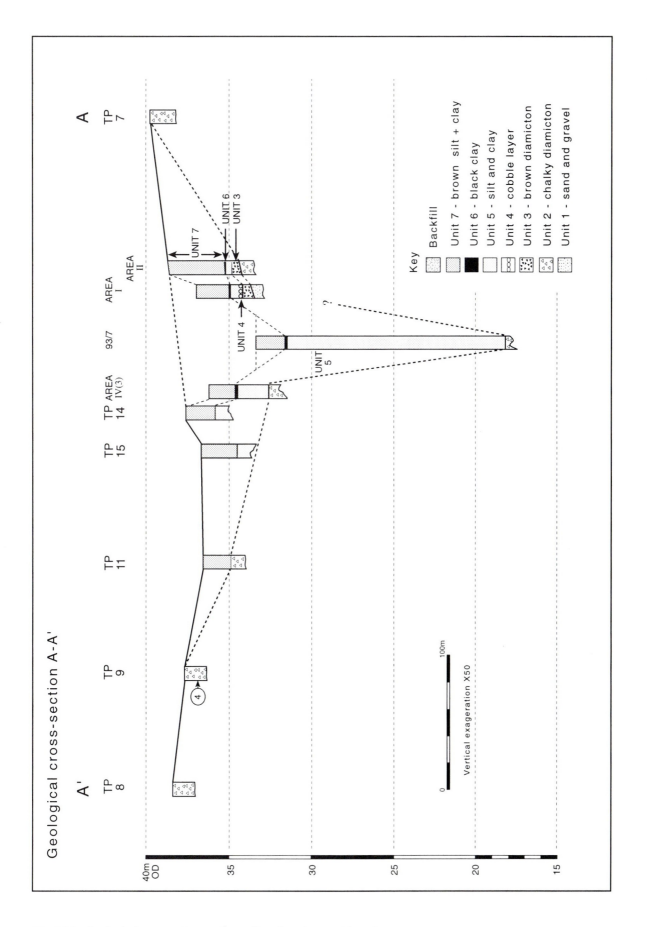

Fig. 4.15a. Geological cross section A-A^1. For line of sections see Fig. 4.3.

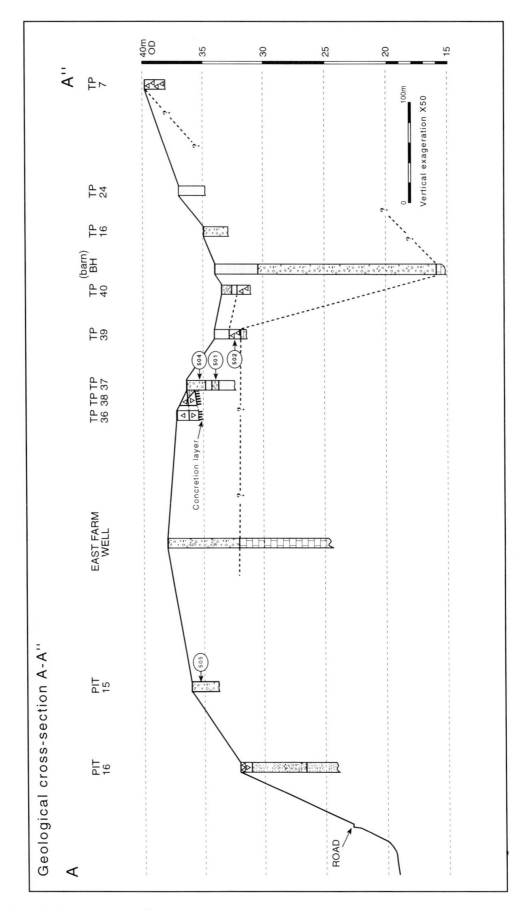

Fig. 15b. Geological cross-section A-A[11]. For line of section see Fig. 4.3.

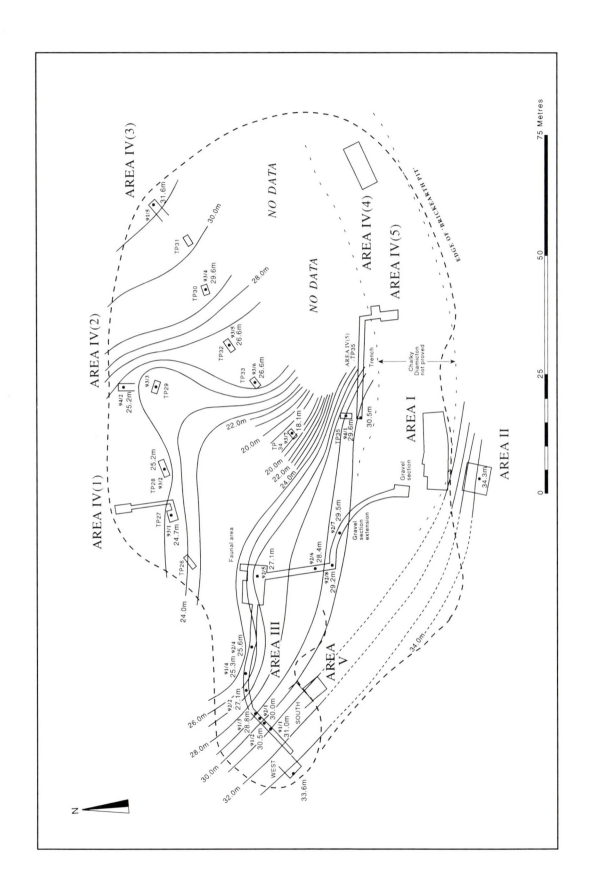

Fig. 4.16. Geometry of the surface of the chalky diamicton (Unit 2).

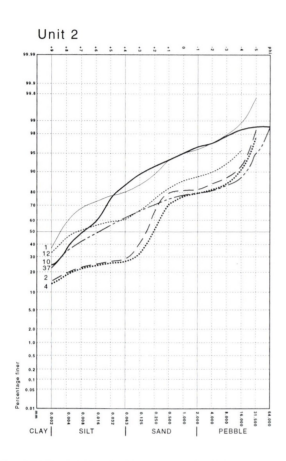

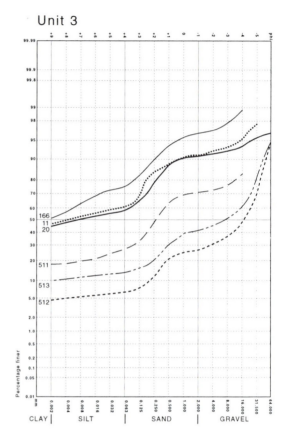

Fig. 4.17. Particle size distributions, Unit 2 and Unit 3.

Unit 5: silt and clay

This unit is distributed across much of the brick pit, forming a major part of the infill of the depression in the surface of the chalky diamicton. It is thin around the edges of the pit but thickens considerably in the centre of the pit, where it attains a maximum recorded thickness of 13.0m in an auger hole (BH 93/7; Fig. 4.4). The auger holes and test pits in the pit indicate that this unit is present beneath the floor of the old brick pit and was largely unexploited by the brick-makers, except for a number of near-rectangular holes dug up to 2m into the upper part of this unit. At the edges of the pit the unit is considerably thinner, forming a 'feather-edge' to the infill of the depression in the upper surface of the chalky diamicton. The distribution of the unit outside the pit is unknown, though it may be present at depth, beneath 'brickearth' (Unit 7) and slopewash.

In the centre of the brick pit the unit overlies chalky

diamicton (Unit 2), demonstrated in a number of auger holes. The surface of the chalky diamicton forms a depression elongated in a west-east direction (Fig. 4.16). The silt and clay has infilled this feature. At the edge of the pit in Area I this unit overlies the cobble layer (Unit 4) and is less than 1m thick. The unit is represented by a thin (c.20cm) layer in Area II (Fig. 4.19). In Area III the unit is again present and is much thinner than in the central part of the pit. Here it is 2-3m in thickness, thinning in a southerly direction (ie towards the edge of the channel feature).

A number of distinct lithofacies can be identified within this unit. These can be differentiated on the basis of colour and texture. However, they do not form a vertical succession of sediments, rather the unit is laterally variable across the area of the pit. The lithofacies described below display the variations in sediments at the margin and centre of an infilling depression.

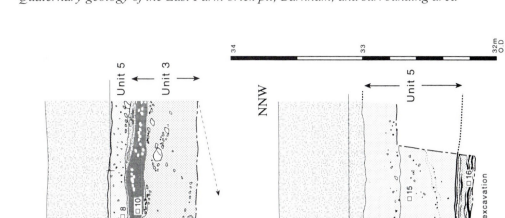

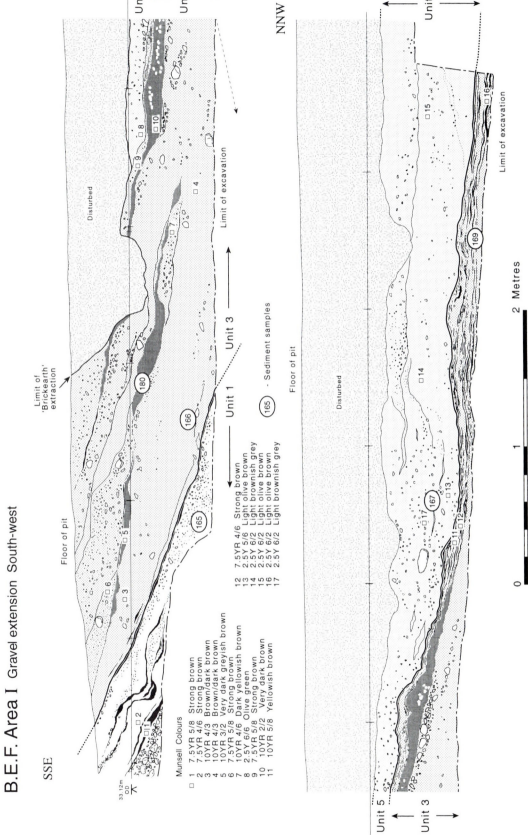

B.E.F. Area I Gravel extension South-west

Fig. 4.18. Area I gravel extension, south-west section.

Munsell Colours

1 7.5YR 5/8 Strong brown
2 7.5YR 4/6 Strong brown
3 10YR 4/3 Brown/dark brown
4 10YR 4/3 Brown/dark brown
5 10YR 3/2 Very dark greyish brown
6 7.5YR 5/8 Strong brown
7 10YR 4/6 Dark yellowish brown
8 2.5Y 6/6 Olive green
9 7.5YR 5/8 Strong brown
10 10YR 2/2 Very dark brown
11 10YR 5/8 Yellowish brown

12 7.5YR 4/6 Strong brown
13 2.5Y 5/6 Light olive brown
14 2.5Y 6/2 Light brownish grey
15 2.5Y 6/2 Light olive brown
16 2.5Y 6/2 Light olive brown
17 2.5Y 6/2 Light brownish grey

165 - Sediment samples

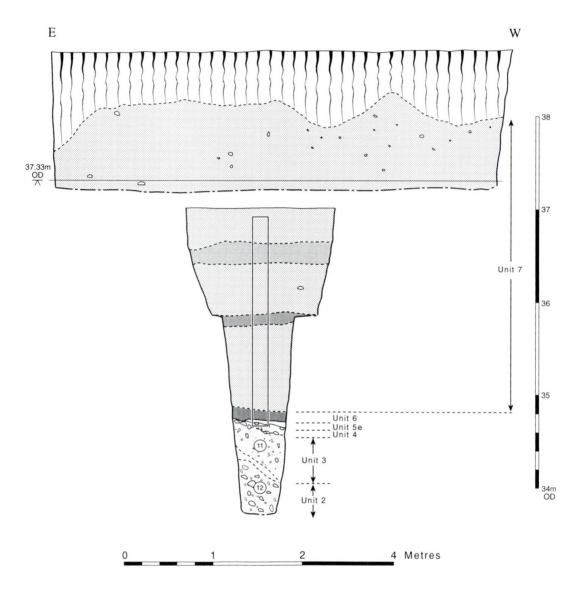

Fig. 4.19a. Area II south section.

Unit 5a: brown silt and clay. The basal contact of this lithofacies is with the chalky diamicton in the centre of the pit, recorded in a number of boreholes across the pit (Fig. 4.4). The unit varies in recorded thickness from 13m in the centre of the depression to less than 1m at the edges. The unit consists of a variety of stoneless silt and clay deposits, with beds of fine sand and silt, the thickest of which is up to *c*.1m thick in Area III (south) (Fig. 4.13) and is laterally continuous at least as far as auger hole BH 92/5 (Fig. 4.4). The bulk of the unit is

made up of sily clay (Fig. 4.20; samples 152, 153, 157, 158). The sandy facies consist dominantly of fine sand (samples 154, 155, 156) towards the margins in Area III (south), with a mode in the 0.063-0.125mm fraction (Fig. 4.20), becoming somewhat finer in the centre of the channel (samples 120, 126), where they are predominantly a silty texture (Fig. 4.20). The silt and clay is clearly laminated in places, with fine sand laminae visible in some of the auger samples. The sand layers in Area III (south) (Fig. 4.13) also show evidence

B.E.F. Area II East section

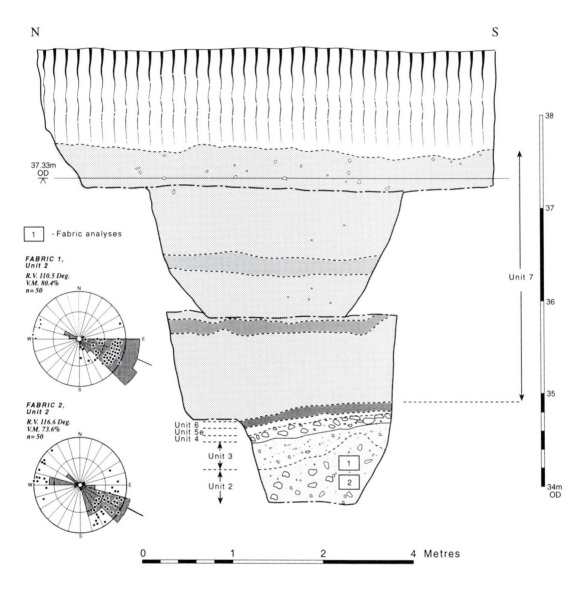

Fig. 4.19b. Area II east section.

of bedding. The sediments are predominantly brown in colour, colours range typically from light yellowish brown (2.5Y 6/4) to light olive brown (2.5Y 5/6), though occasional brown layers (10YR 4/4) are present.

This part of Unit 5 is interpreted as the infill of a depression in the chalky diamicton surface, which took place under still water or very low energy moving water conditions. The fine-grained texture and evidence of laminated sediment may suggest lacustrine conditions, though higher energy regimes causing influxes of sand into the basin suggest occasional fluvial influences. It is probable that the infill of the depression began at the end of the glaciation that deposited the chalky diamicton, while the channel formed in the surface of the chalky diamicton may have been created by meltwater flow. It is also possible that dead-ice processes may have operated particularly to form the very deep part of the chalky diamicton surface, as demonstrated by BH 93/7 (Fig. 4.4).

51

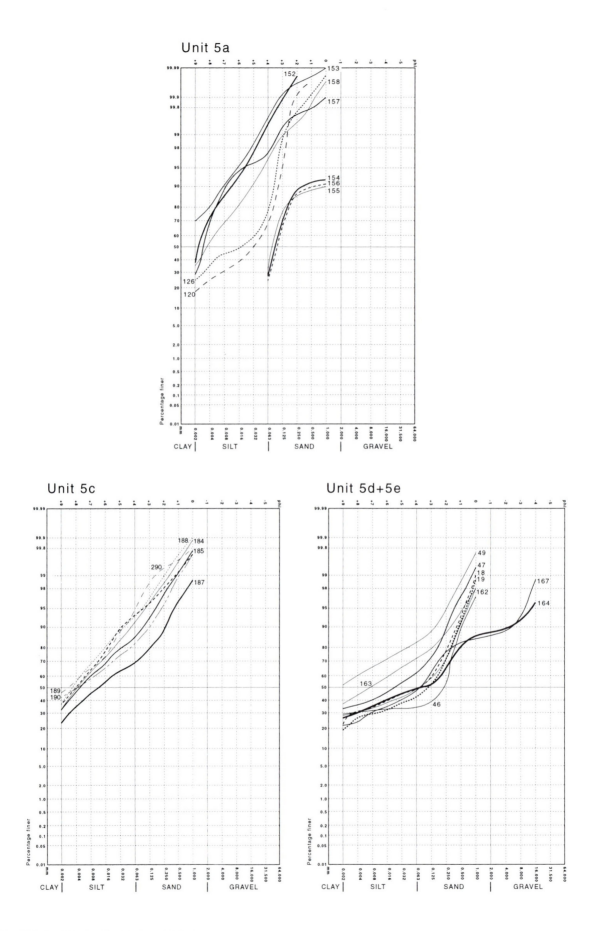

Fig. 4.20. Particle size distributions, Unit 5.

Unit 5b: grey chalky clay. This facies can be recognised particularly on the northern side of the pit in test pits and auger holes (Fig. 4.4) and in sections in Area IV(1) (Fig. 4.21) and IV(2) (Fig. 4.22). The facies is characterised by small chalk pebbles in a greyish clay matrix. The thickness of this facies is variable, being 0.6m thick in Area IV(1). In the side (west) section of Area IV(1) the unit dips southwards into the centre of the depression over the upper surface of the chalky diamicton (Fig. 4.21). This facies appears to interdigitate with Unit 5a; a number of distinct layers of chalky clay are present in BH 93/2, separated by stoneless silt and clay.

The absence of this facies in the central part of the channel suggests that it represents deposition at the margins of the infilling depression, with coarser chalky material incorporated into these sediments probably as a result of reworking from chalky diamicton down the local slopes.

Unit 5c: grey silt and clay. The upper 2-3m of the fine-grained infill of this channel consists of a series of predominantly grey, calcareous clays. The unit is thickest in the central part of the pit around the Area III (faunal area) (Fig. 4.4), thinning towards the edges, to feather out completely around the margins of the channel. As a whole, the unit can be traced laterally from the Area III (faunal area) in the centre of the pit towards Area III (south), though it wedges-out at the western end of the 'slit trench' joining Area III with Area I, as shown in cross-section B-B[1] (Fig. 4.24). A north-south cross-section C-C[1] (Fig. 4.25) through the brick pit also shows that the unit thins out in a northerly and southerly direction.

A number of sections created along the 'slit trench' showed the lateral variability of this unit and the relationship of the deposits in the central part of the pit to the more marginal facies. This unit is about 3m thick in the centre of the pit and thins towards the edges. Its texture is consistent across the exposures (Fig. 4.20) with only one facies, at the top of pit 4 (sample 187) standing out as being slightly coarser (Fig. 4.20). Sediment from BH 93/7 (sample 290) 1.5m below the black clay of Unit 6 (see below) has a similar texture to the pit 4 and pit 9 exposures (Fig. 4.20).

In the centre of the pit (Area III, faunal area), where the unit is at its thickest, it consists of (from the base of the section; Figs 4.27, 4.28) a sequence of light brownish grey clay (2.5Y 6/2), a discontinuous dark brown/black clay (10YR 2/1-10YR2/2), a light olive brown shelly clay (2.5Y 5/4) and a brown gritty clay (10YR 4/3). In a small part of the section in pit 8/9 a small remnant of black clay (probably Unit 6) was observed to overlie this sequence. The lateral relationships between the exposures in Pit 9 and Pit 4 are difficult to establish precisely. The brown gritty clay

thins out to the west towards Area III (south) and disappears in between pits 5 and 6 where it is underlain by grey shelly clay. The lowest facies in pit 9 (brownish grey clay) is visually and texturally very similar to the upper part of the sequence in pit 4. The pit 4 sequence consists of calcareous light brownish grey silt and clay (2.5Y 6/2), with shells, mottled in places with laminations. At the base of the section in pit 4 is a 10cm layer of concentrated shell debris in a series of brown and grey laminations. This concentrated shell layer can be traced west into pits 1 and 2, where it rises gradually to finally thin and disappear in Area III (south). These lateral relationships established in the sections cut in the 'slit trench' suggest that the sequence in pit 4 underlies that in pit 9, though it is not possible to determine whether the two sequences overlap or whether there is a gap between the top of pit 4 and the base of pit 9.

This unit represents continued infilling of the channel with predominantly fine-grained sediments. The facies is distinguished from the underlying Unit 5b by its grey colour and the conspicuous presence of mollusc remains and other faunal debris.

Unit 5d: grey/brown stony clay. This facies is present in Area III (south) and in Area I (gravel extension) (Figs 4.13, 4.18). The unit is predominantly made up of fine-grained sediments (Fig. 4.20) but with a coarse component, consisting mainly of flint pebbles (sample 164, Table 4.1, Fig 4.20). In Area III (south) it forms a *c.*1m thick unit above the conspicuously shelly equivalent of Unit 5c (Fig. 4.13). The unit thins towards the right of the section and continues into the Area III (west) section, cutting out the underlying Unit 5a. The upper and lower contacts dip towards the centre of the channel. The unit is also present in Area I (gravel extension) where it consists of a brownish grey stony silt/clay, with the pebbles being predominantly flint (sample 167, Table 4.1, Fig. 4.20).

This unit, like Unit 5b, is interpreted as a marginal facies, deposited at the edge of the channel, and as a consequence is somewhat coarser than the lateral equivalents in the centre of the channel (Units 5a and 5c). The gravel fraction is likely to be reworked from the durable component of the sand and gravel, and diamictons.

Unit 5e: yellow silty sand. This unit is present in Area I (Fig. 4.6) where it overlies the cobble layer (Unit 4) and forms the interstitial material for much of that unit, and in Area II where it is *c.*0.2m thick and again overlies a layer of flint cobbles (Fig. 4.19). In Area I the yellow silty sand is 0.3-0.4m in thickness, varying slightly over the undulating surface of the cobbles, being generally thinner on the higher parts and thicker on the lower parts of the cobble layer.

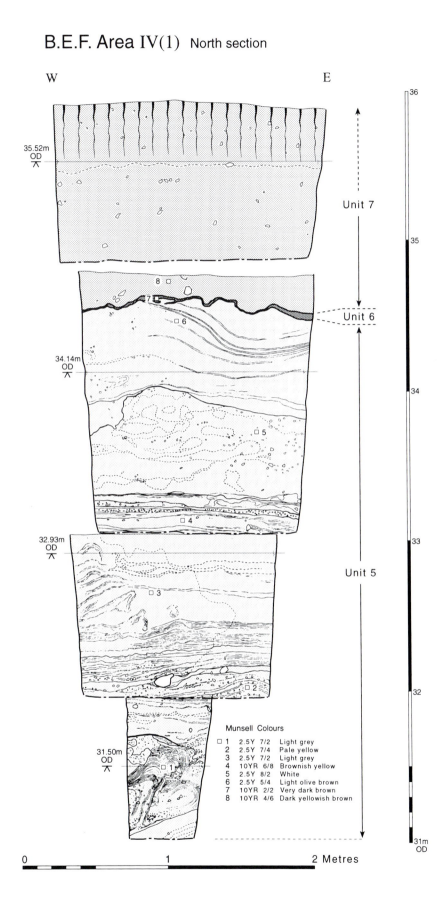

B.E.F. Area IV(1) North section

Munsell Colours

☐ 1 2.5Y 7/2 Light grey
  2 2.5Y 7/4 Pale yellow
  3 2.5Y 7/2 Light grey
  4 10YR 6/8 Brownish yellow
  5 2.5Y 8/2 White
  6 2.5Y 5/4 Light olive brown
  7 10YR 2/2 Very dark brown
  8 10YR 4/6 Dark yellowish brown

Fig. 4.21b. Area IV(1) north section.

B.E.F. Area IV(2)

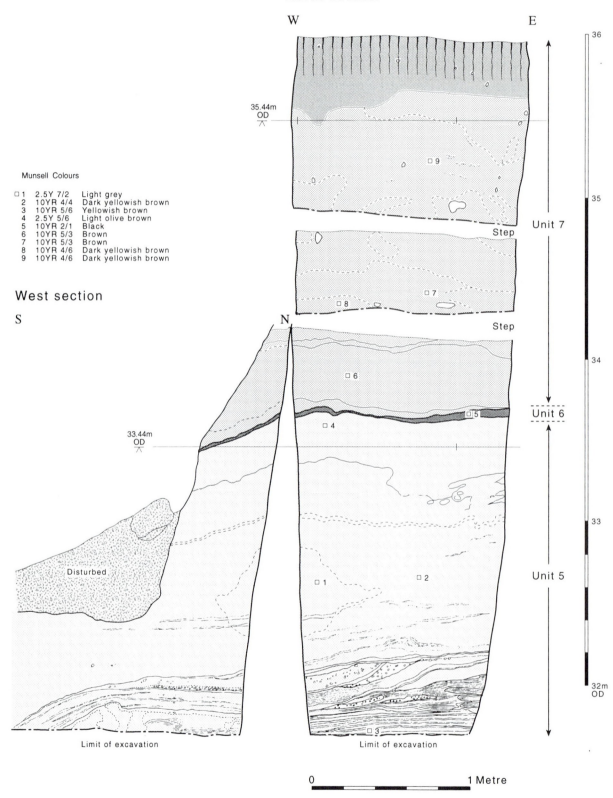

North section

West section

Munsell Colours

☐ 1 2.5Y 7/2 Light grey
2 10YR 4/4 Dark yellowish brown
3 10YR 5/6 Yellowish brown
4 2.5Y 5/6 Light olive brown
5 10YR 2/1 Black
6 10YR 5/3 Brown
7 10YR 5/3 Brown
8 10YR 4/6 Dark yellowish brown
9 10YR 4/6 Dark yellowish brown

Fig. 4.22. Area IV(2) north and west sections.

B.E.F. Area IV(3) North section

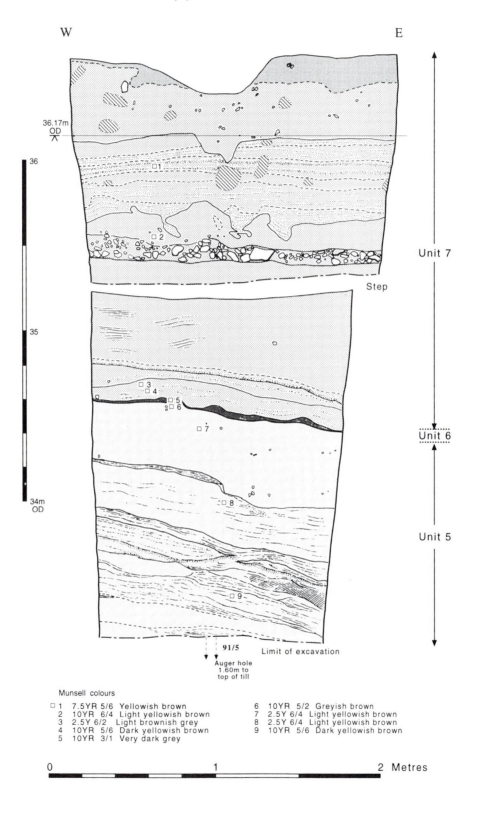

W   E

36.17m
OD

36

35

34m
OD

Unit 7

Step

Unit 6

Unit 5

91/5
Auger hole
1.60m to
top of till

Limit of excavation

Munsell colours

□ 1	7.5YR 5/6	Yellowish brown	6	10YR 5/2	Greyish brown
2	10YR 6/4	Light yellowish brown	7	2.5Y 6/4	Light yellowish brown
3	2.5Y 6/2	Light brownish grey	8	2.5Y 6/4	Light yellowish brown
4	10YR 5/6	Dark yellowish brown	9	10YR 5/6	Dark yellowish brown
5	10YR 3/1	Very dark grey			

0   1   2 Metres

Fig. 4.23. Area IV(3) north section.

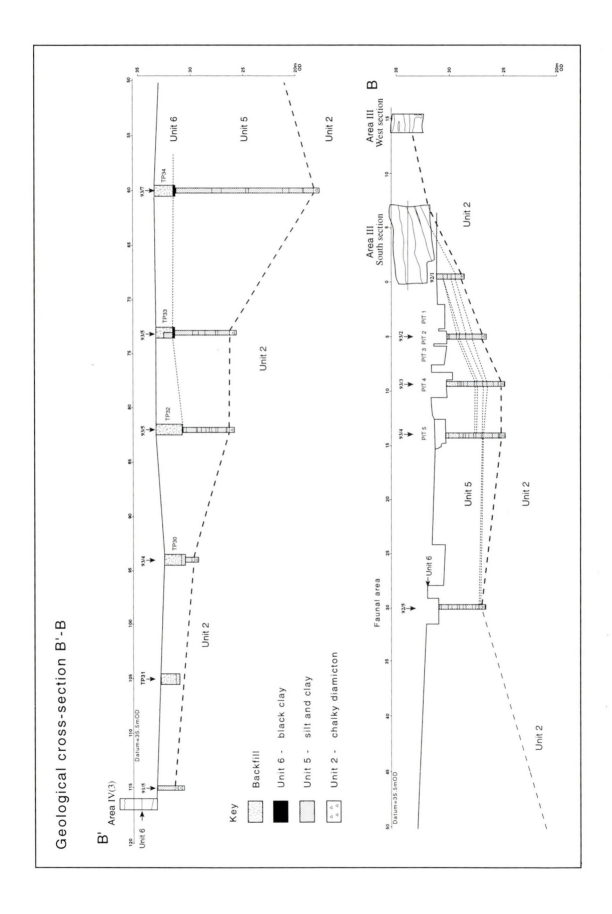

Fig. 4.24. Geological cross-section B¹-B through the East Farm brick pit. For line of section see Fig. 4.4.

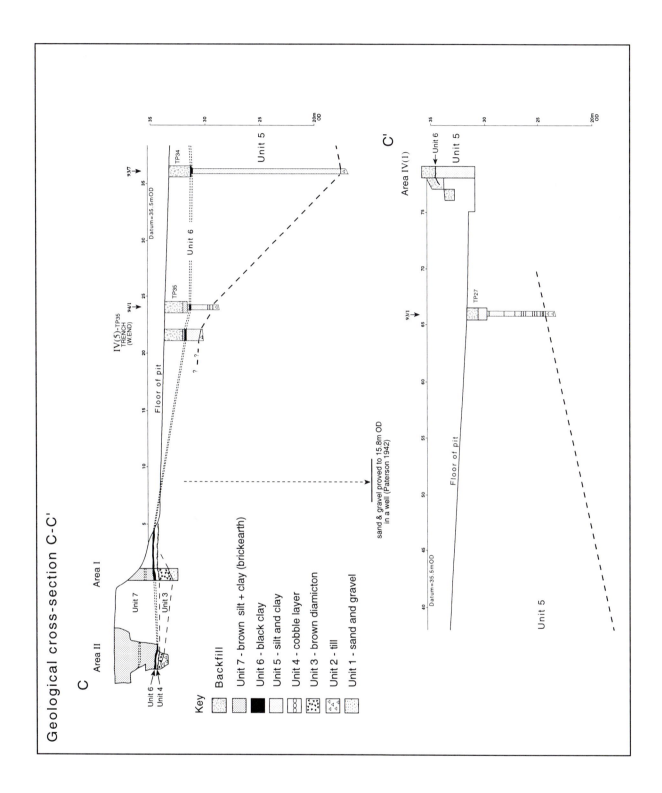

Fig. 4.25. Geological cross section C-C¹ through the East Farm brick pit. For line of section see Fig. 4.4.

Unit 5e is also present in Area IV(4) where it again overlies the cobble layer (Unit 4) and forms a *c*.0.4m thick unit (Fig. 4.8). The unit is at a similar altitude (*c*.35.0-35.5m OD) in both Area I and Area IV(4). A similar unit is also present overlying cobbles *c*.1m lower in altitude in Area IV(5) (Fig. 4.9), which is located between Area I and Area IV(4). The unit is light yellowish brown (2.5Y 6/4) in colour, and has a silty sand texture (samples 18, 19), with around 55% sand, 30% silt and 15% clay (Fig. 4.20).

In Area III (south) the upper part of Unit 5d is a yellowish brown sandy, silty, clay facies (Fig. 4.13) that is very similar to the yellow silty sand in Area I. The upper contact is marked by a number of artefacts found in section in Area III (south) (Fig. 4.13) lying on an undulating surface that was exposed in controlled excavations in the adjacent Area V. Similar sediments are also present in Areas IV(1), IV(2) and IV(3), up to 0.6m thick and ranging in colour from light yellowish brown (2.5Y 6/4) to light olive brown (2.5Y 5/6) (Figs 4.21, 4.22, 4.23).

There are no sedimentary structures within this unit particularly diagnostic of its origin. The fine texture suggests a low energy environment, and it is possible that this unit formed as the cobble surface was periodically inundated by gently flowing water. Flow strength was low, but sufficiently great to lift small flint flakes from the cobble surface and rework them into the silty sand.

Summary of Unit 5. Taken together the various facies that make up Unit 5 are interpreted as a vertically and laterally variable sequence infilling the channel in the chalky diamicton. Sedimentation commenced, probably under cold climate conditions, with fine grained facies deposited in a still and slow flowing water regime, and coarser material deposited around the margins. Sedimentation continued into the subsequent warm phase when the fossiliferous silts and clays were deposited in the centre of the channel. As the channel progressively infilled with sediments, inundation of the marginal areas occurred and the cobble layer in Areas I and II was covered with a sequence of silty sand, which also occurs in Area III.

Unit 6: black clay

This unit forms a distinctive layer in Area I, where it overlies the yellow silty sand (Unit 5e) (Fig. 4.6). It is also present in Area IV(4) and Area IV(5) where it again overlies yellow silty sand (Figs 4.8, 4.9). In Area II, on the edge of the brick pit adjacent to Area I, this unit overlies Unit 5e (Fig. 4.19). Elsewhere in the brick pit equivalent black clay has been identified in TP 33 and 34 (Fig. 4.26), where it overlies grey silt and clay (Unit 5c). It is also present in the trench joining Area IV(5) and TP 35 (Fig. 4.11). The unit is also present, in a much degraded state, in Area III where it was observed to overlie grey silt and clay (Unit 5c) in the centre of the pit and in Area III (south) it overlies the coarser grey/brown stony clay facies (Unit 5d) (Fig. 4.13). In Area IV(1) and IV(2) thin horizons of black clay are thought to be equivalent to this unit (Figs 4.21, 4.22). In Area IV(3) there is a further thin black sandy clay layer that may represent this unit (Fig. 4.23). TP 14 in the field to the north of Area IV(3) (Fig. 4.15) also

revealed a black sandy clay unit 0.4m thick. The locations, upper surface heights and recorded thickness of this unit are shown in Fig. 4.29. The black clay is generally up to 0.3m in thickness, being thicker in the marginal locations in Area I and Area IV(4) along the southern edge of the pit. The altitudinal range of the unit is between 31.6m OD and 35.9m OD (Fig. 4.29), with the lowest point in the centre of the pit (TP 33) and the highest point in Area I. The unit is at a consistent level along the southern margin of the pit between Area I and Area IV(4), while the section in Area IV(5) shows the unit dipping steeply to the north into the pit (Fig. 4.8), following the dip of the underlying yellow silty sand (Unit 5e) and cobble layer (Unit 4).

The colour of the unit is somewhat variable; in Area II it is dark brown (10YR4/3) in colour, whereas in Area I it is dark yellowish brown (2.5Y 3/2). The unit is noticeably blacker in the centre of the pit; in TP 33 and 34 it is black (10YR 2/1), and where observed in auger holes (BH 92/6, 92/7, 94/1; Fig. 4.4) it is very dark greyish brown (10YR 3/2) to black (10YR 2/1).

The texture of the unit (Fig. 4.30) consists dominantly of clay (40-55%), with lesser quantities of sand (15-35%) and silt (20-30%). A sequence of 16 contiguous samples through this unit and the deposits immediately above and below (Fig. 4.30) in Area I shows that the particle size distribution displays some variability, with the sand content increasing towards the base of the unit. There is a marked textural break at the top of Unit 6, which contains significantly more sand than the overlying Unit 7 (Fig. 4.30). This may suggest that there is a break in sedimentation at this point. The values for organic carbon content are uniformly low, though somewhat higher than the overlying and underlying units (Fig. 4.30). Values for iron and manganese content through this section (determined by atomic absorption spectrophotometer) show no marked variations and, despite the colouration of the unit, are not significantly higher than the underlying and overlying sediments (Fig. 4.30). However, in Area II, manganese levels associated with Unit 6 are markedly higher than those for the overlying 'brickearths' (Unit 7), though iron content shows little systematic variations (Fig. 4.31).

The colour and textural properties of this unit suggest that it is the result of post-depositional processes acting upon the sediments immediately beneath (Unit 5). The nature of these processes cannot be determined by examination of the macro-scale features of the unit, and therefore a detailed micromorphological investigation was undertaken (see Chapter 6). It is apparent, however, that there is a marked textural change at the top of this unit, which suggests that there is an unconformity at this point. This has some bearing upon the interpretation of the archaeology from Units 5 and 6.

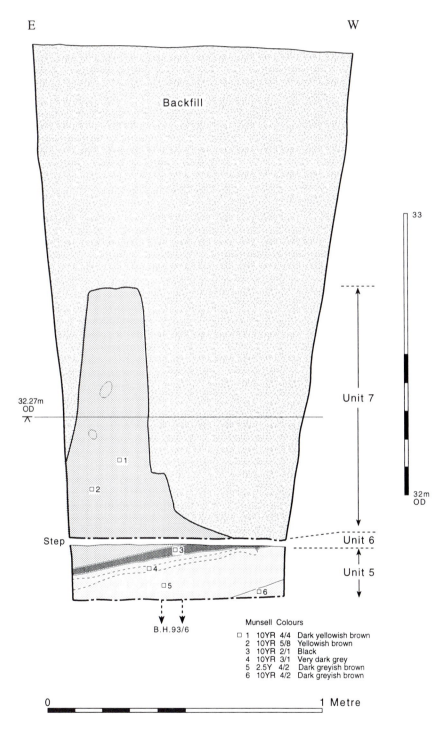

B.E.F. Area IV Test Pit 33 South face

E

W

Backfill

33

32.27m
OD

Unit 7

32m
OD

Step

Unit 6

Unit 5

B.H.93/6

Munsell Colours
☐ 1 10YR 4/4 Dark yellowish brown
2 10YR 5/8 Yellowish brown
3 10YR 2/1 Black
4 10YR 3/1 Very dark grey
5 2.5Y 4/2 Dark greyish brown
6 10YR 4/2 Dark greyish brown

0   1 Metre

Fig. 4.26. Test pit 33 south face.

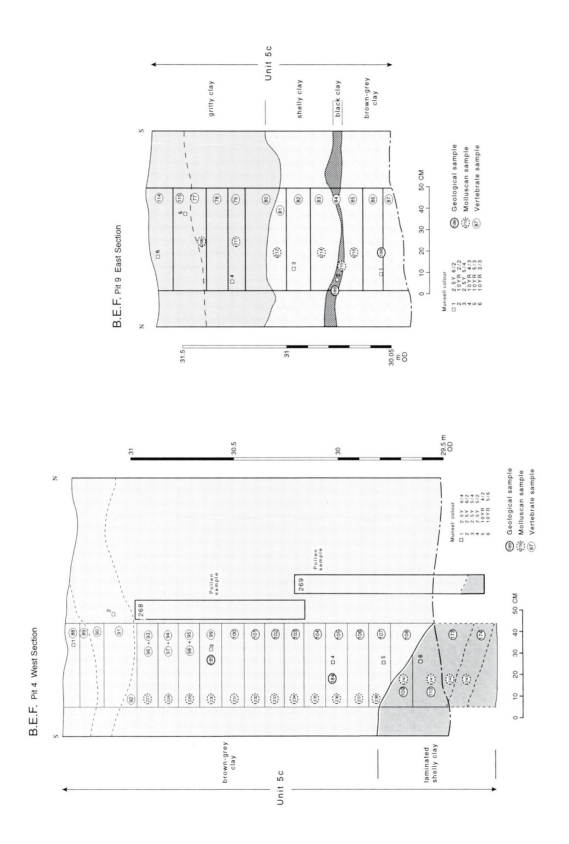

Fig. 4.27. Pit 4 west section and Pit 9 east section in Area III.

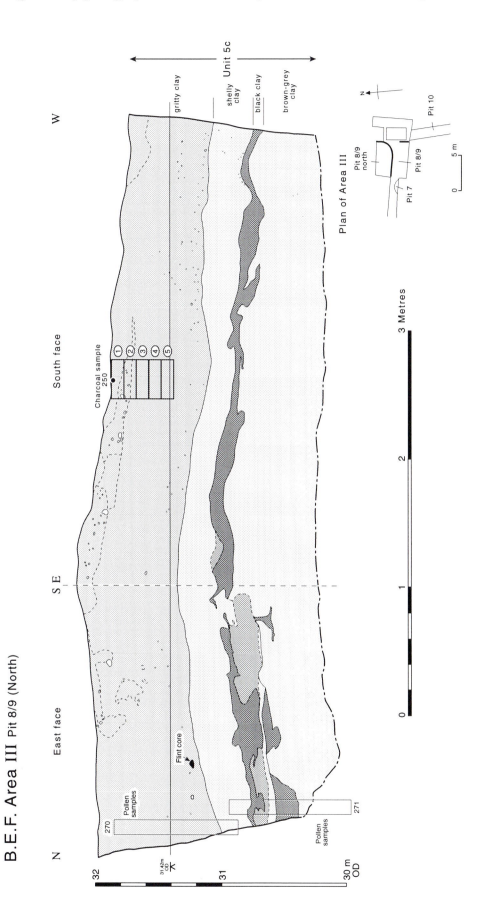

Fig. 4.28. Area III Pit 8/9 (north) east and south faces.

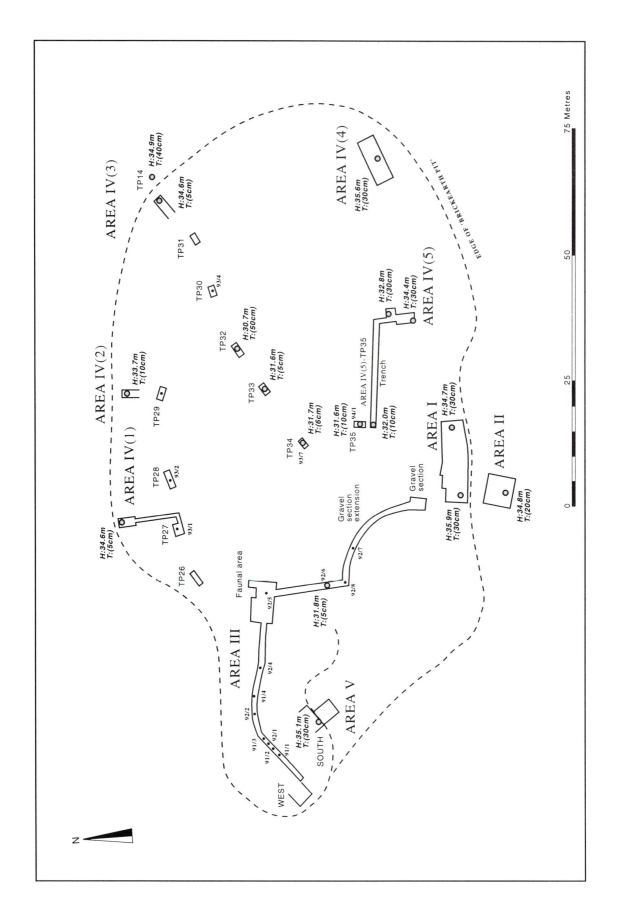

Fig. 4.29. Location of exposures showing the black clay (Unit 6) around the East Farm Pit, with the height of the upper surface(m OD) and unit thickness (cm in brackets).

Unit 7: brown silt and clay ('brickearth')

This is the uppermost unit in the sequence in the brick pit. It is present in Area I and Area II, where it overlies the black clay (Unit 6) (Figs 4.6, 4.19). The unit is also recognisable in Area III (west) (Fig. 4.14) and in Area IV(4) (Fig. 4.8). Outside the brick pit the unit is recognisable in a number of trial pits (Fig. 4.3). In Areas I, II, III and IV(4) this unit overlies the black clay (Unit 6). The unit is *c*.4m thick in Area I and Area IV(4). The unit is predominantly brown (10YR 5/3) to yellowish brown (10YR 5/8) in colour with prominent darker horizons visible in Area I, Area II and Area IV(4), which are dark brown (7.5YR 4/4) or dark greyish brown (10YR 4/2) in colour. The sediments consist typically of around 5-10% sand, 30-40% silt and 50-65% clay, though the upper part of the sequence contains considerably more sand, with up to 46.4% sand at the top of the sequence in Area II (Fig. 4.31). A series of samples taken at 10cm intervals though this unit in Area II (south section; Fig. 4.31) shows no clear vertical trend other than becoming progressively sandier towards the top. No significant variations in the texture of the unit are apparent across the darker horizons within Unit 7 (Fig. 4.31). The marked textural change at the base of the unit takes place between sample 200 and 210, which coincides with the contact with Unit 6. The uppermost *c*.1m of the sequence in Area II consists of stony sandy clay with many flints, which shows signs of disturbance both by periglacial processes and by ploughing.

Organic carbon levels in Unit 7 are very low throughout (Fig. 4.31), with no clear relationship between percentage organic carbon and the dark brown horizons within Unit 7. Indeed some of the highest values occur just above these horizons (Fig. 4.31). The values are consistent with those reported by Kemp (Chapter 6). Iron and manganese levels in this unit show some variations, though there is no clear relationship between these properties and the observable colour and textural variation in the unit (Fig. 4.31).

This unit is thought to be the result of progressive accumulation of fine-grained sediments mainly as a result of slope-wash into the valley bottom. Contributions to the sediment may also have occurred through fluvial and aeolian processes. The sandy laminations present in the upper part of the sequence suggest that low energy fluvial processes may have become more significant as deposition progressed. The darker layers within the unit reflect periodic stability when soil-forming processes operated on the land surface, followed by further deposition and burial of the incipient soils. These features and processes are considered in detail in Chapter 6.

Paterson (1942) identified a decalcified 'boulder clay' overlying these deposits, (bed (f) of Paterson 1942). It is the case that the upper *c*.1m of Unit 7 is made up of stony sandy material, which has been heavily affected by periglacial activity, biological processes and by ploughing. However, there is no evidence to suggest that this unit constitutes a glacial deposit, and as discussed above, it cannot be traced laterally into the quartzite-bearing glacial deposits that occur north of the brick pit as suggested by Paterson (1942). It is more likely that this sediment is the result of mass movement of sediment down the slopes, reworking gravel-sized material from glacial sediment on the dry valley sides and disturbance of the underlying 'brickearth' by periglacial processes.

SUMMARY OF THE GEOLOGICAL SUCCESSION IN THE EAST FARM BRICK PIT

The lowest two units in the pit are of glacial origin. Ashton *et al*. (1994a) suggested that the first unit to be deposited was chalky diamicton. However, for reasons outlined above, it is probable that the sand and gravel was deposited first, followed by the chalky diamicton. The sequence in the brick pit therefore begins with glaciofluvial sand and gravel, deposited in a steep-sided channel incised into the underlying Chalk bedrock. On top of this lies a sheet of chalky diamicton deposited by an ice-sheet. On retreat of the ice-sheet, a channel was cut into the upper surface of the chalky diamicton, which immediately began to be infilled. The deposits filling the channel consist of solifluction diamictons (Unit 3), and a variety of fine-grained facies (Unit 5). On the margins of the channel the surface of the gravel (Unit 1) was periodically inundated by flowing water to produce a winnowed surface of coarse flint cobbles, which were overlain by the yellow silty sand (Unit 5e). As filling of the channel progressed and it started to dry out, the land surface became more stable, allowing soil formation to take place, to form the black clay (Unit 6) over much of the site. Periodic phases of sedimentation and land surface stability created a sequence of fine grained 'brickearth' (Unit 7) within which are a number of weakly developed soil horizons (Chapter 6). A diagrammatic representation of the geological sequence is shown in Fig. 4.32.

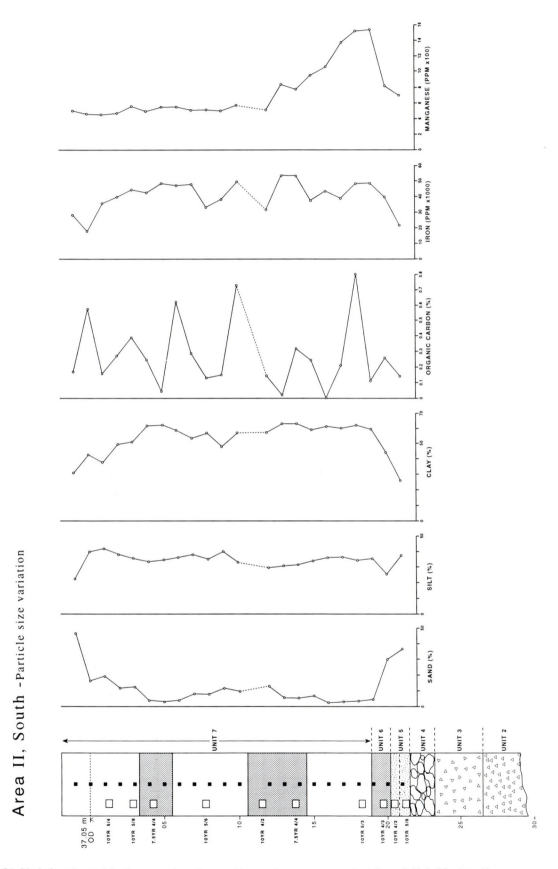

Fig. 4.31. Variations in particle size, organic carbon and iron and manganese content through Unit 7 in Area II.

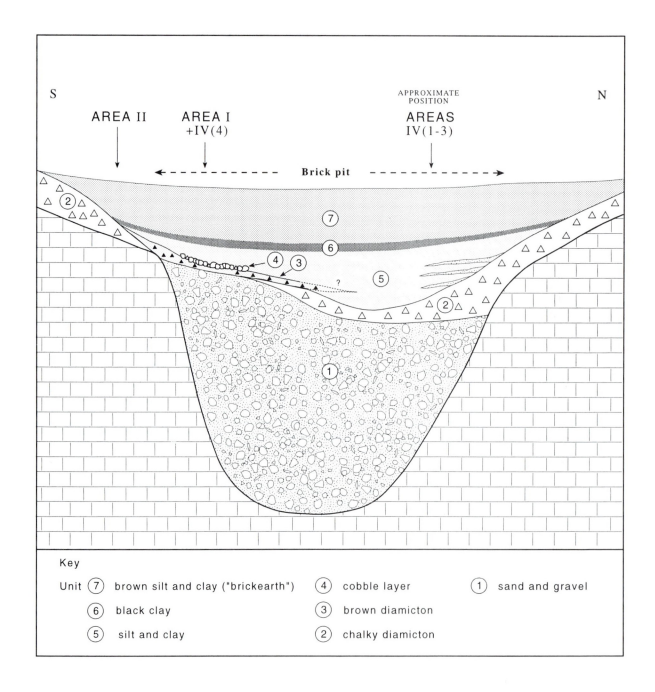

Fig. 4.32. Schematic diagram of the sequence in East Farm brick pit.

ADDITIONAL EXPOSURES IN THE SURROUNDING AREA

In addition to the East Farm Pit and adjacent sites described above, sections were recorded at a number of localities, somewhat further afield (Fig. 4.3), which provide additional information on the local geological sequence. One of these was described by Paterson (1942) and is located in woods known as 'Kidney Plantation'. It is an old gravel pit, located north of the Barnham-Euston road about 1km north-east of the brick pit (Fig. 4.3). Three further sites were investigated, that were commercial sand and gravel extractive operations, operated by A.R. Tilbrook, and were active during the 1989-94 field excavations. The first of these closed in 1989, the second was open briefly in 1991, and the third was opened in 1992 and has recently closed. They are referred to as Tilbrook's 1st, 2nd and 3rd pits respectively. They are all south of the Barnham-Euston road and are some 400-800m east of the brick pit (Fig. 4.3).

Kidney Plantation Pit

Sections in this pit were described by Paterson (1942) as showing a sequence of coarse sand and gravel, including large flint cobbles and 'boulder clays'. The latter unit was described as 'brown boulder clay, weathering green' (1942, 18-19) and correlated with a deposit referred to as a 'solifluxion-boulder clay-conglomerate' described elsewhere (pit 15 and 16, Fig. 4.3). It was clearly thought by Paterson (1942) to be the result of glacial activity, though the possibility that it had 'slipped' down slope to its present position was recognised. The largely inferred stratigraphic relationship between this unit and the brown Bunter-rich 'boulder clays' seen on the Farm Ridge is difficult to substantiate. However, Paterson (1939, 1942) suggested that it represented the youngest of three glacial incursions into the Breckland.

In 1993 five sections were exposed in the pit (Fig. 4.33). The pit has been partly in-filled with rubbish, but the south-western end, where Paterson's (1942) sections were located, has been completely backfilled. The sections described here are from the central part and from the south-western perimeter of the pit, as the eastern end is heavily overgrown.

The sequence exposed in these sections consists of coarse gravel, with beds of fine sand and silt, showing horizontal lamination and ripple cross stratification, resting on Chalk. In sections 2 and 3 within the pit the surface of the Chalk is between 20.5-22.0m OD. In sections 4 and 5, to the south-west of the pit some 200m west of sections 1-3, the Chalk surface is between 26.7-27.8m OD.

The clast lithology of the gravel (Table 4.2) is dominated by flint (55.8-61.7%) and chalk (19.1-22.9%), together with lesser quantities of quartz and quartzite. Among the minor constituents (Table 4.2) are *Rhaxella* chert, limestone, Jurassic shell fragments, igneous lithologies and glauconitic sandstone, all of which are typical of glaciofluvial gravel in western Suffolk.

The deposits in Kidney Plantation pit are most probably of glaciofluvial origin, resulting from deposition by outwash streams in a highly variable discharge regime. They occupy a channel-like feature in the Chalk bedrock that, at its lowest observed point is at *c*.20m OD; this is an altitude that is, coincidentally, similar to the probable base of sand and gravel in the channel to the south of the Chalk ridge that separates Kidney Plantation pit from East Farm brick pit. The gravel is also very similar in clast composition to the sand and gravel (Unit 1) in the channel beneath the brick pit. It is therefore possible that deposition of glaciofluvial gravel was taking place both south of the Chalk ridge within a tunnel valley and as a more extensive spread of gravel to the north of the ridge. However Paterson (1942) suggested that the Kidney Plantation gravel was outwash from the second glaciation in his sequence, characterised by the presence of Bunter pebbles, which were deposited only on the north side of the Chalk ridge. This gravel was then overlain by a 'brown boulder clay', though the evidence for this relationship is extremely tenuous (believed by Paterson to be visible in pit 12).

Unfortunately the occurrence of any glaciogenic units in this pit could not be verified, partly because the sections described by Paterson no longer exist and partly because the relevant deposits occur in the upper part of the sequence which is now inaccessible. It would not be unexpected to find glacial deposits in close association with outwash, although this interpretation and the somewhat tortuous arguments deployed by Paterson (1942), on which the separation of glacial deposits into three distinct glacial phases was based, are open to question. In the first description of the Barnham sequence Paterson (1937) did not include a third glacial episode, though the occurrence of solifluction deposits is indicated. Paterson (1942, 24) conceded that the 'boulder clay' in Kidney Plantation pit may be a slope deposit resulting from solifluction down slope. Concerning its relationship to the rest of the sequence, Paterson (1942) considered that this unit was a continuation of similar sediments found on the north side of the Chalk ridge 1km to the west (pit 16), where it overlies chalky sand which was, in turn, thought to be banked up against older glacial sediments ('brown boulder clay'), therefore separating the deposits into distinct glacial phases. The juxtaposition of the latter two deposits was not observed by Paterson, but was inferred from their respective altitudes.

In the light of the reinterpretation of the glacial deposits in the immediate vicinity of the East Farm brick pit as the product of a single glacial episode (see above), but in the absence of new information concerning this part of the sequence, it is considered unlikely that these deposits are *in situ* glacial sediments and are probably the result of mass movement processes. The sequence in Kidney Plantation pit probably represents deposition by outwash at the same time as the deposition of gravel in the channel beneath the brick pit, with deposition of a diamicton unit over the gravel as a result of solifluction (or gelifluction) processes.

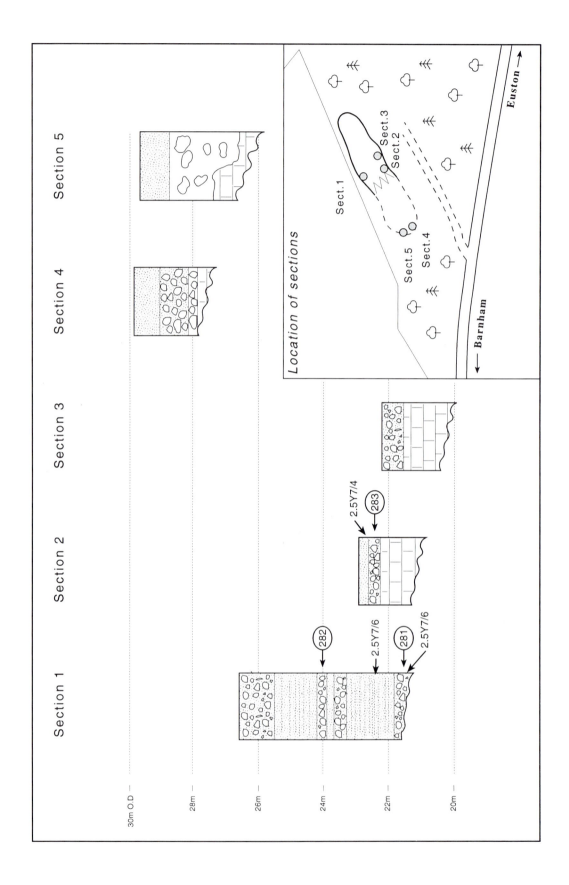

Fig. 4.33. Sections in Kidney Plantation Pit.

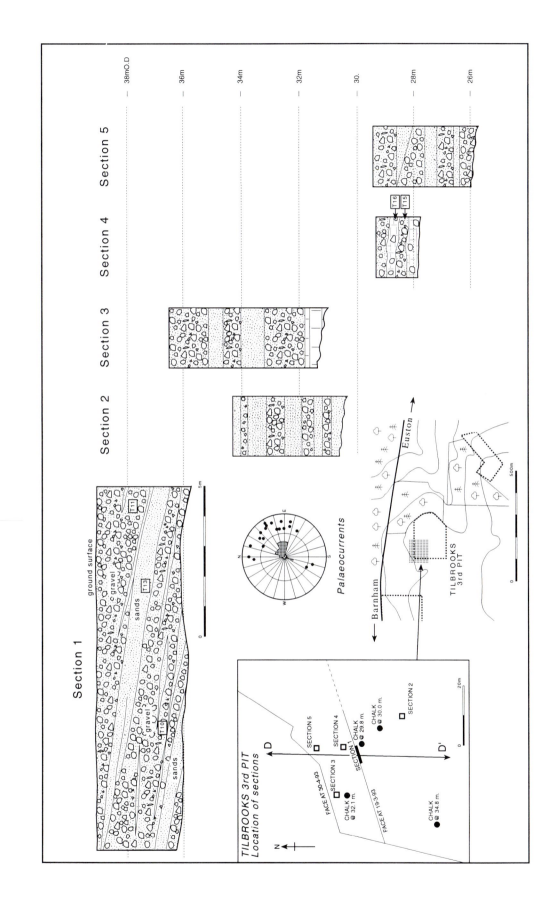

Fig. 4.34. Tilbrook's 3rd pit, sections 1-5.

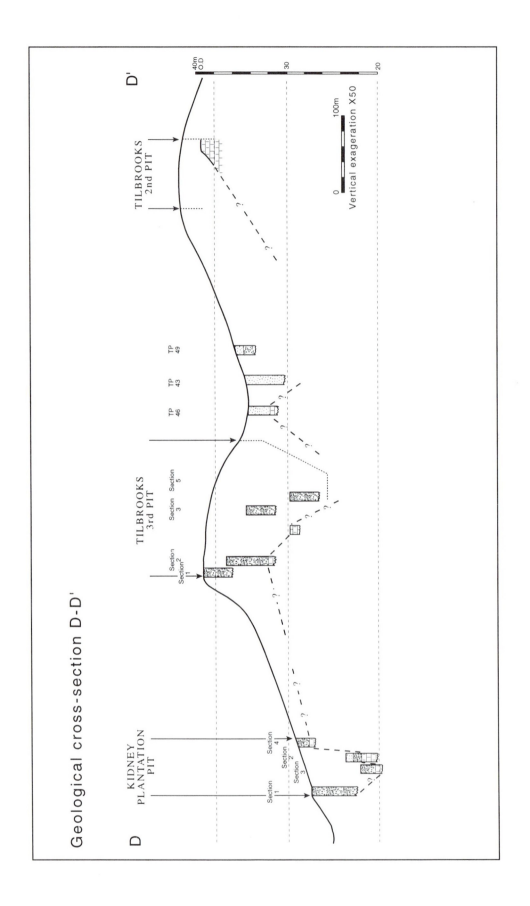

Fig. 4.35. Cross section D-D[1]. For line of section see Fig. 4.3.

Tilbrook's 1st gravel pit

This gravel pit is located close to Paterson's (1942) pit 14, to the south of the Barnham-Euston road some 500m north-east of the East Farm brick pit and 300m south-west of Kidney Plantation pit (Fig. 4.3). It is an extension of a pit first opened in 1941 and referred to by Paterson (1942) as the 'new pit'. Gravel then exposed in this pit, to a thickness of *c*.6m was thought to be a continuation of the Kidney Plantation sequence. A single exposure was recorded here in 1989 as back-filling of the pit with rubbish was nearing completion.

The section (Fig. 4.5) revealed *c*.2m of sand and gravel resting on a sloping Chalk surface, which dipped northwards. This gravel is overlain by 0.45m of yellowish brown (10YR 5/4 - 4/6) sand and silty sand. Above this is a thin light olive brown (2.5Y 5/4) chalky diamicton, containing large chalk pebbles and displaying crude sub-horizontal layering. Above this is a 0.8m thick unit of dark yellowish brown (10YR 4/4) sandy diamicton, with prominent sand layers 1-3cm in thickness. The upper contact is undulating and it is overlain by disturbed material.

The clast lithology of the basal gravel (Table 4.2) is predominantly flint (77.8%), with quartz and quartzite present in minor quantities. The overlying chalky diamicton consists mainly of chalk and flint. Only very few clasts were recovered from the brown sandy diamicton. Of these 72.4% were flint, with chalk (17.2%) and quartzose pebbles (8.6%) making up the remainder.

The sand and gravel is probably of glaciofluvial origin, their lithology being consistent with that of Unit 1 in the brick pit sequence. The chalky diamicton above is similar to chalky tills in the area and it is probably of glaciogenic origin. The laminations in the

unit are difficult to interpret from the small exposures available. They may result from either sub-glacial deformation processes, or from sediment gravity flows. Whichever is the case, the unit indicates glacial activity at or near the locality. The overlying brown-coloured diamicton is unlike the brown diamicton (Unit 3) described in the East Farm brick pit. It is not decalcified and contains relatively few flint pebbles. Its mode of origin is difficult to ascertain from the limited exposure available. It may be of glacial origin, though there is nothing diagnostic in the section to confirm this. The two sandy horizons within the unit suggest that water-lain sediments form at least part of this unit. The dissimilarity of this unit to the chalky diamicton below it and elsewhere in the area may indicate that, if it is the product of glacial deposition, it relates to a different ice sheet traversing different source sediments to that which deposited the chalky diamicton.

This pit lies to the north of the Chalk ridge that runs West to east across the area. The Chalk surface is at *c*.35m OD at this point and slopes northwards and it is possible that the gravel here forms part of the same sand and gravel deposit as that exposed in Kidney Plantation pit only some 300m to the north-east, overlying Chalk at a height of *c*.20m OD.

Tilbrook's 2nd gravel pit

This pit, located 1km east of East Farm brick pit (Fig. 4.3), was open only briefly in 1991, closing as the gravel deposits were quickly exhausted. No sections were recorded in the pit, though gravel was observed directly overlying Chalk bedrock. The surface of the Chalk rose rapidly to the south, suggesting that the southern edge of a gravel-filled channel occurs at this point.

sample number	qtz	qtzte	sst	glauc sst	Carb chert	*Rhaxella* chert	flint	chalk	lst	soft sst	ironst	Jurassic shell	ign	meta	other	n
281	2.5	9.0	1.1	0.4	1.4	0.0	58.5	19.1	4.7	0.0	0.0	0.4	1.8	0.0	1.1	277
	3.1	*11.2*	*1.3*	*0.4*	*1.8*	*0.0*	*72.3*	*(23.7)*	*5.8*	*0.0*	*0.0*	*0.4*	*2.2*	*0.0*	*1.3*	
282	1.8	5.0	1.8	0.0	2.5	0.5	61.7	22.9	1.4	0.0	0.5	0.2	0.9	0.0	0.9	441
	2.4	*6.5*	*2.4*	*0.0*	*3.2*	*0.6*	*80.0*	*(29.7)*	*1.8*	*0.0*	*0.6*	*0.3*	*1.2*	*0.0*	*1.2*	
283	4.2	10.8	1.7	0.0	0.4	0.4	55.8	19.2	0.8	0.0	2.9	0.8	0.4	0.0	2.5	240
	5.2	*13.4*	*2.1*	*0.0*	*0.5*	*0.5*	*69.1*	*(23.7)*	*1.0*	*0.0*	*3.6*	*1.0*	*0.5*	*0.0*	*3.1*	
T8	2.7	6.3	0.0	0.0	2.4	0.0	77.8	0.0	9.2	0.0	0.0	0.0	0.0	0.0	1.7	415
T10	5.1	7.4	0.6	0.0	2.3	0.0	83.7	0.0	0.0	0.0	0.0	0.0	0.0	0.0	0.9	661
T11	6.8	6.5	0.0	0.0	1.7	0.0	83.3	0.0	0.0	0.0	0.0	0.0	0.0	0.0	1.7	587
T15	5.7	11.3	0.0	0.0	1.1	0.0	50.9	29.8	0.0	0.0	0.0	0.0	0.0	0.0	1.1	265
	8.1	*16.1*	*0.0*	*0.0*	*1.6*	*0.0*	*72.6*	*(42.5)*	*0.0*	*0.0*	*0.0*	*0.0*	*0.0*	*0.0*	*1.6*	
T16	6.3	13.0	0.0	0.0	1.0	27.4	51.4	0.0	0.0	0.0	0.0	0.0	0.0	0.0	1.0	208

Table 4.2. Clast lithological analysis of deposits at Kidney Plantation Pit and Tilbrook's Pits, Barnham. 11.2-16.0mm size fraction counted from sands and gravels, 8.0-16.0mm fraction counted from diamicton units. Percentages calculated excluding the non-durable chalk component are also shown (in italics) for those samples containing chalk pebbles.

Tilbrook's 3rd gravel pit

This pit, the largest of the three, was opened in 1992. It lies adjacent to Gravelhill Plantation, 300m east of the 1st pit and 300m south of Kidney Plantation pit (Fig. 4.3). The ground surface at this point is *c*.39m OD. A number of sections were recorded in this pit during 1993 and 1994 (Fig. 4.34).

Section 1, located on the northern edge of the pit (Fig. 4.34), shows the upper part of the sequence. It consists of a series of large gravel and sand beds dipping in an easterly direction (Fig. 4.34). The gravel facies are up to *c*.1m in thickness and bedding within each facies is parallel with the upper and lower contacts (Fig. 4.32). Palaeocurrent measurements (Fig. 4.34) from the gravel deposits indicate an easterly flow direction (n=20). The top of this section is the ground surface at 39m OD.

Section 2 is located in the central part of the pit, where the Chalk surface is somewhat lower. The surface of the Chalk slopes southwards into the centre of the pit, and in the vicinity of this section is at 29.8m OD. Section 2 consists of coarse chalky gravel with beds of horizontally bedded sand, and occasional ripple drift silty sand with fine-grained drapes over ripple surfaces (Fig. 4.34). Section 3 on the northern edge of the pit displays 4.7m of sand and gravel overlying Chalk bedrock at an altitude of 32.0m OD.

Sections 4 and 5 are also located within the deeper part of the pit. Section 4 records chalky gravel inter-bedded with rubbly chalk containing flint, quartz and quartzite pebbles (Fig. 4.34). The base of this section is at *c*.27.8m OD. Section 5 shows coarse gravel, with crude horizontal bedding at the base and foreset beds higher up the sequence. A concave-up (channel) erosion surface is overlain by trough cross-stratified sand and pebbly sand (Fig. 4.34). The base of this section is at 26.6m OD. Chalk bedrock was not recorded beneath these sections, but must be below *c*.26m OD at this point.

A number of bulk samples were taken from these sections. The gravel is dominated by flint (Table 4.2), with samples T10 and T11 containing over 80% flint, with 12-13% quartz and quartzite. Chalk is absent. Sample T16 is conspicuously chalky, with 50.9% flint and 17% quartz and quartzite (Table 4.2). A bulk sample of the rubbly chalk in section 4 yielded a small number of clasts in the 11.2-16mm fraction, which consist of flint, quartz and quartzite, together with rounded chalk pebbles. The lack of chalk in samples T10 and T11 is probably the result of weathering and decalcification close to the ground surface.

The sand and gravel in this exposure is probably of glaciofluvial origin. The coarse nature, clast lithology and geometry of the gravel are not inconsistent with such an interpretation. The palaeoflow direction of these deposits is towards the east.

The sequence in this pit records a thick series of sand and gravel occupying a channel cut into the Chalk bedrock, down to at least 26m OD (Fig. 4.35). Chalk bedrock at the northern edge of the channel is at *c*.32m OD, dropping rapidly to the south to below 26m OD in the area of sections 4 and 5. The southern edge of this channel is probably located in the vicinity of Tilbrook's 2nd pit (Fig. 4.35). The sand and gravel may be the continuation of the gravel in East Farm brick pit (Unit 1) which is known to occupy a steep-sided channel in the Chalk. The probable configuration of the channel is indicated in Fig. 4.3, based upon these observations and on the geophysical data (see Chapter 5). It is also possible that this channel may be continuous with the tunnel valley feature identified at Euston (Woodland 1970). The Chalk ridge that separates the East Farm pit from the modern River Little Ouse is not a prominent feature at this point and the gravel exposed in the pit may form a continuous spread either side of the ridge, associated with a marked channel feature, but also forming a more extensive spread of gravel northwards at least as far as Kidney Plantation pit.

THE BARNHAM SEQUENCE

The foregoing descriptions of the Quaternary geology of the East Farm brick pit and a number of other localities in the area allow a complete reassessment of the Quaternary succession of the district. Paterson (1937, 1942) undertook a detailed investigation of the geological succession and suggested a complex sequence of events (Fig. 4.36). The current investigations have re-examined some of the critical localities and key stratigraphical relationships in this sequence and on this basis a major revision of the Barnham sequence is proposed (Fig. 4.32).

The first recognisable event in the area is the erosion of a steep-sided channel in the Chalk bedrock. This probably occurred beneath an ice-sheet (cf. Woodland 1970). This channel was filled with glaciofluvial sand and gravel (Unit 1), followed by deposition of a sheet of chalky diamicton (till) over the area (Unit 2) by an ice sheet moving across the region from the west. It is possible that, during an early stage of glaciation, this ice-sheet interacted with another ice-sheet in this area; the section in Tilbrook's 1st pit suggests that two distinct glaciogenic units may be present at that site. On the basis of observations and analysis of samples from this site during the 1979 excavations by Wymer, Prof. J. Rose arrived at a similar conclusion and suggested that deposits in this pit were of 'Cromer till type' (J. Rose, unpublished data and pers. comm.). Deposition of sand and gravel appears to have been extensive to the north of the site in the area now occupied by the Little Ouse valley. It is possible that outwash deposition took place roughly simultaneously over much of this area. However the deposition of the gravel at Kidney Plantation pit may have taken place as the ice retreated.

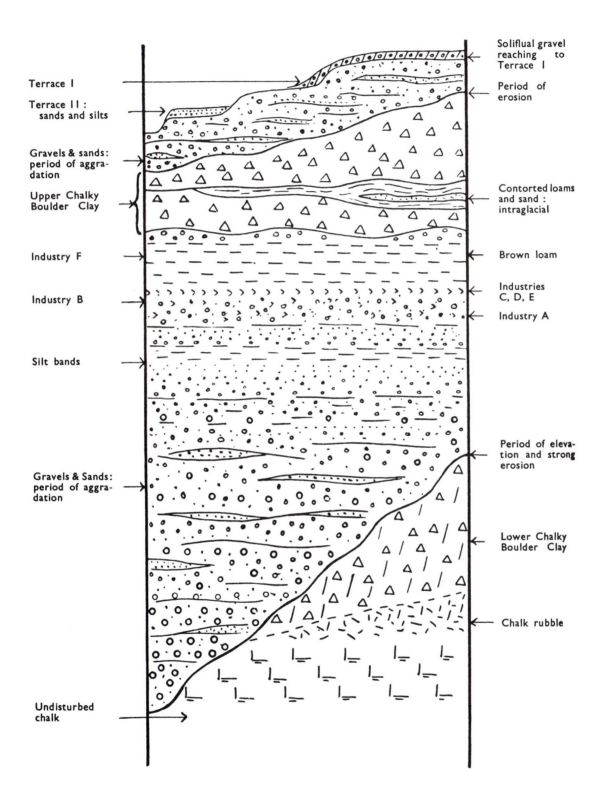

Fig. 4.36. The Barnham sequence according to Paterson (1937). Reproduced by kind permission of the Prehistoric Society.

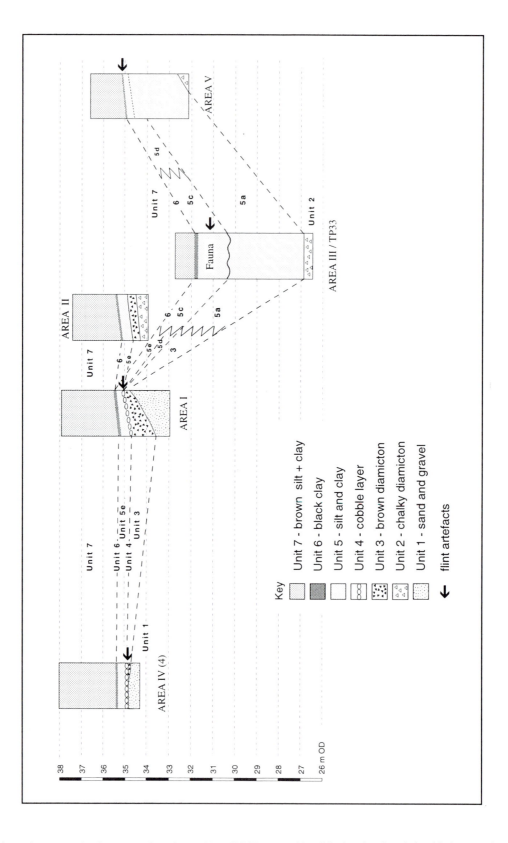

Fig. 4.37. Schematic cross section from approximately east (Area IV(4)) to west (Area V), showing the relationship between the main artefact bearing units, modified from Ashton *et al.* 1994b.

At the end of the glacial episode continued fluvial activity led to the incision of a channel in the surface of the chalky diamicton in the area of the East Farm brick pit. On the edges of the channel decalcification and mass movement processes led to the formation of brown diamicton (Unit 3) which extends a few metres into the channel. Gravel deposits (Unit 1) exposed along the margins of the channel formed a surface over which water occasionally flowed, winnowing fine grained sediments away to leave a coarse layer of flint cobbles (Unit 4). The channel began to fill with fine-grained sediments (Unit 5), consisting of a number of facies reflecting deposition at the margins and in the centre of the channel. In the centre of the channel the sequence consists of mainly silts and clays, occasionally laminated, with layers of fine sand, suggesting still water conditions, with periodic low energy moving water. Along the margins of the channel the sediments are coarser and occasionally stony, suggesting inputs from the channel sides. The sediments filling this channel become progressively more organic and fossiliferous up through the sequence, suggesting a change in the environment during deposition of the sequence.

This sequence appears to be sealed across much of the pit by a thin dark brown or black clay layer (Unit 6). This unit has been studied through micro-morphological investigations, which indicate that it is a weakly developed soil (Chapter 6). Above this, the remainder of the sequence consists of brown, oxidised silt and clay ('brickearth') (Unit 7) which complete the infill of the channel feature. This unit probably formed as a result of alluvial and colluvial processes, and its deposition is punctuated by periods of land surface stability and incipient soil formation (Chapter 6).

This revised sequence differs substantially from that proposed by Paterson (1937, 1942). In particular, only one glacial episode is recognised, rather than the three proposed by Paterson (1942). This glacial episode is followed by sedimentation in a channel during the subsequent temperate phase. There is no evidence for glacial activity at this site after the infilling of the channel took place. The fine-grained, fossiliferous deposits in the centre of the channel can be associated with the archaeological horizons on the margins of the channel, where the geological sequence is greatly condensed. This revised geological succession provides a framework in which the archaeological evidence can be reassessed:

THE RELATIONSHIP OF THE PRINCIPAL ARTEFACT LOCATIONS WITHIN THE BARNHAM SEQUENCE

The key locations from which artefacts have been recovered are: (1) Area I, on and within the cobble layer (Unit 4) and from within the overlying yellow silty sand (Unit 5e); (2) Area IV(4), within and on the cobble layer (Unit 4) and the base of the overlying yellow silty sand (Unit 5e); (3) Area V, from the upper part of Unit 5 (Unit 5d); (4) Area III (faunal area) in the centre of the pit. A small number of artefacts have been recovered from other locations across the site, although only the localities listed above will be considered further below. Full details of the artefact assemblages are given in Chapters 19-23. The position in the geological succession as a whole and the relationship of these assemblages to each other underpin the interpretation of the archaeological information (Fig. 4.37). A number of observations of particular importance, are discussed briefly below.

The artefact assemblages in Area I and Area IV(4) occur in the same stratigraphic position; they are both found within and on the cobble layer (Unit 4) and in the case of Area I from the base of the overlying yellow silty sand. This unit is capped in both areas by the black clay of Unit 6. Ashton *et al.* (1994b) argued on this basis for the contemporaniety of the artefact assemblages from these two areas. Although they are some 50m apart, there is a remarkable similarity in the two sequences, an observation supported by sections in Area IV(5), which also show a similar stratigraphy, suggesting that the sequence is continuous along that part of the south-eastern pit edge, though with some height variability. Thus, given this level of stratigraphic resolution, it is reasonable to suggest that the assemblages are broadly contemporaneous. However, the problems created by the episodic deposition and erosion that must have occurred during the accumulation of the sequence, the sporadic nature of human occupation of the site during that period and the small amount of reworking of artefacts from the surface of the cobbles into the overlying yellow silty sand make it impossible to determine more precisely the nature of the relationship between the two assemblages. While this is a key problem to be addressed at this site, contemporaneity can only be demonstrated within the stratigraphic resolution of the sequence.

The small assemblage of artefacts found in Area III occurs at various points over a depth of 60cm within the sediments (Unit 5c) that filled the channel during the temperate episode. It has been shown above that this channel fill sequence thins towards the margins and passes laterally into Unit 5e (Fig. 4.37). It is therefore possible to demonstrate that these sediments, which overlie the cobble layer in Area I and Area IV(4), equate with the thicker channel fill sequence (Unit 5c) in the centre of the pit. This suggests that the archaeology associated with Unit 5e is contemporaneous with the filling of the channel during the temperate episode and with the artefacts that occur within that channel-fill. The artefacts from the centre of the channel may be considered as in primary context and their presence here is of some significance in relating the main artefact assemblages in Area I and Area IV(4) to the floral and faunal data derived from the thicker channel-fill sequence in Area III.

Artefacts recovered from Area V are associated with Unit 5d, and occur beneath a darker horizon that is equated with the black clay (Unit 6) in Area I. This assemblage is therefore also associated with marginal facies of the channel-fill sequence and is located at the edge of the channel feature with Unit 5d being laterally equivalent to Unit 5e in Area I (Fig 4.37). In this respect it shows similarities with the Area I and Area IV(4) assemblages. Its relationship to the underlying and overlying deposits also demonstrates that it can be considered to be contemporaneous with the assemblages from Area III, Area I and from Area IV(4).

It can be shown that the four main locations from which significant quantities of artefacts have been recovered occur within the same part of the sequence in different areas of the site, namely the fine-grained sediments that fill the channel cut into the glacial deposits. The altitudinal position of the sequences from these areas (Fig. 4.37) indicates that, while there is some variation in the altitude of the artefact-bearing sediments, this is consistent with the variations in height that would be expected between the centre and the margins of the channel. The height and thickness of the overlying black clay (Unit 6) also varies across the site (Fig. 4.29) and is lowest in the centre of the channel.

Taken together the stratigraphic and sedimentological information from this site clearly suggests that all the archaeology can be considered to be contemporaneous, as it occurs within laterally equivalent deposits. It is not possible to state any more precise relationships as the stratigraphic resolution is too coarse to allow more detailed assessment, nor can the archaeology be related to any specific part or parts of the interglacial sequence as the palaeo-environmental information is derived from Area III and the majority of the archaeology from Area I and Area IV(4). It is within this stratigraphic context and these constraints that the archaeology must be interpreted.

CORRELATION WITH THE REGIONAL SUCCESSION

The Barnham sequence can be related to the regional Quaternary succession in East Anglia firstly through correlation of the glaciogenic sediments. The chalky diamicton (Unit 2) can be correlated with the Lowestoft till: the regionally extensive till sheet deposited over much of eastern England (Perrin *et al.* 1979). The brown sandy diamicton observed in Tilbrook's 1st pit has been tentatively interpreted as a glaciogenic unit and may be correlated with the suite of deposits known as the North Sea Drift. The unit identified here may be equivalent to the Starston till, recognised in the lower Waveney valley (Lawson 1982; Auton *et al.* 1985) which has been correlated with the Norwich brickearth, a weathered facies of the North Sea Drift. The Lowestoft till has been defined as a member (Lowestoft Till Member) of the Lowestoft Formation and the Starston till as the Starston Member of the North Sea Drift Formation (Bowen *et al.* in press). Both the Lowestoft and the North Sea Drift Formations are of Anglian age (Mitchell *et al.* 1973).

Overlying the glaciogenic succession at Barnham is a series of fine-grained deposits. These deposits have been collectively termed the Barnham Formation (Bowen *et al.* in press) and comprise Units 3-7. The deposition of these sediments probably began at the end of the Anglian Stage, but continued into the subsequent temperate episode. There is no indication of a major hiatus in this sequence of deposits which fill the channel cut into the top of the chalky diamicton. These sediments, which contain floral and faunal remains and archaeological material, may therefore be assigned to the Hoxnian Stage as this is the temperate stage immediately following the Anglian glaciation (Mitchell *et al.* 1973). However it should be noted that it has been suggested that the type site for the Hoxnian Stage is separated from the Anglian by a cold-warm climate cycle (Bowen *et al.* 1989). This raises the question of time-equivalence of this sequence with that at the Hoxnian stratotype. This will be considered further (Chapter 24) in the light of the palaeontological and geochronological information presented in Chapters 11 and 16-18.

5. GEOPHYSICAL INVESTIGATIONS

Clive Roberts

INTRODUCTION

During 1992 and 1993 a resistivity survey was undertaken across the dry valley around the East Farm Pit. It was hoped that use of this technique might distinguish between the four basic geological units known from the site - fine-grained clay and silt, sand and gravel, chalky diamicton and solid Chalk.

It has long been appreciated that there is a significant geophysical contrast between Cretaceous Chalk and overlying sediments, mostly in terms of conductivity/resistivity and density. Electrical surveying techniques, particularly resistivity, have been successfully used by geologists and archaeologists to examine sub-surface features of both natural and unnatural origins (Aspinall & Walker 1975; Barker & Harker 1984; Cornwell & Carruthers 1991; Noel 1992). Vertical electrical sounding (VES) is a simple technique used to give high quality information about lithological variations or interface boundaries with sub-horizontal attitudes. Although computer modelling can give detailed information on such lithological and thickness variations, there are two important points to consider.

First, as electrical currents are transferred through the sub-surface strata by the movement of ions in waters held within pores and fissures, resistivity generally increases as porosity increases and decreases as water content increases. Such characteristics can also be influenced by groundwater geochemistry and sediment grain morphologies. Consequently, a heterogenous sand unit may have resistivity values that deviate from an average value depending on its local composition. Second, it is vital to obtain good quality borehole data for ground truthing purposes, so that quality interpretations can be inferred from both observed and computed information.

METHODOLOGY

The main method of data collection used at this site concentrated on the Offset Wenner system of measurement (Barker 1981) with a multicore cable length of 256m and an ABEM Terrameter SAS 300 as the field power source. Standard Wenner arrays use a collinear array of four equally spaced electrodes, where a direct current is applied to the outer two electrodes and a resultant potential difference is measured across the inner two electrodes after a short time interval. Increasing the electrode spacing allows the current to penetrate deeper into the sub-surface strata and hence provides an indication of any change in ground characterisation. An offset switch is used to negate the influence of near-surface anomalies caused by the effects of boulders or other similar sized objects. For a 256m cable, an average depth of penetration would be expected in the order of 40-45m. In practice, this figure could increase or decrease due to a number of factors, not least being the depth to the water table.

RESISTIVITY SURVEY

A total of nine linear soundings were carried out along a general north-south trend in order to study the thicknesses of lithologies around the brick-pit area. Individual arrays were aligned east-west to parallel not only the contour features of the dry valley but also the postulated position of the channel and to allow the traverse to extend to the north and south of the pit (Fig. 5.1). The arrays were also aligned east-west to minimise the probability of cutting across different geological units. The plough soil allowed easy penetration for the electrodes and there was very little disturbance to the electrical signal from chalk/flint cobbles or boulders.

RESULTS

Field Data

Most of the readings of apparent resistivity obtained from field measurements fell within the range 40-125Ωm. Logarithmic plots of the derived data displayed changes in the gradient of the plots to suggest lithological variation below ground level. Overall sampling errors were estimated at less than 2% from repeatability measurements and so reasonable confidence can be placed on resistivity values obtained. The range of true resistivity values for individual layers is likely to be beyond the ranges measured in the field due to a variety of reasons, but generally would be reflected in the slope changes in plotted data. Computer modelling procedures can utilise the gradient of slopes and provide absolute resistivity values with thickness information of individual layers.

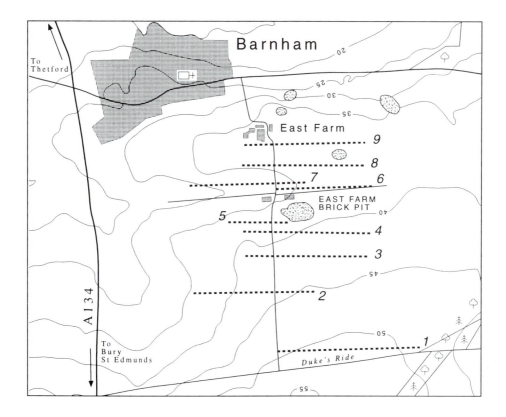

Fig. 5.1. Plan of the survey area. Dashed lines numbered 1 to 9 indicate the location of individual resistivity arrays.

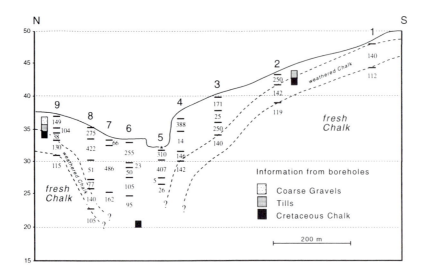

Fig. 5.2. Idealised north-south cross section. Numbers above ground level refer to numbered traverses in Figure 5.1. Numbers below ground level indicate true resistivity values of individual layers with appropriate thicknesses from computer modelling. The symbol * below traverse 5 represents a value of 940Ωm. Dashed lines represent the fresh and weathered Chalk boundaries.

Computer Modelling

Toggling of observed data was undertaken using "RESIX" software, which uses the observed slope of profiles and compares them to the computed slopes of data entered by the operator. A close fit between the two indicates a reasonable model of resistivity values and layer thickness. The results are given in Figure 5.2, which shows the projected computed values from the linear arrays. Fitting errors between the observed and computed curves for all nine locations were 1.2% ± 0.5%, which indicates a relatively high level of precision. However, some degree of caution should be considered when a large number of layers are inferred (e.g. under location 6), as these may not be geologically justifiable. Nevertheless, true resistivity values in the range 5-407Ωm probably indicate good lithological variation. One thin high resistivity layer of 940Ωm (marked *, Fig. 5.2) is required to explain a relatively steep gradient in the plotted data associated with location 5.

LITHOLOGICAL INTERPRETATION

At localities 1, 2, 3, 4, 8 and 9 (where depth to Cretaceous Chalk bedrock is probably shallowest) two resitivity values are postulated for the solid geology, i.e. an upper layer of 130-142Ωm (around 2.5 to 3m in thickness) and a lower layer of 105-119Ωm. The lower layer represents fresh Cretaceous Chalk that is relatively unfissured with an absence of both solutional cavities and probably significant flint bands. The upper layer may reflect a degree of weathering in the same lithological unit, resulting in either a higher clay content in the matrix or possibly increased fissuring. A large range of values is obtained for the superficial deposits, indicating four potential lithological types. Very low values in the range 5-25Ωm may be a clay-rich layer and are probably best correlated with the brickearths previously quarried in the area. Values in the range 25-100Ωm indicate a larger clast size associated with an increased bulk porosity, probably reflecting silt to fine sand types of lithologies. Medium to coarse sands and gravels with a higher bulk porosity are interpreted for values in the range 100-275Ωm. The highest resistivity values of 388-940Ωm are indicative of cobble and boulder layers with a more prominent open framework. Stabilised water levels in old farm wells below 20m OD in the immediate vicinity indicated that the regional water table was too low to have influenced the results during the survey period. However, perched water could have been contained within the Pleistocene sequence. As the survey followed a prolonged dry spell and no water problems were reported during excavations, resistivity values in the four main lithological units are perceived as being unaffected by groundwater.

DISCUSSION

Corroborative information from boreholes indicates that depth to the Chalk bedrock can be modelled to a high degree of accuracy by resistivity sounding. A deep sediment filled channel clearly occupies the present-day dry valley, but the precise nature and exact depth of the main channel is poorly constrained by this survey, although the peripheral aspects are reasonably well modelled. Deep penetration and characterisation of the solid geology below the channel is theoretically possible using the Wenner array, but the lateral extent of the linear spread required is hampered by interference from farm buildings, old foundations, made ground and inhomogenous superficial deposits. However, a suitable model of the channel configuration may be possible using electrical imaging techniques with an array perpendicular to the present survey. A north-south gravity survey by CLR (unpublished) over the same site reveals negative Bouguer anomalies along three independent traverses perpendicular to the present-day dry valley. Such observations are consistent with a sequence of sand and gravel deposits infilling an incised valley in the Chalk, where the infilling sequence is less dense than the host Chalk rock. There may be some advantage in undertaking further geophysical investigations to delineate channel characteristics and so further gravity and electrical imaging will be undertaken in the future to model such features over a wider area.

The rapid lithological changes within the channel configuration, suggested by lateral and vertical resistivity contrasts, is not best explored using Wenner techniques. Nevertheless, considerable variation in ground conductivity is apparent and so electrical imaging using a 50-electrode array may provide the increased internal definition required. Layers of argillaceous material in the stratigraphic column will probably argue against the use of ground penetrating radar (GPR) techniques to provide further detail, as clay absorbs a significant amount of the signal energy and hampers adequate penetration. However, a focus for future research must be to provide more detail on the internal stratigraphy of the channel as well as further constraining the overall dimensions of large scale sedimentary structures.

6. MICROMORPHOLOGY OF THE AREA I SEQUENCE AT EAST FARM, BARNHAM

Rob A. Kemp

INTRODUCTION

The Lower Palaeolithic site at East Farm, Barnham has been investigated by a number of archaeologists and Quaternary scientists over the last 60 years. The 1989-94 excavation re-exposed and enlarged a section (Area I) containing artefact-bearing strata which had been previously described by Wymer (1985). The section (Fig. 6.1) is fully described in Chapter 4. Briefly it consists of glaciofluvial sand and gravel (Unit 1) overlain by a brown diamicton (Unit 3) that probably owes its origin to mass movement processes. This unit is itself covered by fluvial cobble lag (Unit 4) and yellow silty sand (Unit 5e) deposits. The sequence is completed by a thin black clay layer (Unit 6) overlain by several metres of brown silt and clay ('brickearth') (Unit 7) containing laterally continuous, darker brown bands. It is suggested that this 'brickearth' probably accumulated by a combination of low-energy fluvial deposition and sheet wash from adjacent slopes.

Wymer (1985) introduced the possibility that the black clay beneath the 'brickearth' might be a buried palaeosol, in which case, similar origins could be invoked for the darker bands within the 'brickearth' itself. Field examination of the units has been inconclusive, however, so it was decided to utilise a micromorphological approach based upon detailed characterisation of thin sections from throughout the sequence. Previous micromorphological studies of similar sequences have been successful not only in clarifying the status of such units, but also reconstructing relevant pedosedimentary formative stages (Kemp 1985a, 1985b; Kemp *et al.* 1994; Preece *et al.* 1995).

METHODS

A series of bulk samples were taken from several of the units as indicated in Figure 6.1 and their organic carbon contents determined using the wet oxidation method outlined by Bascomb (1982). Undisturbed blocks were collected within Kubiena tins (7 x 5 x 4cm) at irregular intervals down the sequence (Fig. 6.1). Each block was air-dried, impregnated with polyester resin and made into a thin section according to standard procedures (Lee & Kemp 1992). Thin sections were described at 10-400x magnification under a polarising microscope using terminology modified from Bullock *et al.* (1985)

and Kemp (1985a). Semi-quantitative estimates of the areal cover of key micromorphological features were made by reference to previously point-counted thin sections (Murphy & Kemp 1984) and standard frequency charts (Bullock *et al.* 1985).

MICROMORPHOLOGICAL FEATURES

The main micromorphological features recorded within the sequence are illustrated in Plate 6.1. The ratio of coarse to fine material (c:f 10μm) in the groundmass is generally between 3:2 and 1:2, with the size of the coarse particles ranging from 10-500μm (Pls 6.1a & 6.1b). These variations are clearly a function of changing depositional regimes. The colour of the fine material mainly reflects the dominating influence of redox processes (Vepraskas *et al.* 1994) associated with periodic anaerobic conditions, which have led to the redistribution of iron (Fe) and manganese (Mn) oxides and creation of irregular mottling patterns comprising grey depleted zones (<1-2cm) and orange-brown zones (<1-2cm) of concentration (Pl. 6.1c). Further evidence of these hydromorphic processes is provided by Fe/Mn pure coatings (<100μm) and root pseudomorphs (<100μm) around and within voids, and hypocoatings (<200μm) of Fe/Mn oxides superimposed upon groundmass in zones parallel to planar voids and channels (Pl. 6.1d).

The composition of these redox concentration features can be crudely estimated by observing them under oblique incident light whereby shades of yellowish brown, orange and red colours are often taken to indicate the presence of various iron oxides, and black colours are attributed to manganese oxides, although it is likely that many features contain both components in differing proportions (Bullock *et al.* 1985). Under these light conditions, parts of the groundmass sometimes has a greyish brown pigment. Again, although not completely diagnostic, these colours are often caused by concentrations of small quantities of organic substances superimposed upon the fine material of the groundmass (Bullock *et al.* 1985). Organic staining of this kind, associated with very low bulk organic carbon contents, has been reported from buried A horizons of palaeosols within colluvial sequences in the Isle of Wight (Preece *et al.* 1995). Close examination of some thin sections from Barnham under oblique incident light also reveals the presence of greyish brown (organically-stained?) rounded, equant aggregates (<2mm) embedded within non-organically-pigmented groundmass. These aggregates are interpreted as remnants of a granular soil structure formed in a pre-existing A horizon which has partially survived diagenetic compaction, ageing and disintegration.

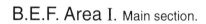
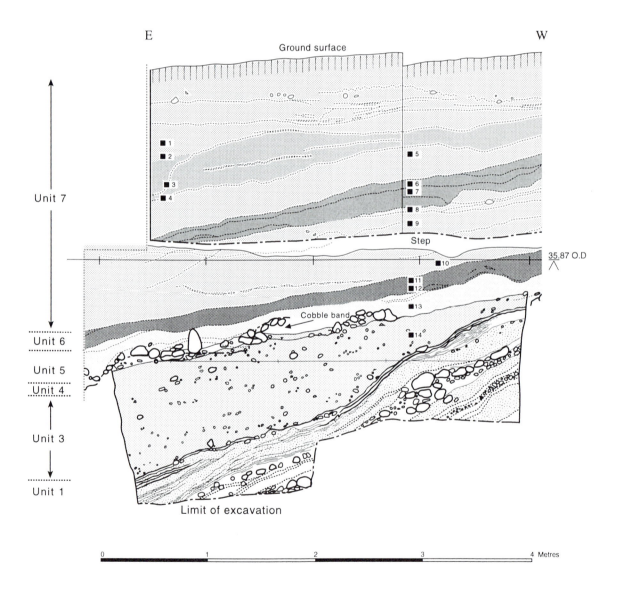

B.E.F. Area I. Main section.

Fig. 6.1. Area I, part of main section showing location of thin sections.

The other main micromorphological features in the thin sections from Barnham are the continuously oriented, micro-laminated and non-laminated, speckled and limpid clay coatings (50-250µm) around channels and packing voids (Pls 6.1e & 6.1f). These are pedogenic in origin, resulting from the accumulation of clay-size particles moved down in suspension from an overlying soil horizon (McKeague 1983; Kemp 1985a). Sometimes the coatings are deformed (Pl. 6.1g), perhaps in response to biotic or even freeze-thaw disruptive processes. The well-developed monostriated, granostriated and random striated b-fabrics of the associated groundmasses (Bullock *et al.* 1985), however, tend to support a shrink-swell mechanism for the deformation. The few sharply bounded, rounded fragmented coatings embedded within some groundmasses, sometimes where there are no other illuvial clay features (Pl. 6.1h), are similar to features described from sediments at Northfleet (Kent) by Kemp (1991). They are interpreted as representing clay coatings originally formed in a soil at another location. The soil was then eroded with the coatings being fragmented, transported and incorporated into the deposited sediment.

DEPTH DISTRIBUTION OF KEY MICROMORPHOLOGICAL FEATURES

The depth distribution of some key micromorphological features is summarised in Figure 6.2. The presence of embedded, rounded fragmented clay coatings within the groundmass of the brown diamicton towards the base of the sampling profile adds support to the interpretation that this unit originated by erosion and mass movement of adjacent soils and sediments.

The vertical trend in c:f 10µm ratios above suggests that the yellow silty sand and black clay represent a fining-up fluvial sequence which culminated in establishment of a relatively 'stable' land surface and soil development. The black clay is in essence the A horizon of a palaeosol, the colour reflecting the pigmenting influence of very small amounts of finely-divided organic matter mixed in, or superimposed upon, the groundmass. Further evidence for the pedogenic modification of this unit is provided by the organically-stained granular aggregates.

Despite its clear macro- and micromorphological expression, this 'palaeo'. A horizon contains very little organic carbon (0.3%), certainly nothing approaching typical organic carbon values of present-day topsoils in the region (ca. 2-5%). Furthermore, there is only a limited vertical trend in terms of contrasts in contents between the A horizon(s) and over/underlying sediments, although this may be a consequence of a limited number of samples analysed and the problems of chemically differentiating fossil humic material from

modern root contaminants. Similar low values reported from the Late-glacial Pitstone Soil in the Isle of Wight were attributed to post-burial oxidation (Preece *et al.* 1995). The frequent reported absence of A horizons within buried palaeosols is often conveniently attributed to a phase of pre-burial erosion, whereas in many places they may be present but simply not recognised due to diagenetic oxidation, compaction and alteration or, where covering sediment thicknesses are minimal or aggradation rates slow, transformation into B horizons of subsequent soils.

Clay coatings in the yellow silty sand at Barnham may have formed during this phase of pedogenesis with clay being translocated down from the A horizon into an underlying B horizon. The presence of clay coatings throughout the whole vertical sequence, however, makes it difficult to apportion the features to specific phases of translocation, particularly as they do not appear in obvious superposition. In any case, interpretations based upon subtle vertical trends in illuvial clay contents would have to be treated with caution, due to the high levels of stress reorganisation which make recognition and accurate quantification of illuvial clay difficult (McKeague 1983). Nevertheless, the clay coatings within and above the A horizon (black clay) clearly must have resulted from translocation processes active at higher land surfaces once aggradation had been initiated and presumably then diminished again. It is logical to correlate these land-surfaces with the dark bands within the overlying 'brickearth'; these have the previously-discussed micromorphological characteristics of A horizons of soils.

There is a clear sedimentary break between the soil developed in the fluvial sediments and the overlying 'brickearth', as shown by a marked fining in c:f 10µm ratios and the smaller size of coarse particles. The complex origin of the 'brickearth' is confirmed by the layers of different textures towards the top of the unit, some of them containing embedded fragmented clay coatings presumably eroded from soils at other locations. Undisturbed or deformed clay coatings and redox concentration/depletion features are ubiquitous throughout the 'brickearth', further confirming the influence of *in situ* pedogenic processes at various stages during its accumulation. The lack of any consistent superposition of these features precludes the opportunity to reconstruct an ordered process sequence. However, the frequent occurrence in the same thin section of ferrimanganiferous depletion and concentration features either superimposed on (i.e. postdating), or coated by (i.e. predating), illuvial clay features indicates a complex and perhaps varying pedogenic environment with both redox and translocation processes active throughout the development of the pedosedimentary complex.

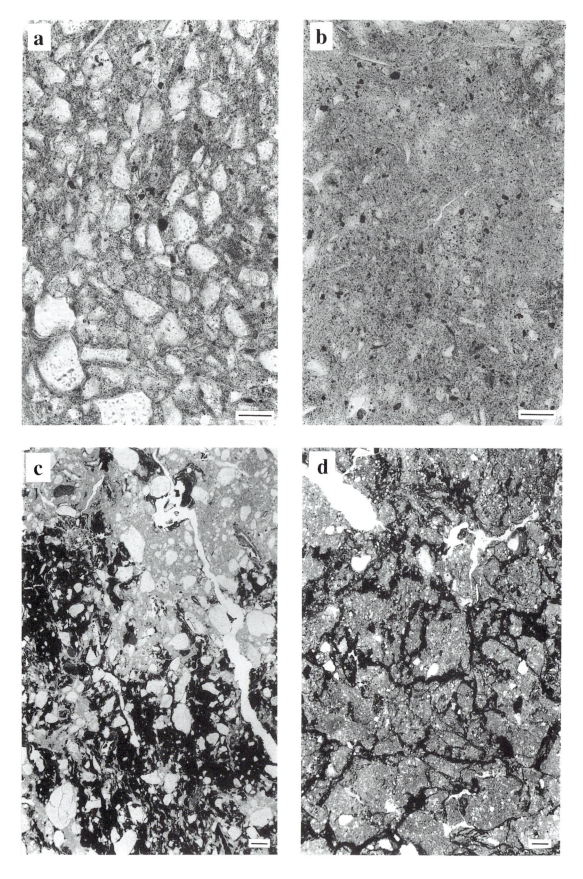

Plate 6.1. Photomicrographs of major micromorphological features. Plane polarised light; scale bar = 250µm. a. Groundmass with a c:f ratio = 3:2; b. Groundmass with a c:f ratio = 1:2; c. Ferrimanganiferous concentration and depletion mottles extending across the groundmass; d. Ferrimanganiferous hypocoatings, coatings and root pseudomorphs lining and infilling voids.

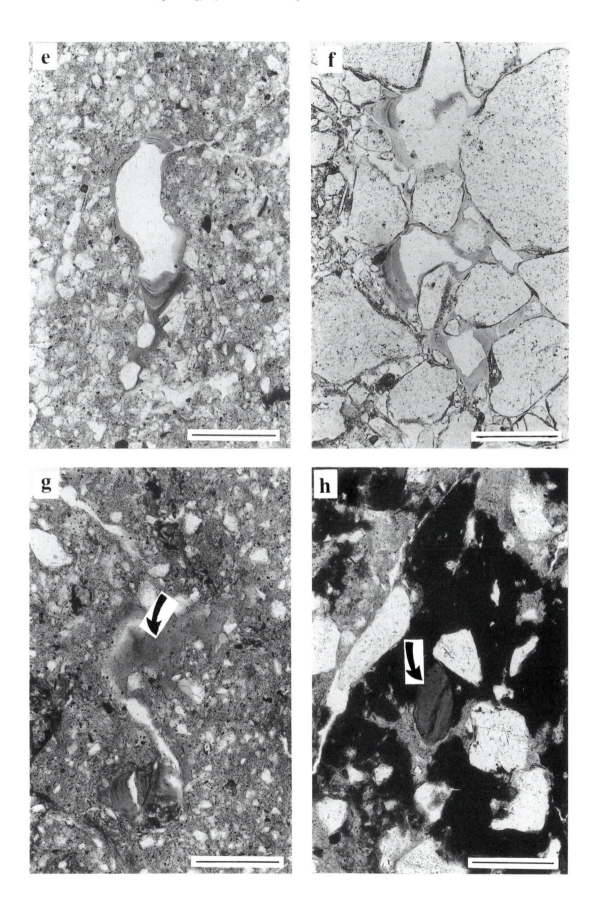

Plate 6.1 cont. e. Undisturbed clay coatings around channels; f. Undisturbed clay coatings around sand grains; g. Deformed clay coatings (arrowed); h. Rounded fragmented clay coatings (arrowed) embedded within the groundmass.

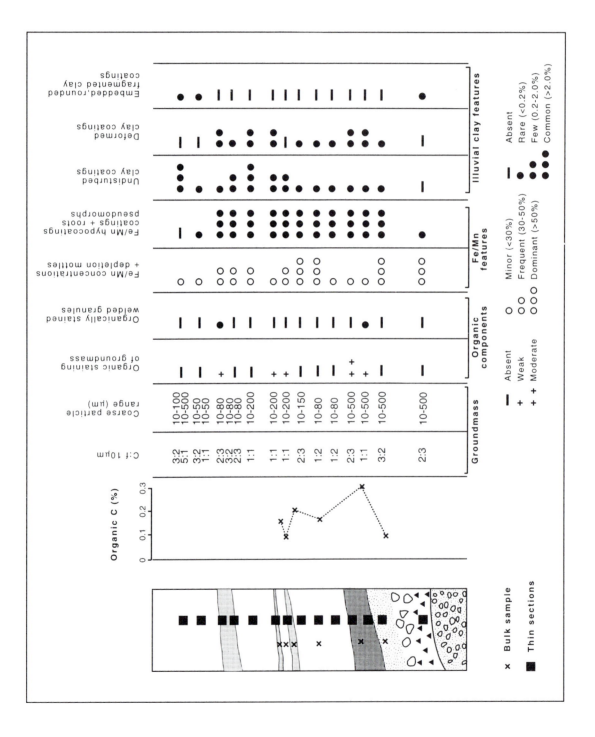

Fig. 6.2. Composite log of Area I section against depth functions of organic carbon and micromorphological features.

CONCLUSIONS

Analysis of 14 thin sections from throughout the Area I section at Barnham suggests a complex pedosedimentary history. The sediments were apparently deposited in stages separated by phases of relative stability when land surfaces were established and soils developed. The oldest soil, recognised mainly by the remnant characteristics of its A horizon, formed in the fluvial deposits above the brown diamicton and fluvioglacial sands and gravels. Several darker bands within the overlying 'brickearth' probably also represent A horizons of soils. Each sedimentary unit was insufficiently thick to bury the underlying soil and isolate it from the effects of pedogenesis associated with the next landsurface(s). The whole vertical sequence has been pedogenically-altered with illuvial clay coatings and ferruginous mottles extending above, within and below these buried A horizons . The complete sequence could therefore be considered as a complex 'welded' soil consisting of a series of overlapping sola.

7. INTRODUCTION TO THE VERTEBRATE ASSEMBLAGES

Simon Parfitt

INTRODUCTION

Although faunal remains were reported from East Farm Pit, Barnham, through eyewitness accounts in the earlier part of this century, both Paterson (1937, 1942) and Wymer (1985) were unable to locate the deposits in which they were contained (also see Appendix VII). It was only during the current excavations in 1991 that fragmented shell was found on the western edge of the Area III south section, and in corresponding deposits in the Area III west extension trench. The expansion of this trench towards Area I in 1992, revealed a series of pits and sections, originally cut during the clay extraction, through the calcareous grey silt and clay. It was clear that these sediments contained an abundant microfauna, and so Pits 4 and 9 were selected and column samples were taken from their west and east sections respectively. In 1993 a 2m x 3m area, adjacent to Pit 9, was selected for area excavation, being completed in 1994.

From this sampling and excavation programme, over nine tonnes of sediment was sieved and a vast quantity of small vertebrate fauna was recovered. This chapter provides an introduction to this work, in particular the context and location of the sampled sediments, but also the methodologies used in their extraction and processing. It is concluded with some preliminary comments on the taphonomy of the vertebrate assemblages. The detailed reports on the vertebrate fauna are given in Chapters 8 - 11.

THE GREY SILT AND CLAY

All the faunal remains were recovered from the grey silt and clay (Unit 5c; see Chapter 4). This sub-unit forms part of the channel sediments (Unit 5) that were laid down under slow-flowing to still water conditions and postdate the glacial to late glacial sequence (Units 1 - 3; see Chapter 4). The channel sediments reach a maximum depth of 14m, but it is the top 2-3m of this fill, in the middle of the channel, that forms the grey silt and clay. Lateral equivalents of the sub-unit are found at the edges of the channel, in the form of the brown stony clay (Unit 5d) in Area III south section, and in the flint artefact-bearing yellow silty sand (Unit 5e) in Areas I and IV(4). All these units (5c - 5e) are sealed by the black clay (Unit 6; see Chapters 4 and 6) which formed after the silting-up of the channel and represents the formation of a stable landsurface.

Study of the sections revealed in Pits 1 to 9 showed stratigraphic variation in the composition of the grey silt and clay, and also showed that these sediments dipped to the north-west towards the centre of the channel. As a result, the sediments on the present surface of the clay pit become progressively younger towards the centre of the channel, with those revealed in Pit 4 being stratigraphically lower than those in Pit 9 (for full discussion see Chapter 4). Although the exact relationship between the two pits has not been established, due to the complexity of the lateral variations, it is argued that the sediments in Pit 4 and Pit 9 form a semi-continuous sequence through the grey silt and clay.

The subdivisions of the grey silt and clay, used in Chapters 8 - 12, from top to bottom are as follows:

gritty clay (Pit 9)

shelly clay (Pit 9)

black clay (Pit 9)

brown-grey clay (Pits 9 and 4)

laminated shelly clay (Pit 4 and Area III south)

basal silt

These subdivisions form the basic units of analysis for demonstrating variation through the sequence, which was initially examined through two column samples taken from Pit 4 (west section) and Pit 9 (east section).

PITS 4, 8 AND 9

The two column samples from Pit 4 (west) and Pit 9 (east) were taken down, over a 50 x 20cm area, by 10cm spits, but also respecting natural stratigraphic boundaries (Fig. 7.1, 7.2). Pit 4 (west) was taken down 21 spits through the brown-grey clay and into the laminated shelly clay, while Pit 9 was taken down 13 spits through the gritty clay, black clay, shelly clay, and into the top of the brown-grey clay. To supplement the column samples an additional seven samples were also taken from Pit 4 (east) and Pit 8 (west), through the brown-grey clay and gritty clay respectively.

The sediment was carefully excavated by hand (the few large faunal remains being recorded *in situ*), bagged on site, and then later weighed, dried and wet-sieved at 0.5mm mesh. The residues were sorted and all bone, tooth and antler extracted with the help of a variable magnification binocular microscope. The vertebrate material was then subdivided into fish, herpetofauna, birds and mammals, and given to the respective specialists.

conditions of the majority of the *Hyla* fossils compared with the fragmentary nature of the fossils of most of the other herpetological species at Barnham is unexplained.

Although this is the first record of *Hyla arborea* as a British fossil, *Hyla meridionalis* has been reported from the Ipswichian Itteringham Site in Norfolk (Holman, 1992a), and *Hyla* sp. has been reported from Cudmore Grove in Essex (Holman *et al.* 1990).

Currently, the genus *Hyla* does not occur naturally in Britain, although *Hyla aborea* has been introduced from time to time in southern England and on the Isle of Wight. *Hyla arborea* presently ranges widely across temperate western and central Europe except for southern France and Iberia (Arnold & Burton 1978; Escriva 1987). *Hyla arborea* is usually found in well-vegetated habitats and prefers places with bushes, trees or reed beds (Arnold & Burton 1978).

In addition, there are two elements of *Hyla* that are too fragmentary to determine to the specific level, but there is no reason to believe that they do not also represent *Hyla arborea*.

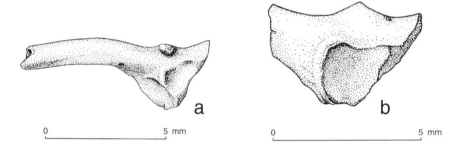

Fig. 9.1. Amphibians from the gritty clay. a. left illium in lateral view of *Hyla arborea* (common tree frog); b. left ilium in lateral view of *Bufo calamita* (natterjack toad). Each scale line = 5mm (illustration: J. Alan Holman).

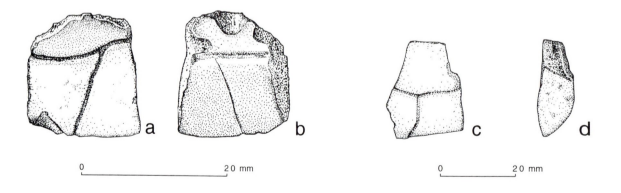

Fig. 9.2. *Emys orbicularis* (European pond terrapin) from the gritty clay. a. Peripheral bone in external view; and b. in internal view; c. second peripheral bone in external view; and d. in posterior view. Each scale line = 20mm (illustration: J. Alan Holman).

Anura: Bufonidae

Bufo bufo (Linnaeus 1758), common toad. There are 46 skeletal parts from all four of the fossiliferous stratigraphic units at Barnham. Holman (1989) gave criteria for separating the ilia of *Bufo bufo* from that of *Bufo calamita*, although only a small sample of modern *Bufo* skletons was available. However, in 1992 a large series of *Bufo* skeletons was studied by the author at the Museo National de Ciencias Naturales in Madrid. It was found that the structure of the dorsal prominence of the ilium is the most diagnostic feature in the identification of the three European species of *Bufo*. A low, undivided dorsal ilial prominence is diagnostic for *Bufo bufo*.

A block (sample B701) was lifted in the field, which contained the partial skeletons of at least two large *Bufo bufo* as well as many tiny bone fragments, and a fish scale. These bones may represent the stomach contents of a small predator, possibly a grass snake, *Natrix natrix*. The grass snake is by far the most common reptile in the fauna, and the bones in the nodule, including the fish scale, appear. to be etched as if by the powerful digestive juices of a snake.

I have observed *Natrix natrix* feeding upon large toads in a herpetological locality near Oxford University (pers. observ. summer 1984), and Smith (1964) reports that this snake eats common toads as well as fish. Rollinat (1934) indicates that in central France, where *Rana temporaria* is not the common frog in the area, common toads (as well as natterjacks, spadefoots, and edible frogs) are the preferred food of grass snake.

The common toad is a very common fossil in British Pleistocene sites. Presently, common toads occur in a variety of habitats, some of them rather far from water. *Bufo bufo* is presently common in East Anglia (Cooke & Scorgie 1983).

Bufo calamita Laurenti 1768, natterjack (Fig. 9.lc). This species is represented by a mere four ilia from the gritty clay. They all have the high, triangular ilial prominence that is diagnostic of *Bufo calamita* (Holman 1989, fig. 1). This species presently occurs in scattered localities in England and south-west Scotland as well as in south-western Ireland. In England the natterjack is mainly confined to coastal dunes, but occurs in a few inland heath sites. A few populations presently exist in coastal dune sites in East Anglia (pers. observ.), but the author is not aware that this species occurs in any inland sites in the region. This is the first record of natterjack from the Hoxnian Interglacial.

Bufo viridis Laurenti 1768, green toad. With only four ilia from the black, shelly and gritty clays, this is the first record of this continental anuran species from Britain. It is not, however, an unexpected record considering the other exotic herptiles that have been reported from the British Pleistocene. The ilia of *Bufo viridis* may be separated from the other two European species of *Bufo* on the basis of its bilobed, relatively low ilial prominence (Sanchiz 1977). At present the species occurs in Europe (including the southern tip of Sweden, but excluding the rest of Fennoscandinavia, the British Isles and Europe, west of the Rhine), the northern coast of Africa, and then eastward to western China (Frost 1985).

In Europe, green toads are usually found in lowland areas, often in sandy habitats (Arnold & Burton 1978). Presently the three *Bufo* species above, may be found together in Germany in the Rhine Valley (Günther 1996, figs. 123, 131 and 146).

Anura: Ranidae

Rana arvalis Nilsson 1842, moor frog. This species is represented by 17 ilia from all the units except the black clay. Holman (1987) has given characters that separate the ilia of *Rana arvalis*, a brown frog species, from other British and European *Rana*. Presently the moor frog is found in damp fields and bogs, often in association with *Rana temporaria*, but it is said to prefer wetter habitats (Arnold & Burton 1978). The moor frog presently does not occur naturally in Britan, but ranges from western France across middle and northern Europe.

Rana (ridibunda) sp. water frog of the *Rana ridibunda* species complex. The 27 ilia (from the black, shelly and gritty clays) of species of the *Rana ridibunda* complex of water frogs are relatively easy to identify (Holman 1998), but problems arise when one attempts to identify ilia of the individual species of this group. Most of these frogs are found in or near permanent low energy bodies of water.

Rana temporaria Linnaeus 1758, common frog. This species is represented by ten skeletal elements from all four stratigraphic units. Holman (1985) has pointed out characters that are diagnostic of the ilia of *Rana temporaria*, a brown frog species, and Holman *et al.* (1988) pointed out diagnostic characters of the sacrum of this species. This is a species that is presently characteristic of many moist habitats in Britain and Europe. The common frog is often found in drier meadows than is the moor frog (Arnold &Burton 1978). *Rana temporaria* is currently widespread but not common in East Anglia (Cooke & Scorgie 1983).

Over 330 *Rana* elements are too fragmentary for specific identification. It appears that most of them have undergone some sort of pre-depositional erosion and perhaps were stomach contents of small carnivores.

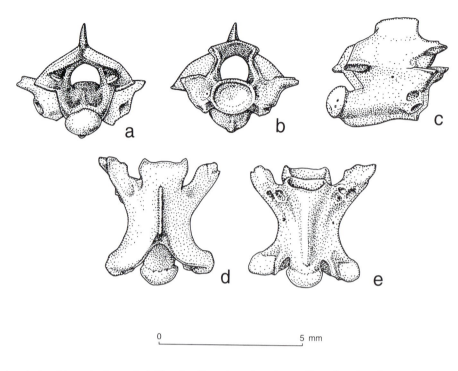

Fig. 9.3. *Elaphe longissima* (Aesculapian snake). Vertebra from the gritty clay. a. Posterior view; b. anterior view; c. lateral view; d. dorsal view; e. ventral view. The scale line equals 5mm and applies to all figures (illustration: J. Alan Holman).

REPTILIA

Testudines: Emydidae

***Emys orbicularis* (Linnaeus 1758), European pond terrapin (Fig. 9.2).** *Emys orbicularis* is represented by many skeletal fragments, mainly of the carapace, which occur principally within the gritty clay, but also in the units beneath. This species has been recorded from all of the interglacial stages of the Middle and Upper Pleistocene in Britain and also from the warmest portion of the Flandrian (Holocene) (Stuart 1979, 1982). Presently, the species ranges widely through temperate Europe, but it is absent from the British Isles, northern France, the Alpine region, Fennoscandinavia, the Low Countries and part of Germany (Stuart 1982, fig. 5.3). In its present European range (Arnold & Burton 1978, map 48), *Emys orbicularis* is found in still or slow-moving water with abundant aquatic vegetation.

Squamata: Anguidae

***Anguis fragilis* Linnaeus 1758, slow worm.** The 40 vertebrae from this species were recovered from all four stratigraphic units. Its osteological elements are very characteristic and it has been identified from several British Pleistocene interglacial sites (Holman 1993, 1998). Presently the slow worm prefers well-vegetated, often damp habitats with ample ground cover (Arnold

& Burton 1978). It is widespread but not common in East Anglia (Cooke & Scorgie 1983).

Squamata: Lacertidae

***Lacerta* sp. small *Lacerta* species.** The two vertebrae from the gritty and the black clays, appear to be indistinguishable from several small *Lacerta* species, but probably represent *Lacerta vivipara*, a species that is presently widespread and fairly common in East Anglia (Cooke & Scorgie 1983).

Squamata: Colubridae

***Natrix natrix* (Linnaeus 1758), grass snake.** There are 52 vertebrae of this species from all four stratigraphic units at Barnham. Szyndlar (1984) has shown that the trunk vertebrae of *Natrix natrix* may be distinguished from the other European genera of *Natrix* (*N. maura* and *N. tesselata*) on the basis of their less acutely pointed hypapophyses and more robust parapophyseal processes. Several of the above *Natrix* vertebrae lack complete hypapophyses, but they have the robust parapophyseal processes of *Natrix natrix*. At present the grass snake is usually found near water in a variety of habitats (Arnold & Burton 1978). The grass snake is currently widespread but not common in East Anglia (Cooke & Scorgie 1983).

***Natrix maura* or *tesselata*, viperine or dice snake.** It was possible to ascertain whether six vertebrae from the gritty and the black clay represent *Natrix maura* or *Natrix tesselata*. Both of these snakes occur on the continent of Europe but are presently absent from Britain (Arnold & Burton 1978). Of the two species, *Natrix maura*, which ranges into north-western France, presently occurs nearest to Britain.

There are many vertebrae of *Natrix* (387) that are very eroded and fragmentary, and lack the diagnostic processes for specific identification.

***Elaphe longissima* (Laurenti 1768), Aesculapian snake (Fig. 9.3).** This species is represented by only five vertebrae from the gritty clay, and is only the third record of this genus and species in the fossil record of Britain. The identification of individual trunk vertebrae of *Elaphe longissima* has been discussed by Szyndlar (1984) and Holman *et al.* (1990). The two previous records were from Beeches Pit, Suffolk and Cudmore Grove, Essex. The Aesculapian snake is absent from the modern fauna of Britain. Its present distribution is somewhat similar to that of *Emys orbicularis*, but it does not generally range as far north as *Emys orbicularis*. At present, the Aesculapian snake is usually found in dry habitats such as open woods with shrubby vegetation (Arnold & Burton 1978).

Squamata: Viperidae

***Vipera berus* (Linnaeus 1758), adder.** There are only six vertebrae of this species from Barnham, which were recovered from the gritty clay and the brown-grey clay. Szyndlar (1984) discusses the identification of indivudual vertebrae of *Vipera berus*. Presently, the adder is local and not common in East Anglia, except for parts of the Essex coast, the Suffolk coastal heaths, and Norfolk (Cooke & Scorgie 1983). It currently occupies a wide variety of habitats in Britain (Arnold & Burton 1978).

DISCUSSION

The Barnham herpetofauna (at least 17 taxa) has exceeded the number of herpetological species that are recorded from the Middle Pleistocene Cudmore Grove herpetofauna of Essex, heretofore the richest in Britain (Table 9.1). Moreover, the Barnham site has yielded the largest number of amphibian species (10) ever recorded from a single British locality. This is noteworthy, as only six amphibian species currently occur in Britain (Cooke & Scorgie 1983). All of the species of amphibians that presently occur naturally in Britain occur at Barnham plus the exotic species *Bufo viridis, Hyla arborea, Rana arvalis* and *Rana (ridibunda)* sp.

Barnham, Suffolk	Cudmore Grove, Essex
Triturus cristatus	*Triturus cristatus*
Triturus helveticus	
Triturus vulgaris	*Triturus vulgaris*
Hyla arborea	*Hyla* sp. indet.
Bufo bufo	*Bufo bufo*
Bufo calamita	
Bufo viridis	
Rana arvalis	*Rana arvalis*
Rana (ridibunda) sp.	*Rana (ridibunda)* sp.
Rana temporaria	
Emys orbicularis	*Emys orbicularis*
Anguis fragilis	*Anguis fragilis*
Lacerta sp.	*Lacerta* sp.
Elaphe longissima	*Elaphe longissima*
Natrix maura or *tessellata*	*Natrix maura* or *tessellata*
Natrix natrix	*Natrix natrix*
Vipera berus	*Vipera berus*

Table 9.1. The two largest Pleistocene herpetofaunas in Britain compared.

This is the first fossil record of *Bufo viridis* and *Hyla arborea* in Britain, and only the third fossil record of *Elaphe longissima* and *Triturus cristatus* in these islands. Moreover, the Barnham Site has produced the first fossil record of *Bufo calamita* from the Hoxnian of Britain. This inland fossil record of the natterjack is of considerable interest in that most modern British records of this species are from coastal dunes (Holman & Stuart 1991).

This complex of fossil amphibian and reptile species indicates a rather wide range of habitats. A body of still or slowly moving water is indicated by the presence of the water frog *Rana (ridibunda)* sp. and *Emys orbicularis*, and the water snakes. Wetlands are indicated by *Triturus cristatus, Triturus helveticus, Rana arvalis, Rana temporaria, Natrix natrix*, and a damp habitat with low bushes is suggested by *Triturus vulgaris, Bufo bufo, Rana temporaria, Anguis fragilis*, probably *Lacerta* sp. and *Natrix natrix*. Finally, a rather open, dry, sandy upland habitat is indicated by *Bufo calamita, Bufo viridis*, and *Elaphe longissima*.

Indications are that wetter habitats gave way to drier ones through time at the Barnham site, as the last four species in the above paragraph are found predominantly in the gritty clay. A discussion of the stratigraphhic distribution of the Barnham amphibians and reptiles is provided in Chapter 15.

Based on the modern distribution of the Barnham exotic species, *Hyla arborea, Bufo viridus, Emys orbicularis, Elaphe longissima*, and *Natrix maura* or *tesselata* (especially *Emys orbicularis, Elaphe longissima*, and the water snakes) a warmer climate than presently occurs in East Anglia is strongly suggested. The modern limit of the range of *Emys orbicularis* is thought to be controlled by temperature and days of sunshine in the summer months. A mean

July temperature in excess of 17-18°C, combined with sunshine and few humid, cloudy days appears necessary for its eggs to hatch (Stuart 1979). Thus, individuals released into the wild in England have been able to survive for some years, but have not been able to sucessfully breed in England's cool, equable climate.

Elaphe longissima is also an egg-laying species (Escriva 1987), and it may be that in the northern part of its range it faces problems similar to *Emys orbicularis*. At present the Aesculapian snake does not range as far north in Europe as *Emys*, and nowhere does its range extend as far north as Britain (Arnold & Burton 1978, map 112). The author is not aware that any individuals released in the wild in Britain have ever survived for even a few years. The nearest that water snakes presently occur to Britain is in north-western France.

10. THE AVIFAUNA

John R. Stewart

INTRODUCTION

The Middle Pleistocene avifauna from Barnham Palaeolithic site is not particularly rich as is often the case with open air sites, as opposed to cave sites. However, bird fossils of this date are not very well represented in Europe and therefore faunas such as this are important. When the Barnham fauna is added to others it will hopefully allow this gap in our knowlege to be filled. Other Middle Pleistocene sites of about this age in Britain which have yielded birds are Swanscombe (Harrison 1979b; Parry 1996), Hoxne (Stuart *et al.* 1993) and Cudmore Grove.

Identification of the remains was achieved by the use of the osteological collections at the sub-department of Ornithology of the Natural History Museum at Tring (Hertfordshire). Literature dealing with the identification of the various taxa was consulted (Stewart & Hernandez Carrasquilla 1997). However, previously described diagnostic characters were not taken as read, and were checked prior to their application to the Barnham bird fossils.

SYSTEMATIC DESCRIPTION

The systematic attributions made here follow the guidelines set out in the report on the birds from Torbryan Valley (Stewart in prep.). The material is listed in Appendix III.

Anseriformes: Anatidae

Anas **sp., dabbling duck.** Only two elements of *Anas* sp. have been identified. They were recovered together from a sieved sample and appear to belong to the same individual. The generic identification is based on the proportions of the synostosis metacarpalis distalis (Woelfle 1967). Due to the overlap in skeletal size and shape of many species within this genus further diagnosis is not possible. All that can be said is that this is a large member of the genus.

Undetermined anatidae, ducks. Sixteen further specimens can clearly be identified as anatids, athough determination beyond that level has not been possible at this stage. Factors contributing to this are the fragmentary nature of the assemblage as well as the number of taxa within this family today. Despite this, inferences can be made regarding the affinities of some of the specimens and the assemblage as a whole. First, two specimens clearly do not belong to either the genus *Netta* or *Aythya*. They are the distal fragment of a left coracoid from Area III (E7) and the fragmentary left coracoid from Area III Pit 5 (black clay). These specimens differ from those genera in that their facies articularis clavicularis protrude medially with respect to their sulcus m. supracoracoidei (Woelfle 1967). Second, the assemblage appears to be divisible into two size classes. The first size class, to which the second coracoid mentioned above belongs, is within the range of the mallard *Anas platyrhynchos*; while the second size class, to which the first coracoid belongs, lies between that of the mallard and the teal *A. crecca*.

Columbibormes: Columbidae

Columba **cf.** *palumbus*, **wood pigeon?** There is only one specimen of a columbiforme and from its proportions would appear to be referable to the largest species in the western Palaearctic, the wood pigeon (*C. palumbus*). The determination of the specimen was achieved on morphological and metrical grounds as described by Fick (1974). While the specimen clearly belongs to a columbiforme its specific status must remain uncertain. During the Quaternary certain bird species are known to have changed in size which sheds doubt on the use of size for species identification (Stewart 1992).

Contrary to Parry (1996) *C. palumbus* was not described by Mourer-Chauviré (1975) as 'having remained relatively constant'. Its presence was merely noted at a number of sites, including some of Middle Pleistocene age and these remains were said to be indistinguishable from modern specimens. Mourer-Chauviré (1975) does describe different forms of *C. livia* which can be more readily studied due to the greater abundance of fossils. The large number of fossils of this species is no doubt related to their regular use of rocky outcrops and the use of caves as nest sites. In contrast, *C. palumbus* lives in and near woodlands and nests in trees and consequently is rarer as a fossil. The scarcity of their fossils makes it difficult to establish whether the species has undergone change during the Quaternary. So the lack of comment by Mourer-Chauviré should not be taken as an indication that she regards the taxon as 'having remained relatively constant'. It simply means that nothing unusual was noted amongst the material available to her.

Together with the specimen described from Swanscombe (Parry 1996), this is the oldest probable record of *C. palumbus* from the British Pleistocene. The wood pigeon today is found in boreal to warm temperate zones and is associated with broad leaf or coniferous woodlands. It may be resident or a migrant (Harrison 1982).

Passeriformes: Turdidae

***Turdus* cf. *philomelos/iliacus*, song thrush? or redwing?** The two specimens of the genus *Turdus* have been identified from the relative size of the second pneumatic fossa in the humerus (Janossy 1983) and the discontinuity on the facies articularis ulnocarpalis of the carpometacarpus (Stewart 1992). They are the size of the two smallest members of this genus in Europe, *T. philomelos* or *T. iliacus* (Stewart 1992). It should be noted that due to a lack of available comparative material no comparison of the above material has been made with the two European species of rock thrush *Monticola saxatilis* or *M. solitarius* which must therefore remain possibilities.

Undetermined Passeriformes, song birds. In addition, there are several specimens that clearly belong to passerines, although the number of taxa which could be represented and the fragmentary nature of the remains prevents further identification.

TAPHONOMY AND PALAEOECOLOGY

The recovery method for the fauna at Barnham has followed recent precedents discussed by Harrison and Stewart (in press) in that fine meshed sieves (0.5mm) were used extensively. This is reflected in the number of small skeletal elements recovered such as phalanges, os carpi ulnare and taxa such as passerines, which would doubtless not be recovered without sieves.

Preservation is very good, as exemplified by the presence of an immature anatid tarsometatarsus. Immature bird remains are uncommon in Quaternary fossil faunas, presumably because of their lesser degree of ossification rendering them less prone to preservation. Furthermore, none of the bones examined show any signs of being water worn which is typical of the sediment type in which the fossils occur i.e. fine grained sediments deposited in gentle slow flowing waters. The remains of an associated carpometacarpus and phalange 1 of digit 2, presumably belonging to a single individual probably implies a relatively fast sedimentation rate. Situations where articulated bird wings remain for some time (Parry 1996), usually involve desiccated carcasses in environments such as strand lines and are therefore probably not relevant here.

The avifauna at Barnham agrees well with other forms of evidence for the nature of the local palaeoenvironment. Anatids make up the bulk (69%) of the material recognisable to family level or beyond. This is not surprising given the nature of the deposit, representing a relatively slow moving watercourse and the other animal remains such as freshwater fish and amphibians, which give similar indications. This phenomenon has been remarked upon by Harrison (1988), who mentioned that most Pleistocene avifaunas from the south-east of England are from fluvial deposits and are thus dominated by water birds and in particular anatids. Other such sites are West Runton (Harrison 1979a), Boxgrove (Harrison & Stewart in press), Cudmore Grove (unpublished) and Swanscombe (Harrison 1979b; Parry 1996). This contrasts with most of the rest of Britain, where Pleistocene avifaunas are from cave deposits and where faunas are often more species-rich. Another factor related to this phenomenon is that the south-east of England generally produces older faunas. There is only one significant Late Pleistocene avifauna in south-eastern England, which is from Ightham Fissure in Kent (Newton 1894, 1899).

The other elements of the fauna may indicate the presence of boreal to warm temperate woodland. Of particular importance in this respect is the wood pigeon (*Columba* cf. *palumbus*) as these birds are generally restricted to wooded environments today. The small thrush (*Turdus* sp.) would give a similar indication if the remains are of the song thrush (*Turdus philomelos*). However, if they belong to the redwing (*T. iliacus*) a different, more open wooded environment would be invoked unless the birds were wintering in the area. Caution should be exercised here as the species have been identified on the basis of size because other members of the genera *Columba* and *Turdus* are indistinguishable in terms of non-metric characters (Fick 1974; Stewart 1992); there is a possibility that during the Quaternary the modern species were differently sized or that extinct birds in these genera may have existed. This would signify that size may give a misplaced sense of security during identification. It is tempting to interpret the presence of the other, smaller passerines at the site as further evidence for woodland, although this diverse order can be found in many other habitats.

A further cautionary note should be made about the use of birds in reconstructing palaeoenvironments; as correctly pointed out by Parry (1996), there is a significant possibility that birds today do not occupy precisely the same ecological situations as they did in the past. However, it is unlikely that the general conclusion that the site was surrounded by woodland would be put seriously in doubt. The other vertebrate evidence concurs with the interpretations based on the bird remains.

No signs of the cause of death are present on the specimens in the form of raptor or carnivore damage, digestive corrosion such as described by Mayhew (1977) and Andrews (1990) for rodents. Similarly, no evidence such as butchery by humans, or gnaw marks by mammalian predators was found. Little can be said of the taphonomy of the avian remains prior to deposition, except that none of the specimens show signs of having been exposed to weathering for any length of time implying rapid burial.

CONCLUSIONS

In conclusion, this small assemblage contributes to two areas of knowledge. First, it adds to the rare body of data of Middle Pleistocene birds in Britain. Perhaps more importantly, from the perspective of this volume, it provides confirmation of the palaeoenvironmental results suggested by the other lines of evidence. The bird assemblage is consistent with the interpretation of slow-flowing, or still-water, within proximity to woodland.

11. THE INTERGLACIAL MAMMALIAN FAUNA FROM BARNHAM

Simon Parfitt

INTRODUCTION

Until recently the only substantial information on British Hoxnian terrestrial vertebrates came from several fossil assemblages collected from sediments associated with the ancestral river Thames at Swanscombe (Sutcliffe 1964; Schreve 1996), Ingress Vale (Sutcliffe & Kowalski 1976), and Clacton (Singer *et al.* 1973), and from lake deposits such as at Copford (Brown 1852) and Hoxne (Stuart *et al.* 1993) both in East Anglia, and from Hitchin, Hertfordshire (Holyoak *et al.* 1983). Despite sizeable collections of large mammals from these sites, with the exception of Hoxne, none has produced large quantities of small vertebrates. This represents a substantial gap in our knowledge of Middle Pleistocene mammal evolution. Due to the scarcity of Hoxnian small mammals, the discovery and intensive sieving of new Hoxnian fossiliferous deposits in fluvio-lacustrine deposits at Barnham provides an important addition to the British Middle Pleistocene fossil record.

The fossiliferous deposits were discovered in 1991. The subsequent excavation in Area III, the column sampling of Pits 4 and 9 and the washing of the samples through fine-meshed sieves, are fully described in Chapter 7. The vertebrate remains were found exclusively within the grey silt and clay (Unit 5c), which is the upper 2-3m of a series of fluvio-lacustrine deposits, laid down in a deep channel overlying Anglian glacio-fluvial deposits (see Chapters 4 and 7). The fossiliferous sequence seems to represent a single cycle of deposition that must correspond to a brief interval of geological time. Pollen evidence from the lowest part of the fossiliferous deposit suggests that the fauna accumulated during the early temperate stage of an interglacial. The geological context (Chapter 4) and other biota (Chapters 8-10, 13) therefore suggest that the bones were deposited in a large slow-moving river with well-vegetated banks and marshes flanked by a mosaic habitat of temperate open-grassland and forest. Towards the top of the sequence the water-body became more stagnant and parts of the channel probably dried-up periodically at the end of the deposition of the grey silt and clay, leading to the formation of the overlying palaeosol (Unit 6; see Chapters 4 and 6).

Unit 5c has itself been divided into six fossiliferous levels (from the base: basal silt, laminated shelly clay, brown grey clay, black clay, shell clay and gritty clay; see Chapters 4 and 7). Mammal bone abundance is very low in all of Unit 5c except for the gritty clay at the top of the sequence. This deposit is richly fossiliferous and yielded most of the mammalian fossils in which the bones and teeth of small and very small mammals predominate. The upper part of the fossiliferous sequence has also yielded some rare and fragmentary large mammal remains.

The number of microvertebrate fossils collected at Barnham East Farm is by far the largest yet recovered from any British Hoxnian locality and the collection has significantly increased our knowledge of the diversity of the Hoxnian mammal community. This fauna is also notable as it occurs in a stratified sequence allowing the study of faunal change through time on a scale which has seldom been attempted for a non-cave site. However, the most significant aspect of the fauna concerns the reconstruction of the setting for early hominid occupation at the site, and for dating of the sequence by biostratigraphic correlation with other Middle Pleistocene localities.

This chapter focuses on the taxonomy of the mammal remains and summarises the implications of the fauna for palaeoecological reconstruction. In the concluding section, the age implications of the mammalian fauna are also investigated.

METHODS

Taxonomic determinations are based on comparisons with modern specimens housed in the osteological comparative collections at the Natural History Museum, London; where appropriate, comparisons were made with identified material from other Pleistocene sites.

Measurements of the large mammal bones were taken using sliding callipers and recorded to the nearest 0.1mm. Unless otherwise stated, measurement methods follow von den Driesch (1976). Microvertebrate remains were measured to the nearest 0.01mm with a Nikon binocular microscope fitted with a calibrated eyepiece graticule. Measurement protocol and dental terminology follow Reumer (1984) for mandibles and teeth of the Soricidae, van der Meulen (1973) for the Arvicolidae, and van der Weerd (1976) for the Muridae. All measurements are quoted in mm and those prefixed by 'e' are estimated values.

The mammalian remains are listed by taxon and measurements of individual specimens tabulated in Appendix IV. Detailed descriptions of the material are kept with the vertebrate collection in the Department of Palaeontology, Natural History Museum, London.

Direct morphological and size comparisons have

been made with British material from the following Middle Pleistocene localities: West Runton Forest Bed, Norfolk (Cromerian *sensu stricto*); Sugworth, Oxfordshire and Little Oakley, Essex, of probable Cromerian age; Boxgrove, West Sussex, Ostend, Norfolk, and Westbury-sub-Mendip, Somerset dating to the later part of the 'Cromerian Complex' (tentatively assigned to oxygen isotope stage 13 by Bishop 1982 and Roberts *et al.* 1994). Hoxnian localities include: Beeches Pit and Hoxne, Suffolk; and Swanscombe, Kent. Faunas which may date to the first temperate stage of the 'Saalian Complex' (correlated with oxygen isotope stage 9 by Bridgland 1994) incude Purfleet, Grays Thurrock, and Cudmore Grove, all Essex. Comparisons were also made with the following Late Pleistocene Ipswichian faunas: Joint Mitnor cave, Devon; and Swanton Morley and Barrington, Cambridgeshire.

SYSTEMATIC PALAEONTOLOGY

Chiroptera: Vespertilionidae

***Plecotus* sp., long-eared bat.** The only specimen of a bat from Barnham is an isolated M^2 from the shelly clay. The anterobuccal portion is broken away, but otherwise the tooth is intact (Pl. 11.1). The molar is clearly assignable to *Plecotus* on the basis of morphology (Menu & Popelard 1987; Sevilla & Lopez-Martinez 1986; Sevilla-Garcia 1986) and is similar in size and shape to the M^2 of modern *P. auritus*.

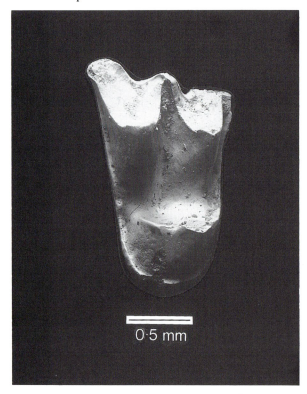

0·5 mm

Plate 11.1. *Plecotus* sp.: occlusal view of right M^2 (shelly clay, BEF 726).

However, the upper molars of the two Palaearctic species of *Plecotus* (*P. auritus* and *P. austriacus*) cannot be distinguished on the basis of morphology. Although *P. auritus* is on average larger than *P. austriacus* there is overlap in dental measurements. The problem of identifying isolated teeth is further compounded by the larger size of Pleistocene *P. auritus*. For these reasons the long-eared bat from Barnham is referred to generic level only.

	N	Mean ± SD	Range
Plecotus auritus			
Recent, Britain	9	1.83 ± 0.06	1.69 - 1.88
Boxgrove	1	-	(1.96)
Plecotus austriacus			
Recent, Britain	6	1.98 ± 0.06	1.93 - 2.09
Plecotus sp.			
Barnham	1	-	**(1.89)**

Table 11.1. Buccolingual width (in mm) of the second upper molar of *Plecotus* from Barnham, and a comparison with Recent and Pleistocene material.

Insectivora: Soricidae

***Sorex minutus* L. 1766, pygmy shrew.** Two partial mandibles and a number of isolated teeth of pygmy shrew have been recovered from the black clay, shelly clay and gritty clay. The mental foramen is situated below the trigonid of the M_1, which excludes reference to *S. minutissimus* in which the mental foramen lies below the buccal re-entrant valley of the M_1 (Rzebik-Kowalska 1991). In *S. minutissimus*, too, the condyle is relatively short with a wide interarticular area, and the upper incisor is non-bifid. Comparisons between measurements of the Barnham mandibles and teeth with those given by Reumer (1984) show that the Barnham specimens fall close to the lower limit of the recorded range observed in Recent *S. minutus*.

	N	Mean ± SD	Range
Recent			
Germany [1]	15	3.16 ± 0.11	2.8-3.3
Poland [2]	40	3.12 ± 0.08	2.90-3.25
Greece [1]	4	3.83 ± 0.14	3.5-4.1
British Middle Pleistocene			
Barnham	2	-	**(2.99, 3.09)**
Boxgrove [3]	2	-	(2.9, 3.0)
Westbury-sub-Mendip [4]	2	-	(e 2.8, 3.1)
West Runton [3,5]	3	-	(3.07, 3.07, 3.14)

Table 11.2. Height of the coronoid process (in mm) in Pleistocene and Recent samples of *Sorex minutus*. Data from: [1] Hutterer (1990), [2] Rzebik-Kowalska (1991), [3] Personal observation, [4] Bishop (1982), [5] Harrison & Clayden (1993).

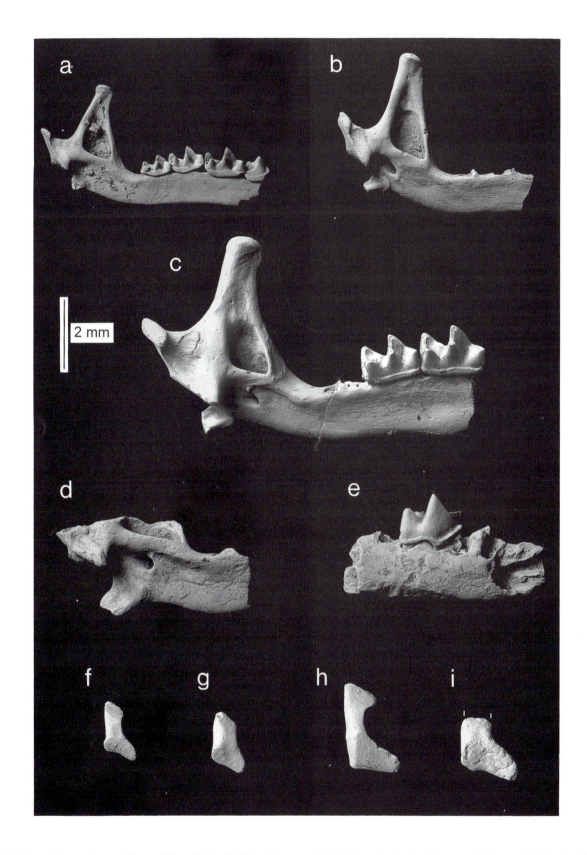

Plate 11.2. a: *Sorex minutus*: left mandible with P_4 - M_3 (black clay, BEF 1445), lingual view; b: *Sorex* sp. 1: left mandible (gritty clay, BEF 826), lingual view; c: *Neomys* sp.: left mandible with M_1 - M_2 (gritty clay, BEF 827), lingual view; d - e: *Crocidura* sp.: left mandible (gritty clay, BEF 1047), lingual view; e: right mandible with M_1 (gritty clay, BEF 907), buccal view; f: *Sorex minutus*: caudal view of condyle (black clay, BEF 1445); g: *Sorex* sp. 1: caudal view of condyle (gritty clay, BEF 826); h: *Neomys* sp.: caudal view of condyle (gritty clay, BEF 827); i : *Crocidura* sp.: caudal view of condyle (gritty clay, BEF 1047).

113

The pygmy shrew has a long evolutionary history going back to the late Pliocene (Reumer 1984) and in the British Isles it is first recorded from early Middle Pleistocene deposits at Sugworth (Stuart 1980) and West Runton (Harrison & Clayden 1993). It has been recorded from a number of Middle Pleistocene localities including Hoxnian records from Beeches Pit and Hoxne (Stuart *et al.* 1993) where it is a rare component of the small mammal assemblage.

***Sorex* sp.1, shrew.** A medium-sized species of *Sorex*, represented by 30 isolated teeth and 17 mandibles (most of which are edentulous), it is the most common insectivore in the Barnham deposits. The mandibles are readily referable to *Sorex* on the basis of morphology.

Although the mandibular ramus shows some morphological variability, the differences are not sufficient to demonstrate the presence of more than one species of medium-sized *Sorex*. In addition, the variation in the size of the mandibular ramus is equivalent to the range found in extant western Palaearctic *Sorex* of equivalent size (Niethammer & Kraap 1990).

	N	Mean + SD	Range
Height of coronoid process (H)	8	4.07 ± 0.10	3.95-4.23
Height of condyle (HC)	7	1.73 ± 0.09	1.58-1.88
Length of upper condylar facet (LUF)	8	0.76 ± 0.05	0.66-0.85
Length of lower condylar facet (LLF)	10	1.00 ± 0.15	0.60-1.10

Table 11.3. Measurements (in mm) of the mandibular ramus of *Sorex* sp. 1 from Barnham. Measurements follow Reumer (1994).

Height of coronoid process	N	Mean	Range
S. araneus			
Recent, Britain	12	4.40	4.25-4.60
Sorex sp. 1			
Barnham	**8**	**4.07**	**3.95-4.23**
Sorex runtonensis			
Boxgrove	30	4.01	3.82-4.20
Westbury-sub-Mendip [1]			3.8-4.4
West Runton	10	4.04	3.92-4.17

Table 11.4. Coronoid height (in mm) of *Sorex* sp.1 of the mandibles from Barnham, and a comparison with Recent and Pleistocene species of medium-sized *Sorex*. [1] Data from Bishop (1982).

The dimensions of the teeth and mandible are smaller than the common shrew *Sorex araneus* but larger than the pygmy shrew *S. minutus*. Amongst the extant western Palaearctic species of *Sorex* it is closest

to Laxmann's shrew *S. caecutiens*, the Iberian shrew *S. granarius*, and the alpine shrew *S. alpinus* (Niethammer & Kraap 1990). In comparison with British Pleistocene *Sorex*, Early and Middle Pleistocene *S. runtonensis* is almost identical as far as size is concerned (Table 11.4). The characteristics of the Barnham mandibles are as follows. The ascending ramus is slender with an evenly tapering apex and a rounded tip (Pl.11.2b). The external temporal fossa is generally large, although somewhat variable in size, and coronoid spicule is often poorly developed and indistinct on some specimens. The condylar process is relatively narrow with a broad trapezoidal interarticular area which separates a narrow upper and lower facet (Pl. 11.2g, Table 11.3). The mental foramen of the horizontal ramus is situated below the M_1 between the anterior corner of the tooth and the buccal re-entrant valley.

Fossil *Sorex* is a particularly difficult group as fossil and extant species are characterised by great individual variation in mandible morphology (van der Meulen 1973). Many morphological features which are commonly used to distinguish fossil forms, such as the shape of the ascending ramus, are found to be variable in Recent populations and this range of variability is often not taken into account in the description of new Pleistocene species. The distribution of pigmented areas used to distinguish Recent forms (Dannelid 1989) is of less use when identifying fossil material as it is rarely preserved. As the morphological variation among *Sorex* species is so small, species of similar size tend to look very much alike and are difficult to distinguish on fragmentary material. Accordingly, this has led to the description of a profusion of European Pleistocene species; many of these are of uncertain validity or based on very scant material.

One feature which has been used with reference to extant medium-sized *Sorex* is the ratio of height to breadth of the mandibular condyle (Condyle index). This has been studied by Handwerk (1986) who was able to separate the sibling species *S. araneus* and *S. coronatus* using the condyle index. In an attempt to better identify the Barnham material, the condyle index was plotted against condyle height for five species of Recent European *Sorex*, together with early Middle Pleistocene *S. runtonensis* from West Runton and Boxgrove, Middle Pleistocene *Sorex* sp. from Beeches Pit and Late Pleistocene *S. 'kennardi'* from Ponder's End, Middlesex (Harrison 1996). Figure 11.1 shows that the extant species are separated into discrete clusters on the basis of size and condyle shape. The Barnham sample forms a discrete cluster which overlaps with the other British Pleistocene samples and with that of extant *S. caecutiens*. This cluster is characterised by mandibles with small condyles which are relatively narrow in relation to their height. In contrast to this group, the other extant species (*S. alpinus*, *S. araneus*, *S. coronatus* and *S. isodon*) vary considerably in size between species but all have condyles that are relatively broad in relation to their height. It is interesting that the Pliocene and Pleistocene medium-sized species of *Sorex* (such as *S. bor*, *S. casimiri*, *S. praealpinus*, *S. polonicus*, and *S. subaraneus*) described by Rzebik-Kowalska (1990) from Poland, all fall within this second cluster. The only species described by Rzebik-Kowalska which falls within the other group is *S. runtonensis*; Late Pleistocene *S. 'kennardi'* described by Harrison (1996) from Conningbrook, Kent and Obłazowa, Poland also cluster with this group. The broad similarity between *S. runtonensis*, *S. kennardi* and the Barnham group in condyle morphology also extends to such features as their size, and to dental and mandibular ramus morphology. Indeed, Harrison (1996) has suggested that *S. kennardi* and *S. runtonensis* 'appear virtually indistinguishable and the conclusion is inescapable that they represent a lineage which persisted throughout the Pleistocene'; in his opinion these forms are conspecific. The Barnham sample is important as it appears to link

early Middle Pleistocene *S. runtonensis* with Late Pleistocene *S. kennardi* which may be ancestral to the living, European *S. caecutiens*. However, the author is reticent at making a specific determination until more detailed information is available on the dental morphology of these forms. Consequently the medium-sized shrew from Barnham is referred to *Sorex* sp. 1. Whether these forms represent a single lineage or separate but closely related species, is not yet possible to tell. However, they are so similar that there is little doubt that they are closely related.

***Neomys* sp., water shrew.** Water shrew remains are rather scarce in the sample from Barnham. One of the mandibles is illustrated in Plate 11.2c and 11.2h, and measurements of specimens from Barnham and several other localities are compared with the two living species of *Neomys* in Table 11.5. The Barnham mandibles are larger than those from the 'Cromerian Complex' and fall broadly within the zone of size overlap of Recent *N. fodiens* and populations of large body size of Miller's Water shrew (*N. anomolus*).

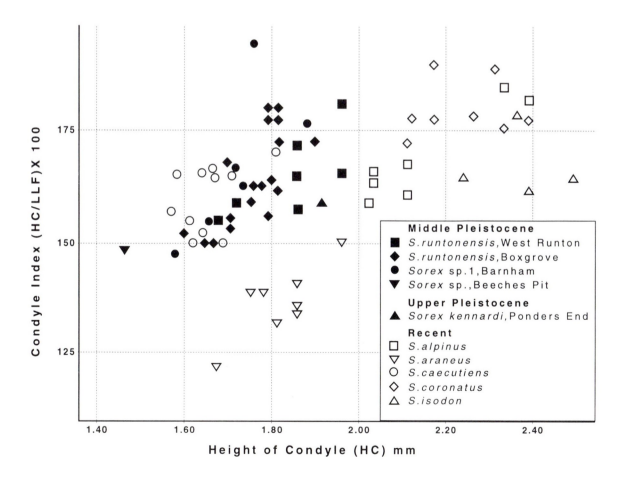

Fig. 11.1. Relationship between height of the mandibular condyle and condyle index of various species of *Sorex* from British Pleistocene localities (solid symbols) and Recent European *Sorex* (outline symbols).

	N	Mean + SD	Range
Recent			
Neomys fodiens			
Britain	10	4.71 ± 0.14	4.51 - 5.00
Austria [1]	14	4.67 ± 0.04	4.45 - 4.90
Neomys anomolus			
Austria [2]	9	4.19 ± 0.04	4.00 - 4.40
Spain	10	4.47	4.21 - 4.61
British Middle Pleistocene			
Neomys browni			
Grays Thurrock	3	-	(e 4.15, 4.29, 4.46)
Neomys sp.			
Boxgrove	4	4.22 ± 0.06	4.15 - 4.30
Barnham	**5**	**4.51 ± 0.13**	**4.41 - 4.70**
Neomys newtoni			
Westbury-sub-Mendip [3]	3	-	(e 4.1, 4.2, 4.3)
West Runton	19	4.03	3.82 - 4.26

Table 11.5. Height of the coronoid process (in mm) of Recent *Neomys fodiens*, *N. anomolus*, and a comparison with temporal samples of British Pleistocene *Neomys*. Data from: [1] Spitzenberger (1990a), [2] Spitzenberger (1990b), [3] Bishop (1982).

The taxonomy of British Pleistocene water shrews and their relationships to living forms is currently rather uncertain. Hinton (1911) described two new species of *Neomys* from the British Middle Pleistocene (*N. newtoni* from the Freshwater Bed, West Runton, and *N. browni* from Grays Thurrock) which he distinguished from *Neomys fodiens* on size and on minor characters of the mandible. Hinton based his descriptions of these forms on a small number of specimens and it is now apparent from an examination of the much larger samples available from West Runton, as well as from comparisons with Recent *Neomys*, that the characters used to distinguish the two fossil forms are variable in Recent *Neomys* and do not provide adequate taxonomic characters. In addition, morphometric and multivariate analysis of Recent and fossil *Neomys* (Parfitt & Rosas unpublished) failed to find any features which separate Middle Pleistocene *Neomys* from Recent *Neomys fodiens*.

Crocidura sp., white-toothed shrew.

The record of white-toothed shrew is of particular interest as *Crocidura* was previously thought to be an important biostratigraphic indicator species restricted to oxygen isotope stage 7 in the British Isles (Currant 1989). Although *Crocidura* is rather infrequent in British small mammal assemblages, there is now evidence that it was present during oxygen isotope stage 9 at Purfleet (Parfitt in Bridgland *et al.* 1995), and the material from Barnham records its first occurrence in the British Hoxnian.

	L	TRW	TAW	LLF	h/ M$_2$
M$_1$ (BEF 1105)	1.75	1.08	1.18	-	-
Mandible + M$_2$ (BEF 907)	1.70	1.07	1.03	-	1.84
Mandible (BEF 1047)	-	-	-	1.56	-

Table 11.6. Measurements (in mm) of *Crocidura* sp. from Barnham. Measurements follow Reumer (1984), h/M$_2$ is the height of the mandibular ramus below the M$_2$ measured lingually. TRW = trigonid width; TAW = talonid width; LLF = length of lower condylar facet

	N	Mean	Range
Recent			
Crocidura leucodon	11	1.75 ± 0.08	1.64-1.88
Crocidura suaveolens	10	1.30 ± 0.06	1.20-1.40
Crocidura russula	10	1.60 ± 0.08	1.52-1.76
British and French Middle Pleistocene			
Aveley (*C.* cf. *C. suaveolens*)	1	-	(1.40)
Tornewton Cave (*Crocidura* sp.) [1]	12	1.72 ± 0.16	1.54-2.08
La Fage, France (*Crocidura* sp.) [2]	15	1.43 ± 0.11	1.22-1.56
La Fage, France (*C. zorzii*) [2]	8	1.82 ± 0.06	1.75-1.92
Barnham (*Crocidura* sp.)	**1**	**-**	**(1.84)**

Table 11.7. Measurements (in mm) of the height of the mandibular ramus below the M$_2$ (measured lingually) in samples of *Crocidura*. Data from: [1] Rzebik (1968) Vivien's Vault, [2] Jammot (1974).

The material consists of three specimens, a lower first molar (BEF 1105), a mandibular ramus with M$_2$ (BEF 907), and a fragment of the posterior part of another mandible (BEF 1047), all from the gritty clay. While incomplete, the specimens are easily separable from other British Pleistocene soricids and they can be identified as white-toothed shrew on the basis of morphological features. Today, three species of the genus *Crocidura* inhabit continental Europe. These are the lesser white-toothed shrew *C. suaveolens*, the greater white-toothed shrew *C. russula*, and the bicoloured white toothed shrew *C. leucodon*. Several species have been described from the European Pleistocene but their validity and relationships to the extant species are currently under debate (Reumer 1986; Rzebik-Kowalska 1995).

Measurements are given in Table 11.6, and the mandible fragments are illustrated in Plate 11.2, c, d and i. The morphology of the lower first and second lower molars (BEF 1105 and 907), with a broad buccal cingulum, low entoconid crests and a buccal re-entrant valley, which is situated high above the cingulum, is typical for *Crocidura*. The lingual cingulum is indistinct and the buccal cingulum of the M$_1$ is constricted below the trigonid where the lower margin of the crown is undulate. In this feature, the specimen compares well with *C. leucodon* rather than with *C. russula* in which the buccal undulation and constriction of the cingulum are generally more pronounced on both the M_1 and M_2.

Of the two mandible fragments BEF 907 is the most complete and comprises the horizontal ramus with M_2 (Pl. 11.2e). The mental foramen is not preserved, although what remains of the horizontal ramus shows that it must have been located anterior to the M_1. The other mandible fragment (BEF 1047) lacks the coronoid process and the dorsal half of the condyle (Pl. 11.2d); the horizontal ramus is broken infront of the M_3 alveolus. The shape of the lower facet of the condyle, the position of the mental foramen, and the protruding ridge below the internal temporal fossa are characteristic of a member of the genus *Crocidura*.

The Barnham white-toothed shrew remains are unfortunately too fragmentary for specific designation, although they indicate a large form. Measurements of the mandibular ramus (Table 11.6) and of the lower molars (compared with measurements given by Krapp 1990) fall close to the upper limit of the size range for Recent *C. leucodon*, the largest of the extant European white-toothed shrews.

The presence of *Crocidura* in the gritty clay at Barnham is the earliest record of the genus in Britain, with the previous earliest record being that in the Corbets Tey Formation from Purfleet, Essex (Parfitt in Bridgland *et al*. 1995). In addition to the record from Purfleet, which probably correlates with oxygen isotope stage 9, white-toothed shrew has been recovered from broadly contemporaneous Thames terrace deposits at Grays Thurrock (Hinton 1901) and at Cudmore Grove, both in Essex (Bridgland *et al*. 1988). A third group of sites record its presence during a later temperate event that predates the Ipswichian and is widely believed to correlate with part of marine oxygen isotope stage 7. These late Middle Pleistocene occurrences are from: Aveley (Stuart 1982; Sutcliffe 1995) and the Ebbsfleet Valley (Parfitt pers. observ.) in Essex; Itteringham, Norfolk (correlated with this group by Currant (1989) on the basis of the mammalian fauna); and the enigmatic fauna from the 'Otter Stratum', Tornewton Cave, Devon (Rzebik 1968; Sutcliffe 1976; Currant 1996). It is clear from these finds that a number of species of white-toothed shrew were present in Britain during the late Middle Pleistocene. The mandible from Aveley was identified as *C.* cf. *suaveolens* on the basis of its small size (Table 11.7) and morphology. On the basis of the large range in size of the mandibles (Table 11.7) described by Rzebik (1968) from Vivien's Vault, Tornewton Cave there are almost certainly two species of *Crocidura* from the 'Otter Stratum'. As noted by Stuart (1982) the Tornewton Cave white-toothed shrews are similar in size to the extant *C. russula* and *C. leucodon*, although one specimen is exceptionally large and probably represents a second species.

What is now abundantly clear is that *Crocidura* existed in at least three separate temperate episodes during the British Middle Pleistocene. It has yet to be recorded from a well dated Last Interglacial context. Whether this reflects a real absence during oxygen isotope stage 5e is unknown as few sites of this age have been adequately sieved. To date *Crocidura* has not been found in any deposits pre-dating the Anglian stage and it was probably absent from Britain during the 'Cromerian Complex' as represented by the deposits at West Runton, Westbury-sub-Mendip and Boxgrove. It is important to note that these sites have been extensively sampled for small mammals and have produced large samples of soricids.

The British records of *Crocidura* represent the final stages in the progressive north-western expansion of the genus which took place during the Late Pliocene to the Holocene (Reumer 1984). The rarity of *Crocidura* in British Pleistocene deposits reflects the fact that it is a warm adapted species, which is found across much of central and southern Europe, but no farther north than 53°N at the present day. Consequently, it was probably restricted to the warmest temperate stages of the Middle Pleistocene in Britain.

Insectivora: Talpidae

***Talpa minor* (Freudenburg 1914), extinct mole.** The small, now extinct mole, *Talpa minor* is relatively common. Fossil evidence suggests that two species of mole occurred in north-western Europe during the Middle Pleistocene. These were *T. minor*, a small mole, and the western mole *T. europaea*, now common throughout large parts of central Europe. The bones and teeth of these two species can be distinguished as *T. europaea* is considerably larger than *T. minor*, and there is little size overlap in the dimensions of their bones and teeth (Fig. 11.2). No talpid remains were found at Barnham which can be identified as *T. europaea*.

T. minor is probably closely related to the blind moles (*T. caeca*) which today inhabit the Mediterranean region of Europe from south-east Spain to Greece (Niethammer & Krapp 1990). Their remains are not uncommon in Pliocene and Pleistocene deposits in north-western Europe where they range in time from the Late Pliocene to the Holsteinian/Hoxnian Interglacial. In the British Isles , *T. minor* has been recorded from the Cromerian of West Runton (Stuart 1996) and Sugworth (Stuart 1980), and in deposits of late 'Cromerian Complex' age at Boxgrove and Westbury-sub-Mendip (Bishop 1982) where it co-occurs with *T. europaea*. In the Hoxnian, *T. minor* has been recorded from Hoxne (Stuart *et al*. 1996), Swanscombe (Stuart 1982; Schreve 1996), Barnham, Beeches Pit (Preece *et*

	Humerus SD			Humerus Bd		
	N	Mean	Range	N	Mean	Range
T. minor						
Barnham	**8**	**3.05**	**2.87-3.25**	**6**	**5.94**	**5.37-6.39**
Boxgrove (Unit 5a)	15	3.14	2.84-3.50	11	6.63	5.88-7.44
T.europaea						
Recent, Britain (male)	14	4.35	4.05-4.64	14	9.17	8.67-9.55
Recent, Britain (female)	14	4.11	3.87-4.39	12	8.59	8.09-9.14
Boxgrove (Unit 5a)	16	3.90	3.68-4.30	14	8.26	7.73-8.85

Table 11.8. Humerus measurements (in mm) of *Talpa europaea* and *T. minor*. SD is the smallest breadth of the diaphysis, Bd is the breadth of the distal epiphysis.

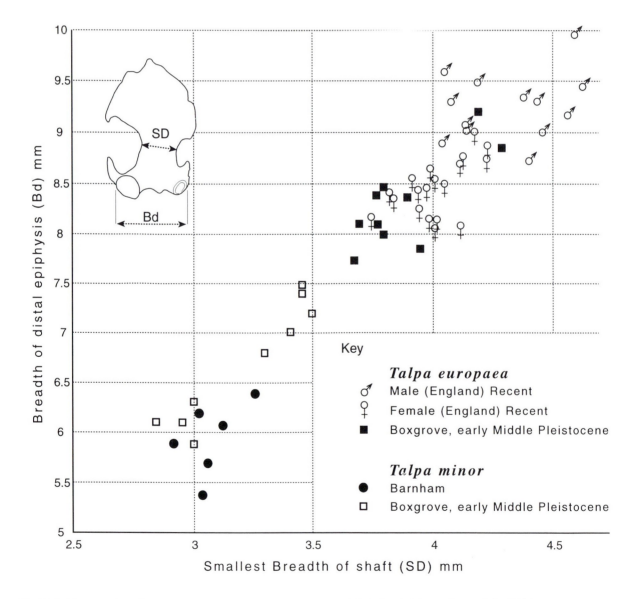

Fig 11.2. Bivariate plot of humerus distal breadth against smallest breadth of the shaft in modern and fossil *Talpa*.

al. 1991) and also probably at Woodston (Horton *et al.* 1992). Schreve (1996) has tentatively identified *T. europaea* from the Lower Loam of Swanscombe based on an M_1 (erroneously identified as an M_2). This tooth is 25% smaller than the mean of a sample of 20 females of the corresponding tooth in *T. europaea* and most probably *T. minor* on the basis of its small size (Table 11.9). To date no British Hoxnian site has produced remains of *T. europaea*, and it is therefore possible that this reflects a real absence from Britain during the Hoxnian.

Radius Bp.	N	Mean	Range
T. minor			
Barnham	4	2.68	2.33-3.20
Swanscombe (Lower Loam)	1	2.82	-
Boxgrove (Unit 5a)	4	3.24	2.73-3.56
T.europaea			
Recent, Britain (male)	14	4.43	4.00-4.93
Recent, Britain (female)	14	4.07	3.69-4.44
Boxgrove (Unit 5a)	4	4.12	4.00-4.40

Table 11.9. Radius measurements (in mm) of *Talpa europaea* and *T. minor*. Bp is the breadth of the proximal articular surface.

A comparison may be made with measurements of early Middle Pleistocene *T. minor* from Boxgrove with those of the Barnham specimens. The two most commonly represented bones for which comparative measurements are available are the humerus and the radius. Measurements for these elements are therefore compared with various fossil and Recent *Talpa* in Tables 11.8 and 11.9 and Figure 11.2. It can be seen from these data that on size the humeri from Barnham are relatively small and fall close to the lower end of size variation for this element in *T. minor* from

Boxgrove. The small size of the Barnham humeri is presumably due to small sample size and to the absence of males which are larger than females in both *T. europaea* and *T. minor*. Measurements of the Barnham radii show a broader spread, probably reflecting the presence of both males and females for this element.

***Desmana moschata* (L. 1758), Russian desman.**
Russian desman is represented by a P^1 and a mandible fragment from the shelly and gritty clays respectively. Measurements of the Barnham specimens are compared with those of Recent and fossil *Desmana moschata* in Table 11.10.

Stuart *et al.* (1993) have shown that the Hoxne desman is larger than that from West Runton, and data given in Table 11.10 shows the Hoxne desman was comparable in size to the Recent Russian desman. In contrast to Hoxne, the Barnham specimens are distinctly smaller and fall within the range of variation observed in the West Runton sample. Unfortunately the sample size is too small to provide detailed comparisons between the British samples or to confirm the apparent trend for increasing size in this lineage through the Pleistocene.

The Russian desman is a highly specialised semi-aquatic insectivore which is facing extinction in its rapidly shrinking range. While today it is confined to the basins of the Don, the Volga and the Ural rivers, fossil remains (Jánnosy 1965) indicate a former distribution which extended as far as the British Isles in the Middle Pleistocene. Records of Russian desman from the British Pleistocene are uncommon and range in age from the early Middle Pleistocene Cromerian Interglacial (Harrison *et al.* 1988) to the late Middle Pleistocene at Chislet (see Bridgland *et al.* 1998 for a discussion of the conflicting views of the age of Chislet).

	Recent Russia			Hoxne	Barnham	W-s-M	Ostend	West Runton		
	N	Mean	Range	Range	Range	Range	Range	N	Mean	Range
Dentition:										
P^1 length	7	185	1.80-1.96	-	1.58	-	-	2	-	1.81, 1.83
P^1 width	7	170	1.60-1.76	-	1.57	-	-	2	-	1.58, 1.63
Mandible:										
Ramus depth behind M_3	7	5.62	5.23--6.08	5.90	4.97	4.75	4.70	12	5.05	4.50-5.56
M_1-M_3 (alveolar)	8	9.81	9.17-10.65	10.12, 10.00[1]	-	-	-	10	8.93	8.54-9.38[1]
P_3-M_3 (alveolar)	8	16.37	15.40-16.87	15.76, 15.82[1]	-	-	-	10	15.06	14.82-15.29[1]

Table 11.10. Comparative measurements (in mm) of mandible and dentition in samples of *Desmana moschata*. [1] Data from Stuart *et al.* (1993). W-s-M = Westbury-sub-Mendip.

		MD Length		BL Breadth		Incisor Index	
	N	Mean	Range	Mean	Range	Mean	Range
Oryctolagus cuniculus							
Recent, Britain	11	2.80	2.50 - 3.34	2.00	1.55 - 2.35	72	59 - 81
Swanscombe [1]	5	2.71	2.54 - 2.76	1.92	1.80 - 2.04	71	66 - 74
Barnham	**1**	-	**(2.7)**	-	**(1.8)**	-	**(67)**
Boxgrove	1	-	(2.6)	-	(1.85)	-	(71)
Lepus timidus							
Recent, Scotland	13	2.56	2.19 - 2.74	2.27	1.81 - 2.55	88	81 - 97
Lepus europaeus							
Recent, Britain	11	3.19	2.98 - 3.46	2.08	1.93 - 2.44	65	60 - 71

Table 11.11. Measurements (in mm) of the upper incisor of Recent and Pleistocene *Oryctolagus* and *Lepus*. The incisor index (mesiodistal length x 100/buccolingual breadth) is the relative length of the crown expressed as a percentage. [1] Data from Mayhew (1975). MD length = mesiodistal length; BL breadth = buccolingual breadth.

Lagomorpha: Leporidae

***Oryctolagus* cf. *O. cuniculus* L. 1758, rabbit.** A single upper incisor fragment collected from the gritty clay is the only evidence of a rabbit in the Barnham fauna. The I^1 is rectangular in cross section (length to width ratio = 1.5) with a rounded medial lobe, a shallow mesial groove and a pronounced longitudinal depression on the posterior face which clearly identify this specimen as *Oryctolagus*. Metrical characters, in particular the cross sectional dimensions of the I^1, are also characteristic of *Oryctolagus* . This is shown by the length and width of the I^1 compared with those of Recent *Lepus timidus* and *L. europaeus* and fossil and Recent *Oryctolagus cuniculus* given in Table11.11. The measurements show a clear separation in cross sectional dimensions between the three lagomorph species, with the Barnham measurements falling within the range for *O. cuniculus*.

Fossil finds of *Oryctolagus* are largely confined to the Iberian Peninsula, southern France and Italy, and it is probable that the genus originated in the western Mediterranean region during the Late Pliocene (Rogers, P.M. *et al*. 1994). According to Donard (1975), the earliest record of *Oryctolagus cuniculus* is from the early Middle Pleistocene (Mindel) of Montousse in southern France. In Britain, rabbit was present in two temperate episodes of the Middle Pleistocene; during the 'Cromerian Complex' where it is found at Boxgrove (Currant in Roberts 1985), and in the Hoxnian where it is known from Barnham, and at Swanscombe where it occurs in abundance in the Lower Loam (Mayhew 1975). With the exception of these finds, the rabbit is not recorded from northern and central Europe during this period.

In the context of its Pleistocene distribution, the presence of the rabbit in Britain during two separate temperate episodes is remarkable. The apparent absence of the rabbit from continental Europe may be explained if the rabbit migrated north along coastlines, rarely penetrating far inland. Today, coastal habitats, with open grassland and sandy soils are often ideal for the rabbit, and, in the northern part of its range, it may have favoured these areas in preference to densely wooded hinterland of the interglacials. The find of rabbit from Boxgrove, a coastal site, would seem to support this scenario; the records from Barnham and Swanscombe (both inland sites) show that it made incursions inland perhaps along grassy floodplains of large rivers. Although the natural distribution of the rabbit has been greatly influenced by human introductions, it is apparent from its present day range that it is not able to survive far into eastern Europe or in the extreme north. This suggests that it prefers an equable maritime climate with mild winters; a combination of both climate and the distribution of grasslands/open woodland may have acted together to determine the distribution of the rabbit during the Pleistocene

Rodentia: Sciuridae

***Sciurus* sp. Squirrel.** A distal fragment of a left tibia from the grey clay represents the sole record of a squirrel from Barnham. The distal breadth of the tibia (4.78 mm) is smaller than those of Recent red squirrels measured (mean = 5.43 mm, range = 5.06-5.70 mm, N = 9), but this may reflect the limited geographical range of the small comparative sample (Britain, France and Belgium). Today, the red squirrel, *S. vulgaris*, shows considerable geographic variation in body size with a decline in body size from relatively large in the south to relatively small in the north of its European range.

Squirrels are exceptionally rare as Pleistocene fossils in the British Isles. Hinton (1914) described an extinct squirrel, *Sciurus whitei*, from a single tooth from the Cromerian 'Monkey Gravel' overlying the Freshwater Bed at West Runton. The relationship of *Sciurus whitei* to later Middle Pleistocene records of *Sciurus* from Westbury-sub-Mendip (Andrews 1990), Boxgrove,

Ostend (Sutcliffe & Kowalski 1976) Beeches Pit and Barnham is uncertain as these remains are either too sparse, or fragmentary, to assign with confidence to a particular taxon.

Rodentia: Arvicolidae

***Clethrionomys glareolus* (Schreber 1780), bank vole.**
The bank vole, *Clethrionomys glareolus*, is represented by 87 isolated molars (Fig. 11.3a-b) which are morphologically identical with Recent European *C. glareolus*. In young individuals the molars are unrooted, but the pulp cavities close in the early stage of growth to form roots. The adult molars have rounded salient angles, thick enamel and crown cementum in the re-entrant valleys.

Measurements of the Barnham sample are given in Table 11.12, and the length of the first lower molar is compared with that from other British Pleistocene localities and a Recent sample of *C. glareolus* in Table 11.13. The measurements for the Barnham sample fall well within the range for this species from Boxgrove, but are noticeably smaller than the Recent sample. Van Kolfschoten (1991) has noted the generally small size of north-west European Middle Pleistocene *C. glareolus*, and this observation is supported by the sample from Barnham and the other British localities included in Table 11.13.

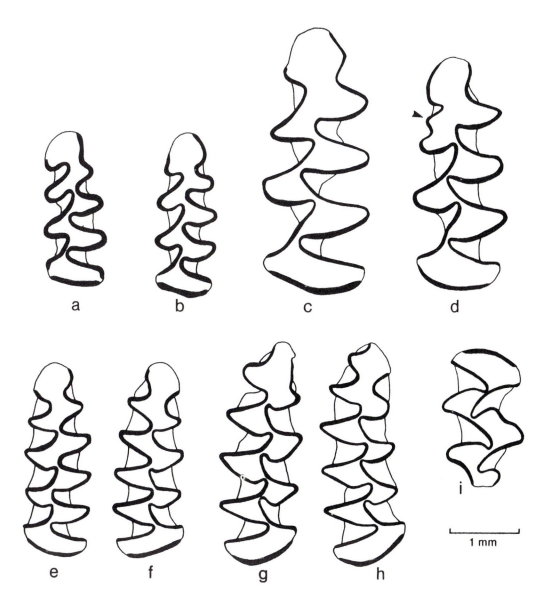

Fig. 11.3. a-b: *Clethrionomys glareolus*: a: left M$_1$ (brown-grey clay, BEF 602); b: left M$_1$ (brown-grey clay, BEF 528); c-d: *Arvicola terrestris cantiana*: c: left M$_1$ (black clay, BEF 1486); d: left M$_1$ (gritty clay, BEF 465), arrow indicates '*Mimomys* fold'; e-f: *Microtus (Terricola)* cf. *Subterraneus*: e: left M$_1$ (gritty clay, BEF 940); f: right M$_1$ (shelly clay, BEF 1307); g-i: *Microtus agrestis*: g: right M$_1$ (gritty clay, BEF 788); h: right M$_1$ (gritty clay, BEF 1306); i: right M^2 (gritty clay, BEF 943). (illustration: Simon Parfitt).

	N	Mean ± SD	Range
M^1 Length	11	1.73 ± 0.07	1.63-1.86
M^1 Width	5	0.79 ± 0.01	0.78-0.80
M^2 Length	11	1.32 ± 0.10	1.20-1.56
M^2 Width	7	0.75 ± 0.02	0.65-0.82
M^3 Length	9	1.59 ± 0.13	1.31-1.78
M^3 Width	7	0.76 ± 0.03	0.73-0.80
M$_1$ Length	6	2.05 ± 0.11	1.87-2.21
M$_1$ Width	4	0.81 ± 0.06	0.73-0.87
M$_2$ Length	13	1.33 ± 0.06	1.24-1.48
M$_2$ Width	11	0.73 ± 0.05	0.66-0.81
M$_3$ Length	7	1.21 ± 0.07	1.12-1.28
M$_3$ Width	7	0.61 ± 0.06	0.53-0.68

Table 11.12. Measurements (in mm) of molars of *Clethrionomys glareolus* from Barnham.

M$_1$ Length	N	Mean	Range
Recent			
Poland [1]	25	2.29	2.07-2.55
British Pleistocene			
Joint Mitnor Cave	1	-	(1.88)
Swanton Morley [2]	5	2.12	2.06-2.26
Grays Thurrock	10	1.94	1.81-2.04
Barnham	**6**	**2.05**	**1.87-2.21**
Swanscombe (Lower Loam)	1	-	(1.98)
Boxgrove	130	2.05	1.65-2.31
Sugworth [3]	4	2.03	1.94-2.14
West Runton	12	2.02	1.85-2.21

Table 11.13. Comparative measurements (in mm) of the first lower molar of *Clethrionomys glareolus*. Data from: [1] Nadachowski (1982), [2] Coxon *et al.* (1980), [3] Stuart (1980).

Remains of the bank vole referred to the living species are well represented in British sites ranging in age from the Cromerian (Freshwater bed at West Runton) to the Holocene. They are nearly always found in British temperate small mammal faunas, which accords with their modern preference for closed woodland and densely overgrown scrub. Although it occurs in small numbers at most Hoxnian localities (Hoxne, Beeches Pit, Swanscombe, Lower Loam, Clacton, Ingress Vale and Woodston) it is never abundant. This is no doubt a reflection of the scarcity of deposits which have been collected for small mammals.

***Arvicola terrestris cantiana*, water vole.** The water vole is the largest and the most abundant of the voles present at Barnham. In all, 599 remains (predominantly isolated molars) were identified. This represents one of the largest samples of Middle Pleistocene *Arvicola* from Britain. In Britain today, the water vole (*Arvicola terrestris*) is closely associated with water edge habitats, preferring well-vegetated banks of slow-flowing rivers, streams and ponds. As at Barnham, it tends to be common in Pleistocene fluvial and lacustrine deposits suggesting it was probably also adapted to an aquatic lifestyle during this period (Stuart 1982).

The water vole lineage is perhaps one of the best known examples of phyletic evolution in a Quaternary mammal (Sutcliffe 1985). Because of its abundance in fossil assemblages and its rapid evolution during the Pleistocene, it is an ideal tool for biostratigraphic correlation (von Koenigswald 1973; Sutcliffe & Kowalski 1976). Until recently, it was generally believed that the water vole lineage underwent gradual, unidirectional change since the early Middle Pleistocene. However, it now appears that the evolution of *Arvicola* was more complex than originally thought, with variable rates of change and important reversals in the assumed trend (Kratochvil 1981; van Kolfschoten 1990; von Koenigswald & van Kolfschoten 1996). Consequently, it was deemed necessary to reassess the pattern of change in British *Arvicola* before applying these data to the correlation of Barnham. Disagreement on the taxonomy and phylogenetic relationships of Recent and fossil *Arvicola* led van Kolfschoten (1990) to propose that all fossil and Recent central and north-west European members of the genus *Arvicola* should be considered as belonging to a sub-species of *Arvicola terrestris*. In this taxonomy, the British early Middle Pleistocene *Arvicola*, which is distinguished by '*Mimomys* - type' enamel differentiation, relatively small size, high frequency of the '*Mimomys* fold', and a relatively short M$_1$ anteroconid complex is referred to *Arvicola terrestris cantiana*. This taxonomy is the one adopted here.

Models of evolution and the taxonomy of Pleistocene Arvicola. The living water vole, *Arvicola terrestris*, evolved from its ancestor, *Mimomys savini* during the 'Cromerian Complex' (von Koenigswald & van Kolfschoten 1996). The *Mimomys* lineage is characterised by a gradual increase in crown height of the molars which culminated in the development of unrooted, continuously-growing molars. The transition from *Mimomys*, with rooted molars, to *Arvicola* with continuously-growing molars is documented in western European sites to have taken place after the Brunhes-Matuyama boundary but before Interglacial IV of the 'Cromerian Complex' (von Koenigswald & van Kolfschoten 1996). The subsequent evolution of *Arvicola* in north-western Europe is characterised by an increase in body size, a reduction of the thickness of enamel on trailing edges of the molar triangles, an elongation of the anteroconid complex (ACC) of the M$_1$, and by the loss of the '*Mimomys* fold' (Stuart 1982).

Following the work of von Koenigswald (1972, 1973), enamel thickness has been the principal criteria for identifying water voles to species. For the *Arvicola* lineage, a succession of species has been established, based primarily on the relative thickness of the molar enamel, progressing from *Arvicola cantiana* with *Mimomys* type enamel differentiation in the early part of the Middle Pleistocene, to '*Arvicola cantiana - terrestris*' with undifferentiated enamel (late Middle Pleistocene) and finally to *Arvicola terrestris* (Late Pleistocene to Recent) with thinner enamel on the trailing edges of the molar salient angles (Stuart 1982). For the British Pleistocene, these successive changes were first described in detail by von Koenigswald (1972, 1973). Subsequently, Sutcliffe and Kowlaski (1976) used the differences in the stage of evolution of British Pleistocene *Arvicola* in support of their argument for an additional temperate stage between the Hoxnian and the Ipswichian. This model of gradual, unidirectional change in the water vole lineage evolution has now been tested with new samples from stratified sequences in Germany and The Netherlands which demonstrate that the trend in enamel thickness was not a simple progressive one but included at least one reversal in the trend (Kolfschoten 1990). This reversal in the European sequence is thought to result from the immigration of less-derived populations from southern Europe during the climatic amelioration at the end of the Saalian, implying that evolution progressed at different rates in different geographical areas. In addition, studies of living water voles have shown that this assumed geographical cline in enamel differentiation exists today, with the living water voles in southern Europe resembling those found in north-western Europe during the Middle Pleistocene (Kratochvil 1981). Because of these complicating factors, the thickness of the enamel in *Arvicola* must be used with caution when correlating Pleistocene sites. Nevertheless, when used in combination with molar size, frequency of '*Mimomys* fold', and occlusal morphology, the evolutionary stage of *Arvicola* may still be a useful biostratigraphic tool.

In order to evaluate the significance of this sequence of changes in the British water vole lineage for biostratigraphic correlations, representative samples of British water voles have been examined from a series of localities spanning the Middle and Late Pleistocene. The size of the M_1, the enamel thickness, and the '*Mimomys* fold' frequency are described for the Barnham assemblage, and comparisons have been extended to the samples given in Tables 11.14-17 and Figure 11.4. The approximate chronological order of the sites is also shown in Figure 11.4; Westbury-sub-Mendip (Calcareous Member), Ostend and Boxgrove have been correlated with oxygen isotope stage 13 (Bishop 1982; Roberts *et al.* 1994), the Hoxnian localities with oxygen isotope stage 11, Purfleet, Grays Thurrock and Cudmore Grove with oxygen isotope

stage 9 (Bridgland 1994), Aveley with oxygen isotope stage 7 (Sutcliffe 1995; Bridgland 1994) and the Ipswichian is correlated with oxygen isotope stage 5e (Gascoyne *et al.* 1981).

Size of the molars. Stuart (1982) has demonstrated a trend towards increasing size of the British water vole during successive temperate stages since the Cromerian. Based on measurements of the teeth, early Middle Pleistocene *Mimomys* was 30% smaller than the living British water vole (Stuart 1982; Martin 1993).

Measurements of the Barnham water vole molars are given in Table 11.14 and the length of the first lower molar is compared with various samples in Table 11.15. The sample from Barnham agrees closely with that from Swanscombe, and both are intermediate in size between early Middle Pleistocene *Arvicola* and Late Pleistocene samples given by Stuart (1982).

	N	Mean ± SD	Range
M^1 Length	77	3.12 ± 0.14	2.80-3.41
M^1 Width	56	1.46 ± 0.09	1.25-1.63
M^2 Length	69	2.37 ± 0.15	2.02-2.74
M^2 Width	52	1.34 ± 0.08	1.20-1.51
M^3 Length	53	2.31 ± 0.14	2.10-2.58
M^3 Width	44	1.23 ± 0.09	1.02-1.43
M_1 Length	77	3.57 ± 0.17	3.14-4.01
M_1 Width	61	1.43 ± 0.07	1.28-1.58
M_2 Length	81	2.21 ± 0.12	1.98-2.64
M_2 Width	63	1.24 ± 0.07	1.08-1.38
M_3 Length	46	2.18 ± 0.14	1.83-2.41
M_3 Width	35	1.09 ± 0.07	0.95-1.24

Table 11.14. Measurements (in mm) of molars of *Arvicola terrestris cantiana* from Barnham.

M_1 Length	N	Mean	Range
Arvicola			
Recent			
Poland [1]	20	4.18	3.90-4.44
British Pleistocene			
Swanton Morley [2]	3	-	(3.44, 3.50, 3.76)
Joint Mitnor Cave	3	-	(3.59, 3.76, 3.95)
Grays Thurrock	7	3.60	3.54-3.74
Purfleet	2	-	(3.30, 3.40)
Barnham	**77**	**3.57**	**3.14-4.01**
Hoxne [3]	3	-	(3.44, 3.46, c. 3.48)
Swanscombe (Lower Loam)	7	3.55	3.43-3.72
Boxgrove	80	3.40	2.84-3.92
Mimomys savini			
West Runton	20	3.22	3.07-3.40

Table 11.15. Comparative measurements (in mm) of M_1 length of *Arvicola* and *Mimomys savini*. Data from: [1] Nadachowski (1982), [2] Coxon *et al.* (1980), [3] Stuart *et al.* (1993).

123

M₁ Length	N	Mean ± SD	Range
Gritty clay	61	3.59 ± 0.18	3.14-4.01
Shelly clay	6	3.57 ± 0.08	3.47-3.66
Black clay	9	3.46 ± 0.14	3.24-3.70
Brown-grey clay	1	-	(3.46)

Table 11.16. Measurements (in mm) of M_1 of *Arvicola terrestris cantiana* from the main fossiliferous units at Barnham. The units are in stratigraphic order with the oldest at the bottom.

Although samples from individual units of the lower part of the fossiliferous sequence at Barnham are small, they nevertheless appear to indicate a small increase in size of the water voles during the deposition of the fossiliferous deposits (Table 11.16).

Relative length of the anteroconid complex (ACC). Water vole molar evolution is also characterised by a progressive increase in the length of the anterior part of the M_1 and of the posterior part of the M^3. For the M_1, these differences can be quantified by measuring the distance along the midline of the M_1 from the anteriormost point of the buccal re-entrant angle (BRA) 2 to the anterior tip of the molar. These measurements are given expressed as a ratio (A/L) which quantifies the relative length of the anteroconid complex (ACC) in comparison to occlusal length (van der Meulen 1973). The mean A/L values for the fossil samples (*Mimomys*

savini: West Runton mean 38.6 ± 2.28 (N=20), pre-Anglian *Arvicola*: Westbury-sub-Mendip (Calcareous Member, Bishop Collection) 38.8 ± 2.14 (N=21), Ostend 39.3 ± 2.28 (N=8), post-Anglian *Arvicola*: Barnham 39.6 ± 3.03 (N=73), Grays Thurrock 40.51 ± 2.28 (N=7), Joint Mitnor Cave 40.0 ± 0.65 (N=3)) are smaller than the Recent mean (42 ± 0.01 (N=20), Nadachowski 1982), showing that Pleistocene *Mimomys* and *Arvicola* possessed a relatively short anteroconid complex. The mean ACC length in available post-Anglian *Arvicola* samples is slightly higher than those of the pre-Anglian *Arvicola* sample. The differences between the post-Anglian samples appear to show a slight shift to larger values with time, although larger samples are required to test this.

Enamel thickness. The relative thickness of the enamel on the trailing and leading edges of the molars also changed in sequence during the Pleistocene (Heinrich 1978, 1987, 1982a, 1982b; van Kolfschoten 1990; von Koenigswald & van Kolfschoten 1996). For the British localities given in Figure 11.4, the differences in enamel thickness between the leading and the trailing edges of the triangles was measured using the methods developed by Heinrich (1978, 1987, 1982) and van Kolfschoten (1996). In this method, the relative thickness of the enamel on the trailing and leading molar triangles is expressed as a quotient (SDQ) for the sample of molars.

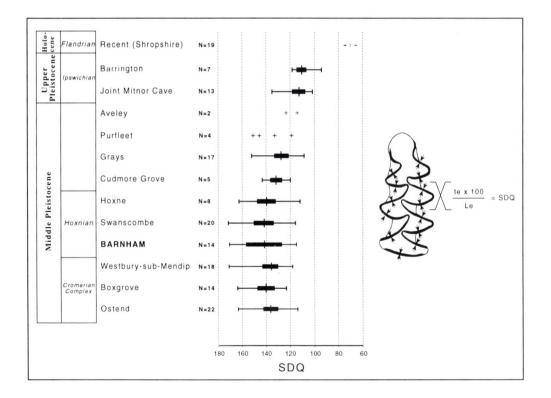

Fig. 11.4. Enamel thickness quotient (SDQ values) of British Pleistocene and Recent *Arvicola* molars. For the larger samples, the mean is indicated by a vertical line, the standard deviation by a solid bar, and the observed range by a horizontal line. The inset shows the location of measurements taken for the lower first molar (after van Kolfschoten 1990).

The SDQ values have been measured for the British water vole lineage and are summarised for the first time in Figure 11.4. The diagram shows that there was no significant change in the SDQ ratio during the early part of the Middle Pleistocene. During this period of stasis SDQ values fluctuates around a mean value of 140. The value for Barnham is close to this value, consistent with a Hoxnian age for the deposits. A trend towards decreasing SDQ values is seen during the later part of the Middle Pleistocene at Cudmore Grove, Grays Thurrock and Purfleet where the mean values for SDQ are 130. The greatest change in the SDQ values, however, occurred between the end of the Middle Pleistocene and the Holocene, a period of time for which there are few large assemblages of *Arvicola*.

'Mimomys fold' frequency. The '*Mimomys* fold' is a ridge of enamel on the anterior edge of the buccal salient angle (BSA) 4 (Fig. 11.3d) which is relatively common in most earlier populations of *Arvicola* and *Mimomys* but is exceptionally rare in living populations of *Arvicola terrestris* (Table 11.17). The presence or absence of a '*Mimomys* fold' on the M_1 is biostratigraphically important as the frequency of this feature decreases through time (Stuart 1982).

'*Mimomys* fold'	N	Present	Freq. %
Arvicola			
Recent, Britain	50	0	0
Barrington	1	0	0
Joint Mitnor Cave	3	0	0
Swanton Morley [1]	4	0	0
Cudmore Grove	11	0	0
Grays Thurrock	12	1	8.3
Purfleet	2	0	0
Barnham	**121**	**37**	**30.6**
Hoxne[2]	5	1	20.0
Beeches Pit	12	4	33.3
Swanscombe	9	5	55.5
Boxgrove	354	35	9.9
Mimomys savini			
West Runton	100	27	27

Table 11.17. Frequency of the '*Mimomys* fold' in British Recent and Pleistocene populations of *Arvicola* and *Mimomys savini*. Data from [1] Coxon *et al.* (1980); [2] Stuart *et al.* 1993.

The data presented in Table 11.17 shows that this trend was not one of gradual decrease in '*Mimomys* fold' frequency over the last 0.5 myr. During the Middle Pleistocene, for example, there was an abrupt decline in frequency from around 30% cent during the Hoxnian, to 4% in the subsequent interglacial as represented by the deposits at Cudmore Grove, Grays Thurrock and Purfleet. Unfortunately, the fossil record of the water vole is very poor in the late Middle and

Late Pleistocene. However, the '*Mimomys* fold' was not observed in the Ipswichian or the Recent sample, so if present, it is very rare.

In the time period encompassing the Hoxnian and the Cromerian, there is no evidence for a steady decline in '*Mimomys* fold' frequency. Instead, the highest values are found in the youngest samples (32% in the Hoxnian) with slightly lower values in the Cromerian (27%), and the lowest values are found in deposits of intermediate age at Boxgrove where just 35 (10%) of the 354 M_1's have a '*Mimomys* fold'. The exceptionally high frequency of the '*Mimomys* fold' in the British Hoxnian water vole is not observed in broadly contemporary European samples (van Kolfschoten pers. comm. 1998), and may be a biostratigraphically significant feature of British Hoxnian *Arvicola*.

Summary. The changes in the occlusal pattern of British Middle Pleistocene water vole molars are summarised in Figure 11.4. Although the elucidation of the trends will require the study of larger samples, especially for the late Middle and Late Pleistocene, some general comments on the nature and the rate of change in this lineage can be outlined. In summary, for the temperate stages, size increases from the Cromerian to the present, and is accompanied by a tendency towards a relatively longer anteroconid complex. The '*Mimomys* fold' is only common in early Middle Pleistocene *Mimomys* and *Arvicola* from the late 'Cromerian Complex' and the Hoxnian. Thereafter, it is either absent or present at very low frequencies. The trend in enamel differentiation, previously characterised as undergoing gradual unidirectional change, instead shows a prolonged period of stasis for much of the Middle Pleistocene. There is a gradual increase in SDQ values towards the end of the Middle Pleistocene with a period of rapid change during the late Middle and Late Pleistocene. The reversal in SDQ values at the transition from the Saalian to the Eemian, recognised in Germany and the Netherlands, may provide an important means for correlating sites. However, the possibility that this reversal occurred in Britain cannot be investigated at present because of the poor record of *Arvicola* in Britain for this period.

The British Hoxnian samples are characterised by relatively small molars with a short anteroconid complex, a high SDQ value and a very high prevalence of the '*Mimomys* fold'. In all of these features, the *Arvicola* sample from Barnham is consistent with a Hoxnian age.

***Microtus (Terricola)* cf. *subterraneus*, common pine vole.** The 'pine vole' *Microtus (Terricola)* sp., is represented by 14 first lower molars. In the M_1 (Fig. 11.3e-f) the dentine fields of the T4 and T5 are broadly confluent, forming a '*Pitymys* rhombus' which is well separated from an 'arvalid' type AC2 (*sensu* van der Meulen 1973). Living voles, with a broadly confluent T4 and T5 of M_1, have traditionally been placed in the genus (or subgenus) *Pitymys* which includes both the Nearctic and the Palaearctic pine voles. Although most authorities now include the western Palaearctic 'pine voles' in the genus (or subgenus) *Terricola* as distinct from the Nearctic pine voles of the genus *Pitymys* (Chaline *et al.* 1988), the taxonomy of this group is far from being resolved. Krystufek *et al.* (1996) have expressed doubts as to the validity of *Terricola* and they question whether the western Palaearctic 'pine voles' are a monophyletic group, suggesting that the dental similarities between them is a result of parallelism.

The specific identity of the Barnham pine vole is uncertain as the occlusal pattern of the M_1 in species of European 'pine voles' is very similar. Nevertheless, the small size of the teeth and their close morphological resemblance to the extant common pine vole *M. (T.) subterraneus* suggest a direct relationship with the common pine vole, and this seems the most likely hypothesis. Measurements of the first lower molar (Table 11.18) show that the Barnham 'pine vole' was intermediate in size between the early Middle Pleistocene form from Boxgrove, and Recent *M. (T.) subterraneus*. Size change appears to have been particularly pronounced in the common pine vole as evidenced by the large increase in size observed between the Holocene and the present day in Poland (Nadachowski 1982).

Differences in the relative length of the anteroconid of M_1 were also investigated to see if there were differences between the British Pleistocene and Recent 'pine vole' samples. The relative length of the anteroconid complex (ACC) in Barnham *M. (T.)* cf. *subterraneus* (N=13, mean 52.1, range 47.5-56, standard deviation 2.51) is almost identical to the mean of Recent *M. (T.) subterraneus* from the Pieiny Mountains, Poland (N=20, mean 52, range 50-54, standard deviation ±0.01) given by Nadachowski (1982). The West Runton 'pine vole' (*Pitymys arvaloides* Hinton 1923 but referred to common pine vole by Stuart 1982) is, however, distinct from Hoxnian and late 'Cromerian Complex' (Boxgrove, Westbury-sub-Mendip, Calcareous Member) material on account of its shorter anteroconid Complex (N=19, mean 51.3, range 48-55, standard deviation 1.91).

Today, the common pine vole is found in grassland and open woodland throughout central and eastern Europe with the exception of southern France, the Mediterranean region, and the British Isles. During the early Middle Pleistocene *Microtus (Terricola)* cf. *subterraneus* is consistently represented in British small mammal faunas, particularly during the temperate stages of the 'Cromerian Complex' (Andrews 1990). In Britain it is last recorded in the Hoxnian (Stuart 1982),

and it appears not to have recolonised in subsequent warm stages. This is surprising as it is found in contemporary sites on the continent.

M_1 Length	N	Mean	Range
Recent, Poland [1]	20	2.62	2.49-2.72
Holocene, Poland [1]	30	2.48	2.31-2.70
Hoxne [2]	3	-	(c. 2.12, 2.28, 2.62)
Swanscombe	3	-	(2.31[a], 2.41[b], 2.54[b])
Barnham	**14**	**2.53**	**2.13-2.79**
Boxgrove	32	2.40	2.11-2.61
West Runton	19	2.42	2.15-2.67

Table 11.18. Comparative measurements (in mm) of first lower molar length of British Pleistocene *Microtus (Terricola)* cf. *subterraneus* and Recent and Holocene *M. (T.) subterraneus*. Data from: [1] Nadachowski (1982), [2] Stuart *et al.* (1993). The Swanscombe sample derives from [a] the Upper Middle Gravel and [b] the Lower Loam.

***Microtus agrestis* (L. 1761), field vole.** The field vole, *Microtus agrestis*, is the most abundant of the small voles at Barnham. It is identified by the presence of M^2 with an additional postero-lingual salient angle ('*agrestis*' loop) which readily distinguishes it from other species of *Microtus*. The first lower molars are notoriously difficult to distinguish from those of the closely related common vole, *M. arvalis*, since the occlusal morphology and dimensions of the M_1 of both species overlap to a large degree. However, Nadachowski (1984) has shown that the M_1 of the two species can be separated using M_1 length and the degree of asymmetry of the M_1 triangles. Plots of M_1 length against LT4/LT5 index (which measures molar asymmetry) show a clear discrimination between the two species for Recent populations. In *M. agrestis*, the M_1 is on average larger with asymmetrical triangles. In comparison, the M_1 of *M. arvalis* is on average smaller with more symmetrical triangles. Plots of M_1 length against LT4/LT5 index for the *Microtus agrestis/arvalis* group from Barnham shows the presence of two clusters (Fig. 11.5) consistent with the two extant species *M. arvalis* and *M. agrestis*.

As can be seen from Table 11.19, the mean occlusal length of the M_1s from Barnham is much larger than that of Boxgrove, but comparable with Recent *M. agrestis*. This difference indicates that *M. agrestis* significantly increased in size between the 'Cromerian Complex' and the Hoxnian.

In addition to length of the M_1, the relative length of the anteroconid complex (ACC) of M_1 also changes with time. To investigate this change the A/L values (van der Meulen 1973) of fossil *M. agrestis* from West Runton (Upper Freshwater Bed), Boxgrove (late 'Cromerian Complex'), Grays Thurrock (early 'Saalian Complex', correlated with oxygen isotope stage 9 by

	N	Mean	Range
M²			
Recent, Britain	11	1.54	1.45-1.63
Grays Thurrock	17	1.61	1.49-1.73
Hoxne [1]	6	1.48	1.34-1.76
Barnham	**8**	**1.65**	**1.51-1.81**
M₁			
Recent, Britain	20	2.65	2.44-2.89
Recent, Poland [2]	30	2.94	2.50-3.30
Grays Thurrock	10	2.63	2.48-2.81
Purfleet	2	-	(2.84, 2.87)
Barnham	**16**	**2.91**	**2.58-3.22**
Boxgrove	24	2.70	2.30-2.95
M₁ A/L			
Recent, Poland [2]	30	54 ± 0.02	50-61
Grays Thurrock	9	52.7 ± 1.12	51.5-55.2
Barnham	**16**	**52.1 ± 1.91**	**48.7-55.0**
Boxgrove	11	51 ± 0.03	47-56
West Runton [3]	30	50.6 ± 1.50	47.5-53.8

Table 11.19. Length measurements (in mm) of M₁ and M² and anteroconid length index (A/L) of *Microtus agrestis* from Barnham compared with Recent and Pleistocene samples. Data from: [1] Stuart *et al.* (1993), [2] Nadachowski (1982), *M̃.* cf. *agrestis*

Bridgland 1994), and samples of extant European populations, were compared. The A/L values for these assemblages are given in Table 11.19.

The increasing values of A/L with geological time (Table 11.19) show that *M. agrestis* evolution (as in other species of *Microtus*) is characterised by a progressive increase in the relative length of the anteroconid complex. In this scheme, the mean of the Barnham sample falls between those of Boxgrove and Grays Thurrock. These differences may have biostratigraphic value if the analysis of further samples show that this trend is both progressive and unidirectional.

***Microtus arvalis* (Pallas 1779), common vole.** The common vole is represented by only three lower first molars, the measurements of which are given in Table 11.20. This species is typically found in short grazed grassland and it avoids areas of tall ungrazed, wet grassland particularly when the field vole is present (Bjärvall & Ullström 1986). Competition between the two species, and the predominance of marshy grassland habitat at Barnham, probably account for the low numbers of common vole in the fauna.

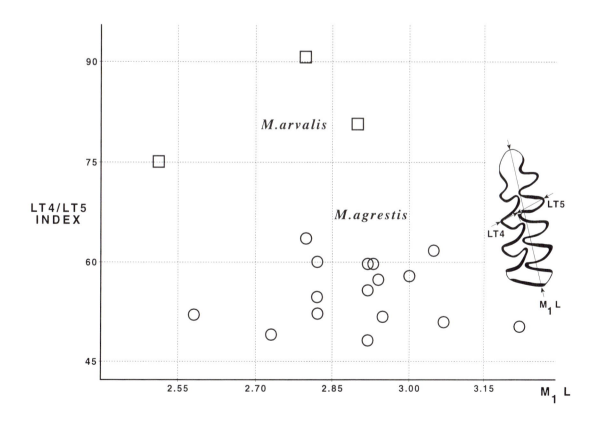

Fig. 11.5. Relationship between M₁ length and LT4/LT5 index in *Microtus agrestis* and *Microtus arvalis* from Barnham

M₁ Length	N	Mean	Range
Recent, Poland [1]	30	2.67	2.48-2.84
Barnham	**3**	-	**(2.51, 2.80, 2.90)**
Boxgrove	24	2.40	1.99-2.71

Table 11.20. Length measurements (in mm) of the first lower molar of *Microtus arvalis* from Barnham compared with an early Middle Pleistocene sample from Boxgrove and a Recent Polish population. [1] Data from Nadachowski (1982).

Rodentia: Muridae

Apodemus sylvaticus (L. 1758), wood mouse. Based on size and morphology, two species of *Apodemus* appear to be represented in the Barnham assemblage. Of these, the larger and most abundant form is identical in morphology to the closely related living species, the yellow-necked mouse *Apodemus flavicollis* and wood mouse *A. sylvaticus*. The smaller of the two species at Barnham, *A. maastrichtiensis*, is easily identified due to a combination of its distinctive morphology and smaller size.

On the basis of biometric criteria, both *A. sylvaticus* and *A. flavicollis* species are known to have co-existed since the Early Pleistocene in Europe (Michaux & Pasquier 1974), but *A. flavicollis* has not been found as a securely dated Pleistocene fossil in the British Isles (Sutcliffe & Kowalski 1976). Although it is generally assumed that medium sized species of *Apodemus* found in British Pleistocene sites are wood mouse rather than yellow-necked mouse, this has rarely been tested. This is because, although *A. flavicollis* is on average larger than *A. sylvaticus*, there is considerable overlap in

measurements and there are no reliable morphological characters of the dentition which would facilitate identification of fragmentary palaeontological material.

The problems of using absolute size to distinguish between *A. flavicollis* and *A. sylvaticus* are compounded as the size of both species varied considerably during the Pleistocene as noted by Michaux and Pasquier (1974) and by Tchernov (1979). Also, in Recent populations, differences in competition and levels of predation between populations can have a profound effect on the body size of the two species. This is illustrated by isolated island populations of *A. sylvaticus* which, in the absence predators and of competition from other small mammals, can be as large as *A. flavicollis* (Angerbjörn 1986).

Although it may not be possible to use absolute size alone to identify which of the two species is represented in a fossil assemblage, it should be possible to recognise assemblages where the two species co-occur. For instance, large samples should show a bimodal distribution for dental measurements if both *A. sylvaticus* and *A. flavicollis* are present. With small sample sizes, an increase in the range of the measurements relative to samples in which only one of the species is present would indicate the presence of more than one species.

For the British Pleistocene samples of *Apodemus*, the number of species was investigated by utilising a range based coefficient of variation developed by Freudenthal (Freudenthal & Cuenca Bescos 1984; Freudenthal & Martín-Suárez 1990). This coefficient (V') may be used to estimate the degree of variation of a sample, and to determine whether the sample is composed of material of more than one species.

	N	Length Mean ± SD	Range	N	Width Mean ± SD	Range
A. sylvaticus						
M¹	22	1.89 ± 0.07	1.73-2.03	24	1.19 ± 0.04	1.13-1.26
M²	10	1.28 ± 0.04	1.23-1.35	10	1.12 ± 0.04	1.04-1.18
M₁	20	1.78 ± 0.05	1.66-1.86	20	1.04 ± 0.03	0.98-1.12
M₂	16	1.21 ± 0.04	1.15-1.30	16	1.03 ± 0.04	0.95-1.09
A. maastrichtiensis						
M¹	3	-	(1.51, 1.61, 1.63)	3	-	(1.03, 1.03, 1.08)
M²	2	-	(1.07, 1.10)	2	-	(1.04, 1.18)
M₁	4	1.50 ± 0.09	1.38-1.59	4	0.91 ± 0.07	0.83-1.00
M₂	1	-	(1.01)	1	-	(0.91)
Apodemus sp.						
M³	2	-	(0.83, 0.87)	2	-	(0.84, 0.87)
M₃	1	-	(0.90)	1	-	(0.88)

Table 11.21. Dimensions (in mm) of *Apodemus sylvaticus*, *A. maastrichtiensis* and *Apodemus* sp. molars from Barnham.

	N	M[1] Length Mean	Range	V' [a]		N	M[1] Length Mean	Range	V' [a]
Recent									
A. sylvaticus, Britain	17	1.84	1.69-1.96	15.9		20	1.71	1.61-1.79	10.6
A. flavicollis, Britain	18	1.96	1.83-2.12	-		18	1.82	1.70-1.90	11.1
British Pleistocene									
Swanton Morley [1]	-	-	-	-		3	-	1.82, 1.84, 1.88	-
Grays Thurrock	4	1.80	1.61-2.03	23.1		8	1.74	1.61-1.89	16
Barnham	22	1.89	1.73-2.03	15.9		20	1.78	1.66-1.86	11.4
Westbury-sub-Mendip [2]	1	-	1.85	-		-	-	-	-
Little Oakley [3]	2	-	1.72, 1.79	-		-	-	-	-
Sugworth [4]	-	-	-	-		5	1.80	1.72-1.86	7.8
West Runton	5	1.78	1.75-1.82	3.9		2	-	1.69, 1.78	-

Table 11.22. Length and coefficient of variation (V') for first upper and lower molars of Recent *Apodemus sylvaticus* and *A. flavicollis* compared with samples of British Pleistocene *Apodemus* (excluding *A. maastrictiensis*). [a] Variation (V') = 100 R/M, where R is the range, and M is the median (Freudenthal & Cuenca Bescos (1984); Freudenthal & Martín-Suárez (1990)). Data from: [1] Coxon *et al.*(1980), [2] Bishop (1982), [3] Lister *et al.* (1990), [4] Stuart *et al.* (1980).

	Barnham *Apodemus sylvaticus*			Recent, Britain *Apodemus sylvaticus*			Recent, Britain *Apodemus flavicollis*		
	N	Mean	Range	N	Mean	Range	N	Mean	Range
M^1 L	22	1.89	1.73-2.03	17	1.84	1.69-1.96	18	1.96	1.83-2.12
M^1 W	22	1.19	1.13-1.26	17	1.18	1.14-1.12	18	1.28	1.22-1.33
M^2 L	10	1.28	1.23-1.35	17	1.23	1.11-1.33	18	1.29	1.24-1.34
M^2 W	10	1.12	1.04-1.18	17	1.15	1.09-1.19	18	1.21	1.16-1.26
M_1 L	20	1.78	1.66-1.86	17	1.71	1.61-1.79	18	1.82	1.70-1.90
M_1 W	20	1.04	0.98-1.12	17	1.05	0.98-1.08	18	1.09	1.02-1.16
M_2 L	16	1.21	1.15-1.30	17	1.16	1.07-1.28	18	1.29	1.24-1.34
M_2 W	16	1.03	0.95-1.09	17	1.02	0.97-1.07	18	1.10	1.05-1.16

Table 11.23. Measurements (in mm) of Barnham *Apodemus sylvaticus* compared with Recent *A. sylvaticus* and *A. flavicollis* from Britain.

The coefficient V' was calculated for samples of British Pleistocene *Apodemus*, and these values were compared with the plots V' of fossil and Recent murids given by Freudenthal and Martín-Suárez (1990) with values for samples of Recent *Apodemus*, in Table 11.22. Using this method, the samples from the British Pleistocene localities (with the exception of Grays Thurrock) are shown to be homogeneous with no evidence of more than one species of medium-sized *Apodemus*. The size of upper and lower first molars of this group, although variable, fall within the range of Recent *A. sylvaticus*. In contrast to these assemblages, the sample from Grays Thurrock (Hinton 1901) shows a very high value for V' which falls outside the range for single species samples given by Freudenthal and Martín-Suárez (1990). The Grays Thurrock sample probably consists of two species of *Apodemus*, of which the larger is probably *A. flavicollis*. This may, therefore, represent the first Pleistocene record of yellow-necked mouse in the Britain.

The wood mouse has a very wide geographical and stratigraphical range and it is a common rodent in Pleistocene temperate stages (Currant 1986) and today it is closely associated with woodland or grassy scrub (Bjärvall & Ullström 1986). It is also found in Pleistocene cold stages in Britain. This is not unexpected as today its range extends into the arctic circle and it is able to survive in sparsely vegetated montane habitats (Wilkinson 1987).

***Apodemus maastrichtiensis* van Kolfschoten 1985, extinct mouse.** Pleistocene and Recent *Apodemus* are generally characterised mainly on the basis of size and molar structure (Niethammer & Krapp 1978). *Apodemus maastrichtiensis* from Barnham differs from specimens attributed to *A. sylvaticus* in having an M^1 with three roots, a t9 which is smaller than the t6, a narrow elongated t7 (Fig. 11.6) and an M^2 (Pl. 11.3) with an incipient t3 and a much reduced t9 and t7 (dental terminology follows van der Weerd 1976). In the M_1 and M_2, the cusp pairs form chevrons with wide angles. Additionally, molars of *A. maastrichtiensis* differ from those of *A. sylvaticus* in their smaller size (Pl. 11.3, Table 11.24).

129

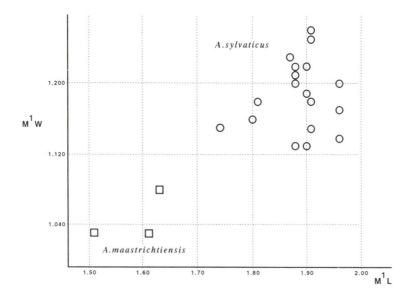

Fig. 11.6. Bivariate plot of length against width in M¹ of *Apodemus sylvaticus* and *Apodemus maastrichtiensis* from Barnham.

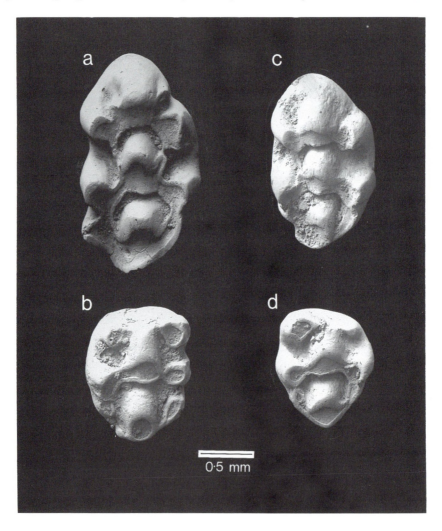

Plate 11.3. a-b: *Apodemus sylvaticus*: a: right M¹ (gritty clay, BEF 768); b: right M² (gritty clay, BEF 427); c-d: *Apodemus maastrichtiensis*: c: right M¹ (gritty clay, BEF 403); d: left M² (gritty clay, BEF 406).

		Barnham			Maastricht-Belvédère 4 [1]			Boxgrove	
	N	Mean	Range	N	Mean	Range	N	Mean	Range
M^1 L	3	-	(1.51. 1.61, 1.63)	7	1.67	1.51-1.82	4	1.71	1.62-1.82
M^1 W	3	-	(1.03, 1.03, 1.08)	7	1.06	1.02-1.09	4	1.06	1.01-1.11
M^2 L	2	-	(1.07, 1.10)	10	1.10	0.94-1.19	3	-	(1.11, 1.16, 1.18)
M^2 W	2	-	(1.04, 1.18)	10	1.02	0.99-1.08	3	-	(0.97, 1.03, 1.08)
M$_1$ L	4	1.50	1.38-1.59	11	1.50	1.37-1.60	4	1.61	1.56-1.66
M$_1$ W	4	0.91	0.83-1.00	11	0.91	0.84-0.95	4	0.91	0.89-0.93
M$_2$ L	1	-	(1.01)	8	1.03	0.94-1.16	1	-	(0.98)
M$_2$ W	1	-	(0.91)	8	0.94	0.88-0.98	1	-	(0.98)

Table 11.24. Comparative measurements (in mm) of *Apodemus maastrichtiensis* molars. [1] Data from van Kolfschoten (1985).

The features cited above clearly show that this material resembles Middle Pleistocene *A. maastrichtiensis* from the type locality at Maastricht-Belvédère (van Kolfschoten 1985). Tooth size falls within the range of the Maastricht-Belvédère sample, and also agrees with the small sample of *A. maastrichtiensis* from Boxgrove (Table 11.24).

In Britain, *A. maastrichtiensis* has been found at five other localities which range in age from Cromerian to probable oxygen isotope stage 7 age. The earliest evidence for its occurrence in Britain comes from channel deposits at Little Oakley in Essex of probable Cromerian age (Lister *et al.* 1990). Although this specimen has been previously identified as *Apodemus* cf. *sylvaticus*, the small size and the angle of the chevrons show that it is probably a lower first molar of *A. maastrichtiensis*. *A. maastrichtiensis* is also known from Westbury-sub-Mendip (Calcareous Member), and it occurs in some numbers in the main fossiliferous deposits at Boxgrove. Both sites are of Pre-Anglian age and probably date to the end of the 'Cromerian Complex'. Post-Anglian records are sparse. The only other Hoxnian record is from Beeches Pit, Suffolk (Preece *et al.* 1991), and the latest known occurrence is from late Middle Pleistocene (oxygen isotope stage 7) channel deposits at West Wittering, Sussex (Parfitt 1998). On the continent, the species has a similar stratigraphic range with a last known occurrence in the Eemian (van Kolfschoten 1990; Benecke & Heinrich 1990; van Kolfschoten & Turner 1996).

The taxonomic relationships of *A. maastrichtiensis* are unclear, although several authors (van Kolfschoten 1991; Martín & Mein 1998) have suggested that it may be related to '*Parapodemus*' *coronensis* described by Schaub (1938) from the Early Pleistocene of Brassó (Hungary). Martín and Mein (1998) have suggested that both species are possibly related to the living pygmy field mouse *A. microps*. Unfortunately, the sample of *coronensis*, which has been transferred to *Apodemus* by Martín and Mein (1998), is scant and its relationship to either species is unclear.

Carnivora: Ursidae

Ursus sp., bear. The P^2 of a bear was recovered from the brown-grey clay. Unfortunately the tooth is undiagnostic and cannot be identified to species. Anterior premolars (P $^{1-3}$) are often present in brown bear (*Ursus arctos*) but are generally absent in the cave bear *Ursus spelaeus*, though the Hoxnian sample is too small to determine their prevalence in this species. To date, *Ursus spelaeus* is the only species of bear recorded from the Hoxnian in Britain (Kurtén 1959).

Carnivora: Mustelidae

Mustela cf. *M. putorius* L. 1758, polecat. A polecat is represented by a lower carnassial from the gritty clay. Table 11.25 shows measurements of this specimen compared with a sample of the western polecat *Mustela putorius*, steppe polecat *M. eversmanni* and early Middle Pleistocene *M.* cf. *stromeri* from Hundsheim, Austria. The lower carnassial from Barnham is morphologically very similar to *M. putorius*, although it is clearly smaller than Recent *M. putorius* from western Europe. As many species of mustelid show significant geographical differences in size and marked size fluctuations during the Pleistocene, the relatively small size of the Barnham polecat may not be significant.

The relative length of the talonid is an important taxonomic feature which has been used to distinguish the Early and Middle Pleistocene species *M. stromeri* from Recent polecat. This species was described by Kormos (1934) from the Villafranchian of Beremend (Hungary) and material from Betfia, Erpfingen and Hundsheim (Heller 1958; Thenius 1965) was subsequently referred to this taxon. According to these authors, the lower carnassial of *M. stromeri* has a relatively long talonid. This observation is confirmed by the data given in Table 11.25 which shows that the talonid index for *M. stromeri* falls close to the lower limit of variation of Recent *M. putorius*. In this feature, the Barnham carnassial is identical to Recent *M. putorius* and *M. eversmanni*.

	M₁ L			**M₁ W**			**M₁ talonid L**			**Talonid index [1]**	
	N	Mean	Range	N	Mean	Range	N	Mean	Range	N	Mean	Range
M. putorius												
Recent, Europe	31	7.98	7.00-9.50	31	3.15	2.63-3.75	29	1.96	1.50-2.62	29	24	20-29
Barnham	**1**	**-**	**(6.75)**	**1**	**-**	**(2.4)**	**-**	**-**	**(1.7)**	**-**	**25**	**-**
M. eversmanni												
Recent, Europe	7	8.06	7.63-8.50	7	3.04	2.75-3.13	7	1.96	1.63-2.13	7	24	21-26
M. cf. *stromeri*												
Middle Pleistocene, Hundsheim [2]	2	-	(7.7, 7.5)	2	-	(3.1, 3.0)	2	-	(2.2, 2.1)	2	-	(28, 28)

Table 11.25. Comparative measurements (in mm) and talonid index of the lower carnassial in samples of *Mustela putorius*, *M. eversmanni* and *M.* cf. *stromeri*. [1] (Talonid length) x 100 / length. [2] Data from Thenius (1965).

Polecats are rather scarce in the British Pleistocene, and the only well dated remains are of a robust form of *M. putorius* found in cave faunas of Devensian age (Reynolds 1912; Jacobi *et al.* 1998).

Carnivora: Felidae

***Panthera leo* (L. 1758), lion.** Lion is represented in the assemblage by five bones from the gritty clay. It is very likely that they come from the same individual, for they were found in close proximity to each other, and all are of the same size class. The astragalus (BEF 351) and the partial axis vertebra (BEF 294) are illustrated in Figure 11.7 and measurements of the astragalus are compared with Recent and Pleistocene *Panthera leo* in Table 11.26.

In Britain, the earliest well-dated occurrence of lion is from the late 'Cromerian Complex' deposits at Westbury-sub-Mendip (Calcareous Member) and Boxgrove. Finds from the East Anglian coast at Pakefield and Cromer (Turner 1995) may represent a presence during earlier stages of the 'Cromerian Complex', but the bones from these localities are either poorly provenanced or inadequately documented.

The earliest representatives of the European lion lineage were considerably larger than modern African lions, as discussed by Kurtén and Poulianos (1977) and Bishop (1982). In Table 11.26, the extremely large size of the Barnham lion is illustrated by the greatest length of the astragalus which compares closely with the large, early Middle Pleistocene, lion from the Calcareous Member of Westbury-sub-Mendip (Bishop 1982). These bones are larger than the comparative sample of modern African lion (Table 11.26), and indicate a lion of considerable size. The Barnham specimen is also larger than a small sample from the Last Glaciation from France and Germany (Table 11.26).

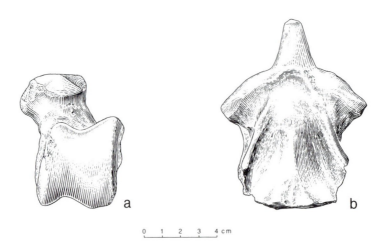

Fig. 11.7. *Panthera leo*: a: right astragalus (gritty clay, BEF 351), dorsal view; b: axis vertebra (gritty clay, BEF 294), ventral view.

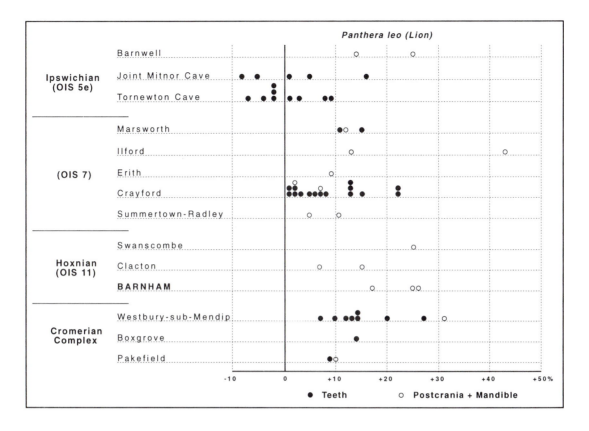

Fig. 11.8. Measurement comparisons of British Pleistocene *Panthera leo* with a Recent African male. The fossil specimens are plotted as a percentage deviation from the African male 'standard' (vertical line), and the sites are arranged in an approximate temporal sequence.

	N	Mean + SD	Range
Recent			
Africa [1]	8	53.1 ± 3.59	47.5-59.2
German / French Weichselian			
Gailenreuth, Germany	2	-	(67.1, 67.4)
Jaurens, France [2]	5	60.9 ± 5.18	56.0-67.0
British Middle Pleistocene			
Hoxnian, Barnham	1	-	**(70.1)**
Westbury-sub-Mendip	1	-	(73.5)

Table 11.26. Greatest length (in mm) of the astragalus of Recent and Pleistocene *Panthera leo*. [1] Sample comprises 4 males and 4 females, [2] Data from Ballesio (1980).

Unfortunately, it is not possible to make direct size comparisons between Barnham and other British Pleistocene lion fossils as few sites have produced large samples which would allow the dimensions of individual bones to be compared between sites. This problem can, however, be resolved by comparing the dimensions of the specimens in the fossil sample with those of homologous elements in a 'standard' skeleton. Although there are several problems with this approach, it has been used here as it allows broad trends in body

size to be examined. In Figure 11.8 size change in British Pleistocene lion is shown by comparing measurements of the fossil sample against a recent skeleton of a large male African lion in the Natural History Museum collection. The sizes of the fossil specimens are plotted as percentage differences from the modern standard (0%). The figure shows a clear decrease in size since the early Middle Pleistocene. Lion from the 'Cromerian Complex' and the Hoxnian seems, on average, slightly larger in dimensions than that from the late Middle and Late Pleistocene. This indicates that lions from successive temperate episodes tended to decrease in size during this time period.

Proboscidea: Elephantidae

***Palaeoloxodon antiquus* Falconer & Cautley 1845, straight-tusked elephant.** Elephant material is unfortunately very scanty at Barnham. Paterson (1937) records a large piece of elephant bone recovered by the clay pit workers which was kept for many years in the grounds of Euston Hall. Unfortunately this cannot now be traced and the only identifiable fragments from the recent excavation consist of a single plate of a cheek tooth and a fragment of tooth enamel. In the more

133

complete piece (BEF 99), the enamel of the lamella is relatively thick, strongly folded, and the enamel outline approximates a lozenge-shape. These features are characteristic of *Palaeoloxodon antiquus*, the straight-tusked elephant.

Straight-tusked elephant is known widely from the 'Cromerian Complex' onwards; the earliest finds are from various British deposits of the Cromer Forest Bed Formation (Lister 1996), and on the Continent they have been recovered in early Middle Pleistocene deposits at Mosbach, Germany. It probably frequented open woodland subsisting on a diet of browse and grasses (Stuart 1982), and in Britain it is generally found in interglacial stages, associated with regional woodland interspersed with more open areas of grassland.

Perissodactyla: Rhinocerotidae

***Stephanorhinus* sp., rhinoceros.** The remains of rhinoceros comprise a lower molar fragment (BEF 357) and the distal portion of a right metacarpal IV (BEF 316) from the gritty clay. Due to the fragmentary nature of the specimens it is not possible to identify them with certainty beyond the level of *Stephanorhinus* sp.

Artiodactyla: Suidae

***Sus scrofa* L. 1758, wild boar.** Only three specimens can be ascribed to wild boar, all from the gritty clay. The two tooth fragments are unworn, and the proximal end of the phalanx is unfused indicating that they are from a juvenile. As the specimens were recovered from a localised area it is possible that they derive from one individual.

Today, wild boar is closely associated with woodland and is found throughout much of the Mediterranean, deciduous and mixed woodland zones of Eurasia and North Africa. Its northern distribution is limited by thick snow cover and deep ground frost which prevents the animals from searching for underground food (Bjärvall & Ullström 1986). Not surprisingly, Pleistocene records in Britain are restricted to the major temperate episodes (Stuart 1982). The earliest British record of *Sus scrofa* is from the Freshwater Bed (Cromerian) at West Runton, and it occurs in all of the major temperate episodes of the Middle and Late Pleistocene.

Artiodactyla: Cervidae

***Dama dama* (L. 1758), fallow deer.** The only fallow deer bones from the site are the distal end of a humerus (BEF 352, Fig. 11.9) from the brown-grey clay, and a cuneiform (BEF 332) and unciform (BEF 340), which can be articulated, from the black clay. Both sets of bones are large in comparison with modern British fallow deer and probably represent an animal closer in size to the large Hoxnian fallow deer from Swanscombe, Clacton, and Hoxne. Illustrating this difference, the greatest breadth of the unciform is 35% larger than the corresponding value in modern *Dama*, and the trochlear breadth of the humerus is 35% larger than the mean of a sample of 12 Recent Richmond Park deer given by Lister (in Stuart *et al.* 1993).

Lister (1986; in Stuart *et al.* 1993) notes that the body size of Hoxnian fallow deer is significantly larger than modern British and Ipswichian ones. Hoxnian fallow deer, assigned to the subspecies *Dama dama clactoniana* by some authors, are also distinguished by the form of the antlers, which possess a narrower palmation and an additional tine on the anterior border of the palmation (Sutcliffe 1964; Leonardi & Petronio 1976; Lister 1986). While the Barnham fallow deer appears to have large body size suggesting affinities with the distinctive Hoxnian/Holsteinian form, the sample is small, and size alone is insufficient for subspecies diagnosis (Lister in Stuart *et al.* 1993).

Fallow deer is an important palaeoecological indicator as it is intolerant of cold climates and its distribution is closely associated with deciduous and mixed woodland today. The earliest known British appearance of the fallow deer is in the type Cromerian fauna of West Runton (Lister 1984). It appears in most of the subsequent Middle and Late Pleistocene interglacials with the probable exception of oxygen isotope stage 7 where it has yet to be identified (Sutcliffe 1996).

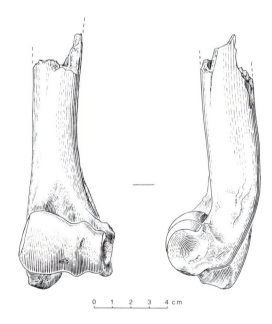

0 1 2 3 4 cm

Fig. 11.9. *Dama dama*: distal end of left humerus from the brown-grey clay (BEF 352) in cranial (left) and lateral (right) view.

***Cervus elaphus* L. 1758, red deer.** The red deer is represented in the assemblage by a lower third deciduous premolar (BEF 966), and the basal part of a shed antler (BEF 349, Fig. 11.10). Morphologically and metrically these bones are not distinguishable from the corresponding bones of Recent British red deer.

Red deer makes it first appearance in north-western Europe in the West Runton Freshwater Bed fauna (Lister 1986), and is a relatively frequent find in British Pleistocene deposits. Lister (1984) has drawn attention to the ecological plasticity of the species which enabled it to survive in varied habitats and under contrasting climatic regimes. The red deer is also characterised by pronounced variation in body size between populations which is reflected in the size and form of the antlers. Within species, differences in body size between populations of herbivores are often a reflection of disparity in habitat quality (Guthrie 1984). Lister (1984) has suggested that this factor probably accounts for differences in body size between contemporary populations of red deer living in contrasting habitats but within a restricted geographical region.

Although the dimensions of the Barnham fossils correspond to those of early Holocene *C. elaphus*, the sample size is unfortunately too small to make detailed size comparisons with other Hoxnian localities. Until further Hoxnian samples are available, the possibility that the population differences noted by Lister (in Stuart *et al.* 1993) represent a temporal sequence of size change must be left open.

Artiodactyla: Bovidae

***Bos/Bison* sp., a bovine.** The sole bovid bone is a fragment of right femur shaft (Fig. 11 a-b, BEF 315), which matches aurochs or bison in size. Although this fragment is nondescript, it is the only bone amongst the fauna which exhibits clear evidence of human alteration. This alteration takes the form of two conspicuous linear marks, apparently caused by a sharp-edged stone artefact, and a percussion impact notch (*sensu* Binford 1981), produced by direct impact to extract bone marrow. The anatomical location of the bone fragment is illustrated in Figure 11.11 c, which shows that the cut-marks are located close to the lower border of lesser trochanter. The lesser trochanter is a rough tuberosity which is the zone of attachment for the psoas major, quadratus femoralis and iliacus muscles (Sisson & Grossman 1956). Binford (1981) records cut-marks in an equivalent location which he attributes to filleting of muscles attached to the femur.

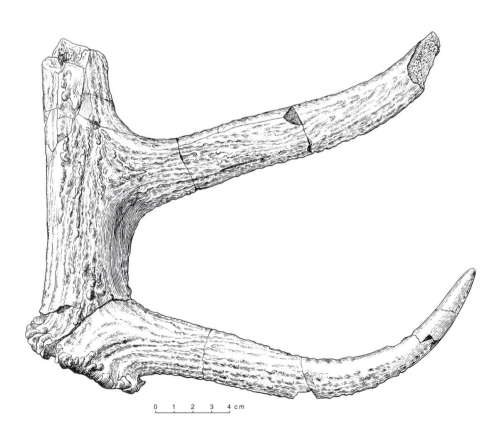

0 1 2 3 4 cm

Fig. 11.10. *Cervus elaphus*: shed antler from the gritty clay (BEF 966).

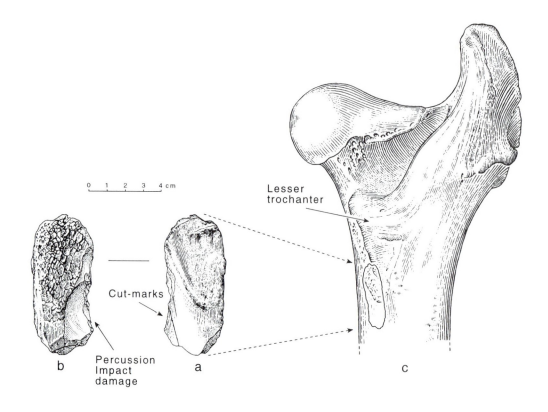

Fig. 11.11 a-c. Fragment of bovid right femur showing cut-marks (a) and lunate fracture scar on the medullary surface (b). The location of the piece is shown superimposed on the outline of a comparative proximal femur in (c) (posterior view)

The cut-marks are bisected by a curved fracture and a semi-circular region of incipient cracks. On the medullar surface this takes the form of a lunate fracture scar (Fig. 11.11.b) typical of the type of damage produced by direct percussion with a blunt object. The impact damage was most probably produced during marrow extraction. As described by Binford (1981), the Inuit extract marrow from the femur by holding the bone near the distal end and striking the proximal end of the shaft against a hand-held anvil. This process produces damage which exactly replicates the form and position of the impact damage found on the proximal femur shaft from Barnham.

PALAEOENVIRONMENTAL AND CLIMATIC SIGNIFICANCE OF THE MAMMAL FAUNA

The species list given in Table 11.27 summarises the presence of the mammals in the various beds of Unit 5c. Table 11.28 quantifies the relative abundance of the smaller mammals using numbers of identifiable specimens (NISP) and estimates of the minimum number of individuals (MNI). Large mammals have not been quantified in the same way as they were generally

collected using manual excavation and coarse mesh sieving; only very rarely were their remains found in the samples sieved through fine meshes which have been used to quantify species abundance.

Taken together, the mammals indicate an environment of deciduous or mixed woodland with dense ground-level cover and areas of more open grassland or marsh bordering a large body of water. Semi-aquatic and wetland species are well represented, and these include the Russian desman, water shrew and water vole. Their presence confirms the geological and other faunal evidence pointing to a large body of standing water. The Russian desman *Desmana moschata* is a bizarre and highly specialised semi-aquatic talpid which is endangered and survives only in disjunct, relict populations in southern Russia and the Ukraine. It is highly adapted for an amphibious life, and although a powerful swimmer, it avoids rapid currents, preferring marshes, slow-flowing rivers and streams, and the rank waters of stagnant lakes and ponds (Gorman & Stone 1990). It digs extensive burrow systems in soft, steep banks above the level of seasonal flooding.

	brown-grey clay	black clay	shelly clay	gritty clay
Chiroptera				
Plecotus sp., long-eared bat	-	-	+	-
Insectivora				
Sorex minutus, pygmy shrew	+	+	+	+
Sorex sp.1, shrew	+	+	+	+
Neomys sp., water shrew	+	+	+	-
Crocidura sp., white-toothed shrew	-	-	-	+
Talpa minor, extinct mole	-	+	+	+
Desmana moschata, Russian desman	-	-	+	+
Primates				
Homo sp., (artefacts) hominid.	-	+	+	+
Lagomorpha				
Oryctolagus cf. *O. cuniculus*, rabbit	-	-	-	+
Rodentia				
Sciurus sp., squirrel	-	-	-	+
Clethrionomys glareolus, bank vole	+	+	+	+
Arvicola terrestris cantiana, water vole	+	+	+	+
Microtus (Terricola) cf. *subterraneus*, common pine vole	+	+	+	+
Microtus agrestis, field vole	+	-	+	+
Microtus arvalis, common vole	-	-	-	+
Apodemus sylvaticus, wood mouse	+	+	+	+
Apodemus maastrichtiensis, extinct mouse	-	-	+	+
Carnivora				
Ursus sp., bear	+	-	-	-
Mustela cf. *M. putorius*, polecat	-	-	-	+
Panthera leo, lion	-	-	-	+
Proboscidea				
Palaeoloxodon antiquus, straight-tusked elephant	-	-	-	+
Perissodactyla				
Stephanorhinus sp., rhinoceros	-	-	-	+
Artiodactyla				
Sus scrofa, wild boar	-	-	-	+
Dama dama, fallow deer	+	+	-	-
Cervus elaphus, red deer	-	-	+	-
Bos/Bison sp., a bovine	-	-	-	+

Table 11.27. Mammalian fauna list and stratigraphic occurrence at Barnham.

For this reason, the Russian desman avoids areas of low-lying river floodplains which are subject to winter flooding. The diet of the Russian desman consists mainly of aquatic invertebrates such as insect larvae, leeches and molluscs that it locates amongst stones and rotting vegetation with its sensitive proboscis-like snout. Although the climatic tolerances of the Russian desman are poorly known as its distribution is now severely restricted, it is unable to thrive in regions where the water is ice covered for prolonged periods, or in dry areas where waterbodies are subject to seasonal desiccation (Gorman & Stone 1990).

The glacially eroded landscape formed by the Anglian ice sheets left vast areas of lakes which would have provided suitable habitat for the Russian desman during the Hoxnian. It is therefore rather surprising that desman is so poorly represented in the Barnham fauna.

The water shrew and water vole are both amphibious mammals that are generally closely associated with water to varying degrees. In northern Europe, the water shrew (*Neomys* sp.) is typically a lowland species that colonises banks of well-vegetated clear, often fast-flowing, rivers and streams. Ponds, lakes and marshes are less frequently inhabited, and it will spread to other habitats, especially woodland, often at considerable distances from water. In the Barnham sequence the water shrew declines steadily in abundance from 12% of the small mammal assemblage in the black clay to 3% in the gritty clay (Table 11.28). This may be a reflection of the increasing stagnation of the waterbody water which would have been less favourable to *Neomys*.

Being semi-aquatic in lifestyle, the water vole *Arvicola* sp. prefers a variety of habitats close to water, including densely vegetated banks of slow-flowing rivers, streams, and lakes and ponds. As with the water shrew, it is also found away from water, generally in damp grassland but also, particularly in the southern part of its range, in drier grassland often at considerable distances from water. In Pleistocene faunas the water vole is often abundant in waterlain deposits indicating that it was closely associated with aquatic habitat during this period. Nowadays, its range extends from the edge of the Arctic to the Mediterranean apart for parts of France and the Iberian peninsula where it is replaced by the closely related southern water vole (*Arvicola sapidus*). As would be expected from a highly adaptable and widely distributed species, it is found in both warm and cold stage small mammal assemblages in the British Isles. At Barnham, the water vole is the most common mammal in the fossil assemblage as one might expect in an environment close to permanent water with open herbaceous vegetation.

Species which point to the presence of open terrain include the field vole, common vole, rabbit and probably also the white-toothed shrew. The field vole *Microtus agrestis* indicates the presence of rough, ungrazed grassland in the vicinity of the site. This species, although preferring grasslands, is also found in open woodland providing there is a dense ground cover of herbaceous vegetation. Unlike the common vole *Microtus arvalis*, the field vole is particularly common in marshes, river banks and other damp habitats.

The common vole is also a characteristic inhabitant of open herbaceous vegetation, but it avoids damp,

ungrazed grasslands particularly when the field vole is numerous. As the common vole lives in an extensive tunnel system just below the soil surface (unlike the surface runways of the field vole), it survives better in areas that are heavily grazed. At Barnham the common vole is very rare, represented by only three teeth from the gritty clay. Both species of vole are found throughout central and northern Europe, but are absent in large areas of the Mediterranean; the northern limit of the field vole extends to the Arctic Circle, while the common vole is found only as far north as 60°N in western Europe.

Perhaps the best indication of grassland is provided by the rabbit *Oryctolagus* cf. *O. cuniculus*. Rabbits are found in most open grassland habitats, preferring warm, dry short turf grassland where they reach very high population densities (Morrison 1994). They favour grassland fringed by scrub or woodland as this provides some protection against aerial predators. The rabbit feeds mainly on shoots of grasses and other herbaceous vegetation; it inadvertently maintains its grassland habitat by feeding on young trees thus inhibiting the spread of dense woodland and scrub.

	brown-grey clay		black clay		shelly clay		gritty clay		Total	
	NISP	MNI	NISP	MNI	NISP	MNI	NISP	MNI	NISP	MNI
Chiroptera										
Plecotus sp., long-eared bat	-	-	-	-	1 (0.9)	1 (3.1)	-	-	1	1
Insectivora										
Sorex minutus, pygmy shrew	1 (1.6)	1 (6.7)	4 (3.7)	1 (4)	4 (3.4)	2 (6.3)	5 (1.1)	2 (2.3)	14	6
Sorex sp. 1, shrew	4 (6.3)	2 (13.3)	11 (10.2)	2 (8)	14 (12.1)	2 (6.3)	16 (3.5)	4 (4.6)	45	10
Neomys sp., water shrew	-	-	10 (9.3)	3 (12)	4 (3.4)	2 (6.3)	16 (3.5)	4 (4.6)	30	9
Crocidura sp., white-toothed shrew	-	-	-	-	-	-	2 (0.4)	1 (1.1)	2	1
Talpa minor, extinct mole	-	-	1 (0.9)	1 (4)	1 (0.9)	1 (3.1)	16 (3.5)	3 (3.4)	18	5
Desmana moschata, Russian desman	-	-	-	-	1 (0.9)	1 (3.1)	-	-	1	1
Lagomorpha										
Oryctolagus cf. *O. cuniculus*, rabbit	-	-	-	-	-	-	1 (0.2)	1 (1.1)	1	1
Rodentia										
Clethrionomys glareolus, bank vole	22 (34.9)	5 (33.3)	19 (17.6)	5 (20)	9 (7.6)	2 (6.3)	30 (6.6)	8 (9.2)	80	20
Arvicola terrestris cantiana, water vole	28 (44.4)	4 (26.7)	53 (49.1)	9 (36)	57 (49.1)	10 (31.3)	290 (64)	36 (41.4)	428	59
Microtus (Terricola) cf. *subterraneus*, common pine vole	1 (1.6)	1 (6.7)	1 (0.9)	1 (4)	5 (4.3)	3 (9.4)	7 (1.5)	6 (6.9)	14	11
Microtus agrestis, field vole	2 (3.2)	1 (6.7)	-	-	3 (2.6)	2 (6.3)	16 (3.5)	5 (5.7)	21	8
Microtus arvalis, common vole	-	-	-	-	-	-	1 (0.2)	1 (1.1)	1	1
Apodemus sylvaticus, wood mouse	5 (7.9)	1 (6.7)	9 (8.3)	3 (12)	16 (13.8)	5 (15.6)	42 (9.3)	12 (13.8)	72	21
Apodemus maastrichtiensis, extinct mouse	-	-	-	-	1 (0.9)	1 (3.1)	10 (2.2)	3 (3.4)	11	4
Carnivora										
Mustela cf. *M. putorius*, polecat	-	-	-	-	-	-	1 (0.2)	1 (1.1)	1	1
Total	63	15	108	25	116	32	453	87	740	160

Table 11.28. The Number of Identifiable Specimens (NISP) / Minimum Number of Individuals (MNI) by which mammalian species are represented in the various stratigraphic units at Barnham. The counts are derived from bulk samples sieved to 0.5 and 1 mm. Note that only the smaller mammals are tabulated. Numbers in parenthesis are percentages of the NISP and MNI calculated for each unit.

The presence of rabbit at Barnham is intriguing as its Pleistocene distribution was confined mainly to southern Europe. However, during the Boxgrove interglacial and the Hoxnian, it expanded into the British Isles reaching its northernmost point at Barnham. To have survived during interglacials in the British Isles, the rabbit would have needed suitable conditions which combined relatively warm temperatures, in addition to, and perhaps more importantly, an environment of extensive areas of linked grassland habitat. Although interglacial landscapes are usually characterised as monotonous blankets of deciduous woodland, this interpretation is often not supported by the mammalian evidence. Many animals which are commonly found in British interglacials such as the fallow deer, horse, straight-tusked elephant and lion are more typical of a diverse patchwork of habitats combining tracts of woodland interspersed with open grassland. This interpretation has important implications for the Palaeolithic archaeological record which is further discussed in Chapters 23 and 24.

Dry open conditions are also the preferred habitat of the European white-toothed shrews (*Crocidura* sp.). They are occasionally found in open woodland, but dry scrubland, heath and grassland are favoured habitats. Ground cover is an important habitat requirement as it provides some degree of protection against predators. Shrews of the genus *Crocidura* are among the least cold-adapted of the European small mammals (Rzebik-Kowalska 1996); today, their northern limit in Europe largely follows the 19° C July isotherm. The presence of white-toothed shrew in the gritty clay can reasonably be taken as an indication of relatively warm conditions.

Areas of dry ground are also indicated by the small mole *Talpa minor* which is present in the upper part of the fossiliferous sequence (Table 11.28). Ecologically moles are important as they are highly adapted to a burrowing mode and thus provide information about soil conditions. Although *T. minor* is extinct (unless it is related to the blind mole *T. caeca*), its skeleton is identical, apart from its smaller size, to the living European mole *T. europaea* and it was clearly adapted to a burrowing mode of life. It was probably similar in appearance and habitat to the living species of *Talpa*. Today, moles are distributed throughout most of Europe, as far north as northern Scandinavia where seasonally frozen ground impedes burrowing. Moles also avoid dry sandy soils which cannot support burrows; similarly waterlogged soils and areas liable to prolonged periods of flooding are also avoided. The population density of the mole is largely determined by the abundance of soil invertebrates, particularly of earthworms that are the main component of the moles diet. Consequently it tends to be common in open deciduous woodland and grassland pastures with rich humic soils and rare in nutrient poor soils that support coniferous woodland and acidic heaths and moorland (Gorman & Stone 1990).

The red deer, common pine vole and the pygmy shrew are undemanding in terms of vegetation, and these adaptable species can be found in a wide range of habitats. Although the red deer *Cervus elaphus* is often typified as a woodland deer, it can adapt to an extremely varied range of habitats. While woodland and woodland-edge habitats provide optimal conditions (reflected in the large body size of these populations), other habitats such as treeless grassland, heather, moorland and montane areas may also support large populations of red deer. The great ecological plasticity of this species is also reflected in its fossil distribution that encompasses both warm and cold stages and habitats as varied as dense deciduous woodland and open steppe-like environments (Stuart 1982). On its own, the presence of red deer in the gritty clay provides little palaeoecological information. Likewise the common pine vole *Microtus* (*Terricola*) *subterraneus* is found in many different habitats but it tends to be common in grassland as well as in open woodland. The pygmy shrew *Sorex minutus* is another species which is found in almost all habitats, although it is often less frequent in woodland and scrub than in open habitats, providing the latter has some cover and an abundance of invertebrates. It is a voracious insectivore, and each day it must consume more than its own body weight in prey to maintain its metabolism.

Open woodland and scrub habitats are indicated by the lion (*Panthera leo*), straight-tusked elephant, long-eared bat and the wood mouse. Like its modern-day counterparts the European Pleistocene lion probably preferred open, lightly wooded areas, avoiding densely forested conditions (Stuart 1982). The modern distribution of the lion has been greatly reduced by the activities of man and today viable populations are found only in Africa south of the Sahara and the Gir Forest near the north-west coast of India. During the Pleistocene, however, it had a continuous range which also encompassed much of the Nearctic, the Oriental Region and Palaearctic from Siberia in the east to the British Isles in the west. The ecological flexibility of the lion is illustrated by its ability to survive in both warm and cold stages in the British Pleistocene. Lions hunt, either individually or as a co-ordinated group depending on the type of habitat and prey behaviour. The immense size of the Barnham lion would have enabled it to feed on a wide variety of large herbivores. Carnivore tooth damage is rare on the Barnham large mammal bones; the only gnawed fragment (a piece of a limb-bone shaft) may derive from a lion kill or from some other large carnivore not represented in the assemblage.

The extinct straight-tusked elephant *Palaeoloxodon antiquus* to judge from associated floral and faunal evidence probably also favoured a mixed habitat of woodland and more open parkland. In Britain, it is typically found in interglacial faunas in association with temperate regional forests (Stuart 1982).

The wood mouse *Apodemus sylvaticus* is well represented in the Barnham assemblage and it increases in abundance from the brown-grey clay to the gritty clay (Table 11.28). It is the most common small rodent in woodland (other than purely coniferous forest) and scrub, but it is found in nearly all habitats, including open grassland, providing it can conceal itself in dense vegetation. The wood mouse is found throughout central and southern Europe as far north as the boundary between the mixed deciduous and coniferous forest zone; its northernmost range is probably determined by the scarcity of suitable food in the taiga and tundra rather than directly by climate.

The record of long-eared bat is particularly interesting, as bats are generally completely absent in faunas from 'open' sites. This is unfortunate as bats often have very specific habitat requirements and their distributions are controlled by climate to a greater extent than are most mammals. The Barnham bat is unfortunately not identified to species, although it is clearly a long-eared bat. Today, there are two species of long-eared bat (*Plecotus auritus* the common long-eared bat and *Plecotus austriacus* the grey long-eared bat) which together are distributed through most of Europe except for the far north. The grey-long eared bat has a more southerly distribution of the two, but, in large areas of central and western Europe the two species are found together, often hibernating in the same roost. Ecologically, they are very similar and both prefer open woodland and parkland habitat. Like many woodland species of bat their flight is slow and fluttering and their aerial manoeuvrability allows them to glean moths, caterpillars, beetles and other invertebrates from tree trunks and foliage.

A number of species are closely associated with mature woodland to varying degrees. These include the squirrel, polecat, bank vole, wild boar and the fallow deer. These species are more typical of mixed and deciduous temperate woodland than of pure coniferous forest; the distribution of many of these species, with the notable exceptions of squirrel and bank vole, extend only as far as the northern coniferous forest zone.

The squirrel *Sciurus* sp. is the only arboreal species represented at Barnham. Squirrels are essentially forest animals which are generally found in mature mixed or conifer-dominated woodland which provides them with a constant food supply such as seeds, fruits, berries and fungi. They are skilful climbers, and their agility and arboreal habitat protects them from most predators. The low level of predation may explain why squirrels are poorly represented in fossil small mammal assemblages which are generally derived from predator action. At present, the European red squirrel has a wide distribution in Europe from the Mediterranean to the Arctic Circle; its northern distribution is limited by the lack of continuous tree cover, and where it is common its numbers are controlled by the availability of tree seeds particularly during the Autumn.

Polecat (*Mustela putorius*) also frequents habitats with plenty of cover and it is principally found in deciduous and mixed woodland, well-vegetated river banks, marshland and other low-lying damp environments. These habitats provide it with a rich source of food such as small mammals, fish, birds, reptiles and amphibians and large invertebrates. It is widely distributed in Europe today, and can be found from the coast of the Mediterranean to the edge of the coniferous forest zone in western Europe.

The bank vole *Clethrionomys glareolus* is a rodent that is closely associated with woodland from the Arctic Circle in the north to northern Spain, northern Italy, Greece and the Balkans in the south. It prefers mature deciduous and mixed woodland with a luxuriant scrub or herb layer. Although woods of various kinds are its primary haunt, it can also be found in dense scrubland and less commonly in open herbaceous vegetation. Its food consists almost entirely of vegetable matter. Unlike *Microtus*, which has continuously growing molars adapted to abrasive vegetation, the molars of the bank vole are rooted, and better suited to its less abrasive diet of berries, nuts, roots and leaves.

At Barnham, the relative abundance of bank vole decreases from 33 and 20% of the smaller mammals in the brown-grey clay and black clay respectively to 6 and 9% in the shelly and gritty clay. This decline in the bank vole's abundance perhaps indicates a decline in dense vegetation cover; the concomitant increase in the water vole (a semi-aquatic and grassland species) provides support for this interpretation.

The wild boar *Sus scrofa* is another species that is closely associated with deciduous and mixed woodland. Swampy lowland, woodland and reed beds are particularly favoured as the wild boar likes to wallow in mud. Nowadays, it can be found throughout much of central and southern Europe as far north as the coniferous woodland zone. Wild boar are omnivores feeding on anything edible off the surface of the soil using their powerful flexible snouts to grub for rhizomes and tubers. Their fossil record is confined to interglacial periods in north-western

Europe, and today the limiting factors to the wild boars northernmost range are a combination of deep ground frost and snow cover which prevents it searching for food (Bjärvall & Ullström 1986)

Like wild boar, the fallow deer *Dama dama* is intolerant of cold climate and its fossil record shows that it was restricted to temperate woodland episodes in northern Europe during the Pleistocene (Stuart 1982). The reproductive biology of the fallow deer, notably the relatively late rut which leaves the males in poor condition during the winter, and the birth of the fawns relatively late in the summer, both appear to be important factors limiting the distribution of fallow deer in northern latitudes.

Typical fallow deer habitat is mature deciduous or mixed woodland with dense undergrowth interspersed with open ground which provides grazing. At Barnham, fallow deer is recorded in the lowermost fossiliferous deposit (the brown-grey clay), thus providing compelling evidence for temperate conditions during its deposition.

BIOSTRATIGRAPHIC IMPLICATIONS OF THE MAMMALIAN FAUNA

Introduction

The mammalian fauna from Barnham provides a number of species which are biostratigraphically significant. The known chronological range of these species is summarised in Figure 11.12 along with the range of other temporally significant taxa. Information on evolutionary transitions, size and morphological change, as well as potentially significant non-occurrence of taxa, are also summarised. The time period represented encompasses part of the Middle Pleistocene from the Cromerian *sensu stricto* to the first interglacial of the 'Saalian Complex' (*sensu* Bridgland 1994). The rationale for the subdivision of the 'Cromerian Complex' faunas can be found in Turner (1996) and the post-Anglian interglacial sites are described briefly below. This scheme of Middle Pleistocene faunal change provides the model for assessing the likely date of the Barnham fauna.

British Hoxnian and early 'Saalian Complex' faunas

Hoxnian mammals have been recorded from a total of eight localities in the British Isles. Mammalian faunal lists for the most significant sites are given in Table 11.29. The best known and most extensive Hoxnian mammalian fauna occur in the Orsett Heath Gravel exposed at Barnfield Pit Swanscombe and an adjacent quarry at Ingress Vale, Kent (Sutcliffe 1964; Lister

1986; Currant 1996; Schreve 1996). The fluvial deposits at Swanscombe form a terrace contained within a broad channel cut by the ancestral River Thames following its diversion by Anglian ice into its present day course (Bridgland 1994; Gibbard 1994,). The principal collections derive from the Lower Loam and Gravel, and from the stratigraphically higher Middle Gravels. The earliest deposits are fully temperate in character (probably Ho II), whereas molluscan and mammalian evidence from the upper part of the Middle Gravel, which according to Kerney (1971) did not begin to accumulate until the late temperate substage (zone III), indicates a period of climatic deterioration heralding the onset of periglacial conditions. The fluvial and estuarine Thames-Medway deposits at Clacton-on-sea, Essex, have also produced an abundant fauna dominated by large mammals (Warren 1955; Stuart 1982). Palynological evidence suggests a correlation with the type site of the Hoxnian at Hoxne and indicates that the vast majority of the bones and the artefacts probably derive from the early temperate zone of this interglacial (Pike & Godwin 1952; Turner & Kerney 1971). The distinctive 'Rhenish' molluscan fauna found in the estuarine beds at Clacton is also found in the Middle Gravel of Swanscombe and provides an important biostratigraphic 'link' between these sequences (Meijer & Preece 1995).

At Hoxne, Suffolk, a sequence of interglacial organic lake muds occupying a basin in Anglian Chalky Boulder Clay has yielded a small mammalian fauna (Stuart *et al.* 1993). The poorly fossiliferous lake muds are in turn overlain by a series of fluvio-lacustrine deposits which contain the Upper and Lower Industries, and from which most of the faunal remains have been excavated (Stratum C and Bed 4, Table 11.29). The stratigraphic position of the faunal horizon above the lacustrine deposits of zone IIIa indicate that they accumulated during the later part of the interglacial. Two other Hoxnian lacustrine sequences which occupy depressions in the Anglian till have produced mammal remains, at Hitchin, Hertfordshire (Boreham & Gibbard 1995) and Copford, Essex (Sutcliffe & Kowalski 1976; Wymer 1985). Both sites have yielded limited mammalian faunas that have been pollen-dated to Hoxnian zones II and IIIb respectively. A small Hoxnian fauna has been recently described from the Woodston Beds near Peterborough. At this site abundant biological evidence indicates that the fluvial and estuarine beds containing the mammal remains accumulated during zone II of the Hoxnian (Horton *et al.* 1992).

A further important group of Hoxnian fossiliferous deposits are the spring and tufa sequences that stratigraphically overlie Anglian till, at Hitchin, Hertfordshire and Beeches Pit, Suffolk. Both sites

	Barnham (HoII)	Beeches Pit[1]	Clacton[2] (HoIIb/I-IIIa)	Hitchin[3]	Hoxne[4] (Stratum C)	Hoxne[4] (Bed 4)	Ingress Vale[5] (HoIII?)	Swansc.L. Loam[6] (HoII?)	Swansc. UMG[6] (HoIII-IV?)	Woodston[7] (HoII)
Chiroptera										
Plecotus sp., long-eared bat	+	-	-	-	-	-	-	-	-	-
Insectivora										
Sorex minutus, pygmy shrew	+	+	-	-	cf.	cf.	-	-	-	-
Sorex sp.1, shrew	+	+	-	-	+c	+c	-	-	-	-
Neomys sp., water shrew	+	+	-	-	-	+	-	-	-	-
Crocidura sp., white-toothed shrew	+	-	-	-	-	-	-	-	-	-
Talpa minor, extinct mole	+	+	-	-	-	+	-	+	-	-
Talpa sp., mole	+	-	-	-	-	-	-	-	-	+
Desmana moschata, Russian desman	+	-	-	-	+	+	-	-	-	-
Primates										
Macaca sylvanus, macaque	-	-	-	-	+	+	-	+	-	-
Homo sp., hominid	+	+	+	+b	+	+	+	+	+	-
Lagomorpha										
Oryctolagus cf *O. cuniculus*, rabbit	+	-	-	-	-	-	-	+	-	-
Lepus timidus, mountain hare	-	-	-	-	-	-	-	-	+	-
Rodentia										
Sciurus sp., squirrel	+	+	-	-	-	-	-	-	-	-
Trogontherium cuvieri, extinct beaver-like rodent	-	-	+	-	+	-	+	-	-	-
Castor fiber, beaver	-	-	+	-	+	-	-	+	-	-
Lemmus lemmus/Myopus schisticolor, Norway or wood lemming	-	-	-	-	+	+	-	-	+	-
Clethrionomys glareolus, bank vole	+	+	+	+ab	+	+	+	+	-	+
Arvicola terrestris cantiana, water vole	+	+	+	+a	+	+	+	+	-	+
Microtus (Terricola) cf. *subterraneus*, common pine vole	+	+	-	+a	+	+	-	+	-	+
Microtus agrestis, field vole	+	+	-	-	+	+	-	+	-	-
Microtus arvalis, common vole	+	+	-	-	-	cf.	-	cf.	cf.	-
Microtus agrestis/M. arvalis, common or field vole	+	+	+	-	-	-	-	-	-	-
Microtus oeconomus, northern vole	-	-	-	-	-	-	+	+	-	-
Apodemus sylvaticus, wood mouse	+	+	-	+a	-	+	cf.	+	-	+
Apodemus maastrichtiensis, extinct mouse	+	+	-	-	-	-	-	-	-	-
Eliomys quercinus, garden dormouse	-	+	-	-	-	-	-	-	-	-
Carnivora										
Canis lupus, wolf	-	-	-	-	-	-	+	+	+	-
Ursus spelaeus, extinct cave bear	-	-	-	-	-	-	-	+	-	-
Ursus sp., bear	+	+	-	+b	+	-	-	-	-	-
Mustela cf. *M. putorius*, polecat	+	-	-	-	-	-	-	-	-	-
Meles sp., badger	-	-	-	+	-	-	-	-	-	-
Martes martes, pine marten	-	-	-	-	-	-	-	+	-	-
Lutra lutra, otter	-	-	-	-	+	-	-	-	-	-
Felis sylvestris, wild cat	-	-	-	-	-	-	-	+	-	-
Panthera leo, lion	+	-	+	-	+	-	+	+	+	-
Proboscidea										
Palaeoloxodon antiquus, extinct straight-tusked elephant	+	-	+	+b	+	-	+	+	+	-
Perissodactyla										
Equus ferus, horse	-	+	+	-	+	-	+	+	+	-
Equus hydruntinus, extinct equid	-	-	-	-	-	-	-	-	-	-
Stephanorhinus kirchbergensis, Merck's rhinoceros	-	-	+	-	-	-	+	+	+	-
Stephanorhinus hemitoechus, narrow-nosed rhinoceros	-	-	+	-	-	-	+	+	-	-
Stephanorhinus sp., rhinoceros	+	-	+	+b	+	-	-	+	+	-
Artiodactyla										
Sus scrofa, wild boar	+	-	+	-	-	-	+	+	-	-
Megaloceros giganteus, extinct giant deer	-	-	-	+b	+	-	-	+	+	-
Dama dama, fallow deer	+	+	+	+b	+	-	+	+	+	-
Cervus elaphus, red deer	+	+	+	+b	+	-	+	+	+	-
Capreolus capreolus, roe deer	-	-	-	+b	+	-	-	+	-	-
Bos primigenius, extinct aurochs	-	+	+	-	-	-	+	+	+	-
Bison priscus, bison	-	-	+	-	-	-	-	+	-	-
Bos/Bison sp., a bovine	+	-	-	+b	+	-	-	-	+	-

Table 11.29. See opposite for caption

have yielded a remarkable molluscan fauna in association with vertebrate remains. As discussed by Preece *et al.* (1991) and Rousseau *et al.* (1992), the molluscan fauna comprises a unique combination of species (the so called *Retinella* (*Lyrodiscus*) fauna) which have been found at a number of sites from eastern England to southern Germany. The *Retinella* (*Lyrodiscus*) fauna is probably of Hoxnian/Holsteinian age, and has been correlated with oxygen isotope stage 11 by Rousseau *et al.* (1992).

The molluscan fauna and the vertebrate remains from Beeches Pit (Holyoak *et al.* 1983; Preece *et al.* 1991; Holman 1994) and the Hitchin tufa (Kerney 1959, 1976b) indicate that the tufa sequences developed under forested conditions in a warm climate.

The sites listed above have been ascribed a Hoxnian age on lithostratigraphic grounds and, for the majority of sites, by palynology. The sites are also characterised by a distinctive mammalian fauna that distinguishes this period from other British interglacials. Biostrati-graphically significant occurrences for the Hoxnian include the first appearance of the rhinoceros *Stephanorhinus hemitoechus* and *S. kirchbergensis*, the cave bear *Ursus spelaeus*, and aurochs *Bos primigenius*. Giant deer *Megaloceros giganteus* is also recorded for the first time from an interglacial context during the Hoxnian. A number of species have their last appearance in the Hoxnian including the extinct beaver-like rodent *Trogontherium cuvieri*, and the small extinct mole *Talpa minor*. The common pine vole *Microtus* (*Terricola*) cf. *subterraneus* is a common component of the British Hoxnian small mammal fauna which is not found in later deposits. The distinctive fallow deer *Dama d. clactoniana* and a 'primitive' form of water vole *Arvicola terrestris cantiana* are also distinctive for the Hoxnian.

The interglacial following the Hoxnian is characterised by the faunas from Purfleet and Grays Thurrock, Essex; a diverse vertebrate fauna from the Cudmore Grove Channel, Essex, probably also correlates with these sites as suggested by Currant (in Bridgland *et al.* 1988) and Roe (1995). Bridgland's (1994) model of the Thames terrace stratigraphy, based principally on geomorphology, places the Corbets Tey Gravel, of which the Purfleet and Grays Thurrock deposits are part, within the first interglacial of the 'Saalian Complex' which he correlates with oxygen isotope stage 9. This episode is characterised by a quite different mammalian fauna from either the Hoxnian or the later 'Saalian Complex' temperate episodes. Biostratigraphically significant taxa include brown bear *Ursus arctos* which replaces the cave bear in this fauna, and the presence of the spotted hyaena *Crocuta crocuta* which is found for the first time in a post-Anglian temperate context at Grays Thurrock. The small mammal fauna lacks *Microtus* (*Terricola*) cf. *subterraneus* and *Talpa minor*, and the water vole from this stage is a more 'advanced' form of *Arvicola*, which is morphologically different from the Hoxnian population (Bridgland *et al.* 1995).

Age of the Barnham mammalian fauna

The Barnham fauna is readily distinguished from earlier British interglacials. Species characteristic of the early Middle Pleistocene 'Cromerian Complex' such as the extinct shrew *Sorex* (*Drepansorex*) *savini*, and the rodents *Pliomys episcopalis* and *Microtus gregalis* (*gregaloides* morphotype) are absent in the Barnham fauna. These species are well represented in British 'Cromerian Complex' small mammal faunas, for example at Ostend, Westbury-sub-Mendip and Boxgrove, but are unknown from post-Anglian/Elsterian contexts. The fact that the post-Anglian mammal assemblages are so different from late 'Cromerian Complex' faunas from Britain and north-west Europe (Fig. 11.15) highlights the severity of faunal turnover during the period from the late 'Cromerian Complex' to the Hoxnian.

The small extinct mole *Talpa minor* and the pine vole *Microtus* (*Terricola*) cf. *subterraneus* are important for determining the relative age of the site as both species are known only from Hoxnian and

Table 11.29. Comparison of the Barnham fauna with those of selected British Hoxnian localities. ([1] Beeches Pit fauna from Preece *et al.* 1991, Parfitt unpublished. [2] Clacton faunal list combines material from Jaywick, the Golf Course excavation (Singer *et al.* 1973), the Freshwater Beds of Channel 1 exposed on foreshore, and the former Butlin's Holiday Camp (Bridgland *et al.* in prep.). Data from Sutcliffe (1964); Singer *et al.* 1973; Wymer 1985. [3] Hitchin faunas from [a] Hitchin tufa (Kerney 1959; Holyoak *et al.* 1983) and [b] the Hitchin lake deposits (Boreham & Gibbard 1995). [4] Hoxne (Stratum C and Bed 4) data from Stuart *et al.* 1993, [c] fragmentary remains of a medium-sized species of *Sorex* referred to *Sorex* cf. *araneus* by Stuart *et al.* 1993. [5] Ingress Vale (Dierden's Pit) fauna from Sutcliffe 1964. [6] Swanscombe (Lower Loam and (U.M.G.) Upper Middle Gravel) fauna based on Sutcliffe 1964; Stuart 1982; Schreve 1996; Parfitt unpublished data. [7] Woodston fauna from Horton *et al.* 1992).

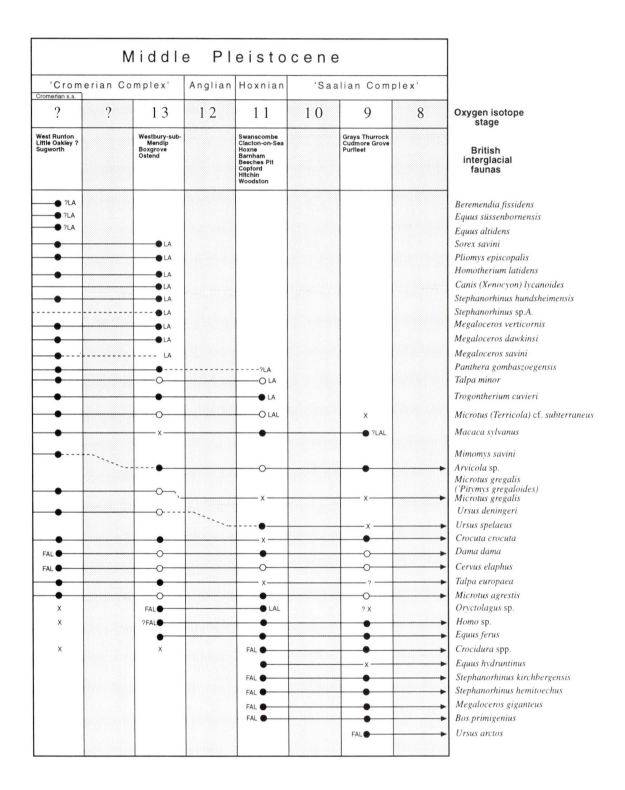

Fig. 11.12. Range chart showing temporally significant taxa for British Middle Pleistocene temperate stages. Stippled columns denote cold stages. Correlation with the deep-sea oxygen isotope record is based on Bridgland (1994) and Roberts *et al.* (1994, 1997). O and ● indicate a species is present (O--●--O) denotes a size and/or morphological shift within a lineage). X shows a genuine absence in the British fauna, although the species is recorded from broadly contemporary deposits in continental north-western Europe. Range bars terminating with an arrow denote the species is found in later British faunas. Abbreviations are as follows: LA last appearance (extinction), LAL last appearance locally, FAL first appearance locally.

earlier Middle Pleistocene interglacial periods in the British Isles. *Microtus* (*Terricola*) cf. *subterraneus* has previously been recorded from a number of Hoxnian deposits, such as the tufa at Hitchin (Kerney 1959), Beeches Pit (Preece *et al.* 1991), the Lower Loam at Swanscombe (determined as *Pitymys arvaloides* by Sutcliffe & Kowalski 1976) and Woodston (Horton *et al.* 1992). Its latest occurrence in Britain is in the main faunal horizons (Stratum C and Bed 4) at Hoxne which date to the closing phase of the Hoxnian (Stuart *et al.* 1993).

The small mole *Talpa minor* has a similar stratigraphic range in Britain to the pine vole. It is abundant in the British pre-Anglian deposits at West Runton (Stuart 1995), Westbury-sub-Mendip (Bishop 1982; Andrews 1990; Stringer *et al.* 1996) and Boxgrove (Currant in Roberts 1996; Parfitt 1998) where it occurs together with the larger mole *Talpa europaea*. In the Hoxnian, *Talpa minor*, but not *Talpa europaea*, is documented from the Swanscombe Lower Loam (Schreve 1996), the fluviatile freshwater and estuarine deposits at Woodston (Horton *et al.* 1992), and from the spring and tufa deposits at Beeches Pit (Preece *et al.* 1991). Currently there is no evidence for its presence in Britain later than the Upper Sequence of Hoxne (Stuart *et al.* 1993). Similarly, in north-western Europe it is not known from sites younger than the Holsteinian (Reumer 1996).

Russian desman is also generally believed to have its last occurrence in Britain during the Hoxnian (Stuart *et al.* 1993; Bridgland *et al.*1998). It is well represented in the type Cromerian of West Runton and from post-Cromerian *sensu stricto* deposits at Westbury-sub-Mendip and Ostend. The failure to recover Russian desman from sites, such as Boxgrove, is presumably due to ecological and taphonomic factors as it has been recorded in broadly contemporaneous deposits at Westbury-sub-Mendip and Ostend. It has previously only been recorded once in the British Hoxnian, from the Upper Sequence at Hoxne (Stuart *et al.* 1993). The biostratigraphic significance of Russian desman must however be treated with caution as it is a habitat specialist which was evidently a rare component of the small mammal community during the British Middle Pleistocene. Recently, Russian desman has been recorded from cold stage deposits of probable post-Hoxnian age at Chislet, Kent (Bridgland *et al.* 1998). This discovery highlights the incompleteness of our knowledge regarding the stratigraphic distribution of this elusive animal and underlines the general scarcity of small mammal faunas in the fossil record from certain stages of the British Pleistocene. Until its stratigraphic range is better known, its utility for precise biostratigraphic correlation is questionable.

Another species which may have potential biostratigraphic value is the rabbit *Oryctolagus* cf. *cuniculus*. In addition to the single record from Barnham, rabbit is recorded in some numbers from the lower part of the Swanscombe sequence (Mayhew 1975) and from the late 'Cromerian Complex' at Boxgrove (Currant in Roberts 1986). This species appears to have colonised northwestern Europe only twice until reintroduced from southern Europe in recent times. The ecological niche of the rabbit was apparently occupied by the mountain hare *Lepus timidus* during the interglacial episodes when the rabbit was not a member of the British fauna.

Until recently, the field vole *Microtus agrestis* was known only from Hoxnian and later contexts in Britain (Stuart *et al.* 1993). More recently, however, it has been identified in pre-Anglian contexts at Boxgrove and Westbury-sub-Mendip (Currant pers. comm.) where it has been identified from second upper molars with an '*agrestis* loop' characteristic of the living field vole. It appears that *Microtus agrestis* was also present in the earlier type Cromerian fauna of West Runton, although this form lacks the distinctive second upper molar morphology found in most later populations.

The presence of white-toothed shrews *Crocidura* sp. in the British Pleistocene was also considered to be biostratigraphically significant by Currant (1989) who suggested that *Crocidura* was prevalent in Britain during a temperate period in the late Middle Pleistocene. Recent work has shown that white-toothed shrew was also present during an earlier temperate stage at Purfleet (Bridgland *et al.* 1995), and the new record from Barnham records an even earlier occurrence. That *Crocidura* represents a hitherto unrecorded species for the British Hoxnian highlights the rarity of soricids in deposits of Hoxnian age and the incompleteness of our knowledge about them. It now seems likely that white-toothed shrews first appeared in Britain during the Hoxnian, and that its presence characterises this and later peak interglacial periods of the Middle Pleistocene. It is highly probable that white-toothed shrews were not present during the Cromerian *sensu lato* as represented by the deposits at West Runton, Westbury-sub-Mendip and Boxgrove as the very large collections from these localities do not contain *Crocidura*. Among the Barnham microtine rodents, the most interesting biochronologically are the water vole *Arvicola terrestris cantiana* and field vole *Microtus agrestis* because both are geographically widespread species which underwent rapid evolution during the Pleistocene.

For the water vole lineage, the morphological transitions in the British Quaternary succession are now understood in some detail, particularly for the early part of the Middle Pleistocene as discussed above. A notable feature of the Barnham water vole population is the atypically high frequency of the '*Mimomys* fold', a feature which is characteristic of British Hoxnian *Arvicola*. In addition to this, a combination of small size, a relatively short M_1 anteroconid complex, and *Mimomys* enamel differentiation (mean SDQ 140.5) together distinguish the Barnham and other Hoxnian water voles samples from those of any other interglacial recognised in Britain.

A Hoxnian age is also consistent with the morphology of the field vole *Microtus agrestis* molars. This lineage is characterised by the acquisition of the '*agrestis* loop' of the second upper molar in the early Middle Pleistocene, by changes in size (probably resulting from climatic or other environmental fluctuations), and by the relative length of the anterior part of the first lower molar (as measured by the A/L Index) which increases in successively later populations. In the Barnham sample, the mean value of A/L is intermediate between the values measured for *Microtus agrestis* from Boxgrove and Grays Thurrock. This is consistent with a Hoxnian age for Barnham.

Hoxnian Faunal Succession

Stuart (1982; Stuart *et al.* 1993) has argued that British Hoxnian mammal assemblages can be subdivided into two broad chronological groups. Most Hoxnian mammalian assemblages belong to the early part of this interglacial as inferred from the palynological data. This group includes the faunas from Clacton-on-Sea (pollen-dated to Ho II, or I-IIIa), Woodston (Ho II), Swanscombe (Lower Gravel and Lower Loam) (Ho II ?), the Hitchin lacustrine beds (Ho II) and Barnham (Ho II); the tufa deposits at Beeches Pit and Hitchin probably also the belong to the early part of the interglacial. The second group is composed of the fauna from the Middle Gravels at Swanscombe which according to Stuart *et al.* (1993) agrees closely with the mammalian faunas associated with the Hoxne Lower and Upper Industries. Importantly, the Hoxne upper sequence fauna overlies the lacustrine beds (the upper part of which belongs to pollen zone IIIb) thus providing strong evidence that this group dates to the closing phase of the Hoxnian (Stuart *et al.* 1993).

Although these faunal groups show strong similarities, and both are fully temperate in character, there is evidence for faunal differences between the early and later parts of the Hoxnian. The most striking difference between the faunas from the early and later part of the Hoxnian is the presence of lemming (either Norway lemming *Lemmus lemmus* or wood lemming

Myopus schisticolor) in both the Swanscombe Upper Middle Gravel (Sutcliffe & Kowalski 1976) and in Stratum C and Bed 4 at Hoxne (Stuart *et al.* 1993). Lemming is absent from the large small mammal sample at Barnham and therefore it probably colonised Britain during the later part of the Hoxnian. It may be significant that lemming is also found in the closing stages of the Boxgrove interglacial. In the Boxgrove deposits, *Myopus schisticolor* is found in the top of the marine deposits and in the lower part of the terrestrial sequence in association with a temperate fauna indicating deciduous or mixed woodland conditions. Later, *Myopus schisticolor* is replaced by *Lemmus lemmus* in the cold stage brickearths and gravels which overlie the temperate beds (Parfitt 1998). The co-association of lemming with an otherwise temperate mammalian fauna may, therefore, be a peculiarity of the latter part of some British Middle Pleistocene interglacial cycles.

The suggestion of a faunal shift in the later part of the Hoxnian is also reflected in a decrease in the relative abundance of obligate woodland mammals and an increase in more open country species observed by Sutcliffe (1964) and others (Lister 1986, Schreve 1996) for the Swanscombe sequence. These changes have been attributed to an opening up of the woodland as a consequence of climatic deterioration.

Among the mammals, the best evidence for faunal evolution within the Hoxnian comes from size changes in some of the mammals common to both groups. This has previously been described for red deer by Lister (in Stuart *et al.* 1993) who noted that the Hoxne upper sequence red deer were significantly larger than those from the early part of the Hoxnian as represented at Swanscombe and Clacton. Similarly, the Russian desman from Hoxne represents a large animal, comparable in size to extant populations, while early Hoxnian material from Barnham (Ho II) is exceptionally small. Conversely, the field vole decreased in size between the beginning and end of the Hoxnian. As discussed by Stuart *et al.* (1993) the Hoxne field vole is significantly smaller than the extant form. In contrast that from Barnham is significantly larger and similar in size to the extant British field vole.

These size changes, as discussed by Lister for Hoxnian red deer (in Stuart *et al.* 1993), were probably driven by climatic or other environmental changes. This pattern of size change is entirely consistent with evidence for vegetational change and for climatic deterioration recorded for the later part of the Hoxnian as recognised in the Marks Tey pollen sequence (Turner 1970) and in the molluscan fauna from the Swanscombe Middle Gravel (Kerney 1971). Such changes need not imply any great difference in age between the two faunal groups.

Biostratigraphic summary

From the foregoing discussion it is clear that the Barnham mammalian fauna shows the strongest affinities with the early part of the Hoxnian; a conclusion convincingly supported by lithostratigraphy and palynological evidence. Confirmation of a post-Anglian age, as indicated by the stratigraphic position of the fossiliferous beds above Anglian Lowestoft Till, is provided by the composition of the mammal fauna which contains none of the characteristic 'Cromerian' species commonly found in British pre-Anglian contexts. Based on the occurrence of *Talpa minor*, *Microtus* (*Terricola*) cf. *subterraneus* and possibly also *Oryctolagus* the temperate sediments were deposited during the Hoxnian as none of these species are found in post-Anglian stages later than this stage. Similarly, the stage of evolution of the Barnham water vole *Arvicola terrestris cantiana* and the field vole *Microtus agrestis*, relative to those of other British Interglacial localities, confirms this age assignment.

12. MOLLUSCA FROM THE LOWER PALAEOLITHIC SITE AT BARNHAM

M.B. Seddon

INTRODUCTION

Non-marine molluscs occur frequently in Middle and Late Pleistocene deposits in Britain, especially in southern and eastern England. These fossils provide an indication of the local environment, although they are less valuable as indicators of temperature, given their often widespread geographic distributions. Within the Middle to Late Pleistocene some species do provide evidence of thermal regime, for example *Belgrandia marginata*, with a present distribution which is southern European and *Clausilia pumila*, a continental European species, are both thought to indicate warmer conditions than at present (Kerney 1977; Keen 1990).

Some species are at present only known from sites of specific ages, and these provide the possibility of use for correlation between sites. Although freshwater fauna from interglacials often show little variability through the Middle to Late Pleistocene, the Cromerian Interglacial deposits at West Runton are typified by the occurrence of such species as *Valvata goldfüssiana*, *Tanousia runtoniana* and *Bithynia troscheli* (Sparks 1980). Some of these species are also recorded at Little Oakley (Preece 1990) and Sugworth (Gilbertson 1980; Preece 1989), both of which are probably also Cromerian in age.

Freshwater species from the late Middle Pleistocene deposits at Swanscombe show some changes in the sequence (Kerney 1971; Meijer & Preece 1995). The Lower and Middle Gravels contain taxa such as *Corbicula fluminalis*, *Valvata naticina* and *Belgrandia marginata*; but it is the appearance of *Theodoxus danubialis (= serratiliniformis)*, at the top of the Lower Loam that helps to infer that the Thames and Rhine river systems became linked at this time (Kennard 1942; Meijer & Preece 1995).

At Barnham, the occurrence of shells within the faunal deposits of Unit 5c (grey silt and clay) in Area III, therefore, provided the possibility of shedding light on several avenues of study. Palaeoenvironmental and biostratigraphic information might be obtained, that itself could be directly related with the other faunal and floral data from the site (see Chapters 7-11, 13 and 15), but also potentially important data on fluvial colonisation histories and the inferred links with the rivers of continental Europe. The latter might also be deduced from study of the fish (see Chapter 8).

METHODS

Samples were taken during the period 1991-93, the two key sampling locations being in Pit 4 and the stratigraphically higher Pit 9 (see Chapter 7, Figs 7.1 and 7.2). The pits were sampled at 10cm intervals through a total of 3.3m of the grey silt and clay, each sample being approximately 2kg in weight. The grey silt and clay can itself be divided from the base into the laminated shelly clay, the brown-grey clay, the black clay, the shelly clay and the gritty clay

All samples except the dated materials (see Chapter 16) were broken down in a weak calgon solution, the shells floated off and the residue passed though 2mm and 0.5mm sieves. The coarse and fine residues were handpicked under a stereomicroscope (x6 magnification). All nomenclature follows Kerney and Cameron (1979) and Kerney (1976a).

RESULTS

The numbers of shells for each species by sample number from Pits 4 and 9 are given in Appendix V, and a summary is shown in Table 12.1. The greatest concentrations of shells were found in the brown-grey clay from samples 233-236 in Pit 4, and in the shelly clay from samples 92-96 in Pit 9. The majority of shells recovered from the site were freshwater in origin, although there was a small proportion of terrestrial shells. Despite sampling for larger shells it should be noted that a high percentage of the shells recovered were broken fragments, either shell apices or body fragments typically 0.5mm to 1.5mm in diameter.

Freshwater molluscs

The assemblage was typified at most levels by a dominance of *Bithynia tentaculata* (L.), present as both shell apices and opercula. The opercula were examined to check for the presence of *Bithynia leachii*, but most adult opercula have the characteristic oval form of *B. tentaculata*. In the laminated shelly clay (Pit 4, samples 240-241), the opercula of *Bithynia* formed dense thick lenses (see Chapter 7, Fig. 7.1). The highest density of opercula recorded from this analysis came from the brown-grey clay (Pit 4, sample 235) where over twice the number of discs were obtained than at any other level.

Habitat type			gritty clay	shelly clay	black clay	brown-grey clay	laminated shelly clay	Total
Freshwater Gastropods								
Moving Water	*Bithynia tentaculata* (L.)	opercula	3	283	57	7368	1054	9003
		shells	2	107	6	869	0	984
	Valvata piscinalis (Müller)	shells	0	6	0	20	0	26
	Lymnaea cf. *stagnalis* (L.)	shells	0	1	0	22	0	23
	Unionidae	shell frags	0	0	0	*	0	*
Ditch group	*Valvata cristata* (Müller)	shells	0	70	1	114	0	185
	Gyraulus laevis Alder	shells	0	3	0	0	0	3
	cf. *Planorbis planorbis* (L.)	shells	0	19	0	4	0	23
Catholic group	*Armiger crista* (L.)	shells	0	10	0	13	0	23
Slum group	*Lymnaea truncatula* (Müller)	shells	0	0	0	2	0	2
	Undet.		0	0	0	182	0	182
Freshwater Bivalves								
Catholic group	*Pisidium* cf.*milium*	valves	0	0	0	1	0	1
Land Gastropods								
	Succineidae sp.	shells	0	14	0	1	0	15
	Clausilidae	apices	0	0	0	2	0	2
	Ceciliodes acicula	shells	1	0	0	0	0	1
	Helicellidae	apices	0	0	0	4	0	4
	Cepea/Arianta spp.	shell frags	0	*	0	*	0	*

Table 12.1. Quantities of shells by species from Unit 5c. * = shell fragments.

There are three possible explanations for the predominance of opercula within the brown-grey clay and laminated shelly clay.

(1) Post-depositional weathering. The opercula of *Bithynia* spp. have a different shell composition being formed from calcite not aragonite like the shells. This means that the opercula may survive in partly decalcified deposits.

(2) Fluvial sorting. The opercula are flat discoid shapes which give rise to different behaviour compared to the shells during transportation by the river. It is possible to find concentrated beds of opercula and other light shells along the strandline at the edge of river channels.

(3) 'Splitting'. Sparks (1961, 1964) reported that the opercula may appear to be more common as they split into several layers. This can give discrepancies between shell counts and opercula counts in some deposits.

Shells formed *c.* 20% of the sum of opercula and shells present in the brown-grey clay in Pit 4 (samples 233-237) suggesting that the predominance of opercula may be the result of splitting, although sorting may also have been involved. At a higher level in the same unit

in Pit 4 (samples 229-232) many opercula were recorded, but few shells suggesting fluvial sorting or splitting. At still higher levels in the brown-grey clay only opercula were preserved, which may suggest post-depositional decalcification. Thus at Barnham, all three of the different theories on the causes of predominance of opercula may have been operative at different stages.

B. tentaculata has been recorded through most interglacial stages of the British Pleistocene since the Norwich Crag. There are also cold-stage records which appear to be mainly late-glacial warming or interstadials. *B. tentaculata* is widespread in the British Isles and has a wide habitat tolerance. It avoids waters that are soft or poorly oxygenated, living in lakes, rivers and streams usually associated with stagnant to moderately fast-flowing water with scanty or dense vegetation. As this species is frequent throughout Pleistocene deposits it is used for relative and absolute dating techniques, and at this site provides one source for amino-acid racemisation ratios (see Chapter 16). The sediments suggest (see Chapter 4) that the deposition of the unit took place under still or low energy water conditions. This species could be found in either of these conditions, although the low energy moving water would provide a better explanation of the predominance of opercula at some levels. Care was taken in examination of the larger shells collected at the site, to check whether other Bithynia species (e.g. *B. troscheli*) were present.

Other freshwater species present within Unit 5c include *Valvata piscinalis* (Müller) and *Lymnaea* cf. *stagnalis* (L.). Both of these species are again indicative of slow moving water. Although *Lymnaea stagnalis* (L.) is viewed as one of the species typically associated with moving water and large ponds, it lives in a wide range of hard-water habitats, preferring rivers, lakes and large ditches, but can withstand slight salinity and occasionally occurs in small pools. The species has been recorded from Cromerian and later interglacials and from a few interstadial deposits. *Lymnaea* cf. *stagnalis* (L.) is only recorded from the brown-grey clay (Pit 4, samples 234 and 236) whereas *Valvata piscinalis* is recorded from both the brown-grey clay (Pit 4, samples 234 and 236) and the shelly clay (Pit 9, sample 212). *Valvata piscinalis* is a common freshwater snail which is very variable in shell size and form. This species is present in almost all glacial and interglacial stages since the Norwich Crag. The normal range of habitats includes lakes, running water of streams and rivers, rarely in small ponds or small ditches as it has a poor tolerance to poorly oxygenated water or base-poor sites. None of the larger shells matched the more distinctive forms such as *V. p.* var. *antiqua*. recorded at Swanscombe.

Valvata cristata (L.), is one of the 'Ditch' group (Sparks 1961). The species prefers still or slow-flowing water with at least a moderate base content, often in dense submerged vegetation, although it can be found in backwaters of large rivers. Some of the shells in these samples were very small and broken, hence have been placed with the undetermined group, due to the presence of *Gyraulus laevis* and young *V. piscinalis*. A few shells of *Planorbis planorbis* (L.) have also been found in the brown-grey clay (Pit 4, samples 231, 234 and 236) and in the shelly clay (Pit 9, sample 212). The species has been found in most interglacial stages since the Norwich Crag, and the habitats where it can be found include streams, rivers, lakes and fen-ditches, preferring places with plenty of vegetation.

By contrast *Armiger crista* (L.) is also present in the brown-grey clay (Pit 4, samples 231 and 236) and in the shelly clay (Pit 9, sample 212) and this was classified as one of the 'Slum' species (Sparks 1961) as it will tolerate a wide range of habitats, does not require clean water, generally being associated with a muddy organic substrate.

Terrestrial molluscs

There are terrestrial species present in some levels; apices of the spindle-shaped Clausiliidae family were recovered from the brown-grey clay (Pit 4, samples 234 and 236). When compared, the shape of the apices are similar to *Ruthenica* and *Clausilia*, but broader than *Laminifera*. These shells, although having small apices, do not appear to have been reworked, but this possibility cannot be discounted. The presence of this family suggests an interglacial woodland fauna. Species of both genera are present at Beeches Pit (Preece *et al.* 1991) although *Clausilia* spp. are present in most interglacial and postglacial sequences, *Ruthenica* has only been recorded from Hoxnian deposits, for example at Beeches Pit (Preece *et al.* 1991) and Hitchin (Holyoak *et al.* 1993).

The presence of a species from the subfamily Helicellidae, would point to open environments, possibly grassland. These may be *Candidula* spp. but the shell fragments were too small for confirmation.

Cecilioides acicula (Müller) found in the gritty clay (Pit 9, sample 209) is discounted from the analysis as it is normally found living in soil.

Apical fragments of a large Helicid the size of *Cepaea* or *Arianta* were recovered as well as fragments of the columella axis and lip from the brown-grey clay in Pit 4. These are most likely to have been present in temperate woodland, although they may have been present in more open areas

DISCUSSION

The extreme fragmentation of the freshwater shells has hampered investigation, as there may well be more taxa present, some of which may well be more diagnostic than, those presented here. Such a situation is not infrequent in fluvial sediments as commented on by Green *et al.* (1997).

All of the species identified could be found in slow-flowing water, possibly as a backwater to a main channel, or a large pool, surrounded by temperate woodland, with some open ground. The presence of *Valvata cristata* (L.) and *Planorbis planorbis* (L.) suggest that the habitat had submergent weeds, possibly throughout the period of deposition. Many of these species normally avoid poorly oxygenated water.

Generally, little can be said about changes in habitat through the sequence. There is, however, a slight a suggestion of increasing siltyness in the upper part of the brown-grey clay (sample 231) where *Armiger crista* is present, but other species such as as *Lymnaea stagnalis* are absent. However, the low numbers of species analysed (other than *B. tentaculata*) mean that the data are inconclusive.

All of the species recorded are found in most interglacial deposits and therefore little can be said about correlation with other sites.

13. PALYNOLOGY OF THE BARNHAM SEQUENCE

Chris Hunt

INTRODUCTION

The application of pollen analyis to the Barnham investigation was hoped to offer an assessment of the regional and local patterns of vegetation surrounding the site, while the analysis of algal and fungal microfossils was intended to provide indications of the local depositional environment. The pollen-rich sediments were located in the grey silt and clay (Unit 5c, see Chapter 4) in Area III, sediments that have been interpreted independently as being laid under slow-flowing or still water conditions. These units also contained rich faunal remains, which it was hoped would provide an independent assessment of the environment surrounding the site during this time (see Chapters 7-12). Laterally equivalent sediments (grey/brown stony clay - Unit 5d, and the yellow silty sand, Unit 5e) were located in the archaeologically-rich Areas I, III, IV(4) and V, so that reconstructions of the environment have a direct bearing on the biotope of these early people.

The dating of Barnham to oxygen isotope stage 11 (Ashton *et al.* 1994a; see Chapter 16) also provided the opportunity to compare the Barnham pollen sequence to other sites attributed to this stage (Swanscombe and Clacton), and those assigned more generally to the Hoxnian (Hoxne and Marks Tey), to investigate the similarities or differences between their palynological signatures. This is discussed in detail in the final section.

SAMPLING AND SAMPLE PREPARATION

The Barnham Quaternary deposits were sampled for palynology using a number of grab samples from the archaeologically-important contexts in Area I (brown diamicton, yellow silty sand and black clay), but of these only sample 172 from the brown diamicton produced pollen (see Chapter 4, Fig. 4.7). In addition four monoliths, two from Pit 4 (monoliths 269 and 268 - see Chapter 4, Fig. 4.28), and two from Pit 9 North (monoliths 271 and 270 - see Chapter 7, Fig. 7.2). The monoliths were subsampled at approximately 0.1m intervals over a total depth of 3.6m, though sampling intervals were varied to take advantage of suitable lithologies. Following unsatisfactory preparations at a number of intervals, a further twelve samples were reprepared to give larger pollen counts. In all, samples taken from 41 levels in the monoliths plus the five

samples from other contexts were prepared for palynology.

In the laboratory, the monoliths and grab samples were carefully cleaned by scraping away the outer few centimetres of sediment and initially samples of 2ml volume were cut using cleaned scalpels. In the resampling, samples of 4ml volume were taken. The samples were boiled in 5% potassium hydroxide for five minutes, then sieved on a nominal 10μm nylon mesh to remove fines. The fraction retained on the sieve was 'swirled' on a clock-glass to remove silt and sand. The resulting organic concentrate was stained with safranin and was mounted in glycerol gel for examination. Slides were logged at 400x magnification, and difficult grains identified at 1000x, using phase contrast and Nomarski interference contrast as appropriate. All palynomorphs in the samples were identified (or noted as unidentifiable) and counted. Figures given for number of grains refer to absolute counts. The pollen diagram (Fig. 13.1) is calculated as percentages of total pollen and spores. Algal and fungal micofossils and spines of *Ceratophyllum* were not included in the percentage calculation but are plotted as percentages of total pollen. Pollen taxonomy generally follows Moore *et al.* (1991), except where this is superseded by the nomenclature changes of Bennett *et al.* (1994). Taxonomic notes at the end of the chapter deal with problematical taxa. Assemblages were also examined under ultraviolet light, so that recycled or contaminant grains could be identified by their different fluorescence colour and intensity.

RESULTS

The results of the palynological analyses were extremely variable. The assemblages varied in composition and preservational characteristics. The samples from the monoliths contained between 0 and 567 pollen grains and plant spores, and between 0 and 2991 algal microfossils. Those from the grab samples were mostly barren, with only sample 172 containing 6 poorly preserved pollen grains. Three recent grains were identified by their cell contents, staining and preservational characteristics and were verified by their fluorescence colour; these were omitted from the counts and are not discussed further. The pollen spectra were grouped into a number of assemblage-biozones, which are described below and shown in Figure 13.1. The depths given are from the top of the conjoined monoliths. It will be seen in Figure 13.1 that the pollen diagram is plotted in two halves. This is because of incompatabilities between counts from the top of monolith 271 and the base of monolith 270. Further comments are made about this phenomenon below.

LPAZ Barnham 1
3.60-3.21m. *Betula-Corylus-Quercus-Alnus*-Poaceae

Pollen is extremely sparse except in the basal sample, where it is sparse. Preservation is good, but palynomorphs are flattened and of a translucent pale yellow colour, taking stain poorly. The fluorescence colour is a dull slightly reddish brown for virtually all palynomorphs. The only exception was a three-dimensional grain of *Glaux* in one sample, with a fluorescence colour of bright pinkish-orange.

The basal assemblage is dominated by *Betula* (16%), *Quercus* (18%), *Corylus* (16%), *Alnus* (12%) and Poaceae (12%). *Tilia* and Type X are present. The aquatic *Myriophyllum* is present, together with sedge pollen and the damp meadow species *Filipendula*. The other samples contain virtually no pollen though recycled pre-Quaternary palynomorphs are present and algal microfossils are rare.

A very sparse pollen assemblage (sample 172), consisting of poorly preserved single grains of Poaceae, *Centaurea*, *Plantago*, *Sphagnum*, *Lycopodium* and Filicales was recovered from the top of the brown diamicton in Area I, gravel section (see Chapter 4, Fig. 4.7). The diamictons are solifluction deposits and lithostratigraphically equate approximately with this biozone. The very sparse pollen assemblage probably equates approximately with the even sparser assemblages near the base of monolith 269.

LPAZ Barnham 2
3.21-2.90m. *Pinus-Corylus-Betula*-Poaceae

Pollen is sparse and well-preserved in three dimensions, but did not take stain. The fluorescence colour is bright pinkish-orange for pollen and Zygnemataceae, and bright white for *Sigmopollis* and Leiosphaerids.

The assemblages are dominated by *Pinus* (falling from 26 to 15%), *Corylus* (rising from 21 to 27%), *Betula* (falling from 12 to 11.5%), Poaceae (falling from 21 to 11.5%), with a little *Quercus* (rising from 2.4 to 5%) and with the incoming of *Ulmus* and *Tilia*. *Picea*, *Populus*, Lactucae, *Rumex* and recycled pre-Quaternary microfossils are sporadically present. Sedges, *Typha* and the aquatic *Myriophyllum* are present in all samples. Algal microfossils are present, with assemblages dominated by *Sigmopollis*.

LPAZ Barnham 3
2.90-1.66m. *Corylus-Quercus*-Poaceae

Pollen is sparse to common in this biozone, with most samples containing around 100 grains and a few containing more than 200. Pollen is generally well-preserved in three dimensions, but took stain poorly. The fluorescence colour is bright pinkish-orange for pollen and Zygnemataceae, bright yellow for *Botryococcus* and *Pediastrum*, and bright white for *Sigmopollis* and Leiosphaerids.

The samples are dominated by *Corylus* (15-51%), *Quercus* (2-27%), *Alnus* (1.3-24%) and Poaceae (2-29%) with generally low incidences of *Betula*, *Ulmus* and *Pinus* and the occasional occurrence of *Tilia*, *Carpinus*, *Acer*, *Ilex*, *Salix*, *Juniperus*, Type X, *Ulex*, *Hedera* and Rosaceae. *Pinus* and *Betula* have small peaks toward the middle of the biozone. A variety of herbaceous taxa, notably *Artemisia* and Lactucae, are present. Sedges, *Ranunculus*, *Typha* and the aquatics *Myriophyllum*, *Nymphaea* and *Potamogeton* are present. Filicales, *Pteridium* and *Sphagnum* spores are present in low numbers. Algal microfossils are present in most samples, but the planktonic *Botryococcus* and also *Sigmopollis* and the Leiosphaerids and to a lesser extent the benthic Zygnemataceae become very abundant near the top of the biozone.

LPAZ Barnham 4
1.66-0.86m. *Quercus-Corylus-Alnus*-Poaceae

Pollen is generally abundant in this biozone, with samples containing between 132 and 658 grains. It is generally 'thin' and moderately preserved, and most samples took stain. In samples which did not take stain, particularly near the top of the biozone, grain outlines are slightly 'fuzzy'. The fluorescence colour is bright pinkish-orange for pollen and Zygnemataceae, bright yellow for *Botryococcus* and *Pediastrum*, and bright white for *Sigmopollis* and Leiosphaerids.

The samples are dominated by *Quercus* (2-30%), *Corylus* (13-54%) and Poaceae (15-30%). *Alnus* rises gently to 20% and then declines to 0.7%. *Pinus*, *Ulmus*, *Acer*, *Tilia*, and Type X are regularly present, other species such as *Betula*, *Picea*, *Carpinus*, *Fraxinus*, *Taxus*, *Juniperus*, *Ilex*, *Hedera* and *Ulex* are present occasionally. Herbaceous taxa, especially *Artemisia* and *Rumex*, but also *Galium*, Caryophyllaceae, *Thalictrum* and *Filipendula* are present. Wetland species - Cyperaceae, *Ranunculus*, *Typha* - are relatively abundant and a variety of pollen of aquatics are present. Counts for Filicales are fairly low in most samples. The planktonic algal microflora, especially *Sigmopollis*, *Pediastrum* and *Botryococus*, are extremely abundant in the middle and top of the biozone.

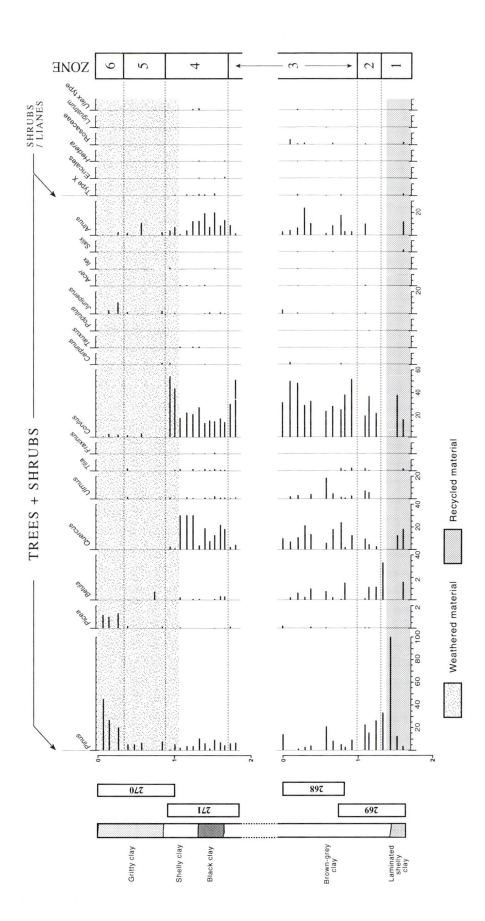

Fig. 13.1. Pollen diagram through the Barnham sequence.

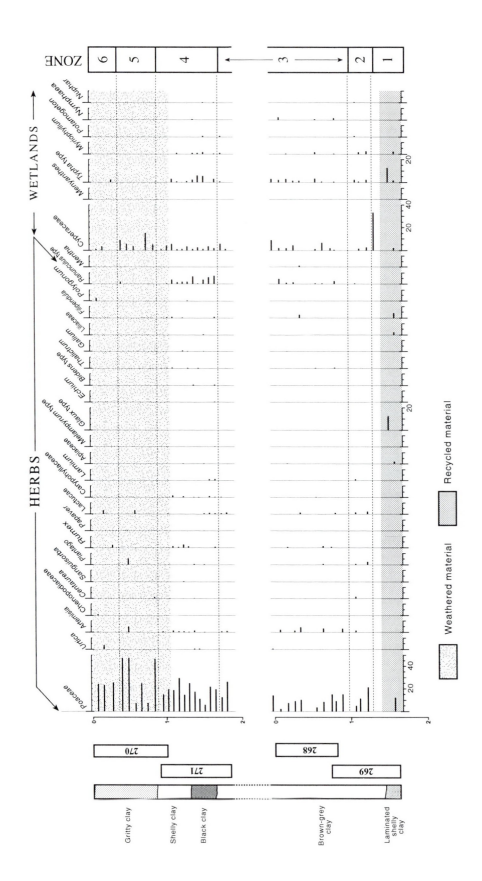

Fig. 13.1 cont.

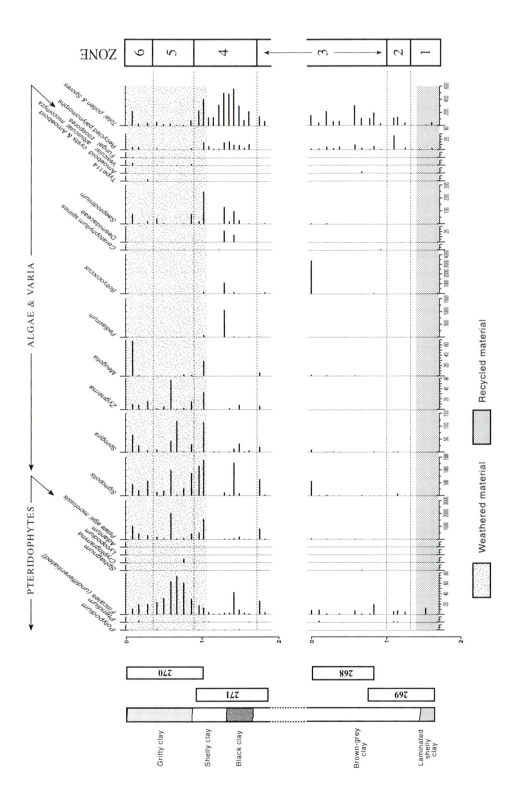

Fig. 13.1 cont.

LPAZ Barnham 5
0.86-0.32m. Poaceae-Filicales

Pollen is sparse and especially so in the middle part of this biozone. Preservation is good and in three dimensions. The fluorescence colour is bright pinkish-orange for most pollen, *Saeptodinium* and Zygnemataceae, while it is dull orange-red for most Filicales, and bright white for *Sigmopollis* and Leiosphaerids.

The assemblages are dominated by pollen of Poaceae (46-47%) and Filicales spores (24-31%), with occasional *Artemisia, Plantago,* Cyperaceae. The highest sample from this biozone contains occasional grains of *Pinus, Picea, Juniperus, Alnus, Betula, Corylus, Ulmus* and *Tilia,* together with *Polypodium* and *Lycopodium* spores. Leiosphaerids (344-940%) and *Sigmopollis* (260-2420%) are extremely abundant, and both the small (11-120%) and the large (40-100%) *Saeptodinium* spp. are common, though of lesser importance towards the middle of the biozone. Vesicular arbuscular micorrhyza are sometimes present.

LPAZ Barnham 6
0.32-0.00m. *Pinus-Picea*-Poaceae-Filicales

Pollen is fairly rare at the base of this biozone but abundant at the top. Preservation is moderate to good, but saccate pollen is often torn. The fluorescence colour is bright red for most pollen, *Saeptodinium* and Zygnemataceae, but dull orange red for grains of *Corylus, Alnus,* a few *Pinus* and some Filicales. *Botryococcus* is bright yellow and *Sigmopollis* and Leiosphaerids are bright white.

The assemblages are dominated by pollen of *Pinus* (rising from 21 to 45%), *Picea* (10-13%), Poaceae (23-26%) and spores of Filicales (11-21%). *Juniperus* falls towards the top of the biozone (to 10%); *Alnus* and *Corylus* are present. Herbaceous taxa other than Poaceae (23-26%) are generally sparse and wetland taxa are virtually absent. Algal microfossils, especially *Sigmopollis* (205-1500%) and Leiosphaerids ((370-1390%), and to a lesser extent the small *Saeptodinium* species (95-179%), are extremely abundant in this biozone. Vesicular arbuscular micorrhyza and fungal zoospores are present.

TAPHONOMY AND PALAEOECOLOGY

The palynology of the Barnham site is complex, but interpretation of the taphonomic pathways is aided by reference to the preservation and fluorescence characteristics of the palynomorphs. The sequence is interpreted here using the biozones that have been described above.

LPAZ Barnham 1

The palynomorphs in this assemblage biozone have unusual preservation characteristics, having a translucent pale yellow colour in transmitted light and a dull reddish-brown fluorescence colour. These characteristics are comparable with those of many thermally mature Mesozoic and Tertiary grains and are consistent with these grains having a long history, probably including some exposure to a relatively high heat flow as a result of burial. Taken at face value, this assemblage is typical of interglacial conditions, but the preservational and fluorescence characteristics lead to the recognition of this assemblage as recycled. The one exception is the grain of *Glaux*, which has preservation and fluorescence characteristics comparable with those of pollen in the overlying biozones and is therefore regarded as *in situ*. It is thus suggested that the virtual absence of *in situ* pollen and the presence of recycled pollen points to an environment with low biological productivity and high sedimentation rates, probably as the result of a cold climatic regime at the end of a cold stage. A similar conclusion can be derived from the very sparse assemblage recovered from the top of the brown diamicton in Area I (see Chapter 4, Fig. 4.7). An alternative explanation is also possible: that conditions during this biozone were hostile to the preservation of pollen and that only thermally mature recycled palynomorphs could be preserved. There is, however, no trace of the weathering which might be expected in the monolith sediments at this point.

LPAZ Barnham 2

The uniform preservation and fluorescence characteristics of palynomorphs in this biozone indicate that they form coherent *in situ* assemblages unaffected to any significant extent by contamination or recycling. The different fluorescence colours of some algal microfossils reflects only differences in chemical composition.

The abrupt base of this biozone and the absence of typical herb-rich late-glacial and earliest interglacial boreal forest biozones are strongly indicative of a significant hiatus in the sampled sequence. The assemblages of this biozone are rather sparse, with *Pinus* and herbaceous taxa and Poaceae declining, *Corylus* dominant and rising, *Quercus* low and rising and *Betula* significant. They point to an early-interglacial fairly open boreal forest being invaded by mixed oak forest taxa, with a consequent closing of the canopy and exclusion of herbaceous taxa. Such a situation might approximate to early in zone II of the Turner and West (1968) model. The small pollen counts and the fairly high counts for *Pinus* and Filicales are consistent with deposition in a fluvial regime (Hunt 1994); and it is thus possible that these taxa are 'overrepresented'. *Typha,* some Cyperaceae and *Myriophyllum* are marginal and shallow aquatic plants and consistent with a water body less than a metre deep, fringed by marshy places. Little indication of water depth can be gained from the algal microflora, but the low number of algal microfossils point to the water body not being strongly eutrophic.

LPAZ Barnham 3

The uniform preservation and fluorescence characteristics of palynomorphs in this biozone point to the assemblages being substantially *in situ* and unaffected by contamination and recycling of older material.

The dominance of *Corylus, Quercus* and *Alnus,* together with the presence of *Ulmus, Tilia, Betula,* and a variety of other tree species are consistent with a regional mixed oak forest vegetation, a fully temperate climatic regime and zone II of an interglacial in the Turner and West (1968) model. *Ilex* and *Hedera,* in particular, can be taken as evidence of a mild climatic regime. The high *Corylus* counts and the presence of shrubs such as *Juniperus* and *Ulex,* together with the Poaceae and herbaceous taxa such as *Artemisia, Rumex, Galium* and *Filipendula,* is consistent with forest-margin, scrubland and grassy habitats, probably maintained along the river corridor by the grazing pressure of large mammals. Habitats enriched by animal dung are perhaps indicated by the pollen of *Urtica*; and the high counts for *Botryococcus, Pediastrum, Sigmopollis* and Leiosphaerids towards the upper part of the biozone point to considerable eutrophication of the water body, probably also by animal droppings. The presence of *Typha, Ranunculus* and Cyperaceae probably reflects shoreline vegetation, while the abundance of planktonic algal microfossils and virtual absence of pollen of aquatics and benthonic algae may reflect some combination of eutrophication and/or deep, slow-moving water. Early in the biozone, the presence of *Ceratophyllum* spines certainly points to deeper water. The peaks of *Pinus* and Filicales probably reflect fluvial taphonomic processes rather than the common occurrence of these taxa.

LPAZ Barnham 4

The uniform preservation and fluorescence characteristics of the palynomorphs in this biozone indicate that the assemblages are *in situ* and unaffected by recycling of older pollen. Although the palynomorphs are 'thin' there is no evidence (such as raised frequencies of resistant taxa such as *Pinus,* Lactucae or fern spores; Hunt 1994) for the selective loss of taxa through fluvial taphonomic or pedogenic

processes. Similarly 'thin' pollen are typical of some calcareous depositional environments, such as tufas and some caves.

The dominance of broad-leaved tree pollen and the presence of *Hedera* is consistent with a fully-interglacial climate and a regionally forested landscape. The overall characteristics of the biozone equate with late in zone II of the Turner and West (1968) model. The fall of *Alnus* and the rise of *Quercus* probably reflects a successional change, but might also be climatically controlled, perhaps by declining rainfall. The high counts for *Corylus* are perhaps consistent with nearby forest-edge habitat or polyclimax mosaic features - glades or scrub woodland following fire or treefall. The substantial counts for Poaceae and the presence of herbaceous taxa such as *Artemisia, Rumex, Galium, Thalictrum, Sanguisorba, Filipendula* and Caryophyllaceae are indicative of local wet and dry grassland, presumably maintained by grazing and trampling by large herbivores. The presence of *Urtica* in this biozone is also consistent with the presence of large mammals since nettles prefer nutrient-enriched habitats. The pollen of *Typha, Ranunculus* and Cyperaceae reflect shoreline vegetation. The pollen of *Myriophyllum, Nymphaea* and *Menyanthes* indicate water depths in the region of at least half a metre. Deeper water, perhaps as much as 2m, may be indicated by the presence of *Ceratophyllum* spines and the relative importance of planktonic algae, notably *Pediastrum* and *Botryococcus.* The high counts for algal microfossils indicate eutrophication, possibly because the water body was enriched by animal dung, but also possibly as the result of algal blooms in mineral-rich groundwater.

There are incompatabilities between counts at the top of monolith 271, and counts from the same levels in the base of monolith 270. *Quercus* is high at the top of 271, while *Corylus* is high in the base of 270. It is suggested that this phenomenon is the result of the irregular approach of a weathering front (see following section). *Corylus* is more weathering-resistant than *Quercus* (Havinga 1984) and it is argued that some *Quercus* and other grains were eliminated by pedogenic processes from the base of 270, while these species were unaffected by weathering in the nearby top of 271.

LPAZ Barnham 5

The abrupt change between assemblages in LPAZ Barnham 4 and this biozone might reflect a depositional hiatus. This is most likely to reflect significant oxidation and microbial damage by pedogenic processes operating down to a marked weathering front. The fluorescence colours indicate that some Filicales spores throughout the biozone and pollen of broad-leaved trees and spores of *Polypodium* at the top of this biozone are significantly damaged, presumably by pedogenic processes. The peak in Filicales may be explained by fern spores being more resistant to pedogenic degradation than are most pollen grains. Fern spores tend, therefore, to become concentrated in soils as the pollen is eliminated by weathering (Dimbleby 1985; Havinga 1984). The occasional vesicular arbuscular micorrhyza are also consistent with pedogenesis.

Poaceae and herb pollen shows 'fresh' fluorescence colours and may have infiltrated from the contemporaneously accreting soil surface into the deposit during and possibly after pedogenesis (cf. Keatinge 1983; Dimbleby 1985). The continuing high counts for algal microfossils point to sustained eutrophic conditions, prior to pedogenesis, while the rise of the benthic Zygnemataceous algae indicate that the water body was very shallow. The presence of large counts for algal microfossils in strongly weathered sediments is not surprising; Hunt (1994) has pointed out that many algal microfossils are known to be more weathering-resistant than pollen. It can thus be hypothesised that deposition of this interval took place in a shallowing, eutrophic water body. The climatic conditions under which this occurred are, on palynological evidence, uncertain. After deposition of the sediments, the water table must have fallen significantly and pedogenic alteration and partial destruction of the pollen assemblages took place. This is the type of process which operates to produce a welded soil, and is compatible with the sediment characteristics of this interval.

LPAZ Barnham 6

Two components can be recognised on their fluorescence characteristics in this biozone. The dull orange fluorescence colours allow the recognition of a pedogenically damaged component - notably pollen of *Alnus* and *Corylus*, some *Pinus* and Filicales spores. The wetland flora is poorly and irregularly represented, but the water body appears to have been highly eutrophic, with massive algal blooms. The benthic Zygnemataceous algae are significant, consistent with the water body being very shallow. The algal blooms and the presence of *Urtica* most probably reflect nutrient input to the water body and land-surface from dung of large animals. This component was probably deposited with the sediment, sometime late in the temperate phase of the interglacial, and it is perhaps consistent with the presence of European pond tortoise in this horizon.

The pollen which fluoresces bright red, dominated by Poaceae, *Pinus, Picea,* and with falling *Juniperus,* most probably reflects open boreal woodland, perhaps spruce-dominated as this species is not a significant producer of pollen, and with substantial areas of grassland and scrub. *Juniperus* probably reflects summer warmth, but the overall aspect of this assemblage, including its low diversity, is consistent with winter cold. This component thus probably equates to zone IV of an interglacial in the Turner and West (1968) model and is rather reminiscent of the biotype of High Lodge (Hunt 1992, 1994). The red fluorescence colour of this component seems to be typical of assemblages which have been subjected to repeated wetting and drying cycles after deposition, as might be expected in a soil profile where microbial activity was insufficient to eliminate the pollen. The distribution pattern of this component, with numbers rising upwards in the section, is typical of the patterns of infiltrating pollen in soils recorded by Keatinge (1983) and Dimbleby (1985). This is consistent with the presence of fungal zoospores and vesicular arbuscular micorrhyza (both are fungal entities typical of soils), and with a stillstand in deposition at or just above this horizon and the intermittent, but continuing formation of a welded soil.

The assemblage of this LPAZ Barnham 6 can therefore be regarded as a palimpsest, with an earlier component laid down in temperate conditions and then pedogenically damaged and a later component which infiltrated into the deposit during the post-temperate zone, from an open boreal woodland. Infiltration into these deposits would have ceased either because they became too deeply buried for material to reach them from the surface or because rising water tables prevented further downward movement.

BIOSTRATIGRAPHY

It is becoming unfashionable to use pollen for biostratigraphic purposes, partly because it has become clear that it is unrealistic to expect identical vegetational development during any given temperate phase across a large region and partly as the result of the development of new geochronometric techniques. Nevertheless, the Barnham palynological sequence arguably contains important evidence concerning the age and correlation of the site. The sequence contains pollen reflecting most of zone II and at least a part of zone IV of an interglacial (using the conventions of Turner & West 1968), though it must be pointed out that the pollen counts in some parts of the sequence are very small. Zones I and III of the interglacial seem to be missing or poorly preserved. This is unfortunate, since zone III is often held to be the most distinctive part of interglacial pollen sequences. Nevertheless, some comparisons can be made and some tentative conclusions drawn.

Post-Anglian palynological record

Four sites (Swanscombe, Clacton, Hoxne and Marks Tey) have produced palynological signatures that can be compared to that from Barnham. However the dating of these sites is problematic. Aminostratigraphy has been used by Bowen *et al.* (1989) to assign Swanscombe and Clacton to oxygen isotope stage 11, but Hoxne to stage 9. This dating of Swanscombe and Clacton is supported by Bridgland (1994) but opposed by Gibbard (1994) on their individual assessments of the lithostratigraphical evidence in the Thames basin. Hoxne has also been assigned to stage 11 on stratigraphic grounds, as the lake beds rest on Lowestoft Till, attributed to stage 12 (Singer *et al.* 1993). Marks Tey has been widely attributed to the same temperate phase as Hoxne, based on the similarity of the palynology and thus described as Hoxnian (Turner & West 1968; West & Gibbard 1995).

The palynology of these sites has been studied by a variety of specialists which has led to further disagreements. The Lower Loam at Swanscombe was first investigated by Mullenders and Desair-Corremans and described by Wymer (1974), while this and other units were later investigated by Hubbard (1982, 1996). The cliff section at Clacton was described by Pike and Godwin (1953) and lower levels beneath the clifftop sequence were later described by Turner and Kerney (1971). Wymer (1974) also briefly described work carried out by Mullenders and Desair-Corremans on a sequence from the Golf Course at Clacton. The palynology at Hoxne was described by West (1956), while that at Marks Tey was investigated by Turner (1970).

The disagreement over the palynology stems from severe criticisms by Turner (1985) of the pollen work undertaken by Mullenders and Desair-Corremans (in Wymer 1974), and by Hubbard (1982). This criticism is based on the 'unusual' pollen assemblages at Swanscombe and Clacton compared to the typical Hoxnian spectra from Hoxne and Marks Tey. Thus he suggested that the assemblages from Swanscombe and Clacton Golf Course must have resulted from weathering or contamination.

It is possible that Turner (1985) was correct in suggesting that these sites were contaminated. However, Wymer (pers. comm. 1995) maintains that Mullenders was emphatic that this was not the case, and Hubbard (pers. comm. 1995) is also clear that his samples were not contaminated. (It is worth pointing out that contamination is usually visible to the alert palynologist as differences in compression, preservational state and staining characteristics of the pollen grains.) It is also clear that weathering, as a process, could never be possible for the *appearance* of species like *Fagus* in the assemblages - weathering can only *remove* grains! Weathering, however, does tend to produce a

characteristic 'signature' in pollen assemblages (Havinga 1967, 1984; Hunt 1994), with abnormally high percentages of resistant taxa such as *Pinus*, Lactucae and fern spores. This was not the case at Clacton Golf Course or Swanscombe (Wymer 1974; Hubbard 1982).

Some of the differences between the lacustrine deposits at Hoxne and Marks Tey and the fluvial units at Swanscombe and Clacton Golf Course may be taphonomic. Although this could have a significant effect (cf. Hunt 1994), it cannot account for the very real differences between the sites, particularly the presence at Swanscombe and on Clacton Golf Course of *Fagus*, which is otherwise unknown in Britain in the Later Middle Pleistocene until stage 7.

The considerable similarity between Clacton Golf Course and the Swanscombe Lower Loam, and their differences with the Hoxne and Marks Tey, thus might support the aminostratigraphic interpretation, that these sites were laid down during an interglacial period separate from the Hoxnian (Bowen *et al.* 1989). The Barnham site, associated with amino-acid ratios indicative of stage 11 (Ashton *et al.* 1994a) offers the possibility of testing the hypothesis of a palynologically distinct stage 11 interglacial and thus of throwing light on this problem.

Comparisons with Barnham

Comparison of the Barnham interglacial with pollen diagrams of known Hoxnian age, notably those from Hoxne (West 1956) and Marks Tey (Turner 1970), shows some similarities and some important differences. Like the Hoxnian sites, Barnham has the extinct Type X, long thought to be a good marker for the Hoxnian (Turner 1970) but also present at Swanscombe (Hubbard 1982, 1996). It should also be noted that Type X is present in the recycled assemblage in the lowest part of the Barnham pollen diagram. Type X is, incidentally, an important component of the pollen spectra in an interglacial of probable 'Cromer-complex' age at Walton-on-the-Naze (Boatman *et al.* 1973; Bowden *et al.* 1995) so it cannot be used as an exclusive 'guide fossil' for the Hoxnian.

Zone I of the Turner and West (1968) model is missing at Barnham, so this sequence cannot be compared with the Hoxnian biozone HoI. In biozone HoII at Hoxne and Marks Tey, *Quercus* expands before *Corylus* (West 1956; Turner 1970), but at Barnham *Corylus* is already important as the expansion of *Quercus* starts. It should be noted that this part of the Barnham diagram is based on low counts and this observation should therefore be regarded with some caution. The characteristic NAP peak and fall in *Corylus* in biozone HoIIc at Hoxne and Marks Tey is not present at Barnham. *Taxus* is present in HoIIIb and HoIVa at

Marks Tey (Turner 1970), but is present in LPAZ Barnham 4, equivalent to late in zone II of the Turner and West (1968) model.

There appears to be strong weathering of assemblages in LPAZ Barnham 5 and a complex taphonomic history for LPAZ Barnham 6 including a possible non-deposition episode at the top of the latter biozone, which means that all of zone III of the Turner and West (1968) model is unrecognisable at Barnham. (It is, of course, possible that this zone was not well developed in the Barnham interglacial.) It is thus impossible to make comparisons with Biozone HoIII, with its very characteristic peak in *Abies.* This species was not present at all at Barnham, however. It could, perhaps, be argued that such a weathering-resistant species should have survived in this interval if it was initially present, given that some (comparably resistant) *Pinus* grains did survive.

Abies, however, persists through HoIV and into the following glacial period at Marks Tey (Turner 1970). The comparable biozone at Barnham, LPAZ Barnham 6, differs significantly from the late Hoxnian sequences, since *Abies* is completely absent and there is instead a strong peak in *Picea.* This biozone is also distinctive since it contains virtually no *Betula*, which is fairly common in biozone HoIV and the following early glacial biozone (Turner 1970).

Although the evidence is equivocal in places, there are sufficient differences to suggest that Barnham LPAZ 2-6 represents an interglacial which is palynologically distinct from the Hoxnian of Hoxne and Marks Tey.

The three published accounts of the palynology of the Clacton channel deposits have each dealt with different parts of the extensive sequence. The assemblages reported by Turner and Kerney (1971) beneath the cliff-top, contain Type X and are comparable in a general way with assemblages from LPAZ Barnham 3 and LPAZ Barnham 4, though they differ in having higher percentages of *Alnus* and lower percentages of *Corylus* than Barnham. This difference *could* be a localised phenomenon relating to local vegetational patterns. However, if these samples are part of the same interglacial cycle as the stratigraphically higher late interglacial sequence from the cliff-top, then there are some marked differences with Barnham. The assemblages on the cliff-top are marked by high percentages of *Abies* (Pike & Godwin 1953; S. Hall pers. comm. 1997) and it is very unlikely that they are equivalent to part of the interglacial at Barnham.

The assemblages reported in outline by Wymer (1974) from the Golf Course at Clacton are also unlike those from Barnham, but the presence of *Fagus* and mixed oak forest species in the basal gravel invites comparison with assemblages from the lower part of the Lower Loam at Swanscombe which also contain mixed oak forest taxa and *Fagus* (Hubbard 1982, 1996; R.

Hubbard, pers. comm. 1995). The pollen diagram from the overlying marl at the Clacton Golf Course (Wymer 1974) is not dissimilar to the upper part of the pollen diagram from the Lower Loam at Swanscombe figured by Wymer (1974), though the analyses of Hubbard (1982, 1996), appear to have come from a different lithological unit.

Thus, the pollen diagrams from Clacton Golf Course and Swanscombe are only broadly comparable with the equivalent part of the pollen diagram from Barnham. Type X is present at Barnham and Swanscombe, but the Swanscombe and Clacton Golf Course deposits contain more *Pinus* and *Betula* and distinctly less *Corylus* than does the sequence at Barnham. More significantly, the Lower Loam at Swanscombe and the gravels at Clacton Golf Course contain *Fagus*, but *Fagus* is completely absent at Barnham, (and in the Hoxnian of Hoxne and Marks Tey). It is thus probable that the Barnham interglacial is not closely comparable with the interglacial represented by the Lower Loam at Swanscombe and the Clacton Golf Course sequence.

There is, therefore, a distinct probability that the period following the Anglian Glaciation is much more complex than previously suggested. The Clacton Golf Course and the Swanscombe Lower Loam sequence probably contain the early stages of the interglacial whose later stages can be seen in the Clacton cliff section. It is also just possible that two interglacial sequences are represented at Clacton, one at the Golf Course equivalent to the Lower Gravel and parts of the Lower Loam at Swanscombe, and another in the cliffs. The alternative hypothesis follows the argument of Turner (1985) and dismisses the Clacton Golf Course and Swanscombe pollen records as unreliable. Such a hypothesis is open to testing using fluorescence microscopy, and should not be allowed to outweigh the hypothesis of a palynologically distinct Swanscombe-Clacton interglacial until such a test has been made.

The interglacial at Barnham is arguably distinct from both the Hoxnian of Hoxne and Marks Tey and from the Swanscombe Lower Gravel/Lower Loam and Clacton pollen-based interglacial sequences. This conclusion is difficult to reconcile with current models of the post-Anglian Middle Pleistocene, which either encompass one interglacial before the Ipswichian (Gibbard 1994), or three interglacials (the Swanscombe, Hoxnian and Stanton Harcourt interglacials) before the Ipswichian (Bowen *et al.* 1989; Bridgland 1994). The first of these models reflects a strongly traditional viewpoint which is coming under increasing pressure as new discoveries are made and old sites are reassessed. The latter model, currently fashionable among British Quaternary specialists, is an approach to stratigraphy based on radiometric comparisons with the deep sea oxygen isotope record, and the sometimes problematical aminostratigraphic technique. The model relies on the accurate identification of events which are manifested in completely different ways in the terrestrial and marine realms. It also relies on the assumption that a single oxygen isotope stage in the deep sea is equivalent to a single interglacial episode on land. Some of the oxygen isotope stages in the Middle Pleistocene, notably stage 7, but also stage 11, are not simple events but each contain two or more marked temperature peaks. Three stage 7, stage 9 and two or three stage 11 interglacial events are suggested by long cores in the Velay and cross-European correlations (Andrieu *et al.* 1996; de Beaulieu, pers. comm. 1996).These authorities contend that the Holsteinian stratotype, with its characteristic late interglacial *Abies* peak, can be assigned to stage 11. It is therefore distinctly possible that the 'three interglacial model' is too simplistic to encompass the complexity of events in the British Middle Pleistocene.

It is thus tentatively suggested that there is now evidence for at least four interglacial episodes - Barnham, Swanscombe/Clacton, Hoxne/Marks Tey and Stanton Harcourt - between the Anglian Glaciation and the Ipswichian Interglacial. There are, inevitably, considerable reservations, concerning poor preservation of assemblages, small pollen counts, taphonomic factors and local ecological patterning. Nevertheless, the differences, particularly in the late-interglacial stages, are marked enough to be confident that Barnham is not equivalent to Hoxne or Marks Tey, thus reinforcing the aminostratigraphical evidence. The differences in the late interglacial assemblages also preclude correlation with the cliff section at Clacton, which may now be tentatively suggested to be equivalent in age to the Holsteinian stratotype. Differences between the Barnham and the Clacton Golf Course site and the Lower Gravel and Lower Loam at Swanscombe are less marked, but if only one interglacial is present at Clacton, it is (on grounds of the late interglacial assemblages) most unlikely to be equivalent to Barnham. Resolution of the actual number of interglacial episodes involved and their correlation is, however, vastly beyond the scope of this report and must await the testing of the Swanscombe Lower Loam and Clacton pollen with fluorescence microscopy and/or the evolution of more sensitive dating techniques than are currently available.

CONCLUSIONS

The silts and clays at Barnham contain evidence for an episode of interglacial status. The basal part of the silts and clays was laid down rapidly in cold conditions. A hiatus separates these deposits from the main part of the sequence, which was laid down in fairly deep, sometimes eutrophic water during zone II of an interglacial. The regional vegetation was species-rich mixed oak forest, with areas of scrub and wet and dry grassland probably maintained by some combination of polyclimax successional forces and grazing pressure.

The water body shallowed considerably during Zone III of the interglacial. Pollen from this zone was virtually all eliminated by later weathering, but the algal microfossils, which are more weathering-resistant water than the pollen, show that the water body was relatively shallow at this time and strongly eutrophic as a result of nutrient flux, perhaps from animal dung. It eventually dried out, and strong pedogenic alteration of the upper part of the waterlain sediments occurred during a period approximately equivalent to part of zone IV of the interglacial period. Zone IV is characterised by a distinct peak of *Picea*. It shows indicators of pedogenesis and the intermittent but continuing formation of a complex welded soil. The regional vegetation was open boreal forest with pine, spruce and juniper and intervening grassland areas.

The interglacial at Barnham is palynologically relatively well characterised, and cannot be closely compared with either the Hoxnian or with the Clacton/Swanscombe interglacial(?s). If the Barnham interglacial *is* truly distinctive, as suggested above, and the Clacton and Swanscombe pollen sequences *are* valid, then the reassessment of the currently understood post-Anglian sequence of interglacials in the British Isles will become urgently necessary.

Taxonomic notes

Corylus. Grains logged as '*Corylus*' have a morphology which is compatible with both *Corylus* and *Myrica* pollen. Attribution to *Corylus* is on the grounds that environments suitable for *Myrica* were not present at Barnham during the sampled interval.

Type X. Grains logged as Type X conform in every way to the descriptions and illustrations in Turner (1973).

Zygnemataceae. In this group are grouped spores of the zygnemataceous benthonic algae *Spirogyra*, *Zygnema* and *Meugotia*. These all have broadly similar habitat requirements.

Saeptodinium spp. These dinoflagellate cysts correspond closely to specimens described as *Saeptodinium skipseaense* by Hunt *et al.* (1985). They are large, often around 80μm long, with psilate endophragm and ectophragm and a transapical, compound archaeopyle. A small *Saeptodinium* species is also present in some samples. These dinoflagellate cysts are smaller, usually between 20 and 30μm long, with a rounded to peridinioid outline, and most have only a single surviving wall layer. They have a transapical, compound archaeopyle.

Leiosphaerids. In this category are lumped a variety of psilate, approximately spherical microfossils, some with an equatorial split, and varying in size from about 8μm to around 15μm. Most have a test wall less than 0.5μm thick and virtually none take stain. They appear to be the spores of freshwater benthonic algae.

Type 114. These are psilate, pale yellow ?algal spores with a subcircular pylome.

VAM. These are vesicular arbuscular micorrhyza, fungal structures symbiotic with the roots of higher plants. They were discussed recently by Hunt (1994).

14. THE WOOD CHARCOAL FROM BARNHAM

Caroline Cartwright

Samples from a variety of contexts were taken for the extraction of wood charcoal or charred plant macrofossils from Areas I and III. Only a small quantity of wood charcoal was recovered, this being from the black clay (Unit 6) in Area I, from a grey band within the brown silt and clay or 'brickearth' (Unit 7) also in Area I, and from the black clay (Unit 6) in Area III (faunal area).

THE WOOD CHARCOAL

The wood charcoal was extracted by flotation, and standard procedures by optical microscopy were adopted for the identification to taxon. Reference was made to the collection of macro-specimens of wood charcoal and thin-sections of British woods collected for comparative purposes in the Barnham area by the author and held in reference collections of the Department of Scientific Research, British Museum.

Area I

A very small quantity of wood charcoal (1.5g) was retrieved from samples taken from the black clay in Area I (sample 29a; see Chapter 4, Fig. 4.6). The fragments were all identified as *Corylus* sp., hazel.

A larger quantity of wood charcoal (3.8g) was also recovered from a grey layer within the overlying brown silt and clay (sample 29b; see Chapter 4, Fig. 4.6). This consisted of *Corylus* sp. (1.5g), *Quercus* sp., oak, (1.2g) and *Taxus* sp., yew (1.1g).

Area III (faunal area)

Samples from the black clay at the top of the faunally-rich calcareous grey silt and clay in Area III (faunal area) produced 5.0g of wood charcoal fragments (sample 250; see Chapter 4, Fig. 4.28). Although in poor condition, these have been identified as *Corylus*

sp. (2.2g), *Fraxinus* sp., ash (1.2g), *Quercus* sp. (1.1g) and *Betula* sp., birch (0.5g).

DISCUSSION

Although the quantity of wood charcoal at Barnham is low (10.3g), some cautious observations may be made regarding the arboreal taxa present. They are all taxa that occur in temperate periods both past and present. In particular the occurrence of *Corylus* sp. and *Quercus* sp. is mirrored by the pollen found in the underlying grey silt and clay (see Chapter 13). These are key elements of a highly recognisable vegetational community. At the present day the components of the oak-hazel wood community in the British Isles are very diverse; rich understorey and sub-community vegetation develops according to local soil and topographical features (Rodwell 1991). Most commonly found on the more calcareous sediments including clays and glacial drift, oak-hazel woods often represent the climax forest type in areas continuously wooded for long periods of time (*ibid.*). Such woods occur in regions in which the annual rainfall does not exceed 1000mm (*ibid.*); heavy waterlogging which might inhibit the beneficial effects of active invertebrates to the soil and leaf litter can hinder the development of a healthy, diverse oak-hazel woodland community (*ibid.*).

The absence of pollen from the black clay and the severe weathering of pollen in the top metre of the underlying grey silt and clay, gives the wood charcoal an added significance, even though the quantities are small. The taxa present suggest the continuation of temperate conditions to the top of the black clay in Area III. This would support the palaeoenvironmental interpretation of the faunal sequence, where the occurrence of species such European pond terrapin and Aesculapian snake are strongly indicative of warm conditions (see Chapter 9).

15. PALAEOECOLOGICAL SUMMARY OF UNIT 5C

INTRODUCTION

In this chapter the palaeoenvironment of the site during the deposition of Unit 5c is discussed. This layer contains an abundant molluscan and vertebrate fauna and the palynological analyses were also undertaken on samples collected from this unit. Environmental evidence as such is unfortunately not preserved in the deposits associated with the main archaeological areas. The sediments at the margins of the basin, where the archaeological evidence is concentrated are decalcified, thus calcareous fossils are not preserved. Similarly oxidation and microbial damage have depleted the fossil pollen in these areas. However, the clay pit does have a small portion of fine-grained sediments (Unit 5c) that contain molluscs, vertebrates and pollen in varying degrees of abundance and preservation. These deposits have been extensively sampled for environmental evidence as an aid to more accurately understanding the contemporary hominid environment.

Vertebrate remains are by far the most commonly preserved and comprehensively sampled. Molluscan remains are also abundant in parts of the sequence although they are generally crushed which has selectively destroyed larger shells. Plant remains (charcoal) and pollen provide information on vegetational conditions, but differential preservation and low numbers of palynomorphs in certain layers means that the apparent palynological signal from deposits with poor pollen preservation and low concentrations must be interpreted with caution.

The study of one stratigraphic section does not allow us to propose a sedimentological, palaeoenvironmental, and palaeogeographic reconstruction of the whole basin. Nevertheless, some generalisations about the palaeoenvironmental evolution in the area of the site, during part of the Hoxnian, can be obtained. This summary of the evidence from Unit 5c contributes important information that is pertinent to understanding the ecological changes that took place in this basin during part of the Hoxnian. As the fossiliferous units were deposited at the same time as the archaeology-rich horizons at the margins of the waterbody, the results presented here are of direct relevance to the interpretation of the early hominid palaeoenvironment at the site. In this section we aim to integrate the faunal evidence with sedimentological and palynological data for the fossiliferous deposits.

EVIDENCE FOR PALAEOENVIRONMENTAL AND ECOLOGICAL CHANGE IN UNIT 5C

The facies association described for Area III Unit 5c strongly indicates a fluvio-lacustrine origin for these fossil-rich deposits. The 2-3m of fossiliferous deposits consist solely of fine-grained sediments (clay and clayey sandy silt). The succession consists of six sub-units: (the basal silt, laminated shelly clay, brown-grey clay, black clay, shelly clay and gritty clay) from which the majority of the Mollusca, vertebrate remains and palynological record is derived. The faunal and floral remains, except for the recycled palynomorphs from the laminated shelly clay, represent autochthonous assemblages which therefore reflect the plants and animals living in close proximity to the site.

THE VERTEBRATE FAUNA

Intensive sampling of the deposits has yielded an extensive vertebrate fauna. In terms of species richness, the Barnham vertebrate assemblage is among the highest for Middle Pleistocene faunas from a single fossiliferous bed. Minimally, the assemblage includes 25 species of mammals, 3 species of birds, 10 amphibians, 1 terrapin, 2 lizards, 4 snakes, and 13 species of fish (Table 15.1).

Sampling of Unit 5c for vertebrates was undertaken at a number of sites within Area III. The most complete sequence through the deposits is exposed in Pits 4 and 9, and the samples from these columns were examined in detail to determine the broad trends in the composition of the vertebrate faunas through the sequence. The sediment samples obtained from the columns were wet-sieved through a 0.5mm mesh and the concentration of bones and counts of the numbers of fish, amphibian, and reptile and small mammal bones were determined for each sample. These data are plotted in Figure 15.1. This diagram shows that there was a pronounced increase in the number of bones between the top of the brown-grey clay and into the base of the gritty clay, this was followed by a decline in bone concentration towards the top of the gritty clay. A more dramatic change is seen in the marked decrease in fish at the top of the shelly clay. This trend continues in the gritty clay, where the samples are dominated by amphibians, reptiles and small mammal remains.

	basal silts	laminated shelly clay	brown-grey clay	black clay	shelly clay	gritty clay
Pisces						
Salmo trutta, trout	-	-	+	-	+	-
Salmonidae gen. et sp. indet., salmonid	-	-	+	-	-	+
Esox lucius, pike	+	+	+	+	+	+
Gobio gobio, gudgeon	-	-	+	-	-	+
Tinca tinca, tench	-	-	+	+	+	+
Blicca bjoerkna or *Abramis brama*, silver or common bream	-	-	+	-	-	-
Alburnus alburnus, bleak	-	-	+	-	+	+
Scardinius erythrophthalmus, rudd	-	-	+	+	+	+
Rutilus rutilus, roach	-	-	+	+	+	+
Leuciscus sp. indet., chub, orfe or dace	-	-	+	-	-	-
Anguilla anguilla, eel	-	-	+	-	+	+
Gasterosteus aculeatus, three-spined stickleback	-	+	+	+	+	+
Lota lota, burbot	-	+	-	-	-	-
Perca fluviatilis, perch	-	-	+	-	-	-
Amphibia						
Triturus cristatus, warty newt	-	-	+	+	+	+
Triturus helveticus, palmate newt	-	-	-	-	-	+
Triturus vulgaris, common newt	-	-	-	+	+	+
Triturus sp. indet., indeterminate newt	-	-	+	+	+	+
Hyla arborea, common tree frog	-	-	-	-	+	-
Hyla sp. indet., indeterminate tree frog	-	-	-	-	-	+
Bufo bufo, common toad	-	-	+	+	+	+
Bufo calamita, natterjack	-	-	-	-	-	+
Bufo virdis, green toad	-	-	-	+	+	+
Bufo sp. indet., indeterminate toad	-	-	+	+	+	+
Rana arvalis, moor frog	-	-	+	-	+	+
Rana (ridibunda) sp. water frog of the *R. ridibunda* species group	-	-	-	+	+	+
Rana temporaria, common frog	-	-	+	+	+	+
Rana sp. indet., true frog, species indeterminate	-	+	+	+	+	+
Reptilia						
Emys orbicularis, European pond terrapin	-	-	-	-	-	+
Anguis fragilis, slow worm	-	-	+	+	+	+
Lacerta sp., small *Lacerta* species	-	-	-	+	-	+
Natrix natrix, grass snake	-	-	+	+	+	+
Natrix maura or *tesselata*, viperine or dice snake	-	-	-	+	-	+
Natrix sp., grass or water snake	-	-	+	+	+	+
Elaphe longissima, Aesculapian snake	-	-	-	-	-	+
Vipera berus, adder	-	-	+	-	-	+
Aves						
Anas sp. indet, indeterminate dabbling duck	-	-	-	+	-	-
Columba cf. *palumbus*, wood pigeon	-	-	-	-	-	+
Turdus cf. *philomelos* or *T.* cf. *iliacus*, song thrush or redwing	-	-	-	+	+	-
Mammalia						
Plecotus sp. indet., indeterminate long-eared bat	-	-	-	-	+	-
Sorex minutus, pygmy shrew	-	-	+	+	+	+
Sorex sp. 1, shrew	-	-	+	+	+	+
Neomys sp. indet., indeterminate water shrew	-	-	-	+	+	+
Crocidura sp. indet., indeterminate white-toothed shrew	-	-	-	-	-	+
Talpa minor, extinct mole	-	-	-	+	+	+
Desmana moschata, Russian desman	-	-	-	-	+	+
Homo sp. indet., (artefacts) hominid.	-	-	-	+	+	+
Oryctolagus cf. *O. cuniculus*, rabbit	-	-	-	-	-	+
Sciurus sp. indet., indeterminate squirrel	-	-	-	-	-	+
Clethrionomys glareolus, bank vole	-	-	+	+	+	+
Arvicola terrestris cantiana, water vole	-	-	+	+	+	+
Microtus (Terricola) cf. *subterraneus.*, common pine vole	-	-	+	+	+	+
Microtus agrestis, field vole	-	-	+	-	+	+
Microtus arvalis, common vole	-	-	-	-	-	+
Apodemus sylvaticus, wood mouse	-	-	+	+	+	+
Apodemus maastrichtiensis, extinct mouse	-	-	-	-	+	+
Ursus sp. indet., indeterminate bear	-	-	+	-	-	-
Mustela cf. *M. putorius*, polecat	-	-	-	-	-	+
Panthera leo, lion	-	-	-	-	-	+
Palaeoloxodon antiquus, straight-tusked elephant	-	-	-	-	-	+
Stephanorhinus sp. indet., indeterminate rhinoceros	-	-	-	-	-	+
Sus scrofa, wild boar	-	-	-	-	-	+
Dama dama, fallow deer	-	-	+	+	-	-
Cervus elaphus, red deer	-	-	-	-	-	+
Bos or *Bison* sp., aurochs or bison	-	-	-	-	-	+

Table 15.1. The vertebrate fauna from Barnham Unit 5c.

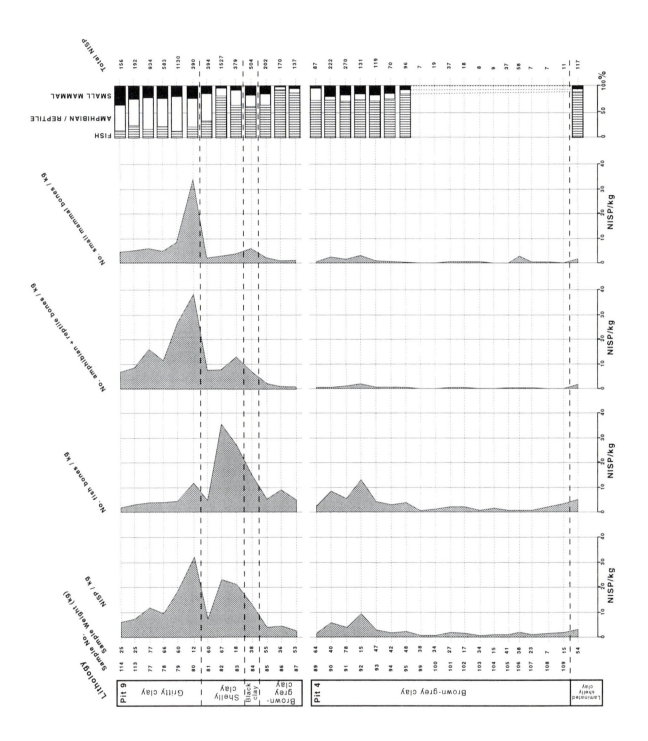

Fig. 15.1. Summary of the vertebrate fauna from Unit 5c compiled from the column samples excavated in Pits 4 and 9. The histograms show changes in bone concentration (NISP/kg, number of identifiable specimens per kg of sediment) and in the absolute abundance of fish, amphibians and reptiles, and small mammals. The numbers of identifiable fragments for the main vertebrate groups are summarised as percentages in the block diagram.

169

Changes in abundance of main vertebrate groups thus indicate a decline in strictly aquatic elements, and a greater input of terrestrial vertebrates into the depositional site. These changes show that wetter habitats gave way to increasingly drier ones through time, reflecting the gradual infilling and shallowing of the basin which eventually led to the formation of a stable landsurface (unit 6). Dramatic changes in the species composition of the fish fauna (see Chapter 8, Fig. 8.1) provide important information on the changing nature of the aquatic environment. In the brown-grey clay, a high diversity fauna indicative of clear, well-oxygenated, flowing freshwater is replaced by one of low diversity dominated by tench, stickleback and lesser numbers of pike and rudd. This low-diversity fauna is found in the black, shelly and gritty clays and is composed of fish species which are tolerant of poor-water conditions. The faunal change at the boundary between the brown-grey and black clay reflects a decrease in water-flow, and a waterbody that may have been oxygen-depleted and prone to eutrophication.

The herpetofauna is the most taxonomically diverse for any known British Pleistocene locality. Of all the vertebrates, the amphibian and reptile fauna seems to be the best indicator of climatic conditions. The high diversity (at least 17 taxa) and the presence of a number of cold-intolerant species both reflect a climate that was warmer than the present. Using modern distributions of the species, the climate may have been similar to the warm continental climate of southern and central France as all of the amphibian and reptile species can be found in this region today.

Amphibians and reptiles increase in abundance and diversity with the most species being found in the gritty clay. The abundance of pond terrapin in this unit indicates slow-flowing still water with a mild climate, whilst the other species indicate a diversity of local habitats that must have included areas of open water, wetlands and damp terrestrial habitats. Drier open grassland or sunny woodland clearings are indicated by both the natterjack and the Aesculapian snake.

The sparse bird fauna is also dominated by aquatic species (dabbling duck) which prefer slow-flowing or standing water.

The mammalian assemblage consists of an abundance of small mammals. Importantly, many of the most abundant of the small mammal species are extremely rare or unknown from other Hoxnian localities in Britain.

The most common small mammal at Barnham is the water vole. This is followed in importance by bank vole and wood mouse. The other microtine rodents and insectivores are, by contrast, quite rare. The composition of the assemblage is similar throughout the sequence, greater numbers of identifiable fragments

from the gritty clay accounting for the greater number of species in this unit. There are, however, trends in the relative abundance of certain species which may indicate habitat change. A steady increase in the relative abundance of the water vole and wood mouse and a decrease in bank vole may indicate a decrease in woodland and dense ground cover. It is equally possible that these changes are due to differences in the way the bones were accumulated. However, this suggestion needs to be tested further with a detailed analysis of the small mammal taphonomy.

The presence of one exclusively forest species, the squirrel also indicates that woodland habitat was in close proximity to the site. The local habitat from the small mammal evidence can be characterised as woodland habitats interspersed with more open ground.

Large mammals are also present, but rare, in all of the Unit 5c beds except for the shelly clay. The large mammal faunal composition with the occurrence of wild boar, fallow and red deer, straight-tusked elephant, a rhinoceros and bovid, is indicative of open habitats immediately contiguous with scrub and deciduous woodland habitats interspersed with more open ground. Climatically the mammals indicate peak interglacial conditions, and the mammal community is entirely consistent with the early temperate stage of an interglacial as inferred from the palynological data.

MOLLUSCS

Molluscs (see Chapter 12) are very rare in the gritty clay and were probably lost as a result of the partial decalcification of this horizon. Lower in the stratigraphic section, shells are abundant in the shelly clay and the brown grey clay. The molluscan fauna from these levels is a very restricted one, partially due to difficulties involved in identifying extremely fragmentary material. Freshwater molluscs dominate the assemblage and consist of species generally found in slow-flowing but well-oxygenated waters. Rare terrestrial molluscs indicate that the waterbody was surrounded by temperate woodland interspersed with some open ground. Low numbers of land molluscs are a common feature of molluscan remains from modern large lakes and stable rivers. The paucity of land molluscs in the brown-grey clay and shelly clay, therefore, indicates a large perennial waterbody that did not receive a significant input of terrestrial molluscs either from bank collapse or inwash from the land during flood events.

WOOD CHARCOAL AND POLLEN

Direct evidence for the vegetational conditions comes from wood charcoal and pollen evidence (see Chapters 13 and 14). Wood charcoal occurs in low quantities, from two units which are stratigraphically above the fauna-rich horizon. That from the black clay of Unit 6, which directly overlies the fossiliferous deposit in Area III is important as it provides evidence for the continuation of temperate woodland conditions into the terrestrial sequence.

Analysis of the pollen from the brown-grey clay, black clay (of Unit 5) and shelly clay indicates that the trees and herbaceous vegetation that produced them formed mixed oak woodland bordered by scrub and open grassland during the early temperate stage of an interglacial. Algal spores indicate that the brown-grey clay was deposited in fairly deep water which shallowed and became increasingly eutrophic as freshwater sedimentation came to an end. Hunt (Chapter 13) has interpreted the palynological record as indicating an initial period of cold climate followed by an amelioration to temperate conditions followed by a later cooling at the end of the interglacial. However, the virtual absence of non-recycled pollen at the base of the sequence, and the weathering and overprinting of pollen signatures at the top of the sequence make this interpretation suspect. What is clear, however, is the evidence from the pollen of temperate conditions during the accumulation of the grey-brown, black and shelly clays.

SUMMARY

The palaeoenvironmental data discussed above for Unit 5c provides a remarkably consistent picture of the local and regional environment during the deposition of the fluvio-lacustrine sequence. The lowest part of the sequence for which large quantities of molluscs, vertebrates and pollen have been recovered is the brown-grey clay. A large perennial, slow-flowing, waterbody is indicated which supported a species rich, temperate fish fauna. Palynological data from the middle and upper part of the brown-grey clay (LPAZ Barnham 3 & 4) indicates a regional environment of mixed oak forest with a diversity of open and forest-edge vegetational communities. Terrestrial vertebrates and land Mollusca are very sparse in this horizon indicating that the river was of a substantial size, and did not receive a significant input of terrestrial material into the system either from bank collapse or from inwash during flood events.

In the overlying black clay, remains of exclusively aquatic vertebrates again predominate, although the molluscan assemblage is very sparse. In this horizon, the taphonomy of the vertebrate remains indicates still, probably shallowing-water, and relatively fast sedimentation which has preserved fragile and associated skeletal material. The environment of deposition may have been a river backwater, or, the waterbody may have become isolated from the river during this stage. This horizon, therefore, represents an important change in the palaeodrainage regime from that of the brown-grey clay. Notably, the black clay is the lowest part of Unit 5c to have produced flint artefacts, which, although sparse, are in mint condition. There is little evidence for change in vegetational conditions from the top of the brown-grey clay, which probably represents the later part of the early temperate zone of the interglacial. However, the fish fauna from this horizon shows a reduction in species-diversity, a trend which is intensified in the overlying deposits.

A return to flowing-water is seen in the deposition of the shelly clay which contains abundant molluscan remains and a vertebrate assemblage dominated by freshwater fishes. Although certain of the Mollusca indicate a substantial body of flowing water, the flow was probably slower than during the deposition of the brown-grey clay. The low-diversity fish fauna, and high numbers of algal microfossils indicate that the waterbody was subject to low-oxygen conditions, perhaps as a result of eutrophication.

The gritty clay shows evidence for a major change in the local environment which developed from an essentially aquatic one to a fully terrestrial one during the deposition of this horizon. Although pollen and Mollusca are unfortunately poorly preserved due to pedogenic processes, vertebrate remains are both abundant and well-preserved, and provide a clear picture of the sequence of environmental change. During the deposition of the gritty clay, the aquatic vertebrate component became increasingly less important, and small mammals increased steadily in abundance. The fish fauna is a low-diversity one which is composed of species able to tolerate oxygen-depleted and eutrophic waters. The driving force behind these changes was the infilling of the basin which precipitated a change from a perennial waterbody to a more ephemeral one which eventually dried up or migrated away from the site. The type of terrestrial habitat which surrounded this diminishing waterbody can be inferred from the mammal community which indicates a 'patchwork' of deciduous woodland, marsh and open grassland and a climate warmer than present day.

The association of fresh condition flint artefacts with Unit 5c, provides an important link with the more prolific archaeological assemblages at the edges of the channel. This, together with the stratigraphic correlation between Units 5d and 5e in Areas I, IV(4) and V, with Unit 5c in Area III create a detailed environmental background for the human activity at the site.

16. AMINOSTRATIGRAPHY AND AMINO ACID GEOCHRONOLOGY

D.Q. Bowen

Amino acids contained in the indigenous protein preserved in the carbonate remains of fossil bivalves and gastropods degrade progressively with time. Such changes may be used to estimate the time that has elapsed since the death of the organism (Miller & Brigham-Grette 1989; Wehmiller 1989). Racemization refers to the time-dependent progressive inversion of L amino acids to the D configuration, but in the case of the protein amino acid L-isoleucine racemization occurs about only one of two chiral carbon atoms. This reaction, epimerization, proceeds from an initial D/L ratio close to zero to an equilibrium ratio of about 1.3. The reaction rate is also controlled by, temperature and taxonomy, but by using monospecific samples, or several species known to epimerize at the same rate, these effects may be minimised.

The integrated temperature at a site is the most important control on the reaction rate and thus the resolving power of the method. For example, at tropical sites with mean annual temperatures exceeding 25°C, age differences of *ca.* 1 ka can be resolved within the Holocene, and between 5 to 10 ka for older samples; but equilibrium is reached after only 150-300 ka. At Arctic sites the mean annual temperatures of less than 10°C no measurable racemization is detected in Holocene samples, and equilibrium is reached in less than 10 Ma. At mid-latitude sites, such as the USA, Britain and New Zealand, with mean annual temperatures greater than 10°C, the reaction rate is substantially lower and equilibrium takes about 2 Ma. If the amino acid relative timescale can be calibrated by other independent dating methods it may be converted to an amino acid geochronological scale.

The method has been widely applied to marine bivalves and gastropods for correlation and geochronological purposes in the USA (Kennedy *et al.* 1982, Wehmiller & Belknap 1982), Europe (Miller & Mangerud 1985), the Mediterranean (Hearty e*t al.* 1986), New Zealand (Bowen *et al.* 1998) and Britain (Bowen *et al.* 1985; Bowen & Sykes 1988). It has also been applied to terrestrial bivalves and gastropods in Britain (Bowen *et al.* 1989), the USA (Oches *et al.* 1996) and Europe (Oches & McCoy 1995).

Bowen *et al.* (1989) converted their British terrestrial amino acid scale using a variety of dating methods and then correlated it with oxygen isotope stratigraphy. Thus individual stratigraphical units could be correlated not only throughout Britain but with the global oxygen isotopic stratigraphical standard. This model (Bowen *et al.* 1989) was subsequently tested and found robust:

in the Avon Valley (Maddy *et al.* 1992), Severn Valley (Maddy *et al.* 1996), Thames Valley (Bowen *et al.* 1996; Bridgland 1996), and Ouse Valley (Green *et al.* 1997), as well as at other locations (Keen *et al.* 1996).

Type-site	D-alle/L-Ile	Correlation ($\delta^{18}O$)	Age (ka)
Halling	0.036 ± 0.01 (3)	2	-12.25
Upton Warren	0.07 ± 0.01 (3)	4	-57
Cassington	0.08 ± 0.01 (6)	5a	74-83
Trafalgar Square	0.1 ± 0.01 (11)	5e	114-127
Strensham	0.17 ± 0.01 (29)	7	186-242
Hoxne	0.26 ± 0.02 (14)	9	312-334
Swanscombe	0.3 ± 0.017 (34)	11	364-427
West Runton	0.35 ± 0.01 (9)	13	474-528
Waverley Wood	0.38 ± 0.026 (15)	15	568-621
cf. Boxgrove	0.29 ± 0.025 (27)	11	346-427

Table 16.1. Up-dated and revised amino acid geochronological model (Bowen *et al.* in press). Geochronology of oxygen isotope stratigraphy from Basinot *et al.*(1994).

The original model (Bowen *et al.* 1989) has been modified by the inclusion of additional data for Waverley Wood and Swanscombe; new data on samples with a more precise provenance at Hoxne; and substitution of Strensham (de Rouffignac *et al.* 1995) for Stanton Harcourt, and Trafalgar Square (Bridgland 1994) for Bobbitshole because of their superior stratigraphical relationships (Table 16.1). The Cassington site at which the D-aIle/L-Ile ratios are calibrated by OSL dating (Maddy *et al.* 1998) is correlated with oxygen isotope sub-stage 5a. Thus Upton Warren, previously correlated with sub-stage 5a (Bowen *et al.* 1989) is, on the basis of epimerisation kinetics, dated as *ca.* 57 ka (Bowen *et al.* in press). Further calibration is available from OSL dating at West Runton and, through correlation, with Chlorine-36 rock exposure dating for Strensham (Bowen *et al.* in press).

Lab. No.	Stratig. unit	Species	D-alle/L-Ile	Age (ka)	δ^{18}O stage
ABER 1188	Unit 5c (72)	*B. tentaculata*	0.31	364-427	11
ABER 1189	Unit 5c (71)	*B. tentaculata*	0.29	364-427	11
UKAL 65	Unit 5c (83)	*V. piscinalis*	0.27±0.01(2)	364-427	11
UKAL 65	Unit 5c (18)	*B. tentaculata*	0.31±0.2 (3)	364-427	11

Table 16.2. Lab numbers refer to the Amino Acid Geochronological Laboratory when it was at Aberystwyth (analyses in 1992) and Cardiff (UKAL - analyses in 1995); n refers to the number of analyses on the same shell. *Bithynia tentaculata and Valvata piscinalis* both epimerize at the same rate

D-alle/L-Ile measurements on samples from Barnham, Unit 5c (Table 16.2) may be correlated with those at Swanscombe and Beeches Pit at West Stow. Independent age estimates based on TL and Uranium-series at West Stow support the correlation on these D-alle/L-Ile ratios with oxygen isotope stage 11 (364-427 ka).

The D-alle/L-Ile ratios from Barnham are distinct from those at Hoxne and represent an earlier event. It has been suggested that the Hoxnian (Hoxnian lake beds) immediately followed the Anglian glaciation, but evidence in the Lower Thames shows that the Swanscombe 'interglacial' event occurred between the Hornchurch Till (Anglian) and Hoxnian interglacial deposits, correlated by D-alle/L-Ile ratios at Purfleet and Belhus Park (Bowen *et al.* 1996; Bridgland 1994).

The correlation proposed between Swanscombe (and, therefore Barnham) and Boxgrove in Sussex (Bowen & Sykes 1994) is controversial (Roberts *et al.* 1994). Workers at Boxgrove prefer correlation with oxygen isotope stage 13 ('Cromerian'), rather than stage 11, on the basis of microtine rodent fossil correlation with Europe (Roberts *et al.* 1994). But the ongoing debate about how the Cromerian of West Runton, Norfolk, should be correlated with the Cromerian 'complex' of the Netherlands, that contains four 'Cromerian' interglacials (Turner 1996), illustrates some of the uncertainties. The principal problem arises because the microtine rodent biochronology is not tied, anywhere, to an independent geochronological scale.

17. THERMOLUMINESCENCE DATING OF BURNT FLINT

Nick Debenham

The thermoluminescence (TL) method has been used to date the burning of five pieces of natural flint from East Farm Pit, Barnham. The flints derived from three locations in Area I, Area III and Test Pit 34 are labelled as follows:

TL Ref	Site Ref	Location
BEF11	BEF92 24	Area I, top of black clay
BEF12	BEF92 26	Area I, top of black clay
BEF13	BEF92 51	Area I, 15cm below black clay in yellow silty sand
BEF21	BEF93 A4 FL31	Area III faunal area, black clay
BEF22	267	Test Pit 34, black clay

The three flints from Area I are from the black clay and the upper part of the yellow silty sand (see Chapter 4, Fig. 4.6). The main *in situ* artefact-bearing horizons come from immediately below these units, from the base of the yellow silty sand, and on and within the cobble layer (see Chapter 19). The flints from Area III and Test Pit 34 also come from the black clay, which in Area III is at the top of the faunal sequence (see Chapter 4).

A general description of the TL method of dating is given by Aitken (1985). As is common with most archaeological flint, a major part of the radiation dose received by these samples was carried by gamma rays from the surrounding sediments. The intensity of the gamma radiation was measured on site by means of a portable spectrometer. In Area I, the measurements showed that the dose rate was uniform in the horizontal plane, but that significant variations occurred in the vertical direction. The cause of this variation appeared to be the cobble layer which had relatively low natural radioactivity, and therefore reduced the gamma intensity in its vicinity. The gamma dose rates experienced by the flint samples, BEF11-13, were estimated by interpolating the trend of the data measured at different heights above the cobble layer to the sample locations. Imprecision in relating the vertical positions of the gamma measurements to those of the flints inevitably led to uncertainties in the gamma dose rate assessments. For sample BEF13, which lay only 20cm above the cobble layer, this uncertainty amounted to ±10%, and was the dominant source of error in its TL date.

For the other two flints, BEF21 and 22, the local stratigraphies were much more uniform. The environmental gamma dose rate of BEF21 was measured within a surviving section of the layer in which the flint was found. Because clay around the find location had been removed by quarrying, the measured section was at a distance of approximately 3m from the flint. However, it is safe to assume horizontal uniformity of the original gamma dose rates across this part of the site. The flint, BEF22, was found at the bottom of Test Pit 34. Its environmental dose rate was assessed by direct measurement close to the find position.

In the laboratory, the flints were prepared for TL measurement by first cutting away the outer 2-3mm. This removed material that had been exposed to light and to short-ranged radiations (alpha and beta) originating in the soil. The remaining interior part of the flint was then crushed and sieved to select grains of approximately 100µm size. Following treatment with dilute hydrochloric acid, and washing in distilled water, methanol and acetone, these grains were deposited onto lightly oiled stainless steel discs. Half of the sample discs were left unirradiated, and the rest were given differing amounts of beta dose in order to increase their TL responses. The unirradiated discs yielded measurements of the natural TL intensity, while a comparison of this intensity with those from the irradiated discs formed the basis of the archaeological dose assessment. Collectively, these data are referred to as first glow measurements. Despite the old age of the flints, the natural TL intensity was not close to the saturation level. In fact, the added beta doses increased the TL to more than three times the natural intensity without saturating the response. Nevertheless, the growth of the first glow TL versus dose showed a departure from linearity which was clearly due to the onset of saturation.

The radiation dose received by the flint during its burial is called its palaeodose, and was determined by extrapolating the first glow growth curve with a non-linear curve. The form of the curve used to perform the extrapolation was obtained from the second glow growth curve; i.e. the curve of TL growth versus radiation dose in discs which had previously had their natural TL removed by the first heating. The second glow growth curve was measured over a range of doses that approximately matched the effective dose range of the first glow data. The second glow measurements were first fitted with a saturating exponential curve. The shape of this curve was then fitted to the first glow data by translating it along the dose axis and adjusting its scale on the intensity axis. The off-set of the dose axis translation corresponds to

Sample Ref.	Site Ref.	Palaeo-Dose (Gy)	Alpha dose rate (GY/ka)	Beta dose rate (Gy/ka)	Env. dose rate (Gy/ka)	TL Age (ka)
BEF11	Area I; BEF92 24	372±18	0.135	0.074	1.030	300±32
BEF12	Area I; BEF92 26	355±15	0.106	0.079	1.030	292±31
BEF13	Area I; BEF92 51	273±14	0.071	0.060	0.810	290±39
BEF21	Area III; A4 FL31	353±12	0.098	0.055	1.004	305±28
BEF22	Test Pit 34; (267)	324±14	0.109	0.060	1.060	264±25

Table 17.1. Palaeodoses, dose rates and TL dates from the burnt flints at Barnham. Uncertainties in alpha dose rates range from ±0.015 to ±0.028 Gy/ka; for beta dose rates, from ±0.025 to ±0.036 Gy/ka; environmental dose rate uncertainties are approximately ±0.086 Gy/ka.

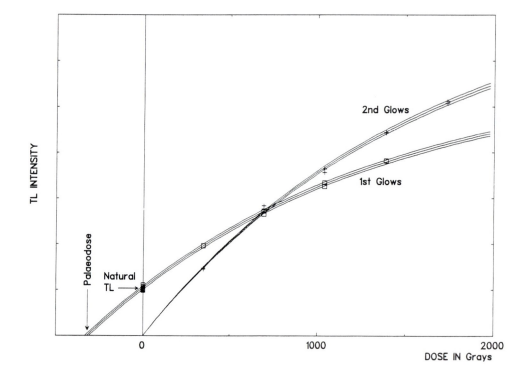

Fig. 17.1. TL growth curves fitted to first glow data (squares) and second glow data (crosses measured from aliquots of the flint sample, BEF22. The palaeodose is determined by extrapolating the first glow data by means of a non-linear curve. The form of this curve is obtained by fitting a saturating exponential curve to the second glow data, which show the growth of TL versus dose in previously heated aliquots. The vertical scale of the extrapolation curve has been adjusted to allow for the change of TL sensitivity that has occurred during the first heating (illustration: Nick Debenham).

the palaeodose of the flint, while the scale adjustment allows for any alteration of the sample's sensitivity to TL due to the first heating. In all cases, the second glow growth curve gave a good description of the form of the first glow data. Figure 17.1 illustrates the method of palaeodose measurement.

Further TL measurements were carried out on the grains of 2-10μm size in order to determine the efficiency of alpha irradiation in producing TL. The alpha and beta radiation received by the samples originated entirely within the flints themselves. The relatively low internal radioactivity of the flints meant that, at most, 16% of the natural TL was due to these short-ranged radiation components. The internal dose rates were assessed by means of alpha counting and potassium analyses of the flints.

Table 17.1 presents the measured palaeodoses and dose rates, together with the TL dates for the burning of the five flints. The date error limits, which result largely from environmental dose rate uncertainties, express the overall random and systematic age uncertainties at the 68% confidence level. Within these uncertainties, there are no significant differences between the five dates. It should be noted that the TL date determinations of samples BEF11, 12 and 13 share environmental dose rate data, and are therefore not fully independent measurements. Allowing for this fact, a weighted mean date of 295 ± 27 ka BP is calculated for the three flints from Area I. This averaged date for Area I and the measured dates of BEF21 and BEF22 are largely independent of each other. From these three date measurements, a weighted mean age of 286 ± 18 ka BP is obtained as the best estimate for the burning of the flints.

18. OPTICALLY-STIMULATED LUMINESCENCE AND ESR DATING AT BARNHAM: PRELIMINARY RESULTS

E. J. Rhodes

INTRODUCTION

Eight sediment samples were collected from the Palaeolithic site of Barnham in order i) to assess the feasibility of luminescence dating of Middle Pleistocene fluvial sediments, and ii) to provide chronological constraints for the site. Subsequently a fragment of elephant tooth from Area III was also submitted for ESR dating. These samples form part of an ongoing research program at Royal Holloway College (University of London), attempting to develop useful chronological tools for the British archaeological and Quaternary communities, particularly beyond the range of radiocarbon dating.

Sediment samples were collected from a range of sedimentary depositional environments, including medium/coarse sands and gravels (probably glaciofluvial in origin), medium/fine laminated fluvial sands, and fluvial and lacustrine silts. A range of environmental radiation measurements was made at different locations around the site, with a Harwell portable gamma spectrometer.

PRELIMINARY LUMINESCENCE MEASUREMENTS

Two sand-rich sediment samples were prepared for assessment of their luminescence characteristics. These were from sands within gravels stratigraphically beneath Area I (lab. code 283, field code sample B), and from sands within Area IV(3) (lab. code 285, field code sample D).

For both samples, a normal luminescence quartz separation procedure was adopted. However, IRSL measurements on the separated sample 283 displayed high count rates, associated with a significant feldspar content (Rhodes & Pownall 1994). The observation of feldspar grains not being removed fully from certain samples following extended (40 mins or 1 hour) treatment in 40% HF (hydrofluoric acid) has now been made regularly within the laboratory. This phenomenon, presumably associated with the presence of highly resistant feldspar phases, is particularly prevalent for glaciofluvial sediment samples, although virtually never observed for aeolian samples. (Rhodes & Bailey 1997). This sample was reprocessed, but still retained high IRSL signals, possibly associated with a high concentration of feldspar inclusions within the quartz grains (Huntley et al. 1993).

In contrast, sample 285 displayed negligible IRSL signals after separation, associated with good quartz separation. OSL measurements, using blue/green stimulation wavelengths from a filtered halogen lamp (420-560 nm) were made, and a naturally-normalized additive growth curve constructed. It was expected that this plot would display either no increase in luminescence with added dose (saturated behaviour, characteristic of old samples beyond the maximum age range of luminescence dating), or an increasing signal in the form of a single saturating exponential function, allowing extrapolation to zero intensity and the estimation of an equivalent dose (D_E) value, and the calculation of an age estimate. In the former case, it is not possible to derive an additive dose age estimation, although it may be possible to estimate a minimum age from the regenerated signal. In the latter case, an age estimation is made by dividing the extrapolated D_E value by the measured dose rate.

However, the form of growth displayed by this sample was interesting and somewhat bizarre (Fig. 18.1). Although associated with relatively low scatter between aliquots, the growth curve displayed a systematic series of steps, or alternate peaks and troughs. Such behaviour has not previously been widely observed in OSL studies, besides lower magnitude 'kinks' apparent in the growth curves of some samples (e.g. Spooner & Questiaux 1989), although such effects have been recorded in TL studies. It is likely that this effect results from some form of sensitivity change or competition between trapping sites (e.g. dose quenching, Huntley et al. 1996), possibly involving diffusion effects, either during the laboratory (and/or natural) dosing stage, or during luminescence measurement, or possibly during both (Bailey et al. 1997). Understanding and mitigating the effects of such phenomena will play a major role in the development of luminescence dating techniques extending to several hundred thousand years in the future.

While this sample represents an extremely valuable tool in the development of such long range archaeological and Quaternary dating techniques, it is unfortunately not possible at present to derive a luminescence age for it

Sub-sample	t μm	U EN ppm	U DE ppm	D sed μGya⁻¹	D_E Gy	EU Age ka	LU Age ka
A1	3650	1.51	41.6	880 ± 55	429 ± 14	205 ± 14	293 ± 18
A2	2400	0.41	41.6	880 ± 55	380 ± 8	194 ± 15	271 ± 18

Table 18.1. Sub-sample thickness (t), U concentration in enamel (EN) and dentine (DE), external dose rate (D sed), equivalent dose (D_E), Early U uptake model age (EU) and linear U uptake model age.

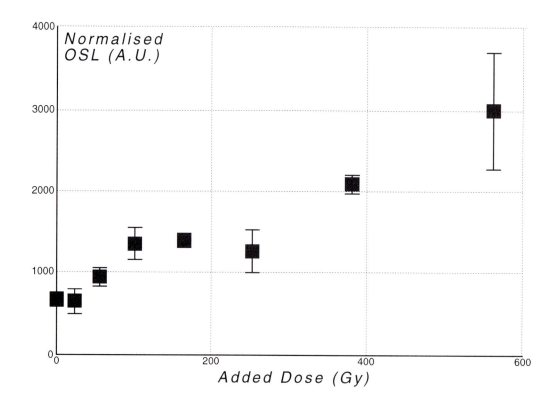

Fig. 18.1. 'Stepped growth curve observed for the naturally normalised total integral OSL for sample 285 from Barnham, UK. The form of growth is clearly not characterised by a single saturating exponential curve.

ESR DATING

The fragment of elephant tooth, from Area III (BEF 93, D4 F99), was rather small for conventional ESR dating (Grün 1989). Two ESR enamel subsamples were separated from the tooth, powdered, and each was weighed into 10 identical aliquots of approximately 12 and 20mg respectively. These were given a range of laboratory gamma doses up to a maximum of 6.3 kGy, and the ESR signal at g=2.00018 measured for each, using an overmodulation technique (Rhodes & Grün 1991). Owing to the small size of each aliquot, a multiple scan data collection procedure was adopted, using a Bruker 106 ESR spectrometer. The signals were filtered using a reverse fourier transform procedure, and fitted with a single saturating exponential function, weighting inversely proportional to the square of intensity (Grün & Rhodes 1992). Determination of the uranium content for both enamel and dentine was performed using ICP-MS on small samples (<100mg). By combining the novel approach of reverse fourier filtering, multiple scanning of powder samples and ICP-MS analysis, it has been possible to determine age estimates for both subsamples with no loss of precision, in comparison to conventional ESR techniques, despite the very small aliquot size.The results shown in Table 18.1 include both early uptake and linear uptake models for the U content. When significant concentrations of uranium are present within the enamel and dentine, the manner in which the uranium content was acquired by the tooth becomes significant. The 'true' sample age is expected to lie between the dates calculated for the two extreme uptake models. In the present case, this would suggest a date between approximately 200 and 300ka. In terms of correlation with warm oxygen isotope stages, this would suggest that the most likely age would be either oxygen isotope stage 7 or 9.

However, it has recently been observed for several samples, that teeth with significant concentrations of uranium appear to provide age underestimations (Zhou *et al.* 1997). Tentative interpretation of this effect suggests that it might be due to incorrect assumptions concerning the distribution of uranium within the enamel and dentine, and local saturation effects. In this case, absolute maximum age estimates can be made by assuming a zero U concentration (recent U uptake). In the present case this gives maximum dates of 417 ± 17 and 432 ± 29 ka for samples A1 and A2 respectively. It should be stressed that this is an extremely unlikely scenario, and that the "true" ages are likely to be somewhat younger.

It is possible that the present uncertainty in sample age might be resolved by combined ESR/TIMS U-series dating (McDermott *et al.* 1993). However, this technique still relies on correct assumptions in the calculation of the ESR age component (Zhou *et al.* 1997). Detailed fission track mapping, SEM analysis, laser ablation ICP-MS or microprobe analysis combined with suitable modelling might resolve the issue of uranium distribution and local saturation, and further research on this sample is underway at present.

SUMMARY

At present the luminescence measurements have not been able to estimate the age of the site, owing to the irregular luminescence characteristics of the material measured.

The ESR tooth enamel measurements suggest a date between *ca.* 200 and 300ka. However, as the U concentration in this tooth is relatively high, some caution needs to be exercised in this interpretation. A maximum age estimate, provided by a recent uptake model for U, places a limit at around 430ka.

19. THE TAPHONOMY OF THE FLINT ASSEMBLAGES

Nick Ashton

INTRODUCTION

The study of artefact taphonomy has become an increasingly important aspect of lithic analysis, particularly for the earlier periods. Studies by Isaac (1967), Shackley (1974), Rick (1976), Schick (1986), Schiffer (1983), Chase *et al.* (1994) and Dibble (1995b), to cite but a few, have shown the importance of understanding the effects that the natural environment has on the type of archaeological signatures recovered. These natural processes include the effects of various types of fluvial environment (from flood plain to gravel bar and braided channel) and of solifluction on the movement and composition of lithic artefact assemblages. The understanding of these processes forms an essential pre-cursor to the interpretation of any human behaviour at a site. This chapter studies the effects of these processes on the artefact assemblages at Barnham.

The taphonomy of the artefact assemblages can be studied from six angles. The interpretation of the sediments and depositional environments provide a key to the types of movement that might have affected the assemblages, while study of the condition, orientation, spatial distribution, refitting, technology and size distributions of the artefacts gives direct evidence of the degree of disturbance in these environments. It was hoped that by study of the taphonomy certain key questions could be answered concerning the formation of the artefact assemblages.

(1) What post-depositional processes, if any, have the various artefact assemblages undergone? In particular, are the fresh artefacts from the yellow silty sand in Area I and from the surface of the grey/brown stony clay in Area V *in situ*, or if not by what processes have they been moved?

(2) If artefact assemblages have moved, from where do they derive? For example, do the fresh artefacts from the yellow silty sand in Area I originate from the cobble layer?

(3) If they have moved, what effect has this had on the composition of the assemblages? More specifically are the assemblages fully representative of complete knapping sequences?

(4) Can separate groups of artefacts be distinguished on the basis of their condition, orientation, or spatial distribution? In particular, can the biface manufacturing debitage be distinguished from the hard hammer debitage in Area IV(4)?

Depositional environments

Most of the artefact bearing deposits at Barnham were laid down under fluvial conditions. The exceptions are the upper part of the Area I (gravel section) which is interpreted as a solifluction deposit (see Chapter 4), and the top of the grey silt and clay in Area III which was probably laid down under still water or near-still water conditions. Within these sediments it should also be realised that hiati in deposition might exist with the formation of temporary landsurfaces. These too will have an effect on artefact distribution and condition. These depositional envirnments are discussed below.

Fluvial environments. The effect of fluvial environments on stone tool assemblages has been extensively studied by Schick (1986) through experimentation and on-site observation. Although, much of this work was specifically geared towards East African palaeoenvironments, many of the results and conclusions are relevant to European situations. This work is important for showing the complexity of fluvial contexts and in acting as a cautionary tale for the over-interpretation of artefact assemblages.

There are clearly many factors that influence the degree and type of movement of flaked stone artefacts under fluvial conditions. These would include velocity of water flow, degree of slope, and size of the artefact, but also other factors that might be less obvious. The shape of the artefacts is also of importance. Flakes, for example, are often less prone to movement when resting on the sediment because of their lenticular shape, whereas cores, despite being heavier, will move under slower water velocities. Natural obstacles will also halt the movement of artefacts. Equally, where one object has come to rest, this may act as an impediment to other artefacts and natural clusters can form. The type of sediment can also play a role, so that softer sediments are more likely to bury artefacts, particularly flakes, in contrast to more consolidated sediments.

The type of movement is also dependant on these factors. Sliding occurs more often to flatter objects, under slower water flows, while rolling is more likely to happen to more globular objects, and under conditions of faster water flow. Whether objects slide or roll will also affect their orientation. The long axes of objects that slide are likely to be parallel to the direction of flow, whereas those that roll are usually perpendicular to the flow. However, the latter once deposited, or immediately prior to deposition, will often be nudged into a parallel direction. When objects come to rest, particularly on softer sediments, the sediment at the upstream end is sometimes washed away to form a hollow into which the artefact becomes embedded, at an angle against the flow. This type of dip is termed imbrication.

It is well recognised that fluvial movement will also cause microscopic and macroscopic damage to artefacts, particularly in coarser sediments. Gravel will cause abrasion and rounding of artefact edges, together with scratching of their surfaces (Harding *et al.* 1987).

Fluvial movement will also affect the distribution of artefacts. Not only will distinct knapping scatters usually become more dispersed, but size sorting will affect the type of dispersal, with smaller artefacts tending to travel further. This winnowing effect can produce natural associations of smaller artefacts, or leave as a lag the larger objects.

Although the importance of some of these factors is difficult to assess at a site, fluvial movement will still produce distinct patterns. These patterns include the condition of the artefacts, their orientation, and evidence of redistribution and size sorting. This evidence is discussed below.

Still-water. In still-water or near still-water conditions minimal movement or re-orientation of artefacts would be expected. Equally, there should be minimum damage to artefact edges or surfaces.

Solifluction. Movement in solifluction is an equally complex subject, dependant on variables such as slope, type of substrate, climate, ground water and many others (Harris 1987; Catt 1988). With only 23 artefacts from the brown diamicton (Area I, gravel section) there has been no study of orientation, artefact size or distribution, but simply of condition. In particular, scratching of a flint surface is often attributed to movement in solifluction (Paterson 1937; Stapert 1976, 1979).

Depositional hiati. Although hiati in sediment deposition may be difficult to recognise in the field, they may play a significant part in artefact distribution and condition. In a subaerial context artefacts are prone to slope movement, or disturbance through trampling by large mammals. The latter process, although not limited to landsurfaces, is likely to have a greater effect where sedimentation is slow, particularly around the edges of a water body. The effect of trampling has been

largely studied on bone (Andrews 1990), but artefacts are subject to the same processes. It may cause edge damage and breakage and, in softer sediments, vertical dipping and displacement.

THE EXCAVATED ASSEMBLAGES

The site was excavated in seven main areas producing 12 artefact assemblages, some of which come from very similar contexts. These areas and the assemblages are summarised below. The exact quantities from each area and context are given in Table 19.1.

Area I

Cobble layer (Unit 4). 502 cores, flakes and flake tools from the surface to a maximum depth of 20cm.

Yellow silty sand (Unit 5e). 657 cores, flakes and flake tools from the basal 20cm.

Black clay (Unit 6). One biface and two flakes from the base.

Brown silt and clay ('brickearth') (Unit 7). One biface thinning flake and one flake from just above the black clay.

Area I (gravel section)

Brown diamicton (Unit 3). 24 cores, flakes and flake tools from the top 30cm.

Area II

Yellow silty sand (Unit 5e). 43 cores, flakes and flake tools from the surface to a maximum depth of 15cm.

Brown silt and clay ('brickearth') (Unit 7). 5 flakes from the basal 1m.

Area III

Grey silt and clay (Unit 5c). 16 cores, flakes and flake tools from the top 65cm.

West Section and Slit Trench. 30 cores, flakes and flake tools found through section cutting in the base of the brown silt and clay and top of grey/brown stony clay.

Area IV(4)

Cobble layer (Unit 4). 623 cores, flakes, flake tools, biface manufacturing flakes with one biface from the surface and to a maximum depth of 20cm.

Area IV(5)

Cobble layer (Unit 4). 61 cores and flakes from the surface to a maximum depth of 20cm.

Area V

Grey/brown stony clay (Unit 5d). 52 flakes, with one biface manufacturing flake and one flake tool, from the top 30cm.

Surface of grey/brown stony clay. 135 cores, flakes and biface manufacturing flakes.

Area Context Spit	I y.s.sand	I cobble	IGS solif	II y.s.sand	III g.silt	IV(4) cobble surf,1,2	IV(4) cobble 3,4	IV(5) cobble	V st.clay surface	V stclay
Cores	27	58	1	2	3	20	11	7	4	-
Hard hammer flakes	600	428	22	39	12	168	148	54	80	52
Flake tools	30	16	1	1	1	2	5	-	-	1
Soft hammer flakes	-	-	-	-		166	102	-	51	1
Chips	939	141	3	5	93	43	51	15	36	16
Bifaces	-	-	-	-	-	-	1	-	-	-
Biface roughouts	-	-	-	-	-	1	-	-	-	-
Total	1596	643	27	47	109	400	318	76	171	70

Table 19.1. Quantities of artefact types from the principle contexts in Areas I, II, III, IV(4) and V. y.s.sand = yellow silty sand; cobble = cobble layer; surf,1,2 = surface and spits 1 + 2; 3,4 = spits 3 + 4; solif = solifluction; IGS = Area I (gravel section); g.silt = grey silt and clay; st.clay = grey/brown stony clay.

Area Context Spit	I y.s.sand	I cobble	IGS solif	III g.silt	IV(4) cobble surf,1,2	IV(4) cobble 3,4	V st.clay surface	V st.clay
ROLLING								
1	17.0	5.6	-	75.0	3.9	6.8	5.9	-
2	41.2	18.6	37.5	25.0	58.7	51.5	48.1	11.1
3	16.6	25.7	29.2	-	28.8	26.7	33.3	22.2
4	25.1	50.1	33.3	-	8.7	15.0	12.6	66.7
SCRATCHING								
N	78.8	52.7	37.5	100	81.0	63.9	63.0	38.9
Y	21.2	47.3	62.5	-	19.0	36.1	37.0	61.1
PATINATION								
0	24.0	17.0	33.3	87.5	8.9	25.6	20.7	3.7
1	42.9	26.3	50.0	12.5	26.3	36.1	40.7	18.5
2	33.0	49.7	16.7	-	64.8	38.3	38.5	77.8
STAINING								
0	6.8	3.4	8.3	100	1.7	3.4	7.4	1.9
1	28.0	26.3	20.8	-	30.4	28.9	37.8	29.6
2	65.1	70.3	70.8	-	67.9	67.7	54.8	68.6
SURFACE								
1	3.2	7.4	12.5	-	5.0	24.1	9.6	5.6
2	96.5	92.4	87.5	100	95.0	75.9	90.4	94.4
3	0.3	0.2	-	-	-	-		
n	657	502	24	16	357	267	135	54

Table 19.2. Rolling, scratching, patination, staining and surface sheen by area and context. y.s.sand = yellow silty sand; cobble = cobble layer; surf,1,2 = surface and spits 1 + 2; 3,4 = spits 3 + 4; solif = solifluction; IGS = Area I (gravel section); g.silt = grey silt and clay; st.sand = grey/brown stony clay.

Several of these assemblages are too small to justify statistical comparison, but in most cases they appear to reflect the larger assemblages from similar contexts. On this basis the assemblages from the 'brickearth' and the black clay in Area I, from Area II and from Area IV(5) are not included in the following discussion. The assemblages from Area I (gravel section) and from Area III are included, however, because they derive from different contexts to the remaining assemblages and are also in different condition. The assemblage in Area I includes the artefacts excavated by Wymer in 1979 (Wymer 1985; see Chapter 2).

CONDITION

Methods

The condition of the artefacts from the different contexts and areas is given in Table 19.2. This includes abrasion, scratching, patination, staining and surface sheen.

The degree of rolling and abrasion on artefacts was noted on a scale of 1 to 4, 1 being very fresh with no traces of abrasion, and 4 being pieces with considerable edge damage and rounding of the ridges on the dorsal face. Macroscopic scratching was noted seperately as being present or absent.

The surface colouration of flint is altered by both patination and staining. The term patination has been used by different authors in different ways, and has been claimed by Shepherd (1972) to be confused with 'cortication'. He argues that the latter process involves the release of water and silica from the surface down through the flint, opening up a porous surface. Conversely, patination (the pale-creamy colouration) on a flint surface, is formed by the infilling of these pores by silica from soil water. This may account for the occurrence of patination on one side of a flint, and its absence on the opposite side (Sturge 1911; Stapert 1976), with protection of the underside from percolating ground water. However, Sturge attributed this to the subaerial exposure of flint. The latter would explain the frequently observed, and apparently rapid, patination of a flint surface on exposure to daylight.

The degree of patination is often difficult to assess because of the frequent overprinting by surface staining. Staining is thought to be caused generally by iron-rich or sometimes manganese-rich water, which creates an orange-brown, occasionally black, surface colouration to flint (Stapert 1976). Patination and staining were each noted on a scale of 0 to 2, 0 being unpatinated and unstained, 2 being considerably patinated and stained.

The artefacts were also recorded as having a matt, silk or gloss surface sheen. At many sites the more rolled artefacts have often aquired a surface gloss. The vast majority of artefacts at Barnham simply had a silk surface sheen, with little variation. This is not commented on further.

Results

Area I and Area IV(4) and Area I (gravel section).

In Areas I and IV(4) the abrasion and rolling of the artefacts varies considerably both in the yellow silty sand and in the cobble layer (Table 19.2) with both stratigraphic units containing rolled and fresh material. Many of the more abraded artefacts are also scratched. Most of the artefacts are typically patinated and stained, but to varying degrees. Unlike Area I, Area IV(4) was excavated in spits (surface and 1 to 4) each about 5cm in depth. The higher spits and lower spits, however, contained both fresh and rolled material, supporting the view that the spits were an arbitary division of the gravel. Artefacts from the Area I (gravel section) also vary in condition, and although the numbers are low, a few comments can be made. They are generally less rolled than those in the cobble layer, but are also more scratched. Their patination and staining is similar to the artefacts from the other units.

The strong correlation between edge abrasion and scratching (Fig. 19.1) suggests that the rolled and abraded artefacts and those that are scratched have undergone similar processes. The relatively higher incidence of scratching on artefacts from the brown diamicton (Area I gravel section, see Table 19.2), but

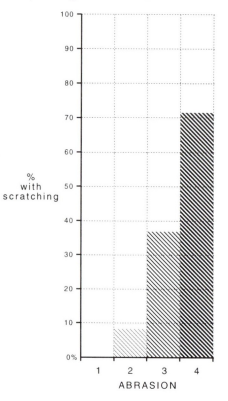

Fig. 19.1. Percentage of flakes with scratching by abrasion types 1-4 (see Appendix VI).

the lower degree of edge abrasion and rolling, suggests that at least one cause of scratching was movement in solifluction, whereas the rolling and edge abrasion was principally caused by movement in the cobble layer under fluvial conditions.

This together with the admixture of fresh and rolled artefacts suggests the following hypothesis. The rolled and scratched artefacts in the cobble layer were in part derived from the underlying brown diamicton, and perhaps from other adjacent areas. They underwent considerable further movement in the cobble layer, and during the later stages of this process became progressively intermixed with more recently knapped artefacts from the surface of the cobble layer. An element of both the fresher and more rolled artefacts was then incorporated into the overlying yellow silty sand through further fluvial reworking.

Although distinctions have been made between artefacts that are fresh and those that are rolled and scratched, there is no clear grouping into seperate assemblages, rather there is a continuum of variation in the degree of rolling, abrasion and scratching. This distinction acts, however, as a convenient, if arbitary, division of material that was produced over slightly different lengths of time. As a further check on this division, the fresh and rolled groups from each context and area were compared in terms of patination and

staining. Figures 19.2 and 19.3 indicate that there is little variation between the groups, all artefacts being moderately stained and patinated. This suggests that patination and staining in Areas I and IV(4) cannot be used to divide the material further into temporally discrete assemblages.

Finally, there are slight differences between Areas I and IV(4). The Area I material tends to have greater proportions of both fresher and of more rolled material. This probably reflects a greater quantity of material being derived from the brown diamicton beneath, but also the more rapid burial of later knapped material by the overlying yellow silty sand. This may also explain the increase in refitting in Area I (see refitting below). In addition, the Area IV(4) artefacts have a characteristic mottled staining, which appears to overlie the patination, and they also tend to have a slightly more matt surface sheen. The variation in surface condition is likely to be due to slight differences in very localised ground water conditions, and therefore of minor significance (see also Chapter 22). One other distinction that can be made is that Area IV(4) contains biface manufacturing debitage. This is virtually all in fresh condition, whereas the core and flake working varies considerably. The patination and staining is very similar for all groups in Area IV(4) (Fig. 19.3).

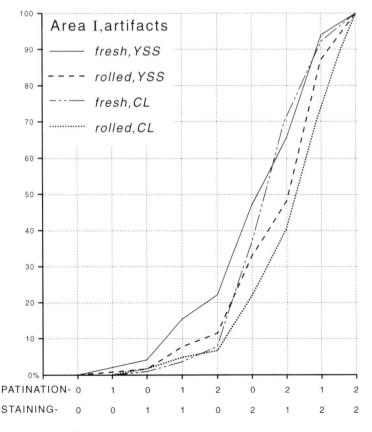

Fig. 19.2. Cumulative frequency graph showing the percentage of fresh and rolled flakes from the yellow silty sand and the cobble layer in Area I by patination and staining type (0-2). Also see Appendix VI.

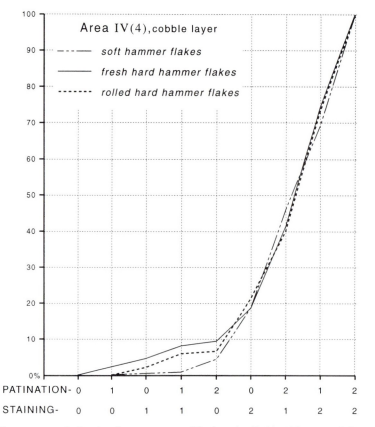

Fig. 19.3. Cumulative frequency graph showing the percentage of fresh and rolled hard hammer flakes, and soft hammer flakes from the cobble layer in Area IV(4) by patination and staining type (0-2). Also see Appendix VI.

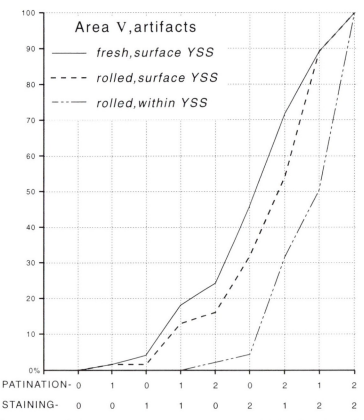

Fig. 19.4. Cumulative frequency graph showing the percentage of fresh and rolled flakes from the surface of the grey/brown stony sand and from within the grey/brown stony sand in Area V by patination and staining type (0-2). Also see Appendix VI.

Area III. The condition of the larger artefacts (> 20mm) from Area III is completely different to others from the site. Without exception they are very fresh, unpatinated and unstained. They appear to have undergone very little movement, and were probably quickly buried resulting in little patination. The smaller chips and spalls from this area are slightly more rolled, although unstained and only slightly patinated. They have probably been washed in with the sediment, and some may well have been caused by natural clast collision.

Area V. In Area V the artefacts both from the surface and from within the grey/brown stony clay form two distinct groups, based on condition. These are a fresh group with little abrasion and scratching, and a rolled group with considerable abrasion and scratching. Unlike Area I and IV(4) there is no continuum of variation between the two groups. The biface manufacturing debitage was, virtually without exception, in a fresh condition, whereas the core and flake working was both fresh and rolled. Like Areas I and IV(4) all the artefacts are moderately patinated and stained. This is the case for both the fresh and the rolled artefacts from both within and on the grey/brown stony clay although those from the latter tend to be slightly more affected by both processes.

ORIENTATION

Methods

The orientation of all artefacts with a maximum dimension greater than 4cm was recorded in the field by logging the location of each end of the long axis resulting in a direction of dip of the longest axis (horizontal orientation in a downslope direction) and degree of dip (vertical orientation). Although measurements were made on all these artefacts, on many it was difficult to determine the long axis, and subsequent analysis has shown that only 27% have a marked elongation (length/width > 1.5). To use only these artefacts would reduce all samples to less than 50 measurements, so reluctantly all measurements have been used, but with some reservations as to their value.

The measurements were plotted out on rose diagrams to summarise the trends in the data. It was principally the artefacts in fresh condition that were of interest, to assess whether they were *in situ*, or had been moved fluvially. It was initially assumed that if the artefacts were *in situ* there should be a random orientation, whereas movement within a fluvial system would produce a preferred orientation. Unfortunately, it was soon realised that this argument could not be sustained; most of the artefact groups (including the rolled ones where there should have been a preferred orientation) showed little evidence of patterning. This could be explained in several ways, such as other clasts in the cobble layer determining orientations, or the overprinting of several directions of flow, or simply the methodological problems (see comments above). This implies that the absence of a preferred orientation cannot be taken as evidence of a lack of movement.

Despite these problems, the fresh group from Area I did show some patterning. This is discussed below. The assemblage from Area III was not assessed because of insufficient numbers. Again the numbers from Area V were too small, but some observations were noted during excavation. These are discussed below.

Results

Area I. The pattern from the fresh artefacts in the cobble layer are the clearest, showing a horizontal orientation in two axes (Fig. 19.5a). The orientation towards the east-south-east corresponds with the fall in slope at this point (Fig. 19.6) and the possible direction of flow. The second horizontal orientation is at right angles to this, as might be expected from some fluvial systems. The interpretation of the dip of the long axis is more complex, with the strongest dip being towards the south-south-west. The implication of this not clear. What is important, however, is that the artefacts have a preferred orientation, implying that despite their freshness, they have been moved.

The fresh artefacts from the yellow silty sand show a more random pattern (Fig. 19.5b). In an attempt to refine the analysis, the group was split into two weight catagories (< 50g and ≥ 50g). It was hoped that the lighter element might show more evidence of movement than the larger element. The patterns are indeed clearer (Figs 19.5c-d). The lighter group appears to have a preferred orientation along three axes. Two of these can be accounted for by orientation with the flow, and at right angles to the flow. Whether the third axis indicates flow in a slightly different direction is not clear. In contrast, the heavier element has a preferred orientation principally along one axis (east-west), in what may be the direction of flow. The lack of orientation at right angles might indicate that flow was sufficient to orientate the artefacts with the flow, but was not strong enough to roll them at right angles. It is likely then that very few of the artefacts are absolutely *in situ*, a conclusion that is consistent with the interpretation that the artefacts in the yellow silty sand derive from the surface of the cobble layer.

Area V. There are only 19 artefacts with a measured orientation from the fresh group on the surface of the grey/brown stony clay, a number insufficient for analysis. The only other information from the orientation and dip that can be used, are observations made during excavation. Here, it was noted that without exception the fresh artefacts rested on and parallel with the undulating surface of the grey/brown stony clay. This might suggest that they are *in situ*. For further discussion see spatial distribution and refitting below.

In conclusion, the orientation data from Area I suggests that none of the artefacts are absolutely *in situ*. Unfortunately, no conclusions can be drawn about the artefacts in Areas III and IV(4), while observation during excavation might suggest that those in Area V are *in situ*.

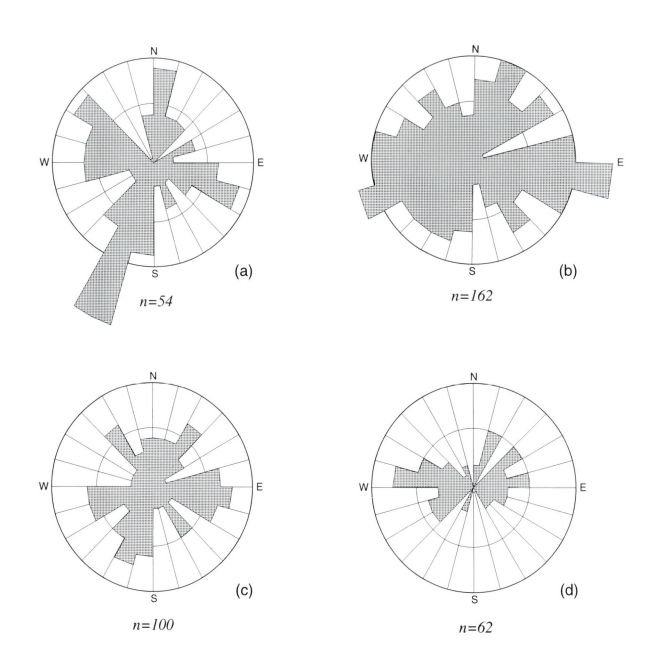

Fig. 19.5. Rose diagrams for the orientation of maximum dips of flakes. a. Fresh artefacts from Area I, cobble layer. b. Fresh artefacts from Area I, yellow silty sand. c. Fresh artefacts from Area I, yellow silty sand < 50g. d. Fresh artefacts from Area I, yellow silty sand ≥ 50g.

SPATIAL DISTRIBUTION AND REFITTING

Methods

Study of the spatial distribution of the artefacts can potentially distinguish between artefacts that are *in situ* and those that have moved post-depositionally. Discrete scatters of artefacts would be expected from *in situ* knapping groups, which can be confirmed by refitting. In situations where there has been some movement of the artefacts, refitting can also show the direction and degree of the disturbance.

A total of 20 person-weeks was spent by several people over three years on the refitting programme, which concentrated on the fresh artefacts from each of the areas. The spatial distribution of the artefacts was ignored, so as not to bias the outcome of the refitting programme. As a result the distribution of the refits should be representative of the movement of the artefacts or of any potential knapping scatters.

Results

Area I. The analysis of the spatial distribution of the artefacts in Area I was limited to the fresh material from the yellow silty sand, as it was this group of material that was more likely to be *in situ*. Generally the distribution shows a broad spread of material, with only one reasonably discrete scatter to the west of the main distribution (Fig. 19.6). Much of this scatter is composed of refitting Group A (Fig. 19.7), and therefore it does suggest that this group of material is *in situ*. The absence of material to the west of this scatter is probably in part due to the thinness of the yellow silty sand, only 5 to 10cm thick here, compared to up to 35cm in the eastern part of the area.

The three major refitting groups are plotted out with the other refits in Figures 19.7-8, and apart from Group A, appear not to be *in situ* and to have moved post-depositionally. The main axis of movement seems to be in a down-slope direction towards the east, which may also be the direction of water flow.

There are also six examples of refitting between the yellow silty sand and the cobble layer, supporting the interpretation (see above) that the fresh artefacts originate principally from the surface of the cobble layer and have become incorporated both into the cobble layer and into the overlying yellow silty sand.

Area III. The 16 artefacts from Area III are thinly scattered horizontally over 7m and vertically over 65cm. The condition of the material, the fine sediment in which they occur, and the absence of other clasts suggests that the artefacts are probably *in situ*, although dispersal through trampling cannot be ruled out. However, the distribution of the material together with the absence of refitting indicates that the artefacts were introduced into the grey silt and clay through human means, already knapped. This is discussed further in Chapter 23.

Area IV(4). As all the artefacts from Area IV(4) were from the cobble layer, they have probably all undergone varying degrees of movement. However, it was thought worthwhile comparing the fresh biface manufacturing debitage with the fresh core and flake working, on the basis that differences in distribution might show the discreteness of the technologically distinct episodes of working. These are shown in Figure 19.9, which indicates that the two distributions are very similar. Because they are fresh in condition, and have probably undergone comparatively little movement, this evidence supports the interpretation that they were knapped at the same time in the same area.

Refitting shows no distinctive pattern, except it further suggests that the artefacts have moved post-depositionally (Fig. 19.10). Six examples of refitting between the different spits also support the interpretation that there has been considerable admixture of material vertically, and that the spits have no stratigraphic significance. The refits are principally of biface manufacturing debitage.

Area V. Although it has been suggested above that the fresh material on the surface of the grey/brown stony clay in Area V might be *in situ*, this is not supported by the spatial distribution or refitting (Fig. 19.11). The lack of distinct knapping scatters, the general similarity in distribution between the hard and soft hammer flakes, and the low quantity of refitting, suggests that either there has been some movement of the artefacts, or that they have been brought into the area already knapped. The one refitting group (Group D) consists of four small hard hammer flakes, removed as a sequence, and possibly knapped from core P1993.3-1.xx (see Chapter 20). The distances between the refits also suggest some limited movement, be it human or otherwise. The problems of the interpretation of this area are discussed further below.

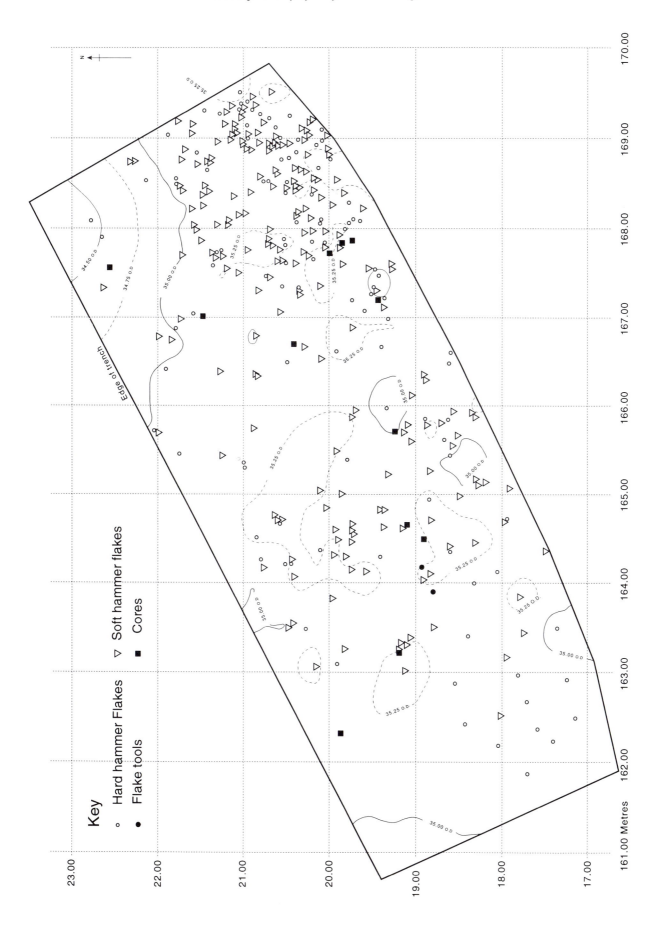

Fig. 19.9. Distribution of artefacts in Area IV(4).

TECHNOLOGICAL COMPARISONS

Methods

Technological comparisons can also be used to support some of the inferences drawn from the various site formation studies. Technological similarities between different stratigraphic units can help infer the origin of some of the groups. This is particularly pertinent to the artefacts from Areas I, IV(4) and V. For the purposes of this study, two main technological measures have been used, namely butt type and dorsal scar pattern (see Chapter 20 and Appendix VI).

Results

Area I. Comparison between the two assemblages from the cobble layer and the yellow silty sand in Area I show that there are few technological differences between them (Table 19.3). The technological similarity is consistent with the interpretation that there has been admixture between the artefacts in the two sediment units.

Area IV(4). It has already been shown that the spits in the cobble layer in Area IV(4) were arbitary divisions. Comparison of the technology shows first that both the higher and lower spits contain biface manufacturing debitage, as well as core and flake working (Table 19.1), and furthermore that more detailed comparisons of the butts and dorsal scar patterns on the hard hammer flakes show distinct similarities. This supports the notion that the assemblage from the cobble layer can be taken as a single unit, with varying artefact conditions.

Area Context Spit	I y.s.sand	I cobble	IV(4) cobble surf,1,2	IV(4) cobble 3,4	V st.clay surface	V st.clay
L.	48 ± 29	57 ± 26	57 ± 26	54 ± 22	45 ± 23	51 ± 22
W.	40 ± 19	48 ± 21	50 ± 21	47 ± 19	37 ± 14	42 ± 15
Th.	15 ± 8	19 ± 11	18 ± 11	17 ± 9	14 ± 7	17 ± 13
Wt.	44 ± 92	83 ± 178	70 ± 95	56 ± 62	31 ± 63	42 ± 41
n	630	444	170	153	80	53
BUTT						
1	73.6	75.9	76.8	67.0	78.8	72.1
2	8.7	4.0	2.0	5.7	9.6	-
3	14.1	18.2	17.2	25.5	5.7	23.3
4	2.1	0.6	4.0	1.9	1.9	4.7
6	1.4	1.2	-	-	3.8	-
n	424	324	99	106	52	43
DORSAL SCAR PATTERN						
1	51.6	48.3	55.9	48.6	44.8	48.9
2	11.2	13.0	7.9	9.7	20.9	6.4
3	0.5	0.9	1.3	0.7	-	2.1
4	0.9	0.2	0.7	0.7	1.5	-
5	14.0	13.3	8.6	10.4	13.4	27.7
6	0.7	0.7	1.3	0.7	3.0	-
7	2.5	1.2	2.0	2.8	1.5	-
8	1.3	3.1	0.7	2.8	1.5	-
10	15.8	18.7	19.7	22.9	13.4	12.8
11	0.4	0.2	0.7	-	-	-
12	1.1	0.2	1.3	0.7	-	2.1
n	556	422	152	144	67	47

Table 19.3. Size, butt types and dorsal scar patterns by area and context. y.s.sand = yellow silty sand; cobble = cobble layer; surf,1.2 = surface and spits 1 + 2; 3,4 = spits 3 + 4; st.clay = grey/brown stony clay.

Area V. There do seem to be some differences between the core and flake working on the surface of the grey/brown stony clay and that within it. Some of these differences may be due to the low artefact numbers. Other variation might also be accounted for by the difference in formation of the two groups. The majority of fresh material occurs on the surface of the grey/brown stony clay, and is probably attributable to specific knapping events, or selected, transported elements, whereas the rolled element, much of which occurs within the grey/brown stony clay is likely to reflect more generalised knapping. This for example might explain the similarity in the butt types between the assemblage from within the grey/brown stony clay and the assemblages from Areas I and IV(4). In terms of the biface manufacturing debitage, virtually all this occurs on the surface of the grey/brown stony clay.

SIZE SORTING

Methods

As a final analysis, the influence of size sorting has been assessed to guage whether the rolled and fresh groups from each area are representative of complete knapping sequences. Complete knapping sequences normally consist of large amounts of smaller debitage with decreasing amounts of the larger elements (Schick 1986). Experiments were conducted using raw material from Barnham to investigate the size distributions of both hard hammer and soft hammer debitage and through comparison with the archaeological assemblages assess the degree of disturbance. For the analysis, debitage smaller than 2cm maximum dimension has been excluded due to the difficulties of distinguishing between smaller knapped chips and those created through clast collision. However, broken flakes have been included. Clearly size distributions are dependant on the amount of breakage. If breakage, however, is due to the knapping process rather than post-depositional effects, then comparison between distributions and with experimental results should not be affected. The similarity in breakage patterns between the rolled and fresh elements (Table 19.4) suggests that most of this is caused during the knapping, and not

through movement in a fluvial environment. Although the level of breakage in the experimental assemblage is quite high it is still within the range shown by the archaeological assemblages. For this study, therefore, all artefacts, including broken ones, have been included. Other details of the experiments are fully described in Chapter 21.

Results

Core and flake experiments. The technological analyses in Chapter 20 show that the experimental assemblage effectively mimicks the archaeological assemblage. In accordance with the results obtained by Schick (1986) the experimental assemblage show a decrease in the quantity of flakes through increased size (axial length).

Comparisons between the Areas I and IV(4) rolled and fresh groups, together with the experimental assemblage, are shown in Figures 19.12a and b. These indicate that the rolled groups are lacking in smaller elements, suggesting that the smaller debitage has been winnowed away. The fresh groups, however, have comparable size distributions to the experimental assemblage, suggesting that they consist of largely complete knapping episodes. Such differences between the rolled and fresh groups are also reflected in the higher proportion of cores and the lower proportion of chips in the former (Table 19.6).The size distributions for the Area V groups are more complex (Fig. 19.12c). The hard hammer debitage rolled group has a similar profile to the rolled groups from Areas I and IV(4), suggesting that the smaller element has been winnowed away. The fresh hard hammer debitage distribution poses more difficult interpretational problems. It has a completely different type of profile, with a large number of smaller elements, but also a peak in the medium size range. This type of profile is neither typical of a complete knapping sequence nor of a winnowed assemblage. The presence of medium size-ranged pieces together with the presence of several cores might suggest that these pieces were humanly introduced into the area, already knapped. Although the distribution may also simply reflect the small sample size. These problems are discussed in Chapter 23.

| Area | I | I | IV(4) | IV(4) | V | V | Exper. |
Condition	fresh	rolled	fresh	rolled	fresh	rolled	
BROKEN							
No	53.5	57.2	38.2	51.5	51.9	53.8	43.4
Yes	46.5	42.8	61.8	48.5	48.1	46.2	56.6
n	475	590	123	200	27	206	106

Table 19.4. Breakage of hard hammer flakes by area and degree of abrasion.

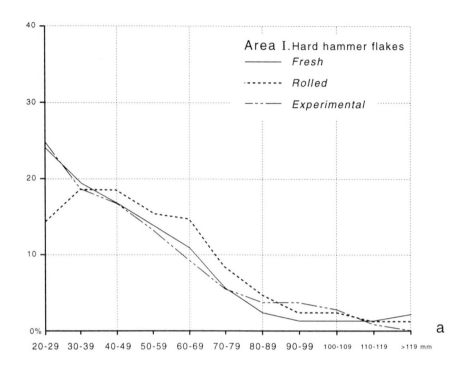

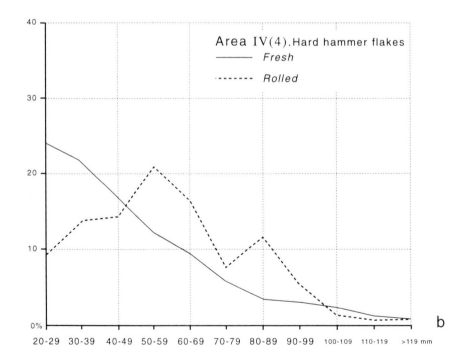

Fig. 19.12 a-d. Percentage of flakes by 10mm size catagories (maximum length).

Biface manufacturing experiments. The technological analysis of the biface experiments was a by product of a study conducted for the raw material chapter. For this reason there are differences between the experimental and archaeological assemblages which are discussed fully in Chapter 20. Despite these problems, some observations can still be made in terms of size distribution.

The biface debitage from both areas shows the characteristic decrease in quantity with size, suggesting that neither of the assemblages have been the subject of winnowing. There are differences in size distribution, however, between the experimental and archaeological assemblage, with the Area V material and to some extent the experimental debitage lacking the larger flake element. In the case of the experimental debitage this is due to the difference in knapping technique which is fully discussed in Chapter 20. The situation in Area V could be interpreted in several ways. It could be seen as the winnowed, smaller element from a complete knapping sequence, although this is unlikely because of the much larger size of the hard hammer cores and flakes also found in the area. Alternatively, it might be argued that a different knapping technique was adopted in Area V, compared to Area IV(4), with the use of a soft hammer only in the final stages. This might be the case, although there is a complete absence of hard hammer debitage that bears any of the signs of biface manufacture. A more economic explanation would be that the assemblage is simply the final stages of the knapping process, with the initial stages being undertaken elsewhere. This is discussed more fully in Chapter 20.

SUMMARY

From the above discussion of condition, orientation, spatial distribution, refitting, technology and size distributions, eight main assemblages can be distinguished at Barnham. In several instances divisions are made on the basis of condition, which is merely a convenient way of distinguishing between those artefacts that have undergone comparatively little movement, and those that have moved much further. Apart from Area V, this division is regarded as artificial, but nonetheless probably reflects groups of material that were knapped together over a more limited timespan. These assemblages are discussed below.

Area I

The assemblages in Area I are divided on the basis of condition rather than context, thus giving an Area I rolled group and an Area I fresh group. This is supported to an extent by the orientation data, but principally by the refitting and technology. It is argued

that knapping took place on or near the cobble layer over some length of time. Periodic reworking of the material took place causing abrasion and edge damage and admixture of the material within the deposit, with some being derived from the underlying brown diamicton. The final knapping events on that surface became both incorporated into the cobble layer, through slight reworking, and together with more rolled elements, into the overlying yellow silty sand. The rolled group appears to have been size-sorted and only consists of the larger elements. The fresh group seems to be representative of the full knapping sequence.

Area I (gravel section)

Most of the 24 artefacts from this area have been scratched and have some edge abrasion and rolling, although there are several fresh pieces. Although their condition varies they are regarded technologically as a single group, and are interpreted as being moved to a varying extent as part of the solifluction process.

Area III

Only 16 artefacts larger than chip size (maximum dimension > 20mm) were excavated from Area III, or from adjacent areas. Although they came from varying depths within the grey silt and clay (the top 65cm), they can be treated as a single assemblage in terms of condition and technology. They are all regarded as being *in situ*, but do not appear to have been knapped within the area.

Area IV(4)

The artefacts from the cobble layer in Area IV(4) can be divided on technological grounds into two groups; one group is the result of hard hammer core and flake working, while the second is the debitage and on occasion the endproduct of biface manufacture. These two groups are treated separately for the purposes of the technological analysis, although they are clearly, on the grounds of condition and context, part of the same assemblage. In terms of condition, the biface manufacturing debitage seems to form a single group (see Table 20.9, Chapter 20), whereas the core and flake working can be divided into a rolled and fresh group, similar to Area I. The abandonment of the division by spits is supported by the orientation, spatial distribution, refitting and technology of the material.

As with Area I, the core and flake working is regarded as being knapped on the surface of the cobble layer over some length of time. The fresh core and flake working and the fresh biface manufacturing debitage are regarded as contemporary and are interpreted as the final knapping events on that surface. All of the fresh

Area Condition	I fresh	I rolled	IGS mixed	III fresh	IV(4) fresh	IV(4) rolled	V fresh	V rolled
Evidence for movement from								
Size-sorting	N	Y	Y	N	N	Y	N	Y
Refitting	N	Y	Y	Y	N	Y	N	Y
Rolling	N	Y	Y	N	N	Y	N	Y
Distribution	Y	Y	Y	N	Y	Y	Y	Y
Orientation	Y	Y	Y	?	Y	Y	?	Y

Table 19.5. Evidence for movement from size-sorting, refitting, rolling, redistribution and re-orientation for each artefact group. IGS = Area I (gravel section).

Area Condition	I fresh	I rolled	IGS mixed	III fresh	IV(4) fresh	IV(4) rolled	V fresh	V rolled
Cores	29	56	1	3	13	18	4	-
Hard H. flakes	443	585	22	12	121	195	27	106
Fl.tools	32	14	1	1	2	5	-	-
Soft H. flakes	-	-	-	-	241	27	48	4
Bifaces	-	-	-	-	1	-	-	-
Biface roughouts	-	-	-	-	1	-	-	-
Total	504	655	24	16	379	245	79	110

Table 19.6. Quantities of artefact types by artefact groups (area and degree of abrasion). IGS = Area I (gravel section).

material has been reworked into the cobble layer.

From the size distributions, the fresh groups seem to be fully representative of the complete knapping sequences, whereas the rolled group is missing the smaller elements, and appears to have been size-sorted.

Area V. The artefacts from the surface of the grey/brown stony clay, like Area IV(4), can be divided into those resulting from core and flake working, and those related to biface manufacture. The soft hammer debitage was virtually all in fresh condition (see Table 20.9, Chapter 20), but the hard hammer debitage formed two distinct groups, fresh and very rolled. The artefacts from within the grey/brown stony clay were all from core and flake working with only one possible soft hammer flake. They were principally in a rolled condition, with just five fresh flakes. Although there is less justification for joining artefacts from the surface of

the grey/brown stony clay with those found within it, due to the low quantities they have been grouped together and then divided into fresh and rolled catagories. The rolled group is regarded as being derived probably from a gravel context elsewhere. Occasional rolled pebbles within the grey/brown stony clay were presumably transported with the artefacts.

The interpretation of the fresh groups is more complex. Although their orientation and condition suggest that they are *in situ*, the low quantity of refitting and dispersed distribution point towards at least some movement. The size distribution profiles show that they are principally composed of the smaller knapping elements which might suggest that they have been winnowed out from a knapping group elsewhere. However, the presence of several cores and several larger flakes implies that this is not the case, and that at least some of the artefacts have been humanly introduced into the area. Although there may be some movement of the artefacts, this has probably not affected the composition of the assemblage. The nature of this movement is probably best explained through slight fluvial reworking on the surface of the grey/brown stony clay, sufficient to blur any knapping scatters, but not strong enough to rework them into the grey/brown stony clay. The artefacts are regarded, therefore, as being in primary context, if not quite *in situ*.

The assemblages outlined above form the basis for the study of the technology in Chapter 20. The taphonomic evidence, discussed in this chapter, is summarised in Table 19.5, while the composition of these assemblages is given in Table 19.6.

20. THE TECHNOLOGY OF THE FLINT ASSEMBLAGES

Nick Ashton

This chapter is primarily designed to describe the technology of the assemblages, but in so doing to draw attention to differences in the assemblages that reflect variation in human behaviour. This variation in human behaviour is studied in more detail in Chapter 23. The assemblages discussed below, also include those excavated by Wymer in 1979. The latter were excavated from the same location as Area I and can be attributed to the same sequence of contexts. Their main value is in adding several flake tools, and in particular a sequence of refitting flakes and a core (Group A).

SITE FORMATION AND RAW MATERIALS

A full discussion of the site formation is given in Chapter 19, but Table 20.1 shows the eight artefact groups deduced from this study with the quantities of artefact types. They form the basis of the technological study. Between and within these groups a basic distinction can be made between the core and flake technology and the biface manufacturing technology. These are described and discussed separately below.

The study of the raw material is discussed in Chapter 21, but here a few observations are made which can be deduced from a study of the artefacts and which are pertinent to the understanding of the technology. The raw material source for both Areas I and IV(4) was the cobble layer within which and on which the flint artefacts were found. This consisted of flint cobbles, derived from an outwash gravel, ranging in size from less than 5cm up to 25cm across, and occasionally as large as 45cm maximum dimension (see Chapter 4). In Area V there is no immediate source of raw material within the area, but its condition suggests it came from a nearby location, similar to that of Area I. The term 'immediate' in this context means actually within the area of excavation. Equally, the artefacts in Area III have no obvious source within the area, but presumably originated from a gravel on the edge of the channel. As far as the excavations could ascertain, there were no other sources of raw material in the immediate area.

CORE AND FLAKE TECHNOLOGY

The system used to understand the core and flake technology is the same as that used in the Swanscombe report (Ashton & McNabb 1996). The methodology was developed as a system to describe the reduction processes apparent on the refitting flakes and cores from High Lodge, Swanscombe and Barnham. The system is summarised briefly here and is described in full in Appendix VI.

The flaking of cores is often characterised by a series of removals that form a sequence. Such a sequence is termed a *core episode*. Often there will be several independant sequences or core episodes on a single core, where the core has been turned and a different part has been worked. The methodology used here relies on identifying and summarising these core episodes. The simplest is a *single removal* (type A) which is one flake removed independantly of other removals. If a single removal is followed by one or more removals in the same direction and from the same or adjacent platforms in the same plane, then this is termed *parallel flaking* (type B). A single removal or a sequence of parallel flaking often develops into a more complex sequence, termed *alternate flaking* (type C), where the core is turned and the proximal ends of the flake scar or scars act as the platform for one or more further removals (type Ci). The sequence can develop further by the core being turned back to the original direction, with the second set of removals being the platform for one or more removals (type Cii). Where alternate flaking incorporates one or more series of parallel flaking the core episode is given as Cip or Ciip. Type D is given when remnants of previous flaking can be recognised, but it cannot be related to a specific core episode (also see Appendix VI). By using this methodology, it is possible to describe and summarise the reduction processes for each core, rather than naming it as a static endform which often bears little relationship to its previous history. The processes described are, of course, the final phases of core reduction, and it is only through refitting that the complete sequence can be understood.

The method of recording the flakes is designed to provide support for the interpretation of the cores. Of particular importance are the butt types, the dorsal scar patterns, the amount of cortex and the relict core edges. The measures are fully explained in Appendix VI, but the relict core edges require some explanation here. Relict core edges 1, 2 and 3 are remnants of an old core edge that is no longer being worked and shows a sequence of removals that are not directly related to the removal of the actual flake (*passive* relict core edge). They indicate the passive use of parallel flaking (B), simple alternate flaking (Ci) and complex alternate flaking (Cii) respectively. Relict core edges 4, 5 and 6 are part of the core edge that is still being worked with the removal of the flake being part of that sequence (*active* relict core edge). They indicate the active use of parallel flaking, simple and complex alternate flaking

Area Condition	I fresh	I rolled	IGS mixed	III fresh	IV(4) fresh	IV(4) rolled	V fresh	V rolled
Cores	29	56	1	3	13	18	4	-
Hard H. flakes	443	585	22	12	121	195	27	106
Fl.tools	32	14	1	1	2	5	-	-
Soft H. flakes	-	-	-	-	241	27	48	4
Bifaces	-	-	-	-	1	-	-	-
Biface roughouts	-	-	-	-	1	-	-	-
Total	504	655	24	16	379	245	79	110

Table 20.1. Quantities of artefact types by artefact groups (area and degree of abrasion). IGS = Area I Gravel Section.

respectively. The difference between them is that the passive relict core edges reflect a full sequence of removals on that part of the core, whereas the active relict core edges may form only the first part of a sequence. For this reason parallel flaking is likely to have a higher representation among the active relict core edges.

These technological measures are a direct reflection of what has happened on the cores. At Barnham there are sometimes insufficient quantities of cores to justify a statistical analysis. The flakes, therefore, often provide the only means of understanding and comparing the technology.

The cores

Only the cores from Area I and Area IV(4) are of sufficient numbers to merit any form of statistical analysis, and even then the numbers are low. For this reason both the fresh and rolled element from each area are combined to form a more meaningful sample. The justification for combining the cores in this way is provided by the technological analysis of the flakes (see below). This shows that the technology between the fresh and rolled groups is similar, even though the rolled groups have been naturally sorted by size. The cores from Areas III and V, although small in number, are put alongside for comparison. The latter are all from the fresh assemblage.

The technology of the cores from the two main assemblages is summarised in Table 20.2. All the core episode types are represented, although there is some variation in the relative proportions, possibly due to the low numbers. When the core episodes are summarised as A, B, C and D, then the percentages of each type are similar. One possible difference is the higher

percentage of D in Area I at the expense of C. This seems to reflect slightly more intensive flaking in Area I, where previous core episodes have been obscured by more recent reduction (see below). The number of flakes per core episode is also similar between the areas, again suggesting technological similarity.

Where slight differences do occur, is in the sizes and weights of the cores; those from Area IV(4) are slightly larger on average than those from Area I. Whether this is significant or not, is discussed below.

The analysis can be taken further by considering the amount that each nodule was reduced. This can be measured in several ways. Table 20.2 shows the mean and range of the number of scars on the cores. This clearly indicates that fewer flakes were removed from the cores in Area IV(4) than in Area I, and is also reflected by the number of core episodes recorded on each core, there being far fewer in Area IV(4). It is further suggested by the amount of cortex retained on the cores with those from Area IV(4) generally being more cortical. One final measure is the ratio of flakes to cores. To be meaningful this can only be assessed from complete knapping sequences, in other words only the fresh cores and flakes from Areas I and IV(4). This shows that the ratio of flakes to cores is lower for Area IV(4), supporting the interpretation that there has been less reduction in Area IV(4).

All these measures suggest that the amount of reduction was greater in Area I than Area IV(4), perhaps also reflected by the slightly larger cores. However, one other factor that should also be considered is the size of the original nodules; smaller nodules would also produce a smaller number of flakes, and higher levels of cortex retention. Although the original size of the nodules is difficult to guage, one measure which should broadly reflect it, is the

Area	I	IV(4)	V(fresh)	III	Exper
CORE EPISODES WITH SUBTYPES					
A	22.2	20.5	25.0	25.0	20.0
B	14.2	13.6	-	-	-
C	19.1	31.8	50.0	-	20.0
Ci	8.0	6.8	25.0	25.0	-
Cip	5.6	2.2	-	-	40.0
Cii	13.6	11.4	-	-	10.0
Ciip	6.2	9.1	-	50.0	-
Ciii	1.2	-	-	-	-
D	9.9	4.5	-	-	10.0
CORE EPISODES					
A	22.2	20.5	25.0	25.0	20.0
B	14.2	13.6	-	-	-
C	53.7	61.4	75.0	75.0	70.0
D	9.9	4.5	-	-	10.0
n	162	44	4	4	10
FLAKE SCARS/CORE EPISODE					
Mean	4.0	3.9	3.0	3.5	4.3
SIZE					
L	97 ± 38	115 ± 36	66 ± 17	75 ± 17	105 ± 23
W	79 ± 30	91 ± 23	79 ± 21	66 ± 16	82 ± 23
Th	57 ± 28	62 ± 18	38 ± 13	39 ± 16	68 ± 14
Wt	599 ± 1003	638 ± 716	171 ± 121	209 ± 147	632 ± 571
n	85	31	4	3	6
SCARS/CORE					
Range	1-20	1-11	1-5	4-5	2-11
Mean	7.6	5.6	3.0	4.7	7.3
CORE EPISODES/CORE					
1	40.0	70.4	100	66.7	50.0
2	37.6	22.7	-	33.3	33.3
3	15.3	6.8	-	-	16.7
4	5.9	-	-	-	-
5	1.2	-	-	-	-
Mean	1.9	1.4	1.0	1.3	1.7
CORTEX					
1	-	-	-	-	-
2	27.1	38.7	25.0	33.3	33.3
3	68.2	54.8	75.0	66.7	66.7
4	4.7	6.5	-	-	-
RATIO OF HH FLAKES:CORES (fresh groups only)					
	16.3	9.5	6.7	4.3	17.7

Table 20.2. Technological attributes of the cores from Areas I, IV(4), III and V (fresh) and the experimental group.

combined weight of the cores and flakes divided by the number of cores. If this is calculated just on the fresh artefacts (as the rolled flakes have probably been size-sorted, see Chapter 19), the figures produced are 1.092kg for Area I and 1.236kg for Area IV(4). Although these figures suggest that the selected nodules in Area I were slightly smaller than those in Area IV(4), the raw material study (Chapter 21) shows the converse, with the nodules in Area IV(4) being slightly smaller. This data combined, provides little solid evidence to suggest that there are significant differences in raw material selection between the areas. This probably supports the interpretation that nodules of broadly similar size ranges were selected in Areas I and IV(4), but that those in Area IV(4) were reduced less, producing larger cores and fewer, more cortical flakes.

Although there are only four cores from the fresh assemblage in Area V, and three from Area III, some comments can still be made. There appear to be few differences in the technology, which is supported by the refitting group from Area V (see refitting below). However, with the cores from Area V, there are also some clear differences with the other areas. Two of the cores are made on small pebbles, the third is on a natural flake, while the last is made on a thick flake, effectively a split, medium-sized cobble (about 15cm across). Technologically, this could be interpreted as a flaked flake (see Group D, below). The four cores have probably had little more than twelve flakes removed in total. This proportion of flake scars to cores is much lower than Areas I and IV(4) (Table 20.2). In addition the number of core episodes per core is also much lower. This is also reflected by the proportion of hard hammer flakes to cores, which is also much lower than the other areas. However, it is equally clear that the four cores would not have been sufficient to provide the 27 flakes recovered from the fresh assemblage in Area V. The implications of this are discussed further below and in Chapter 23. The absence of any cores in the rolled assemblage from Area V may be significant, but is more likely to be due to fluvial size-sorting.

Some of these differences are also reflected in the Area III cores. They all seem to have been made on small to medium sized pebbles, but unlike Area V they would have been sufficient in theory to have produced all the flakes. However, the large size of some of the flakes and the low proportion of cortex suggests that they were not knapped from these cores.

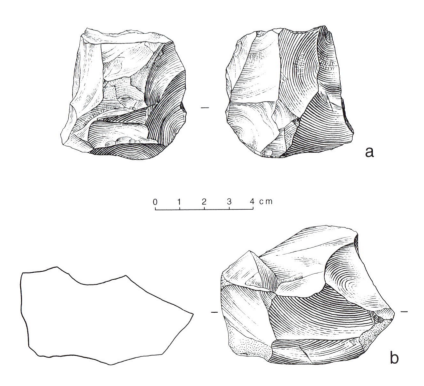

Fig. 20.1. a. Core (P1990.10-7.1056) from Area I, cobble layer, showing two episodes of alternate flaking (Cpii) and several previous removals (D). b. Core (P1990.10-7.611) from Area I, yellow silty sand, showing one episode of alternate flaking (Cpi).

The flakes

For the analysis of the flakes, the full range of artefact groups has been used. The observations from the flakes help to support the interpretation of the core technology (Table 20.3). By definition the flakes studied under this section should have been produced by hard hammer percussion, but the interpretation of flakes is never clearcut. Within Area I there are several flakes that could be interpreted as soft hammer flakes, but without clear supporting evidence from the remainder of the debitage it is difficult to be certain. Equally, within Areas IV(4) and V some of the flakes that have been categorised as hard hammer, may infact derive from biface manufacture. It is hoped, however, that a high percentage have been correctly attributed.

In most of the technological measures there appear to be few differences between the separate areas, or where differences do occur, it can probably be attributed to small sample size. As would be expected with simple hard hammer technology, only a small percentage of the flakes from each area bear evidence of platform adjustment, and there is little variation between the groups. The platform adjustment usually took the form of several very small flakes being removed immediately below the platform on the dorsal face, prior to the removal of the main flake. In no instance was there any evidence of preparation flaking on the platform or of facetting.

The relict core edges are also similar between the areas, although comparisons are only statistically meaningful between Areas I and IV(4). Generally they support the interpretation of the cores, in that parallel flaking and alternate flaking predominate. In addition, there appear to be few differences between Areas I and IV(4). As predicted, there is a much higher percentage of parallel flaking in the active relict core edges, but it is also important among the passive relict core edges. This is at variance with the evidence from the cores which indicates that alternate flaking was used to a greater extent. The difference might be accounted for by the fact that cores are likely to show more of the sequence, and are probably a more accurate reflection of the relative importance of the two techniques. This can be confirmed by the refitting evidence (see below).

Generally the frequency of different flake-butts from all the excavated areas are similar and support the evidence from the cores of their reduction by parallel and alternate flaking. The predominance of plain and cortical/natural butts would be expected from such flaking. One difference between the areas is the higher percentage of cortical/natural butts (type 3) in Area IV(4), and the lower percentage in Area V fresh group. Edge and bifacial butts (types 4 and 6) are also more frequent in the fresh groups from Areas IV(4) and V, which probably reflects the difficulties of distinguishing some biface thinning flakes.

The percentages of different dorsal scar patterns show little variation between the areas. They all show a predominance of types 1, 2, 5 and 10, indicating that the majority of flakes were either cortical/natural or were preceded by flakes that were removed either in the same direction or from a lateral edge. This range of dorsal scar pattern types is typical of parallel and alternate flaking. Again, one difference is the slightly higher percentage of cortical/natural flakes in Area IV(4) fresh group and rather fewer in Area V fresh group (see below).

The cortex on the flakes and their size show much clearer differences between the areas. The flakes from Area IV(4) have a higher percentage of cortex than those from Area I, while those from Area V have a much lower percentage. In terms of size, the flakes from Area IV(4) are slightly larger than those from Area I, although the size distributions (see Chapter 19, Figs 19.12a, 19.12c) are similar. In contrast, the average size of the flakes is significantly smaller in Area V. This is also reflected by the size distributions (see Chapter 19, Fig. 19.12c)

The technological analysis shows two principal differences between the areas. The cortical butts, number of purely cortical flakes, and the amount of cortex on the flakes, all suggest that the flakes in Area IV(4) were knapped from cores that were less reduced than those in Area I. The original nodules appear to have been of similar sizes (see above). In contrast, these same measures, in addition to the small size, suggest that the flakes from Area V are from the final stages of the knapping process. These conclusions support the interpretation of the cores.

Reduction stages. The presence of numerous cores in Areas I and IV(4) suggests that the complete knapping process took place in those areas, but the question arises as to whether different stages of knapping can be isolated, by comparison with Area V. The two measures used so far to assess the knapping stage are cortex and size. The quantity of cortex is probably the best guage of knapping stage, although with this type of knapping it will directly relate to the stage within a core episode, as opposed to the complete core reduction; if a second core episode is undertaken on an otherwise unworked part of the core, then the initial flakes will be cortical even though the core is midway through reduction. Nonetheless, five main flake types can be created which show a reduction in cortex retention on the dorsal face and butt (see Appendix VI) and broadly reflect arbitary stages in the progressive reduction of a core episode. Within broad terms it can still be stated that the degree of cortex retention on a whole assemblage of flakes reflects knapping stage.

This is illustrated in Figure 20.2, where the basic proportions of cortex retention are shown, as indicated by the five flake types, between Areas I, IV(4) and V.

Size, however, is a far cruder measure of knapping stage. If the five cortex flake types are used as stages of reduction of a core episode, then although the average size of flakes will tend to be smaller in the final stages, the size ranges show considerable overlaps (Table 20.4). This makes the attribution of individual flakes to a particular stage difficult if not impossible. The size of each range is presumably due to variation in the size of the nodules. The table also shows that the initial, cortical flakes to be removed from a core are in fact on average smaller than those removed in the middle phases. This may be due to the difficulties of creating a working edge, particularly on rounded nodules, leading to the selection of a narrow part of the core for initial knapping.

These problems highlight the difficulties of isolating individual flakes, or of dividing assemblages, into a particular stage of reduction. It is only through the characteristics of complete assemblages where cortex and size can be used to assess what stages of reduction are represented.

Other attributes are equally difficult to use for the isolation of reduction stages; as demonstrated with the analysis of the Areas I, IV(4) and V assemblages, all the other technological attributes are broadly similar between the areas. What this does suggest, however, is that a similar knapping procedure is adopted right the way through the reduction sequence, with no apparent stages.

On this basis, it must be concluded that although the later stages of knapping are almost certainly present in Areas I and IV(4), they cannot be isolated from the complete assemblages, even by comparison to Area V.

Fresh and rolled groups. The differences within each area between the fresh and rolled groups is sometimes quite marked, for example the cortical dorsal surfaces in Areas IV(4) and V, or the differences in size in Area I. This variation can probably be explained by the differences in formation of the two groups. The fresh groups are regarded as broadly *in situ* and are fully representative of the specific knapping events, whereas the rolled groups are derived, perhaps from different knapping locations and then have undergone natural selective processes, such as size sorting, prior to final deposition. This may explain some of the differences between the groups, which are not regarded as significant to the interpretation of the technology.

Area Condition	I fresh	I rolled	IV(4) fresh	IV(4) rolled	V fresh	V rolled	Exper. core	Exper. biface
FLAKE TYPE								
Hard	84.2	95.8	91.1	98.0	88.9	96.2		85.0
Indet	15.0	4.0	8.9	2.0	11.1	3.8		15.0
Soft	0.8	0.2	-	-	-	-		-
n	475	599	123	200	27	106		147
PLATFORM ADJUSTMENT								
No	89.7	98.5	94.2	91.9	94.7	96.1		81.9
Yes	10.3	2.0	5.8	8.1	5.3	3.9		18.1
n	349	399	69	136	24	76		116
RELICT CORE EDGE								
1	6.6	15.2	5.2	12.5	-	-	6.7	11.1
2	3.3	2.2	5.2	6.2	-	-	-	-
3	1.7	-	-	-	-	-	-	-
4	75.2	78.3	84.2	65.6	66.7	94.1	80.0	87.0
5	8.3	2.2	5.2	9.4	33.3	-	6.7	-
6	5.0	2.2	-	6.2	-	5.9	6.7	1.9
n	121	92	19	32	3	17	30	54

Table 20.3. See opposite

Area	I	I	IV(4)	IV(4)	V	V	Exper.	Exper.
Condition	fresh	rolled	fresh	rolled	fresh	rolled	core	biface
BUTTS								
1	75.1	74.2	69.6	72.8	57.9	80.3	64.6	55.2
2	7.2	6.3	2.9	4.4	15.8	2.6	6.3	11.2
3	14.3	17.3	20.3	22.1	5.3	15.7	24.0	24.1
4	2.3	0.8	7.2	0.7	10.5	1.3	3.8	3.4
5	-	-	-	-	-	-	-	1.7
6	1.1	1.5	-	-	10.5	-	1.3	4.3
n	349	399	69	136	19	76	79	116
DORSAL SCAR PATTERNS								
1	50.2	50.1	47.3	54.8	45.8	46.7	54.3	36.7
2	13.4	10.8	8.0	9.1	29.2	11.1	15.2	20.4
3	0.9	0.5	-	1.6	-	1.1	1.0	0.7
4	0.5	0.7	1.8	-	-	1.1	-	-
5	14.8	12.8	7.1	10.8	12.5	21.1	10.5	15.6
6	0.7	0.7	0.9	1.6	8.3	-	-	-
7	1.4	2.4	1.8	2.7	-	1.1	1.9	2.7
8	2.1	2.0	1.8	1.6	-	1.1	-	0.7
9	-	-	-	-	-	-	-	0.7
10	14.6	19.1	28.6	17.2	4.2	15.6	17.1	18.4
11	0.5	0.2	0.9	-	-	-	-	0.7
12	0.9	0.5	1.8	0.5	-	1.1	-	3.4
Distal index (4+6+7+9 +11+12)	4.0	4.5	7.1	4.8	8.3	3.3	1.9	7.5
n	432	545	112	186	24	90	105	147
CORTEX								
1	9.4	8.2	17.9	9.0	3.7	4.7	16.0	17.0
2	19.0	13.4	19.5	24.0	11.1	17.0	23.6	22.4
3	41.2	42.2	39.0	44.0	48.1	40.6	46.2	49.7
4	30.3	36.2	23.6	23.0	37.0	37.7	14.2	10.9
Cortical index	35.7	31.2	43.9	39.7	27.1	28.9	47.0	48.4

The cortical index is $(x_1 \times 1) + (x_2 \times 0.67) + (x_3 \times 0.33)$ where x is the cortex catagory (see Appendix VI).

	I	I	IV(4)	IV(4)	V	V	Exper.	Exper.
n	468	597	123	200	27	106	106	147
L	49 ± 31	53 ± 25	52 ± 27	59 ± 22	45 ± 24	49 ± 22	48 ± 22	44 ± 19
W	41 ± 21	46 ± 20	47 ± 24	49 ± 17	37 ± 17	39 ± 14	43 ± 23	39 ± 18
Th	15 ± 10	18 ± 10	16 ± 10	19 ± 9	14 ± 9	15 ± 10	13 ± 8	11 ± 6
Wt	48 ± 106	70 ± 154	61 ± 101	65 ± 67	31 ± 54	37 ± 56	37 ± 57	21 ± 31
n	468	597	123	200	27	106	106	147
BROKEN								
No	53.5	57.2	38.2	51.5	51.9	53.8	43.4	51.0
Yes	46.5	42.8	61.8	48.5	48.1	46.2	56.6	49.0
n	475	590	123	200	27	106	106	147

Table 20.3. Technological attributes of the hard hammer flakes by Area and degree of abrasion, and from the core and flake experiments and the biface experiments.

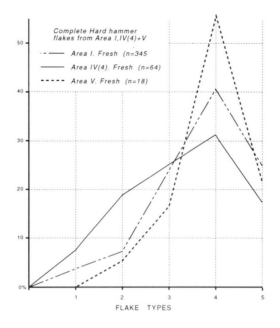

Fig. 20.2. Percentage of fresh condition flake types 1-5 (see Appendix VI) from Areas I, IV(4) and V.

Flake type	1	2	3	4	5
Area I					
Mean & s.d	42 ± 71	37 ± 41	68 ± 144	59 ± 125	33 ± 79
Range	1-266	2-170	1-950	1-1133	1-477
Area IV(4)					
Mean & s.d	12 ± 12	115 ± 154	110 ± 84	52 ± 50	38 ± 56
Range	1-33	2-473	10-288	2-175	3-194

Table 20.4. Means, standard deviations and ranges for Areas I and IV(4) cortical flake types (see Appendix VI).

Refitting groups

Three groups of refitting flakes were found in Area I (Groups A, B and C), and a small additional group in Area V (Group D). There are also several refitting pairs of flakes, three of which incorporate flake tools. The latter are discussed under flake tools, below, while the distribution and spatial organisation of the refitting is discussed in Chapter 19.

Group A. This group was excavated by Wymer (1985) and consists of 16 pieces, namely one core and 14 flakes (one broken in two) (Fig.20.3). The flint was originally a 'cannon-shot' nodule, was severely battered on the outside, and at some point had been split into two, probably naturally. The sequence consists of one core episode of alternate flaking (type

Ciip) which migrated around part of the ridge created by the split in the nodule.

Initially one missing flake was removed in direction A, followed by three existing flakes and one missing flake in direction B (Wymer # 82 [+ 3-part of 82], 10, and 17). This was followed by a sequence of five existing and two missing flakes in direction A, removed from the platform created by the scar of flake 17 (Wymer # 6, 5, 7, missing, 11, 26, and missing). The core was turned and two missing flakes and one existing flake were removed in direction B (Wymer # 1). This was followed by a missing flake in direction A, flake 88 in direction B, and four existing and two missing in direction A (missing, Wymer # 8, 81, 9, missing, and 30). For the disribution see Figure 19.7, Chapter 19.

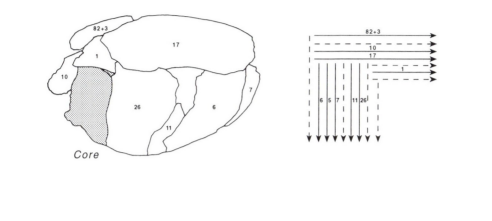

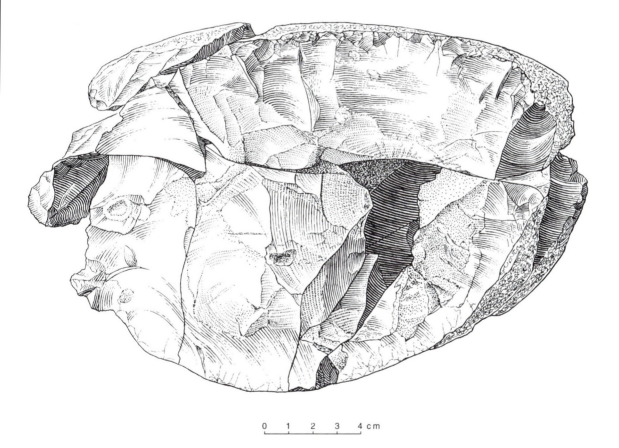

0 1 2 3 4 cm

Fig. 20.3a.-d. Refitting Group A from Area I, excavated by Wymer (1985). Schematic diagrams show the numbering of the flake removals, and the sequence and direction in which they were removed.

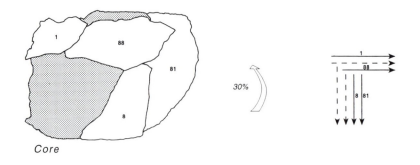

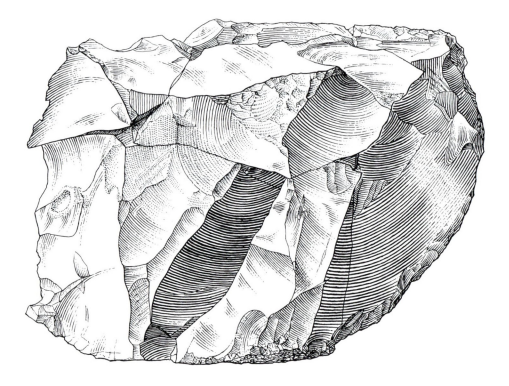

Fig. 20.3b

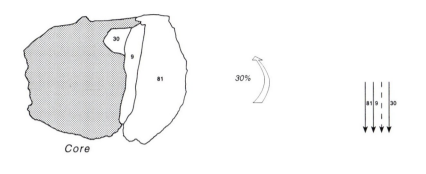

Core

30%

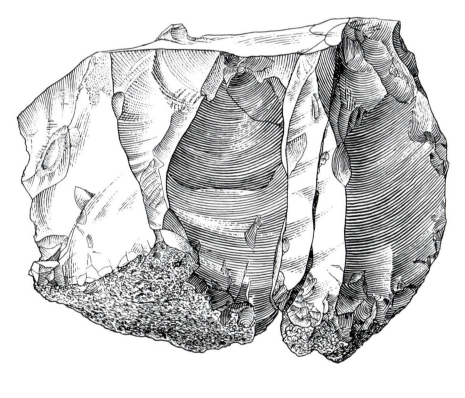

0 1 2 3 4 cm

Fig. 20.3c

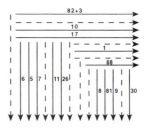

Core

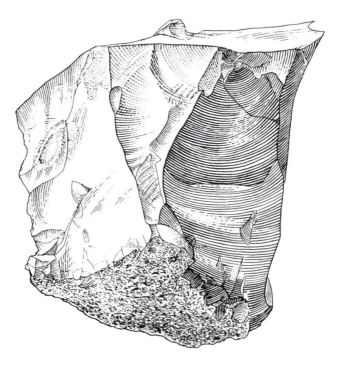

0 1 2 3 4 cm

Fig. 20.3d.

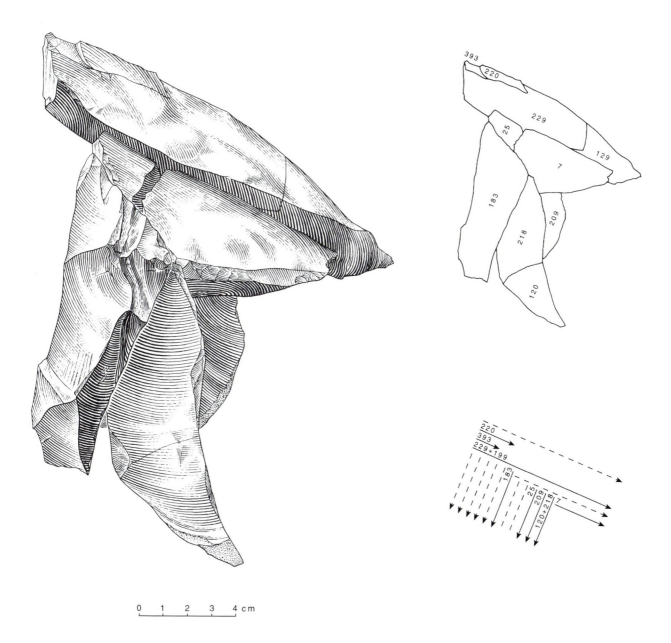

0   1   2   3   4 cm

Fig. 20.4. Refitting Group B from Area I. Schematic diagrams show the numbering of the flake removals, and the sequence and direction in which they were removed.

Group B. This group from Area I consists of eight flakes, two of which broke on knapping into two pieces (Fig. 20.4). Nine of the pieces were recovered in the current excavations, the last flake being recovered by Wymer. The group comprises one long sequence of alternate flaking (type Ciip). An initial missing flake was removed in direction A, followed by a single flake (P1990.10-7.229 and 199) in the same direction, and probably from the same platform. On knapping the flake broke laterally in two, and two small additional flakes were removed spontaneously from the platform on the dorsal surface (P1990.10-7.220 and 393). The core was turned and six flakes were removed from direction B, five of which are missing, but the last flake being P1990.10-7.183. The core was turned again to remove a missing flake in direction A, followed by two missing and three existing flakes in direction B (Wymer # 25, P1990.10-7.209 and 218). The latter flake broke spontaneously on knapping (P1990.10-7.120). The core was turned once more to remove one flake (P1990.10-7.7) in direction A. This last flake was retouched (see flake tools below; also see Fig. 19.7, Chapter 19).

217

Group C. The four flakes and a core which form this group were all recovered in the current excavations from Area I and one sequence of alternate flaking can be identified (Fig. 20.5). Because many of the flakes are missing, much of the sequence is difficult to reconstruct in detail, but the flaking is concentrated along a single ridge around 180° of the core. There are at least five flakes in direction A, and probably several in direction B, but the precise sequence is not known. This is followed by one flake in direction A (P1990.10-7.938), possibly a missing flake in direction B, and then two further flakes (P1990.10-7.472 and 478) in direction A, but further round the ridge. Finally a missing flake is removed in direction B, a further missing one from direction A, and then P1990.10-7.476 also in direction A from core P1990.10-7.616. The distribution of the flakes is given in Figure 19.7 (Chapter 19).

Group D. This group from Area V consists of four flakes, with again one sequence of alternate flaking

(type Ciip) represented. The first flake (P1994.3-1.119) appears to be a soft hammer removal in direction A, while the following two flakes are missing, with the first in direction B, followed by one in direction A. This sequence is followed by four hard hammer flakes in direction A (P1994.3-1.76, P1994.3-1.93, one missing, and P1994.3-1.52). In terms of raw material, cortex and condition, the three flakes appear to be a part of a core from Area V (P1994.3-1.82), which itself has one refitting flake (P1994.3-1.106). This core is a large, thick flake from a medium sized nodule. The flake appears to have split the nodule into two. The four refitting flakes could either be an earlier sequence from the core, or from the other half of the nodule. The distribution of the scatter is given in Figure 19.9 (Chapter 19). The initial flaking with a soft hammer suggests that there was an attempt to make a biface. This attempt appears to have been quickly abandoned after the first few removals, with the flaking switching to hard hammer mode.

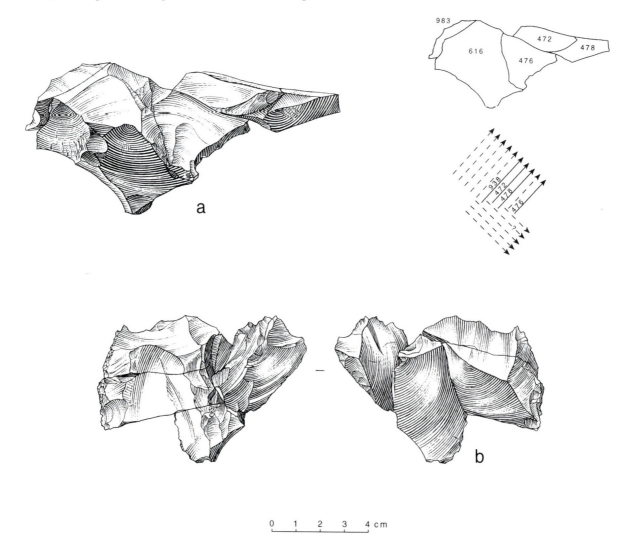

Fig. 20.5a. Refitting Group C from Area I. b. Refitting Group D from Area III. Schematic diagrams show the numbering of the flake removals, and the sequence and direction in which they were removed.

Core and flake knapping experiments

Core and flake knapping experiments were conducted (by the author), first to compile size distribution profiles for the study of the taphonomy, but also to compare with the technological analysis of the archaeological assemblages. Six nodules were selected from the cobble layer in Area I which were thought to reflect the size-range of nodules represented by the debitage in the assemblages. Their weights varied from 589g to 5,031g (mean 1,528g). Two flint hard hammers were used (also from Area I), weighing 270g and 342g. The purpose was to reduce the nodules by methods recognised in the assemblages, principally by parallel and alternate flaking. Although these techniques formed the basis of the knapping, they did not predetermine the fluidity of the knapping process. This was guided by the availabilty of platforms as knapping progressed, with the main aim of obtaining a range of large to medium size flakes.

The success of the knapping experiments in mimicking the archaeological assemblages can be assessed by comparing the technological measures. Table 20.2 shows that the characteristics of the experimental cores are similar to those from Areas I and IV(4). This includes the average size measurements together with analysis of the core episodes, scars and amount of cortex retention. One slight difference is the ratio of hard hammer flakes to cores, which is 17.7 for the experimental assemblage, compared to 16.4 and 9.5 for the fresh artefacts from Areas I and IV(4). The low figure for Area IV(4) is probably accounted for by the argued decrease in core reduction in that area (see above).

Technological comparisons of the flakes also show a similarity between the experimental and archaeological assemblages from Areas I and IV(4). There are, however, some differences. Cortex/natural surface retention is generally higher on the experimental flakes as expressed through percentage of cortical/natural butts (type 3) and through the cortical index. This might be explained by the ease of distinguishing natural surfaces (stained) and flaked surfaces (unstained) in the experimental assemblage compared to the archaeological material. One other difference is the lower weight of the experimental flakes. This appears to be mainly due to a decrease in thickness. This itself probably indicates a slight difference in knapping style, perhaps with the use of a lighter hammer. Thinner flakes might also explain the slight increase in breakage. Despite these small variations, the experiments support what is known from the refitting, that the principal methods used were parallel and alternate flaking.

Flake tools

The flake tools from Areas I, IV(4) and V can be divided into scrapers, denticulates, retouched notches, flaked flakes and retouched flakes. In addition, the spalls from flaked flakes have been recorded. They are summarised in Table 20.5. Although the range of flake tools is similar between the areas, and there are no noticable differences in their general form, there is considerable variation in the overall proportion of flake tools to flakes. Many of these differences may be due to the low counts, particularly in Area V, or the differences between the rolled and fresh groups is almost certainly due to the difficulties of distinguishing natural edge abrasion from retouch. However, the low proportion of tools in Area IV(4) compared to Area I is difficult to explain in this way. The possible significance is discussed in Chapter 23, as is the apparent absence of tools from the fresh assemblage in Area V. Each category of flake tool is discussed below, together with the refitting flake tools and evidence of resharpening.

Scrapers. There are a total of 18 scrapers, most showing a variation in form (Fig. 20.6). The retouch appears to be placed on the most convenient edge available, whether it be lateral or distal, and in one case on the butt of the flake. The retouch is usually limited to one edge, and in only one case is it longer than 50mm, averaging at 41mm. It is usually semi-invasive or sometimes marginal, and quite often producing a semi-denticulated edge. The angles vary between 38° and 86°, and averages at 67°. The edges are generally convex, but occasionally straight or slightly concave. The mean size and standard deviation of the scrapers (Table 20.6) shows that the selected blanks tend to be from the larger of the flakes. In five cases the scrapers have also been modified as flaked flakes.

Denticulates. Although some of the scrapers could perhaps be described as denticulates, there are only two clear examples. These pieces have had two or three clear, sequential notch spalls removed, but importantly with some additional retouch (Fig. 20.7a).

Retouched notch. The one retouched notch could almost be described as a concave scraper, the only difference being that it is slightly more concave, and has a shorter edge (25mm).

Flaked flakes. The flaked flakes are by far the largest category of tool at the site, in all areas (total 34, with an additional 6 on scrapers) (Figs 20.6-8). They have been defined by Ashton *et al.* (1991) and consist simply of flakes that have had further flakes removed. At

Barnham they vary, as at other sites, in that they are flaked from distal, lateral and proximal edges, and from both ventral and dorsal faces. Occasionally only one flake has been removed, but more frequently two to three flakes, and occasionally up to nine. In some instances, particularly where the original flakes are large, they could be interpreted as cores. However, in the absence of microwear, any assessment of this is limited to an intuitive guess as to whether the flaked flakes could be used as tools, or whether the flaked flake spalls would have been functionally too small (see refitting below). The average size of the pieces is similar to the scrapers (Table 20.6), again being selected from the larger of the flakes. This in itself might support the notion that the majority were used as tools.

The spalls removed from flaked flakes have also been recovered and total 29. They are often difficult to identify, but where flakes have been removed from the ventral surface, they can often be recognised by the presence of the original ventral surface, and occasionally by the presence of the original bulb of percussion. However, where flakes have been removed from the dorsal surface, identification is more problematic. This is dependant on recognising part of the ventral surface on the butt of the flake, which is often associated with a low platform angle.

Retouched flake. The one retouched flake is considerably larger than most of the flake tools (maximum length 161mm), has two long unretouched edges, and has retouch in at least one, and possibly two places. There is marginal, sporadic retouch at the apex of the two, unretouched edges, with probable retouch on the dorsal face, but removed from the butt. The latter has created a concave, retouched edge. This area of the retouch could theoretically have been removed prior to the removal of the flake, although this is unlikely.

Area Condition	I fresh	I rolled	III fresh	IV(4) fresh	IV(4) rolled	V fresh	V rolled
Scrapers	10	4	1	2	-	-	1
Denticulates	2	-	-	-	-	-	-
Ret. Notches	-	1	-	-	-	-	-
Ret. Flake	1	-	-	-	-	-	-
Flaked Flakes	19	9	-	-	5	-	-
Flk.Flk.Spalls	24	4	-	-	-	1	-
Total	56	18	1	2	5	1	1
% Flk Tools/ Hard H.Flakes	6.7	2.3	7.7	1.6	2.5	0	1.0

Table 20.5. Quantities of flake tools and flaked flake spalls by artefact groups

	Scrapers	Flaked flakes	Flaked flake spalls
L	65 ± 21	67 ± 21	37 ± 16
W	65 ± 34	61 ± 19	32 ± 8
Th	24 ± 9	29 ± 11	11 ± 6
Wt	106 ± 101	128 ± 129	14 ± 14
n	18	33	29

Table 20.6. Length, width, thickness and weight of scrapers, flaked flakes and flaked flake spalls from Areas I, IV(4) and V.

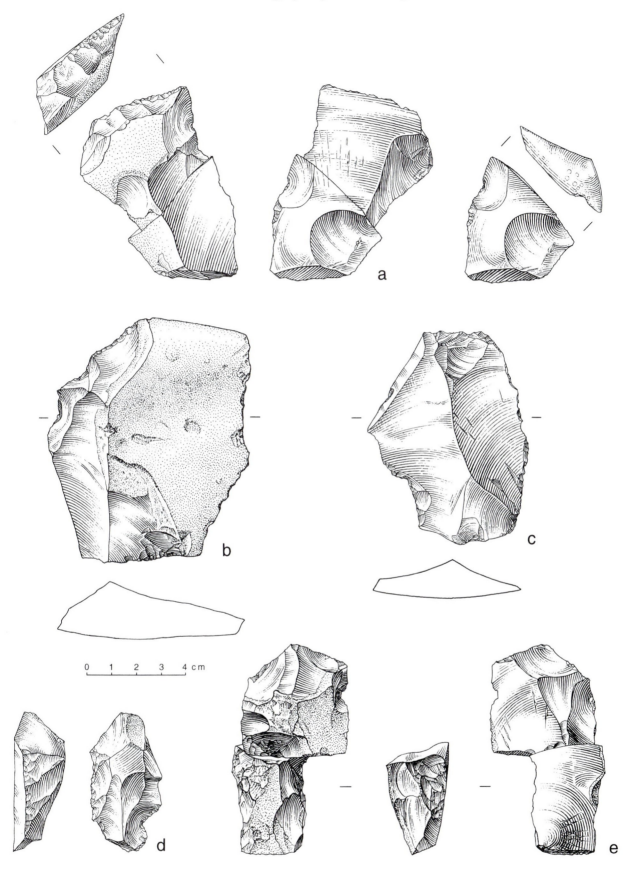

0 1 2 3 4 cm

Fig. 20.6. Scrapers, denticulates and flaked flakes from Area I, yellow silty sand: a. Scraper and flaked flake (P1990.10-7.9). b. Flake broken as knapping accident in two; proximal end (P1990.10-7.20) subsequently made into flaked flake, and distal end (P1990.10-7.11) made into scraper and flaked flake. c. Denticulate (P1990.10-7.16). d. Scraper (P1990.10-7.15). e. Flake broken as knapping accident in two; proximal end (P1990.10-7.12) subsequently made into intensively retouched double scraper, and distal end (P1990.10-7.28) made into flaked flake.

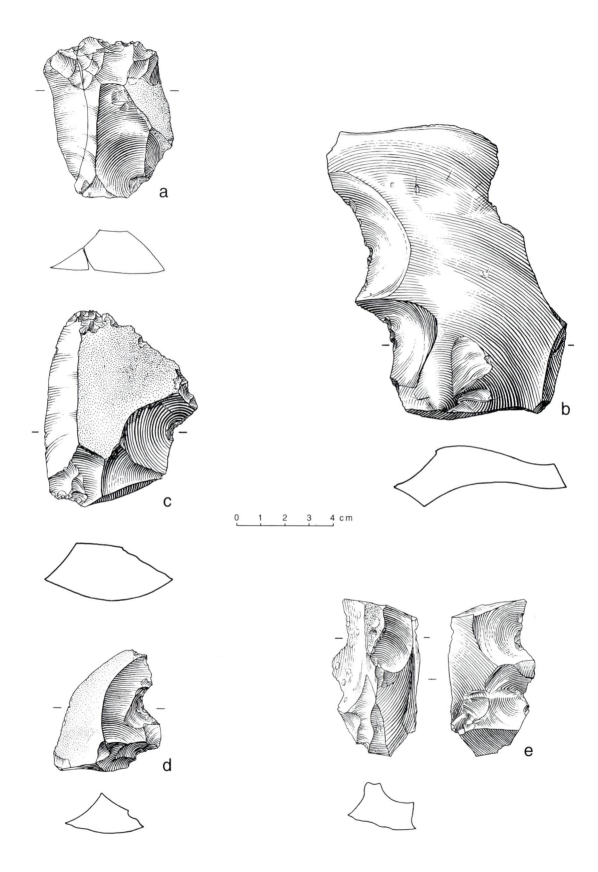

Fig. 20.7. Denticulates and flaked flakes from Area I: a. Denticulate (P1990.10-7.6) from yellow silty sand. b. Flaked flake (Paterson, Industry E). c. Flaked flake (Wymer # 2) from yellow silty sand. d. Flaked flake (P1990.10-7.25) from yellow silty sand. e. Flaked flake (P1990.10-7.644) from cobble layer.

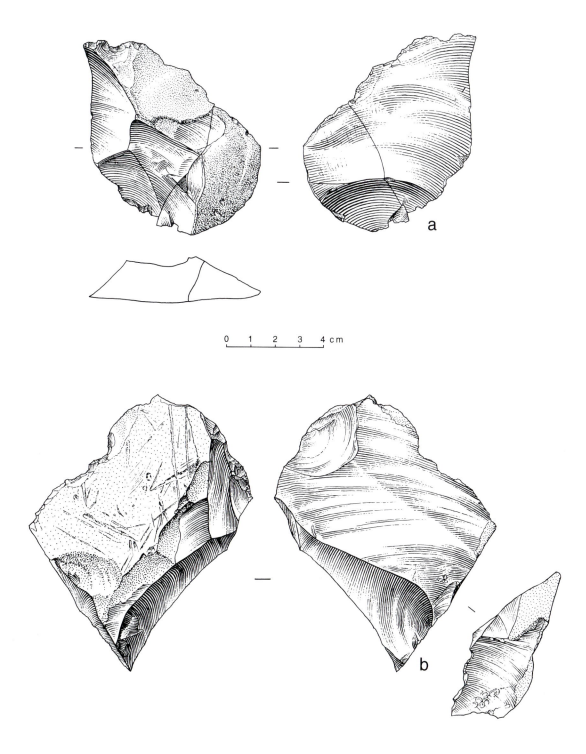

0 1 2 3 4 cm

Fig. 20.8. a. Flaked flake from Area I (P1990.10-7.41 from yellow silty sand and P1990.10-7.638 from cobble layer) broken accidentally from Area I. The latter has had further flake removed. b. Flaked flake with scraper retouch (P1990.2-6.1) from Area III, grey silt and clay.

Refitting. There are three examples where flake tools refit, and they all consist of refitting broken flakes. In the first example, a flake has accidentally broken in two (Fig. 20.6b). One half (P1990.10-7.20) has been modified on the ventral surface into a flaked flake with two removals. The second half (P1990.10-7.11) has been retouched into a scraper on the distal end and has then had four flaked flake spalls removed from several edges and both ventral and dorsal faces. The scraper could have been made prior to the flake breaking.

In the second example a flake has had one flake removed from the proximal end on the ventral surface (Fig. 20.8a). Probably as an attempt to remove a second flake, the piece has broken in two. One half (P1990.10-7.41) had no further modification, while the second half (P1990.10-7.638) had one further flake removed on the dorsal surface from a lateral edge.

The third example is again a flake that has probably broken accidentally during knapping (Fig. 20.6e). The distal half (P1990.10-7.28) had nine flakes removed to create a flaked flake, with the removals occurring on lateral, distal and proximal edges, and also from both dorsal and ventral faces. This could be interpreted as a core, although the largest of the flake removals is only 33mm in maximum dimension, and most are considerably smaller. The proximal end of the flake (P1990.10-7.12) was also modified by steep retouch along both lateral edges to create a scraper. On one of these edges the retouch has removed 20mm from the thickness of the original flake, and is probably a good example of resharpening (see below).

Resharpening. Although resharpening is often difficult to recognise or distinguish from initial manufacture, there are at least seven cases at Barnham where resharpening or remodification is the most likely explanation (for review see Dibble 1995). These are limited purely to Area I. In the three refitting examples, in each case there was certainly modification after the initial flake was broken, and in at least one case (possibly all three) this modification took place after the initial flake had already been retouched (P1990.10-7.41 and 638; Fig. 20.8a). Whether the flakes were used prior to breaking, is difficult to assess. However, in one of the refitting examples (P1990.10-7.12) the retouch was clearly intense, removing 20mm from the edge, and was probably caused by resharpening (Fig. 20.6e). There is one other flake tool where there is intensive scraper retouch that may be resharpening (P1990.10-7.9, Fig. 20.6a). The opposite edge had at least two flakes removed to form a flaked flake.

In addition to these examples there are two instances of scrapers being reworked into flaked flakes. This is also suggestive of resharpening or reuse. Equally, the reason why flaked flakes often have several flakes removed, might be for the creation of a new edge. If some denticulates could be included within the general catagory of flaked flake, then this might also explain this tool's form.

Although there appear to be examples of resharpening at Barnham, the majority of flake tools have only limited modification to their edges. This probably reflects the abundant, if poor raw material available at the site, where there is no shortage of large and medium flakes as blanks for flake tools. The examples that do appear to exist of resharpening or maintenance seem almost to reflect the obsessive reuse of one particular flake. None of these flakes are remarkable in terms of size, nor do they seem to possess other particularly desirable features.

Summary of the core and flake technology

The core and flake technology in all the areas is dominated by parallel and alternate flaking. This is supported by the study of the cores, flakes, refitting groups and experiments. The principal difference between the areas is the reduction in size and number of cortical flakes in Area V, compared to Areas I and IV(4), suggesting that the Area V assemblage is from the later stages of knapping. The type of cores in Area V suggest that either partially knapped cores were transported to the area, knapped, and then taken away again, or that previously knapped flakes were selectively brought in. Although the knapping in Area I and IV(4) was similar, the cores in Area IV(4) were less reduced than those from Area I.

The flake tools are dominated by flaked flakes, some scrapers, and rare examples of denticulates, retouched notches, and retouched flakes. Differences in quantity of flake tools exist between the areas. There are far more flake tools, with some evidence of resharpening in Area I, whereas there are far fewer in Area IV(4), and none in Area V. In contrast, there are few differences in the range of flake tools between the areas.

BIFACE TECHNOLOGY

The biface assemblages

There are two assemblages that result from biface manufacture, one from Area IV(4) and the other from Area V. Table 20.7 gives the technological attributes for the flakes from these areas. The distinction between these and the technological attributes for the hard hammer flakes are clear, in particular the increase in the breaks, the platform preparation, and in butt types 4 and 5, together with a slight increase in dorsal scar pattern types 3, 4 and 7, and finally a marked reduction in size. This supports the original separation of the flakes into hard and soft hammer, which as has been emphasised throughout is an approximation to any real division.

Area V and the smaller element from Area IV(4). Of more interest is the distinction between Area IV(4) and Area V. It has already been argued that the hard hammer debitage is from the later stages of reduction in Area V. This also appears to be the case for the soft hammer debitage, which can be seen by a significant decrease in size and in the amount of cortex (see cortical index). In addition there is a slight increase in knapping breaks (as shown by the knapping break index) compared to Area IV(4). All of these appear to be characteristic of the later stages of biface manufacture. Other variations between the two data sets may also be indicative of final biface production. In the dorsal scar patterns, the distal index (the combination of scar pattern types 4, 6, 7, 9, 11 and 12) is lower for Area V. Effectively this indicates that the dorsal scars show less knapping from the distal end. The possible reasons for this are discussed below. In addition, the number of dorsal scars, as reflected by the dorsal scar index, is also lower for Area V (for discussion also see below). Finally, the butt types also vary. This may not be a statistically viable comparison due to the small numbers from Area V, although the complete absence of cortical butts and the increase in marginal butts may be significant.

Although it is possible that several of the flakes in Area V might be from resharpening, the majority appear to be an integral part of the initial production. This is reflected in their size and occasional retention of cortex, characteristics that would not normally be associated with resharpening flakes.

With the general absence of bifaces in Area IV(4) (see below), the question is immediately raised as to whether the assemblage in that area represents the complete reduction sequence, or whether only the initial stages of the process are present (see experiments below). Unlike core and flake working, with biface manufacture there is a much better correlation between flake size and reduction stage. Therefore, to answer this the range of flake sizes in the two assemblages has been compared (Table 20.8). An initial comparison of length, width and weight shows that the Area V flakes fall towards the smaller end of the Area IV(4) flake range. A more detailed examination of the lighter (< 20g) and smaller flakes (< 50mm in length), however, shows a far clearer pattern. Here there is a good similarity in the distributions between Areas IV(4) and V (Fig. 20.9). This similarity in size is clearly supported by the means and standard deviations of all the size measurements (Table 20.7). This suggests that the total knapping sequence is represented in Area IV(4), rather than only the initial stages.

The similarity in sizes is also generally supported by the technological observations. Both the Area V assemblage and the smaller element from Area IV(4) (< 20g) are characterised by having a greater number of knapping breaks (see knapping break index), a higher percentage of missing butts, a lower percentage of cortex (see cortical index), a lower distal index for the dorsal scar patterns, and a lower number of dorsal scars (see dorsal scar index), in comparison to the larger element from Area IV(4) (> 20g).

There are, however, two possible technological differences. First, the butt types vary between the two groups (for example types 1 and 3). However, as indicated above, this is probably due to the small number of flakes with butts from Area V. Second, some of the dorsal scar patterns appear to vary in a more random manner (for example types 2 and 5). This may be partly due to the combination of the high number of categories and the low numbers from Area V. Therefore, perhaps the best indications are gained by using the distal index, as above.

On the basis of the technological data, therefore, it can be argued that the two groups from Area IV(4) broadly reflect different stages of the knapping process. However, within the larger group, there will inevitably be elements from the final stages, and within the smaller group elements from the initial stages. It might be argued that further refinement of the smaller element from Area IV(4) could be achieved by removing the flakes with more cortex. However, there is tabular flint within the cobble layer that could have been used for biface manufacture. The final finishing flakes on these blanks would have retained a high proportion of cortex. For this reason it is probably better to keep the few cortical flakes within the smaller element from Area IV(4).

As a further support for the division between the two size groups in Area IV(4), there are also significant differences in condition (Table 20.9). The group with the smaller flakes is slightly less abraded, is less scratched and has fewer flakes with a matt surface. In addition, the group is markedly less stained and slightly more patinated. These contrasts suggest slightly different histories of deposition for the two groups either spatially or temporally. The increased abrasion and scratching for the larger group probably reflect greater movement in a fluvial context, also mirrored by the higher amount of staining. Therefore, the difference in condition might be explained, for example, by the final knapping of a biface roughout taking place slightly higher up the river bank, on drier land, and later becoming incorporated into the general assemblage. This must remain a speculation, but nonetheless can be presented as a plausible explanation.

It should be emphasised that this separation into reduction stages is probably an arbitrary division of a knapping continuum. The only hint that the division might represent a distinct stage in the minds of the knappers is from the spatial distinction. This is the complete spatial separation in Area V, and inferred from condition in Area IV(4).

Area	IV(4)	V	IV(4)(<20g)	IV(4)(>20g)	IV(4)(>20g) less cortex	IV(4)(>20g) more cortex	Exper.
FLAKE TYPE							
I	32.1	28.8	31.5	33.3	28.2	56.2	34.7
S	67.9	71.2	68.5	66.7	77.8	43.8	65.3
n*	268	52	181	87	71	16	176
L	47 ± 27	36 ± 14	36 ± 11	67 ± 19	66 ± 19	71 ± 21	39 ± 15
W	41 ± 20	33 ± 11	32 ± 17	58 ± 14	57 ± 13	66 ± 16	34 ± 12
Th	9 ± 6	6 ± 3	7 ± 3	15 ± 6	14 ± 5	21 ± 9	5 ± 3
BTh	5 ± 4	6 ± 3	4 ± 3	8 ± 5	7 ± 4	10 ± 6	3 ± 2
Wt	22 ± 36	7 ± 7	7 ± 5	55 ± 48	47 ± 34	93 ± 77	6 ± 7
BROKEN							
No	14.6	13.5	8.3	27.6	26.8	31.2	22.7
Yes	85.4	86.5	91.7	72.4	73.2	68.8	77.3
KNAPPING BREAKS							
0	22.0	11.5	14.9	36.8	38.0	31.2	22.2
1	44.0	32.6	43.6	44.8	42.2	56.2	46.6
2	27.2	42.3	32.6	16.1	16.9	12.5	27.8
3	6.0	13.5	7.7	2.3	2.8	-	3.4
4	0.4	-	0.6	-	-	-	-
5	0.4	-	0.6	-	-	-	-
Knp.brk.index	23.9	31.5	27.5	16.8	18.6	16.2	22.5

The knapping break index is $\sum xp_{(x)}/5$ where x is the number of knapping breaks and p is the percentage of the knapping break frequency - ie for IV(4) it is $[(22.0 \times 0) + (44.0 \times 1) + (27.2 \times 2) + (6.0 \times 3) + (0.4 \times 4) + (0.4 \times 5)]/5$. See Appendix VI.

Area	IV(4)	V	IV(4)(<20g)	IV(4)(>20g)	IV(4)(>20g) less cortex	IV(4)(>20g) more cortex	Exper.
BUTTS							
1	39.7	46.1	32.9	48.3	42.0	80.0	51.8
2	11.0	7.7	7.9	15.0	16.0	10.0	6.1
3	14.0	-	13.2	15.0	16.0	10.0	2.6
4	21.3	38.5	31.6	8.3	10.0	-	25.4
5	12.5	7.7	13.2	11.7	14.0	-	14.0
6	1.5	-	1.3	1.7	2.0	-	-
% miss. butts	49.3	75.0	58.0	31.0	29.6	37.5	35.2
n	136	13	76	60	50	10	114
No Cone	83.8	84.6	89.5	76.7	80.0	60.0	54.4
Cone	16.2	15.3	10.5	23.3	20.0	40.0	45.6
n	136	13	76	60	50	10	114
No Platf.adjust.	54.4	61.5	55.3	53.3	46.0	90.0	39.5
Platf.adjust.	45.6	38.5	44.7	46.7	54.0	10.0	60.5
n	136	13	76	60	50	10	114

Table 20.7. See opposite.

Area	IV(4)	V	IV(4)(<20g)	IV(4)(>20g)	IV(4)(>20g) less cortex	IV(4)(>20g) more cortex	Exper.
CORTEX							
1	4.1	1.9	4.4	3.4	-	18.7	0.6
2	8.6	3.8	5.5	14.9	-	81.3	8.5
3	41.4	17.3	36.5	51.7	63.4	-	39.8
4	45.9	76.9	53.6	29.9	36.6	-	51.1
Cortical index	23.6	10.2	20.3	30.5	21.1	72.9	19.4

The cortical index is $(x_1 \times 1) + (x_2 \times 0.67) + (x_3 \times 0.33)$ where x is the cortex catagory. See Appendix VI.

Area	IV(4)	V	IV(4)(<20g)	IV(4)(>20g)	IV(4)(>20g) less cortex	IV(4)(>20g) more cortex	Exper.
DORSAL SCAR PATTERN							
1	56.9	58.3	65.3	40.7	42.2	33.3	48.9
2	17.0	18.7	11.4	27.9	32.4	6.7	29.0
3	3.2	4.2	4.2	1.2	1.4	-	4.0
4	2.8	2.1	2.4	3.5	4.2	-	4.0
5	5.5	10.4	5.4	5.8	5.6	6.7	4.5
6	1.6	-	1.8	1.2	1.4	-	-
7	4.3	4.2	2.4	8.1	5.6	20.0	5.7
8	1.2	-	-	3.5	4.2	-	1.1
9	1.2	-	0.6	2.3	2.8	-	0.6
10	5.1	2.1	5.4	4.6	-	26.7	0.6
11	-	-	-	-	-	-	1.1
12	1.2	-	1.2	1.2	-	6.7	0.6
n	253	48	167	86	71	15	176
Dist.index =4+ 6+7+9+11+12	11.1	6.3	8.4	16.3	14.1	26.7	12.0

Area	IV(4)	V	IV(4)(<20g)	IV(4)(>20g)	IV(4)(>20g) less cortex	IV(4)(>20g) more cortex	Exper.
NO. DORSAL SCARS							
0	6.0	1.9	6.1	5.7	1.4	18.7	0.6
1	21.6	23.1	27.6	9.2	5.6	31.2	5.1
2	27.6	28.8	31.5	19.5	15.5	37.5	34.7
3	17.9	30.8	18.8	16.1	16.9	12.5	34.7
4	12.7	11.5	8.3	21.8	26.8	-	19.3
5	8.2	3.8	4.4	16.1	19.7	-	4.0
6	3.4	-	2.2	5.7	7.0	-	1.1
7	1.1	-	1.1	1.1	1.4	-	0.6
8	0.7	-	-	2.3	2.8	-	-
9	0.7	-	-	2.3	2.8	-	-
Scar index	26.2	23.8	22.3	34.5	39.9	14.4	28.7
Scar index whole flakes (n)		20.0 (7)	20.7 (15)			25.8 (19)	16.0 (5)

The scar index is $\sum x p_x / 10$ where x is the number of dorsal scars and p is the percentage of each dorsal scar frequency. See Appendix VI.

Table 20.7. Technological attributes for the soft hammer flakes from Areas IV(4) and V shown by percentages. * Unless stated otherwise these are totals for all other measures.

Area	IV(4)	V	IV(4)(<20g)	IV(4)(>20g)	IV(4)(>20g) less cortex	IV(4)(>20g) more cortex
CONDITION						
1	8.2	5.7	9.9	4.6	4.2	6.2
2	81.6	86.5	81.2	82.8	81.7	87.5
3	10.1	7.7	8.8	12.6	14.1	6.2
PATINATION						
0	18.3	25.0	16.0	13.8	16.9	-
1	19.8	32.7	19.9	27.6	29.6	23.1
2	61.9	42.3	64.1	58.6	53.5	76.9
STAINING						
0	3.3	5.8	5.5	-	-	-
1	36.2	38.5	32.6	18.4	16.9	25.0
2	60.4	55.8	61.9	81.6	83.1	75.0
SURFACE						
1	13.8	3.8	10.5	20.7	18.3	31.2
2	86.2	96.2	89.5	79.3	81.7	68.8
SCRATCHING						
No	89.9	96.2	97.2	74.7	74.6	75.0
Yes	10.1	3.8	2.8	25.3	25.4	25.0
n	268	52	181	87	71	16

Table 20.9. Condition, patination, staining, surface sheen and scratching for the soft hammer flakes from Areas IV(4) and V.

The larger element from Area IV(4). A further question that can be asked, is whether the very initial stages of biface knapping are represented in Area IV(4). It has been demonstrated above that a good way of distinguishing the later stages of biface manufacture is by using weight. Although this method might also distinguish the earlier stages of the process, probably a more reliable way is by looking at the cortical and semi-cortical flakes (cortex categories 1 and 2). The larger element ($\geq$ 20g) was selected from Area IV(4) and cortex categories 1 and 2 were compared to categories 3 and 4, in an attempt to isolate the early and middle stages of production. Unfortunately there are only 16 flakes from categories 1 and 2, but despite the low number, there are some clear indications from the data. First there is a striking contrast in size, the more cortical flakes being considerably larger on average than the less cortical ones. In addition, the more cortical flakes have a higher number of flakes with an indeterminate hammer mode, a lower number of breaks

and knapping breaks, a higher number of incipient cones on the butts, and considerably less platform preparation. The butts and dorsal scars also appear to have significant differences. The butts are exclusively plain, dihedral or cortical, with no marginal or classic soft hammer butts, while the number of dorsal scars is lower, as would be expected from more cortical flakes.

Finally, for the more cortical flakes, the distal index is considerably higher, showing far more flaking from the distal end. It is worth comparing this to the hard hammer, cortical flakes from Area IV(4), where the distal index is 2.7 compared to 26.7 for the soft hammer flakes (Table 203). The implication is that these soft hammer flakes are genuinely distinct from other cortical flakes and the high amount of distal flaking suggests that the nodule is being worked from opposite edges for the initial shaping and roughing out.

Any comparison between the condition of the two groups is again prone to the problems of small sample size. As shown in Table 20.9, although there are one or two differences between the cortical groups, it is difficult to draw a valid distinction between them. This might suggest that the two groups have undergone similar if not identical depositional and post-depositional histories.

One of the measures above, shows a correspondence between the reduction of flake size and the number of breaks. This relationship is naturally a consequence of breakage, where an increase in breaks will reduce the size of the artefacts. However, it is worth investigating whether it is more than this. From a visual inspection of the flakes, it can be seen that where flakes have been broken, their thickness has been largely unaffected. If thickness is used as a crude measurement of size, then it can be shown that whether broken or whole, the more cortical flakes are thicker. Although the size of the complete flakes can also be compared, unfortunately the numbers are very small, with a mere five from the more cortical group. The average weight for this group is 135g, compared to 60g for the less cortical group. Because of the low numbers these figures may not be significant.

On this basis the biface assemblages can be divided into four groups - one group from Area IV(4) that broadly reflects the initial stages of biface production, a second group from the same area that appears to be the middle stages, and a further two groups from Area IV(4) and V that seem to be from the later stages of manufacture. Again, it should be emphasised that the division of the Area IV(4) material into reduction stages is an approximation, but also that these stages are probably an arbitary division of a knapping continuum. Particularly, for the initial and middle stages of the knapping sequence there is no evidence that they represent real divisions in method. Nonetheless they provide a convenient means of showing how knapping progressed through the reduction sequence.

Refitting. There are only eight pairs of refitting pieces from Area IV(4), and all but two of these are proximal to distal joins. Unfortunately, neither these, nor the two dorsal to ventral refits add anything to an understanding of the technology. There are no refits from the soft hammer debitage from Area V.

Biface manufacturing experiments

As a by-product of the experiments for the raw material study (see Chapter 21) the debitage from these experiments was used for size-distribution and technological comparisons. The experiments were undertaken by Francis Wenban-Smith and are fully described in Chapter 21. The debitage from nodules 10, 12, 15 and 18 in stage 1 of the experiments was used. Three of these nodules produced successful bifaces,

and the fourth was semi-successful. Because the main purpose of the experiments, in the context of the raw material study, was to assess the suitability of the nodules for biface manufacture and to produce bifaces by the most effective means possible, there was no attempt to imitate the techniques used in the archaeological assemblage. The result is that there are some distinct differences between the archaeological assemblage from Area IV(4) and that from the experimental assemblage.

The principal difference in approach appears to be the stage at which the soft hammer (red deer antler) was adopted in the experimental knapping which was usually between a quarter and a third of the way through the reduction sequence. In addition the hard hammer was also used on occasions in the later stages of reduction, so that in total 38% of the flakes were hard hammer removals. In contrast to this, it has been argued above that in the assemblage from Area IV(4), use of a soft hammer was adopted from the earliest stages of reduction. Comparison between the archaeological and experimental assemblages provides support for this, which is discussed below.

For the initial analysis, the experimental assemblage was treated as an archaeological group of material, and so only those flakes that were interpreted as being soft hammer, or as probably soft hammer, were included. Comparison with the known hammer mode shows that 17% of soft hammer flakes were wrongly attributed. This was expected as most of these flakes lacked the essential characteristics of soft hammer debitage, often due to breakage. These flakes were included in the hard hammer category, and the majority were classed as indeterminate. Only 8% of hard hammer flakes were wrongly attributed, most of these being due to the dorsal scar pattern and the thinness of the flakes.

Comparison between the soft hammer debitage from the experimental and archaeological assemblages is given in Table 20.7. In terms of size, the experimental assemblage is directly comparable with the assemblage from Area V, and the smaller element (<20g) from Area IV(4). As it is known that the experimental assemblage is from the later stages of knapping, this provides support for the interpretation that the Area V assemblage and the smaller element from Area IV(4) are also from the later stages of biface manufacture. It is of relevance here that 95% of the soft hammer experimental assemblage weighs less than 20g. Other technological measures show a general similarity with Area V and all the Area IV(4) groups, with many of the indices falling between the earlier stage and later stage knapping groups. This includes the percentage of breakage, the knapping break index, the cortical index, distal index and scar index, but is also shown in the size distribution in Figure 19.12d (Chapter 19). This seems to support the conclusion that the assemblages from

Areas V and IV(4)(<20g) come from the later stages of the reduction process. Notable differences include the percentage of butts with a marked incipient cone, and the number of platforms with edge adjustment. Both of these indicate a variation in knapping style, possibly with a difference in the type of soft hammer.

A second part of the analysis involves study of those flakes attributed to hard hammer knapping. The question arises as to whether these flakes are technologically distinguishable from core and flake working, and if not whether this might have had an effect on what has been attributed to this technology in Area IV(4). Table 20.3 compares the fresh core and flake working from Areas I and IV(4) with the hard hammer experimental debitage from biface manufacture. This shows that for most measures, the assemblages are indistinguishable, but there are also two important distinctions. First, the size of the artefacts are much lighter in the experimental group. This implies that if hard hammer flakes from biface manufacture had become intermixed in any significant quantities with the core flake debitage from Area IV(4), that this would have the effect of making the flakes

from that assemblage lighter. This appears not to be the case, with the hard hammer flakes from Area IV(4) being heavier than those from Area I (see Table 20.3). A lesser difference is the greater incidence of platform preparation in the experimental assemblage. This might be simply due to knapping technique, but equally might be taken as an indication of biface manufacture. These differences together with the low proportion of flakes to core in the Area IV(4) assemblage suggests that there are very few flakes within that assemblage that ought to be attributed to biface manufacture.

Despite the differences in technique, the biface experiments indicate three things. First, the analysis supports the interpretation that the assemblage from Area V and the lighter group from Area IV(4) are from the later stages of biface reduction. Second, the division between biface manufacturing debitage and core and flake working debitage in Area IV(4) is supported by the analysis of hard hammer debitage from the experimental assemblage. Finally, the experiments also show that there is great scope for investigating differences in biface knapping technique, that goes beyond the bounds of this report.

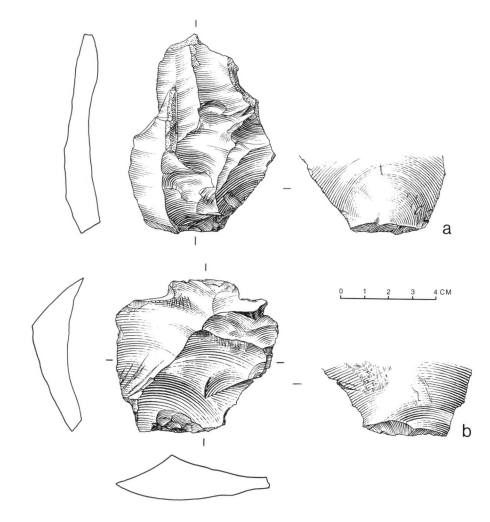

Fig. 20.10. a. Biface manufacturing flake (P1993.3-1.356) from Area IV(4), cobble layer. b Biface manufacturing flake (P1993.3-1.367) from Area IV(4), cobble layer.

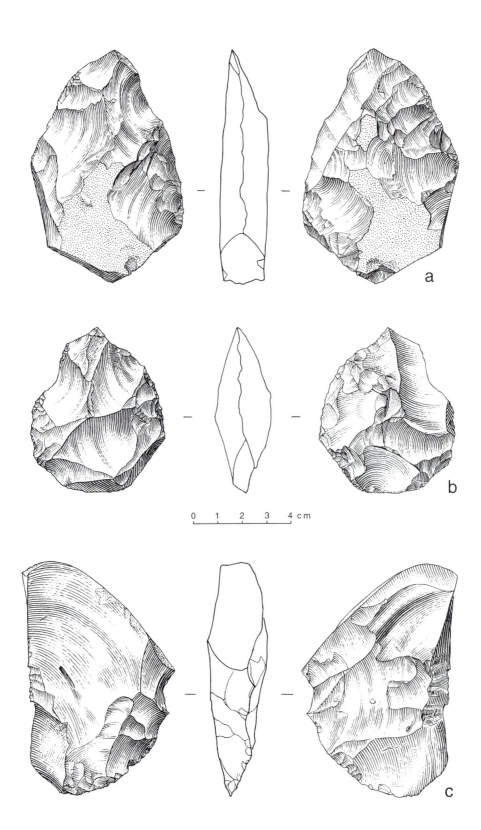

Fig. 20.11. a. Biface (P1990.10-7.3) made on tabular flint from Area I, black clay. b. Biface (P1993.3-1.1) from Area IV(4), cobble layer. c. Broken biface (P1993.3-1.2) made on flake from Area IV(4), cobble layer.

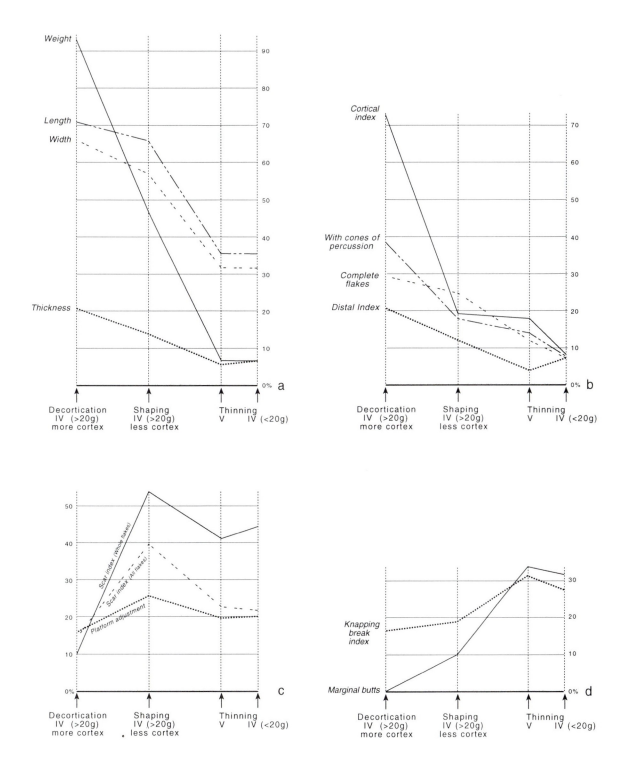

Fig. 20.12a-d. Measurements, and percentages of attributes and indices of decortication, shaping and thinning flakes from Area IV(4) cobble layer, and thinning flakes from Area V. See Table 20.7 and Appendix VI for further explanation.

Biface reduction

The process of biface manufacture has often been described through experimental work (Coutier 1929; Bordes 1947; Knowles 1953; Crabtree 1970; Newcomer 1971; Jones 1979; 1981; Bradley & Sampson 1986), but only rarely has the technology been described from archaeological evidence. Newcomer described from experiments, three distinct stages in the manufacturing process, with the use of different methodologies for the shaping, thinning and finishing of bifaces. In contrast, Austin (1994) from biface refitting work at Boxgrove, argued that no distinct stages could be recognised, and that the process was one continuous reduction.

At both Boxgrove and Barnham, however, it can be argued that at least in terms of spatial organisation, and therefore, also perhaps in terms of perception, it was not one continuous process. At Boxgrove, the reduction can be traced from roughing out areas near the flint source below the cliff, to distinct biface thinning and finishing areas up to 400m from the cliff (Austin 1994). At Barnham, Area V appears to be distinct from Area IV(4), containing as noted above smaller flakes from the later stages of the reduction process. This may also be the case for the smallest element (< 20g) from Area IV(4). To take the groups from Areas IV(4) and V is perhaps a good starting point for examining both the technological and spatial stages in the reduction.

Decortication and initial flaking. The cortical group from the larger element in Area IV(4) probably represents the initial stages of production. Unfortunately, the group only numbers 16, and of these only 11 are complete flakes. However, there are still some comments that can be made. As shown above the flakes are larger in size. The fact that they tend to be thicker probably accounts for the lower proportion of breakage. They also bear some of the features that are more akin to hard hammer flakes, such as thicker butts, more distinct incipient cones on the butts, and less platform preparation. There are other features, however, that mark them out as probably being soft hammer flakes; the bulbs of percussion are more diffuse, they have occasional lips below the butt, and in terms of their ventral surface morphology, bear the undulating wave pattern that is characteristic of soft hammer debitage. The experiments clearly show that incipient cones on the butts can be produced with an antler hammer used with force.

The flakes are further characterised by having simple butts (plain, dihedral and cortical) as would be expected from initial flaking of a nodule, but also a higher proportion of dorsal flake scars from the distal end. The high amount of distal flaking suggests that the nodule has been worked from opposite edges for the initial shaping and roughing out.

Middle stage flaking. The next stage of the reduction, but one that probably runs as a continuous process from the initial roughing out, in the past has been described as the shaping (Newcomer 1971). However, there is no evidence that this stage is methodologically distinct from the initial flaking. A much larger number of flakes (the less cortical flakes from the larger element (> 20g) in Area IV(4)) can probably be attributed to this stage. They are smaller in size and due to the decrease in thickness have more knapping breaks. They also have clearer indications of soft hammer use which include fewer incipient cones on the butt, more platform preparation, a greater number of marginal and bifacial butts, and usually the curved profile of soft hammer flakes. The dorsal scar patterns indicate a lower number of dorsal flake scars from the distal end, the majority being removed from the proximal and lateral edges. The reason for this is probably due to a greater intensity of flaking along a single edge prior to working the piece either bifacially along that edge or working from the opposite edge. A final characteristic of these flakes is the higher number of flake scars. This would partly be expected from largely uncortical flakes, but also from the increased intensity of flaking.

Final flaking. The final stage of manufacture, described by Newcomer (1971) as thinning, is represented by two groups of flakes - the smaller element (< 20g) from Area IV(4) and the group from Area V. Again, there is no evidence that this stage is methodologically distinct from the earlier stages. The flakes are characterised by being smaller in size which again due to the reduction in thickness probably led to more knapping breaks. There is again an increase in the features associated with soft hammer working, such as a further decrease in the number of incipient cones on the butt, an increase in marginal butts, and the curved profile of soft hammer flakes. One exception to this trend is the decrease in the number of prepared platforms. This is probably due to the high frequency of marginal butts, where crushing of the edge during the flake removal has obscured any previous preparation.

The dorsal scar patterns also show a decrease in the amount of flaking from the distal end. As discussed above, this decrease probably reflects more concentrated flaking along a single edge prior to flaking other areas. The dorsal scar count is one of only two measures that goes against the trends established between the initial and middle stage flakes. For the final stage flakes the scar count decreases, which might be against expectations. At least some of this decrease is due to the increased amount of breakage, although when whole flakes are compared (Table 20.7), the decrease is less marked, but still apparent. This variation may, however, be due to the small sample size. Therefore, what can be said is that if entire groups are considered, the number of flake scars on thinning flakes is lower than on shaping flakes, with most of the reduction being due to increased breakage.

The bifaces and biface roughout

Two bifaces and one biface roughout were recovered from the excavation. These are described below.

Area I, black clay, P1990.10-7.3. (L. 92mm, W. 63mm, Th. 17mm, Wt. 121g; Fig. 20.11a). This biface is made on a thin piece of tabular flint. Up to a third of the cortex has been retained on both faces, while the butt end is formed by vertical breaks through the tabular flint. At least one of these breaks occurred after the start of the knapping process. The piece has been minimally worked on both faces with use of a soft hammer, but removing little more than 15 flakes. A tranchet flake was removed towards the end of the process, producing a relatively sharp, straight edge along one side of the piece. There are at least two smaller flakes removed from the same direction after the removal of the tranchet flake.

Area IV(4), cobble layer spit 4, P1993.3-1.1. (L. 64mm, W. 55mm, Th. 24mm, Wt. 72g; Fig. 20.11b). There is no cortex retained on this piece, so the original size of the nodule cannot be guaged. The piece has been worked bifacially around all the edges, again with what seems to be a minimum of flaking. One of the final flakes to be removed has created a notch along one edge.

Area IV(4), surface of cobble layer, P1993.3-1.2. (L. 93mm, W. 60mm, Th. 22mm, Wt. 128g; Fig. 20.11c). This biface roughout appears to have been made on either a knapped or natural flake. It has been worked bifacially along one edge, with the removal of at least nine flakes. The focus of the knapping appears to have been the removal of an area of cortex along the edge of the piece. During this process the piece seems to have broken through endshock, and was abandoned.

Summary

The reduction sequence has been divided into the three stages of roughing out, shaping and thinning. This may well form one continuous process,and in some respects, the technological divisions between them may well be arbitary. However, the various measures of the technology show distinct trends as reduction proceeds, which illustrate the changes in approach to the knapping. These are summarised in Figure 20.12. It should also be noted that the final stage of knapping appears to have taken place in distinct locations, which indicates at least a geographical distinction in the manufacture.

CONCLUSION

The aim of the technological analysis has been to describe the variations in human activity at Barnham. This variation can be summarised as differences in the presence or absence of biface manufacturing debitage, in the proportion of flake tools, but also in differences in the stages of reduction (both core and flake, and biface manufacture) found in the various areas. The interpretation of the variation in human activity, and in particular how this was distributed within the landscape is the subject of Chapter 23.

21. RAW MATERIAL AND LITHIC TECHNOLOGY

Francis Wenban-Smith and Nick Ashton

INTRODUCTION

The objective of this contribution is to investigate the extent to which the raw material characteristics at East Farm Pit, Barnham, influenced or constrained the knapping strategies practised and the debitage produced. It has recently been suggested (McNabb 1992; Ashton *et al.* 1994) that the long-standing distinction in the British Lower Palaeolithic between Clactonian and Acheulian industrial traditions (Wymer 1974; Roe 1981) is a misconception based on the inappropriate pigeon-holing into one or other tradition of a fundamentally similar technological record whose main element of variability is the proportion of bifaces in assemblages (cf. Wenban-Smith 1995). Ashton & McNabb (1994) have suggested that the absence or scarcity of bifaces in so-called Clactonian assemblages is due primarily to constraints imposed by local raw material characteristics, rather than a technological repertoire lacking bifacial production. The reinvestigation of levels previously interpreted as Clactonian at the East Farm Pit enabled the raw material available to be assessed for its possible influence on the knapping technology applied.

Area I of the East Farm Pit (see Chapter 3) was originally investigated by Paterson (1937) and subsequently by Wymer (1985). The assemblages recovered by Paterson and Wymer, identical to those from the current excavations (see Chapter 20), consisted of cores, flakes and flake-tools, and were regarded by them as representing a Clactonian industry. Current work, including refitting, has shown that the fresh condition artefacts from within and on the cobble layer in Area I, and from the basal part of the overlying yellow silty sand, form a single assemblage, largely in primary context (see Chapter 19). As the cobble layer was the probable source of raw material for this assemblage, a research programme was carried out to investigate the suitability of this source of raw material for biface manufacture.

In the final season of excavations, evidence of biface manufacture was discovered on and within the same cobble layer in Area IV(4), 50m to the east of Area I. Therefore the raw material from Area IV(4) was also examined to investigate whether there were any contrasts with the raw material from Area I, and whether the characteristics of the raw material from the two different locations correlated in any degree with the associated differences in knapping strategy.

AREA I: RAW MATERIAL SUITABILITY FOR BIFACE MANUFACTURE

The main questions in Area I were: (1) could typical Lower Palaeolithic bifaces be made from the available raw material on the surface of the gravel? (2) how suitable was the available raw material for biface manufacture? and (3) could empirical criteria for the suitability of raw material for biface manufacture be established?

Methodology

Experimental knapping (Coutier 1929; Newcomer 1971), debitage analysis (Ohnuma & Bergman 1982; Wenban-Smith 1989) and archaeological finds (Spurrell 1884; Parfitt pers. comm.) have shown that Lower Palaeolithic knappers were using both hard percussors (rolled flint or quartzite pebbles, small flint nodules with thick cortex) and soft ones (ends of long-bones or shed antler beams). Therefore the knapping tools used in the experimental programme were the basal 15cm of a beam of shed red deer antler and a rolled quartzite pebble. The knapper (FW-S) has had over 10 years of experience using these tools attempting to replicate Lower Palaeolithic bifaces from a variety of raw materials. Therefore, while not being as habitual or proficient a knapper as most in the Lower Palaeolithic, a reasonable level of competence and experience was present. The model for the intended shape of the finished bifaces was based on the slightly pointed ovates from the Lower Industry at nearby Hoxne, an assemblage dated to broadly the same age as the primary context archaeological horizon at Area I (Singer *et al.* 1993).

Experimental knapping

As the first stage of the Area I investigation, the excavated surface of the cobble layer in Area I, which spread over 30m^2, was searched for raw material potentially suitable for biface manufacture; nine pieces were easily found which were regarded as suitable (nodules 1-9). A further nine nodules were then selected from the second Area I raw material sample, discussed below. The second group of nodules (10-18) were all considered at least adequate for biface manufacture, although they were generally less suitable than the first group of nodules. Therefore a total of 18 knapping experiments were carried out, attempting to produce bifaces from a raw material sample whose suitability ranged from adequate to ideal. The dimensions and weights of the selected raw material were recorded before knapping (Table 21.1), and whilst knapping was taking place characteristics affecting the successful production of bifaces were noted. This information is summarised below and also shows the outcome of the attempted biface production.

Nodule	L.mm	W.mm	Th.mm	Wt.kg
1	275	182	103	3.69
2	271	190	63	3.24
3	193	192	63	2.82
4	227	165	65	2.79
5	242	201	86	2.65
6	319	274	159	9.91
7	278	240	90	5.76
8	250	190	95	4.82
9	470	310	80	11.55
10	172	157	133	2.39
11	169	145	106	1.99
12	185	135	73	2.06
13	205	132	115	2.35
14	178	152	84	2.33
15	168	121	40	1.06
16	156	143	94	2.52
17	177	131	73	2.16
18	140	118	55	2.15

Table 21.1. Size and dimensions of nodules selected for knapping experiments

1. Failure. The size of the nodule and its lenticular shape seemed ideally suited for biface manufacture. However, the flint was shot through with frost-fractures making production of a biface impossible.

2. Success. The nodule had been formed as a large pot-lid from a much larger nodule, reflecting the effect of severe cold conditions upon the raw material at some stage. The condition of the flint in the pot-lid itself had not been damaged by the frost and its lenticular shape was ideally suited to successful biface manufacture.

3. Success. The lenticular shape and size of the nodule were ideally suited to biface manufacture. A single frost-fracture was found shortly after knapping began. This caused the nodule to break into two pieces. However a successful biface was produced from the larger of these two pieces without difficulty.

4. Success. The shape of the main body of flint in this nodule was more globular than lenticular, making it potentially adequate but not ideal for biface manufacture. The flint was not frost-fractured which enabled the nodule to be thinned during knapping and a successful biface produced.

5. Success. The shape of the main body of flint in this nodule was very globular, making it awkward for biface manufacture. However the good quality of the flint itself enabled bifacial thinning, and a successful biface was produced.

6. Failure. This had a suitable lenticular shape, but was very large and had very rounded edges, both factors not ideal for biface manufacture. The flint quality was generally high although there were several frost-fracture planes. The combination of the rounded edges and the frost-fractures made it impossible to thin the nodule and so produce a successful biface.

7. Failure. This nodule had the right lenticular shape for biface manufacture, although it was a little too large and thick to be considered ideal. The flint quality turned out to be poor - hard to flake and yet at the same time brittle, making it impossible to produce thinning flakes which travelled any distance. A very crude biface was produced with great difficulty.

8. Failure. As with nodule 7, this nodule was too large and thick to be ideal for biface manufacture although its generally lenticular shape made it potentially adequate. Its surfaces also showed some signs of frost-fracturing. As knapping began it became clear that this frost-fracturing continued through the heart of the nodule, making successful production of a biface impossible.

9. Success. This nodule was very large and both faces were flat. The size of the nodule meant that a large amount of flint had to be removed to reduce the biface being made to a manageable size, although the large size meant that if the nodule broke then the pieces could also have been used for biface manufacture. The flint was tough near the heart of the nodule but it was still possible to produce a successful biface.

10. Success. The nodule was of medium size and its generally rounded shape made it awkward to thin and shape bifacially. However, the good quality of the flint made successful production of a biface possible.

11. Failure. The nodule was of medium size and fairly lenticular, but had thick cortex and showed signs of frost-fracturing. The thick cortex hindered bifacial thinning, and after about 20 flake removals a major frost-fracture caused abandonment of the biface-making attempt.

12. Success. The nodule was fairly small, but had a lenticular heart of flint. There were signs of potential frost-damage, and the cortex was quite thick. The internal flint quality proved good, and it was possible to make a biface despite some minor frost-fractures.

13. Failure. The size and shape of the nodule were suitably lenticular, but there were external signs of frost-fracture. The first flake revealed the whole nodule to be highly frost-fractured, and the biface-making attempt was abandoned.

14. Failure. The size and shape of the nodule were suitably lenticular, and the flint quality appeared good. However, the flint quality turned out to be poor, not allowing invasive bifacial thinning, despite the absence of major frost-fractures. Production of a biface proved impossible.

15. Success. This nodule was a piece of tabular flint, and such pieces despite being already quite thin often prove hard to shape into bifaces. In this case the internal quality of the flint was sufficiently good for a successful biface to be produced.

16. Failure. The heart of this nodule was rounded and globular, making it barely adequate for biface manufacture. It also proved to contain frost-fractures, and the attempt to make a biface was quickly abandoned.

17. Failure. This nodule was a bit rounded at the edges making it awkward to thin the biface without making it too small. Some minor frost-fractures also hindered bifacial thinning, and although a small, crude biface was produced the experiment was counted as a failure.

18. Failure. This nodule had a very suitable lenticular shape, with no obvious flaws in the raw material. However, frost-fracture flaws appeared as knapping progressed, and it was only possible to produce a very crude biface; as for experiment 17, this was counted as a failure.

Of the 18 selected nodules eight successful bifaces were produced and there were ten failures, three of which were nonetheless crude but serviceable bifaces. The failures were due in all cases to frost-fracturing or poor flint quality within nodules whose shape was at least adequate, if not always ideal, for biface manufacture. The experiments showed that good quality and fracture-free flint was necessary for the successful production of bifaces. The presence of frost-fractures in some of the experimental raw material made it impossible to thin and shape those nodules bifacially and hence produce bifaces. Frost-fracturing had visibly affected many of the nodules on the surface of the lag gravel. However, there still remained sufficient good quality raw material for several successful bifaces to be produced, and in the case of nodule 2 the effect of frost action in producing a giant pot-lid had helped create suitable raw material for biface manufacture.

The quality of the raw material of each experimental nodule was assessed before knapping began on a scale of 1-3 (poor-good). Of the eight successful bifaces, six were made on good quality raw material and two on medium quality raw material. Of the ten failures, four were on raw material thought to have been good quality, five were on medium quality raw material and one was on poor quality raw material. These results suggest that approximately 40% of the available raw material in the cobble layer in Area I which appears good quality will probably have sufficient flaws to hinder biface manufacture. Conversely, approximately 25-30% of raw material which appears of medium quality may, given a suitable shape, in fact be adequate for biface manufacture.

Suitability for biface manufacture

In order to investigate further the prevalance of suitable raw material for biface manufacture in the Area I cobble layer a larger sample of raw material was studied. All flint pieces over 150mm maximum dimension were collected from four arbitrarily chosen metre-squares. In total, 97 pieces of raw material were collected. The dimensions and weight of each piece were recorded, and its suitability for biface manufacture assessed on a scale of 1 (useless) to 5 (ideal) (see below). This assessment was based on the size and shape of each piece, and took no account of the condition of the flint, which was assessed separately. This enabled the actual prevalence of suitable pieces of raw material for biface manufacture to be recorded, whilst distinguishing the

relative contributions of nodule shape and flint condition to the result.

1. Useless. Some nodules were too small, too spherical or had too mis-shapen a heart of flint to contemplate making a biface.

2. Just feasible. Nodules which were just big enough to contain a biface-size heart of flint, but whose shape made the production of the biface extremely difficult. A globular nodule is awkward to thin, and other awkward features on a nodule could be either very rounded edges or edges marked by steep vertical faces, both of which make shaping and thinning difficult.

3. Adequate. Nodules with plenty of flint for a biface but whose shape is still globular or otherwise awkward as described above. Very large flint nodules would also mostly be in this category as although a biface could almost certainly be produced, they would require time-consuming reduction and thinning, or the production of large flakes as blanks - a difficult task.

4. Suitable. Nodules with plenty of flint for a biface and whose shape does not pose any major problems. Good shapes for bifaces are nodules with a lenticular shaped heart of flint with quite sharply rounded edges making it easy to a) initiate knapping and b) thin the biface.

5. Ideal. Nodules which are lenticular and well-proportioned as described above. Nodules in this category would often be smaller and thinner than those in category 4, and so require less material to be knapped away and less thinning.

In the Area I raw material sample studied here, 21 nodules were initially (based on shape, before considering flint condition) regarded as adequate for biface manufacture (22%), 13 as suitable (13%) and 4 as ideal (4%). The stage 1 experiments proved that good quality flint is essential for successful biface manufacture, as any flaws caused invasive thinning flakes to fail, and made production of a bifacial tool impossible. The proportions of nodules which were adequate or better for biface manufacture, and which were also of good quality flint are summarised below (Table 21.2). This table shows that poor flint quality made many otherwise suitable nodules inadequate for biface manufacture. Despite this reduction, 17% of the Area I sample were adequate or better for biface manufacture and 10% were suitable or ideal. The stage 1 knapping experiments showed that several nodules which appeared in good condition were in fact sufficiently flawed to disrupt biface production. The small number of nodules actually knapped (18) makes quantification of this factor unreliable, but a 40% wastage rate was indicated. However, the stage 1 experiments also indicated that 25% of material assessed as medium quality may in fact be adequate for biface manufacture. At a location where so much material is frost-fractured, but where good quality raw material can be found, it is doubtful how much time or energy Palaeolithic knappers would have invested in raw material which appeared dubious. Therefore this positive factor has been discounted in the following assessment of the overall prevalence of suitable raw material available in Area I for biface manufacture. These results suggest that at least 10% of the raw material over 150mm exposed during deposition of the so-called Clactonian assemblage in Area I would have been adequate or better for biface production. Suitable pieces of raw material were, therefore, available in the cobble layer in Area I at a frequency of between 1 and $2/m^2$.

Category	3	4	5
Total	21	13	4
Good condition	7	7	3
% original sample	7	7	3

Table 21.2. Percentage of good condition raw material adequate or better for biface production in Area I sample. 3 = adequate, 4 = suitable, 5 = ideal.

Measuring the suitability

In order to investigate whether suitability of raw material shape for biface manufacture could be related to a simple combination of empirical measurements, the dimensions and weights of each piece of raw material in both the Area I sample and also the stage 1 knapping experiments were recorded and compared with their estimated biface-manufacturing suitability. The average dimensions and weight of raw material in each suitability category are summarised in Table 21.3 below. This table also shows the average value of a thinness ratio for each nodule (width/thickness). This statistic would be expected to reflect biface-making suitability since it measures thinness in relation to plane-size. It can be seen that increasing biface-making suitability corresponds consistently with increasing overall dimensions up to and including category 4

(suitable), and then category 5 (ideal) nodules are distinguished by i) being large but smaller than those of category 4, and ii) being thinner in relation to plane-size. The thinness ratio on its own correlates even more consistently with biface-making suitability, with a perfect correlation from low to high. There is a marked increase in thinness ratio values between category 4 (suitable) and category 5 (ideal) nodules, suggesting that this may be a key statistic in identifying nodules of particularly suitable shape for biface manufacture. These results suggest that such simple empirical data may, with a minimum of statistical manipulation, be able to reflect biface-making suitability of raw material. However, although the means are indicative of broad trends, the standard deviations reveal a certain amount of overlap between the characteristics of successive grades of suitability, particularly for weight due to the influence of a few very large nodules. Since the five variables studied cannot be illustrated simultaneously, it is necessary to reduce the dimensionality of the data for display. The two main empirical characteristics which affect suitability for biface manufacture are absolute size, as there must be enough flint for a biface, and shape - more suitable nodules are thinner in relation to length and width. Absolute size is directly reflected in the weight of a nodule, and thinness can be represented by width/thickness, which it has already been shown correlates well with suitability for biface manufacture. Therefore width/thickness was plotted against weight, and the clustering on this diagram of biface-making suitability examined (Fig. 21.1a). Four outlying nodules weighing over 10kg were excluded, to enable the variation within the rest of the data to be shown more clearly. Once a nodule reaches this size it will always be adequate for biface manufacture whatever its shape due to the large volume of flint; conversely it will rarely be suitable and never ideal due to the problems and labour involved in knapping such a heavy nodule.

Category	1	2	3	4	5
Length (mm)	192 ± 60	183 ± 27	200 ± 44	271 ± 112	230 ± 59
Width (mm)	116 ± 45	136 ± 22	145 ± 40	173 ± 50	184 ± 34
Thickness (mm)	88 ± 33	90 ± 21	91 ± 31	108 ± 41	76 ± 21
Thinness (W/T)	1.34 ± 0.26	1.57 ± 0.33	1.70 ± 0.40	1.80 ± 0.81	2.51 ± 0.48
Weight (g)	2765 ± 4225	2232 ± 1065	2987 ± 2577	4907 ± 3987	3544 ± 2313
Quantity	37	22	31	17	8

Table 21.3. Means and standard deviations of size, weight and thinness for nodules of different categories of biface-making suitability (Area I).

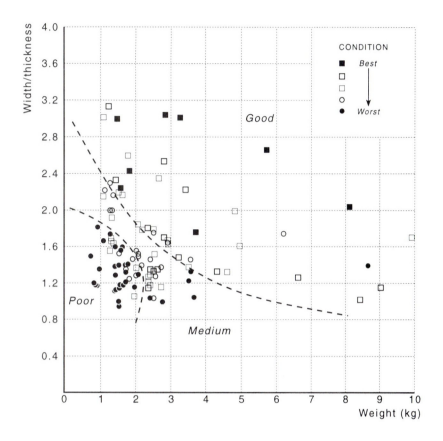

Fig. 21.1. Suitability of raw material for biface manufacture in relation to width/thickness and weight.

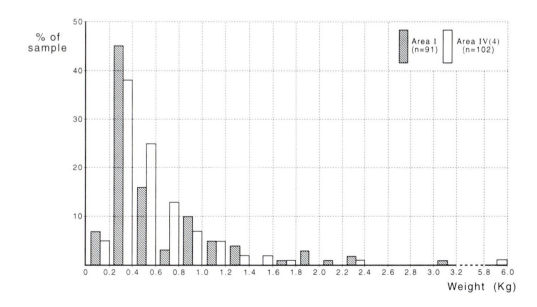

Fig. 21.2. Distribution of raw material weight for second Area I and Area IV(4) samples.

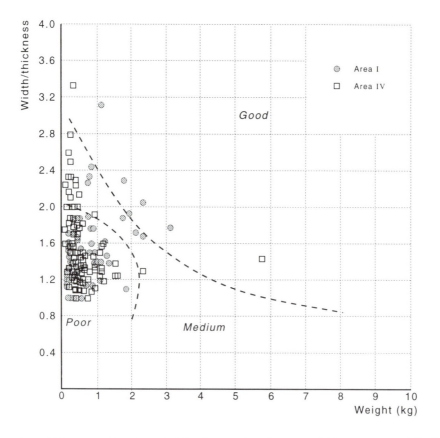

Fig. 21.3. Comparison of biface manufacturing suitability for samples of raw material from Areas I and IV(4).

Figure 21.1 shows that individual nodules of a particular biface-making suitability can vary quite widely in the variables analysed. However this figure also shows different zones where nodules are consistently more or less likely to be adequate or better for biface manufacture; in the 'good' zone the probability of adequate or better raw material is over 85%, in the 'medium' zone it is approximately 50%, and in the 'poor' zone it is less than 15%. The diagram shows that for smaller raw material a higher thinness ratio is necessary for successful biface production; however, as raw material size increases a lower thinness ratio becomes more acceptable.

Approximately 30% of the raw material is in the medium zone, where there is a 50-50 chance of material being adequate for biface manufacture. This uncertainty is not surprising considering the vagaries of shape which may influence i) the suitability for biface manufacture, and ii) the value of a simple empirical measurement. For instance a minor depression in the middle of a lenticular nodule would render it useless for biface manufacture without greatly altering its weight or its maximum width and thickness; conversely, a fairly minor protrusion out of one face of an otherwise lenticular nodule would significantly alter its width/thickness ratio without greatly affecting its suitability for biface manufacture.

The uncertainty of the medium zone is offset by the certainty of the good and poor zones, in which there is a high probability of a piece of raw material being good or bad respectively for biface manufacture. The presence of approximately 70% of the sample in one or other of these two zones suggests that the simple empirical variables used in the construction of Figure 21.1 can be used by any researcher, independently of any knapping expertise, to i) assess the general suitability for biface manufacture of a large sample of raw material from a horizon or site, and/or ii) identify some specific nodules from a sample which are either good or bad for biface manufacture.

COMPARISON OF RAW MATERIAL FROM AREAS I AND IV(4)

In the final season of excavations, biface-making debitage was recovered from within and on the surface of the cobble layer in Area IV(4), about 50m to the east of Area I. In contrast, the extensive excavation of Area I over four seasons failed to produce any unambiguous evidence of biface manufacture at the level of the cobble layer. In order to investigate whether this contrast in lithic technology may have been influenced by the immediately available raw material, the raw material from Areas I and IV(4) was compared by collection of two further samples, one from each area. Unfortunately the samples collected did not include enough nodules greater than 150mm for a valid statistical comparison, so a lower cut-off point for maximum dimension of 75mm was used. Although these samples are, therefore, not directly comparable with that discussed above from Area I, they nonetheless provide a direct comparison between Areas I and IV(4).

The means and standard deviations of the dimensions, weight and thinness of these samples are shown in Table 21.4, and Figure 21.2 shows the histograms for the distribution of weight within each sample. The mean values for the weight and dimensions of raw material are consistently larger for Area I, and the average thinness ratio is lower. However, the distribution within each sample of weight shows that the samples from both areas have similar quantities of smaller raw material (ie. approximately 70% less than 600g), but that larger nodules are slightly more frequent in Area I, with 10% greater than 1.5kg compared to 4% for Area IV(4), leading to the higher mean value.

	Area I	Area IV(4)
Length (mm)	116 ± 38	110 ± 27
Width (mm)	82 ± 30	77 ± 21
Thickness (mm)	55 ± 16	52 ± 18
Weight (g)	622 ± 586	578 ± 640
Thinness (W/T)	1.51 ± 0.38	1.57 ± 0.43
Quantity	91	102

Table 21.4. Means and standard deviations of size, weight and thinness (W/T) for second sample from Area I and sample from Area IV(4)

The raw material from Area IV(4) was also compared with that from Area I by plotting thinness versus weight for both samples (Fig. 21.3), which enabled the suitability of the Area IV(4) sample for biface production to be i) assessed by comparison with the results discussed above, and ii) compared with that of Area I.

The bulk of the raw material from the Area IV(4) sample falls well outside the zone of good biface-making raw material. However, there is a cluster of pieces in the medium zone which have higher weight/thickness ratios (between 2 and 3), but which weigh 500g or less. Half of these pieces should be adequate or better for biface manufacture, although the small amount of flint in these nodules would limit the size of any finished biface. This result suggests that, although a small proportion of raw material from Area IV(4) was probably suitable for biface manufacture, the biface-manufacturing activity at Area IV(4) was not due to the immediate availability of particularly suitable raw material.

Figure 21.3 shows that the second sample from Area I includes several nodules weighing over 1kg, and with a high enough weight/thickness ratio to put them in the good zone for biface manufacture, in contrast to the sample from Area IV(4). There are also several nodules weighing over 750g in the medium zone, half of which might, therefore, be expected to be adequate or better for biface manufacture. These results indicate that the Area I raw material was more suitable for biface manufacture than that from Area IV(4), mainly because of the presence in Area I of a greater number of larger nodules, a proportion of which were also suitably shaped. This reinforces the conclusion from the knapping experiments and the analysis of the first Area I raw material sample, that suitable raw material for biface-manufacture is quite readily available in the cobble layer in Area I, as well as demonstrating that it is less common in Area IV(4).

CONCLUSIONS

The knapping experiments showed that it was possible for a modern knapper to make bifaces similar to Lower Palaeolithic examples using the raw material available to the Palaeolithic knappers at the so-called Clactonian horizon in Area I. Refitting material from the Lower Palaeolithic site of Boxgrove, particularly the production of a biface from a fairly spherical flint nodule at GTP17, unit 4b, shows that knappers of this period were highly skilled in producing bifaces from unpromising raw material, suggesting that where a modern knapper can be successful, a Palaeolithic knapper would have had no problems. The main impediment to successful biface production from the raw material in the Area I cobble layer was the prevalence of frost-fracturing. Over half of the knapping experiments carried out failed to produce successful bifaces for this reason, although dubious raw material quality could usually be identifed before, or very shortly after, knapping began.

It was possible, using a simple combination of easily measured data, to establish criteria for the suitability of raw material for biface manufacture. These criteria are somewhat erratic for individual pieces, since it is hard to reduce the subtle variations in shape which affect biface-making suitability to two empirical statistics. Nevertheless, when applied to a large sample of raw material, the two criteria established, width/thickness and weight, did seem in combination to highlight zones where raw material has a either a very high or very low probability of being suitable for biface manufacture. Further experimentation and raw material analysis is required to explore this result further.

The analysis of a large raw material sample from Area I showed almost 40% of the nodules over 150mm long had a shape adequate or better for biface manufacture. Once flint condition, which was generally poor at the horizon studied, is taken into account, it can be suggested that between 5% and 10% of raw material greater than 150mm maximum dimension from the so-called Clactonian horizon in Area I would have been adequate or better for biface production. Such nodules were present at approximately 1-2 per m² over the 10-15cm depth of the cobble layer. This suggests that the lack of biface production was not simply due to the nature of the locally available raw material, presuming the hominids had reasonable access to it. The comparison of raw material samples from Area I where bifaces were not made, and Area IV(4) where they were, showed that the raw material at Area IV(4) was in fact generally less suitable for bifacial technology than that from Area I, with suitably thin nodules mostly being particularly small. The debitage analysis (see Chapter 20) confirms that, nevertheless, these were the nodules used as raw material for bifaces. Taken together, these results strongly suggest that the contrasts in lithic technology between Areas I and IV(4), with biface production at the latter location but not at the former, are not dictated simply by the characteristics of the immediately available raw material.

However, the lack of bifacial production in Area I and its presence in Area IV(4), despite the availability of suitable raw material in Area I and less suitable raw material in Area IV(4), does not necessarily indicate the presence of a distinct Clactonian and Acheulian cultural traditions, respectively lacking or possessing bifacial capability. Knapping strategies serve the purpose of providing tools which aid the survival of a mobile hominid species possibly exploiting a considerable area of the landscape. Explanations for the technological strategies carried out at particular sites need to consider the availability of raw material within the whole landscape being exploited in conjunction with patterns of mobility and the availability of other necessary resources for day-to-day survival (see Chapter 23). What is necessary, therefore, is to develop a broader understanding of the wider landscape around the tiny windows of it investigated as archaeological sites; knapping strategies can no longer be explained simply as responses to immediately available raw material or the mindless repetition of the habits of previous generations.

22. LITHIC MICROWEAR ANALYSIS OF ARTEFACTS FROM BARNHAM

Randolph E. Donahue

A sample of lithic artefacts from a variety of contexts from East Farm, Barnham have been studied using microwear analysis. Principally fresh artefacts were selected, but in addition several rolled artefacts were also included for comparison. The principal aims included: (1) to assess if there was any evidence that these tools were used, and if so, in what manner; (2) to identify the nature and sequence of post-depositional processes that affected the artefacts; (3) to confirm that most artefacts were in primary context; and (4) to compare the results within and among the different sub-assemblages.

LITHIC MICROWEAR ANALYSIS

Lithic microwear analysis is the microscopic examination of surface wear and fracture scars that form along the edges of fine-grain silicious stone such as flint and chert. Experimental studies demonstrate that microscopic wear and fracture scar characteristics result from tool use and vary systematically according to the worked material (e.g. hide, wood, meat, bone) and to the applied forces and motions (e.g. cutting, scraping, wedging, etc.). Understanding of these principles and relationships permits microwear analysts to infer past uses of lithic artefacts with a greater degree of precision and accuracy than through reliance on either macroscopic attribute analysis or ethnographic analogues of tool form. Natural processes also produce systematic microwear features which can often make inferences about tool use more difficult (Shackley 1974; Keeley 1980; Levi-Sala 1986a, 1986b), but can aid the understanding of site formation processes (Donahue 1994).

METHODOLOGY

The selected sample included 28 artefacts from Areas I, III, IV(4) and V (Chapter 19). From these a sample of 18 artefacts was selected for microscopic investigation: eight from Area I; all four artefacts from Area III; and three artefacts each from Areas IV(4) and V.

Sampling and cleaning

A preliminary inspection of the artefacts was made prior to cleaning and then a sample of the better quality specimens was gently cleaned with ethyl alcohol on ventral surfaces (on the bulb of percussion) and on dorsal ridges. These surfaces were then observed at 200x magnification. This was to assess the condition and characteristics prior to cleaning with harsher chemicals, particularly hydrochloric acid.

Each artefact was bathed in a solution of 12% HCl for 15 minutes, followed by multiple baths in water for 30 minutes. The artefacts were then patted dry with paper towel. During the cleaning process it was noted that some artefacts were substantially 'dirtier' than others, particularly P1992.2-6.16 and P1992.2-6.1, and some labels disintegrated during the acid bath. The acid bath appeared to have little effect on the artefacts' surfaces: there were no colour changes, and surfaces thought to have mineral residues maintained their surface characteristics. In order to assess this further, artefact P1993.3-1.538, characterized by a very reddish surface thought to relate to a build up of iron residues while buried, was placed 20mm up the proximal end in a 12% solution of HCl over an extended length of time, eventually totalling 68 hours. Although the acid bath became tinted, the proximal end displayed no visible differences from the distal end. Because surface gloss was already visible on some artefacts, it was decided that there would be no additional cleaning to the artefacts at this time.

Microwear observation and recording

Artefacts were observed at principally 200x magnification with an Olympus OHM-KLH metallurgical microscope with incident-light. Ventral and dorsal faces, particularly the surfaces of the bulb of percussion and the dorsal ridges, were examined in addition to all edges likely to have been used. Wear and fracture scar characteristics were recorded, and areas of interest were photomicrographed.

RESULTS

The microwear results were generally very consistent. Detailed descriptions of individual artefacts are not included, but these can be obtained from the author. This study will focus on the general patterns and anomalies observed among the artefacts within each site area.

Area III

All Area III artefacts examined have undergone very similar post-depositional processes. The dorsal ridges are mildly rounded with occasional and limited moderate rounding, usually when the ridge line is projected substantially above the rest of the surface. The dorsal ridge is polished, characterised by a narrow, bright line. Such ridge and edge polishing has been noted on artefacts from many prehistoric sites of various ages and is usually related to gentle rubbing by silicious material (Shackley 1974). Potentially usable edges have a similar line of polishing along their length, although it was often interrupted by fracture scars. These lateral edges vary in abrasive rounding depending on 1) edge fracture scarring and 2) the degree to which they protrude. In general, the edges are mildly to moderately rounded and are consistent with what was observed on the dorsal ridges.

Microscopic inspection of the bulbs of percussion, and most other surfaces, shows that they generally display a well defined network of surface polishing. This results when enough protruding points on the grainy flint surface have been polished to link with one another. Only the most protected surfaces do not have this wear effect, and it indicates that a fine abrasive material has been gently rubbing the surface. This networking of polished surface is also generally well developed on both dorsal and ventral faces near the margins of the artefact. This is also to be expected as such surfaces are less protected than others. It is important to note that this is a slight amount of wear, and one could expect to find some kinds of wear from use surviving on the artefacts if an edge has been well used.

On some surfaces, small patches of plastic deformation are evident. These indicate that an object of equal or greater hardness as the flint was being pressed into its surface. Occasionally, striations are observed associated with the plastic deformation indicating the direction of rubbing of the objects. The size, depth, and frequency of these patches indicate that these artefacts did not undergo severe movement. Only one artefact, P1992.2-6.2 displays a high frequency of plastic deformation patches, and even these are quite small and limited to the distal end of the artefact. Associated parallel striations lying oblique to the original plastic deformation striations indicate at least one shift in position of the artefact.

Additional evidence for the kinds of forces applied to the artefacts can be observed from the fracture scars along the edges. All artefacts in the sample have similar post-depositional edge damage of which very little is recent. The degree of damage varies primarily on the basis of the edge angle and the degree to which the edge is sheltered. In general, the damage consists of deep fracture scars of various kinds of initiations and terminations. The fracture scars are of variable size and are discontinuous along an edge. These characteristics suggest that on occasion various forces were being applied in different directions on the artefacts. The

fracture damage is consistent with limited amounts of trampling in soft sediments or small amounts of artefact shifting while in a buried deposit.

The severe abrasion in the form of numerous deep and wide striations on the cortex of artefact P1992.2-6.1 date prior to the tool's manufacture and has nothing to do with its burial environment following hominid discard.

Only artefact P1992.2-6.1 displays possible evidence for tool use (Fig. 22.1). At its distal end there is some retouch (systematic edge fracture scars) and a small concave area. Along the ventral face of the concave edge segment there is a continuous sequence of large, shallow fracture scars with bending initiations and feather terminations. These features are very characteristic of scraping wood with the grain. This is further supported by some striations that lie perpendicular to the edge on the opposite face. There is no surface polishing that can be observed. While it is very possible that this edge was used, the evidence is inconclusive.

In summary, Area III artefacts have consistent wear and fracture damage indicating that they have undergone virtually identical post-depositional processes. They have been only gently modified, likely by fine grain sediments only. They have possibly undergone some mild shifting while in the sediment, but again this would be limited. There is no doubt that they are in primary context.

Area I

Of the Area I artefacts examined, seven of the eight have extremely consistent wear, fracture damage, and chemical alteration. These artefacts consist of a bluish interior (that matches the colouration of Area III artefacts, and are likely to be of the same flint material) with a white granular patina or recortification. Overlying the recortification is a mottled, flesh-colour surface which extends over the older surfaces. What is fascinating about this surface is that it appears to protect the original characteristics of the flint although the underlying white patina has developed quite substantially (averaging about 1.0mm thick) and completely modified the integrity of the original flint structure. It is proposed that, following deposition in this locality, a mineral wash laid a thin deposit on the flint surfaces which 'fossilised' its structure while underlying flint continued to cortify with time. This explanation is not satisfying, but it is difficulty to provide a better one. Analytical and experimental investigations are now underway in an attempt to better understand these features and the mechanisms that produced them.

The seven artefacts from this location with similar characteristics are, in terms of wear and fracture damage, very similar to those recovered in Area III. The dorsal ridges are consistently characterised by mild rounding. They usually have a narrow, brightly polished ridge line. Occasionally, small patches of mild plastic deformation appear along the ridge. On the bulbs of percussion there is mild polishing of higher points to produce a well defined networking of polished surfaces. The network effect varies from being mild and patchy to quite strongly developed. However, the wear never intensifies beyond a network of lines of wear to an extended area of smooth polishing. The networking is most developed on the bulb of percussion and on the surfaces near the margins of the artefacts.

Area	Specimen Examined	Evidence of Use	Degree of post-deposit. modif.
I	P1990.10-7.455	Nil	Mild
I	P1990.10-7.191	Nil	Mild
I	P1990.10-7.216	Nil	Mild
I	P1990.10-7.275	Nil	Mild
I	P1990.10-7.320	Nil	Mild
I	P1990.10-7.370	Nil	Mild
I	P1990.10-7.26	Nil	Mild
I	P1990.10-7.142	Nil	Severe; ancient thermal fracture
III	P1992.2-6.1	?	Mild
III	P1992.2-6.13	Nil	Mild
III	P1992.2-6.16	Nil	Mild
III	P1992.2-6.2	Nil	Mild
IV	P1993.3-1.124	Nil	Severe
IV	P1993.3-1.538	Nil	Mild+
IV	P1993.3-1.547	Nil	Mild
V	P1994.3-1.88	Nil	Mild; heat spall
V	P1994.3-1.35	Nil	Severe
V	P1994.3-1.48	Nil	Mild+

Table 22.1. Summary of microwear results

Occasionally, these surfaces have patches of plastic deformation. For the most part, plastic deformation is extremely limited. Artefact P1990.10-7.26 has the most intensive plastic deformation with numerous small patches extending across both faces at the distal end of the flake. Associated striations are numerous and indicate motion perpendicular to the flake's axis. Nonetheless, while quantitatively more surface damage occurs on this flake than on the others, it is not qualitatively different, and certainly not meaningfully different with regard to post-depositional processes.

Another artefact from this area with interesting wear is P1990.10-7.191. Most of the plastic deformation occurs in small patches across the ventral surface at the distal end. However, there are also areas of plastic deformation on the distal end of the right lateral edge

which is extremely bright and smooth, often somewhat rounded or domed in appearance, and appears to curve around the edge and some arrises. As such it is very similar to wear produced by wood, but among these rather unique characteristics there is a continuation of the flat, less bright plastic deformation features. In the end, it was concluded that the wear had nothing to do with artefact use, but it does indicate how similar natural processes can imitate what are considered to be cultural processes.

Numerous ancient and fresh fracture scars were observed along the edges of these seven artefacts. The fracture scars were discontinuous along the edges, variable in size, deep in cross-section, and of various types (as defined by their cross-sections). Fresh fracture scars were easily identifiable because the fracture scar surface exposed the white patina and in the larger and deeper fracture scars, they exposed the unmodified dark blue flint.

Unique among the examined Area I artefacts is P1990.10-7.142. This is a large and thick cortical flake. Although lacking a non-cortical dorsal ridge, ancient arrises on this surface are extremely rounded and measure more than 10 units at 200x magnification. The dorsal surface has a greater degree of mineral wash than the ventral surface, but both surfaces contain numerous long, wide striations that are filled with white patina. The cortex is extremely pitted. The crater-like pits average approximately 5.0mm in diameter and are most likely the result of thermal stress, not from fire but from natural temperature cycles. It is also possible that the cortex results from an enhanced recortification process induced by the thermal stress.

Most edges are very abrupt on this artefact. The one relatively acute edge appears that it might be retouched; at least the large conchoidal scars here could date to when the flake was manufactured as indicated by the patina. This is not the case for other edges where abrupt fracture scars display a much reduced degree of patina formation. This indicates that some time following deposition the artefact became severely rolled and inflicted with edge fracturing and the formation of the severe striations.

In summary, the artefacts from Area I fall into two groups with distinct post-depositional histories. The group of seven with mild wear have undergone virtually identical post-depositional processes as those artefacts found in Area III, with the exception of the differences in chemical surface alteration. They are characterized by mild rubbing of their surfaces by fine grain sediment, and a very limited amount of shifting within those sediments. The eighth artefact underwent a totally different post-depositional history. Although spatially associated with the other artefacts, there is no wear or fracture scar evidence to suggest it participated in the behavioural system (or systemic context) in which the others participated. Although of hominid manufacture, its wear and fracture damage links it with the cobble layer and indicates it is in secondary context.

Area IV(4)

Three artefacts from Area IV(4) were examined for microwear. Artefact, P1993.3-1.547, is a blade with a white patina formation overlain by a substantial amount of iron oxide mineral residue. Unlike artefacts from Area I, the surfaces of the artefact have not been preserved, but have been substantially altered by the white patina, and this affects a number of key variables, often making them undiscernible.

The dorsal ridge of this artefact is moderately to heavily rounded. Surface wear was not observable on the ridge, ventral surface or near the margins. Fracture scar damage along the edge included medium and large fracture scars. Some of these are recent. The slight increase in size of fracture scars may relate to the thinness of the edge, the weakening of the flint from hydration, or from greater forces applied to this artefact.

Artefact P1993.3-1.538 is a thin lamellar flake with similar wear to P1993.3-1.547, but with a measurable increase in edge fracture damage. This difference can be explained by the very acute lateral edges making them more susceptible to such fracture damage.

Artefact P1993.3-1.124 shows evidence of multiple episodes of surface wear, edge fracture damage, residue development, patina formation and further edge fracture

damage. It has been severely stream rolled prior to its deposition in this area and cannot be considered as being in primary context.

In summary, Area IV(4) contains artefacts in both primary and secondary contexts. The two subassemblages are not likely to be associated behaviourally. The primary context artefacts, although displaying more fracture damage than artefacts in primary contexts in other areas, have edges that are extremely thin and thus may not have undergone greater mechanical processes. It does seem, however, that the geochemical processes have been more active in this area of the site.

Area V

Three artefacts were examined from this area. They include P1994.3-1.36 which is a severely stream rolled flake where patina or recortification is occurring at a rapid rate. Artefact P1994.3-1.88 is a large and very thin flake that is technologically similar to those artefacts found in Area IV(4). It has one thermal fracture scar (a large heat spall) on its cortical surface. This artefact displays very little post-depositional fracture damage or surface wear and is clearly in primary context. The third artefact, P1994.3-1.48, is also in primary context. It is a much thicker flake and technologically similar to those artefacts recovered in Area I.

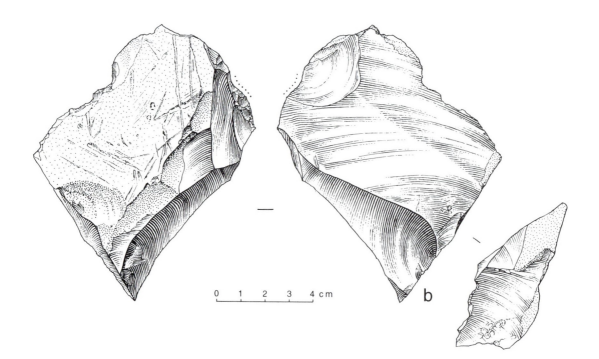

Fig. 22.1. Artefact P1992.2-6.1 showing possible evidence of use-wear on the distal end.

Artefacts with limited post-depositional wear and in primary context		Artefacts with limited post-depositional wear, prob. in primary context		Artefacts with substantial post-depositional wear and in secondary context	
I	P1990.10-7.455	IV	P1993.3-1.538	I	P1990.10-7.142
I	P1990.10-7.191	IV	P1993.3-1.547		
I	P1990.10-7.216			IV	P1993.3-1.124
I	P1990.10-7.275				
I	P1990.10-7.320			V	P1994.3-1.35
I	P1990.10-7.370				
I	P1990.10-7.26				
III	P1992.2-6.1				
III	P1992.2-6.13				
III	P1992.2-6.16				
III	P1992.2-6.2				
V	P1994.3-1.88				
V	P1994.3-1.48				

Table 22.2. Summary of results and implications

Area V appears to contain artefacts that are technologically similar to those found in Areas I and IV(4). It also contains severely modified artefacts that have been stream rolled and redeposited at this locality. This is probably the key area to examine the stratigraphic relationship of the technological, material, and post-depositional modifications of artefacts for Barnham.

With P1994.3-1.35 microwear analysis does not add much that visual inspection would not have observed and inferred. The artefact has been substantially stream rolled. Its relationship to the other artefacts is likely to be coincidental in that it became redeposited in this locality. It is difficult to accept that it was collected by hominids after its original manufacture, discard, and post-depositional damage and then discarded among the other artefacts here without having been further modified. It is most likely that the artefact is derived from, and should be associated with, the cobble layer at the site.

DISCUSSION AND CONCLUSION

Although artefacts from four different areas of the site have been examined, microwear analysis shows that there are at least two distinct and independent artefact histories represented. Otherwise there is no basis to claim that there is any significant mechanically-induced differences between the three areas. Interestingly, each area appears to have a fundamental difference in the formation of surface residues and white patina on the artefacts with the exception of Area V. A visual examination of the artefacts in the sample not studied for microwear indicates that their characteristics are consistent with this overall interpretation.

To the author, these results suggest that artefacts with macroscopically observable damage should be discussed outside the context of the other artefacts; they are not in primary context and have no behavioural relationship to the other artefacts. To combine the two groups together in any analysis is likely to blur rather than clarify spatial and technological patterns at the site.

The remaining artefacts found at the different areas all have similar depositional histories, and in terms of mechanically induced microwear, they are in remarkably good condition. Nonetheless, they have undergone enough post-depositional damage to obscure evidence of any kind of light use and probably heavy use as well. Fracture scar evidence does suggest that some of these tools may have been used.

Finally, although these site areas are some distance apart, the microwear evidence indicates their depositional histories cannot be differentiated. Therefore, although unlikely, there is the possibility that artefacts were transported by the hominids between different areas. This could be checked by refit analysis.

This study represents the first systematic attempt to use microwear analysis to reconstruct artefact depositional histories across multiple localities. As such it is principally dependent on qualitative characteristics as a means of presentation and at times in need of experimentation to confirm the proposed relationships and interpretations. While it is uncertain as to how useful this study has been for the archaeologists interpreting the site, it has been invaluable in providing directions for future experimental research in the application of microwear analysis for interpreting post-depositional processes.

23. THE SPATIAL DISTRIBUTION OF THE FLINT ARTEFACTS AND HUMAN BEHAVIOUR

Nick Ashton

For the study of the spatial distribution, only those artefacts that appear to be broadly *in situ* have been used. This limits the study to the fresh assemblages from Areas I, III, IV(4) and V. Although most of this material has probably moved since it was discarded, refitting indicates that this was only slight. Therefore, at least gross differences in terms of the assemblage variation between areas can be recognised. It is at this level that some aspects of human behaviour might be suggested. Moreover, some inferences can also be drawn from the more rolled material in terms of the duration of human activity in some areas.

ASSEMBLAGE CHARACTERISTICS AND INFERRED HUMAN ACTIVITY

Area I (cobble layer and yellow silty sand)

Due to the varied condition of this assemblage, similar activities probably took place in this area over some length of time. Although there are some technological differences between the rolled and fresh elements, many of these can be attributed to taphonomic factors. It should also be noted that in terms of condition, there is a continuum of variation between the two groups, suggesting periodic if not continuous use of the area.

The artefacts used in this chapter are the fresh assemblages, which consist primarily of complete sequences of core and flake working, where nodules have been selected from the cobble layer and knapped within the area. There is no evidence that other raw material or artefacts were introduced into the area. Some of the flakes (at least 12.3% of flakes > 4cm maximum dimension) were converted into flake tools and discarded within the area. Although most of the flake tools appear to have undergone little resharpening (for review see Dibble 1995), there are several that have had considerable reduction of the edges. This is discussed more fully under flake tools (Chapter 20) where it is suggested that the intensity of the reduction is due to resharpening and modification of these tools, rather than being part of their initial production. The implication from the relatively high percentage of flake tools, together with the instances of more intensive reduction, is that some use of flake tools was also taking place in the area.

Although there is some refitting in Area I, even the larger artefacts, seem to have moved. The three refitting groups are dispersed over distances of up to 6m, with only Group A showing a more distinct concentration (see Chapter 19, Fig. 19.7). Other refits consist of two to three elements and again show varying degrees of dispersal, almost certainly not reflecting their original discard positions (see Chapter 19, Fig.19.8). Equally, there is little patterning in the distribution of cores, flakes and flake tools (see Chapter 19, Fig.19.6). On this basis, little can be inferred about the internal organisation of the area, such as distinguishing between possible manufacturing and use locations. One possible exception is the scraper from Group B, that is found 4m upslope from most of the remaining scatter. It is of a similar size to many of the other flakes, and therefore can probably not be explained away as differential movement of different sized pieces.

Area I, therefore, in its last stages seems to have been a location primarily for manufacture, but also some use. There is also a broad similarity with the rolled element suggesting a continuity of site use over some time

Area III (grey silt and clay)

The assemblage from Area III consists of a large number of chips (< 20mm maximum length) which have probably been washed in with the sediment, but in addition there are 16 larger artefacts in very fresh condition. As discussed in Chapter 19, they appear to have been humanly introduced into the area. Their horizontal distribution spans 7m, and they are concentrated in the top 65cm of the grey silt and clay. This suggests that they have been introduced into the area over some length of time as isolated artefacts, presumably knapped elsewhere. One of the pieces is a scraper that was later modified into a flaked flake. This piece bears some evidence of use on wood, while a second piece may have been damaged through trampling (see Chapter 22).

Three cores were also recovered from the area, but there are no flakes that refit to them. Their occurrence is difficult to interpret. Were they brought into the area, conceivably for use, or were they knapped in the area and the flakes taken elsewhere? In the complete absence of distinct scatters, the latter seems unlikely. Alternatively were they simply thrown into the water? Unfortunately, this cannot be surmised.

Broadly associated with the artefacts is an abundant faunal assemblage (see Chapters 7-13). The vast majority of this is naturally occuring, but several of the larger mammalian bones might have been humanly introduced. On one piece, there are clear cutmarks, indicating butchery (see Chapter 12). This activity, however, cannot be directly attributed to the flint artefacts from the area.

The thin density of artefacts and cut-marked bone from Area III is similar to the 'scatters' of Isaac and Harris (1975) or to the 'veil of stones' of Roebroeks *et al.* (1992). As such it is difficult to infer any direct activity, other than the use of flint for possibly woodworking, and more conclusively butchering within a nearby location. The mechanism by which they were introduced to the area remains unanswered, but could include throwing, dropping, or possibly casual use.

Area IV(4) (within and on cobble layer)

Like Area I, the varied condition of the artefacts suggests use of the area over some length of time, although there are significant technological distinctions between the rolled and fresh elements. Core and flake working appears to have predominated throughout the use of the area, but in the later stages this has been supplemented by occasional biface manufacture. Although these changes in activity should be noted, it is the fresh element that is studied here, being more representative of the immediate location.

As in Area I, for the core and flake working, complete nodules were selected from the cobble layer, and reduced down to the discarded cores. Equally, there is no evidence of other raw material or artefacts being introduced into the area.

In contrast to Area I, there are considerably fewer flake tools (only 3% from flakes > 4cm), and none have been intensively retouched or modified. This might suggest that a greater percentage of flake tools was taken away, rather than used within the area, but there is no conclusive evidence for this. It is likely, however, that use within the area was a less important activity than in Area I.

The principal difference with Area I, is the evidence of biface manufacture. As with the cores, nodules were selected from the cobble layer, and the complete reduction sequence seems to be represented (see Chapter 19). However, there is some evidence that the final stages of knapping were taking place in a slightly separate zone from the initial stages, based on differences in staining and scratching of the artefacts (see Chapter 20).

The biface manufacturing flakes may only represent the production of three to four bifaces, and only one biface and one broken biface roughout were recovered from the area. This implies that perhaps two or three bifaces were removed and presumably used outside the immediate area. The one biface that was recovered (Fig.

20.11b) is only 65mm in length, and has not been extensively worked. This might suggest that it was discarded prior to use, as with the broken roughout.

Although there is some refitting in Area IV(4), like Area I, it implies little about the spatial distribution of artefacts, other than their natural movement.

Throughout its history, Area IV(4) appears to have been an area for the manufacture of flakes and some flake tools from cores, and in its later phases for the occasional production of bifaces. The general paucity of flake tools and bifaces suggests that there was little use of the tools within the area, and that some may have been taken away and used, at least outside the immediate zone of Area IV(4).

Area V (surface of grey/brown stony clay)

The fresh artefacts from Area V were recovered from a distinct undulating surface suggesting a short episode of human activity. Despite this vertical clarity in distribution, the low quantity of refitting and of distinct scatters, suggests that there has been some natural horizontal movement since knapping. However, the size distributions of the artefacts (see Chapter 19, Fig. 19.12), do not suggest that the assemblage has been winnowed, or that it is the winnowed component of a larger assemblage.

Unlike Areas I and IV(4), there is no immediate source of raw material in Area V. The similarity of raw material to Areas I and IV(4) suggests that this came from an exposed area of the cobble layer, nearby. This might have been a matter of a few metres. The artefacts consist primarily of both hard hammer and biface manufacturing flakes. The hard hammer flakes seem to be from the later stages of knapping (see Chapter 20). Although there are four cores, they would not have been sufficient to have produced the number of flakes in the area. This implies that either some cores were taken away from the area, or that some of the larger flakes were introduced into the area already knapped. The one instance of refitting (Group D; see Chapter 20, Fig. 20.5b) suggests that at least some knapping was taking place in the zone. With this group the first flake appears to be a soft hammer removal, but the following three flakes are undoubtedly produced with a hard hammer. There may have been the initial intention to produce a biface, which was soon abandoned in favour of core reduction.

Although there are no formal flake tools in the area, there is some evidence of tool manufacture. There is at least one flaked flake spall, with one other possible example. These cannot be refitted to the flaked flakes from which they were removed, so the tools were presumably taken from the immediate area.

The only possible evidence of tool use in the area is in some or all of the cores. One of the cores is made on a thick flake, in effect a split nodule, and could be classified as a flaked flake. It was catagorised as a core on the basis of the number of flakes removed (at least four and probably several more), and the fact that the original flake comprised the larger part of a nodule. There is just one flake that refits to this nodule. The four refitting flakes (Group D, see Chapter 20) also seem to come from the same nodule, and possibly even the same core. A second core is made on a natural flake and has had five flakes removed, while the remaining two cores are both made on small nodules and have had a maximum of three flakes removed in total. It could be argued that in terms of morphology, the minimum amount of working, and in perhaps two cases, the blank form, that these pieces could be classified as tools. This is an interpretation that should be considered, but unfortunately there is not enough evidence either to support or negate it.

The biface manufacturing flakes also appear to be from the later stages of knapping. The technology suggests that most of these are from the final stage of the production of bifaces, rather than from resharpening (see Chapter 20). No bifaces were recovered from the area, but whether they were used there prior to being removed cannot be established.

Area V, is probably the most complex of the areas to understand, despite showing only a brief episode of activity. There appears to have been the final production of both bifaces and flakes in the area, and also the occasional manufacture of flake tools. Unfortunately, there are also some imponderables. Some cores may have been taken away from the immediate area, or alternatively some larger flakes introduced. Nor can it be established whether bifaces and flake tools were used within the excavation area.

Area V (within grey/brown stony clay)

Only six artefacts in fresh condition were excavated from this unit, and they were dispersed over 2.4m and a depth of 20cm. Other than one biface manufacturing flake, they consist exclusively of hard hammer flakes. There are no clear knapping scatters within the area, and their distribution suggests random deposition over some length of time. This location, like Area III, is probably best interpreted as one of the 'scatters' of Isaac and Harris (1975). For a fuller discussion see below.

Area I (black clay)

A single biface was found in the black clay in Area I, with two hard hammer flakes over 2m distant. The isolation of the biface suggests that it was manufactured elsewhere, brought into the area, possibly used, and then discarded. The association with the black clay,

interpreted as a palaeosol, might be significant. Other locations were probably being periodically inundated by the river, during, or at least after the various knapping episodes.

THE PROBLEM OF CONTEMPORANEITY

The areas of human activity, discussed above, represent different lengths of time, and can only be argued to be broadly contemporary. The issue of contemporaneity has only occasionally been discussed in the literature (Stern 1993, 1994). In the absence of refitting, where it is reasonably assumed that a single sequence probably occurred within a short period of time (ie days or less, rather than months), it is impossible to demonstrate.

The measure of contemporaneity is automatically set by the parameters of geological time (see Chapter 4). This is notoriously difficult to measure on a human timescale, where the build-up of 30cm of fine sediment could have taken anything from a few days to several thousand years. Equally, problems exist where sediment deposition, weathering and erosion are seen as uniform, synchronic events, rather than dynamic systems. In reality, the formation of a palaeosol in one part of a landscape may precede the formation of what are interpreted as stratigraphically equivalent palaeosols where, for example, drainage might be different.

In terms of Barnham, then, what parameters can be set? The assemblages on and within the cobble layer in Areas I and IV(4) are from similar deposits and can be argued to be geologically contemporary. From the varying conditions of the artefacts, the knapping took place over a considerable length of time, although the fresh artefacts (paticularly the refitting groups) were probably knapped and quickly covered over by the yellow silty sand. The knapping appears to have only occurred while the cobble layer was exposed. However, it may have been exposed and re-exposed several times, and not necessarily at the same time in each location.

The artefacts from the grey silt and clay in Area III, were again discarded over some length of time. These sediments are a lateral equivalent of the yellow silty sand in Areas I and IV(4), but the upper part in Area III was probably deposited slightly later than in Areas I and IV(4). It is unlikely that the cobble layer at the edge of the channel (Areas I and IV(4)) was reworked to any great extent during the depositon of the top 2m of the grey silt and clay in the centre of the channel (Area III). This suggests that the rolled material from the edges of the channel are contemporary with an earlier phase of sedimentation in the centre of the channel. Equally, if it can be assumed that sedimentation was continuous, the higher level of both the yellow silty sand and palaeosol in Areas I and IV(4) and their position at the edge of the channel suggests that they are earlier than the very top of the grey silt and clay and the palaesosol at the centre of the channel. How much earlier, depends on how quickly the water level dropped and sedimentation ceased.

The deposition of the grey/brown stony clay in Area V is equally difficult to relate to the other artefact locations. Like the yellow silty sand in Areas I and IV(4), it is likely to have been deposited prior to the top of the grey silts and clays in Area III, but its relationship with Areas I and IV(4) cannot be gauged. Even the stabilisation of thegrey/brown stony clay surface in Area V could have occurred before, during or after the depostion of the equivalent deposit in Areas I and IV(4).

The difficulties of refining contemporaneity are not limited to Barnham, but are a problem at all Palaeolithic sites. Stern (1993) argues that at Koobi Fora, Kenya, for example, relating the sites within or eroding out from the lower Okote Member provides a time range ('time average') of up to 90,000 years. Such estimates have been refuted by Bunn and Kroll (1993), but nonetheless the concept of the time average still highlights the difficulties faced by Lower Palaeolithic archaeology in comparing at a human behavioural level broader areas of the landscape. At the other extreme, even sites like Boxgrove (Roberts 1986, 1990; Roberts *et al.* 1997) have difficulties in demonstrating contemporaneity. In the absence of refitting between discrete areas, contemporaneity cannot be refined beyond the geological subunit.

The problems faced at sites such as Koobi Fora are on a different scale to Barnham and Boxgrove, where the time average might be less than a few hundred years, and certainly no more than a few thousand. All the locations at Barnham, although not exactly contemporary, can be regarded as isolated keyholes into a series of activity areas. Some of these keyholes yield only glimpses of activity over a limited period of time, whereas others provide a picture of longer term activitiy.

INTERPRETATIVE FRAMEWORKS

The question now is how the variation in activity can be interpreted. Can the data still support the more traditional, cultural interpretations, or can alternative models be constructed to explain the variation in the stone tool assemblages? These are discussed below.

Cultural models

Traditional approaches to this data would interpret the variation in stone tool assemblages as reflecting different traditions of knapping. In Britain this is formulated as the distinction between the Clactonian (core and flake assemblages) and the Acheulian (core, flake and biface assemblages) (for example Breuil

1932; Warren 1933, 1951; Paterson 1937, 1942; Roe 1981; Wymer 1985). The cultural models rest principally on two bodies of evidence: (1) the differences in the stone tool assemblages; and (2) the chronological separation of these industries. Each of these is briefly examined below in the light of the evidence from Barnham.

The division of British Lower Palaeolithic stone tool assemblages into Clactonian and Acheulian has been argued on the basis of the qualitative variation in the core working and the flake tools and in the presence/absence of bifaces. Recent work has dismissed these claims (McNabb 1992; Ashton 1992; Ashton & McNabb 1992, 1994, 1996; McNabb & Ashton 1992, 1995; Ashton *et al.* 1994b; McNabb 1996) arguing that there are no technological differences in the core working, that the same range of flake tools are present in both industries, and that bifaces are present, albeit in small quantities, in Clactonian assemblages.

Barnham has provided supportive evidence for this view. The assemblages excavated by Paterson (1937, 1942) and Wymer (1985) from the cobble layer in Area I have both been described by those authors as Clactonian. These assemblages come from the same context and area as the assemblage excavated in the current excavations and on this basis should also be regarded as Clactonian. By traditional criteria, the assemblage excavated from Area IV(4) is Acheulian by the mere presence of bifaces and biface manufacturing debitage. The same is true for the assemblage from Area V. Technological comparisons of the assemblages between Areas I and IV(4) (Chapter 20) demonstrate the similarity in the core and flake working. Although there are differences in the quantities of flake tools, the same types of tools are represented. The only marked difference between the areas is the presence of bifaces and biface manufacturing debitage in Area IV(4).

For the proponents of the cultural model, there are two possible interpretations. One view might be that the Area I assemblage was misinterpreted in the past, and is really part of the assemblage from Area IV(4). Although this view might be sustainable, it highlights the weakness and fragility of traditional classification schemes, whereby groups of material, even without bifaces (ie the Area I assemblage) can be regarded as Acheulian. To test such a view, differences in the other artefact catagories would have to be sought, but as argued above it is currently difficult to discern these differences. What is also implied is that marked variations should be expected within separate spatial components of a single assemblage.

An alternative view might be that the assemblages are still regarded as being culturally distinct. To sustain this view it would also be neccessary to explain how different groups of hominids used the same environment and landscape, exploited the same flint sources, and knapped similar cores, flakes and flake tools, over a short period of time.

This leads naturally on to the second body of evidence used to support the cultural model - the chronological separation of the Clactonian and Acheulian assemblage types. It was argued, particularly from the 1950s that the Clactonian pre-dated the Acheulian (Warren 1951; Wymer 1968; Roe 1981).

This was intimately entwined with models of unilinear evolution (McNabb 1996), and was supported by the apparent stratigraphic relationship between the industries at Swanscombe and Barnham. Over the past ten years a growing body of evidence has shown that Acheulian industries occur considerably earlier than Clactonian industries, at sites such as Boxgrove (Roberts *et al.* 1997), High Lodge (Ashton *et al.* 1992) and Warren Hill (Wymer *et al.* 1991). Although the idea of a unilinear evolution has been largely abandoned, environmental models have been developed, that explain the distinction in the industries as being attributable to the exploitation of different landscapes or climatic zones.

One of the first environmental models was developed by Collins (1969) who argued that in the case of Britain, Clactonian assemblages were largely confined to warm, forested environments, whereas Acheulian assemblages were more associated with cool, open, glacial landscapes. It was still explicitly stated that these assemblages represented different cultural groups who were adapted to different environments. More recently a similar theme has been adopted by Mithen (1994) who bolsters the model by combining studies of social learning and primatology. He argues for the same association of industry and environment, but goes on to explain the distinction in the assemblages as due to differences in group size and as a consequence the structure of learning. Open environments, he argues, would be populated by larger social groups, where the channels of social learning would be better defined. As a result information (such as biface manufacture) is more easily transferred, and sustained in a conservative society over long periods of time. In contrast, smaller social groups in forested environments are more likely to have less well-defined channels of learning and as a consequence are unable to maintain key sets of procedures from generation to generation. This is reflected in the absence of bifaces, and also, he argues, in cruder, more haphazard core working.

Although such models are appealing, there is a fundamental problem with the archaeological database. This is demonstrated clearly at Barnham, where biface and non-biface assemblages, but with similar core and flake working, are clearly being made in the same environment. Such evidence is also reflected elsewhere, with a growing list of Acheulian assemblages being associated with interglacial environments (McNabb &

Ashton 1995).

If cultural models are to be sustained, then explanations have to be sought of how different groups of hominids can maintain their distinctions as reflected in stone tools, in the same environments over vast lengths of time. Currently there are no explanations, merely the repetition of long held beliefs.

Technological models

As an alternative to the cultural models Ohel (1979; 1982) put forward the idea that Clactonian assemblages were knapping floors from the initial stages of biface manufacture, and therefore although technologically distinct from Acheulian assemblages, were still part of the same tradition of knapping. He cited as evidence the occurrence of occasional bifaces, backed up by a series of metrical analyses. His ideas were robustly refuted primarily by the lack of evidence for the flakes from Clactonian sites being from the initial stages of biface manufacture (Collins 1979; Newcomer 1979; Roe 1979; Wymer 1979). The difficulties with this model can also be demonstrated at Barnham, where initial biface manufacturing flakes can be distinguished from initial core and flake working, and where the technological studies together with refitting demonstrate that most if not all the knapping in Area I was for the production of flakes from cores.

Resource and landscape models

Studies that reconstruct the distribution of resources in the palaeolandscape have long been applied to the Plio-Pleistocene archaeological record in East Africa (Isaac 1981; Potts 1989, 1991, 1994; Blumenschine & Masao 1991; Bunn 1994; Kroll 1994; Rogers *et al.* 1994), sometimes described as 'off-site' archaeology (Foley 1981). These studies not only chart the use of that landscape by early hominids leading to models of movement, but also provide explanations for the variation in the archaeological record. This approach has been recently criticised because of the difficulties of recognising and comparing discrete behavioural units and of dealing with long time ranges (Stern 1993, 1994), although counter-arguments have robustly defended the studies (Bunn & Kroll 1993; Kroll 1994; also see above). Despite these potential problems, the approach can still be usefully adopted at sites such as Barnham, where much narrower time-ranges can be identified.

At Barnham a small part of a hominid landscape has been identified, where activity in some instances might be measured in centuries, if not decades or less. Over this critical time it can be argued that there were few changes in the distribution of resources or in the configuration of the landscape. It is the relatively constant nature of the landscape that provides the critical backdrop against which hominid activities can be measured. Although it is argued that the activities represented at Barnham are a series of keyholes or photo-shots, by adopting this approach, the information can be interpreted in a way that provides a cohesive behavioural model, or a *photo-montage* of the hominid activities.

The key elements of the landscape consisted of a small stream or river, which on occasions reworked and re-exposed a lag gravel (the cobble layer) on its south margin, providing a natural source of raw material. From the evidence of the fauna and flora, this river valley supported a rich and diverse range of animal and plantlife, much of which could have been exploited by humans. Although there may have been localised changes in the composition of the fauna and flora as the stream dried out, as long as water was available in the area it provided not only a natural focus, but also access to other micro-environments in the surrounding landscape that converged on the water's edge.

The landscape model can be developed by considering a further aspect of the variation in stone tool assemblages - the variation in artefact density. This has been discussed at great length in an East African context, but only rarely applied to Europe. At Koobi Fora, Isaac and Harris (1975) first described the less dense distributions as the 'scatter' between the more dense 'patches'. In similar terms Roebroeks *et al.* (1992) wrote of the 'veil of stones' as the background to the richer 'sites' at Maastricht-Belvedere. The distinction between the two types of distribution has been explained as differences in discard patterns, so that the scatters are a combination of single event discards that occur for a variety of reasons around wide areas of the landscape, whereas the patches are explained as repeated discards in a single location. The reasons for repeated discard in one location can be explained by the positioning of a static resource. In an East African context, the position of a single shade-providing tree

has been put forward as the explanation of repeated actions in one place (Kroll & Isaac 1984; Potts 1991; Kroll 1994). The cobble layer at Barnham provides another example of a static resource.

Perhaps then the variation in distribution can be reduced to the differences between static and mobile resources; static resources would lead to a series of repeated actions in one location, while mobile resources would lead to a series of single event discards over much wider areas. This might be termed the *static resource model* (see Potts 1991). At its basic level this would simply consist of a raw material resource, but through the transport of lithics to other fixed resources (vegetation, water sources, sleeping places) these too would accumulate lithic material by accident and design. As Kuhn (1995) argued 'sites' are where means, motive and opportunity come together most often.

How then can this be applied to Barnham? The most obvious of the static resources is the flint raw material source in Areas I and IV(4). Although accessibilty might have been restricted at times, its location remained the same. Other resources, although static in terms of immediate mobility would be likely to vary location through time. These include woodland and other plant resources, and even the location of the water edge. A prime example of mobile resources would be the location of kill or scavenge opportunities. Not only the initial butchery, but the range of processing activities that stemmed from the butchery, might well be dependant on the initial location.

To take raw material first, it is clear how this had a major effect on the composition and distribution of the assemblages. The assemblages from Areas I and IV(4) sit directly on and within the raw material source. The assemblages have a high density of artefacts (Table 23.1) and consist of complete knapping sequences, core and flake working in Area I, and this combined with biface production in Area IV(4). As a result both areas can be interpreted as primary manufacturing zones with repeated use over some length of time.

Area	I	IV(4)	III	V(surf)	V(within)
Excavation area (m²)	64	26	6	20	20
Total artefacts (>20mm)	504	379	14	74	5
Total HH flakes (>20mm)	475	123	11	23	4
Total flake tools	32	2	1	-	-
Artefacts/m²	7.9	14.6	2.3	3.7	0.2
HH flakes/m²	7.4	4.7	1.8	1.1	0.2
Flake tools/m²	0.5	0.08	0.17	-	-
HH flakes/flake tools	14.8	61.5	11.0	-	-

Table 23.1. Quantities, densities and ratios of artefacts from the fresh assemblages in Areas I, IV(4), III and V (on the surface and within the grey/brown stony clay).

Much of the composition and the artefact density of the assemblage from the surface of the grey/brown stony clay in Area V can also be explained through raw material. The distance from the raw material source is unknown, but could be anything from a few metres to several tens of metres. The assemblage consists of elements from the final stages of both biface production and core and flake working. The initial stages of flaking took place elsewhere, and the most economic explanation is that this was on or nearer to the raw material source. The lower density, the clear association with a distinct horizon, and the general absence of refitting, might also suggest that the assemblage accumulated through a series of single discards, but probably over a short period of time.

The low density of artefacts and the lack of *in situ* knapping in the remaining areas (Area III, Area V within the grey/brown stony clay, and Area I palaeosol) can likewise be explained through distance from raw material. This is particularly the case for the biface and two flakes from the palaeosol in Area I. By this time, the cobble layer, in Area I at least, was concealed and vegetation had begun to encroach along the edges of the channel. Raw material might not have been available for some distance. Certainly the piece was not knapped in the immediate area. Its abandonment on a stable landsurface could imply use and then discard of the piece in that location.

Although raw material as a static resource provides an explanation for the overall pattern of distribution, and the broad composition in terms of *in situ* knapping, mobile resources appear to play an increasingly important role at greater distances from the raw material source. Single discard events can be sometimes isolated (as with the biface from the palaeosol in Area I) and these might be viewed as responses to mobile resource distribution. These could be the location of kill sites, or occurrence of specific vegetation stands. In the case of Barnham, because of the lack of preservation of fauna in most of the archaeological areas, the model is difficult to test.

There are, however, two principal elements of the variation that require further analysis - the occurrence of biface production in Area IV(4) and the higher incidence of flake tools in Area I. Although the poor quality and low quantity or absence of the bifaces from Areas I and IV(4) can be explained through the generally poor quality of the raw material, the difference between the areas is less easy to explain. Here perhaps it is important to recognise as Roebroeks *et al.* (1992) point out that the scatters are not limited to those areas outside the patches, but are likely to overprint the patches, and become archaeologically indistinguishable. Can the presence of biface production be understood in these terms? The biface production appears to be limited to the manufacture of as few as

three or four bifaces, and the artefacts are all in fresh condition. The question arises as to whether it should be regarded as a single event discard, or as repeated activity. If it is repeated activity, then evidence ought to be sought of a permanent change in resource distribution. This might, for example, be a change in the availability of better quality flint resources nearby. If it is a single event, then any number of explanations can be put forward that involve mobile resources, the most obvious one being a scavenge or kill opportunity nearby. Again a lack of faunal preservation means that such explanations cannot be tested at Barnham, but importantly they do provide an interpretative framework for future work.

The higher incidence of flake tools in Area I also needs further assessment. Although the refitting provides no conclusive evidence, the most economic interpretation is that they were manufactured within the area. The fact that they were also discarded in much higher proportions than other areas, also suggests that they were used in that location. A possible explanation for this might be a change in the proximity of the water edge for example, with the cobble layer exposed as dry land. Importantly, however, the use of tools in this area, implies the import of other resources (presumably animal or plant) for processing. This further implies some sort of focus of activity, perhaps a group focus and a faint archaeological signature of social organisation?

Although there may be nothing remarkable in this, there has been reluctance in the recent literature to accept the existence of what Isaac (1978) described as homebases. Schick (1987) for example criticised the term for assuming that early hominid social organisation reflected that seen in modern hunter-gatherers. She preferred a more flexible model whereby the distribution of resources still acted as the key to artefact distributions, but that accumulations at particular sites could be simply interpreted as places where imports exceeded exports. At some sites, however, the archaeological signatures suggest interpretation can be taken further. Perhaps group focus is a less loaded term than homebase, but it still implies the undertaking of several activities in one location, not neccessarily dictated purely by the economy of the resources. The difficulties of identifying these areas is primarily due to the lack of resolution in the archaeology. However, a further example of this can be found at Maastricht-Belvedere (Roebroeks *et al.* 1992) where differences were noted between the scatter of Site N and the patch of Site K. This showed first that formal flake tools were proportionally higher in Site N, but of the still considerable number of flake tools from Site K, virtually none could be incorporated into the large number of refitting or raw material groups. The implication was that they were knapped elsewhere and incorporated into the patch of Site K as part of the scatter of Site N. What is also significant, however, is the marked increase in tool density in Site K (0.37 compared to 0.03 tools/m^2 in Site N) implying tools were being transported there for a specific reason. Roebroeks *et al.* (1992) interpret Site K as a maintenance location, principally on the basis of *in situ* knapping, but it seems to have been more complex than this, acting also as a focus for tool discard.

Although such interpretations go beyond the bounds of the resource and landscape model, what they do illustrate is how evidence of social organisation can be complimentary to this approach. Rather than interpretation being determined by the environment, the approach provides the environmental backdrop against which the archaeological signatures can be measured. Equally, it contributes to the evidence of the broader ecological approaches developed for example by Gamble (1995), where the organisational responses of hominids are viewed against the structure of new and changing environments.

The resource and landscape model provides some of the more obvious answers to the problem of assemblage variation. Although some of the explanations for the variation remain untested, the model does provide a framework for future research. This should be firmly based on a better understanding of the distribution of resources and their possible correlation with archaeological signatures. One of the strengths of the model is the recognition it gives to the mobility of flint and the complexity of the human behaviour that its distribution and composition reflect. The viability of the model to provide solid explanations, however, is dependant on the degree of archaeological and environmental resolution.

CONCLUSION

Various models have been examined in the light of the evidence from Barnham. The cultural models provide a very static view of human behaviour during this period, and take little account of the demonstrable effect that resources and landscape have on assemblage variability. Fundamentally, the models fail to explain how different traditions of toolmaking can survive in the same landscapes over vast periods of time. Recourse to modern ethnographic analogy merely highlights the problems with these models. The technological model again cannot be supported by the evidence from Barnham, or by what is known from other sites during this period in Britain. It too only provides a static, one dimensional interpretation of the variation.

In contrast, the resource and landscape model acknowledges the complexity of the archaeological signatures and the human behaviour they reflect. It also provides testable explanations within a solid framework of interpretation. Some of these explanations have been tested at Barnham and stand up well to the evidence. It is of additional importance that the model is complimentary to the ecological approaches and can potentially provide the basis for a better understanding of social organisation and behaviour during this period. In short, these models highlight the sterility of the Clactonian-Acheulian problem, that may have a place in the history of archaeology, but not as a study for serious debate.

24. SUMMARY

Nick Ashton, Simon G. Lewis & Simon Parfitt

The excavations by the British Museum at Barnham, Suffolk (TL 875787) from 1989-94 investigated a series of geological exposures in and around East Farm Pit, together with detailed archaeological excavations at several locations within the pit. The aim of the work was to: (1) examine the relationship between the Clactonian and Acheulian industries recognised at the site by Paterson (1937, 1942); (2) investigate further the occurrence of refitting cores and flakes that had been recovered by Wymer in 1979 (Wymer 1985); and (3) make a comprehensive study of the geological and environmental context of these industries to understand better the dating of the site, and the landscape in which these industries occurred.

GEOLOGICAL SUCCESSION

The interpretation of the geological succession at the site is based on the series of sections created around the edges of the East Farm Pit, numerous test pits and auger holes in and around the pit, together with sections cuts at three Tilbrooks pits and the Kidney Plantation Pit (see Chapter 4). Geophysical investigations have also contributed to the understanding of the gross sediment body geometry and the nature of the bedrock surface (see Chapter 5).

The East Farm Pit lies in a dry valley, with Chalk rising to the south forming the watershed with the Lark valley, and separated from the present Little Ouse River to the north by another low Chalk ridge. Incised into the Chalk along the axis of the dry valley is a deep (at least 19.5m) channel, which is filled with glaciofluvial sand and gravel (Unit 1) and chalky diamicton (till) (Unit 2). The till forms part of the regionally extensive Lowestoft till, which was deposited during the Anglian Stage. The sand and gravel is probably outwash of that ice sheet, as suggested by the clast lithology of the gravel (see Chapter 4). The exact nature of the relationship between the till and the gravel is difficult to determine (see Chapter 4 for discussion of this problem). The considerable thickness of gravel is suggested by a number of borehole records and geophysics (see Chapters 2, 4 and 5). This and other records suggest that the channel is infilled mainly with sand and gravel, with a layer of chalky diamicton forming the upper part of the infill over most, though not all of the area of the East Farm Pit. Whatever their exact relationship, both units may be interpreted as of glaciogenic origin. Sand and gravel was also observed in the Tilbrook's Pits and

in Kidney Plantation Pit. The gravel appears to fill a series of sub-parallel channels, cut into the Chalk, one or more of which may link up with the channel running beneath the East Farm Pit.

The data from the East Farm Pit indicates that the upper surface of the chalky diamicton is also channeled. This feature reaches a maximum depth of 13.5m and is filled with fine-grained sediments (Unit 5). The considerable depth of this channel over a small area around TP 35 may suggest that its formation is, in part, related to subsidence, possibly as a result of Chalk solution or melt out of dead-ice in the underlying gravel. This cannot be confirmed as no exposures are available. The sediments filling the channel indicate still or slow-flowing water conditions, with mainly laminated silt and clay and a number of persistent bedded sand facies. It is probable that this depression began to fill at the end of the glacial episode and continued into the subsequent temperate phase. This is supported by the appearance of abundant faunal remains and the presence of pollen in the upper 2-3m of sediment (Unit 5c). While the centre of the depression was filling with fine-grained sediment, brown diamicton (Unit 3) formed as a result of mass movement down the slopes around the margin of the channel. These sediments pass laterally into the basal part of the fine-grained channel fill.

The upper fossiliferous part of the channel fill is equated with a period when the surface of the gravel was exposed along the southern edge of the channel, where occasional inundation by water removed finer sediment to leave a coarse 'lag' gravel, consisting of a layer of large flint cobbles (Unit 4). This was ultimately buried by yellow silty sand (Unit 5e), which represents the marginal feather-edge of the channel-fill sequence. The majority of the archaeological assemblages were excavated from within and on the surface of the cobbles layer (Unit 4) and from the overlying yellow silty sand.

The channel fill sequence is covered by black clay (Unit 6) which shows evidence of soil formation (see Chapter 6) and represents a stable land surface formed as the channel finally dried out. This surface was affected to some degree by pedogenesis. The overlying brown silt and clay ('brickearth') (Unit 7) is probably the result of continued deposition by colluvial, alluvial and possibly aeolian processes, with periodic phases of land surface stability allowing weak soil development to occur (see Chapter 6).

Correlation with standard stages	Stratigraphic units		Geological summary		CHANNEL					
							Fish	Herpetofauna	Birds	Mammals
?	7	brown silt and clay 'brickearth'	colluvium with occasional alluvial input, overprinted by weak soil development		black clay					
					gritty clay		Low diversity fauna of still or slow-flowing fresh water, probably poorly oxygenated	Increasing species diversity. Mosaic of wetlands and dry ground habitats. Warmer than today	Sparse fauna. Dabbling ducks indicate still or slow-flowing water	Increasing species diversity. Rare large mammals and diverse small mammal fauna, indicative of temperate deciduous woodland with open areas. Hoxnian-type mammal fauna
					shelly clay					
HOXNIAN *	6	black clay	palaeosol							
	5c	grey silt and clay	slow-flowing to still-water sedimentation		black clay					
	5b/ 5a	grey chalky clay/ brown silt and clay	slow-flowing to still-water sedimentation with influxes of reworked till from margins of channel							
ANGLIAN	2	chalky diamicton	sub-glacial lodgement till		grey-brown clay		Species-rich fish fauna, indicating oxygenated, slow-flowing water			
					laminated shelly clay					
	1	sand and gravel	glaciofluvial outwash gravel		basal silt		Sparse fish remains			

Table 24.1. Summary of the geological, palaeoenvironmental and archaeological information for East Farm, Barnham, showing diagramatically how the thicker channel sequence relates to the channel margin, and their correlation with the standard UK stages. * The aminostratigraphic model of Bowen *et al.* (1989; also see Chapter 16) suggests that the Hoxnian type site is separated from the Anglian by an interglacial represented at Swanscombe and Barnham.

CHANNEL				CHANNEL MARGIN			
Molluscs	**Charcoal & Pollen**	**Geochron-ology**	**Archaeology**	**Archaeology**		**Geological Summary**	**Stratigraphic unit**
	Sparse charcoal, indicating deciduous woodland	TL		Area I - biface and 2 flakes		colluvium with occasional alluvial input, overprinted by weak soil development	brown silt and clay 'brickearth'	7
	Weathered pollen	ESR	Area III - sparse cores and flakes	Area I - cores, flakes and flake tools				
		OSL						
	Pollen zone II, with mixed, deciduous, oak woodland, and open and forest-edge communities	AAR		Area IV(4) - cores, flakes, flake tools and biface manufacturing debitage		palaeosol	black clay	6
Freshwater molluscs, indicative of still or slow-flowing water						low-energy fluvial sedimentation	yellow silty sand/ grey/brown stony clay	5e/5d
						lag gravel	cobble layer	4
				Area V - final debitage from core and flake working, and biface production		solifluction	brown diamicton	3
						sub-glacial lodgement till	chalky diamicton	2
	Recycled pollen							
						glaciofluvial outwash gravel	sand and gravel	1

Table 24.1. cont.

The sequence can be summarised (see Table 24.1) as one of initial incision and filling of a deep channel in the Chalk bedrock during the Anglian glaciation, followed by formation of a second, smaller channel at the end of the glacial episode, which was filled by a series of laterally variable, predominantly fine-grained facies during the latter part of the cold phase and the subsequent temperate episode. The thick sequence in the channel centre can be related to a thinner sequence at the edge of the channel. This is critical as it allows the evidence for human occupation on the channel margins to be related to the environmental information gathered from the upper fossiliferous part of the channel fill sequence. Initial fluvial and lacustrine deposition in the channel is followed by soil development over most of the site as the channel dried out, with continued accumulation of sediments as a result predominantly of colluvial processes.

PALAEOECOLOGICAL STUDIES

The archaeologically-rich horizons in Areas I, IV(4) and V, around the margins of the water body are decalcified and do not contain preserved faunal material. However, laterally equivalent horizons in the centre of the channel contain an abundant molluscan and vertebrate fauna, specifically in the top 2-3m of grey silt and clay (Unit 5c). This unit has been subdivided from bottom to top into laminated shelly clay, brown-grey clay, black clay, shelly clay and gritty clay (see Chapter 7; Table 24.1).

Although the vertebrate material appears to derive from local sources, slight variation in the skeletal elements representation and in the condition, indicate slightly different taphonomies for the bones from the various sub-units. While the bones in the black clay appear to be fresh and rapidly buried, those in the shelly clay have undergone some fluvial sorting. A dual origin is suggested for the bones from the gritty clay, with some having being subject to trampling, while the condition of others indicates more prolonged fluvial movement (see Chapter 7).

Change in the faunal composition through the sequence also reflects change in the depositional environment. Freshwater Mollusca predominate in the laminated shelly clay, brown-grey clay and the shelly clay, indicating slow-flowing water (see Chapter 12). These conditions are also reflected in the diversity of fish in the brown-grey clay. A marked change is indicated by the lower diversity of fish in the overlying black, shelly and gritty clays, with the predominance of tench, stickleback, pike and rudd, suggesting still, or slow-flowing water (see Chapter 8). Still or slow-flowing water is also reflected by the birds, with the presence of dabbling duck in the black clay (see Chapter 9).

The dominance of herpetofauna and mammals in the gritty clay suggests the drying out of the channel. Open-water wetlands and damp terrestrial habitats are indicated by the amphibians, while more specifically, species such as European pond terrapin, the common tree-frog and Aesculapian snake reflect a mild climate with summer temperatures warmer than present (see Chapter 10).

The vegetation beyond the confines of the water-body is reflected by the mammalian fauna, with the range of species such as squirrel, red and fallow deer, boar, together with straight-tusked elephant and bovid suggesting temperate, deciduous woodland habitats interspersed with scrub and more open ground (see Fig. 24.1). The increase in water vole and woodmouse, with the decrease in bank vole towards the top of the gritty clay, might reflect a reduction in woodland or scrub (see Chapter 11).

Pollen is only found in a good preservational state from the upper part of the brown-grey clay through to the shelly clay. This indicates mixed oak woodland with a diversity of open and forest-edge vegetational communities, interpreted as zone II of an interglacial (see Chapter 13). Small amounts of charcoal from the black clay (Unit 6) above the fossiliferous beds shows the continuation of deciduous woodland after the drying-out of the channel (see Chapter 14).

All the environmental evidence contributes to the same picture of a river basin with slow-flowing water that during the early temperate phase of an interglacial slowly changes to a still-water and marsh habitat. The basin is surrounded by mixed deciduous woodland with some areas of open scrub and grassland, in a mild climate, warmer than the present day. This landscape provides the backdrop for the human activity represented around the fringes of the channel.

CORRELATION AND DATING

The geological work has shown that Anglian cold stage deposits (gravels and tills) lie at the base of the sequence. This cold stage is widely attributed to oxygen isotope stage 12 of the deep-sea sequence (427-474ka). In the absence of any major unconformities, the overlying interglacial sediments can be attributed to the warm stage immediately after the Anglian (stage 11, 364-427ka) (see Chapter 4; Bowen *et al.* 1986). AAR ratios, similar to those from Swanscombe, Clacton and Beeches Pit also suggest a stage 11 attribution (see Chapter 16).

The biostratigraphy of the mammals provides support for this date (see Chapter 11). The division of British faunal assemblages into 'Cromerian Complex', Hoxnian and 'Saalian Complex' age provides a model for correlating the site. The absence of species such as the extinct shrew *Sorex (Drepansorex) savini*, and the rodents *Pliomys episcopalis* and *Microtus gregalis* (*gregaloides* morphotype) distinguishes the Barnham fauna from those of 'Cromerian Complex' age. The presence at Barnham of the small extinct mole *Talpa minor*, the pine vole *Microtus (Terricola)* cf. *subterraneus*, and the rabbit *Oryctolagus* cf. *cuniculus*, may also be of biostratigraphic significance, being apparently absent from British assemblages dated to after the Hoxnian. Study of the evolutionary stage of the water vole *Arvicola terrestris cantiana* and the field vole *Microtus agrestis* also support a Hoxnian age (see Chapter 11). In summary, the composition of the mammal fauna suggests affinities with those from the Lower Gravel and Lower Loam at Swanscombe, the Woodston beds near Peterborough, and tufa deposits at Beeches Pit, Suffolk and Hitchin, Hertfordshire. These are all interpreted as being from the early temperate zone of the Hoxnian, which itself is currently attributed to stage 11 (see Chapter 11).

Results of thermoluminescence dating of burnt flint from Area I (Chapter 17) are more problematic. The age estimates range from 305ka to 264ka and suggest attribution of the sequence to stage 9. The apparent discrepancy between these data and the correlation with stage 11, suggested on lithstratigraphic, biostratigraphic and aminostratigraphic grounds, is difficult to resolve. On the basis of the geological observations during these excavations it seems unlikely that the sequence represents two post-chalky diamicton (Anglian), temperate episodes separated by a cold episode, as there are no sediments or structures that could be regarded as indicative of the cold conditions of stage 10 (cf. Sumbler 1994). Neither is there evidence for a significant unconformity below the temperate sequence that could indicate separation from the Anglian glaciation by an entire temperate-cold cycle. However, the burnt flint pieces are, with one exception, associated with Unit 6, whereas the amino acid ratios are on material from Unit 5. One further interpretation is that the underlying glaciogenic sediments should be attributed to stage 10. This interpretation is contrary to that suggested by the amino-acid data from Barnham and the aminostratigraphic model from southern Britain (Bowen *et al.* 1989).

A TL age estimate on burnt flint from the nearby site at Beeches Pit, West Stow of 471 ± 51ka (Lewis 1998) show the potential range of the method and also suggest that the underlying glaciogenic sediments at that site should be correlated with stage 12. The mammalian fauna from Beeches Pit also has marked affinities with that from Barnham (see above and Chapter 11). Thus the correlation between the two sites on geological and biostratigraphic grounds, suggests that caution should be deployed in using the TL age estimates.

Tentative absolute age estimates using ESR have also been obtained (Chapter 18). Initial results suggest an age range of between 200-300ka, based on early uptake and linear uptake of uranium models respectively. An alternative recent uptake model would yield an age estimate of over 400ka. However these estimates must be treated with caution (see Chapter 18 for discussion). On the basis of the data currently available the balance of evidence favours a correlation of the temperate sequence with stage 11 and the underlying glacial deposits with stage 12.

FLINT INDUSTRIES

The flint assemblages were excavated from four main locations (Areas I, III, IV(4) and V), and apart from Area III are all located on the edges of the channel. Although they were excavated from a variety of contexts (Unit 3 - brown diamicton; Unit 4 - cobble layer; Unit 5c - grey silt and clay; Unit 5d - grey/brown stony clay; and Unit 5e - yellow silty sand) the assemblages can be divided broadly into two suites (see Chapters 19 and 20). The first suite (from Areas I, IV(4) and V) consists of artefacts that have undergone varying degrees of rolling and abrasion and indicating in many cases considerable post-depositional movement. They are regarded as a series of knapping events undertaken over some length of time, which have become intermixed and reworked. They primarily occur in the cobble layer, but also in the overlying yellow silty sand and the underlying brown diamicton, and consist of core and flake debitage.

The second suite of assemblages (from all the areas and a similar array of contexts) is composed of artefacts that have little edge abrasion and contain several refitting groups. Although they are interpreted as being in primary context, study of their distribution and orientation suggests that in most cases there has been some limited post-depositional movement. The exception is the small assemblage from Area III (faunal area), where the fine-grained context, the absence of similarly sized clasts and the freshness of the artefacts, suggests that there has been no movement.

The technological analysis is primarily based on the second suite of assemblages, as it is argued that they represent a series of knapping episodes produced over a more limited length of time (see Chapter 19). It is also argued on the basis of their geological context that they are broadly contemporary.

There are significant variations in the technology of each area. The fresh assemblage from Area I rests within, on and above the cobble layer, which appears to have been the source of raw material. The assemblage consists of core and flake working (primarily using alternate platform technique) and from the flakes a variety of flake tools (flaked flakes and scrapers) have been made. Discard of the flake tools (some heavily retouched) within the area might suggest use in that location. Refitting of several sequences supports the technological interpretation.

The fresh assemblage from Area IV(4) also rests on and within the cobble layer, and again this appears to be the source of raw material. Much of the knapping is similar to Area I, consisting of core and flake working with alternate platform technique, although the proportion of flake tools is much lower. In addition, some of the knapping consists of biface manufacturing debitage, together with a single biface. The debitage is interpreted as being from the complete biface knapping sequence, from initial roughing out to final finishing.

The fresh Area V material lies on the undulating surface of the grey/brown stony clay, and a short distance from the presumed source of raw material, the cobble layer. The assemblage consists of core and flake working, together with some biface manufacturing debitage. Both sets of debitage appear to be from the final stages of manufacture. The cores are insufficient to have produced all the flakes, perhaps suggestive of the transport of partially worked cores away from the location. Equally there are no bifaces and very few flake tools, which might imply that Area V was not a use location.

The small, dispersed assemblage from Area III (faunal area) is again a short distance from a source of raw material. Associated with the fauna in the middle of the channel, it seems to be the only strictly *in situ* assemblage. Knapping does not seem to have taken place in the area, implying that the artefacts (all hard hammer flakes and cores) were either brought into the area, dropped or even thrown. One retouched piece bears some evidence of use, perhaps on wood (see Chapter 22).

The variation in assemblage composition between the areas requires explanation (see Chapter 23). Previous models that interpret the variation of British Lower Palaeolithic assemblages are difficult to sustain. In particular, the long held view that core and flake industries (Clactonian) are chronologically and culturally distinct from those that contain bifaces (Acheulian) is not upheld by the evidence from Barnham. Here, the core and flake assemblage from Area I is, within the resolution of the sequence, contemporary with the core, flake and biface assemblage from Area IV(4) and arguably with those from Areas III and V. Other explanations should be sought.

A landscape model provides a more dynamic approach. Here, the distribution of resources is regarded as the critical backdrop which strongly influences the behaviour of early humans. The relatively constant nature of some of these resources over human timespans (decades or perhaps much longer) resolves some of the problems of demonstrating contemporaneity. At Barnham, during the knapping of the flint industries, at least two of these resources were constant - the raw material source and the channel. Therefore, although exact contemporaneity cannot be demonstrated between the areas, or indeed within them, the human signatures that they contain, can be regarded as photo-shots of a range of activities taking place around the channel edge. The photo-montage that they collectively create, provides a much more complete view of the human behaviour.

With this model the distribution of resources provides explanations for some of the variation in assemblage composition. Of particular relevance is the quality, quantity and proximity of the flint raw material. In Areas I and IV(4) the main activity is primary manufacture, easily explained by the presence of abundant raw material within the areas. In Area V the assemblage is from the final stages of knapping, explained by the distance, albeit short, from the raw material source. Area III, in contrast, has no evidence of knapping within the area, but occasional artefacts have been discarded, as part of a dynamic system of artefact movement and use, described by Isaac as the 'scatter' between the patches.

Other variation, in particular the presence of biface manufacture within Area IV(4), and its absence in Area I, require different explanations. Raw material might play some part. Although experiments have shown (see Chapter 21) that there are few differences in the raw material between the areas, they have also shown that only 7% of nodules > 150mm (maximum dimension) are suitable for biface manufacture. As there may be as few as three bifaces manufactured in Area IV(4), the poor quality of raw material may explain the paucity of biface manufacture. As part of this explanation, other resources need to be considered, in particular changes in the less constant resources. These might include changes in accessibility to other flint sources, changes in vegetation, leading to different landscape use, or much more immediate variation in animal resources, such as the chance encounter with a scavenge opportunity. Any one of these factors could explain the presence of a small amount of biface manufacture within Area IV(4) (see Chapter 23 for full discussion). Until the impact of such factors on assemblage composition can be fully understood, it is premature to evoke cultural models for explaining the differences in the industries.

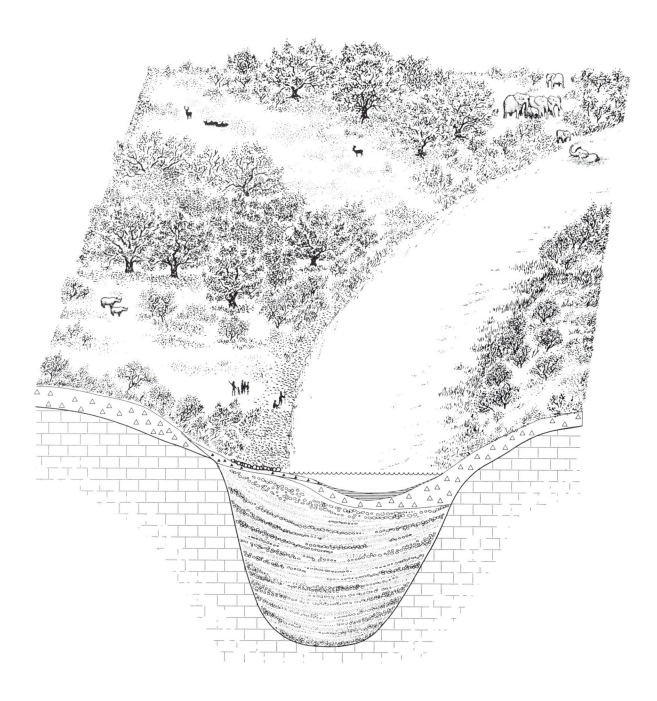

Fig. 24.1. Reconstruction of the Barnham landscape, contemporary with its use by humans, showing the underlying stratigraphy.

PALAEOLITHIC LANDSCAPES

Although this landscape model is only partially tested by the evidence from Barnham, it does provide a framework for future study, and a more flexible and dynamic approach to the study of human behaviour. Above all it demonstrates the need to provide high resolution environmental evidence and a firm understanding of the changing configuration of the landscape to interpret past human behavioural patterns.

Current excavations at Elveden, 7km to the west

(Ashton & Lewis 1997) and Beeches Pit, 10km to the south-west (Wymer *et al.* 1991; Gowlett 1997), together with the results of previous fieldwork in the region, such as at Hoxne (Singer *et al.* 1993), are enhancing the understanding of this landscape. In particular, there is a growing body of data concerning the nature of environmental changes, the implications for the resources the landscape could sustain, and their use by early humans. As such, the story at Barnham and its wider context has perhaps only partially been told.

APPENDIX I. ICHTHYOFAUNA

Brian G. Irving

Number of fish bones recovered from column samples. Totals given for each taxa represent the total number of specimens identified, abundance is calculated as the number of identifiable fish bones (and teeth) per kilogram of sediment.

	Sample No.	NISP/kg	Salmo trutta	Salmonidae	Esox lucius	Gobio gobio	Tinca tinca	Blicca björkna /Abramis brama	Alburnus alburnus	Scardinius erythrophthalmus	Rutilus rutilus	Leuciscus sp.	Anguilla anguilla	Gasterosteus aculeatus	Lota lota	Perca fluviatilis	Total
Gritty clay	114	0.8												15			15
	115	1.5			7		4							16			27
	77	1.9			27		14			4				44			89
	78	2.1			4		43		7				1	57			112
	79	2.1			4		17		4					14			39
	80	5.9		2	4		12		5	4							41
	205	0.8			1	1?	*7*							6			15
	113	1			1		17		5					6			29
	118	3.2			6		35	1	3					7			52
	Total			2	54	1	149	1	24	8			1	179			419
Shelly clay	81	2.1	1		10		50			6	2			13			82
	82	18.1			82					180	234		5	163			664
	83	13.1			39		82		4	21	2			28			176
	192	3.3			8		32		1	5				13			59
	194	17.8			18		97		2	5	6			71			199
	196	14.2			4		44			6	6		1	16			77
	193	2.6			4		14			2	4			8			32
	Total		1		165		319		7	225	254		6	312			1289
Black clay	84	7.6			49		62			3	43			74			231
Brown-grey clay	85	2.5			6		7				24			61			98
	86	4.4		1	14				2	8	28			127		4	184
	87	2.2			7						26		3	78		1	115
	111	1			2			1									3
	112	3.2			13		8			7	10	1		12			51
	112A	2.2			6		14				13			17			50
	89	1			2				2		22			21			47
	90	4.1			9	1	29		2	4	38			45			128
	91	2.4		1	14		8				95			40		1	159
	92	6.4		1	11		1				49			50			112
	93	1.8			4						7			15		1	27
	94	1.3			3						24			11			38
	95	1.7			8		2		4		22	1		32			69
	96	0.3								1	11					1	13
	98	1			1				1		12						14
	99	0.2			2						3						5
	100	0.4			2		1				7						10
	101	1	1		2		2		1		7						13
	102	0.8									4						4
	103	0.1									1						1
	104	0.6			1									8			9
	105	0.3			4												4
	106	0.2			2												2
	107	0.2			1									1			2
	Total		1	3	113	1	72	1	12	20	403	2	3	518		8	1157
Laminated shelly clay	173	0.1			1									4			5
	174	2.8			7									23	3		33
	Total				8									23	3		38
Basal silt	38				2												2
	69				1												1
	69				1												1
	Total				4												4

APPENDIX II. HERPETOFAUNA

J. Alan Holman

AMPHIBIA

CAUDATA

Salamandridae

Triturus cristatus (Laurenti 1768), warty newt

Gritty Clay: 193 vertebrae; 7 right humeri; 2 left humeri; 5 right femora; 1 femur fragment; 3 atlantes; 1 atlas fragment.

Shelly clay: 31 vertebrae; 1 right humerus; 1 right femur; 1 left femur; 1 atlas.

Black clay (Unit 5): 7 vertebrae.

Brown-grey clay: 6 vertebrae.

Triturus helveticus (Razoumowsky 1789), palmate newt

Gritty clay: 7 vertebrae.

Triturus vulgaris (Linnaeus 1758), smooth newt

Gritty clay: 18 vertebrae

Shelly clay: 5 vertebrae

Black clay (Unit 5): 1 vertebra

Triturus sp. Indet., indeterminate newt

Gritty clay: 248 vertebrae; 1 right humerus; 1 left humerus; 7 humeri; 2 femora; 3 atlantes.

Shelly clay: 70 vertebrae; 1 right humerus; 1 humerus; 1 femur.

Black Clay (Unit 5): 10 vertebrae.

Brown-grey clay: 11 vertebrae; 1 atlas.

ANURA

Hylidae

Hyla arborea (Linnaeus 1758), common tree frog

Gritty clay: 5 right ilia; 10 left ilia.

Shelly clay: 1 right ilium; 1 left ilium; 1 left scapula.

Hyla sp. Indet., undetermined tree frog

Gritty clay: 1 right ilium; 1 left humerus.

Bufonidae

Bufo bufo (Linnaeus 1758), common toad

Gritty clay: 9 right ilia; 14 left ilia; 1 left scapula.

Shelly clay: 2 right ilia; 2 left ilia; 2 left scapulae.

Black clay (Unit 5): 5 right ilia; 5 left ilia; 2 partial skeletons.

Brown-grey clay: 2 right ilia; 1 left ilium; 1 right scapula.

Bufo calamita Laurenti 1768, natterjack

Gritty clay: 3 left ilia; 1 right ilium.

Bufo viridis Laurenti 1768, green toad

Gritty clay: 1 left ilium.

Shelly clay: 1 right ilium; 1 left ilium.

Black clay (Unit 5): 1 left ilium.

Bufo sp. Indet., indeterminate toad

Gritty clay: 2 right ilia; 2 left ilia; 1 ilia; 17 right humeri; 23 left humeri; 1 humerus; 1 right scapula; 5 scapulae; 6 sacra; 1 left frontoparietal.

Shelly clay: 1 right ilium; 2 right humeri; 7 left humeri; 1 left femur; 2 right scapulae; 3 scapulae; 6 sacra.

Black clay (Unit 5): 1 left ilium; 5 right humeri; 6 left humeri; 1 humerus; 3 sacra.

Brown-grey clay: 1 right ilia; 1 left humerus; 2 scapulae.

Ranidae

Rana arvalis Nilsson 1842, moor frog

Gritty clay: 7 right ilia; 7 left ilia.

Shelly clay: 1 right ilium; 1 left ilium.

Brown-grey clay: 1 right ilium.

Rana (ridibunda) sp., water frog of the *Rana ridibunda* species complex

Gritty clay: 5 right ilia; 11 left ilia.

Shelly clay: 4 right ilia; 6 left ilia.

Black clay (Unit 5): 2 left ilia.

Rana temporaria Linnaeus 1758, common frog

Gritty clay: I right ilium; 1 left ilium.

Shelly clay: 1 right ilium; 1 left ilium; 1 sacrum.

Black clay (Unit 5): 1 right ilium.

Brown-grey clay: 4 left ilia.

Rana sp. Indet., true frog species, indeterminate

Gritty clay: 96 right ilia; 99 left ilia; 16 right humeri; 8 left humeri; 1 humerus; 5 right scapulae; 4 left scapulae; 16 scapulae; 31 sacra; 1 right frontoparietal.

Shelly clay: 7 right ilia; 6 left ilia; 5 right humeri; 4 left humeri; 2 right scapulae; 2 left scapulae; 1 scapula; 2 sacra.

Black clay (Unit 5): 8 right ilia; 8 left ilia; 1 ilium; 2 right humeri; 1 scapula; 2 sacra.

Brown-grey clay: 5 right ilia; 3 left ilia; 1 right humerus; 1 left scapula; 1 sacrum.

Laminated shelly clay: 1 right ilium.

REPTILIA

TESTUDINES

Emydidae

Emys orbicularis (Linnaeus 1758), European pond terrapin

Gritty clay: 2 vertebrae; 24 shell fragments; 5 peripheral bones; 1 pygal bone; 1 carapace fragment; peripheral and costal fragments.

SQUAMATA

Anguidae

Anguis fragilis Linnaeus 1758, slow worm

Gritty clay: 26 vertebrae; 4 trunk vertebrae; 1 caudal vertebra.

Shelly clay: 1 vertebral fragment.

Black clay (Unit 5): 1 vertebra; 1 caudal vertebra; 1

vertebral centrum fragment; 1 broken osteoscute.

Brown-grey clay: 2 vertebrae.

Lacertidae

Lacerta sp., small *Lacerta* species

Gritty clay: 1 vertebra.

Black clay (Unit 5): 1 vertebra.

Colubridae

Natrix natrix (Linnaeus 1758), grass snake

Gritty clay: 36 vertebrae.

Shelly clay: 2 vertebrae.

Black clay (Unit 5): 7 vertebrae.

Brown-grey clay: 7 vertebrae.

Natrix maura or *tesselata*, viperine or dice snake

Gritty clay: 5 vertebrae

Black clay (Unit 5): 1 vertebra

Natrix sp., grass snake or water snake

Gritty clay: 323 vertebrae.

Shelly clay: 37 vertebrae.

Black clay (Unit 5): 27 vertebrae.

Brown-grey clay: 10 vertebrae.

Elaphe longissima (Laurenti 1768), Aesculapian snake

Gritty clay: 5 vertebrae.

Viperidae

Vipera berus (Linnaeus 1758), adder

Gritty clay: 4 vertebrae.

Brown-grey clay: 2 vertebrae (1 of juvenile).

APPENDIX III. AVES

John R. Stewart

ANSERIFORMES

Anatidae

Anas sp., dabbling duck

>Black clay (Unit 5): 1 left carpometacarpus fragment (two pieces); 1 left phalanx 2 digit 1 of the manus.

Undetermined anatidae, ducks

>Gritty clay: 2 distal left tibiotarsus shaft fragments; 1 proximal left carpometacarpus fragment; 1 distal right carpometacarpus; 1 immature left tarsometatarsus; 1 proximal right humerus caput; 1 proximal right humerus fragment; 1 distal left radius; 1 distal right radius; 2 os carpi ulnare; 1 proximal right scapula; 1 right scapula;1 distal fragment of a left coracoid.

>Shelly clay: 1 distal left radius; 1 proximal left radius. (These two specimens refit).

>Black clay (Unit 5): 1 left coracoid fragment.

COLUMBIFORMES

Columbidae

Columba cf. *palumbus*, wood pigeon?

>Gritty clay: 1 left tarsometatarsus (2 fragments).

PASSERIFORMES

Turdidae

Turdus cf. *philomelos/iliacus*, song thrush? or redwing?

>Shelly Clay: 1 proximal right carpometacarpus.

>Black clay (Unit 5): 1 proximal right humerus.

Undetermined passeriformes

>Gritty clay: 2 distal left tarsometatarsus; 1 proximal right femur; 1 distal left tibiotarsus.

>Black Clay (Unit 5): 1 proximal left carpometacarpus fragment.

>Brown-grey clay: 1 distal right ulna.

Indeterminate aves

>Gritty clay: 1 axis vertebra; 1 damaged thoracic vertebra; 1 damaged cervical vertebra; 1 trochlea of a tarsometatarsus; 2 phalanges of pes.

>Black clay (Unit 5): 2 synsacra fragments; 1 fragment of vertebra fragment; 1 phalanx of pes.

>Brown-grey clay: 1 cervical vertebra fragment; 1 vertebra fragment; 2 phalanges of pes.

APPENDIX IV. MAMMALIA

Simon Parfitt

CHIROPTERA

Vespertilionidae

Plecotus sp., long-eared bat

Shelly clay: 726 R M^2.

INSECTIVORA

Soricidae

Sorex minutus Linnaeus 1766, pygmy shrew

Gritty clay: 783 L upper incisor; 759 R M^1; 652 L mandible frag. with M_1; 866 L mandible; 1277 R mandible frag.

Shelly clay: 534 L mandible with M_1-M_2; 1533 L mandible with P_4-M_3; 0 1561 R mandible with M_2 frag.; 0 1551 R M_1.

Black clay (Unit 5): 1456 R upper incisor; 1464 R M^1; 1 1445 L mandible with P_4 and M_1-M_3; 1448 L lower incisor.

Brown-grey clay: 527 R M^1.

Laminated shelly clay: 381 L P^4 frag.

Sorex sp.1, shrew

Gritty clay: 431 L upper incisor (cf. *Sorex* sp.1); 651 L upper incisor; 784, 1511 R upper incisor; 656 R P^4; 433 L $M^{cf.1}$; 1513 L M^1 frag.; 758 L M^2; 653, 826 L mandible frag.; 746 L mandible frag. with M_1-M_2; 972 L mandible with M_2-M_3 (cf. *Sorex* sp.1); 973, 1278, 1298 R mandible frag.; 1046 R mandible frag. (cf. *Sorex* sp.1); 1279 L mandible frag.; 1303 L mandible with M_2-M_3; 1385 L mandible with M_1-M_2; 400 lower incisor frag.; 782 L lower incisor; 434 P_4.

Shelly clay: 1532 L maxilla with P^4-M^1; 1535 R maxilla with A^{1-2}; 1536 R maxilla with P^4; 1559 L P^4 frag.; 732 L upper incisor; 722 R $M^{cf.2}$; 1538 L M^2; 0 1557 R M^2 frag.; 1399, 1572 R mandible frag.; 1400 L mandible frag.; 1552 R lower incisor; 1537 R lower incisor frag.; 721 L M_1.

Black clay (Unit 5): 1457 L upper incisor; 1458 L P^4; 516 R P^4; 1466 L M^1; 1465, 1467 L M^2; 1446 R mandible frag. with M_1; 1447 L mandible frag. with M_2-M_3; 1454 L mandible frag.; 1443 R lower incisor frag.

Brown-grey clay: 559, 607 L P^4; 548 R M1; 608 L lower incisor; 390 L mandible frag.

Neomys sp., water shrew

Gritty clay: 655 L upper incisor; 760, 1109 R upper incisor; 785 R P^4; 1106 R P^4 frag.; 460 L maxilla with M^1-M^2; 402 R M^1; 968 R M^2; 664 L mandible frag. (cf. *Neomys* sp.); 801 L mandible frag.; 827 L mandible with M_1-M_2; 909 R

mandible frag. with $M_{cf.1}$; 1045, 1103 L mandible frag.; 1104 R mandible frag.; 1514 R M_1; 401 R M_2; 794 L M_2; 786 L P_4 (cf. *Neomys* sp.)

Shelly clay: 1534 R lower incisor; 1368, 1401 L mandible frag.; 1565 L mandible with incisor frag. (cf. *Neomys* sp.); 1560 L P_4

Black clay (Unit 5): 1461 maxilla with A^2 and P^4; 1459 R P^4; 1460 R M^1; 1462, 1463 R $M^{cf.1}$ frag.; 1406 L mandible frag. with P_4; 1442 R mandible with P_4 and M_1-M_2; 1444 R mandible frag.; 1451 R $M_{1\,or\,2}$; 1450 R M_3

Crocidura sp., white-toothed shrew

Gritty clay: 907 R mandible frag. with M_2; 1047 L mandible frag.; 1105 L M_1.

Soricidae gen. et sp. indet., shrew

Gritty clay: 432, 747, 1302 L mandible frag.; 654 mandible frag.; 908 R mandible frag.; 911 L $M_{1\,or\,2}$; 1107, 1108 R $M_{1\,or\,2}$; 910 R M_2.

Shelly clay: 1556 L $M^{1\,or\,2}$; 1578 L mandible frag.; 1554 R lower incisor frag.; 1555 L lower incisor frag.; 1558, 1569 L $M_{1\,or\,2}$.

Black clay (Unit 5): 515 mandible frag.; 1449 R $M_{1\,or\,2}$; 1452, 1453 L $M_{1\,or\,2}$; 1455 P_4.

Brown-grey clay: 542 mandible frag.

Talpidae

Talpa minor (Freudenberg, 1914), extinct mole

Gritty Clay: 611 L upper canine; 430 L P^4 frag.; 906, 1100 R M^2; 1101 R M^3; 1219 L mandible frag.; 799 L P_3; 800 clavicle; 399, 1041, 1091, 1299 R humerus frag.; 899 R humerus; 865, 959 L humerus frag.; 1102, 1213 L humerus; 397 L radius; 482 L radius prox. frag.; 787, 905 R radius prox. frag.; 1097 L radius prox. and shaft frag.; 960 R ulna prox. frag.; 967 R tibia prox. and shaft frag.

Shelly clay: 1553 R M_3.

Black clay (Unit 5): 513 R M_1.

Talpa sp. mole

Gritty clay: 757, 1300 metapodial; 398, 1098 terminal phalanx; 1099 2nd phalanx.

Black clay (Unit 5): 514 molar frag.; 1433 phalanx.

Laminated shelly clay: 389 R upper canine frag.; 380 terminal phalanx.

Desmana moschata (Linnaeus 1758), Russian desman

Gritty clay: 370 L mandible frag.

Shelly clay: 725 P^1

LAGOMORPHA

Leporidae

Oryctolagus cf. *O. cuniculus* (Linnaeus 1758), rabbit

Gritty clay: 459 Upper incisor frag.

RODENTIA

Scuiridae

Sciurus sp., squirrel

Gritty clay: 369 R tibia dist. frag.

Arvicolidae

Clethrionomys glareolus (Schreber 1780), bank vole

Gritty clay: 414, 678, 915, 970, 1125 R M^1; 638 R M^1 frag.; 804 L M^1; 682, 1522 R M^2; 693 L M^2 frag.; 916, 1128 L M^2; 701, 917 R M^3 frag.; 803, 913, 1126 L M_1 frag.; 912, 969 L M_1; 1123, 1124, 1221 R M_1 frag.; 413, 1122 L M_2 frag.; 448, 914, 1121 L M_2; 1127 R M_2 frag.; 449 L M_3 frag.; 689 R M_3; 700 R M_3 frag.

Shelly clay: 1404 L M^1; 1526 R M^1; 1543 L M^2; 707 R M^3; 740 L M^3 frag.; 538 L M_2 frag.; 1548 R M_2; 1549 L M_2; 1550 L M_3 frag.

Black clay (Unit 5): 518 M^1; 1411 R M^2; 1475 L M^2; 1412, 1413, 1472 R M^3; 1468 L M_1; 1469 R M_1; 1407, 1408, 1476 R M_2; 1470, 1471 L M_2; 519, 1409, 1410 R M_3; 520, 1473 R M_3 frag.; 1474 L M_3.

Brown-grey clay: 531 L M^1 frag.; 569, 574 R M^1; 587 L M^1; 567 R M^2; 588, 609 L M^2; 543, 555, 586 R M^3; 549 L M^3 frag.; 589 R M^3 frag.; 528 L mandible with M_1; 602 L M_1; 605 R M_1; 530, 556, 583, 584 L M_2; 571 L M_2 frag.; 578 L M_3; 570 molar frag.

Laminated shelly clay: 82 L M^2; 393, 394 L M^3; 388 R M_1 frag.; 383 R M_3; 395 molar frag.

Arvicola terrestris cantiana, water vole

Gritty clay: 418, 437, 478, 621, 624, 779, 843, 844, 846, 849, 876, 997, 1011, 1017, 1043, 1067, 1076, 1183, 1185, 1212, 1249, 1251, 1252, 1253, 1254, 1255, 1257, 1286, 1287, 1337, 1339, 1340, 1342, 1347, 1349 R M^1; 438, 659, 670, 1025, 1071, 1082, 1085, 1338, 1343, 1346, 1392 R M^1 frag.; 419, 436, 476, 477, 479, 623, 668, 763, 764, 822, 875, 925, 929, 993, 994, 1016, 1060, 1069, 1070, 1094, 1160, 1180, 1247, 1248, 1250, 1256, 1258, 1284, 1285, 1336, 1341 L M^1; 629, 647, 667, 1064, 1167, 1171, 1199, 1204, 1273, 1386 L M^1 frag.; 754, 1515 L M^1 frag. (juvenile); 643, 1198 M^1 frag.

442, 765, 781, 814, 848, 850, 878, 1005, 1007, 1030, 1056, 1062, 1074, 1093, 1168, 1177, 1260, 1262, 1263, 1291, 1292, 1344, 1345, 1348, 1361, 1363, 1390, 1391 R M^2; 454, 823, 882, 883, 887, 1034, 1087, 1096, 1265 R M^2 frag.; 421, 422, 625, 696, 780, 845, 862, 879, 880, 881, 1037, 1057, 1073, 1081, 1084, 1095, 1170, 1172, 1200, 1217, 1261, 1264, 1293, 1294, 1351, 1352, 1353, 1359, 1393 L M^2; 752, 753, 851, 888, 889, 1058, 1163 L M^2 frag.; 931, 939 M^2.

420, 480, 481, 626, 658, 811, 930, 1006, 1008, 1021, 1040, 1072, 1075, 1088, 1089, 1266, 1267, 1274, 1289, 1355, 1356, 1360, 1362, 1369 R M^3; 798, 864, 1020, 1208, 1395 R M^3; 686, 750, 852, 884, 1032, 1165, 1189, 1197, 1207, 1259, 1276, 1288, 1290, 1354, 1357, 1364, 1394 L M^3; 627, 1218 L M^3 frag.

962 R mandible with M_1; 961 L mandible with M_1- M_2; 415, 484, 677, 691, 808, 809, 832, 835, 860, 919, 923, 995, 996, 999, 1001, 1004, 1042, 1092, 1161, 1233, 1234, 1236, 1237, 1281, 1296, 1318, 1319, 1321, 1322 R M_1; 469, 474, 619, 748, 815, 837, 847, 870, 900, 921, 1063, 1077, 1079, 1158, 1166, 1169, 1174, 1178, 1239, 1325 R M_1 frag.; 465, 466, 467, 617, 618, 761, 762, 778, 872, 918, 920, 922, 963, 991, 992, 998, 1000, 1003, 1044, 1066, 1159, 1211, 1214, 1215, 1231, 1232, 1235, 1320, 1323, 1324 L M_1; 441, 468, 792, 833, 834, 836, 838, 859, 869, 871, 874, 924, 1015, 1065, 1068, 1083, 1173, 1179, 1188, 1191, 1192, 1216, 1238, 1272, 1388 L M_1 frag.; 635 M_1 frag.

416, 439, 472, 473, 485, 633, 666, 679, 685, 749, 810, 841, 853, 861, 873, 877, 885, 926, 927, 1012, 1024, 1026, 1033, 1059, 1061, 1078, 1169, 1203, 1243, 1246, 1275, 1327, 1328, 1331, 1334, 1350, 1009 R M_2; 628, 964, 1023, 1028 R M_2 frag.; 417, 440, 445, 447, 470, 471, 690, 812, 839, 840, 842, 928, 1002, 1010, 1013, 1014, 1018, 1019, 1027, 1176, 1182, 1202, 1241, 1242, 1244, 1282, 1283, 1326, 1329, 1330, 1332, 1335, 1365, 1389 L M_2; 645, 813, 1194, 1209, 1245, 1333, 1517 L M_2 frag.

444, 637, 819, 854, 886, 933, 934, 1035, 1086, 1175, 1190, 1201, 1268, 1271 R M_3; 455, 456, 1022, 1195, 1206 R M_3 frag.; 443, 446, 751, 791, 816, 817, 818, 820, 855, 856, 857, 932, 935, 936, 937, 938, 1031, 1090, 1187, 1193, 1269, 1270, 1358, 1397 L M_3; 457, 705, 858, 1080 L M_3 frag.; 475 M_3.; 663, 688, 699, 1164 molar frag.; 766 L lower molar frag.

Shelly clay: 495, 505, 533, 717, 724, 1375, 1402 R M^1; 730, 1527 R M^1 frag.; 1525 R M^1 frag. (juvenile); 506, 507, 729, 1240, 1376 L M^1; 718, 733 L M^1 frag.; 741 M^1 frag.; 498, 500, 1378, 1379 R M^2.; 713, 1381 R M^3; 1528, 1576 R M^3 frag.; 744 R M^3 frag. (juvenile); 1380 L M^3; 1384, 1403, 1571 L M^3 frag.; 532 R mandible with incisor and M_1- M_3; 494, 1369, 1371 R M_1; 743, 1372, 1377 R M_1 frag.; 496 R M_1 or M_2 frag.; 504, 727 L M_1; 497, 501, 711, 1370, 1373 L M_1 frag.; 1575 L M_1 or M_2 frag.; 1374, 1383, 1398 R M_2; 735 L M_2; 731 L M_2 frag.; 712, 720, 1596 R M_3; 1382, 1573 L M_3.

Black clay (Unit 5): 1416, 1418, 1492, 1494 R M^1; 1428 R M^1 frag.; 1 1493 L M^1; 1427, 1429, 1495 R M^2; 1417, 1498 L M^2; 524, 1432, 1499 R M^3; 523 1422, 1423, 1426, 1430, 1497, 1500, 1501 L M^3; 1477 R mandible with M_1; 1414, 1415, 1478, 1479, 1480 R M_1; 1419 R M_1 frag.; 1481, 1482, 1483, 1486 L M_1; 521, 1424, 1484, 1485, 1487 L M_1 frag.;

522, 1421, 1488, 1496 R M_2; 1491 R M_2 frag.; 1420, 1431, 1489, 1490, 1502 L M_2; 525, 526, 1503 R M_3; 1425, 1504 L M_3.

Brown-grey clay: 552, 561 R M^1; 577, 606 L M^1; 562 R M^2; 544, 563 L M^2; 572 L M^2 frag.; 565 R M^3; 598 L M^3; 582 L M^3 frag.; 566 upper molar frag. (juvenile); 551, 573 R M_1; 564 R M_1 (juvenile); 596 R M_1 frag.; 592 L M_1; 560 L M_1 frag.; 553, 554, 597 R M_2; 591 R M_2 frag.; 545, 599 L M_2; 593 L M_3; 576 molar (juvenile); 580 molar; 590 partial skeleton.

Laminated shelly clay: 385 L M^2 frag.; 386 M^3 frag.; 384 L M_1 frag.; 392 molar frag.

Microtus (Terricola) cf.. *subterraneus*, common pine vole

Gritty clay: 1048, 1224, 1307, 1308 R M_1; 641, 1226 R M_1 frag.; 773, 940, 974, 1050, 1304, 1305 L M_1; 942, 975, 1151, 1295 L M_1 frag.

Shelly clay: 723, 1546 R M_1; 738 R M_1 frag.; 491, 716 L M_1.

Black clay (Unit 5): 517 R M_1.

Brown-grey clay: 603 R M_1.

Microtus agrestis (Linnaeus 1761), field vole

Gritty clay: 660, 790, 897, 943, 1210 R M^2; 407, 1129, 1186 L M^2; 461, 463, 788, 890, 1225, 1297, 1306, 1366 R M_1; 462, 829, 941, 1039, 1162, 1222 L M_1.

Shelly clay: 1579 R M^2; 1367 R M_1.

Brown-grey clay: 546 R M_1; 604 L M_1.

Microtus arvalis (Pallas 1779), common vole

Gritty clay: 1049, 1223 R M_1; 977 L M_1.

Microtus agrestis/arvalis, field or common vole

Gritty clay: 435, 657 R M_1; 408, 1310, 1519, 1520 R M_1 frag.; 486, 488, 620, 789, 828, 976, 984, 988, 1152, 1157, 1280, 1309 L M_1 frag.

Shelly clay: 492, 537 R M_1 frag.; 1568 L M_1 frag.

Brown-grey clay: 595 R M_1 frag., 585 L M_1 frag.

Microtus sp., vole

Gritty clay: 632, 634, 648, 704, 774, 795, 797, 806, 821, 825, 896, 945, 946, 948, 978, 1029, 1051, 1052, 1156, 1184, 1205, 1313, 1315 R M^1; 755 R M^1 frag.; 450, 649, 684, 697, 895, 950, 965, 979, 982, 1036, 1053, 1054, 1181, 1229, 1230, 1314, 1316, 1387 L M^1; 863, 1518 L M^1 frag.; 642, 675 M^1 frag.; 453, 644, 669, 702, 793, 981, 1131, 1132 R M^2; 956, 986 R M^2 frag.; 669 R M^2 frag.; 639, 893, 980, 983, 985, 990, 1150 L M^2; 695 L M^2 frag.; 411, 636, 676, 894,

1155 R M^3; 958, 1516 R M^3 frag.; 412, 947 L M^3; 949, 987, 1135, 1227 L M^3; 830, 955 L M^3 frag.

756, 776, 1133, 1136, 1149 R M_1 frag.; 661 L M_1 frag.; 640 R M_1 or M_2 frag.; 409, 458, 464, 777, 796, 892, 1134, 1138, 1153, 1311, 1312 R M_2; 631, 650 R M_2 frag.; 451, 487, 622, 767, 805, 824, 891, 944, 953, 954, 957, 989, 1055 L M_2; 630, 1137, 1154, 1521 L M_2 frag.; 490, 775, 831, 898, 951, 1130, 1228, 1317 R M_3; 410, 452, 489, 646, 683, 807, 952 L M_3; 673 L M_3 frag.

Shelly clay: 508, 510 L M^1; 742, 1574 L M^1 frag.; 509, 1542 L M^2; 719 R M^3; 539 R M^3 frag.; 1545 L M^3 frag.; 709 upper molar frag.; 1577 R M_1 frag.; 728 L M_1 frag.; 493, 734, 737, 1524, 1562 R M_2; 540, 714, 736 L M_2; 708, 1564 R M_3 frag.; 1544, 1570 L M_3; 499 molar frag.

Black clay (Unit 5): 1506 L M^3; 1505 R M_2.

Brown-grey clay: 547 L M^1; L M^2 frag.; 529, 575 R M^3; 579, 600 M^3 frag.; 610 L M_2 frag.; 581 M_3; 541 M_3 frag.

Laminated shelly clay: 387 L M^1; 396 R M^3.

Muridae

Apodemus sylvaticus (Linnaeus 1758), wood mouse

Gritty clay: 425, 698, 768, 901, 971, 1111, 1118, 1119 R M^1; 426, 904, 1120 R M^1 frag.; 423, 424, 681, 703, 769, 867, 868, 1220 L M^1; 1512 L M^1 frag.; 1301 R maxilla with M^1-M^2; 427, 615, 1113 R M^2; 687, 1508, 1509 L M^2; 612, 613 R M_1; 1117 R M_1 frag.; 404, 428, 802, 1110 L M_1; 1038 L mandible with M_1; 405, 680, 1510 R M_2; 429, 614, 671, 674, 770, 1112, 1116 L M_2.

Shelly clay: 1566 R M^1; 535 L M^1; 536, 665 L M^2; 503 L mandible frag.; 710, 739, 1529, 1530 R M_1; 502, 706, 1531, 1539, 1563 L M_1; 715 R M_2; 1541 L M_2

Black clay (Unit 5): 1441 R M^1; 511 L M_1; 1405, 1434 R M_1; 1435, 1436 L M_1; 1437, 1439 R M_2; 1438 L M_2.

Brown-grey clay: 558 R M^1; 557 L M^1; 568 R M^2; 550 R M_1; 594 L M_2.

Laminated shell clay: 391 lower incisor frag.

Apodemus maastrichtiensis van Kolfschoten 1985, extinct mouse

Gritty clay: 403, 692, 1507 R M^1; 771, 1114 R M^2; 406 L M^2; 483, 694, 902 R M_1; 1115 L M_1.

Shelly clay: 1540 L M_2.

Apodemus sp.

Gritty clay: 903 R M^3; 772 L M^3; 672 L M_1 frag.; 616 R M_1 or M_2 frag.

Black clay (Unit 5): 1440 R M_2 frag.; 512 L M_3.

CARNIVORA

Ursidae

Ursus sp., bear

> Brown-grey clay: 378 R P^2.

Mustelidae

Mustela cf. *M. putorius* Linnaeus 1758, polecat

> Gritty clay: 662 L M$_1$.

Felidae

Panthera leo (Linnaeus 1758), lion

> Gritty Clay: 294 axis vertebra; 351 R astragalus; 111 R metacarpal I; 80 R metatarsal III; 132 sesamoid.

PROBOSCIDEA

Elephantidae

Palaeoloxodon antiquus Falconer and Cautley 1845, straight-tusked elephant

> Gritty clay: 99 cheek tooth frag. (destroyed for ESR dating); 183 tooth frag. (Elephantidae)

PERISSODACTYLA

Rhinocerotidae

Stephanorhinus sp., rhinoceros

> Gritty clay: 357 lower molar frag.; 316 R metacarpal IV distal frag. (distal epihpysis unfused)

ARTIODACTYLA

Suidae

Sus scrofa Linnaeus 1758, wild boar

> Gritty clay: 375 cheek tooth frag. (unworn); 113 L lower incisor frag. (unworn); 106 1st phalanx (proximal unfused).

Cervidae

Dama dama (Linnaeus 1758), fallow deer

> Black clay (Unit 5): 332 cuneiform (rearticulates to 340); 340 unciform.

> Brown-grey clay: 352 L humerus distal end.

Cervus elaphus Linnaeus 1758, red deer

> Gritty clay: 349 shed antler frag. (basal region with bez and trez tines); 966 L DP$_3$.

Cervidae indet., deer

> Gritty clay: 2, 3, 10, 13, 21, 30, 34, 63, 91, 114, 126, 145, 181, 199, 203, 211, 213, 216, 217, 219, 224, 225, 226, 228, 236, 239, 356, 363, 366 antler frag.; 272 tooth frag.; 368 molar frag.; 372 upper molar frag.; 377 upper cheek tooth frag.; 358 L I$_1$; 292 L I$_2$; 374 L lower 3rd incisor or canine; 23 metatarsal frag.; 364 metapodial frag.

> Shelly clay: 376 lower molar frag.

> Black clay (Unit 5): 373 vestigial phalanx.

Bovidae

Bos/Bison sp., aurochs or bison.

> Gritty clay: 315 R femur shaft frag. (cutmarks and impact damage).

Unit	No.	Taxa	H	HC	LUF	LLF
BC	1445	SM	2.99	1.39	0.52	0.83
GC	866	SM	3.09	1.35	0.60	0.85
BC	1446	SA	4.12	-	-	1.10
SC	1399	SA	4.23	-	0.75	0.60
SC	1400	SA	4.19	1.74	0.85	1.10
GC	653	SA	-	1.74	0.75	1.07
GC	746	SA	4.07	1.58	0.79	1.07
GC	826	SA	3.96	1.72	0.73	1.03
GC	1278	SA	4.01	1.66	0.55	1.07
GC	1279	SA	3.95	1.76	0.53	0.90
GC	1298	SA	4.04	1.88	0.75	1.06
SB	390	SA	-	-	-	1.03
BC	1444	NS	4.41	2.47	0.93	1.51
SC	1401	NS	4.41	2.28	0.95	1.58
GC	801	NS	4.57	2.38	0.97	1.63
GC	827	NS	4.46	2.38	0.95	1.56
GC	1045	NS	4.70	2.68	1.05	1.56
GC	1103	NS	-	2.33	0.96	1.51
GC	1104	NS	-	2.23	0.85	1.41
GC	1047	CS	-	-	-	1.56

Table 1. Measurements of soricid mandibles. SM = *Sorex minutus*, SA = *Sorex* sp. 1., NS = *Neomys* sp., CS = *Crocidura* sp., H = height of coronoid process, HC = height of condyle, LUF = Length of upper condylar facet, LLF = length of lower condylar facet. All measurements in mm.

Unit	No.	Taxa	Length
BC	1448	SM	2.47
BGC	608	SA	2.99
GC	782	SA	3.24
SC	1534	NS	e 4.16

Table 2. Measurements of soricid lower incisors. SM = *Sorex minutus*, SA = *Sorex* sp. 1., NS = *Neomys* sp.,

Unit	No.	Taxa	M_1 L	M_1 TRW	M_1 TAW
BC	1445	SM	1.18	0.58	0.64
SC	534	SM	-	-	0.65
SC	1533	SM	1.09	0.58	0.65
SC	1551	SM	1.12	0.59	0.66
GC	652	SM	1.12	0.60	0.68
BC	1446	SA	1.51	0.80	0.83
SC	721	SA	1.35	0.70	0.80
GC	433	SA	1.43	0.75	0.79
GC	746	SA	1.41	0.76	0.83
GC	1385	SA	1.38	0.73	0.76
BC	1442	NS	1.56	0.88	0.95
GC	827	NS	1.53	0.87	0.98
GC	909	NS	1.58	0.88	0.95
GC	1514	NS	1.56	0.87	0.89
GC	1105	CS	1.75	1.08	1.18

Table 3. Measurements of soricid M_1. SM = *Sorex minutus*, SA = *Sorex* sp. 1., NS = *Neomys* sp., CS = *Crocidura* sp., TRW = trigonid width, TAW = talonid width.

Unit	No.	Taxa	M_2 L	M_2 TRW	M_2 TAW
BC	1445	SM	1.09	0.60	0.63
SC	534	SM	1.15	0.64	0.61
SC	1533	SM	1.12	0.61	0.64
BC	1448	SA	1.28	0.73	0.74
GC	746	SA	1.25	0.76	0.79
GC	972	cf. SA	1.25	0.73	0.75
GC	1303	SA	1.32	0.75	0.80
GC	1385	SA	1.22	0.69	0.72
GC	410	NS	1.59	0.98	1.03
GC	794	NS	1.57	0.89	0.95
GC	827	NS	1.51	0.84	0.93
GC	1442	NS	1.51	0.83	0.89
GC	907	CS	1.70	1.07	1.03

Table 4. Measurements of soricid M_2. SM = *Sorex minutus*, SA = *Sorex* sp. 1., NS = *Neomys* sp., CS = *Crocidura* sp., TRW = trigonid width, TAW = talonid width.

Unit	No.	Taxa	M_3 L	M_3 W
BC	1445	SM	0.87	-
SC	1533	SM	0.88	0.54
BC	1447	SA	1.00	0.60
GC	972	cf. SA	0.97	0.58
GC	1303	SA	1.02	0.58
GC	1450	NS	1.24	0.70

Table 5. Measurements of soricid M_3. SM = *Sorex minutus*, SA = *Sorex* sp. 1., NS = *Neomys* sp.

Unit	No.	Taxa	Length	LT	H
BC	1456	SM	1.10	0.59	0.74
BC	1457	SA	1.76	1.04	1.14
SC	732	SA	1.66	0.90	1.01
GC	651	SA	1.77	1.09	1.14
GC	1511	SA	1.67	0.95	1.04
GC	431	cf. SA	-	0.80	0.85
GC	655	NS	1.84	0.85	-

Table 6. Measurements of soricid upper incisors. SM = *Sorex minutus*, SA = *Sorex* sp. 1., NS = *Neomys* sp., LT = length of talon, H = height.

Unit	No.	Taxa	P⁴ BL	P⁴ PE	P⁴ LL	P⁴ W
SB	381	SM	-	-	-	1.13
BGC	559	SA	1.46	0.88	-	1.38
BGC	607	SA	1.41	0.85	0.90	1.29
BC	516	SA	1.41	-	-	-
BC	1458	SA	1.40	0.93	0.98	1.29
SC	1532	SA	1.43	0.80	0.88	1.28
SC	1536	SA	1.46	0.95	1.00	1.37
SC	1559	SA	1.41	-	-	-
GC	656	SA	1.37	-	-	-
SC	1459	NS	1.81	1.08	1.13	1.59
GC	785	NS	1.83	1.15	1.26	1.63
GC	1106	NS	1.74	-	-	-

Table 7. Measurements of soricid P⁴. SM = *Sorex minutus*, SA = *Sorex* sp. 1., NS = *Neomys* sp., BL = buccal length, PE = length of posterior emargination, LL= lingual length.

Unit	No.	Taxa	M¹ BL	M¹ PE	M¹ LL	M¹ AW	M¹ PW
BGC	527	SM	1.13	0.85	1.13	1.10	1.23
BC	1464	SM	1.13	1.12	1.16	1.15	1.24
GC	759	SM	1.13	1.18	1.16	1.15	1.30
BGC	548	SA	1.35	-	-	1.31	-
BC	1466	SA	1.35	1.32	1.35	1.23	1.41
SC	1532	SA	1.35	1.22	1.26	1.18	1.41
GC	1513	SA	1.35	-	-	1.38	-
BC	1460	NS	1.58	1.53	1.66	1.75	1.91
GC	402	NS	1.48	-	-	1.73	-
GC	460	NS	1.31	1.33	1.48	1.73	1.62

Table 8. Measurements of soricid M¹. SM = *Sorex minutus*, SA = *Sorex* sp. 1., NS = *Neomys* sp., BL = buccal length, PE = length of proximal emargination, LL = lingual length, AW = anterior width, PW = posterior width.

Unit	No.	Taxa	M² BL	M² PE	M² LL	M² AW	M² PW
BC	1465	SA	1.17	1.09	1.18	1.33	1.37
BC	1467	SA	1.24	1.13	1.20	1.35	1.34
SC	1538	SA	1.16	1.15	1.19	1.38	1.42
SA	1559	SA	1.29	-	-	1.19	-
GC	758	SA	1.22	-	-	1.46	1.46
GC	460	NS	1.53	1.40	1.56	1.67	1.84
GC	968	NS	1.35	1.25	1.32	1.77	1.62

Table 9. Measurements of soricid M². SA = *Sorex* sp. 1., NS = *Neomys* sp., BL = buccal length, PE = length of posterior emarination, LL = lingual length, AW = anterior width, PW = posterior width.

Unit	No.	P⁴L	P⁴W	M¹L	M¹W	M²L	M²W	M³L	M³W
GC	906	-	-	-	-	1.76	1.88	-	-
GC	1100	-	-	-	-	1.98	2.1	-	-
GC	1101	-	-	-	-	-	-	1.60	1.60

Table 10. Measurements of *Talpa minor* upper teeth.

Unit	No.	P₃L	P₃W	M₁L	M₁ TRW	M₁ TAW	M₃L	M₃W
GC	799	0.71	0.40	-	-	-	-	-
GC	513	-	-	1.83	0.95	1.08	-	-
GC	1553	-	-	-	-	-	1.91	0.83

Table 11. Measurements of *Talpa minor* lower teeth. TRW = trigonid width, TAW = talonid width.

Unit	No.	Element	GL	Bp	SD	Bd
GC	865	Humerus	-	-	3.13	-
GC	899	Humerus	-	-	3.12	6.05
GC	959	Humerus	-	-	3.03	6.22
GC	1041	Humerus	-	-	3.25	6.39
GC	1091	Humerus	-	-	3.02	5.37
GC	1102	Humerus	-	-	3.05	5.72
GC	1213	Humerus	11	-	2.96	3.89
GC	1299	Humerus	-	-	2.87	-
GC	482	Radius	-	2.8	-	-
GC	787	Radius	-	3.0	-	-
GC	905	Radius	-	3.2	-	-
GC	1097	Radius	-	2.33	-	-
GC	967	Tibia	-	2.9	-	-

Table 12. Measurements of *Talpa minor* postcrania. GL = greatest length, Bp = breadth of proximal epiphysis, SD = smallest breadth of shaft, Bd = breadth of distal end.

Unit	No.	Element	L	W	Ht. behind M₃
SC	725	P¹	1.58	1.57	
GC	370	Mandible			4.8

Table 13. Measurements of *Desmana moschata*.

Unit	No.	MD L	BL W
GC	459	2.7	1.8

Table 14. Measurements of *Oryctolagus* sp. upper incisor. (MD L = mesiodistal length, BL W = buccolingual breadth)

Unit	No.	M₁L	M₁L-a	M₁w1	M₁c1	M₁b1	M₁Wp
BGC	528	2.01	0.85	0.75	0.13	0.13	0.73
BGC	602	2.03	0.74	0.67	0.15	0.14	0.80
BGC	605	2.21	0.92	0.78	0.12	0.22	0.85
BC	1469	2.09	0.82	0.78	0.15	0.17	-
GC	912	2.09	0.85	0.83	0.06	0.05	0.87
GC	969	1.87	0.61	-	0.18	0.19	-

Table 15. Measurements of *Clethrionomys glareolus*.

Unit	No.	M_1L	M_1L-a	M_1w1	M_1c1	M_1b1	M_1Wp	Notes
BGC	551	3.46	1.48	1.30	0.26	0.43	1.40	Mfa
BGC	564	3.02	-	-	-	-	1.24	Juvenile, Mfp
BC	1414	3.55	1.51	1.18	0.32	0.35	e 1.38	Mfa
BC	1415	3.54	1.40	1.21	0.31	0.40	1.30	Mfa
BC	1477	3.37	1.35	1.25	0.33	0.40	1.38	Mfa
BC	1478	3.24	1.13	-	0.20	0.48	1.39	Mfa
BC	1479	3.70	1.34	1.21	0.28	0.33	1.57	Mfa
BC	1480	3.52	1.51	1.26	0.33	0.46	1.36	Mfa
BC	1481	3.51	1.33	1.20	0.33	0.53	-	Mfa
BC	1483	3.37	1.08	1.35	0.30	0.50	e 1.51	Mfa
BC	1486	3.38	1.39	1.23	0.23	0.34	1.36	Mfa
SC	494	3.49	1.45	1.25	0.29	0.44	1.43	Mfa
SC	504	3.54	1.40	1.29	0.30	0.38	1.35	Mfa
SC	532	3.59	-	-	-	-	1.43	Mfp
SC	727	3.62	1.57	1.31	0.31	0.36	1.43	Mfa
SC	1234	3.66	1.43	1.35	0.31	0.45	1.50	Mfp
SC	1369	3.47	1.44	1.23	0.30	0.39	1.38	Mfp
SC	1371	3.66	1.38	1.24	0.37	0.45	1.43	Mfa
GC	415	3.86	1.63	1.26	0.29	0.33	-	Mfa
GC	465	3.17	1.35	1.35	0.29	0.40	-	Mfp
GC	466	3.61	1.55	-	0.24	0.22	-	Mfp
GC	467	3.22	1.31	1.23	0.28	0.43	-	Mfa
GC	468	-	-	1.21	0.29	0.21	-	Mfa
GC	484	3.14	1.23	-	0.25	0.24	-	Mfa
GC	617	3.59	1.33	1.29	0.25	0.48	1.35	Mfa
GC	618	4.00	1.48	1.40	0.17	0.40	1.56	Mfp
GC	677	3.52	1.44	1.23	0.24	0.32	1.43	Mfp
GC	691	3.56	1.58	1.20	0.27	0.30	1.39	Mfa
GC	761	3.50	1.22	1.35	0.35	0.35	1.56	Mfa
GC	762	3.50	1.34	1.19	0.24	0.48	1.38	Mfa
GC	778	3.41	1.00	1.18	-	-	1.44	Mfa
GC	808	3.82	1.58	1.26	-	0.19	1.44	Mfa
GC	809	3.73	1.57	1.32	0.31	0.30	1.40	Mfp
GC	832	3.72	1.49	1.25	0.19	0.30	1.44	Mfa
GC	834	3.70	1.50	1.27	0.30	0.34	1.43	Mfa
GC	835	3.61	1.48	1.35	0.21	0.35	1.51	Mfa
GC	860	3.68	1.23	1.26	0.36	0.63	-	Mfa
GC	918	3.62	1.43	1.26	0.27	0.36	-	Mfp
GC	919	e 3.27	-	1.37	0.28	0.30	-	Mfa
GC	920	3.37	e 1.25	-	-	-	-	Mfa
GC	922	3.32	1.10	-	0.33	0.43	-	Mfa
GC	923	e 3.15	-	-	0.28	0.28	-	Mfp
GC	961	3.41	1.31	1.28	0.35	0.36	1.38	Mfp
GC	962	3.61	1.25	1.25	0.31	0.53	1.52	Mfa
GC	963	3.50	1.32	1.31	0.20	0.32	1.51	Mfa
GC	991	3.37	1.46	e 1.20	0.22	0.46	1.28	Mfa
GC	992	3.59	1.44	1.28	0.18	0.43	1.35	Mfa
GC	995	3.87	1.58	1.39	0.21	0.24	1.57	Mfp
GC	996	3.37	1.50	1.26	0.31	0.43	1.34	Mfp
GC	998	3.52	1.45	1.32	0.28	0.40	1.38	Mfp
GC	999	3.46	1.42	1.37	0.28	0.38	1.58	Mfp
GC	1000	3.71	1.57	1.36	0.29	0.43	1.48	Mfa
GC	1001	3.57	1.56	1.30	0.31	0.23	1.46	Mfp
GC	1003	3.58	1.41	1.31	0.31	0.28	1.47	Mfp
GC	1004	3.82	1.61	1.35	0.32	0.40	1.48	Mfa
GC	1042	3.83	1.58	1.38	0.10	0.43	1.46	Mfa
GC	1044	3.70	1.46	-	0.27	0.58	-	
GC	1066	3.51	1.43	1.32	0.20	0.48	1.38	Mfa
GC	1092	3.47	1.38	1.28	0.28	0.38	1.43	Mfa
GC	1159	3.71	1.51	1.33	0.24	0.34	1.48	Mfa
GC	1161	3.91	1.51	1.38	0.21	0.38	1.51	Mfa
GC	1211	3.61	1.58	1.31	0.38	0.33	1.38	Mfp
GC	1214	3.55	1.23	1.25	0.30	0.61	1.31	Mfa
GC	1215	3.37	1.38	1.30	0.25	0.38	1.42	Mfa
GC	1231	3.58	1.36	1.35	0.28	0.60	1.41	Mfa
GC	1232	3.56	1.35	1.30	0.25	0.22	1.41	Mfa
GC	1233	3.81	1.38	1.37	0.22	0.40	1.51	Mfa
GC	1235	3.61	1.40	1.34	0.21	0.53	1.48	Mfa
GC	1236	e 3.51	e 1.15	1.25	0.38	-	1.52	Mfa
GC	1237	3.43	1.33	1.14	0.22	0.35	1.35	Mfa
GC	1281	3.80	1.66	1.38	0.35	0.35	1.51	Mfa
GC	1296	3.33	1.23	1.23	0.33	0.40	1.41	Mfa
GC	1318	3.72	1.58	1.28	0.24	0.42	1.46	Mfa
GC	1319	3.81	1.43	1.35	0.32	0.36	1.46	Mfa
GC	1320	3.61	1.45	-	0.23	0.30	-	Mfa
GC	1321	3.56	1.29	1.30	0.34	0.53	1.47	Mfp
GC	1322	3.47	1.58	1.23	0.38	0.55	1.48	Mfa
GC	1323	3.61	1.56	1.28	0.30	0.34	-	Mfp
GC	1324	4.01	1.56	1.36	0.28	0.28	1.38	Mfa

Table 18. Measurements of *Arvicola terrestris cantiana* lower first molar. Mfa = *Mimomys* fold absent, Mfp = *Mimomys* fold present

Appendix IV

Unit	No.	M^1L	M^1W	M^2L	M^2W	M_2L	M_2W	M_3L	M_3W	Notes
BGC	552	2.92	1.35	-	-	-	-	-	-	
BGC	561	2.87	1.38	-	-	-	-	-	-	
BGC	606	3.32	1.52	-	-	-	-	-	-	
BGC	544	-	-	2.11	1.25	-	-	-	-	
BGC	562	-	-	2.16	1.35	-	-	-	-	
BGC	563	-	-	2.17	1.30	-	-	-	-	
BGC	545	-	-	-	-	2.01	-	-	-	
BGC	553	-	-	-	-	2.01	1.08	-	-	
BGC	554	-	-	-	-	2.16	1.25	-	-	
BGC	597	-	-	-	-	2.23	1.24	-	-	
BGC	599	-	-	-	-	1.98	-	-	-	
BGC	593	-	-	-	-	-	-	2.02	-	
BC	1416	3.32	1.51	-	-	-	-	-	-	
BC	1418	2.93	-	-	-	-	-	-	-	
BC	1492	3.18	1.41	-	-	-	-	-	-	
BC	1493	3.05	1.25	-	-	-	-	-	-	
BC	1494	3.13	1.51	-	-	-	-	-	-	
BC	1417	-	-	2.38	e 1.23	-	-	-	-	
BC	1427	-	-	2.26	1.20	-	-	-	-	
BC	1429	-	-	2.23	1.25	-	-	-	-	
BC	1495	-	-	2.61	1.47	-	-	-	-	
BC	522	-	-	-	-	2.12	1.18	-	-	
BC	1420	-	-	-	-	2.24	1.23	-	-	
BC	1421	-	-	-	-	2.06	-	-	-	
BC	1431	-	-	-	-	2.21	-	-	-	
BC	1488	-	-	-	-	2.18	1.21	-	-	
BC	1489	-	-	-	-	2.12	1.23	-	-	
BC	1490	-	-	-	-	2.26	1.23	-	-	
BC	1496	-	-	-	-	2.04	-	-	-	
BC	525	-	-	-	-	-	-	2.08	0.95	
BC	526	-	-	-	-	-	-	1.98	0.98	
BC	1425	-	-	-	-	-	-	2.19	1.06	
BC	1503	-	-	-	-	-	-	2.11	-	
SC	495	3.07	1.39	-	-	-	-	-	-	
SC	533	3.09	-	-	-	-	-	-	-	
SC	506	2.99	1.44	-	-	-	-	-	-	
SC	717	3.19	1.38	-	-	-	-	-	-	
SC	724	3.07	-	-	-	-	-	-	-	
SC	1375	3.41	1.53	-	-	-	-	-	-	
SC	1376	3.08	1.41	-	-	-	-	-	-	
SC	1402	3.02	-	-	-	-	-	-	-	
SC	498	-	-	2.41	1.35	-	-	-	-	
SC	1378	-	-	2.24	1.25	-	-	-	-	
SC	1379	-	-	2.46	1.34	-	-	-	-	
SC	735	-	-	-	-	2.22	1.18	-	-	
SC	1374	-	-	-	-	2.03	1.10	-	-	
SC	1398	-	-	-	-	2.28	e 1.25	-	-	
SC	712	-	-	-	-	-	-	2.13	1.10	
SC	720	-	-	-	-	-	-	1.96	-	
SC	1382	-	-	-	-	-	-	2.26	1.03	
SC	1567	-	-	-	-	-	-	2.16	1.06	
SC	1573	-	-	-	-	-	-	2.28	1.24	
GC	418	3.22	1.51	-	-	-	-	-	-	
GC	436	2.85	1.34	-	-	-	-	-	-	
GC	437	2.80	1.29	-	-	-	-	-	-	
GC	476	2.92	1.39	-	-	-	-	-	-	
GC	477	2.99	1.53	-	-	-	-	-	-	
GC	478	3.12	1.51	-	-	-	-	-	-	
GC	621	2.97	1.39	-	-	-	-	-	-	
GC	623	3.08	1.46	-	-	-	-	-	-	
GC	624	3.08	1.47	-	-	-	-	-	-	
GC	668	2.99	-	-	-	-	-	-	-	
GC	763	3.12	1.45	-	-	-	-	-	-	
GC	764	3.23	-	-	-	-	-	-	-	
GC	779	3.16	1.34	-	-	-	-	-	-	
GC	822	2.81	-	-	-	-	-	-	-	
GC	843	3.37	1.58	-	-	-	-	-	-	

Table 19. Measurements of *Arvicola terrestris cantiana* molars.

279

Unit	No.	M¹L	M¹W	M²L	M²W	M₂L	M₂W	M₃L	M₃W	Notes
GC	1057	-	-	2.56	-	-	-	-	-	
GC	1062	-	-	2.26	-	-	-	-	-	
GC	1073	-	-	2.36	1.30	-	-	-	-	
GC	1074	-	-	2.25	1.41	-	-	-	-	
GC	1081	-	-	2.47	1.38	-	-	-	-	
GC	1084	-	-	2.39	1.28	-	-	-	-	
GC	1093	-	-	2.43	1.41	-	-	-	-	
GC	1095	-	-	2.22	-	-	-	-	-	
GC	1168	-	-	2.41	1.25	-	-	-	-	
GC	1170	-	-	2.33	1.25	-	-	-	-	
GC	1172	-	-	2.33	-	-	-	-	-	
GC	1177	-	-	2.72	-	-	-	-	-	
GC	1200	-	-	2.33	-	-	-	-	-	
GC	1217	-	-	2.23	1.33	-	-	-	-	
GC	1260	-	-	2.49	1.45	-	-	-	-	
GC	1261	-	-	e 2.28	-	-	-	-	-	
GC	1262	-	-	2.24	1.35	-	-	-	-	
GC	1263	-	-	2.16	-	-	-	-	-	
GC	1264	-	-	2.16	-	-	-	-	-	
GC	1291	-	-	2.56	1.28	-	-	-	-	
GC	1292	-	-	2.43	-	-	-	-	-	
GC	1293	-	-	2.46	1.28	-	-	-	-	
GC	1294	-	-	2.20	1.20	-	-	-	-	
GC	1344	-	-	2.46	1.45	-	-	-	-	
GC	1345	-	-	2.18	1.26	-	-	-	-	
GC	1348	-	-	2.38	1.36	-	-	-	-	
GC	1351	-	-	2.55	1.40	-	-	-	-	
GC	1352	-	-	2.52	1.35	-	-	-	-	
GC	1353	-	-	2.51	1.51	-	-	-	-	
GC	1359	-	-	2.50	1.27	-	-	-	-	
GC	1361	-	-	2.54	1.35	-	-	-	-	
GC	1363	-	-	2.48	-	-	-	-	-	
GC	1390	-	-	2.56	1.34	-	-	-	-	
GC	1391	-	-	2.51	1.50	-	-	-	-	
GC	1393	-	-	2.19	-	-	-	-	-	
GC	416	-	-	-	-	2.16	1.15	-	-	
GC	417	-	-	-	-	2.31	1.20	-	-	
GC	439	-	-	-	-	2.13	1.11	-	-	Juvenile
GC	440	-	-	-	-	2.18	1.25	-	-	
GC	445	-	-	-	-	2.01	1.23	-	-	
GC	470	-	-	-	-	2.48	1.34	-	-	
GC	471	-	-	-	-	2.28	1.18	-	-	
GC	472	-	-	-	-	2.40	1.33	-	-	
GC	473	-	-	-	-	2.16	-	-	-	
GC	633	-	-	-	-	2.09	1.23	-	-	
GC	666	-	-	-	-	2.13	-	-	-	
GC	679	-	-	-	-	2.20	1.30	-	-	
GC	685	-	-	-	-	2.07	1.17	-	-	
GC	690	-	-	-	-	2.23	1.31	-	-	
GC	749	-	-	-	-	2.21	1.30	-	-	
GC	810	-	-	-	-	2.23	-	-	-	
GC	812	-	-	-	-	2.21	1.20	-	-	
GC	839	-	-	-	-	2.21	1.28	-	-	
GC	840	-	-	-	-	2.37	1.26	-	-	
GC	841	-	-	-	-	2.15	1.20	-	-	
GC	842	-	-	-	-	2.33	1.34	-	-	
GC	853	-	-	-	-	2.13	-	-	-	
GC	861	-	-	-	-	2.31	1.35	-	-	
GC	873	-	-	-	-	2.34	1.30	-	-	
GC	877	-	-	-	-	2.25	1.18	-	-	
GC	885	-	-	-	-	1.98	1.11	-	-	
GC	926	-	-	-	-	2.26	1.28	-	-	
GC	927	-	-	-	-	2.13	1.30	-	-	
GC	928	-	-	-	-	2.26	1.27	-	-	
GC	1002	-	-	-	-	2.38	1.33	-	-	
GC	1009	-	-	-	-	2.26	1.20	-	-	
GC	1010	-	-	-	-	2.23	1.30	-	-	
GC	1012	-	-	-	-	2.46	1.38	-	-	
GC	1014	-	-	-	-	2.36	-	-	-	
GC	1018	-	-	-	-	2.25	1.29	-	-	

Table 19. Cont.

Unit	No.	M¹L	M¹W	M²L	M²W	M₂L	M₂W	M₃L	M₃W	Notes
GC	1019	-	-	-	-	2.19	-	-	-	
GC	1024	-	-	-	-	2.18	1.30	-	-	
GC	1026	-	-	-	-	2.31	-	-	-	
GC	1033	-	-	-	-	2.21	1.28	-	-	
GC	1059	-	-	-	-	2.06	-	-	-	
GC	1061	-	-	-	-	2.34	1.33	-	-	
GC	1078	-	-	-	-	2.16	1.20	-	-	
GC	1169	-	-	-	-	2.38	1.35	-	-	
GC	1176	-	-	-	-	-	1.23	-	-	
GC	1182	-	-	-	-	2.07	1.20	-	-	
GC	1203	-	-	-	-	2.06	1.10	-	-	
GC	1241	-	-	-	-	2.24	1.18	-	-	
GC	1242	-	-	-	-	2.27	1.32	-	-	
GC	1243	-	-	-	-	2.38	1.35	-	-	
GC	1244	-	-	-	-	2.14	-	-	-	
GC	1246	-	-	-	-	2.29	1.35	-	-	
GC	1275	-	-	-	-	2.36	1.20	-	-	
GC	1282	-	-	-	-	2.36	1.19	-	-	
GC	1283	-	-	-	-	2.08	1.18	-	-	
GC	1326	-	-	-	-	2.64	1.33	-	-	
GC	1327	-	-	-	-	2.18	1.23	-	-	
GC	1328	-	-	-	-	2.19	1.26	-	-	
GC	1329	-	-	-	-	2.31	-	-	-	
GC	1330	-	-	-	-	2.29	1.20	-	-	
GC	1331	-	-	-	-	2.21	-	-	-	
GC	1332	-	-	-	-	2.32	-	-	-	
GC	1334	-	-	-	-	2.13	1.09	-	-	
GC	1335	-	-	-	-	2.09	-	-	-	
GC	1350	-	-	-	-	2.13	1.20	-	-	
GC	1365	-	-	-	-	2.08	-	-	-	
GC	1389	-	-	-	-	2.31	e 1.23	-	-	
GC	443	-	-	-	-	-	-	2.01		
GC	444	-	-	-	-	-	-	1.93	-	
GC	446	-	-	-	-	-	-	1.99	1.04	
GC	475	-	-	-	-	-	-	2.28	0.97	
GC	637	-	-	-	-	-	-	1.83	-	
GC	751	-	-	-	-	-	-	2.13	1.07	
GC	816	-	-	-	-	-	-	2.17	1.05	
GC	817	-	-	-	-	-	-	2.26	1.07	
GC	818	-	-	-	-	-	-	2.15	1.16	
GC	819	-	-	-	-	-	-	2.12	-	
GC	820	-	-	-	-	-	-	2.27	1.02	
GC	854	-	-	-	-	-	-	2.29	-	
GC	855	-	-	-	-	-	-	2.25	1.13	
GC	856	-	-	-	-	-	-	2.29	1.13	
GC	857	-	-	-	-	-	-	2.18	1.10	
GC	886	-	-	-	-	-	-	2.21	1.13	
GC	932	-	-	-	-	-	-	2.37	1.20	
GC	933	-	-	-	-	-	-	2.39	1.10	
GC	934	-	-	-	-	-	-	2.29	1.11	
GC	935	-	-	-	-	-	-	2.11	1.01	
GC	936	-	-	-	-	-	-	2.41	1.18	
GC	937	-	-	-	-	-	-	2.29	1.05	
GC	1031	-	-	-	-	-	-	2.27	1.10	
GC	1035	-	-	-	-	-	-	2.21	1.11	
GC	1086	-	-	-	-	-	-	2.13	1.10	
GC	1090	-	-	-	-	-	-	2.41	1.10	
GC	1175	-	-	-	-	-	-	2.02	-	
GC	1187	-	-	-	-	-	-	2.28	0.98	
GC	1190	-	-	-	-	-	-	2.33	1.09	
GC	1193	-	-	-	-	-	-	2.09	1.17	
GC	1268	-	-	-	-	-	-	2.32	1.17	
GC	1269	-	-	-	-	-	-	2.20	1.15	
GC	1270	-	-	-	-	-	-	2.23	-	
GC	1271	-	-	-	-	-	-	1.88	-	
GC	1358	-	-	-	-	-	-	2.20	1.05	
GC	1397	-	-	-	-	-	-	2.35	1.09	

Table 19. cont.

Unit	No.	M³L	M³L-a	M³w1	M³cl	M³Wa	Notes
BGC	565	2.47	0.92	0.80	0.10	1.22	
BGC	598	2.27	0.80	0.75	0.18	1.30	
BC	523	2.38	1.08	1.05	0.11	1.24	
BC	524	1.98	-	-	-	0.95	Juvenile
BC	1422	2.40	0.97	0.83	0.10	1.23	
BC	1423	2.23	0.68	0.72	0.31	1.28	
BC	1426	2.39	0.92	0.75	0.33	1.33	
BC	1430	2.10	0.77	0.82	0.16	1.20	
BC	1432	2.11	0.91	0.81	0.16	1.09	
BC	1497	2.46	0.97	0.93	0.17	-	
BC	1499	2.18	1.34	0.72	0.29	1.13	
BC	1501	2.13	0.85	0.73	0.22	1.15	
SC	713	2.38	0.98	0.83	0.29	1.24	
SC	1380	2.50	1.00	0.75	0.12	e 1.25	
SC	1381	2.34	0.81	0.83	0.25	1.28	
GC	420	2.31	0.97	0.87	0.25	1.18	
GC	480	2.36	1.03	0.96	0.23	1.26	
GC	481	2.31	0.91	0.88	0.19	1.26	
GC	626	2.48	0.90	0.87	0.08	1.38	
GC	658	2.13	0.83	0.86	0.12	1.23	
GC	686	2.20	0.79	0.76	0.26	-	
GC	750	2.21	-	-	-	1.19	
GC	811	2.51	1.02	0.90	0.16	1.36	
GC	852	2.58	1.09	0.91	0.09	1.43	
GC	884	2.13	0.73	0.85	0.22	1.16	
GC	930	2.29	0.97	0.88	0.18	-	
GC	1006	2.51	1.00	0.85	0.14	-	
GC	1008	2.38	0.92	0.80	0.20	1.21	
GC	1032	2.28	0.98	0.83	0.16	-	
GC	1040	2.23	1.19	0.68	0.14	1.32	
GC	1072	2.53	0.93	0.90	0.04	1.32	
GC	1075	2.23	0.85	0.75	-	-	
GC	1088	2.14	0.88	0.71	0.40	1.20	
GC	1089	2.23	0.85	0.69	0.19	1.18	
GC	1165	2.37	1.00	0.83	0.21	1.33	
GC	1189	2.36	0.94	0.83	0.17	1.15	
GC	1197	2.42	0.89	0.88	0.26	1.28	
GC	1207	2.13	0.88	0.79	0.22	1.10	
GC	1259	2.56	1.01	0.87	0.18	1.29	
GC	1266	2.28	0.88	0.74	0.21	1.23	
GC	1267	2.11	0.88	0.77	0.14	1.02	
GC	1274	2.13	0.75	0.76	0.34	-	
GC	1276	2.33	0.95	0.87	0.11	-	
GC	1288	2.38	1.15	0.93	0.13	1.19	
GC	1289	2.18	0.95	0.88	0.23	1.12	
GC	1290	2.11	0.94	0.85	0.23	1.07	
GC	1354	2.46	0.88	0.83	0.33	1.34	
GC	1355	2.29	0.84	0.82	0.24	1.20	
GC	1356	2.33	0.89	0.80	0.25	1.18	
GC	1357	2.54	1.00	0.86	0.16	-	
GC	1360	2.51	1.03	0.88	0.17	1.31	
GC	1364	2.16	0.85	0.70	0.25	1.03	
GC	1394	2.34	0.95	0.88	0.20	1.30	
GC	1396	2.49	1.01	0.87	0.22	1.31	

Table 20. Measurements of *Arvicola terrestris cantiana* third upper molar.

Unit	No.	M_1L	M_1L-a	M_1w1	M_1c1	M_1b1	M_1w2	M_1c2	M_1b2	M_1Wp
BGC	603	2.26	1.13	-	-	-	-	-	-	-
SC	716	2.57	1.44	0.88	0.08	0.03	0.69	0.15	0.13	0.85
SC	723	2.57	1.33	0.84	0.16	0.03	0.69	0.19	0.15	0.88
SC	1305	2.72	1.46	0.84	0.13	0.03	0.68	0.24	0.25	0.87
SC	1307	2.60	1.41	0.88	0.17	0.03	0.70	0.21	0.22	0.94
SC	1308	2.40	1.14	-	0.15	0.02	-	0.17	0.05	-
SC	1546	2.13	-	-	-	-	-	-	-	-
GC	773	2.48	1.23	-	0.17	0.03	-	0.18	0.24	-
GC	940	2.51	1.36	0.87	0.18	0.03	e 0.73	0.21	0.18	0.90
GC	942	-	-	0.80	0.15	0.05	0.73	-	-	-
GC	974	2.38	1.27	0.75	0.20	0.04	e 0.63	0.23	0.19	-
GC	975	-	1.23	0.78	0.20	0.03	0.66	0.21	0.17	-
GC	1048	2.79	1.39	0.90	0.18	0.02	0.75	0.23	0.22	0.94
GC	1050	2.72	1.45	0.89	0.20	0.03	0.73	0.22	0.17	0.93
GC	1224	2.69	1.35	0.90	0.17	0.03	0.77	0.17	0.20	0.89
GC	1304	2.66	1.45	0.89	0.17	0.02	0.72	0.23	0.22	0.88

Table 21. Measurements of *Microtus* (*Terricola*) sp. lower first molar.

Unit	No.	M^2L	M^2W
SC	1579	1.51	0.80
GC	660	1.66	-
GC	790	1.69	0.98
CG	897	1.53	0.84
GC	943	1.81	1.00
GC	1129	1.58	0.85
GC	1186	1.81	0.98
GC	1210	1.63	-

Table 22. Measurements of *Microtus agrestis* second upper molar.

Unit	No.	M_1L	M_1L-a	M_1w1	M_1c1	M_1b1	M_1w2	M_1c2	M_1b2	M_1Wp	Notes
BGC	546	2.73	1.33	1.01	0.02	0.02	0.80	0.33	0.23	0.94	
BGC	604	2.82	1.46	0.94	0.01	0.02	0.78	0.03	0.25	0.88	
SC	1366	2.94	1.56	0.94	0.01	0.02	0.76	0.22	0.27	-	
SC	1367	2.93	1.48	1.00	0.02	0.01	0.80	0.16	0.25	-	
GC	461	2.92	1.57	1.01	0.03	0.03	0.79	0.20	0.23	-	
GC	462	2.80	1.43	0.98	0.03	0.02	0.78	0.27	0.33	0.94	
GC	463	2.57	-	-	-	-	-	-	-	-	
GC	657	2.30	-	-	-	-	-	-	-	-	Juvenile
GC	788	2.92	1.44	0.99	0.03	0.02	0.80	0.25	0.40	1.03	
GC	829	2.58	1.30	1.00	0.01	0.02	0.77	0.05	0.27	-	
GC	890	2.92	1.57	1.06	0.02	0.02	0.83	0.28	-	1.03	
GC	941	2.82	1.50	0.99	0.002	0.002	0.85	0.20	0.26	-	
GC	1039	3.07	1.53	1.11	0.02	0.02	0.85	0.30	0.30	1.05	
GC	1162	3.22	1.73	1.04	0.03	0.03	0.83	0.14	0.30	-	
GC	1222	3.00	1.62	-	0.02	0.03	0.86	0.02	0.23	-	
GC	1225	3.05	1.58	1.03	0.02	0.02	0.86	0.18	0.30	1.04	
GC	1297	2.82	1.55	0.95	0.03	0.02	0.76	0.18	0.23	-	
GC	1306	2.95	1.56	1.05	0.03	0.02	0.82	0.23	0.21	1.08	

Table 23. Measurements of *Microtus agrestis* lower first molars.

Unit	No.	M_1L	M_1L-a	M_1w1	M_1c1	M_1b1	M_1w2	M_1c2	M_1b2	M_1Wp
GC	977	2.90	1.58	0.87	0.07	0.02	0.73	0.21	0.15	0.98
GC	1049	2.80	1.48	e 0.96	0.02	0.02	0.77	0.30	0.21	-
GC	1223	2.51	1.35	e 0.85	0.04	0.04	0.73	0.18	0.18	0.83

Table 24. Measurements of *Microtus arvalis* lower first molars.

Unit	No.	Taxa	M¹L	M¹W	M²L	M²W	M³L	M³W	M₁L	M₁W	M₂L	M₂W	M₃L	M₃W
BGC	557	AS	1.88	1.22	-	-	-	-	-	-	-	-	-	-
BGC	558	AS	1.73	1.15	-	-	-	-	-	-	-	-	-	-
BGC	568	AS	-	-	1.27	1.18	-	-	-	-	-	-	-	-
BGC	550	AS	-	-	-	-	-	-	1.66	0.98	-	-	-	-
BGC	594	AS	-	-	-	-	-	-	-	-	1.25	1.00	-	-
BC	1441	AS	1.81	1.18	-	-	-	-	-	-	-	-	-	-
BC	1434	AS	-	-	-	-	-	-	1.70	1.05	-	-	-	-
BC	1435	AS	-	-	-	-	-	-	1.74	1.02	-	-	-	-
BC	1436	AS	-	-	-	-	-	-	1.78	-	-	-	-	-
BC	1405	AS	-	-	-	-	-	-	-	-	1.20	1.06	-	-
BC	1437	AS	-	-	-	-	-	-	-	-	1.15	1.08	-	-
BC	1438	AS	-	-	-	-	-	-	-	-	1.30	1.06	-	-
BC	1439	AS	-	-	-	-	-	-	-	-	1.20	1.00	-	-
BC	512	A	-	-	-	-	-	-	-	-	-	-	0.90	0.88
SC	535	AS	1.91	1.18	-	-	-	-	-	-	-	-	-	-
SC	720	AS	1.96	1.20	-	-	-	-	-	-	-	-	-	-
SC	1566	AS	1.96	1.17	-	-	-	-	-	-	-	-	-	-
SC	536	AS	-	-	1.25	1.09	-	-	-	-	-	-	-	-
SC	665	AS	-	-	1.29	1.12	-	-	-	-	-	-	-	-
SC	502	AS	-	-	-	-	-	-	1.83	1.05	-	-	-	-
SC	706	AS	-	-	-	-	-	-	1.76	1.08	-	-	-	-
SC	710	AS	-	-	-	-	-	-	1.83	1.03	-	-	-	-
SC	739	AS	-	-	-	-	-	-	1.86	1.06	-	-	-	-
SC	1529	AS	-	-	-	-	-	-	1.79	1.01	-	-	-	-
SC	1530	AS	-	-	-	-	-	-	1.77	1.03	-	-	-	-
SC	1531	AS	-	-	-	-	-	-	1.81	1.03	-	-	-	-
SC	1539	AS	-	-	-	-	-	-	1.78	1.06	-	-	-	-
SC	1563	AS	-	-	-	-	-	-	1.81	1.07	-	-	-	-
SC	715	AS	-	-	-	-	-	-	-	-	1.24	1.05	-	-
GC	423	AS	1.91	1.25	-	-	-	-	-	-	-	-	-	-
GC	424	AS	2.03	1.25	-	-	-	-	-	-	-	-	-	-
GC	425	AS	2.03	1.25	-	-	-	-	-	-	-	-	-	-
GC	681	AS	1.91	1.26	-	-	-	-	-	-	-	-	-	-
GC	698	AS	-	1.16	-	-	-	-	-	-	-	-	-	-
GC	703	AS	1.80	1.16	-	-	-	-	-	-	-	-	-	-
GC	768	AS	1.90	1.19	-	-	-	-	-	-	-	-	-	-
GC	769	AS	1.90	1.22	-	-	-	-	-	-	-	-	-	-
GC	867	AS	1.88	-	-	-	-	-	-	-	-	-	-	-
GC	868	AS	1.74	1.15	-	-	-	-	-	-	-	-	-	-
GC	901	AS	1.88	1.21	-	-	-	-	-	-	-	-	-	-
GC	904	AS	-	1.24	-	-	-	-	-	-	-	-	-	-
GC	971	AS	1.91	1.15	-	-	-	-	-	-	-	-	-	-
GC	1111	AS	1.88	1.13	-	-	-	-	-	-	-	-	-	-
GC	1118	AS	1.96	1.14	-	-	-	-	-	-	-	-	-	-
GC	1119	AS	1.90	1.13	-	-	-	-	-	-	-	-	-	-
GC	1220	AS	1.87	1.23	-	-	-	-	-	-	-	-	-	-
GC	1301	AS	1.88	1.20	-	-	-	-	-	-	-	-	-	-
GC	1512	AS	-	1.15	-	-	-	-	-	-	-	-	-	-
GC	423	AS	-	-	1.23	1.08	-	-	-	-	-	-	-	-
GC	615	AS	-	-	1.24	1.12	-	-	-	-	-	-	-	-
GC	687	AS	-	-	1.28	1.12	-	-	-	-	-	-	-	-
GC	1113	AS	-	-	1.29	1.15	-	-	-	-	-	-	-	-
GC	1114	A	-	-	1.14	-	-	-	-	-	-	-	-	-
GC	1301	AS	-	-	1.35	1.15	-	-	-	-	-	-	-	-
GC	1508	AS	-	-	1.32	1.04	-	-	-	-	-	-	-	-
GC	1509	AS	-	-	1.31	1.10	-	-	-	-	-	-	-	-
GC	772	A	-	-	-	-	0.87	0.87	-	-	-	-	-	-
GC	903	A	-	-	-	-	0.83	0.84	-	-	-	-	-	-
GC	404	AS	-	-	-	-	-	-	1.73	1.03	-	-	-	-
GC	428	AS	-	-	-	-	-	-	1.81	1.03	-	-	-	-
GC	612	AS	-	-	-	-	-	-	1.86	1.00	-	-	-	-
GC	613	AS	-	-	-	-	-	-	1.76	1.08	-	-	-	-
GC	802	AS	-	-	-	-	-	-	1.77	1.00	-	-	-	-
GC	1038	AS	-	-	-	-	-	-	1.81	1.12	-	-	-	-
GC	1110	AS	-	-	-	-	-	-	1.79	1.03	-	-	-	-
GC	1117	AS	-	-	-	-	-	-	-	1.08	-	-	-	-
GC	405	AS	-	-	-	-	-	-	-	-	1.25	1.02	-	-
GC	429	AS	-	-	-	-	-	-	-	-	1.23	0.98	-	-
GC	614	AS	-	-	-	-	-	-	-	-	1.23	1.09	-	-
GC	671	AS	-	-	-	-	-	-	-	-	1.18	1.02	-	-
GC	674	AS	-	-	-	-	-	-	-	-	1.20	0.95	-	-
GC	680	AS	-	-	-	-	-	-	-	-	1.16	1.00	-	-
GC	770	AS	-	-	-	-	-	-	-	-	1.15	1.03	-	-
GC	1112	AS	-	-	-	-	-	-	-	-	1.26	1.08	-	-
GC	1116	AS	-	-	-	-	-	-	-	-	1.15	1.08	-	-
GC	1510	AS	-	-	-	-	-	-	-	-	1.21	1.05	-	-

Table 25. Measurements of *Apodemus sylvaticus* (AS) and *Apodemus* sp. (A) molars.

Unit	No.	M^1L	M^1W	M^2L	M^2W	M_1L	M_1W	M_2W	M_2W
SC	1540	-	-	-	-	-	-	1.01	0.91
GC	403	1.61	1.03	-	-	-	-	-	-
GC	692	1.51	1.03	-	-	-	-	-	-
GC	1507	1.63	1.08	-	-	-	-	-	-
GC	406	-	-	1.10	1.00	-	-	-	-
GC	771	-	-	1.07	1.03	-	-	-	-
GC	483	-	-	-	-	1.38	0.83	-	-
GC	694	-	-	-	-	1.59	1.00	-	-
GC	902	-	-	-	-	1.50	0.90	-	-
GC	1115	-	-	-	-	1.56	0.93	-	-

Table 26. Measurements of *Apodemus maastrichtiensis* molars.

Unit	No.	L	W
BGC	378	e 6.6	4.7

Table 27. Measurements of *Ursus* sp. P^2.

Unit	No.	M_1L	M_1L tr.	M_1W
GC	662	6.7	5.0	2.4

Table 28. Measurements of *Mustela* cf. *putorius* M_1. L tr. = trigonid length.

Unit	No.	Element	LCDe	BFcd	Gl
GC	294	Axis vertebra	100.2	45.2	-
GC	351	Astragalus	-	-	70.1
GC	111	Metacarpal I	-	-	52.2

Table 29. Measurements of *P. leo* postcrania. LCDe = length in the region of the body including the dens, Bfcd = breadth of the caudal articular articular surface. Gl = greatest length.

Unit	No.	Taxa	Element	BT	Bd	GB	L	W
BGC	352	DD	Humerus	44.2	50.8	-	-	-
BC	340	DD	Unciform	-	-	21.9	-	-
GC	966	CE	DP_3	-	-	-	14.9	7.9

Table 30. Measurements of *Dama dama* (DD) and *Cervus elaphus* (CE) bones and teeth.

Measurement	mm
1. Circumference of burr	215
2. Diameter of burr (anterior - posterior)	70.8
3. Distance from burr to base of brow tine	11
4. Circumference of brow tine, 30mm from point on burr where 2 was measured	86
5. Diameter of brow tine (anterior - posterior)	26.5
6. Distance between edge of the burr and minimum diameter of beam between brow and bez tine	70
7. Circumference of bez tine 20mm from its base	95
8. Diameter of brow tine at 7	34.4
9. Length of brow tine	98
10. Distance from base of brow tine to posterior bez tine	21.5

Table 31. Measurements of *Cervus elaphus* antler (GC,).

APPENDIX V. MOLLUSCA

Mary Seddon

Numbers of shells and opercula by species and sample number (* = shell fragments).

Habitat type	Sample	209	211	212	214	215	216	227	228	229	230	231	232	233	234	235	236	237	238	240	241	242	243	Total
Freshwater Gastropods		1	1	194	22	7	0	2	1	4	2	133	0	164	58	198	149	196	137	0	0	0	0	1269
Moving Water																								
Bithynia tentaculata (L.)	opercula	0	3	96	187	57	238	94	165	50	31	392	290	952	1040	970	2066	717	601	204	296	436	118	9003
	shells	1	1	107	0	6	0	1	0	1	1	86	0	138	6	198	122	179	137	0	0	0	0	984
Valvata piscinalis (Müller)	shells	0	0	6	0	0	0	0	0	0	0	6	0	2	8	0	4	0	0	0	0	0	0	26
Lymnaea cf stagnalis (L.)	shells	0	0	1	0	0	0	0	0	0	0	0	0	0	21	0	1	0	0	0	0	0	0	23
Unionidae	shell frags	0	0	0	0	0	0	0	0	0	*	0	0	0	0	0	0	0	0	0	0	0	0	*
Ditch group																								
Valvata cristata (Müller)	shells	0	0	54	16	1	0	1	0	3	1	28	0	24	21	0	19	17	0	0	0	0	0	185
Gyraulus laevis Alder	shells	0	0	3	0	0	0	0	0	0	0	0	0	0	0	0	0	0	0	0	0	0	0	3
cf. *Planorbis planorbis* (L.)	shells	0	0	16	3	0	0	0	0	0	0	1	0	0	1	0	2	0	0	0	0	0	0	23
Catholic group																								
Armiger crista (L.)	shells	0	0	7	3	0	0	0	0	0	0	12	0	0	0	0	1	0	0	0	0	0	0	23
Slum group																								
Lymnaea truncatula (Müller)	shells	0	0	0	0	0	0	0	1	0	0	0	0	0	1	0	0	0	0	0	0	0	0	2
Undet.		0	0	0	0	0	0	1	0	0	0	0	0	36	43	0	102	0	0	0	0	0	0	182
Freshwater Bivalves																								
Catholic group																								
Pisidium cf.milium	valves	0	0	0	0	0	0	1	0	0	0	0	0	0	0	0	0	0	0	0	0	0	0	1
Land Gastropods																								
Succineidae sp.	shells	0	0	14	0	0	0	0	0	0	1	0	0	0	0	0	0	0	0	0	0	0	0	15
Clausiliidae	apices	0	0	0	0	0	0	0	0	0	0	0	0	0	1	0	1	0	0	0	0	0	0	2
Ceciliodes acicula	shells	1	0	0	0	0	0	0	0	0	0	0	0	0	0	0	0	0	0	0	0	0	0	1
Helicellidae	apices	0	0	0	0	0	0	0	0	2	2	0	0	0	0	0	0	0	0	0	0	0	0	4
Cepea/Arianta spp	shell frags	0	0	*	0	0	0	0	0	0	*	0	0	*	0	0	0	0	0	0	0	0	0	*

APPENDIX VI. FLINT ANALYSIS METHODOLOGY

Nick Ashton

CONDITION

Rolling

1. Mint condition. Sharp edges with no evidence of natural abrasion or edge damage.
2. Fresh condition. Sharp edges with only occasional evidence of natural abrasion or edge damage.
3. Moderately rolled. Edges with clear abrasion and damage. Arrêtes on dorsal surface slightly rounded.
4. Very rolled. Edges considerably rolled and abraded. Clear rounding of arrêtes on dorsal surface.

Patination

0. Unpatinated
1. Moderately patinated
2. Very patinated

Staining

0. Unstained
1. Moderately stained
2. Very stained

Surface sheen

1. Matt
2. Slight sheen
3. Gloss

FLAKES

Cortex

1. Wholly cortical
2. > 50% cortex
3. < 50% cortex
4. No cortex

Cortical index

The cortical index is $(x_1 \times 1) + (x_2 \times 0.67) + (x_3 \times 0.33)$, where x_n is the percentage of cortex category n.

Butt types

1. Plain. Flake removed from a single flake scar.
2. Dihedral. Flake removed from the intersection of two flake scars.
3. Cortical or natural. Flake removed from cortical or natural surface.
4. Marginal. Flake removed from edge of core, forming narrow, indeterminate butt.
5. Soft hammer. Flake removed with antler, bone, or wood hammer forming diffused bulb of percussion, wide point of percussion and often with a lip at the contact between the butt and the ventral surface. The butt is often very thin and in these cases frequently associated with shattering.
6. Mixed. Flake removed from a combination of natural/cortical and flake surfaces.

Dorsal scar patterns (Fig. 1)

Previous flakes, as indicated by the dorsal scar pattern, removed in the following directions.

1. Flakes removed from proximal end only.
2. Flakes removed from proximal and left only, or proximal and right only.
3. Flakes removed from proximal, left and right.
4. Flakes removed from proximal, distal and right only, or proximal, distal and left only.
5. Flakes removed from either left only, or right only.
6. Flakes removed from distal.
7. Flakes removed from proximal and distal.
8. Flakes removed from right and left.
9. Flakes removed from proximal, right, left and distal.
10. Dorsal wholly cortical or natural.
11. Flakes removed right, left and distal.
12. Flakes removed from distal and right only, or distal and left only.

Distal index

The distal index is the combination of dorsal scar pattern types 4, 6, 7, 9, 11 and 12. It is a measure of the amount of flaking from the distal end.

Scar index

The scar index is calculated from the percentages of flakes with x number of scars. Thus the Scar Index = $\Sigma x p_x / 10$ where x is the number of dorsal scars and p is the percentage of each dorsal scar frequency.

For the table below the scar index is:

$$[(6 \times 0) + (9 \times 1) + (30 \times 2) + (35 \times 3) + (16 \times 4) + (4 \times 5)] / 10 = 25.8$$

No. Scars.	0	1	2	3	4	5
%		6	9	30	35	16	4

Knapping break index

The knapping break index is calculated from the percentage of flakes with x number of breaks. Thus the knapping break index = $\Sigma xp_x/5$ where x is the number of knapping breaks and p is the percentage of the knapping break frequency.

For the table below the knapping break index is:

$[(8 \times 0) + (12 \times 1) + (45 \times 2) +(25 \times 3) + (8 \times 4) + (2 \times 5)]/5 = 43.8$

No. Knap. Brks	0	1	2	3	4	5
%	8	12	45	25	8	2

Relict core edges (Fig. 2)

Where a part of a core edge, showing negative bulbs of percussion, is preserved on a flake, this is termed a relict core edge. They can be divided up into two main types: types 1-3 where the core edge is preserved on the dorsal of the flake and forms part of a seperate sequence to that flake; and types 4-6 where the core edge is on the butt of the flake. For the full definition of the core flaking types, see cores, below.

1. Parallel flaking on the dorsal. Two or more flake scars indicating parallel removals from a single or adjacent platforms.
2. Simple alternate flaking on the dorsal. A sequence of flake scars showing that one or more removals formed the platform for one or more further removals.
3. Complex alternate flaking on the dorsal. Similar to 2, but showing evidence of at least one more turn of the core.
4. Parallel flaking on the butt. Similar to 1, but the flake scars indicate removal from the same platform as the actual flake, that flake being the last removal in that sequence.
5. Simple alternate flaking on the butt. Similar to 2, but the sequence is positioned on the butt, with the actual flake forming the last removal in the sequence.
6. Complex alternate flaking on the butt. Similar to 3, but the sequence is positioned on the butt, with the actual flake forming the last removal in the sequence.

Flake types (Fig. 3)

The flake types are designed to give an indication of knapping stage, and are based on the amount of cortex on the dorsal surface and the butt.

1. Cortical dorsal surface and cortical butt.
2. Either > 50% cortical dorsal surface and cortical butt, or cortical dorsal surface and non-cortical butt.
3. Either < 50% cortical dorsal surface and cortical butt, or > 50% cortical dorsal surface and non-cortical butt.
4. Either non-cortical dorsal surface and cortical butt, or < 50% cortical dorsal surface and non-cortical butt.
5. Non-cortical dorsal surface and non-cortical butt.

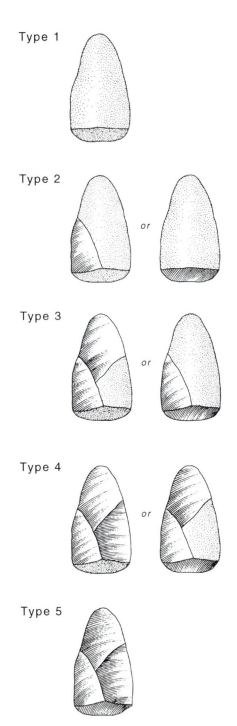

Fig. 3. Flake types 1-5.

CORES

The system of analysis of the cores is based on the notion that core reduction can be divided up into a number of different stages, each described as a core episode. Each core-episode consists of a series of removals that naturally follow on from each other.

Single removal, Type A (Fig. 4.1)

This consists of a single flake removal from a natural surface or from flake scars that are part of a different core episode.

Parallel flaking, Type B (Fig. 4.2)

Two or more flakes removed in a parallel direction from the same or adjacent platforms.

Alternate flaking, Type C

One or more flakes removed in parallel form the platform or platforms at their proximal ends for the next on or more removals. They in turn may form the platform or platforms at their proximal ends for further removals in the same direction as the original set of removals. The core may be turned several times in this way. This can be divided into several types:

Simple alternate flaking, Type Ci (Fig.4.3). The core is turned just once, with one or more removals forming the platform for the second set of removals.

Complex alternate flaking, Type Cii (Fig. 4.4). The core is turned at least twice and consists of at least three sets of removals.

Classic alternate flaking, Type Ciii (Fig. 4.5). A single flake forms the platform for the second flake which in turn forms the platform for the third flake. Several more flakes may be removed in this way.

If episodes of parallel flaking occur as part of Ci or Cii, then they are termed Cip or Ciip.

Where previous flake scars can be recognised, but not attributed to a specific sequence, then **Type D** is recorded.

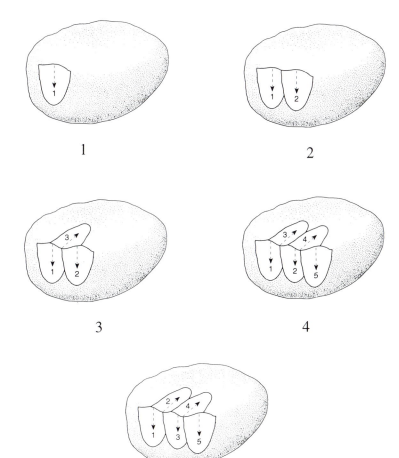

Fig. 4. Core types A-C.

APPENDIX VII. A NOTE ON BRICK MANUFACTURE

Nick Ashton & John McNabb

The earliest history of East Farm Pit is largely unknown, although local tradition asserts that clay was extracted from there as early as the eighteenth century. By 1891, it had certainly been open for some time, as Whitaker *et al.* (1891) describe a large pit, lying half a mile south-east of Barnham St Gregory church. At some point, probably before this, it had became the main source of bricks for the Euston estate, particularly during the rebuilding of Euston Hall in the early 1900s, after the original structure was destroyed by fire. Clay was last extracted in 1927, and several people from Barnham remember the pit being in active use. The late Mr A. Steward, who worked in the brickyard and whose father worked in the pit, recalled the following details in an interview in August 1991.

Clay was dug out during 3-4 weeks around February time, so that bricks could be laid out in the open to dry and there would be no chance of frost damage. This was the slack season for farming, and the farm workers would be deployed for clay digging.

The method used was as follows. Initially a new area was prepared by 'unheading' with the removal of all the top soil and stones from above the clay. A track led into the pit on the south-west side, and the pit was dug from the centre outwards. The method of extraction involved the undermining of the clay face by digging several feet into the base, working from the bottom up, and causing collapse from the top.

The clay was then loaded into a 'tumble' - a large horse drawn cart - and taken to the brickyard in the village (now the site of the RAF married quarters). The carts were only half loaded because of the weight, and even then two or three horses were necessary to pull the carts up the track. At the brickyard the clay was washed and made into bricks.

Most of the flint artefacts were recovered at this point.

White clay was mainly present in the eastern end of the pit, and red clay in the western end. The eastern end was not dug so extensively because the demand for white clay bricks was not so great. The western end was dug seasonally every year. The flint nodules that were exposed by the clay extraction were either taken away and used for building purposes, or were collected into big piles and left on the floor of the pit. It was in the white clay that 'deer bones' were found.

Some details of the method of digging were also gleaned from the current excavations. The brown silty clay ('brickearth'- Unit 7) was cut near-vertically around the edges of the existing clay-pit, down to the top of the black clay (Unit 6) and seems to have been removed at this level across the entire pit. However, the method for removal of the grey silt and clay (Unit 5c) was different. Here, elongated pits, up to 8m in length, and generally between 1m to 2m wide, were dug as parallel trenches, seperated by narrow baulks, less than 30cm wide. Again, they had near-vertical edges and generally were dug up to 2m in depth. Parts of these pits were exposed in the trench cut between Area III and Area I (see Chapter 3, Fig. 3.1), and can be seen in plan in Pit 8/9 (see Chapter 7, Fig. 7.3), and in section in Test Pit 33 (see Chapter 4, Fig. 4.26). This method of digging is reminiscent of the 'stalls' and 'pillars' used in some 19th century coal mining, where each 'stall' would be the working area for one man. After the digging of these pits, they were backfilled with a medium brown sandy loam, which was probably sediment produced from the 'unheading' (see above) consisting of a mixture of ploughsoil and coversand.

BIBLIOGRAPHY

Aitken, M.J. 1985. *Thermoluminescence Dating*. London, Academic Press.

Andrews, P. 1990. *Owls, Caves and Fossils*. London, British Museum (Natural History).

Andrieu, V., Beaulieu, J.L. & Reille, M. 1996. The long pollen sequences from the Velay plateau (Massif Central, France). *Ninth International Palynological Congress: Program and Abstracts, Houston, Texas, June 23-28, 1996*. Abstracts 6.

Angerbjörn, A. 1986. Gigantism in island populations of wood mice (*Apodemus*) in Europe. *Oikos* 47, 47-56.

Arnold, E.N. & Burton, J.A. l978. *A Field Guide to the Reptiles and Amphibians of Britain and Europe*. London, Collins.

Ashton, N.M. 1992. The High Lodge flint industries. In N. Ashton, J. Cook, S. Lewis & J. Rose (eds). *High Lodge: Excavations by G. de G. Sieveking 1962-68 and J. Cook 1988*. London, BMP. 124-63.

Ashton, N.M, Bowen, D.Q., Holman, J.A., Hunt, C.O., Irving, B.G., Kemp, R.A., Lewis, S.G., McNabb, J. Parfitt, S. & Seddon, M.B. 1994a. Excavations at the Lower Palaeolithic site at East Farm, Barnham, Suffolk, 1989-92. *Journal of the Geological Society of London* 151, 599-605.

Ashton, N.M, Bowen, D.Q. & Lewis, S. 1995. Reply to West and Gibbard. *Journal of the Geological Society of London* 152, 571-574.

Ashton, N.M., Cook, J., Lewis, S.G. & Rose, J. (eds) 1992. *High Lodge: Excavations by G. de G.Sieveking 1962-68 and J. Cook 1988*. London, BMP.

Ashton, N.M., Dean, P. & McNabb, J. 1991. Flaked flakes: what, where, why and when? *Lithics* 12, 1-11.

Ashton, N.M. & Lewis, S.G. Elveden, Brickyard Pit (TL8080; ELV006). In E. Martin, C. Pendleton & J. Plouviez (eds), Archaeology in Suffolk 1996. *Proceedings of the Suffolk Institute of Archaeology and History* 109(1), 92-5.

Ashton, N.M. & McNabb, J. 1992. The interpretation and context of the High Lodge flint industries. In N. Ashton, J. Cook, S. Lewis & J. Rose (eds). *High Lodge: Excavations by G.de G. Sieveking 1962-68 and J.Cook 1988*. London, BMP. 164-8.

Ashton, N.M. & McNabb, J. 1994. Bifaces in perspective. In N.M. Ashton & A. David (eds). *Stories in Stone*. London, Occasional Paper of the Lithic Studies Society No. 4. 182-91.

Ashton, N.M. & McNabb, J. 1996. The flint industries from the Waechter excavations. In B. Conway, J. McNabb & N. Ashton (eds). *Excavations at Swanscombe 1968-72*. London, British Museum Occasional Paper 94. 201-36.

Ashton, N.M., McNabb, J., Irving, B.G., Lewis, S.G. & Parfitt, S. 1994b. Contemporaneity of Clactonian and Acheulian flint industries at Barnham, Suffolk. *Antiquity* 68, 585-9.

Ashton, N.M., McNabb, J. & Bridgland, D.R. 1996. Barnfield Pit, Swanscombe (TQ 598743). In D.R. Bridgland, P. Allen & B.A. Haggart (eds). *The Quaternary of the Lower Reaches of the Thames. Field Guide*. Durham, Quaternary Research Association. 129-41.

Aspinall, A. & Walker A.R. 1975. The earth resistivity instrumand its application to shallow earth systems. *Underground Services* 3, 12-15.

Austin, L. 1994. The life and death of a Boxgrove biface. In N.M. Ashton & A. David (eds). *Stories in Stone*. London, Occasional Paper of the Lithic Studies Society No. 4. 119-26.

Auton, C.A., Morigi, A.N. & Price, D. 1985. The sand and gravel resources of the country around Harleston and Bungay, Norfolk and Suffolk. Description of 1:25000 resource sheets comprising parts of TM 27, 28, 38 and 39. *Mineral Assessment Report* 145. Keyworth, British Geological Survey.

Baden-Powell, D.F.W. 1948. The chalky boulder clays of Norfolk and Suffolk. *Geological Magazine* 85, 279-96.

Bailey R.M., Smith B.W. & Rhodes E.J. 1997. Partial bleaching and the decay form characteristics of quartz OSL. *Radiation Measurements* 27, 123-36.

Ballesio, R. 1980. Le gisement Pléistocène supérieur de la grotte de Jaurens à Nespouls, Corrèze, France: les carnivores (Mammalia, Carnivora). *Nouvelles Archives du Muséum d'Histoire Naturelle de Lyon* 18, 61-102.

Barker, R.D. 1981. The offset method of electrical resistivity sounding and its use with a multicore cable. *Geophysical Prospecting* 29, 67-79.

Barker, R.D. & Harker, D. 1984. The location of the Stour buried tunnel-valley using geophysical techniques. *Quarterly Journal of Engineering Geology* 17, 103-15.

Bascomb, C.L. 1982. Physical and chemical analysis of <2mm samples. *Soil Survey Technical Monograph* 6, 14-41.

Bassinot, F.C., Labeyrie, L.D.,Vincent, E., Quidellaeur, X., Shackleton, N.J. & Lancelot, Y. 1994. The astronomical theory of climate and the age of the Brunhes-Matuyama magnetic reversal. *Earth & Planetary Science Letters* 126, 91-108.

Behrensmeyer, A.K., Gordon, K.D. & Yanagi, G.T. 1986. Trampling as a cause of bone surface damage and pseudo-cutmarks. *Nature* 319, 768-771.

Benecke, N. & Heinrich, W-D. 1990. Wirbeltierreste aus interglazialen Beckensedimenten von Grobern (Kr. Grafenhainichen) und Grabschutz (Kr. Delitzsch). *Altenburger Naturwissenschaftliche Forschungen*. Altenburg 5, 231-81.

Bennet, K.D., Whittington, G. & Edwards, K.J. 1994. Recent plant nomenclatural changes and pollen morphology in the British Isles. *Quaternary Newsletter* 73, 1-6.

Binford, L.R. 1981. *Bones: Ancient Men and Modern Myths*. New York. Academic Press.

Bishop, M.J. 1982. The mammal fauna of the early Middle Pleistocene cavern infill site of Westbury-sub-Mendip, Somerset. *Special Papers in Palaeontology* No. 28. London, The Palaeontological Association.

Bjärvall, A. & Ullström, S. 1986. *The Mammals of Britain and Europe*. London & Sydney. Croom Helm.

Blumenschine, R.J. & Masao, F.T. 1991. Living sites at Olduvai Gorge, Tanzania? Preliminary landscape archaeology results. *Journal of Human Evolution* 21, 451-62.

Boatman, A.R.C., Bryant, R.H., Markham, R.A.D, Turner, C. & White, P.C.S. 1973. Walton on the Naze. In J. Rose & C. Turner (eds) *Clacton 1973. Field Guide*. Cambridge, Quaternary Research Association. 21-9.

Bordes, F. 1947. Etude comparative des différentes techniques de taille du silex et des roches dures. *L'Anthropologie* 51, 1-29.

Boreham, S. & Gibbard, P.L. 1995. Middle Pleistocene Hoxnian Stage interglacial deposits at Hitchin, Hertfordshire, England. *Proceedings of the Geologists' Association* 106, 259-70.

Bowden, D.J., Hunt, C.O. & Green, C.P. 1995. The Late Cenozoic deposits at the Naze, Walton, Essex. In D.R. Bridgland, P. Allen & B.A. Haggart (eds). *The Quaternary of the Lower Reaches of the Thames. Field Guide*. Durham, Quaternary Research Association. 298-309.

Bowen, D.Q., Bridgland, D.R., Cameron, T.D.J., Campbell, S., Gibbard, P.L., Holmes, R., Lewis, S.G., McCabe, A.M., Maddy, D., Preece, R.C., Sutherland, D.G. & Thomas, G.S.P. In press. *Correlation of Quaternary deposits in England, Ireland, Scotland and Wales*. London, Geological Society of London, Special Report No. 4, 2nd Edition.

Bowen, D.Q., Hughes, S.A., Sykes, G.A. & Miller, G.H. 1989. Land-sea correlations in the Pleistocene based on isoleucene epimerisation in non-marine molluscs. *Nature* 340, 49-51.

Bowen, D.Q., Pillans, B., Sykes, G.A., Beu, A.G. Edwards, A.R., Kamp, P.J.J. & Hull, A.G. 1998. Amino acid geochronology of Pleistocene marine sediments in the Wanganui Basin: a New Zealand framework for correlation and dating. *Journal of the Geological Society of London* 155.

Bowen, D.Q., Rose, J., McCabe, A.M. & Sutherland, D. 1986. Correlation of Quaternary glaciations in England, Ireland, Scotland and Wales. *Quaternary Science Reviews* 5, 299-340.

Bowen, D.Q. & Sykes, G.A. 1988. Correlation of marine events and glaciations on the north-east Atlantic margin. *Philosophical Transactions of the Royal Society of London* B318, 619-35.

Bowen, D.Q. & Sykes, G.A. 1994, How old is "Boxgrove man"? *Nature* 371, 751.

Bowen, D.Q., Sykes, G.A., Maddy, D., Bridgland, D.R. & S.G. Lewis. 1996. Aminostratigraphy and amino acid geochronology of English lowland valleys: the Lower Thames in context. In D.R. Bridgland, P. Allen & B.A. Haggart (eds). *The Quaternary of the Lower Reaches of the Thames. Field Guide*. Durham, Quaternary Research Association. 61-3.

Bowen, D.Q., Sykes, G.A., Reeves, A., Miller, G.H., Andrews, J.T., Brew, J.S. & Hare, P.E. 1985. Amino acid geochronology of raised beaches in south west Britain. *Quaternary Science Reviews* 4, 279-318.

Bradley, B. & Sampson, C.G. 1986. Analysis by replication of two Acheulian assemblage types. In G.N. Bailey & P. Callow (eds). *Stone Age Prehistory: Studies in Memory of Charles McBurney*. Cambridge, Cambridge University Press. 29-45.

Breuil, H. 1932. Les industries à éclats du Paléolithique ancien. I. Le Clactonien. *Préhistoire* 1, 125-90.

Bridgland, D.R. 1994. *Quaternary of the Thames*. London, Chapman & Hall.

Bridgland, D.R., Allen, P., Currant, A.P., Gibbard, P.L., Lister, A.M., Preece, R.C., Robinson, J.E., Stuart, A.J. & Sutcliffe, A.J. 1988. Report of the Geologists' Association field meeting in north-east Essex, May 22nd-24th, 1987. *Proceedings of the Geologists' Association* 99, 315-33.

Bridgland, D.R., Allen, Patrick, Allen, P., Austin, L., Irving, B., Parfitt, S., Preece, R.C. & Tipping, R.M. 1995 Purfleet interglacial deposits: Bluelands and Greenlands Quarries (TQ 569786). (Part of the Purfleet Chalk Pit SSSI). Also Essex County Council temporary section, Stonehouse Lane. In D.R. Bridgland, P. Allen, B.A. Haggart (eds). *The Quaternary of the Lower Reaches of the Thames. Field Guide*. Durham, The Quaternary Research Association. 189-99.

Bridgland, D.R., Keen, D.H., Schreve, D.C. & White, M.J. 1998. Summary: Dating and correlation of the Stour sequence. In J.B. Murton, C.A. Whiteman, M.R. Bates, D.R. Bridgland, A.J. Long, M.B. Roberts & M.P. Waller (eds). *The Quaternary of Kent and Sussex. Field Guide*. London, Quaternary Research Association. 53-60.

Bridgland, D.R. & Lewis, S.G. 1991. Introduction to the Pleistocene geology and drainage history of the Lark valley. In S.G. Lewis, C.A. Whiteman & D.R. Bridgland (eds). *Central East Anglia and the Fen Basin. Field Guide*. London, Quaternary Research Association. 37-44.

Bridgland, D.R., Lewis, S.G. & Wymer, J.J. 1995. Middle Pleistocene stratigraphy and archaeology around Mildenhall and Icklingham, Suffolk: a report on a Geologists' Association field meeting, 27th June, 1992. *Proceedings of the Geologists' Association*, 106, 57-69.

Bristow, C.R. & Cox, F.C. 1973. The Gipping Till: a reappraisal of East Anglian glacial stratigraphy. *Journal of the Geological Society of London* 129, 1-37.

Brown, J. 1852. On the Upper Teritaries at Copford, Essex. *Quarterly Journal of the Geological Society of London* 8, 184-93.

Bullock, P., Fedoroff, N., Jongerius, A., Stoops, G. and Tursina, T. 1985. *Handbook for Soil Thin Section Description*. Wolverhampton, Waine Research Publications.

Bunn, H.T. 1994. Early Pleistocene hominid foraging strategies along the ancestral Omo River at Koobi Fora. *Journal of Human Evolution* 27, 247-66.

Bunn, H.T. & Kroll, E.M. 1993. Comment on "The structure of the Lower Pleistocene archaeological record: a case study from the Koobi Fora Formation" by N. Stern. *Current Anthropology* 34, 216-7.

Caton, R.B. 1919. Exhibit at meeting at Norwich Museum on March 31st 1919. *Proceedings of the Prehistoric Society of East Anglia* 3, 162-3.

Catt, J.A. 1988. *Quaternarnary Geology for Scientists and Engineers*. Chichester, Ellis Horwood.

Chaline, J., Brunet-Lecomte, P. & Graf, J-P. 1988. Validation de *Terricola* Fatio, 1867 pour les campagnols souterrains (Arvicolidae, Rodentia) paléarctiques actuels at fossiles. *Comptes Rendu de l'Acadamie des Sciences. Paris*. Serié III 306, 475-78.

Chase, P, Armand, D., Debénath, A., Dibble, H., & Jelinek, A. 1994. Taphonomy and multiple hypothesis testing: an object lesson from the Mousterian. *Journal of Field Archaeology* 21, 289-305.

Clarke, M.R. & Auton, C.A. 1982. The Pleistocene history of the Norfolk-Suffolk borderlands. *Institute of Geological Sciences Report* 82/1, 23-9.

Clarke, M.R & Auton, C.A. 1984. Ingham Sand and Gravel. In P. Allen (ed.). *The Gipping and Waveney Valleys, Suffolk. Field Guide*. Cambridge, Quaternary Research Association. 71-2.

Clarke, W.G. 1913. Some Barnham Palaeolithis. *Proceedings of the Prehistoric Society of East Anglia* 1, 300-3.

Collins, D.M. 1969. Culture, traditions and environment of early man. *Current Anthropology* 10, 267-316.

Collins, D.M. 1979. Comment on "The Clactonian: an independant complex or an integral part of the Acheulian?" by M. Ohel. *Current Anthropology* 20, 716.

Conway, B., McNabb, J. & Ashton, N.M. (eds) 1996. *Excavations at Swanscombe 1968-72*. London, British Museum Occasional Paper No. 94.

Cooke, A.S. & Scorgie, H.R.A. 1983. The status of the commoner amphibians and reptiles in Britain. *Focus on Nature Conservation* 3. Shrewsbury, Nature Conservancy Council Report. 1-49.

Corbet, G.B. 1994. Taxonomy and origins. In H.V. Thompson & C.M. King (eds). *The European Rabbit: The History and Biology of a Successful Coloniser.*

Oxford, Oxford University Press. 1-7.

Cornwell, J.D. & Carruthers, R.M. 1986. Geophysical studies of a buried valley system near Ixworth, Suffolk. *Proceedings of the Geologists' Association* 97, 357-64.

Coutier, L. 1929. Expériences de taille pour rechercher les anciennes techniques paléolithiques. *Bulletin de la Societé Préhistorique Française* 26, 172-4.

Coxon, P., Hall, A.R., Lister, A. & Stuart, A.J. 1980. New evidence on the vertebrate fauna, stratigraphy and palaeobotony of the interglacial deposits at Swanton Morley, Norfolk. *Geological Magazine* 117, 525-46.

Crabtree, D.E. 1970. Flaking stone with wooden implements. *Science* 169, 146-53.

Currant, A.P. 1986. Man and Quaternary interglacial faunas in Britain. In S.N. Colcutt (ed.), *The Palaeolithic of Britain and its Nearest Neighbours: Recent Trends*. University of Sheffield, Department of Archaeology and Prehistory. 50-2.

Currant, A.P. 1989. The Quaternary origins of the modern British mammal fauna. *Biological Journal of the Linnean Society* 38, 23-30.

Currant, A.P. 1996. Tornewton Cave and the palaeontological succession. In D.J. Charman, R.M. Newnham & D.G. Croot (eds), *The Quaternary of Devon and East Cornwall. Field Guide*. London, Quaternary Research Association. 174-80

Dannelid, E. 1989. Medial tines on the upper incisors and other dental features used as identification characters in European shrews of the genus *Sorex* (Mammalia, Soricidae). *Zeitschrift fur Säugetierkunde* 54, 205-14.

Dennell, R. 1990. Progressive gradualism, imperialism and academic fashion; Lower Palaeolithic archaeology in the twentieth century. *Antiquity* 64, 549-58.

Dibble, H. 1995a. Middle Paleolithic scraper reduction: background, clarification, and review of the evidence to date. *Journal of Archaeological Method and Theory* 2(4), 299-368.

Dibble, H. 1995b. Introduction to site formation. In H. Dibble & M. Lenoir (eds), *The Middle Palaeolithic Site of Combe-Capelle Bas (France)*. Philadelphia, University of Pennsylvania Museum

Dimbleby, G. 1985. *The Palynology of Archaeological Sites*. London, Academic Press.

Donahue, R.E. 1994. The current state of lithic microwear research. In N.M. Ashton & A. David (eds), *Stories in Stone*. Oxford, Lithic Studies Society Occasional Paper 4. 156-68.

Donnard, E. 1981. *Oryctolagus cuniculus* dans quelques gisements quaternaires Française. *Quaternaria* 23, 145-57.

Driesch, A. Von den. 1976. *A Guide to the Measurement of Animal Bones from Archaeological Sites*. Peabody Museum Bulletin 1, Harvard University.

Ehlers, J. , Gibbard, P.L. & Whiteman, C.A. 1987. Recent investigations of the Marly Drift of northwest Norfolk, England. In J.M.M. van der Meer (ed.). *Tills and Glaciotectonics*. Rotterdam, Balkema. 39-54.

Escriva, L.J.B. l987. *La Guia de Incafo de los Anfibiosy Reptiles de la Peninsula Iberica, Islas Baleares y Canarias.* Madrid, INCAFO SA.

Fick, O.K.W. 1974. *Vergleichend morphologische Untersuchungen an Einzelknochen europäischer Taubenarten.* München, Ludwig-Maximilians-Universität.

Flower, J.W. 1869. On some recent discoveries of flint implements of the drift in Norfolk and Suffolk, with observations on the theories accounting for their distribution. *Quarterly Journal of the Geological Society of London* 25, 449-60.

Foley, R. 1981. *Offsite Archaeology and Human Adaptation in Eastern Africa.* Oxford, BAR International Series 97.

Freudenthal, M. & Cuenca Bescos, G. 1984. Size variation of fossil rodent populations. *Scripta Geologica* 76, 1-28.

Freudenthal, M. & Martín-Suárez, E. 1990. Size variation in samples of fossil and recent murid teeth. *Scripta Geologica* 93, 1-34.

Frost, D.R. (ed.) l985. *Amphibian Species of the World: a Taxonomic and Geographical Reference.* Kansas, Allen Press and the Association of Systematic Collections.

Gamble, C.S. 1995. The earliest occupation of Europe: the environmental background. In W. Roebroeks & T. van Kolfschoten (eds). *The Earliest Occupation of Europe.* Leiden, Analecta Praehistorica Leidensia No. 27. 279-96.

Gascoyne, M.A., Currant, A.P. & Lord, T.C. 1981. Ipswichian fauna of Victoria Cave and the marine palaeoclimatic record. *Nature* 294, 652-4.

Geike, J. 1894. *The Great Ice Age.* London, Macmillan.

Gibbard, P.L. 1994. *Pleistocene History of the Lower Thames Valley.* Cambridge, Cambridge University Press.

Gilbertson, D.G. 1980. The palaeoecology of the Middle Pleistocene Mollusca from Sugworth, Oxfordshire. *Philosophical Transactions of the Royal Society of London* B289, 107-18.

Godwin, H. 1953. British vegetation in the full-glacial and late-glacial periods. In J.E Lousley (ed.), The changing flora of Britain. *Report 1952 Conference of the Botanical Society of the British Isles.* Arbroath.

Gorman, M.L. & Stone, R.D. 1990. *The Natural History of Moles.* London, Christopher Helm.

Goudie, A. 1981. *Geomorphological Techniques.* London, George Allen & Unwin.

Gowlett, J.A.J. & Bell, D.A. S.G. West Stow. Beeches Pit (TL/7971; WSW009). In E. Martin, C. Pendleton & J. Plouviez (eds), Archaeology in Suffolk 1996. *Proceedings of the Suffolk Institute of Archaeology and History* 109(1), 100-3.

Green, C.P., Coope, G.R., Jones, R.L., Keen, D.H., Bowen, D.Q., Currant, A.P., Holyoak, D.T., Ivanovich, M., Robinson, J.E., Rogerson, R.J. & Young, R.C. 1996. Pleistocene deposits at Stoke Goldington, in the valley of the Great Ouse, UK. *Journal of Quaternary Science* 11, 59-87.

Grün, R. 1989. ESR Dating. *Quaternary International* 1, 65-108.

Grün, R. & Rhodes, E. J., 1992. Simulations of saturating exponential ESR/TL dose response curves - weighting of intensity values by inverse variance. *Ancient TL* 10, 50-56.

Gunther, R. (ed.) l996. *Die Amphibien und Reptilien Deutschlands.* Jena, Stuttgart, Lubeck & Ulm, Gustav Fisher.

Guthrie, R.D. (1984) Alaskan megabucks, megabulls and megarams: The issue of Pleistocene gigantism. In H.H. Genoways & M.R. Dawson (eds). *Contributions in Quaternary Vertebrate Paleontology: A Volume in Memorial to John E. Guilday.* Pittsburgh, Carnegie Museum of Natural History Special Publications, Number 8. 482-510

Handwerk, J. 1987. Neue daten zur morphologie, verbreitung und ökologie der spitzmäuse *Sorex araneus* und *S. coronatus* im Rheinland. *Bonner Zoologische Beiträge* 38, 273-97.

Hallock, L.A., Holman, J.A. & Warren, M.R. l990. Herpetofauna of the Ipswichian Interglacial Bed (Late Pleistocene) of the Itteringham Gravel Pit, Norfolk, England. *Journal of Herpetology* 24, 33-9.

Harding, P., Gibbard, P.L., Lewin, J., Macklin, M.G. & Moss, E.H. 1987. The transport and abrasion of handaxes in a gravel bed. In G. de G. Sieveking & M.H. Newcomer (eds). *The Human Uses of Flint and Chert.* Cambridge, Cambridge University Press. 115-26.

Harris, C. 1987. Solifluction and related periglacial deposits in England and Wales. In J. Boardman (ed.). *Periglacial Processes and Landforms in Britain and Ireland.* Cambridge, Cambridge University Press. 209-23.

Harrison, C.J.O. 1979a. Birds from the Cromer Forest Bed Series of the East Anglian Pleistocene. *Transactions of the Norfolk Norwich Naturalist's Society* 24, 277-89.

Harrison, C.J.O. 1979b. Pleistocene birds from Swanscombe, Kent. *The London Naturalist* 58, 6-8.

Harrison, C.J.O. 1980. A re-examination of British Devensian and earlier Holocene bird bones in the British Museum (Natural History). *Journal of Archaeological Science* 7, 53-68.

Harrison, C.J.O. 1982. *Atlas of the Birds of the Western Palaearctic.* London, Collins.

Harrison, C.J.O. 1988. *The History of the Birds of Britain.* London, Collins.

Harrison, C.J.O. & Stewart, J.R. In press. The bird remains. In M.B. Roberts & S. Parfitt (eds). *The Middle Pleistocene Hominid Site at Boxgrove, West Sussex, UK.* London, English Heritage Monograph Series.

Harrison, D.L. 1996. Systematic status of Kennard's shrew (*Sorex kennardi* Hinton, 1911, Insectivora: Soricidae): a study based on British and Polish material. *Acta Zoologica Cracoviensia* 39(1), 201-12.

Harrison, D.L. & Clayden, J.D. 1993. New records of *Beremendia fissidens* (Petenyi, 1864) and *Sorex minutus* Linnaeus, 1766 (Insectivora: Soricidae) from the British Lower and Middle Pleistocene. *Cranium* 10(1), 97-9.

Harrison, D.L., Bates, P.J.J. & Clayden, J.D. 1988. On the occurrence of *Galemys kormosi* (Schreuder, 1940) (Insectivora: Desmaninae) in the British Lower Pleistocene. *Acta Theriologica* 33, 369-78.

Havinga, A.J. 1967. Palynology and pollen preservation. *Review of Palaeobotany and Palynology* 2, 81-98.

Havinga, A.J. 1984. A 20-year investigation into the differential corrosion susceptability of pollen and spores in different soil types. *Pollen et Spores* 26, 541-58.

Hearty, P.J., Miller, G.H., Stearns, C.E. & Szabo, B.J. 1986. Aminostratigraphy of Quaternary shorelines in the Mediterranean basin. *Geological Society of America Bulletin* 97, 850-8.

Heinrich, W.-D. 1978. Zur biometrischen Erfassung eines Evolutionstrends bei *Arvicola* (Rodentia, Mammalia) aus dem Pleistozän Thüringens. *Säugetierkundliche Informationen* 2, 3-21.

Heinrich, W.-D. 1987. Neue Ergebnisse zur Evolution un Biostratigraphie von *Arvicola* (Rodentia, Mammalia) im Quartär Europas. *Zeitsehrift für Geologische Wissenshaften* 15(3), 683-735.

Heinrich, W.-D. 1982a. Ein Evolutionstrend bei *Arvicola* (Rodentia, Mammalia) und seine Bedeutung für die Biostratigraphie im Pleistozän Europas. *Wissenschaftliche Zeitschrift der Humboldt-Universität zu Berlin. Mathematisch-Naturwissenschaftliche Reihe*. 31, 155-160.

Heinrich, W.-D. 1982b. Zur Evolution und Biostratigraphie von *Arvicola* (Rodentia, Mammalia) im Pleistozän Europas. *Zeitsehrift für Geologische Wissenshaften* 10(6), 683-735.

Heller, F. 1958. Eine neue altquartäre Wirbeltierfauna von Erpfingen (Schwäbische Alb) *Neues Jahrbuch für Geologie Paläontologie. Abhandlungen* 107, 1-102.

Hinton, M.A.C. 1901. Excursion to Grays Thurrock. *Proceedings of the Geologists' Association.* 17, 141-4.

Hinton, M.A.C. 1911. The British fossil shrews. *Geological Magazine* 8, 529-39.

Hinton, M.A.C. 1914. On some remains of Rodents from the Red Crag of Suffolk. *Annals and Magazine of Natural History*. London 8(13), 186-95.

Holman, J.A. 1985. Herpetofauna of the late Pleistocene fissures near Ightham, Kent. *Herpetological Journal* 1, 26-32.

Holman, J.A. 1987. Herpetofauna of the Swanton Morley Site (Pleistocene: Ipswichian), Norfolk. *Herpetological Journal* 1, 199-201.

Holman, J.A. 1989. Identification of *Bufo calamita* and *Bufo bufo* on the basis of skeletal elements. *British Herpetological Society Bulletin* 29, 54-5.

Holman, J.A. 1992. *Hyla meridionalis* from the late Pleistocene (last Interglacial Age: Ipswichian) of Britain. *British Herpetological Society Bulletin* 41, 12-4.

Holman, J.A. 1993. British Quaternary herpetofaunas: a history of adaptations to Pleistocene disruptions. *Herpetological Journal* 3, 1-7.

Holman, J.A. 1994. A new record of the Aesculapian snake, *Elaphe longissima* (Laurenti), from the Pleistocene of Britain. *British Journal of Herpetology* 50, 37-9.

Holman, J.A. 1995. Additional amphibians from a Pleistocene interglacial deposit at Purfleet, Essex. *British Herpetological Society Bulletin* 41, 38-9.

Holman, J.A. 1998. *Pleistocene Amphibians and Reptiles in Britain and Europe*. New York, Oxford University Press.

Holman, J.A., Clayden, J.D. & Stuart, A.J. 1988. Herpetofauna of the West Runton Freshwater Bed (Middle Pleistocene), West Runton, Norfolk. *Bulletin of the Geological Society of Norfolk* 38, 121-36.

Holman, J.A. & Stuart, A.J. 1991. Amphibians of the Whitemoor Channel early Flandrian site near Bosley, East Cheshire; with remarks on the fossil distribution of *Bufo calamita* in Britain. *Herpetological Journal* 1, 568-73.

Holman, J.A., Stuart, A.J. & Clayden, J.D. 1990. A Middle Pleistocene herpetofauna from Cudmore Grove, Essex, England, and its paleogeographic and paleoclimatic implications. *Journal of Vertebrate Paleontology* 10, 86-94.

Horton, A., Keen, D.H., Field, M.H., Robinson, J.E., Coope, R.C., Currant, A.P., Graham, D.K., Green, C.P. & Phillips, L.M. 1992. The Hoxnian Interglacial deposits at Woodston, Peterborough. *Philosophical Transactions of the Royal Society of London* B338, 131-164.

Holyoak, D.T., Ivanovich, M. & Preece, R.C. 1983. Additional fossil and isotopic evidence for the age of the interglacial tufas at Hitchin and Icklingham. *Journal of Chonchology* 31, 260-1.

Hubbard, R.N.L.B. 1982. The environmental evidence from Swanscombe and its implications for Palaeolithic archaeology. In P.E. Leach (ed.). *Archaeology in Kent to AD 1500.* London, Council for British Archaeology, Research Report 48. 3-7.

Hubbard, R.N.L.B. 1996. The palynological studies from the Waechter excavations. In B. Conway, J. McNabb & N.M. Ashton. *Excavations in Barnfield Pit, Swanscombe, 1968-72.* London, British Museum Occasional Paper No. 94, 191-9.

Hunt, C.O. 1992. Pollen and algal microfossils from the High Lodge clayey-silts. In N.M. Ashton, J. Cook, S.G. Lewis & J. Rose (eds). *High Lodge: Excavations by G. de G. Sieveking 1962-68 and J. Cook 1988.* London, British Museum Press. 109-15.

Hunt, C.O. 1994. Palynomorph taphonomy in the fluvial environment: an example from the Palaeolithic site at High Lodge, Mildenhall, UK. In O.K. Davis (ed.), *Archeopalynology*. American Association of Stratigraphic Palynologists Contributions Series 29. 115-26.

Hunt, C.O., Andrews, M.A. & Gilbertson, D.D. 1985. Late Quaternary freshwater dinoflagellate cysts from the British Isles. *Journal of Micropalaeontology* 4, 101-9.

Huntley, D.J., Hutton, J.T. & Prescott, J.R. 1993. Optical dating using inclusions within quartz grains. *Geology* 21, 1087-90.

Huntley, D.J., Short, M.A. & Dunphy, K. 1996. Deep traps in quartz and their use for optical dating. *Canadian Journal of Physics* 74, 81-91.

Hutterer, R. 1990. *Sorex minutus*. In J. Niethammer & F. Krapp (eds). *Handbuch der Säugetiere Europas*. Wiesbaden. AULA-Verlag. 183-206.

Irving, B.G. 1996. The icthyofauna from the Waechter excavations, Barnfield Pit, Swanscombe. In B. Conway, J. McNabb & N. Ashton (eds), *Excavations at Barnfield Pit, Swanscombe, 1968-72*. London, British Museum Occasional Paper 94. 145-7.

Isaac, G.Ll. 1967. Towards the interpretation of occupation debris: some experiments and observations. *Kroeber Anthropological Society Papers* 5(37), 31-57.

Isaac, G.Ll. 1978. The food sharing behavior of protohuman hominids. *Scientific American* 238, 90-108.

Isaac, G.Ll. 1981. Stone age visiting cards: approaches to the study of early land-use patterns. In I. Hodder, G.Ll. Isaac & N. Hammond (eds). *Patterns in the Past*. Cambridge, Cambridge University Press. 157-247.

Isaac, G.Ll. & Harris, J.W.K. 1975. The scatter between the patches. Paper presented at Kroeber Anthropological Society, Berkeley, California.

Jacobi, R.M., Rowe, P.J., Gilmour, M.A., Grün, R. & Atkinson, T.C. 1998. Radiometric dating of the Middle Palaeolithic tool industry and associated fauna from Cresswell Crags, England. *Journal of Quaternary Science* 13(1), 29-42.

Jammot, D. 1974. Les Insectivores (Mammalia) du gisement Pléistocène moyen des abîmes de la Fage à Noailles (Corrèze). *Nouvelles Archives Muséum d'Histoire Naturelle de Lyon* 11, 41-51.

Jánnossy, D. 1965. Die Insectivoren-Reste aus dem altspleistozane von Voigtstedt in Thuringen. *Paläontologische Abhandlungen* A 2, 663-78.

Janossy, D. 1983. Humeri of Central European Smaller Passeriformes. *Fragmenta Mineralogica et Palaeontologica* 11, 85-112.

Jones, P.R. 1979. Effects of raw material on biface manufacture. *Science* 204, 835-6.

Jones, P.R. 1981. Experimental implement manufacture and use; a case study from Olduvai Gorge. *Philisophical Transactions of the Royal Society of London* B102, 189-95.

Keatinge, T.H. 1983. Development of pollen assemblages in soil profiles in southeastern England. *Boreas* 12, 1-12.

Keeley, L.H. 1980. *Experimental Determination of Stone Tool Uses: a Microwear Analysis*. Chicago, University of Chicago Press.

Keen, D.H. 1990. Significance of the record provided by Pleistocene fluvial deposits and their included molluscan faunas for paleoenvironmental reconstruction and stratigraphy: case studies from the English Midlands. *Palaeogeography, Palaeoclimatology, Palaeoecology* 80, 25-34.

Keen, D.H., Coope, G.R., Jones, R.L., Field, M.H., Griffiths, H.I., Lewis, S.G. & Bowen, D.Q. 1997. Middle Pleistocene deposits at Frog Hall Pit, Stretton-on-Dunsmore, Warwickshire, English Midlands, and their implication for the age of the type Wolstonian. *Journal of Quaternary Science* 12, 183-208.

Kemp, R.A. 1985a. *Soil Micromorphology and the Quaternary*. Cambridge, Quaternary Research Association Technical Guide 2.

Kemp, R.A. 1985b. The decalcified Lower Loam at Swanscombe, Kent: a buried Quaternary soil. *Proceedings of the Geologists' Association* 96, 343-56.

Kemp, R.A. 1991. Micromorphology of the buried Quaternary soil within Burchell's 'Ebbsfleet Channel', Kent. *Proceedings of the Geologists' Association* 102, 275-287.

Kemp, R.A., Jerz, H., Grottenthaler, W. & Preece, R.C. 1994. Pedosedimentary fabrics of soils within loess and colluvium in southern England and Germany. In A. Ringrose-Voase & G. Humphries (eds). *Soil Micromorphology: Studies in Management and Genesis*. Amsterdam, Elsevier. 207-19.

Kennard, A.S. 1942. Faunas of the High Terrace at Swanscombe. *Proceedings of the Geologists' Association* 53, 105.

Kennedy, G.L., Lajoie, K.R., & Wehmiller, J.W. 1992. Aminostratigraphy and faunal correlations of late Quaternary marine terraces. *Nature* 299, 545-7.

Kerney, M.P. 1959. An interglacial tufa near Hitchin, Hertfordshire. *Proceedings of the Geologists' Association* 70, 322-37.

Kerney, M.P. 1971. Interglacial deposits in Barnfield Pit, Swanscombe, and their molluscan fauna. *Quarterly Journal of the the Geological Society of London* 127, 69-93.

Kerney, M.P. 1976a. A list of the fresh and brackish water molluscs of the British Isles. *Journal of Conchology* 29, 26-8.

Kerney, M.P. 1976b. Molluscs from an interglacial tufa in East Anglia, with the description of a new species of *Lyrodiscus* Pilsbry (Gastropoda: Zonitidae). *Journal of Chonchology* 29, 47-50.

Kerney, M.P. 1977. British non-marine Mollusca: a brief review. In F. Shotton (ed.), *British Quaternary Studies - Recent Advances*. Oxford, Claredon Press.

Kerney, M.P. & Cameron, R.A.D. 1979. *A Field Guide to the Land Snails of Britain and North-West Europe.* London, Collins.

Knowles, F.H.S. 1953. *Stone-Workers Progress.* Oxford, Pitt Rivers Museum Occasional Paper on Technology No. 6.

Koenigswald, W. von. 1972. Sudmer-Berg 2, eine Fauna des frühen Mittelpleistozäns aus dem Harz. *Neues Jahrbuch für Geologie Paläontologie. Abhandlungen* 141, 194-221.

Koenigswald, W. von. 1973. Veränderungen in der Kleinsäugerfauna von Mitteleuropa zwischen Cromer und Eem (Pleistozän). *Eiszeialter und Gegewart.* 23/24, 159-67

Koenigswald, W. von. & Kolfschoten, T. van. 1996. The *Mimomys-Arvicola* boundary and the enamel thickness quotient (SDQ) of *Arvicola* as stratigraphic markers in the Middle Pleistocene. In C. Turner (ed.). *The early Middle Pleistocene in Europe.* Rotterdam, Balkema. 211-26.

Kolfschoten T. van. 1990. The evolution of the mammal fauna in The Netherlands and the middle Rhine area (Western Germany) during the late Middle Pleistocene. *Mededelingen Rijks Geologischen Dienst.* 43 (3), 1-69.

Kolfschoten, T. van. 1991. The Saalian mammal fossils from Wageningen-Fransche Kamp. *Mededelingen Rijks Geologischen Dienst.* 46, 37-53

Kolfschoten, T. van. 1985. The Middle Pleistocene (Saalian) and Late Pleistocene (Weichselian) mammal faunas from Maastricht-Belvédère, (Southern Limburg, The Netherlands). *Mededelingen Rijks Geologischen Dienst.* 39 (1), 45-74.

Kolfschoten T. van & Turner E. 1996. Early Middle Pleistocene mammalian faunas from Karlich and Miesenheim I and their biostratigraphical implications. In C. Turner (ed.). *The early Middle Pleistocene in Europe.* Rotterdam, Balkema. 227-54.

Kormos, T. 1934. Neue und wenig bekannte Musteliden aus dem ungarischen Oberpliozäne. *Folia Zoologica et Hydrobiologica* 5, 129-59.

Kratochvil, J. 1981. *Arvicola cantiana* vit-elle encore? *Folia Zoologica* 30, 289-300.

Krapp, F. 1990. *Crocidura leucodon* (Hermann, 1780) - Feldspitzmaus. In J. Niethammer & J Krapp (eds). *Handbuch der Säugetiere Europas, Band 3/1, Insektenfresser, Herrentiere.* Wiesbaden, AULM-Verlag. 465-84.

Kroll, E.M. 1994. Behavioural implications of Plio-Pleistocene archaeological site structure. *Journal of Human Evolution* 27, 107-38.

Kroll, E.M. & Isaac, G.Ll. 1984. Configurations of artifacts and bones at early Pleistocene sites in East Africa. In H.J.Hietela (ed.). *Intrasite Spatial Analysis in Archaeology.* Cambridge, Cambridge University Press. 4-31.

Krystufek, B., Griffiths, H.I. & Vohralik, V. 1996. The status of *Terricola* Fatio, 1867 in the taxonomy of the Palaearctic 'pine voles' (*Pitymys*) (Rodentia, Arvicolinae). *Bulletin de l'Institute Royal des Sciences Naturelles de Belgique* 66, 237-40.

Kuhn, S.J. 1995. *Mousterian Lithic Technology.* Princeton, Princeton University Press.

Kurtén, B. 1959. On the bears of the Holsteinian interglacial. *Stockholm Contributions in Geology* 2(5), 73-102.

Kurtén, B. & Poulianos, A.N. 1977. New stratigraphic and faunal material from Petralona cave with special reference to the Carnivora. *Anthropos* 4(1-2), 47-130.

Lawson, T.E. 1982. *Geological notes and local details for 1:10,000 sheets TM28 NW, NE, SW, SE (Harleston, Norfolk),* Keyworth, Institute of Geological Sciences.

Lee, J.A. & Kemp, R.A. 1992. *Thin sections of unconsolidated sediments and soils: a recipe.* London, Centre for Environmental Analysis and Management Technical Monograph 2. Royal Holloway, University of London.

Leonardi, G. & Petronio, C. 1976. The fallow deer of the European Pleistocene. *Geologica Romana* 15, 1-67.

Levi Sala, I. 1986a. Experimental replication of post-depositional surface modification on flint. In L. Owen & G. Unrath (eds), *Technical aspects of microwear studies on stone tools. Early Man News* 9/10/11, 103-9.

Levi Sala, I. 1986b. Use wear and post-depositional surface modification: a word of caution. *Journal of Archaeological Science* 13, 229-44.

Lewis, S.G. 1992. High Lodge - stratigraphy and depositional environments. In Ashton, N., Cook, J., Lewis, S.G. & Rose, J. (eds). *High Lodge. Excavations by G. de G. Sieveking, 1962-68 and J. Cook, 1988.* London, British Museum. 51-85.

Lewis, S.G. 1993. The status of the Wolstonian glaciation in the English Midlands and East Anglia. Unpublished PhD Thesis, University of London.

Lewis, S.G. 1998. Quaternary stratigraphy and Lower Palaeolithic archaeology of the Lark valley, Suffolk. In N. Ashton, F. Healy & P. Pettitt (eds), Stone Age Archaeology: Essays in Honour of John Wymer. Oxford, Oxbow Monograph 102, Lithic Studies Society Occasional Paper 6. 43-51

Lister, A.M. 1986. New results on deer from Swanscombe, and the stratigraphical significance of deer in the Middle and Upper Pleistocene of Europe. *Journal of Archaeological Science* 13, 319-38.

Lister, A.M. 1984. Evolutionary and ecological origins of British deer. *Proceedings of the Royal Society of Edinburgh* B82, 205-29.

Lister, A.M. 1996. The stratigraphic interpretation of large mammal remains from the Cromer Forest-bed Formation. In C. Turner (ed.). *The Early Middle Pleistocene in Europe.* Rotterdam, Balkema. 25-44

Lister, A.M. McGlade, J.M. & Stuart, A.J. 1990. The early Middle Pleistocene vertebrate fauna from Little Oakley, Essex. *Philosophical Transactions of the Royal Society of London* B328, 359-385.

Maddy, D., Keen, D.H., Bridgland, D.R. & Green, C.P. 1991. A revised model for the Pleistocene development of the River Avon, Warwickshire. *Journal of the Geological Society of London* 148, 473-84.

Maddy, D., Green, C.P., Lewis, S. & Bowen, D.Q. 1996. The Pleistocene development of the Lower Severn Valley, UK. *Quaternary Science Reviews* 14(3), 209-22.

Maddy, D., Lewis, S.G., Scaife, R.G., Bowen, D.Q., Coope, G.R., Green, C.P., Hardaker, T., Keen, D.H., Rees-Jones, J., Parfitt, S. & Scott, K. 1988. The Upper Pleistocene deposits at Cassington, near Oxford, UK. *Journal of Quaternary Science.* 13(3), 205-33.

Maitland, P.S. 1972. A key to the freshwater fishes of the British Isles. *Scientific Publication of the Freshwater Biological Association* 27, 1-137.

Maitland, P.S. & Campbell, R.N. 1992. *Freshwater Fishes of the British Isles*. London, Harper Collins.

Martin, R. A. 1993. Patterns of variation and speciation in Quaternary rodents. In R.A. Martin & A.D. Barnosky (eds), *Morphological Change in Quaternary Mammals of North America*. Cambridge, Cambridge University Press. 226-80

Martín, S. & Mein, P. 1998. Revision of the genera *Parapodemus*, *Apodemus*, *Rhagamys* and *Rhagapodemus* (Rodentia, Mammalia). *Geobios* 38(1), 87-97.

Maul, L. 1990. Überblick über unterpleistozänen Kleinsäugerfaunen Europaeus. *Quartärpaläontologie* 8, 153-91.

Mayhew, D.F. 1975. The Quaternary history of some British Rodents and Lagomorphs. Unpublished Ph.D. Thesis, University of Cambridge.

Mayhew, D.F. 1977. Avian predators as accumulators of fossil mammal material. *Boreas* 6, 25-31.

McDermott, F., Grün, R., Stringer, C.B. & Hawkesworth, C. J. 1993. Mass-spectrometric U-series dates for Israeli Neanderthal/early modern hominid sites. *Nature* 363, 252-4.

McKeague, J.A. 1983. Clay skins and argillic horizons. In: P.Bullock & C.P.Murphy (eds). *Soil Micromorphology*. Berkhamstead, AB Academic Publishers. 367-87.

McNabb, J. 1992. The Clactonian: British Lower Palaeolithic flint technology in biface and non-biface assemblages. Unpublished Ph.D thesis. London University.

McNabb, J. 1996a. More from the cutting edge: further discoveries of Clactonian bifaces. *Antiquity* 70, 428-36.

McNabb, J. 1996b. Through the looking glass: an historical perspective on archaeological research at Barnfield Pit, Swanscombe, 1900-1964. In B.W. Conway, J. McNabb & N.M. Ashton (eds). *Excavations at the Barnfield Pit Swanscombe, 1968-1972*. London, Occasional Papers of the British Museum No. 94. 31-51.

McNabb, J. & Ashton, N.M. 1992. The cutting edge, bifaces in the Clactonian. *Lithics* 13, 4-10.

McNabb, J. & Ashton, N.M. 1995. Thoughtful flakers. *Cambridge Archaeological Journal.* 5(2), 289-298.

Meijer, T. & Preece, R.C. 1995. Malacological evidence relating to the insularity of the British Isles during the Quaternary. In R.C. Preece (ed.), *Island Britain: a Quaternary Perspective*. Geological Society Special Publication No. 96, 89-100.

Menu, H. & Popelard, J-B. 1987. Utilisation des caracteres dentaires pour la determination des vespertilionines de l'ouest Europeen. *Le Rhinolophe* 4, 1-88.

Meulen, A.J. Van der. 1973. Middle Pleistocene smaller mammals from the Monte Peglia (Orvieto, Italy) with special reference to the phylogeny of *Microtus* (Arvicolidae, Rodentia). *Quaternaria* 17, 1-144.

Michaux, J. & Pasquier, L. 1974. Dynamique des populations de Moulots (Rodentia, *Apodemus*) en Europe durant le Quaternaire. Premières données. *Bulletin de la Sociéte Géologique de France.* 16(4), 431-9.

Miller, G.H. & Brigham-Grette, J. 1989. Amino acid geochronology: resolution and precision in carbonate fossils. *Quaternary International* 1, 111-28.

Miller, G.H. & Mangerud, J. 1989. Aminostratigraphy of European marine interglacial deposits. *Quaternary Science Reviews* 4, 215-78

Mitchell, G.F., Penny, L.F., Shotton, F.W. & West, R.G. 1973. A correlation of the Quaternary deposits in the British Isles. *Geological Society of London, Special Report* 4.

Mithen, S. 1994. Technology and society during the Middle Pleistocene: hominid group size, social learning and industrial variability. *Cambridge Archaeological Journal* 4(1), 3-32.

Moore, P.D., Webb, J.A. & Collinson, M.E. 1991. *Pollen Analysis*. 2nd Edition. Oxford, Blackwell Scientific Publications.

Morrison, P. 1994. *Mammals, Reptiles and Amphibians of Britain and Europe*. London, Macmillan.

Mortillet, G. de 1883. Le Préhistorique. Antiquite de l'Homme. Paris, Reinwald (Bibliothèque des Science Contemporaines VIII).

Mourer-Chauviré, C. 1975. *Les Oiseaux du Pleistocene Moyen et Superieur de France*. Documents de Laboratoire de Géologie de la Faculté de Lyon No. 64, Fascicule 2.

Murphy, C.P. & Kemp, R.A. 1984. The over-estimation of clay and the under-estimation of pores in soil thin sections. *Journal of Soil Science* 35, 481-96.

Nadachowski, A. 1982. *Late Quaternary Rodents of Poland with Special Reference to Morphotype Dentition Analysis of Voles*. Warszawa & Kraków, Panstwowe Wydawnictwo Naukowe .

Nadachowski, A. 1984. Taxonomic value of anteroconid measurements of M_1 in common and field voles. *Acta Theriologica* 29 (10), 123-7.

Newcomer, M.H. 1971. Some quantitative experiments in handaxe manufacture. *World Archaeology* 3, 85-94.

Newcomer, M.H. 1979. Comment on "The Clactonian: an independant complex or an integral part of the Acheulian?" by M. Ohel. *Current Anthropology* 20, 717.

Newton, E.T. 1894. The vertebrate fauna collected by Mr. Lewis Abbott from the fissure near Ightham, Kent. *Quarterly Journal of the Geological Society of London* 50, 188-211.

Newton, E.T. 1899. Additional notes on the vertebrate fauna of the rock-fissure at Ightham (Kent). *Quarterly Journal of the Geological Society of London* 55, 419-29.

Niethammer, J. & Krapp, F. (eds). 1978. *Handbuch der Säugetiere Europas. 1/1 Nagetiere I.* Wiesbaden, Akademische Verlagsgesellschaft.

Niethammer, J. & Krapp, F. (eds). 1982. *Handbuch der Säugetiere Europas. 2/1 Nagetiere II.* Wiesbaden, Akademische Verlagsgesellschaft.

Niethammer, J. & Krapp, F. (eds). 1990. *Handbuch der Säugetiere Europas. 3/1 Insektenfresser, Herrentiere.* Wiesbaden, AULU-Verlag.

Noel, M. 1992. Multicore resistivity tomography for imaging archaeology. In P. Spoerry (ed.), *Geoprospecting in the Archaeological Landscape.* Oxford, Oxbow Monograph No. 18. 89-99.

Oches, E. & McCoy, W.D. 1995. Amino acid geochronology applied to Central European loess deposits. *Quarternary Science Reviews* 14, 767-82.

Oches, E., McCoy, W.D. & Clark, P.U. 1996. Paleotemperature gradient estimates and geochronology of loess deposition for the last glaciation, Mississippi Valley, U.S.A. *Bulletin of the Geological Society of America* 108, 892-903.

Ohel, M.Y. 1979. The Clactonian: an independant complex or an integral part of the Acheulian? *Current Anthropology* 20, 685-713.

Ohel, M.Y. 1982. Is Barnham indeed Clactonian? *Praehistorische Zeitschrift* 57(2), 181-200.

Ohnuma, K. & Bergman, C.A. 1982. Experimental studies in the determination of flaking mode. *Bulletin of the Institute of Archaeology* 19, 127-46.

Parfitt, S.A. 1998. Pleistocene vertebrate faunas of the West Sussex Coastal Plain: their stratigraphic and Palaeoenvironmental significance. In J.B. Murton, C.A. Whiteman, M.R. Bates, D.R. Bridgland, A.J. Long, M.B. Roberts & M.P. Waller (eds), *The Quaternary of Kent and Sussex. Field Guide.* London, Quaternary Research Association. 121-34.

Parry, S. 1996. The avifaunal remains. In B. Conway, J. McNabb & N. Ashton (eds). *Excavations at Barnfield Pit, Swanscombe, 1968-72.* London, British Museum Occasional Paper No. 94. 137-43.

Paterson, T.T. 1937. Studies on the Palaeolithic succession in England No 1, the Barnham sequence. *Proceedings of the Prehistoric Society.* 3(1), 87-135.

Paterson, T.T. 1939. Pleistocene stratigraphy of the Breckland. *Nature* 143, 822-3.

Paterson T.T. 1940-1941. On a world correlation of the Pleistocene. *Philosophical Transactions of the Royal Society of Edinburgh* 60(2), 373-425.

Paterson, T.T. 1942. Lower Palaeolithic Man in the Cambridge District. Unpublished PhD thesis. Cambridge University.

Paterson. T.T. & Fagg, B.E.B. 1940. Studies on the Palaeolithic succession in England. No. II. The Upper Brecklandian Acheul (Elveden). *Proceedings of the Prehistoric Society* 6, 1-29.

Penk, A. & Bruckner, E. 1909. *Die Alpen im Eiszeitalter.* Leipzig.

Perrin, R.M.S., Rose, J. & Davies, H. 1979. The distribution, variation and origins of pre-Devensian tills in eastern England. *Philosophical Transactions of the Royal Society of London* B287, 535-70.

Pike, K. & Godwin, H. 1953. The Interglacial from Clacton-on-Sea, Essex. *Quarterly Journal of the Geological Society of London* 108, 261-72.

Potts, R. 1989. Olorgesailie: new excavations and findings in Early and Middle Pleistocene contexts, southern Kenya Rift Valley. *Journal of Human Evolution* 18, 477-84.

Potts, R. 1991. Why the Oldowan? Plio-Pleistocene toolmaking and the transport of resources. *Journal of Anthropological Research* 47, 153-76.

Potts, R. 1994. Variables versus models of Early Pleistocene hominid land use. *Journal of Human Evolution* 27, 7-24.

Preece, R.C. 1989. Additions to the molluscan fauna of the early Middle Pleistocene depoists at Sugworth, near Oxford including the first British Quaternary record of *Perforatella bidentate* (Gmelin). *Journal of Conchology* 33, 179-82

Preece, R.C. 1990. The Molluscan fauna from Middle Pleistocene interglacial deposits at Little Oakley, Essex and its environmental and stratigraphic implications. *Philosophical Transactions of the Royal Society of London* B328, 387-407.

Preece, R.C., Kemp, R.A. & Hutchinson, J.N. 1995. A Late-glacial colluvial sequence at Watcombe Bottom, Ventnor, Isle of Wight, England. *Journal of Quaternary Science* 10, 107-21.

Preece, R.C., Lewis, S.G., Wymer, J.J., Bridgland, D.R. & Parfitt, S. 1991. Beeches Pit, West Stow, Suffolk. In S.G. Lewis, C.A. Whiteman & D.R. Bridgland (eds). *Central East Anglia and the Fen Basin. Field Guide.* London, Quaternary Research Association. 94-104.

Rage, J-C. 1974. Les batraciens des gisements Quaternaires Européens détermination ostéologique. *Extrait du Bulletin Mensuel de la Société Linnéene de Lyon* 43, 276-89.

Reumer, J.W.F. 1984. Ruscinian and early Pleistocene Soricidae (Insectivora, Mammalia) from Tegelen (The Netherlands) and Hungary. *Scripta Geologica* 73, 1-173.

Reumer, J.W.F. 1986. Notes on the Soricidae (Insectivora, Mammalia) from Crete. I. The Pleistocene species of *Crocidura zimmermanni*. *Bonner Zoologische Beiträge* 37(3), 161-71.

Reynolds, S.H. 1912. *A Monograph of the British Pleistocene Mammalia. The Mustelidae. Volume 2 part 4.* London, Palaeontographical Society.

Rhodes E.J. & Bailey R.M. 1997. The effect of thermal transfer on the zeroing of the luminescence of quartz from recent glaciofluvial sediments. *Quaternary Science Reviews (Quaternary Geochronology)* 16, 291-8.

Rhodes E.J. & Grün R., 1991. ESR behaviour of the paramagnetic centre at g=2.0018 in tooth enamel. *Ancient TL* 9, 14-18.

Rhodes E.J. & Pownall L. 1994. Zeroing of the OSL signal in quartz from young glaciofluvial sediments. *Radiation Measurements* 23, 329-33.

Rick, J.W. 1976. Downslope movement and archaeological intrasite spatial analysis. *American Antiquity* 41(2), 133-44.

Roberts, M.B. 1986. Excavations of a Lower Palaeolithic site at Amey's Eartham Pit, Boxgrove, West Sussex: A preliminary report. *Proceedings of the Prehistoric Society* 52, 215-45.

Roberts, M.B. 1990. Day 3, Stop 6, Amey's Eartham Pit, Boxgrove. In C. Turner (ed.). *SEQS The Cromer Symposium, Norwich 1990. Field Excursion Guidebook September 5th-7th.* Quaternary Research Association. Cambridge. 62-81

Roberts, M.B., Parfitt, S.A., Pope, M., Wenban-Smith, F.F. (with contributions by Macphail, R.I., Stewart, J.R. & Locker, A.) 1997. Boxgrove, West Sussex: Rescue excavations of a Lower Palaeolithic landsurface (Boxgrove Project B 1989-91). *Proceedings of the Prehistoric Society* 63, 303-58.

Roberts, M.B., Stringer, C.B. & Parfitt, S.A. 1994. A hominid tibia from Middle Pleistocene sediments at Boxgrove, UK. *Nature* 369, 311-13.

Rodwell, J.S. (ed.) 1991. *British Plant Communities. Volume 1: Woodlands and Scrub.* Cambridge, Cambridge University Press.

Roe, D.A. 1979. Comment on "The Clactonian: an independant complex or an integral part of the Acheulian?" by M. Ohel. *Current Anthropology* 20, 718-9.

Roe, D.A. 1981. *The Lower and Middle Palaeolithic Periods in Britain.* London, Routledge & Kegan Paul.

Roe, H.M. 1995. The Cudmore Grove Channel (TM 067144). In D.R. Bridgland, P. Allen and B.A. Haggart (eds). *The Quaternary of the Lower Reaches of the Thames. Field Guide.* London, Quaternary Research Association. 258-69.

Roebroeks, W., Loecker, D. de, Hennekens, P. & van Ieperen, M. 1992. 'A veil of stones': on the interpretation of an early Middle Paleolithic low density scatter at Maastricht-Belvédère (The Netherlands). *Analecta*

Praehistorica Leidensia 25, 1-16.

Rogers, M.J., Harris, J.W.K. & Feibel, C.S. 1994. Changing patterns of land use by Plio-Pleistocene hominids in the Lake Turkana Basin. *Journal of Human Evolution* 27, 139-158.

Rogers, P.M., Arthur, C.P. & Soriguer, R.C. 1994. The rabbit in continental Europe. In H.V. Thompson & C.M. King (eds). *The European Rabbit: The History and Biology of a Successful Coloniser.* Oxford, Oxford University Press. 22-63.

Rollinat, R. 1934. *La Vie des Reptiles de la France Centrale: Cinquante Anneés d'Observations Biologique.* Paris, Librairie Delagrave.

Rose, J. 1987. The status of the Wolstonian glaciation in the British Quaternary. *Quaternary Newsletter* 53, 1-9.

Rouffignac, de, C., Bowen, D.Q., Coope, G.R., Keen, D.H., Lister, A.M., Maddy, D., Robinson, J.E., Sykes, G.A. & Walker, M.J.C. 1995. Late Middle Pleistocene interglacial deposits at Upper Strensham, Worcestershire, England. *Journal of Quaternary Science* 10, 15-31.

Rousseau, D-D., Puisségur, J-J. & Lécolle, F. 1992. West-European terrestrial molluscs assemblages of isotopic stage 11 (Middle Pleistocene): climatic implications. *Palaeogeography, Palaeoclimatology, Palaeoecology* 92, 15-29.

Rzebik, B. 1968. *Crocidura* Wagler and other Insectivora (Mammalia) from the Quaternary deposits of Tornewton Cave in England. *Acta Zoologica Cracoviensia* 13(10), 251-61.

Rzebik-Kowalska, B. 1972. The Insectivora from Stránska Skála near Brno. *Anthropos* 20 (New Series 12), 65-70.

Rzebik-Kowalska, B. 1991. Pliocene and Pleistocene Insectivora (Mammalia) of Poland. VIII. Soricidae: *Sorex* Linnaeus, 1758, *Neomys* Kaup, 1829, *Macroneomys* Fejfar, 1966, *Paenelimnoecus* Baudelot, 1972 and Soricidae indeterminata. *Acta Zoologica Cracoviensia* 34(2), 323-424.

Rzebik-Kowalska, B. 1996. Climate and history of European Shrews (family Soricidae). *Acta Zoologica Cracoviensia* 38(1), 95-107.

Sanchiz, F.B. 1977. La Familia Bufonidae (Amphibia, Anura) en el Terciario Europeo. *Trabajos Sobre Neogeno-cuaternario* 8, 75-111.

Schaub, S. 1938. Tertiäre und Quartäre Murinae. *Abhandlungen der Schweizerischen Palaeontologischen Gesellschaft* 61, 1-38.

Schick, K.D. 1986. *Stone Age Sites in the Making: Experiments in the Formation and Transformation of Archaeological Occurrences.* Oxford, BAR International Series 314.

Schick, K.D. 1987. Modeling the formation of early Stone Age artifact concentrations. *Journal of Human Evolution* 16, 789-807.

Schiffer, M.B. 1983. Toward the identification of formation processes. *American Antiquity* 48(4), 675-706.

Schreve, D. 1996. The mammalian fauna from the Waechter excavations, Barnfield Pit, Swanscombe. In B. Conway, J. McNabb & N. Ashton (eds). *Excavations at Barnfield Pit, Swanscombe, 1968*-72. London, British Museum Occasional Paper 94. 149-62

Sevilla, P. & Lopez-Martinez, N. 1986. Comparative systematic value between dental and external/skeletal features in western European Chiroptera. In D.E. Russell, J-P Santoro & D. Sigogneau-Russell (eds). *Teeth Revisited: Proceedings of the VIIIth International Symposium on Dental Morphology, Paris 1986.* Mémoires Muséum National d'Histoire Naturelle, Paris (série C) 53. 255-66.

Sevilla-Garcia, P. 1986. Identificaión de los principales quirópteros ibéricos a partir de sus dientes aislados. Valor sistemático de los caracteres morfológicos y métricos dentarios. *Dõnana. Acta Vertebrata* 13, 111-30.

Shackley, M.L. 1974. Stream abrasion of flint implements. *Nature* 248, 501-2.

Shepherd, W. 1972. *Flint*. London, Faber & Faber.

Shotton, F.W. & Osborne, P.J. 1965. The fauna of the Hoxnian Interglacial deposits at Nechells, Birmingham. *Philosophical Transactions of the Royal Society of London* B248, 353-78.

Singer R., Gladfelter, B.G. & Wymer, J.J. 1993. *The Lower Palaeolithic Site at Hoxne, England.* Chicago, Chicago University Press.

Singer, R., Wymer, J., Gladfelter, B.G., & Wolff, R.G. 1973. Excavations of the Clactonian industry at the Golf course, Clacton-on-Sea, Essex. *Proceedings of the Prehistoric Society* 39, 6-74

Sisson, S. & Grossman, J.B. 1956. *The Anatomy of the Domestic Animals.* Philadelphia & London, W.B. Saunders Company. (Fourth edition, revised).

Smith, G.R. 1981. Late Cenozoic freshwater fishes of North America. *Annual Review of Ecology and Systematics* 21, 163-93.

Smith, M.A. 1964. *The British Amphibians and Reptiles.* London, Collins.

Smith, R.A. & Dewey, H. 1913. Stratification at Swanscombe: report on excavations made on behalf of the British Museum and H.M. Geological Survey. *Archaeologia* 64, 177-204.

Sparks, B.W. 1956. The non-marine Mollusca of the Hoxne Interglacial. In R.G. West (ed.) The Quaternary Deposits at Hoxne. *Philosophical Transactions of the Royal Society of London* B239, 351-4.

Sparks, B.W. 1961. The ecological interpretation of Quaternary non-marine Mollusca. *Proceedings of the Linnean Society of London* 172, 71-80.

Sparks, B.W. 1964. The distribution of non-marine Mollusca in the Last Interglacial in south-east England. *Proceedings of the Malacological Society of London.* 36, 7-25.

Sparks, B.W. 1980. The land and freshwater Mollusca of the West Runton forest bed. In R.G. West (ed.), *The Preglacial Pleistocene of the Norfolk and Suffolk Coasts.* Cambridge, Cambridge University Press. 25-7.

Spitzenberger, F. 1990a.. *Neomys fodiens.* In J. Niethammer & K. Krapp (eds). *Handbuch der Säugetiere Europas.* Wiesbaden, AULA-Verlag. 334-74.

Spitzenberger, F. 1990b. *Neomys anomolus* Cabrera, 1907. In J. Niethammer & K. Krapp (eds). *Handbuch der Säugetiere Europas.* Wiesbaden, AULA-Verlag. 317-33.

Spooner, N.A. & Questiaux, D.G. 1989. Optical dating - Achenheim beyond the Eemian using green and infra-red stimulation. *Long and Short Range Limits in Luminescence Dating.* Oxford, Research Laboratory for Archaeology and the History of Art Occasional Publication No. 9. 97-103.

Spurrell, F.C.J. 1884. On some Palaeolithic knapping tools and modes of using them. *Journal of the Anthropological Institute (GB & Ireland)* 13, 109-18.

Stapert, D. 1976. Some natural surface modification on flint in the Netherlands. *Palaeohistoria* 18, 8-41.

Stapert, D. 1979. The handaxe from Drouwen (Province of Drenthe, The Netherlands) and the Upper Acheulian. *Palaeohistoria* 21, 128-42.

Stern, N. 1993. The structure of the Lower Pleistocene archaeological record: a case study from the Koobi Fora Formation. *Current Anthropology* 34, 201-25.

Stern, N. 1994. The implications of time-averaging for reconstructing the land-use patterns of early tool-using hominids. *Journal of Human Evolution* 27, 89-105.

Stewart, J.R. 1992. The Turdidae of Pin Hole Cave, Derbyshire. Unpublished MSc. Dissertation. City of London Polytechnic.

Stewart, J.R. & Hernandez Carrasquilla, F. 1997. The identification of extant European bird remains: a review of the literature. *International Journal of Osteoarchaeology* 7, 364-71.

Stewart, J.R. In press. Intraspecific variation in modern European birds and its application to the Quaternary avian fossil record: *Lagopus* as a case study. *Smithsonian Contributions to Paleobiology.*

Stuart, A.J. 1979. Pleistocene occurrences of the European pond tortoise (*Emys orbicularis* L.) in Britain. *Boreas* 8, 359-71.

Stuart, A.J. 1980. The vertebrate fauna from the interglacial deposits at Sugworth, near Oxford. *Philosophical Transactions of the Royal Society of London* B289, 87-97.

Stuart, A.J. 1982. *Pleistocene Vertebrates in the British Isles.* London & New York, Longman.

Stuart, A.J. 1996. Vertebrate faunas from the early Middle Pleistocene of East Anglia. In C Turner (ed.). *The early Middle Pleistocene in Europe.* Rotterdam, Balkema. 9-24.

Stuart, A.J., Wolff, R.G., Lister, A.M., Singer, R. & Eggington, J.M. 1993. Fossil Vertebrates. In R. Singer, J.J. Wymer & B.G. Gladfelter (eds). *The Lower Paleolithic site at Hoxne, England.* Chicago, University of Chicago Press. 163-206.

Sturge, W.A. 1911. The chronology of the Stone Age. *Proceedings of the Prehistoric Society of East Anglia* 1, 43-105.

Sumbler, M.G. 1995. The terraces of the River Thame and Thames and their bearing on the chronology of glaciation in central and eastern England. *Proceedings of the Geologists' Association* 106, 93-106.

Sutcliffe, A.J. 1964. The mammalian fauna. In C.D. Ovey (ed.), *The Swanscombe Skull. A Survey of Research at a Pleistocene Site*. Occasional Paper of the Royal Anthropological Institute of Great Britain and Ireland, London, No. 20, 85-111.

Sutcliffe, A.J. 1985. *On the Track of Ice Age Mammals*. London, British Museum (Natural History).

Sutcliffe, A.J. 1996. Insularity of the British Isles, 250, 000 to 30,000 years ago: the mammalian, including human evidence. In R.C. Preece (ed.), *Island Britain: a Quaternary Perspective*. Geological Society Special Publication No. 96. 127-40.

Sutcliffe, A.J. 1995. The Aveley Elephant Pit site, Sandy Lane (TQ 553807). In D.R. Bridgland, P. Allen & B.A. Haggart (eds). *The Quaternary of the Lower Reaches of the Thames. Field Guide*. Durham, The Quaternary Research Association. 189-99.

Sutcliffe, A.J. & Kowalski, K. 1976. Pleistocene Rodents of the British Isles. *Bulletin of the British Museum (Natural History) Geology* 27(2), 31-147.

Szyndlar, Z. 1984. Fossil snakes from Poland. *Acta Zoologica Cracoviensia* 28, 1-156.

Tchernov, E. 1979. Polymorphism, size trends and Pleistocene paleoclimatic response of the subgenus *Sylvaemus* (Mammalia: Rodentia) in Israel. *Israel Journal of Zoology* 28, 131-59.

Thenius, E. 1965. Die carnivoren-reste aus dem altpleistozän von Voigstedt bei Sangerhausen in Thüringen. *Pälaontologische Abhandlungen. Abteilung. A* 2(3), 539-64.

Turner, A. 1995. Evidence for Pleistocene contact between the British Isles and the European continent based on distribution of larger carnivores. In R.C. Preece (ed.). *Island Britain: a Quaternary Perspective*. Geological Society Special Publication No. 96. 141-9.

Turner, C. 1970. The Middle Pleistocene deposits at Marks Tey, Essex. *Philosophical Transactions of the Royal Society of London* B257, 373-440.

Turner, C. 1973. Eastern England. In G.F. Mitchell, L.F. Penny, F.W. Shotton & R.G. West (eds), A correlation of Quaternary deposits in the British Isles. *Geological Society of London Special Report* 4, 8-9

Turner, C. 1985. Problems and pitfalls in the application of palynology to Pleistocene archaeological sites in western Europe. In J. Renault-Miskovsky, Bui-Thi-Mai & M.Girard (eds). *Palynologie Archeologique*. Actes des Journees du 25-26-27 janvier 1984, Paris, Editions du Centre National de la Recherche Scientifique. 347-73.

Turner, C. (ed.) 1996. *The early Middle Pleistocene in Europe*. Rotterdam, Balkema.

Turner, C. & Kerney, M.P. 1971. A note on the age of the freshwater beds of the Clacton Channel. *Quarterly Journal of the Geological Society of London* 127, 87-93.

Turner, C. & West, R.G. 1968. The subdivision and zonation of interglacial deposits. *Eiszeitalter und Gegenwart* 19, 93-101.

Vepraskas, M.J., Wilding, L.P. & Drees, L.R. 1994. Aquic conditions for Soil Taxonomy: concepts, soil morphology and micromorphology. In A. Ringrose-Voase & G. Humphries (eds), *Soil Micromorphology: Studies in Management and Genesis*. Elsevier, Amsterdam. 117-31.

Veracini, C & Galleni, L. 1995. Analysis of teeth from owl pellets for biogeographical studies of the genus *Crocidura* (Insectivora, Soricidae). In J. Moggi-Cecchi (ed.) *Aspects of Dental Biology: Palaeontology, Anthropology and Evolution*. Florence, International Institute for the Study of Man. 357-64

Warren, S.H. 1933. The Palaeolithic industries of the Clacton and Dovercourt districts. *Essex Naturalist* (vol. for 1932-1935) 24, 1-29.

Warren, S.H. 1951. The Clacton flint industry: a new interpretation. *Proceedings of the Geologists' Association* 62, 107-35.

Weerd, A. Van der. 1976. Rodent faunas of the Mio-Pliocene continental sediments of the Teruel-Alfambra region, Spain. *Utrecht Micropaleontological Bulletins Special Publications* 2.

Wehmiller, J.F. 1989. Amino acid racemization: applications in chemical taxonomy and chronostratigraphy of Quaternary fossils. In J.G. Carter (ed.), *Skeletal Biomineralization: Patterns, Processes and Evolutionary Trends*. New York, van Nostrand. 287-318.

Wehmiller, J.F. & Belknap, D.F. 1978. Alternative kinetic models for the interpretation of amino acid enantiomeric ratios in Pleistocene molluscs: examples from California, Washington and Florida. *Quaternary Research* 9, 330-48.

Wenban-Smith, F.F. 1989. The use of canonical variates for determination of biface manufacturing technology at Boxgrove Lower Palaeolithic site and the behavioural implications of this technology. *Journal of Archaeological Science* 16, 17-26.

Wenban-Smith, F.F. 1995. Another one bites the dust. *Lithics* 16, 99-108.

West, R.G. 1956. The Quaternary deposits at Hoxne, Suffolk. *Philosophical Transactions of the Royal Society of London* B239, 265-365.

West, R.G. & Donner, J.J. 1956. The glaciations of East Anglia and the East Midlands: a differentiation based on stone orientation measurements of the tills. *Quarterly Journal of the Geological Society of London* 112, 69-87.

West, R.G. & Gibbard, P.L. 1995. Discussion on excavations at the Lower Palaeolithic site at East Farm, Barnham, Suffolk, 1989-92. *Journal of the Geological Society of London* 152, 570-1.

Wheeler, A. 1977. The origin and distribution of the freshwater fishes of the British Isles. *Journal of Biogeography* 4, 1-24.

Whitaker, W., Woodward, H.B., Bennet, F.J., Skertchly, S.B.& Jukes Brown, A.J. 1891. *The Geology of parts of Cambridgeshire and of Suffolk.* Memoirs of the Geological Survey of England and Wales, explanation of sheet 51NE and part of 51NW.

Wilkinson, D.M. 1987. Montane wood mice *Apodemus sylvaticus* and their relevance to some Quaternary fossils assemblages. *Journal of Zoology* 212, 347-9.

Woelfle, E. 1967. *Vergleichend morphologische Untersuchungen an Einzelknochen des postcranialen Skeletts in Mitteleuropa vorkommender Enten, Halbgänse und Säger.* München, Ludwig-Maximilians-Universität.

Woodland, A.W. 1942. Water supply from underground sources, Cambridge and Ipswich districts. *Geological Survey, Wartime Pamphlet* 20, Part III.

Woodland, A.W. 1970. The buried tunnel-valleys of East Anglia. *Proceedings of the Yorkshire Geological Society* 37, 521-78.

Wymer, J.J. 1968. *Lower Palaeolithic Archaeology in Britain as represented by the Thames Valley.* London, John Baker.

Wymer, J.J. 1974. Clactonian and Acheulian industries in Britain - their chronology and significance. *Proceedings of the Geologists' Association* 85, 391-421.

Wymer, J.J. 1979. Comment on "The Clactonian: an independant complex or an integral part of the Acheulian?" by M. Ohel. *Current Anthropology* 20, 719.

Wymer, J.J. 1985. *Palaeolithic Sites of East Anglia.* Norwich, Geobooks.

Wymer, J.J., Bridgland, D.R. & Lewis, S.G. 1991. Warren Hill, Mildenhall, Suffolk (TL 744743). In S.G. Lewis, C.A. Whiteman & D.R. Bridgland (eds). *Central East Anglia and the Fen Basin. Field Guide.* London, Quaternary Research Association. 50-8.

Zhou, L.P., McDermott, F., Rhodes, E.J., Marseglia, E.A. & Mellars, P.A. 1997. ESR and mass-spectrometric uranium-series dating studies of a mammoth tooth from Stanton Harcourt, Oxfordshire, England. *Quaternary Science Reviews (Quaternary Geochronology)* 16, 445-54.

Zoller, L., Oches, E.A. & McCoy, W.D. 1994. Towards a revised chronostratigraphy of loess in Austria with respect to key sections in the Czech Republic and in Hungary: Quaternary geochronology. *Quaternary Science Reviews* 13, 465-72.